KV-013-276

11E

BUSINESS PRINCIPLES AND MANAGEMENT

Kenneth E. Everard, Ed.D.
The College of New Jersey

James L. Burrow, Ph.D.
North Carolina State University

SOUTH-WESTERN
THOMSON LEARNING

Australia • Canada • Mexico • Singapore • Spain • United Kingdom • United States

Business Principles and Management
by Kenneth E. Everard and James L. Burrow

Executive Editor
Eve Lewis
Project Manager
Carol Sturzenberger
Marketing Manager
Nancy A. Long
Marketing Coordinator
Christian L. McNamee
Production Manager
Patricia Matthews Boies
Manufacturing Manager
Carol Chase

Manufacturing Coordinator
Kevin Kluck
Editorial Assistants
Linda Adams; Stephanie White
Production Assistant
Deb Roark
Consulting Editor
Cinci Stowell, Stowell Editorial Services

Cover/Internal Design
Bill Spencer
Unit Openers and Internal Illustrations
Marjory Dressler, Marjory Dressler Photo-Graphics
Composition/Prepress
Lachina Publishing Services, Inc.
Printer
R. R. Donnelley

ISBN: 0-538-69793-8
Printed in the United States of America

5 6 7 D 05 04 03

For more information, contact South-Western Educational Publishing, 5191 Natorp Blvd., Mason, OH 45040; or find us on the World Wide Web at http://www.swep.com

This book is printed on acid-free paper.

About the Authors:
Kenneth E. Everard, Ed.D., is Professor Emeritus at The College of New Jersey, where he served as professor of management and as developer and administrator of graduate programs in business education, office administration, human resources management, and management. Earlier he taught business education at the secondary level and also taught accounting and management at the University of Maryland in College Park, Europe, and the Far East.

James L. Burrow, Ph.D., is the coordinator of the graduate Training and Development Program at North Carolina State University in Raleigh, North Carolina. He has been a faculty member at the community college and university levels in marketing and human resource development as well as a consultant to business and public organizations.

YOUR COURSE PLANNING JUST GOT EASIER!

- **NEW! Business Principles and Management** by Everard and Burrow
  The eleventh edition of the market-leading text presents the sound fundamental topics needed to manage and operate a successful business. Semester or year-long course.
  0-538-69892-6 Student Workbook
  0-538-69894-2 Student CD
  0-538-69893-4 Printed Tests
  0-538-69891-8 Video Package

- **NEW! International Business** by Dlabay and Scott
  This hardbound text provides the foundation for studying international business and the many aspects of conducting business in the global economy. Semester or year-long course.
  0-538-69855-1 Student Edition
  0-538-69857-8 Student Activities Study Guide
  0-538-69858-6 Printed Tests
  0-538-69859-4 Video

- **NEW! Investing in Your Future** by NAIC
  This text-workbook can teach learners every step of the way toward smart saving and investing. 30+ hours completion time.
  0-538-68607-3 Student Edition (includes Stock Selection Guide Software CD)

- **NEW! Business 2000 Series**
  This exciting new instructional program uses a modular format that allows you to create customized courses or enhance already existing curriculum. Each module includes a Learner Guide, a Video, an Annotated Instructor's Edition, and an instructor's CD.
  0-538-69881-0 E-Commerce Module
  0-538-69876-4 Entrepreneurship Module
  0-538-69866-7 Intro to Business Module
  0-538-69871-3 Advertising Module

- **NEW! SCANS 2000 Virtual Workplace Simulations** in partnership with Johns Hopkins University
  These CDs create a challenging, interactive workplace experience that gives learners a chance to develop and apply their academic and soft skills in a real-world setting.
  0-538-69827-6 Developing a Business Plan
  0-538-69819-5 Developing a Marketing Plan
  0-538-69811-X Building a Problem Solving Team

- **NEW! The 10-Hour Series**
  Become proficient in electronic presentation skills in a short period of time. 10 hours completion time.
  0-538-69849-7 Electronic Business Presentations (softcover text with data disk)

Join Us on the Internet
www.swep.com

HOW TO USE THIS BOOK

Reality Check presents a true story that's tailored to the chapter's contents. By reading the story, you'll have a better understanding of the chapter's main topics.

UNIT 1 CHAPTER 1

CHARACTERISTICS OF BUSINESS

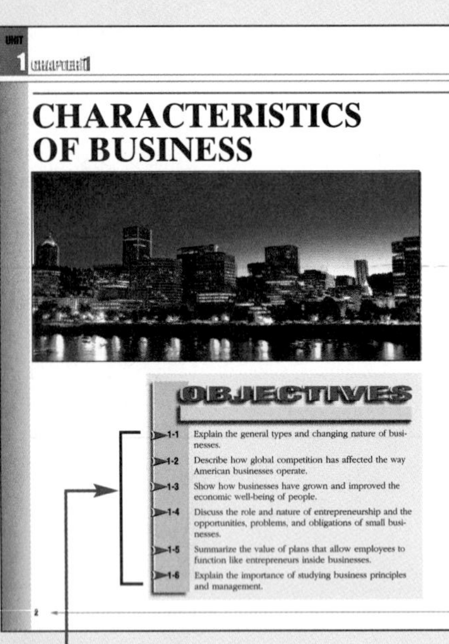

OBJECTIVES

- 1-1 Explain the general types and changing nature of businesses.
- 1-2 Describe how global competition has affected the way American businesses operate.
- 1-3 Show how businesses have grown and improved the economic well-being of people.
- 1-4 Discuss the role and nature of entrepreneurship and the opportunities, problems, and obligations of small businesses.
- 1-5 Summarize the value of plans that allow employees to function like entrepreneurs inside businesses.
- 1-6 Explain the importance of studying business principles and management.

CHARACTERISTICS OF BUSINESS

INCOME VS. OUTGO: A DELICATE BALANCE

American businesses work for Sara Donahue and her family. As the family's financial manager, she pays the bills. Sara and Scott, along with Paul and Marta, are consumers. They buy goods such as clothes, shoes, tricycles, and tents. Likewise, they buy services such as trips to the dentist and to movies. Businesses work very hard to provide the goods and services needed by the Donahue family and everyone else.

The story of American business is a fascinating one. Products found in most homes come from countless producers. The flowering plant in the Donahues' front window could have been purchased from a greenhouse operated by a single person. The light bulbs the Donahue family uses could have been made by a business with 100,000 employees, their carpet from a business with 500 employees, and the cake for Marta's birthday from a bakery with only 10 workers. These and scores of other items found in homes, offices, stores, and factories are produced by many kinds of businesses.

NATURE OF BUSINESS

An organization that produces or distributes a good or service for profit is called a business. *Profit* is the difference between earned income and costs. Every business engages in at least three major activities. The first activity, production, involves making a product or providing a

Over 22 million businesses currently exist in the United States. They vary in size from one employee to nearly 400,000 employees and in assets from a few dollars to billions of dollars. Some of these businesses have only a few customers, while others have millions of customers located throughout the world.

2 3

Facts and Figures introduces interesting statistics and information about business today.

Objectives begin each unit and offer an overview of the information to be studied.

CHAPTER 7 LEGAL ASPECTS OF BUSINESS

LAWYER

Although the popular view of lawyers emphasizes sensational courtroom trials, many lawyers have jobs in government and in business firms, public utilities, banks, insurance companies, real estate agencies, manufacturing firms, and welfare organizations. But no matter what the situation, lawyers hold positions of great responsibility and must adhere to a strict code of ethics.

The more detailed aspects of lawyers' work have been greatly influenced by advances in technology. Software can be used to search legal literature and to organize and index material. Lawyers use the Internet, electronic filing, videoconferencing, and voice-recognition technology. These tools save time and reduce legal costs.

Formal educational requirements usually include a four-year college degree, followed by three years in law school. After that, states require that applicants pass a written bar examination. Persons interested in a particular aspect of law may find related courses useful. For example, tax lawyers must have a broad knowledge of accounting.

For more career information about lawyers, check your library or the Internet for resources.

can set a price that will generate the greatest profit. In a monopoly situation, such as Deion Banks's taxi company, the prices are generally very high. Without competitors to lure customers away with lower prices, the monopolistic company can raise its price as high as it wants. If customers want the product or service, they have no choice but to pay the monopolist's price.

In actual practice, however, few monopolies exist, because of the effectiveness of competition. To illustrate, assume a business offers a new product that no other business has. The product suddenly becomes quite popular. The prospect of profits to be made entices other companies to enter the market to help meet the demand. A temporary monopoly will exist until those competitors can produce and sell similar products. Usually, through competitive pricing, the more efficient companies will attract the greatest number of purchasers, while the less efficient may struggle for survival or go out of business. Even if some competitors fail, however, a monopoly will not exist as long as there are at least two or more producers.

In some situations, however, monopolies may be better for consumers than competition. These situations usually involve providing public services, such as public utilities, which have a fairly stable demand and which are costly to create. A natural gas company, for example, must build hundreds of miles of pipeline along streets and roads in order to deliver gas to homes and industries to fuel furnaces and stoves. If two or three gas companies incurred these same costs to sell gas to a relatively fixed number of customers, the price of gas would be higher than if only one company existed. Also, installing and maintaining so many pipelines would create nuisance problems along crowded streets and highways. In these types of situations, the government grants a monopoly to one company, regulates the prices that the company can charge, and influences other company policies.

Until recently, the federal government had approved of closely regulated monopolies, such as the postal system, utility companies, railroads, and communication firms. However, the trend has shifted from allowing monopolies to weakening or eliminating them in order to encourage competition. No longer, for example, are passenger fares on commercial airlines regulated. As a result, fares have generally dropped. Even telephone service, the trucking industry, and railroads have been deregulated. Today utilities are undergoing deregulation. Firms such as MCI WorldCom and Sprint offer communication services at competitive prices and compete fiercely with the once monopolistic AT&T. The result overall has been that consumers pay lower prices and have more services from which to select.

ILLUSTRATION 7-1 Deregulation of airlines and other industries has helped benefit consumers through lower prices and improved services. Are passenger fares on commercial airlines regulated?

PROMOTING FAIR COMPETITION One way to promote competition is to limit the number of monopolies created and controlled by government. Monopoly conditions can also arise when businesses compete too harshly or unfairly. A large, powerful business can lower its prices deliberately to drive out competitors, thereby discouraging competition. Thus, the federal government supports business practices that encourage competition and discourage monopolies. To achieve this goal, government has passed important laws and created agencies to enforce the laws.

Sherman Act. The first major law promoting competition was the Sherman Antitrust Act of 1890. One of its primary purposes is to discourage monopolies by outlawing business agreements among competitors that might tend to promote monopolies. For example, agreements among competitors to set selling prices on goods are unlawful. If three sellers met and agreed to set the same selling price on the same product each sold, they would all be violating the Sherman Act.

166 167

Career Connection investigates exciting career opportunities related to each chapter's content.

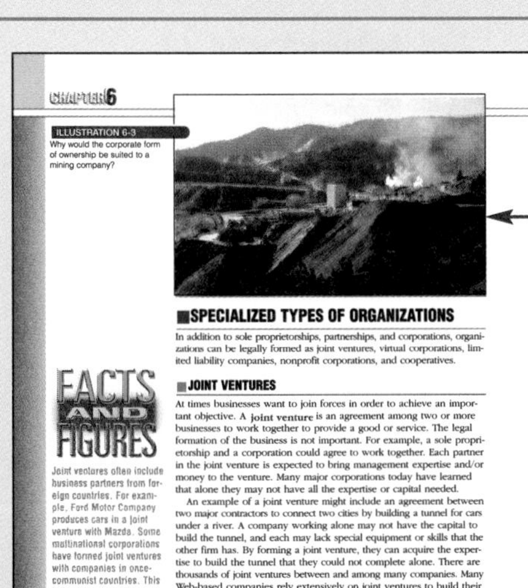

CHAPTER 6

CORPORATE FORMS OF BUSINESS OWNERSHIP

ILLUSTRATION 6-3
Why would the corporate form of ownership be suited to a mining company?

■ SPECIALIZED TYPES OF ORGANIZATIONS

In addition to sole proprietorships, partnerships, and corporations, organizations can be legally formed as joint ventures, virtual corporations, limited liability companies, nonprofit corporations, and cooperatives.

FACTS AND FIGURES

Joint ventures often include business partners from foreign countries. For example, Ford Motor Company produces cars in a joint venture with Mazda. Some multinational corporations have formed joint ventures with companies in once-communist countries. This helps the corporations expand into new markets. At the same time, the joint ventures serve as a way to help companies in the previously communist nations to learn about doing business in a free market economy.

■ JOINT VENTURES

At times businesses want to join forces in order to achieve an important objective. A **joint venture** is an agreement among two or more businesses to work together to provide a good or service. The legal formation of the business is not important. For example, a sole proprietorship and a corporation could agree to work together. Each partner in the joint venture is expected to bring management expertise and/or money to the venture. Many major corporations today have learned that alone they may not have all the expertise or capital needed.

An example of a joint venture might include an agreement between two major contractors to connect two cities by building a tunnel for cars under a river. A company working alone may not have the capital to build the tunnel, and each may lack special equipment or skills that the other firm has. By forming a joint venture, they can acquire the expertise to build the tunnel that they could not complete alone. There are thousands of joint ventures between and among many companies. Many Web-based companies rely extensively on joint ventures to build their businesses.

Because organizations must adapt quickly to compete effectively, a more fluid form of the joint venture, the virtual corporation, is evolving in the world of business. The **virtual corporation** is a network of companies that form alliances among themselves as needed to take advantage of fast-changing market conditions. Puma, the athletic shoe company, for example, is a virtual corporation. Puma markets its shoes in Germany. A small network of Asian companies purchases the materials to make the shoes. Other companies in China, Taiwan, Indonesia, and Korea manufacture the shoes. Then separate companies on all continents sell the shoes. In all, 80 companies worldwide participate in making and selling Puma shoes.

Virtual corporations tend to be more temporary relationships than are joint ventures. Several companies within the network may team up to take advantage of a market opportunity. These same companies may also work with a different combination of partners within the network, depending on the expertise needed to take advantage of a particular market opportunity at that time.

An example of a virtual corporation might include the following situation. Company A wishes to rush to market a new sophisticated computer but needs special parts that it does not produce. Company A learns that Company B produces one part and Company C produces the other needed part. Unfortunately, none of the three companies has customers who would likely have an interest in the new computer. After searching, the firms find that Company D sells computers to customers with special needs. Ultimately, all three companies agree to join with Company A to market the new computer. This virtual corporation situation, which is illustrated in Figure 6-8, makes it possible for all four companies to benefit when no one company could have made and marketed the new computer quickly on its own. Many companies involved in selling the goods of other firms, especially Web-based firms, are virtual corporations.

CYBER COMMUNICATION

Business memos are informal messages sent to persons within an organization. Sending a memo is a quick, easy way to communicate with a colleague or manager within your own department, in another department, or in another company office. The memo is a streamlined, efficient way to send a message to an internal audience.

In many businesses today, e-mail has taken over formal memo writing. E-mail memos are composed, transmitted, and usually read on a computer screen. They can be sent to more than one receiver; they take less time to format and key than letters; and they are less complex and time-consuming than meetings or conference calls.

Before you can organize an effective e-mail message, you must first plan your message. This requires asking yourself four questions: (1) What do I hope to accomplish in sending this message? (2) What do I want the receiver to do or to understand? (3) What does the receiver need to know about the main idea in order to respond to or understand the message? (4) What do I want the receiver to gain from the message?

ACTIVITY Assume that one of your classmates was out sick today. You have volunteered to send the classmate a brief memo describing what happened during the class session. Think about what you want to communicate in your message. Then write your answers to the four questions listed above.

■ LIMITED LIABILITY COMPANIES

Small, growing partnerships are especially attracted to the limited liability company (LLC) form of corporation, which was once called an "S-corporation." The **limited liability company (LLC)** is a special type of corporation that is taxed as if it were a sole proprietorship or

152 153

Cyber Communication explores the pros and cons of e-mail in today's business world. An activity is provided so you can become better acquainted with this critical form of communication.

A variety of **illustrations** (including photographs and art) will enhance your understanding of the text and reinforce important concepts. A discussion question accompanies each photo.

Full-page features on **Business Innovation, Global Perspectives, Ethical Issues,** and **Management Close-Up** will extend your learning by acquainting you with real-world business people, companies, and issues.

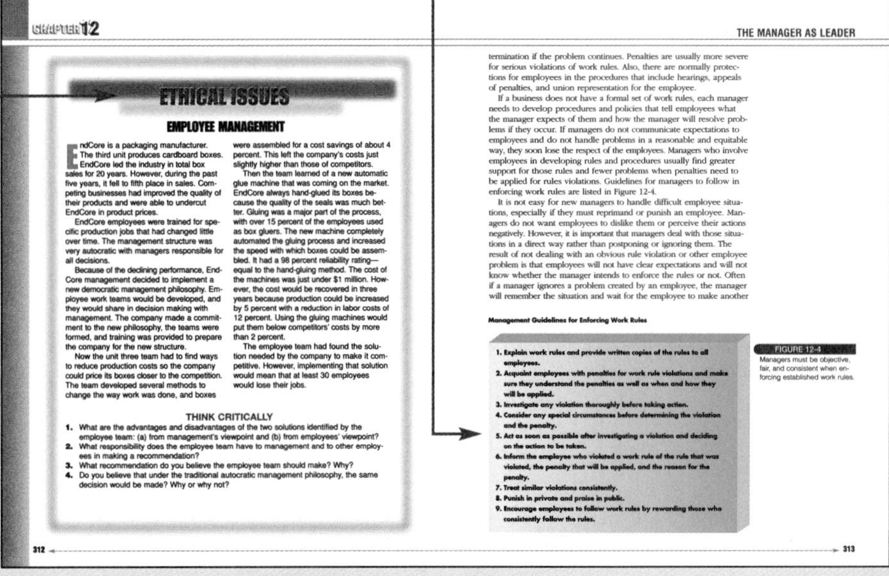

CHAPTER 12

THE MANAGER AS LEADER

ETHICAL ISSUES

EMPLOYEE MANAGEMENT

EndCore is a packaging manufacturer. The third unit produces cardboard boxes. EndCore led the industry in total box sales for 20 years. However, during the past five years, it fell to fifth place in sales. Competing businesses had improved the quality of their products and were able to undercut EndCore in product prices.

EndCore employees were trained for specific production jobs that had changed little over time. The management structure was very autocratic with managers responsible for all decisions.

Because of the declining performance, EndCore management decided to implement a new democratic management philosophy. Employee work teams would be developed, and they would share in decision making with management. The company made a commitment to the new philosophy, the teams were formed, and training was provided to prepare the company for the new structure.

Now the unit three team had to find ways to reduce production costs so the company could price its boxes closer to the competition. The team developed several methods to change the way work was done, and boxes were assembled for a cost savings of about 4 percent. This left the company's costs just slightly higher than those of competitors.

Then the team learned of a new automatic glue machine that was coming on the market. EndCore always hand-glued its boxes because the quality of the seals was much better. Gluing was a major part of the process, with over 15 percent of the employees used as box gluers. The new machine completely automated the gluing process and increased the speed with which boxes could be assembled. It had a 98 percent reliability rating—equal to the hand-gluing method. The cost of the machines was just under $1 million. However, the cost would be recovered in three years because production could be increased by 5 percent with a reduction in labor costs of 12 percent. Using the gluing machines would put them below competitors' costs by more than 2 percent.

The employee team had found the solution needed by the company to make it competitive. However, implementing that solution would mean that at least 30 employees would lose their jobs.

THINK CRITICALLY

1. What are the advantages and disadvantages of the two solutions identified by the employee team: (a) from management's viewpoint and (b) from employees' viewpoint?
2. What responsibility does the employee team have to management and to other employees in making a recommendation?
3. What recommendation do you believe the employee team should make? Why?
4. Do you believe that under the traditional autocratic management philosophy, the same decision would be made? Why or why not?

termination if the problem continues. Penalties are usually more severe for serious violations of work rules. Also, there are normally protections for employees in the procedures that include hearings, appeals of penalties, and union representation for the employee.

If a business does not have a formal set of work rules, each manager needs to develop procedures and policies that tell employees what the manager expects of them and how the manager will resolve problems if they occur. If managers do not communicate expectations to employees and do not handle problems in a reasonable and equitable way, they soon lose the respect of the employees. Managers who involve employees in developing rules and procedures usually find greater support for those rules and fewer problems when penalties need to be applied for rules violations. Guidelines for managers to follow in enforcing work rules are listed in Figure 12-4.

It is not easy for new managers to handle difficult employee situations, especially if they must reprimand or punish an employee. Managers do not want employees to dislike them or perceive their actions negatively. However, it is important that managers deal with those situations in a direct way rather than postponing or ignoring them. The result of not dealing with an obvious rule violation or other employee problem is that employees will not have clear expectations and will not know whether the manager intends to enforce the rules or not. Often if a manager ignores a problem created by an employee, the manager will remember the situation and wait for the employee to make another

Management Guidelines for Enforcing Work Rules

1. Explain work rules and provide written copies of the rules to all employees.
2. Acquaint employees with penalties for work rule violations and make sure they understand the penalties as well as when and how they will be applied.
3. Investigate any violation thoroughly before taking action.
4. Consider any special circumstances before determining the violation and the penalty.
5. Act as soon as possible after investigating a violation and deciding on the action to be taken.
6. Inform the employee who violated a work rule of the rule that was violated, the penalty that will be applied, and the reason for the penalty.
7. Treat similar violations consistently.
8. Punish in private and praise in public.
9. Encourage employees to follow work rules by rewarding those who consistently follow the rules.

FIGURE 12-4
Managers must be objective, fair, and consistent when enforcing established work rules.

312 313

CHAPTER 4 REVIEW

REVIEW

INTERNATIONAL ENVIRONMENT OF BUSINESS

CHAPTER CONCEPTS

- International trade and investment have grown tremendously over the past fifty years, affecting businesses and individuals all over the world. International business occurs in various forms, such as exporting and importing, licensing, joint ventures, wholly owned subsidiaries, and strategic alliances. Multinational firms with operations in multiple countries have emerged.
- International business has some unique challenges, including the need to work within the rules set by more than one government, currency exchange rates, and cultural differences.
- Firms go into international business because of the potential for larger profits and limited opportunities in the home market. Removal of barriers to trade and investment, creation of trading blocs, and technological advances in communication and transportation have created a positive environment for conducting international business.
- Two theories explain international trade and investments. The theory of comparative advantage explains why a particular country specializes in producing a particular product or service. The product life cycle theory explains how a product's life stage encourages international business.
- Data on trade and investment are carefully collected and used to set business and economic policies. In particular, the balance of trade between countries is evidence of a nation's financial strength or weakness.
- Numerous opportunities exist for careers in international business. Colleges and universities offer programs for further study in this field. A multinational firm may fill its positions with managers from the home, host, or even third countries. It is generally very expensive to send managers overseas. Managers with working spouses are often reluctant to go abroad for long periods of time.

BUILD VOCABULARY POWER

Define the following terms and concepts.

1. international business
2. Pacific Rim
3. exporting
4. importing
5. international licensing
6. joint venture
7. wholly-owned subsidiary
8. strategic alliances
9. multinational firms
10. home country
11. host country
12. parent firm
13. subsidiary
14. tariff
15. dumping
16. quota
17. non-tariff barrier
18. embargo
19. sanctions
20. exchange rate
21. culture
22. low-context culture
23. high-context culture
24. World Trade Organization (WTO)
25. euro
26. trading bloc
27. European Union (EU)
28. North American Free Trade Agreement (NAFTA)
29. International Monetary Fund (IMF)
30. World Bank
31. comparative advantage theory
32. product life cycle theory
33. balance of payments
34. current account
35. capital account

REVIEW FACTS

1. What are some of the unique challenges of international business?
2. Why is it easier for a firm to export instead of setting up a wholly-owned foreign subsidiary?
3. What policies can a government adopt to protect domestic businesses from foreign competition?
4. Why are non-tariff barriers harder to remove than tariffs and quotas?
5. How do changes in currency exchange rates affect international business?
6. How do people communicate in low-context and high-context cultures?
7. Give four reasons why a firm may go into international business.
8. What countries are members of NAFTA and the EU?
9. Explain the purposes of the WTO, IMF, and the World Bank.
10. Explain how comparative advantage encourages international trade.
11. How does the product life cycle theory explain international trade and investment?
12. How is the U.S. able to have a deficit in its current account year after year?
13. What qualities do managers need to work in a foreign country?

DISCUSS IDEAS

1. Explain the reasons for the growing importance of international business.
2. The top five countries in which American firms have investments are the United Kingdom, Canada, Netherlands, Germany, and Bermuda. What explains this choice of countries?
3. If a firm sets up a Web page and sells products through the Internet to anyone in the world, is the firm engaged in international business?
4. Why might a company dump its products abroad?
5. Do you believe that some types of businesses in the U.S. should not be owned by foreign firms? Why or why not?
6. If the value of the Canadian dollar continues to rise in relation to the American dollar, what can a Canadian exporter do to keep the price of the goods it sells in the U.S. market competitive?

104 105

Chapter Review will give you the opportunity to tie your learning together. *Chapter Concepts* provides a bulleted summary of the chapter for quick review. *Build Vocabulary Power* will help you acquire a working vocabulary of common business terms. *Review Facts* and *Discuss Ideas* will test your recall of the chapter's main points. *Analyze Information* and *Solve Business Problems* will challenge you to dig deeper into business issues. As you work through the different problems, look for the Internet symbol, which will direct you to the World Wide Web.

CHAPTER 9

REVIEW

E-COMMERCE

ANALYZE INFORMATION

1. A recent report showed the following past and projected growth in business-to-business Internet sales over a 5-year period:

Year	*Total Sales*
1998	$ 45 billion
1999	110 billion
2000	252 billion
2001	499 billion
2002	843 billion

Using those figures, calculate the following amounts:
   a. the amount of increase in sales for each year
   b. the percentage of increase in sales for each year
   c. the total increase in sales for the 5-year period
   d. the total percentage of increase in sales for the 5-year period

Using a computer graphing or spreadsheet program, prepare a bar graph illustrating the year-by-year growth in sales.

2. The use of the Internet varies, based on individuals' ethnic and racial background. The following chart illustrates the number of people in the U.S. based on major ethnic/racial classification and the percentage of that population that use the Internet.

Racial/Ethnic Classification	*U.S. Adult Population (in millions)*	*Percentage of Population Using the Internet*
African-Americans	4.9	28%
Hispanic	3.5	28%
All U.S. ethnic minorities	14.4	31%
Caucasian/White	52.8	37%

   a. Calculate the number of Internet users for each racial/ethnic classification listed. Then determine the total of the U.S. adult population, the total number of Internet users in the U.S. adult population, and the average percentage of the total population using the Internet.
   b. What are some possible reasons why the usage rate of the Internet varies, based on a person's racial/ethnic classification?

INTERNET

3. Go online and find at least three examples of businesses for each stage of e-commerce development: information, interaction, integration. If possible, print a copy of each company's home page. Using that home page, describe why the business fits the stage in which you classified it.

INTERNET

4. Go online and locate examples of advertisements that fit each of the types and sizes listed in Figure 9-5. Prepare an illustration of the advertisements you located by copying, saving, or printing the images or by drawing the ads on a sheet of paper. If you find other commonly used types and sizes of ads, add them to your illustration. Your teacher may ask you and other class members to develop a visual display of all of the illustrations or to make an oral presentation of your illustration.

INTERNET

5. Form a team with other class members. As a team, develop a list of at least five factors that everyone agrees makes an effective e-commerce business. Then, using the Internet and your list of factors, find several e-commerce businesses and rate them using the list of factors. You may want to have each student rate each business and then combine your ratings into a total team rating. Using your results, identify the best and worst e-commerce business. Share your results in a discussion with other teams in your class. Compare the factors your team identified with those of other teams and compare each team's choice of best and worst e-commerce businesses.

SOLVE BUSINESS PROBLEMS

CASE 9-1

Jillian and Dontae were sitting in front of the computer, listening to music they had downloaded and looking at a Web site that identified the top e-tailers for the year.

Jillian: *I really like the idea of shopping on the Web. It seems like you get many more choices, probably lower prices, and it's so convenient.*

Dontae: *I'm not sure I'm convinced yet. Look at the names of some of the businesses on the list. I've never heard of many of them. Do you believe they're all legitimate?*

Jillian: *Well, some of our favorite stores are on the list, so you could start with buying from them.*

Dontae: *But why not just go to the mall and buy from the stores? I'd get the products faster and not have to pay shipping charges. Besides, I don't want to enter my credit card number online, even if it says it's safe.*

Jillian: *But you hand your credit card to a person in every store when you make a purchase. They process it through a telephone line to get the amount approved. Isn't that the same thing?*

Think Critically:

1. Many people do not trust businesses that sell products online, especially if they are not familiar with the company's name. Yet they will walk into a new business in their city and shop without a great deal of concern. What causes the difference in people's view of online businesses compared to traditional businesses?
2. Do you agree with Dontae that it is easier to shop in an actual store in a mall than shop from the same business online? Why or why not?

238 239

CHAPTER 23

REVIEW

PRICING AND PROMOTION

Project: My Business, Inc. will give you the chance to plan your own business. You will gather and analyze data and make decisions as you set up a juice bar.

2. What other products might Kuen carry in addition to grocery items to attract customers from the supermarkets?
3. How should Kuen decide on the prices to charge for the products he carries in his new business?
4. What effect do you think the planned growth in numbers of customers and possible new businesses will have on the decisions Kuen makes about his convenience store?

CASE 23-2

Peter and Torrie were discussing how companies use advertising. Their conversation follows:

Peter: *Companies spend too much money on advertising. If they would spend less, the prices of products would be a lot lower. I heard that companies that advertise on the Super Bowl program spend more than $1 million for one advertisement.*

Torrie: *I agree. It seems that companies advertise to get people to buy products they don't want. I know I've bought some things just because of the ad and regretted it later. I think companies with good products shouldn't have to advertise. People will find out about them from other people who try the products and like them.*

Peter: *The worst thing about advertising is that businesses can say anything they want to about products, even if the statements are untrue. They often criticize their competitors, making you think there's something wrong with the other product. After watching or listening to an ad, you're more confused than ever about what to buy.*

Think Critically:

1. Do you believe product prices would decrease if companies did not advertise? Explain.
2. Do good products need to be advertised? Why or why not?
3. What types of controls are there on what a business can say in its advertising? What can consumers do if they believe they have been misled by advertising?
4. Do you believe advertising results in more confusion than help for consumers? Justify your answer.

PROJECT: MY BUSINESS, INC.

One of the most difficult decisions for a new businessperson is to set prices on products that will provide a reasonable net profit. In addition, a new business needs to carefully plan promotion to introduce people to the business and its products and to encourage customers to visit the new business and try the products. The following activities will help you plan successful pricing and promotion strategies for your juice business.

DATA COLLECTION

INTERNET

1. Many Internet sites offer information on start-up expenses for small businesses in general and the type of juice business you are starting specifically. Locate sources of that information and develop a list of the common types of expenses and the range of costs you might expect to begin your business.
2. Interview one or two small business owners in your community. Ask them to explain the types of promotion they use, what assistance they get to help them with promotional planning, and how they estimate the amount of money they can spend on promotional activities.
3. Collect samples of advertising and promotion that small businesses in your area are using. Analyze their effectiveness in communicating with prospective customers.
4. Check with several media that offer advertising in your community (newspapers, television, radio, etc.). Obtain a price list that indicates the costs of advertising in each medium, based on the size, type, and frequency of the advertising.

ANALYSIS

1. Assume that, in an average month, your sales will include 700 small drinks, 800 large drinks, 900 supplement additions to the drinks (beyond any free supplements), and 2,000 high-energy snack bars. First, determine the price you will charge for each product, being realistic about what you believe customers are willing to pay. Then estimate your monthly expenses for each of the following items: cost of goods sold, inventory spoilage, taxes and fees, equipment expense, interest expense, supplies, repairs and maintenance, salaries, depreciation expense, insurance, advertising, and other expenses. Have several people review your estimates to determine if they are realistic. Then calculate your estimated monthly profit or loss.
2. Is your estimated monthly net profit adequate? If not, consider what changes you could make to improve it. (Do not make any price changes at this time.) Identify which of the possible changes are most likely to be successful and which are least likely to be implemented.
3. Being as creative as possible, list several ways of promoting your new business that would be (a) informative, (b) unique, and (c) affordable. Consider methods in addition to advertising.
4. Develop a three-month promotional plan for your new business. Include methods, media to be used, time schedule, budget, and samples of the promotions.

622 623

REVIEWERS

Krista Anthony
Indianapolis, IN

Bruce J. (Ike) Bergeron
Brattleboro, VT

Cynthia Bertrand
Lake Charles, LA

Cinda M. Blythe
Indianola, IA

Margaret L. Chester
Biloxi, MS

Louis M. DiCesare
Rochester, NY

R. Edward Fielding
Lynchburg, VA

Mrs. Mary A. Gonzalez
Weslaco, TX

Joe Hardesty
Cincinnati, OH

Nancy Jappinen
Oconomowoc, WI

Kelvin M. Meeks
Memphis, TN

Mary Nemesh
Gambrills, MD

John S. Salerno
Newington, CT

Dr. Terry L. Wilson
San Diego, CA

TO THE STUDENT

Welcome to the dynamic and changing world of business and your opportunity to learn more about it! For years, the United States was a country admired for creating valuable new products that provided jobs and an increased standard of living for its people. Later, however, other countries not only copied our business practices but became competitive rivals. Today, global competition is the driving force for survival in world markets.

Change requires that companies adapt to endure. In recent years, global competition has required firms to modify their organizational structures, to learn different ways to satisfy customer needs, and to invent new ways to compete nationally and internationally.

- Would you like to explore the possibility of a career in business?
- Do you plan to enter business as a beginning employee?
- Do you hope to eventually have an opportunity to manage a business for others?
- Ultimately, would you like to own and operate your own business?

This book will provide you with a basic understanding of business principles and management, which is needed by everyone who plans a career in business. Fundamentals related to economic, legal, and social topics are presented, along with information on organizing businesses, marketing products and services, financing operations, managing and developing employees, and making difficult business decisions in a dynamic, competitive atmosphere.

In addition, this text will help you understand various elements of the business world that are particularly important today. These include organizational change, diversity in the workforce, ethics, global competition, the link between business and society, and the critical role played by technology (including the Internet and e-commerce).

To help you learn about business principles and management, this text has a number of special features.

Objectives begins each unit and offers an overview of the information you'll study. Think of the Objectives as goals to achieve as you work through the chapter.

Reality Check presents a true-to-life story that's tailored to the chapter's contents. By reading the story, you'll have a better understanding of the chapter's main topics.

Cyber Communication explores the pros and cons of e-mail in today's business world. An activity is provided so you can become better acquainted with this critical form of communication.

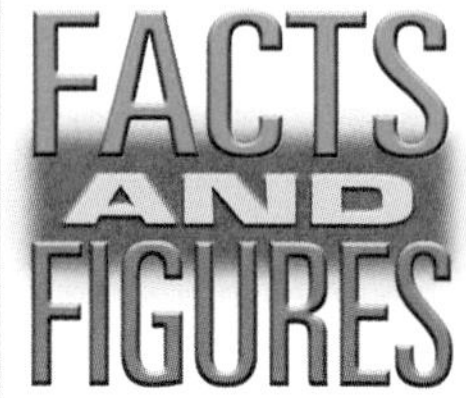

Facts and Figures will introduce you to interesting statistics and information about business today. For example, did you know that one trip to the supermarket can expose you to more than 10,000 marketing messages?

Full-page features on **Business Innovation, Global Perspectives, Ethical Issues,** and **Management Close-Up** will extend your learning by acquainting you with real-life business people, companies, and issues. Critical thinking questions will allow you to research these topics using the Internet.

Career Connection investigates exciting career opportunities related to each chapter's content. For example, if you're interested in becoming a Webmaster, what kind of background will you need?

Chapter Review will give you the opportunity to tie your learning together. *Chapter Concepts* provides a bulleted summary of the chapter's concepts for quick review. *Build Vocabulary Power* will help you acquire a working vocabulary of common business terms. *Review Facts* and *Discuss Ideas* will test your recall of the chapter's main points. *Analyze Information* and *Solve Business Problems* will challenge you to dig deeper into business issues. As you work through the different problems, look for the Internet symbol, which will direct you to the World Wide Web.

PROJECT: MY BUSINESS, INC.

Project: My Business, Inc. will give you the chance to plan your own business, by gathering and analyzing data and making decisions as you set up a juice bar.

Business Principles and Management will give you the information you need to succeed in the world of business. Have a great trip!

CONTENTS

UNIT 7 HUMAN RESOURCES MANAGEMENT 624

UNIT ONE

BUSINESS and its ENVIRONMENT

CHAPTERS

1. Characteristics of Business
2. Social and Ethical Environment of Business
3. Economic Environment of Business
4. International Environment of Business

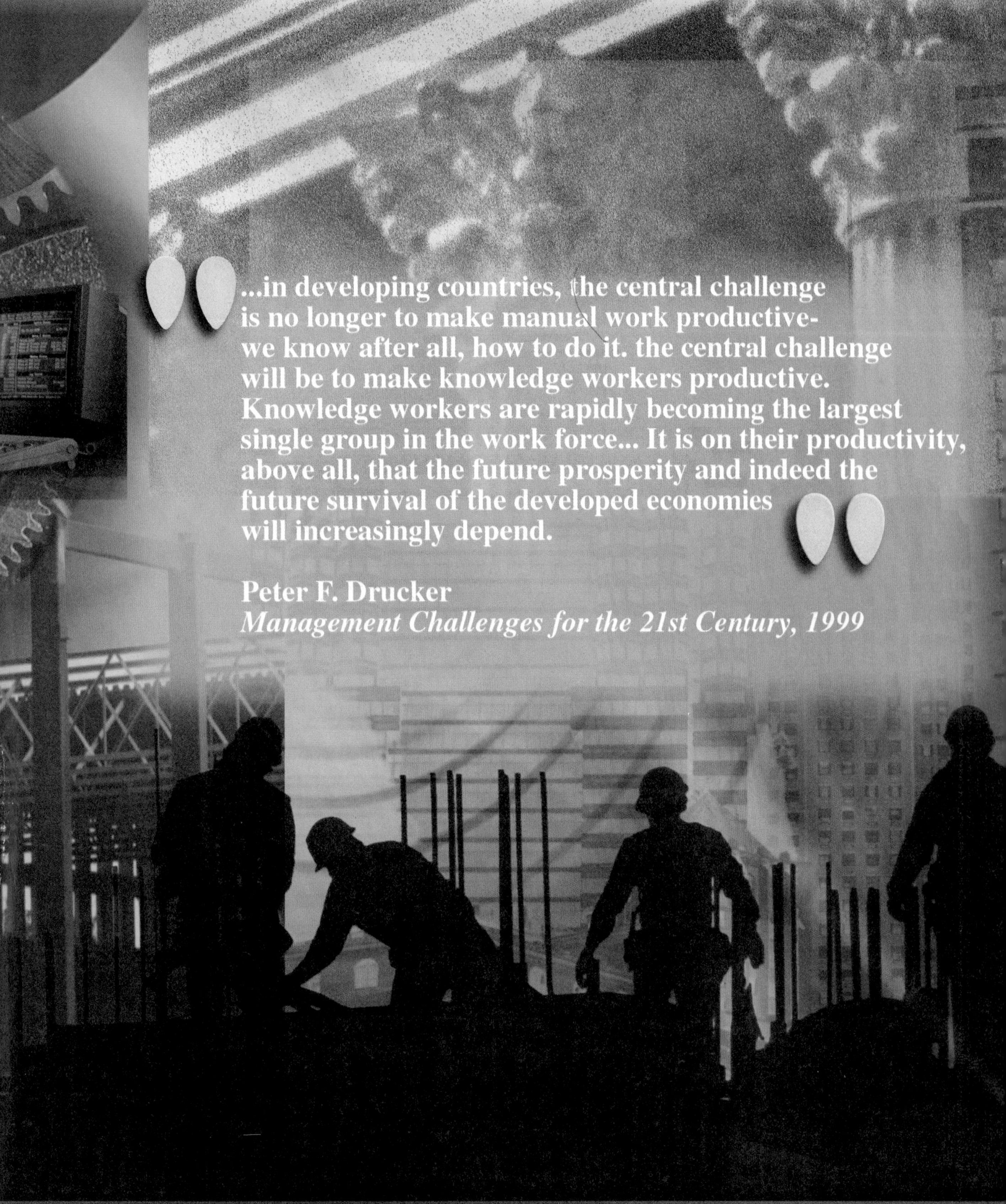
...in developing countries, the central challenge is no longer to make manual work productive- we know after all, how to do it. the central challenge will be to make knowledge workers productive. Knowledge workers are rapidly becoming the largest single group in the work force... It is on their productivity, above all, that the future prosperity and indeed the future survival of the developed economies will increasingly depend.
Peter F. Drucker
Management Challenges for the 21st Century, 1999

CHARACTERISTICS OF BUSINESS

OBJECTIVES

1-1 Explain the general types and changing nature of businesses.

1-2 Describe how global competition has affected the way American businesses operate.

1-3 Show how businesses have grown and improved the economic well-being of people.

1-4 Discuss the role and nature of entrepreneurship and the opportunities, problems, and obligations of small businesses.

1-5 Summarize the value of plans that allow employees to function like entrepreneurs inside businesses.

1-6 Explain the importance of studying business principles and management.

INCOME VS. OUTGO: A DELICATE BALANCE

Sara Donahue waited at the roadside curb for the school bus with her son, Paul. He was growing so fast. It seemed she had to buy something new for him every week—clothes, shoes, school supplies, baseballs, and now a bicycle. Her young daughter, Marta, has similar demands. Last week it was a teddy bear; this week, her first visit to the dentist; and next week, a tricycle.

"When will all these expenses stop?" she wondered.

"What did you say, Mom?" asked Paul.

"I'm just thinking out loud, Paul. Here comes your bus. Don't forget your Little League game later this afternoon."

Paul shrugged. "I won't. And I hope you won't forget that new printer for my computer that's on sale."

Sara had forgotten, but she could always rely on Paul and Marta to remind her of things to buy. Of course, her husband, Scott, was good at sending out "don't forget" signals as well. Fortunately, with his good job at the manufacturing plant and her half-time computer programming job, the family's income was adequate to meet most expenses if they budgeted carefully.

While waving goodbye to Paul as the bus pulled away, she recalled reminding Scott to schedule his vacation time for late June when the family could drive to the mountains and camp out under the stars. "That should keep costs down," she mused, "but I'd better start putting money aside for a new tent, sleeping bags, and gas for the long trip. Maybe the money we make on Saturday's garage sale will pay for some of it."

American businesses work for Sara Donahue and her family. As the family's financial manager, she pays the bills. Sara and Scott, along with Paul and Marta, are consumers. They buy goods such as clothes, shoes, tricycles, and tents. Likewise, they buy services such as trips to the dentist and to movies. Businesses work very hard to provide the goods and services needed by the Donahue family and everyone else.

The story of American business is a fascinating one. Products found in most homes come from countless producers. The flowering plant in the Donahues' front window could have been purchased from a greenhouse operated by a single person. The light bulbs the Donahue family uses could have been made by a business with 100,000 employees, their carpet from a business with 500 employees, and the cake for Marta's birthday from a bakery with only 10 workers. These and scores of other items found in homes, offices, stores, and factories are produced by many kinds of businesses.

Over 22 million businesses currently exist in the United States. They vary in size from one employee to nearly 400,000 employees and in assets from a few dollars to billions of dollars. Some of these businesses have only a few customers, while others have millions of customers located throughout the world.

NATURE OF BUSINESS

An organization that produces or distributes a good or service for profit is called a **business.** *Profit* is the difference between earned income and costs. Every business engages in at least three major activities. The first activity, **production,** involves making a product or providing a

ILLUSTRATION 1-1

Customers are the reason businesses exist. Can a business survive without customers? Does a government have customers?

service. **Manufacturing firms** produce goods, whereas **service firms** provide assistance to satisfy specialized needs through skilled workers, such as doctors, travel agents, and taxi drivers. Today the number of service firms far exceeds the number of manufacturing firms. For this reason, it is sometimes said that we live in a service society.

The second activity that businesses are involved in is marketing. *Marketing* deals with how goods or services are exchanged between producers and consumers. The third activity, **finance,** deals with all money matters related to running a business. Whether a business has one worker or thousands of workers, it is involved with production, marketing, and finance.

The price that Sara Donahue pays for Paul's printer will be based in large part upon supply and demand for the printer. *Supply* of a product refers to the number of similar products that will be offered for sale at a particular time and at a particular price. *Demand,* on the other hand, refers to the number of similar products that will be bought at a given time at a given price.

This book will focus on the various activities involved in managing a business successfully. But before examining those activities in detail, let's take a look at the general nature of business.

TYPES OF BUSINESSES

Generally, there are two major kinds of businesses—industrial and commercial. **Industrial businesses** produce goods used by other businesses or organizations to make things. Companies that mine ore for making metal products, such as printers and tricycles, are industrial businesses. So are companies that construct buildings for other businesses. Highly industrialized nations that produce thousands of products, such as the United States, Japan, and Germany, can be distinguished from **third world nations,** which have few manufacturing firms and a population that is generally poor.

Unlike industrial businesses, **commercial businesses** are engaged in marketing (wholesalers and retailers), in finance (banks and investment companies), and in furnishing services (medical offices, athletic centers, and motels). **Services** are intangible products that use mostly labor to satisfy consumer needs. For example, lawn mowing is a service.

Figure 1-1 shows the number of people employed in selected types of production and service industries. **Industry** is a word often used to refer to all businesses within a category. For example, the publishing industry includes any business that deals with producing and selling books, magazines, newspapers, and other printed documents prepared by authors. Even a government can be considered an industry, because it produces services such as fire and police protection. This industry would include all services provided by local, state, and federal governments.

CHANGING NATURE OF BUSINESS

An important characteristic of business is that it is dynamic, or constantly changing. Most businesses react quickly to the changing nature

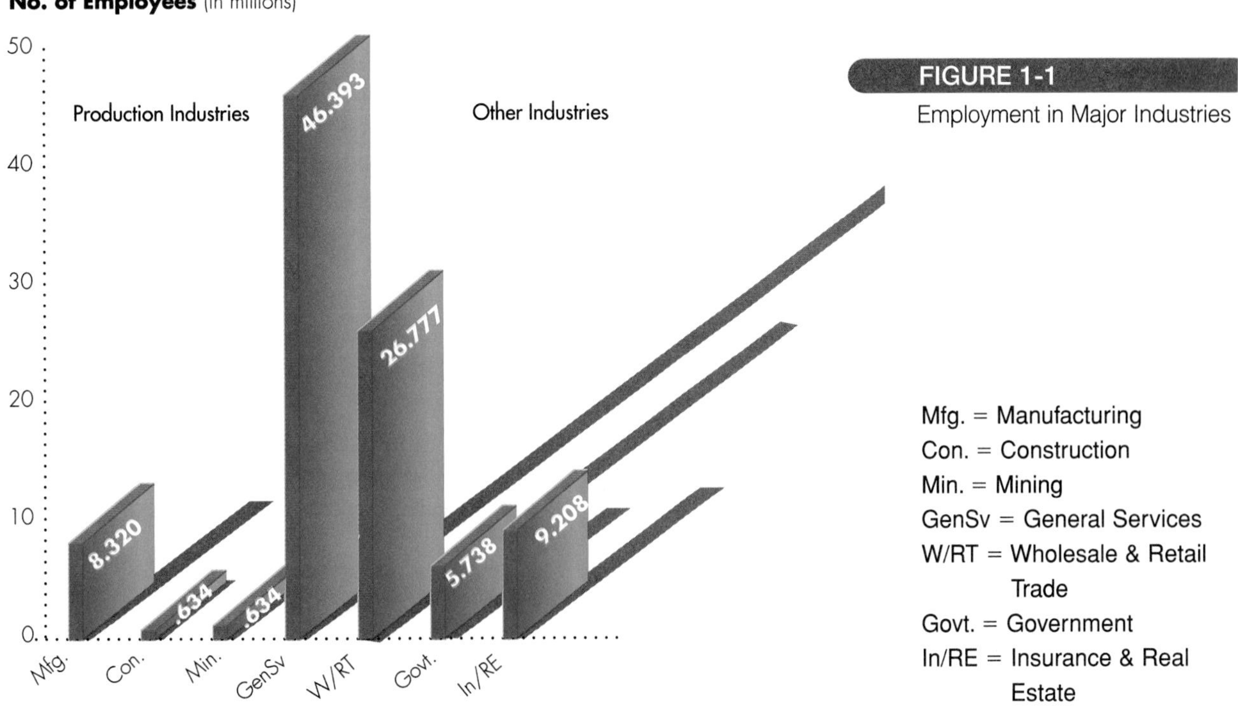

FIGURE 1-1
Employment in Major Industries

Source: *Statistical Abstract of the United States, 1998*

ILLUSTRATION 1-2

Jets that criss-cross countries and oceans can carry people and goods to their destinations in a matter of hours. How have advances in transportation changed the nature of business?

of society. For instance, travel by horse was the principal means of transportation until the invention of steam power. Then, with the emergence of the first cross-country railroad in 1869, goods and services traveled mainly by rail for about 50 years. When the gasoline engine arrived, travel patterns shifted from train to car, bus, and truck. Shortly thereafter, airplanes gliding along at 100 miles an hour were soon replaced by jets criss-crossing countries and oceans, carrying people and goods to their destinations in a matter of hours.

Innovations affect the kinds of products and services offered for sale. For example, clothing used to be made from only natural fibers, such as cotton and wool. Then chemical researchers developed synthetic fibers, such as rayon, nylon, and polyester. Now consumers have more choices in clothing and other fabric products.

Innovations also affect business operations. For example, since Apple Computer built one of the first personal computers about thirty years ago, computers have increasingly influenced the way businesses do business. Computers help businesses produce products as well as keep track of billing, inventory, and customer information. Computers are now involved in most key business functions. Use of the Internet to conduct business has also had a significant impact on business operations large and small. You will learn how innovations affect business operations in many of the chapters in this book.

Figure 1-2 shows the growth in different categories of business in the U.S. since 1980. As you can see, service businesses are increasing in number faster than any other type of business in the U.S.

IMPACT OF GLOBAL COMPETITION ON BUSINESS

For hundreds of years, American businesses have led the way in producing new goods and services for sale around the world. Consumers worldwide eagerly purchased exciting new products that were invented

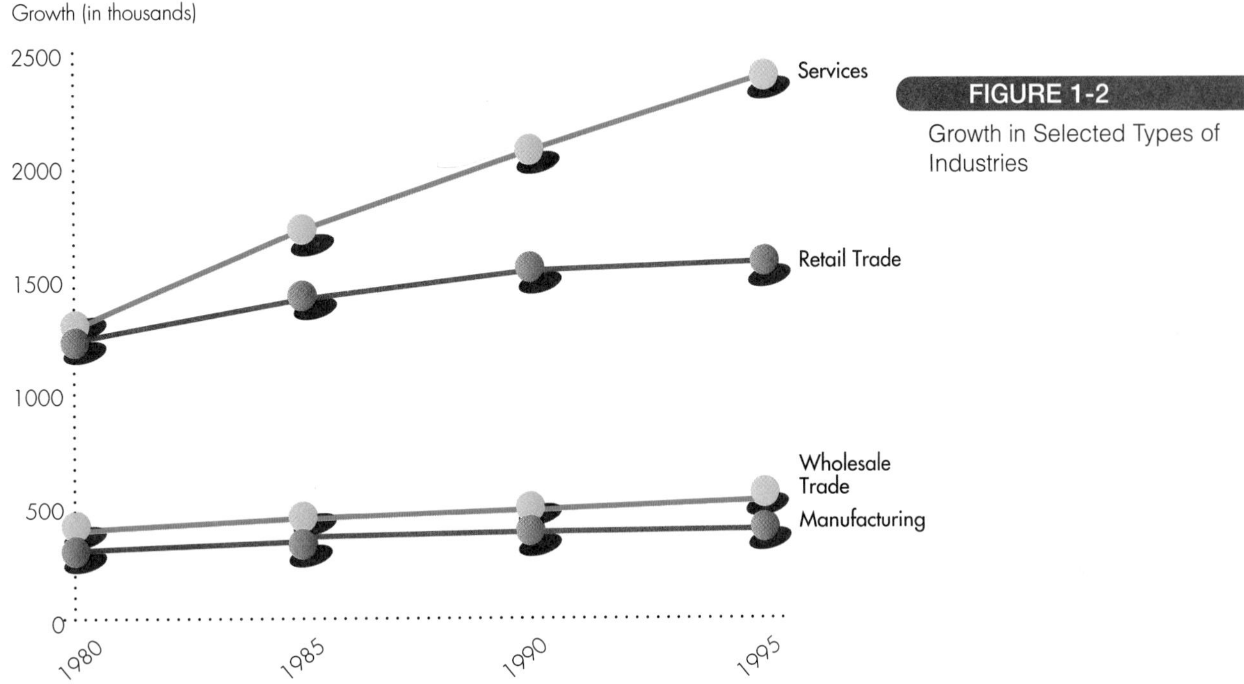

FIGURE 1-2

Growth in Selected Types of Industries

Source: *Statistical Abstract of the United States, 1998*

and made in the United States. Factories hummed with activity, workers from other countries arrived by the thousands to find jobs, and people spent their wages buying the goods that the firms produced. Many leaders from foreign countries also arrived to find out how American businesses were managed.

Over the last 30 years, however, other countries have become more industrialized and have learned how to invent and produce new products for consumers. Americans gradually began to purchase these foreign products. Foreign firms also learned how to make goods efficiently, so they could offer excellent products in greater varieties at lower prices. American business leaders soon realized it was time for change, time to rely on America's abundant human talent to meet the challenge of global competition. **Global competition** is the ability of profit-making organizations to compete with businesses in other countries. Let's look at what is happening to help America compete in a global economy.

FOCUSING ON THE RIGHT THINGS

Businesses often study themselves to determine whether they are doing the right things and doing the right things well. Two terms are used to describe these two points. First, **effectiveness** means making the right decisions about what products or services to offer customers and how to produce and deliver them. Second, **efficiency** means producing needed goods or services quickly and at low cost. Firms that provide products at the lowest cost while maintaining desired quality will succeed. Some firms are extremely efficient but very ineffective, while others are effective but inefficient. Good managers focus on both effectiveness and efficiency.

ACHIEVING EFFECTIVENESS

Making the right decisions requires both common sense and skill. Knowing what customers want is critical to business success and to achieving effectiveness. What kind of tent, for example, will best satisfy the needs of the Donahue family when they take their summer vacation in the mountains? In the past, customers bought whatever was available because there were few brands, colors, and styles from which to select. Today, the choices for most goods have increased because of competition among domestic and foreign firms. **Domestic goods** (products made by firms in the United States) must compete with **foreign goods** (products made by firms in other countries).

Unlike in the past, firms today focus more on gathering information from customers, studying their buying habits, testing new products with customers, and adding new features to existing products. New designs, different shapes and colors, readable instructions, and simplicity of product use are features customers like. Major corporations spend millions of dollars examining customers' preferences. Equally important is that successful firms also invest heavily in keeping customers satisfied after products are sold. Product guarantees and conversations with customers about the product help keep customers loyal.

Customers want not only products that best meet their needs, but also high-quality products. A major new emphasis of American producers is to make products of high quality. Japanese car makers are

ILLUSTRATION 1-3

American car producers have learned to equal or exceed foreign car makers in the quality of their products. Is quality an important factor when you buy a car or other expensive product?

excellent examples of how foreign producers captured a large portion of the market worldwide by providing customers with reliable and attractive cars. In the past, American car producers were not meeting the needs of many buyers. Too many cars had too many defects that required numerous trips to car dealers to correct. On the other hand, Japanese cars had fewer flaws.

American producers learned important lessons about quality from the Japanese. Today, American car producers are building products that equal or exceed Japanese and European standards. American car manufacturers and producers of many other products vigorously stress to their workers the importance of quality. The concept is called **total quality management (TQM),** which is a commitment to excellence that is accomplished by teamwork and continual improvement. Where TQM is practiced, managers and employees receive a great deal of training on the topic of quality from experts. The result is a return to what customers want—well-made products.

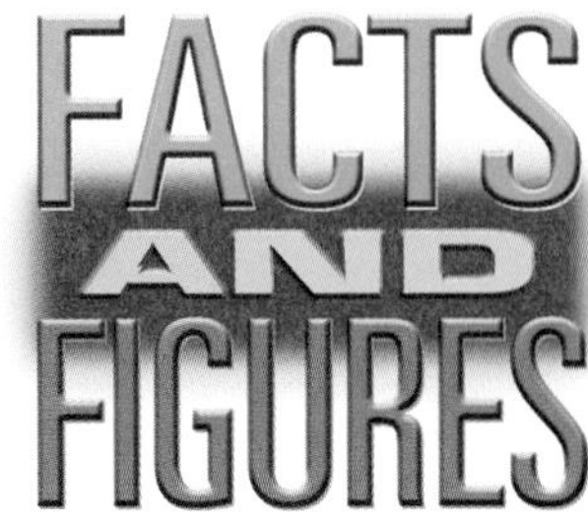

Competition based on quality has grown in importance worldwide. In the United States, the Malcolm Baldrige National Quality Award program is managed by an agency of the federal government. Each year, hundreds of firms apply for this distinctive national honor. Organizations that win an award usually notice an upturn in demand for their products. Quality awards are also offered in other countries. The Japanese offer the Deming Award, which is named after an American who was an expert on quality.

ACHIEVING EFFICIENCY

Not only must firms do the right things, such as offering high-quality products, but they must also produce their products efficiently. Efficiency is measured by **output**—the quantity produced within a given time. **Productivity,** on the other hand, refers to producing the largest quantity in the least amount of time by using efficient methods and modern equipment. Workers are more productive when they are well equipped, well trained, and well managed. Employee productivity has grown over the years in manufacturing firms, as shown in Figure 1-3, but the growth has not been as rapid as in a few other industrialized nations.

Productivity Per Worker in Selected Industrialized Nations

COUNTRY	1980	1985	1990	1996
United States	71.9	87.7	97.7	120.2
France	70.5	83.8	99.1	117.0
Germany	77.3	88.9	99.0	117.0
Japan	63.9	77.3	95.4	114.3
Canada	78.5	94.1	95.8	108.6
England	54.4	71.2	89.3	106.1

Source: *Statistical Abstract of the United States, 1998*

FIGURE 1-3

Output-per-Hour Index for Manufacturing Employees (Index: 1992 = 100)

Efficiency—including improved productivity—can be achieved in three ways:

1. Specialization of effort
2. Better technology and innovation
3. Reorganization.

SPECIALIZATION In any business with more than a few employees, work can be performed more efficiently by having workers become specialists. In a large automobile repair shop, for example, not all workers are general mechanics. Rather, some workers specialize in body repair work while others specialize in repairing transmissions or engines. When workers specialize, they become expert at their assigned tasks. As a result, specialization improves quality while increasing the amount produced. Because specialization improves efficiency, it is no wonder that businesses hire or train employees for many specialized jobs.

Effectiveness can also be improved through **mass production,** the use of up-to-date equipment and assembly line methods to produce large quantities of identical goods. Through mass production, the cost of goods manufactured decreases because it is possible to produce more items in less time. Today, electronically driven equipment, including computers and robots, makes it possible to mass-produce large numbers of items with fewer workers.

TECHNOLOGY AND INNOVATION Effectiveness can also be improved through advanced technology. Technology includes equipment, manufacturing processes, and materials from which products are made. Because of new discoveries and inventions, better-quality goods and services are built at a faster pace and often at a lower cost. Improved materials, for example, may weigh less, last longer, and permit faster product assembly. Examples of new technology are found in everyday items such as cars, clothing, computers, and electronic appliances. Advanced technology helps companies stay ahead of competitors. And because technology has a significant impact on productivity, businesses spend billions of dollars annually on inventing, buying, and using new technology.

Innovation refers to the development of new ideas, products, and processes that contribute to satisfying customers. But creating new products and processes is just the first step. To gain the benefits of innovation, firms must transform their creativity into high-quality products and services or cost-saving benefits.

REORGANIZATION The third and most difficult way to obtain increased efficiency is through reorganizing the way work gets done. From the late 1970s through the early 1990s, companies experienced slow growth, for reasons explained in a later chapter. However, one key reason for the slow growth arose from the competition of other industrialized nations. The typical reaction to slow growth caused by global competition was to cut back production costs by laying off workers. A business would **downsize** by cutting back on the goods and services provided and the number of employees needed to produce them. By laying off workers, dropping unprofitable products or selling them to other firms, or increasing the use of technology, firms were able to cut their costs. But the problem of producing excellent products inexpensively still existed. Better ways were needed to compete with foreign firms, many of which had lower labor costs. Some firms boldly decided to move in a direction that was similar to tearing down the business and rebuilding it.

Many firms arrived at the conclusion that employees are their most important resource. Further, managers learned that by empowering workers, the firm could become more productive. **Empowerment** is letting workers decide how to perform their work tasks and offer ideas on how to improve the work process. Empowerment dramatically changed the role of the worker.

In the past, workers performed narrow tasks on assembly lines and had little decision-making power. After empowering workers, firms found that the quality of work often improved, as did the efficiency of production. Although better-trained and highly skilled workers were required, fewer managers were needed. Companies were able to reduce the number of levels of management by pushing down the day-to-day decisions directly to workers rather than to managers. Workers were taught to use computers, to work in teams, and to be responsible for quality.

While practicing empowerment, some managers were also redesigning the workflow throughout their organizations—a concept sometimes called *reengineering*. Instead of typical assembly lines found in factories and offices, steps were eliminated, abbreviated, or placed entirely in the hands of employees. Customer complaints dropped. Fewer well-trained workers with the help of advanced technology and streamlined work processes could better satisfy customers than could more

CAREER CONNECTION

FINANCIAL MANAGER

Are you good at analyzing detailed financial information? If so, you might want to consider a career as a financial manager. Practically every firm has one or more financial managers, who prepare financial reports, oversee the flow of cash, monitor credit, assess the risk of transactions, raise capital, analyze investments, and evaluate the present and future financial status of the business. In small firms, financial officers usually handle all financial management functions personally. In large firms, these managers oversee financial management departments and help top managers develop financial and economic policy, which is then implemented by employees.

Although financial managers are found in almost every industry, the majority are employed by services industries and financial institutions.

A bachelor's degree in finance or a related field is the minimum educational requirement, but many employers want graduates with master's degrees and a strong analytical background. Continuing education is vital for financial managers, reflecting the growing complexity of global trade, changing state and federal laws and regulations, and varying economic conditions.

For more career information about financial managers, check your library or the Internet for resources.

BUSINESS INNOVATION

EFFICIENCY AND EFFECTIVENESS—DELL DIRECT

Companies can satisfy customers in many ways. Most buyers want a high-quality product at the lowest possible price and a great deal of help when trouble occurs with a product. Successful firms in recent years have introduced innovative ways to meet customer expectations. Domino's Pizza, for example, delivers to your door quickly, as does Lands End. United Parcel Service and Federal Express also come to your door to deliver or pick up packages.

Dell Computer Corporation, however, was the first to do what everyone said would surely fail—sell computers using a toll-free phone number. Michael Dell, the founder of the firm, was told that people want to see, touch, and try highly technical products before they buy. They were wrong.

Michael Dell, who had always looked for easier and faster ways to get things done, got an idea while in college that he believed would serve the computer customer well. He would provide customers with a catalog of computers and computer parts. When they knew what they wanted, they could call his toll-free number, place the order with a credit card, and expect to have the computer shipped directly to their homes or offices within a brief period. Because he didn't incur the expense of maintaining a physical store, Dell was able to keep prices low. He kept no inventory, preferring to make and mail the customer's tailor-made machine soon after receiving the order.

To further make customers happy, he provided a guarantee, and later an extended repair contract offering local service if anything went wrong. The idea worked beyond anyone's imagination. Within a few years his business was profitable and growing rapidly. Dell products are among the highest-rated machines, and satisfied customers spread the good news. Dell is now one of America's largest firms with computers sold around the world using the same ideas that he created in 1983, when the business was launched.

Many other computer firms have copied his low cost, fast service, and customer satisfaction guarantee. Gateway 2000, Compaq, and Micron imitated Dell in selling directly to customers. Dell and its competitors now sell their products over the Internet as well as through toll-free phone calls. Many other firms in different businesses soon adopted Michael Dell's ideas to gain the effectiveness and efficiency that leads to satisfied customers.

THINK CRITICALLY

1. Why do you think buyers like to purchase from Dell Computer Corporation?
2. What specific actions did Dell take to make his company effective?
3. What specific actions did Dell take to make his company efficient?
4. If you don't have Internet access, find a recent magazine or newspaper article dealing with the company and report on it to the class. If you have Internet access, go to the Dell Web site at www.dell.com to gather information about the company and report your findings.

workers using outdated methods and equipment. Most major firms—and many smaller ones—adopted these newer practices and are finding that customer satisfaction has risen along with productivity. The concept of redesigned work and workflow will appear in more detail in a later chapter.

American firms are renewing their position as strong competitors in world business as a result of restructuring and a more intensive focus on quality and customers' needs. Empowering workers has contributed a great deal to the rebuilding. Those firms are now doing the right things well. Furthermore, no large or small businesses in an industrialized society should think only about customers in their own countries. Their customers are located around the corner and around the world. American factories exist in other countries, and businesses in other countries make and sell products in this country.

You will learn more about international business in Chapter 4.

American firms also form joint agreements with domestic and foreign firms. For example, Ford Motor Company and Mazda Motors work with each other to make car parts and entire cars for each other. Similar arrangements exist with European firms. Sony, a large electronics manufacturer in Japan, has formed alliances with many firms in the world, many of which are American.

BUSINESS GROWTH AND PROSPERITY

Overall, the United States is a prosperous nation. Much of its prosperity is due to business growth. Around the world, people admire and envy this country's economic strength. Let's look at two ways in which a nation measures its economic wealth and its benefits to citizens.

GROSS DOMESTIC PRODUCT

The first measure of a nation's economic wealth is the **gross domestic product (GDP).** The GDP is the total market value of all goods and services produced in a country in a year. Whenever products or services are purchased, the total dollar amount is reported to the federal government. The GDP of the United States is compared from year to year and is also compared with the GDP of other countries. These comparisons provide a measure of economic success.

Certain types of transactions, however, are never included in the GDP. These transactions are not recorded because they are unlawful or do not occur as part of normal business operations. For example, when a student is hired to mow lawns, formal business records are not normally prepared and the income is usually unrecorded. When drugs are sold illegally, such transactions are not recorded. Income that escapes being recorded in the GDP is referred to as the **underground economy.** Business transactions that occur in the underground economy have increased in recent years in relation to the total GDP. Some economists believe that estimates range between 5 percent during a brisk economy to 20 percent of the GDP during a lagging economy. The size of the underground economy concerns government officials.

In a recent year, the total known and recorded GDP for the United States reached the staggering $8.8 trillion mark, as shown in Figure 1-4. And in a recent year, the U.S. GDP exceeded the total GDP of four

ILLUSTRATION 1-4

Why could hiring a neighborhood youngster to mow your lawn be considered part of the underground economy?

FIGURE 1-4

U.S. GDP since 1987

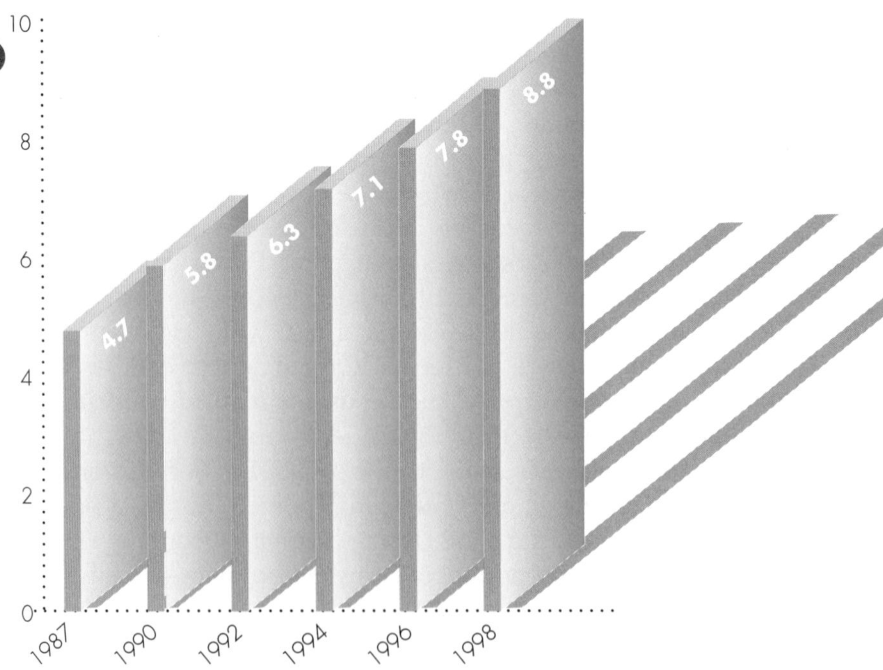

Source: *Bureau of Economic Analysis, 1998*

major countries combined—Japan, Germany, England, and Mexico. The rate of growth and the current size of the GDP indicate, in a rather striking way, the economic strength of the country.

INDIVIDUAL WELL-BEING

A second measure of a nation's wealth is the individual well-being of its citizens. While GDP figures are helpful in judging the overall growth of an economy, such figures by themselves tell little about the economic worth of individuals. However, the U.S. Department of Commerce gathers information that reveals the financial well-being of U.S. citizens.

With increased income, an average family improves its level of living. Over 65 percent of all families live in homes they own. As shown in Figure 1-5, many families now own items once considered luxuries. For example, refrigerators, color televisions, microwave ovens, clothes washers, and cordless phones are found in a majority of households. Over half of all U.S. households have answering machines, and a third own personal computers. In addition, Americans still invest large sums of money in education, with many adults receiving some education beyond high school. Further, individuals invest in life-enrichment

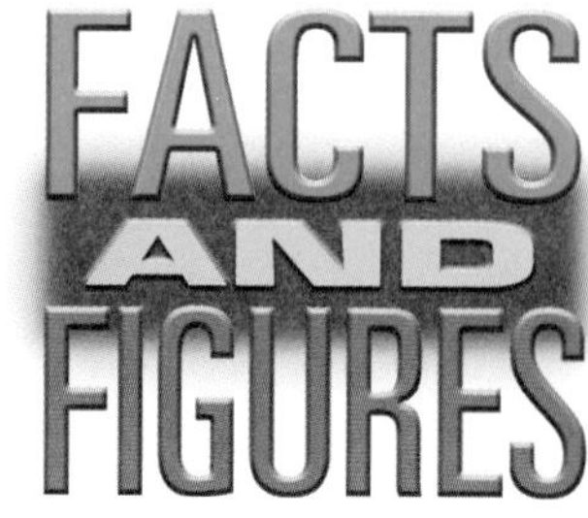

Family income has increased steadily, with the average yearly family income currently exceeding $42,000—much more than it was a decade ago. In a recent year, the average individual yearly income for a male without a high school diploma was $16,000; but for a male with a diploma, it jumped to about $25,000. College graduates earned over $39,000.

Percentage of Households Owning Selected Items

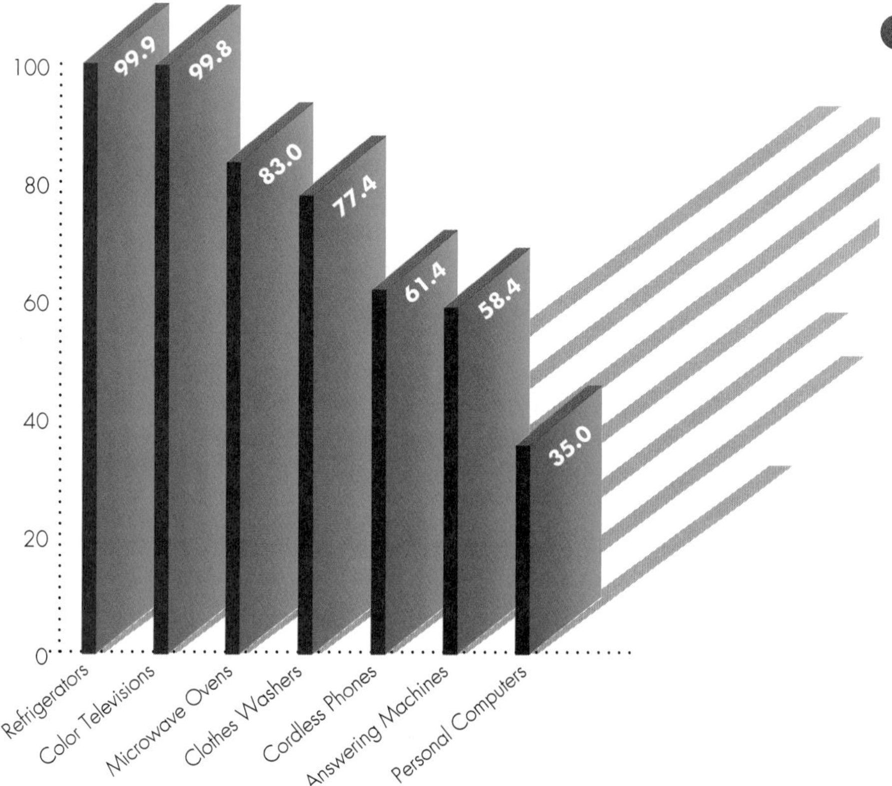

Source: *Statistical Abstract of the United States, 1998*

FIGURE 1-5

Families buy appliances and office equipment with their incomes.

activities by traveling in this country and abroad. Despite these large expenditures on material goods and services, Americans saved nearly $227 billion in a recent year.

Even though the typical American has done well when compared to people in other countries, some problems still exist. For example, slow economic periods may create job shortages, layoffs, and reduced incomes. Some people cannot find employment because of inadequate skills. When incomes drop, it becomes more difficult to buy homes and to send children to college. Lower incomes could also lead to poverty. You will learn more about these and similar problems in later chapters.

ENTREPRENEURSHIP

The successful growth of business in the United States resulted from many factors. Two reasons for business growth are the strong desire by individuals to own their own businesses and the ease with which a business can be started. Someone who starts, manages, and owns a business is called an **entrepreneur.**

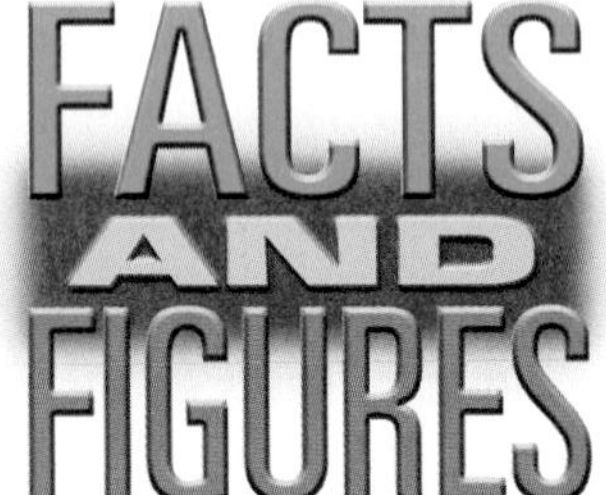

Most small businesses are commonly found in service and retail trade fields that usually employ fewer than 100 people. Nearly 98 percent of all businesses in the country are classified as small. However, over half the total number of workers in this country are employed by businesses with fewer than 500 employees. In addition, the revenue generated from all small businesses accounts for about half of the GDP.

POPULARITY OF SMALL BUSINESS

It is the tradition of this country to encourage individuals to become entrepreneurs. Few government controls, for example, prevent a person from launching a new business. Almost anyone who wishes to do so may start a business. As a result, many new businesses spring up each year. These new businesses may have physical facilities, such as a store in a mall, or they can be individuals working in home offices or businesses that exist only on the Internet.

Small business is the term applied to any business that is operated by one or a few individuals. Because it is normally costly to start a manufacturing business, few small firms produce goods.

In past years, when many large firms were laying off thousands of workers, small businesses with less than 20 employees were hiring in large numbers. Often, the new entrepreneurs were highly skilled managers who were displaced by large firms that were downsizing. Small firms, on the other hand, were reported to be hiring twice as many applicants as the number of employees laid off by large firms. In addition, many of these small firms were adding more high-paying jobs than low-paying jobs.

Many small businesses are one-person or family operations with only a few employees. Examples include restaurants, gift shops, gas stations, and bakeries. Computers have made it possible for small businesses to operate from homes and on the Internet. For example, consultants working from their homes can do much of their work by e-mail with clients, and craftspeople can offer their products for sale on the Internet, without the expense of a storefront. According to the U.S. Department of Commerce, many businesses earn less than $250,000 in yearly revenue, with many of the very small shops earning far less.

ILLUSTRATION 1-5

Many small businesses are one-person or family operations with few employees. Can you name some examples in your community?

GROWTH OF SMALL BUSINESS

Most large businesses today began as very small businesses. Because they supplied products and services consumers desired and because they were well managed, they became larger and larger. For example, Subway began as a small business and now has over 13,000 restaurants around the country. McDonalds and Holiday Inn, once small businesses, now operate worldwide.

GROWTH OF FRANCHISE BUSINESS

For the person with an entrepreneurial spirit, a popular way to launch a small business is through a franchise. A **franchise** is a legal agreement in which a distributor buys the right to sell the franchising company's product or service under the company's name and trademark. Many Docktor Pet Centers, Pizza Huts, and Roy Rogers Restaurants are operated by small business owners under such agreements. The two parties to a franchise agreement are the **franchisor,** the parent company of a franchise agreement that provides the product or service, and the **franchisee,** the distributor of a franchised product or service.

In a typical franchise agreement, the franchisee pays an initial fee to the franchisor and a percentage—usually 3 to 8 percent—of weekly sales. In return, the franchisee gets help in selecting a store site and gets exclusive rights to sell the franchised product or service in a specified geographic area.

The franchisor also provides special training and advice in how to operate the franchise efficiently. These services are particularly valuable to inexperienced entrepreneurs. They give a franchise business a far greater chance of success than a firm starting on its own does. While 5 to 10 percent of franchised businesses fail, the failure rate is far lower than the failure rate of non-franchised businesses.

Prospective franchisees should carefully check out the franchisor. Fraudulent dealers have deceived many innocent people. Franchise agreements may require franchisees to buy all items from the franchisor, often at a price substantially higher than available elsewhere. Some franchisors have been charged with allowing other franchisees to open businesses too close to each other. To avoid these problems, some states have passed laws to protect franchisees. Potential franchisees should seek the help of lawyers and accountants before signing franchising agreements.

In spite of possible dangers, the number of franchises has grown steadily over the years, especially in the retail area. According to a recent report, franchises employ over eight million people and account for nearly half the retail store sales in the country. About 12 percent of all businesses are franchise businesses, such as those listed in Figure 1-6. The two areas with the greatest number of franchises are auto and truck dealerships and gasoline service stations. However, fast food restaurants and convenience shops such as 7-Eleven food stores are also quite popular. In recent years, the number of franchises for service-type businesses that do not require large sums of money to get started have steadily increased.

RISKS OF OWNERSHIP

The success of a business depends greatly on managerial effectiveness. If a business is well managed, it will likely earn an adequate income.

FIGURE 1-6

Many businesses are franchise operations.

Franchises from A to Z

Agway	Nathan's Famous, Inc.
Budget Rent-A-Car	Orange Julius of America
Century 21	Pizza Hut
Denny's	Quik Print, Inc.
Fairfield Inn by Marriott	Roy Rogers
Goodyear Tire Centres	Sbarro, Inc.
Howard Johnson	TCBY Systems
International Dairy Queen	Uniclean Systems
Jiffy Lube	Wendy's Old Fashioned Hamburgers
Kwik Copy	Yogi Bear's Jellystone Park
Lawn Doctor, Inc.	Ziebert Tidycar
Midas International Corp.	

Source: *Bureau of Economic Analysis, 1998*

From an adequate income, it can pay all expenses and earn a profit. If a business does not earn a profit, it cannot continue for long. An entrepreneur assumes the risk of success or failure.

Risk—the possibility of failure—is one of the characteristics of business that all entrepreneurs must face. Risk (which will also be discussed in the credit and insurance chapter) involves competition from other businesses, changes in prices, changes in style, competition from new products, and changes that arise from economic conditions. Whenever risks are high, the risk of failure is also high.

Businesses close for a number of reasons. Thousands fail yearly for financial reasons, as shown in Figure 1-7. One out of every four to five businesses fails within three years, and about half cease operations within six to seven years. However, those figures include firms that voluntarily go out of business, such as by selling to someone else or by adding more owners. The results of a study shown in Figure 1-8 indicate that only 18 percent should fall into the failure category. The reported causes of failures are shown in Figure 1-9. Most often, economic and financial factors cause businesses to fail.

OBLIGATIONS OF OWNERSHIP

Anyone who starts a business has a responsibility to the entire community in which the business operates. Customers, employees, suppliers, and even competitors are affected by a single business. Therefore,

Business Failures: 1985–1996

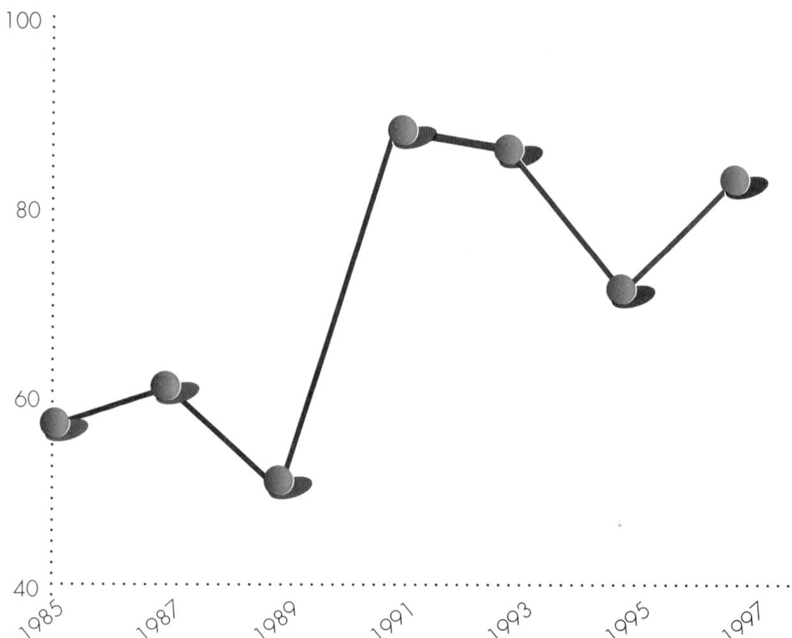

FIGURE 1-7

Number of Businesses that Fail Annually

The Results of 814,000 Firms 8 Years After Starting (in percent)

FIGURE 1-8

Many of the businesses reported as failures are not failures.

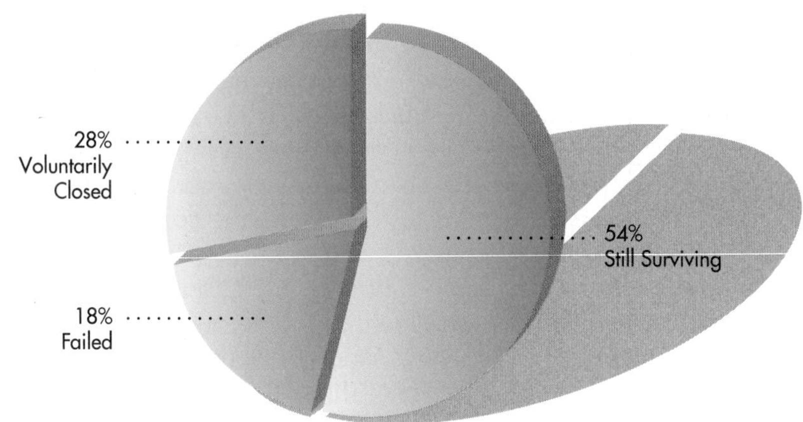

Source: *The Dun & Bradstreet Corporation, 1992*

FIGURE 1-9

Causes of Business Failures

PRIMARY REASONS FOR FAILURES	PERCENT OF FAILURES
ECONOMIC CAUSES Industry weakness, low profits, and low sales	64.1
FINANCE CAUSES Heavy expenses and burdensome debts	23.9
DISASTER AND FRAUD Hurricanes, floods, and theft	6.7
NEGLECT CAUSES Business conflicts, family problems, and poor work habits	3.7
STRATEGY CAUSES Overexpansion and difficulty collecting from customers	0.9
EXPERIENCE CAUSES Inadequate planning and inexperience	0.8

Source: *Adapted from Business Failure Record. The Dun & Bradstreet Corporation, 1992.*

a business that fails creates an economic loss that is shared by others in society. For example, an unsuccessful business probably owes money to other firms that will also suffer a loss because they cannot collect. In fact, a business that cannot collect from several other businesses may be placed in a weakened financial condition and it, too, may fail.

An executive of a major business association pointed out the following obligations of business owners:

1. TO CUSTOMERS: That they may have the best at the lowest cost, consistent with fairness to all those engaged in production and distribution.
2. TO WORKERS: That their welfare will not be sacrificed for the benefit of others, and in their employment relations, their rights will be respected.
3. TO MANAGEMENT: That it may be recognized in proportion to its demonstrated ability, considering always the interest of others.
4. TO COMPETITORS: That there will be avoidance of every form of unfair competition.
5. TO INVESTORS: That their rights will be safeguarded and they will be kept so informed that they can exercise their own judgment respecting their interests.
6. TO THE PUBLIC: That the business will strive in all its operations and relations to promote the general welfare and to observe faithfully the laws of the land.

Just as every business has an obligation to the community, the community has an obligation to each business. Society should be aware that owners face many risks while trying to earn a fair profit on the investment made in the business. Consumers should realize that the prices of goods and services are affected by expenses that arise from operating a business. Employees should also realize that a business cannot operate successfully, and thereby provide jobs, unless each worker is properly trained and eager to work. The economic health of a community is improved when groups in the community are aware of each other's obligations. Some of the social and ethical dilemmas faced by businesses are examined in Chapter 2.

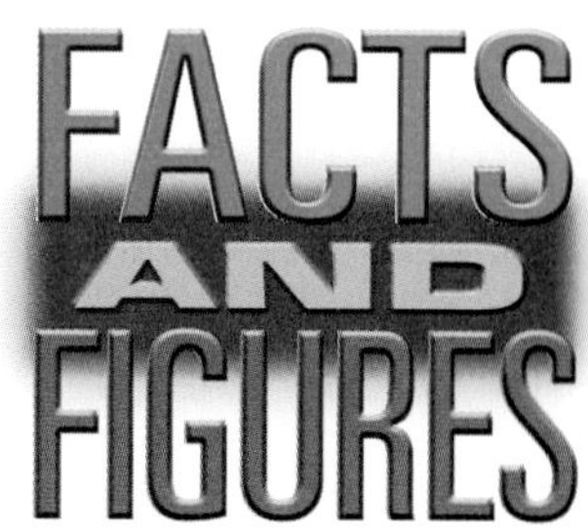

IBM entered late into the personal computer market. When IBM decided to make a small computer, it needed a good product in a hurry. An intrapreneurship unit was created. Within a brief period, the employees who voluntarily joined the unit made a personal computer that soon outsold other brands.

INTRAPRENEURSHIP

Rather than lose creative employees who may quit to start their own businesses, employers now encourage creativity through intrapreneurships. An **intrapreneur** is an employee who is given funds and freedom to create a special unit or department within a company in order to develop a new product, process, or service. Although the main company finances the new venture, intrapreneurs enjoy the freedom of running their operations with little or no interference from upper managers.

Some of the largest corporations in the United States provide intrapreneurship opportunities. By so doing, valuable employees provide the company with innovative products and services.

IBM and other major corporations such as 3M (which makes Scotch tape, Post It Notes, and a variety of other products) and General Electric

FACTS AND FIGURES

Avis, the car rental firm, has an ESOP that created employee participation groups that focused on solving problems. Avis became a more profitable company because employees worked harder and better when they knew they would share in the profits as owners.

have also captured the innovative abilities of employees with entrepreneurial characteristics. Employees benefit because they risk neither their salaries nor their savings to launch a new business. Employers also benefit by keeping creative employees who might have started successful competing businesses. Furthermore, employers and consumers benefit because new and better products, processes, and services are introduced at a quickened pace through intrapreneurships.

In recent years, businesses that struggled for survival in a global economy offered an ownership opportunity to employees. That opportunity became known as an **employee stock ownership plan (ESOP),** which permits employees to directly own the company in which they work by allowing them to buy shares in it. Companies benefit by obtaining funds from employees who buy shares and thereby become highly motivated to make their company a success. ESOPs have been shown to increase productivity.

IMPORTANCE OF STUDYING BUSINESS PRINCIPLES AND MANAGEMENT

Whether you plan to operate a business of your own, move up in a company hierarchy, or simply be a valuable employee for a company, you must be well informed about the production, marketing, and financial activities of a business. As an owner, you must have a complete understanding of all phases of business operations, including employee relations and government regulations. You also need this knowledge to become a competent employee. Moreover, if you expect to become a supervisor or an executive of a company, you must fully grasp how the activities of all departments are coordinated in a smoothly operating business. Even organizations that are not profit-making businesses, such as the government and charitable organizations, operate in a manner similar to businesses. Business knowledge will help you contribute as an employee in one of these organizations as well. You will have an opportunity to learn about career possibilities in the business world in the last chapter of this book.

CHAPTER CONCEPTS

- In recent years, increased global competition has changed greatly the way businesses operate, requiring firms to become more efficient and effective at providing goods and services of high quality at low prices to satisfy customers around the world. Global competition has produced streamlined firms that use new methods to operate. Innovations, such as the development of computer technology, have changed the way businesses run.
- A prosperous business system provides the majority of a country's citizens with a high standard of living. Evidence is shown in a continuously growing GDP and the variety of goods and services that people are able to buy.
- The ease of starting a small business has resulted in many people either becoming entrepreneurs or intrapreneurs, behaving like business owners inside firms. While many small firms fail, a great many become highly successful as independent owners, franchisees, or large international firms.
- An understanding of basic business terms and principles will help you become an effective employee or a successful business owner.

BUILD VOCABULARY POWER

Define the following terms and concepts.

1. business
2. production
3. manufacturing firms
4. service firms
5. finance
6. industrial businesses
7. third world nations
8. commercial businesses
9. services
10. industry
11. global competition
12. effectiveness
13. efficiency
14. domestic goods
15. foreign goods
16. total quality management (TQM)
17. output
18. productivity
19. mass production
20. downsize
21. empowerment
22. gross domestic product (GDP)
23. underground economy
24. entrepreneur
25. small business
26. franchise
27. franchisor
28. franchisee
29. intrapreneur
30. employee stock ownership plan (ESOP)

REVIEW FACTS

1. About how many businesses of all kinds are there in the United States?
2. What three activities do all businesses perform?
3. Which two types of businesses, shown in Figure 1-1, employ the most workers?

4. Which type of business is growing in number faster than any other type of business in the U.S.?
5. Name three techniques that American businesses can use to improve efficiency and productivity.
6. When workers are empowered, what happens in an organization?
7. Why is the gross domestic product (GDP) important?
8. What proof is there that the average American family is financially well off?
9. Is it relatively easy or difficult to start a small business?
10. How much do small businesses contribute to the GDP yearly, and how much of the total workforce is employed by small businesses?
11. In a typical franchise arrangement, what are the advantages to the franchisee?
12. What are the dangers to consider when seeking a franchisor?
13. What are the two main causes for business failure?
14. Why would a large business encourage intrapreneurship?
15. How does a company benefit from having an employee stock ownership plan?

DISCUSS IDEAS

1. How does an industrial firm differ from a manufacturing firm?
2. How have advances in computer technology benefited businesses? Give examples of business tasks that computers could make easier.
3. Study Figure 1-2, which shows changes in the growth of businesses by selected categories. (a) Discuss what is happening to manufacturing when compared to the other categories, (b) offer reasons for the cause of the condition, and (c) indicate what might be done to improve it.
4. Discuss which is more important, effectiveness or efficiency.
5. Discuss a plan of worker specialization and mass production for a company that makes motorcycles.
6. Many new products and methods have been created in this country, but does the number of new inventions always lead to business success over competitors? Explain your answer.
7. Discuss what types of people might prefer to be specialists on an assembly line doing the same tasks continuously, and what types would most prefer to be empowered employees.
8. How might it be possible for the GDP to be larger than the reported amount in a given year? What can be done to prevent inaccurate GDP amounts that are reported?
9. Why might a person who wishes to go into business not want to consider a franchise arrangement?
10. Give examples of risks that the owner of a gasoline service station might have.

11. Not only does the owner of a business have an obligation to employees, but also each employee has an obligation to the employer. Mention some specific obligations that each has.
12. Discuss why it is important for employees, consumers, or citizens to understand how American business operates.

ANALYZE INFORMATION

1. Compare the total of industrial types of businesses in Figure 1-1 with the total of the service industries shown. (a) Approximately what is the total employment for the production industries and for the other industries? (b) By what percentage is the one group larger than the other?
2. Use the actual GDP figures (shown below) to answer these questions: (a) What is the actual number of dollars for 1970? Show all the necessary digits. (b) What is the percent of increase for each decade? (c) Calculate the total percent of increase from 1970 to 1997. (d) Determine the average yearly increase in the GDP for the period shown.

Year	*GDP*
1970	1.036 trillion
1980	2.784
1990	5.744
1997	8.080

3. From his regular job, Ramon earned $25,000 last year, on which he paid his federal taxes. He also paid taxes on a week-long job held before getting his full-time job, from which he earned $600. In addition, Ramon earned $12,500 painting homes for relatives, neighbors, and friends. Early in the year, he bought an antique car in poor condition for $3,500. After spending $6,000 on special parts and many hours remodeling the car, he sold it for $31,000 and received cash for the full amount. Neither the money made when the antique car was sold nor the money earned for painting homes was reported on his income tax return. (a) How much of Ramon's earnings were taxes last year? (b) How much income earned was a part of the underground economy on which no taxes were paid? (c) What percent of his total income for the year was from his underground economy earnings? (d) Does Ramon have a moral obligation to report his underground economy earnings? Explain your answer.
4. You wish to start a small, profitable business in the neighborhood of your school, and you set these guidelines for yourself: The business cannot be a franchise, must be able to operate with only a few workers, must be legal, and must not require an investment greater than $5,000. Either alone or in a group, generate as many creative ideas as possible. Follow instructions set

by your teacher. After developing your ideas, decide which two would have the greatest likelihood of success. Present your ideas to the class.

5. With the help of a librarian or by searching the Internet, find a recent article on productivity or on problems a U.S. company or industry may have when competing with foreign companies. Read the article and make a report following your teacher's instructions.

SOLVE BUSINESS PROBLEMS

CASE 1-1

The Kirk family came to this country early in the 20th century and made a bicycle that soon became known for its quality. Through much of the century, Kirk was the "Cadillac" of American bicycles. In the 1960s, it ran circles around numerous competitors; one in four bikes was a Kirk. Throughout this time, the Kirk family managed the company.

The success of Kirk's line of bicycles gave the company great confidence—perhaps too much confidence. During the last three years sales dropped, slipping from one million bikes sold yearly to 500,000 the next year and 250,000 last year. Three major competitors with nifty lower-priced bikes who sold to K-Mart, Sears, and other large stores were stealing customers. When mountain bikes became popular, Kirk management ridiculed this new fad.

In the meantime, the quality of Kirk bikes faded. To cut costs, employees were let go and lower-quality parts were bought from foreign firms and installed. Kirk managers made no attempt to talk to biking customers. Neither did the managers listen to the hundreds of dealers who sold Kirk bicycles in specialty shops. Loyal dealers started adding competitors' products to survive. Bike deliveries were running late. The changes made to cut costs did not correct the situation. For the last three years, Kirk operated at a loss. Something drastic had to occur.

Recently, Kirk was purchased by another company. Headquarters for the company was set up in Colorado, where biking is popular. Kirk's new managers talked to customers and dealers. As a result, new products rolled off the assembly line that were satisfying loyal dealers and older bikers who recalled the excellent quality of the Kirk two-wheelers. But can the new Kirk adequately rebuild itself to compete in a tough market? Quality Kirk bikes sold only at specialty shops cost $250 to $2,500, which is far more than most bikes purchased at discount stores. Plenty of persuading will be needed to convert the price-conscious casual bikers or the more serious riders who put on 25 to 100 miles a week.

Signs of success appear on the horizon. A small profit is expected this year for the struggling firm. Whether the new managers can reestablish Kirk's earlier lead in the marketplace is yet to be determined.

Think Critically:

1. What was the main reason the old Kirk company failed? Explain your answer.
2. What should the new managers do to help improve Kirk's effectiveness?
3. What might the company do to help improve its efficiency?
4. Create a title for this case that provides the theme to the story.
5. With permission of the instructor, join two other students to discuss and make recommendations for how the Kirk company might expand its business.

CASE 1-2

Fast Food Fellows, often shortened to "Fellows," is a major restaurant franchise that sells outlets to entrepreneurs interested in opening their own businesses. The franchisees are usually quite successful because of the strict rules set by the franchisor. Despite high start-up costs, many applications are rejected.

Emi Tanaka and Rosa Lopez, two friends who have known each other for years, decided they would quit their jobs and go into business for themselves. Neither friend had been a manager or run a business before, but Rosa had worked as a restaurant cashier and Emi's parents ran a small clothing shop where she occasionally worked after school and summers. Both agreed that a new restaurant in their hometown would be an excellent idea and even agreed on a building that had a "for rent" sign. Both liked to cook at home and had visited many restaurants. They agreed that a nice place in the business district of their town would attract shoppers, workers, and others. Both believed they could raise enough money to get started.

Emi and Rosa believed that a franchised business would be the best choice, and both seemed to have adequate money to invest. They checked the local library and Internet resources for franchising information and found a long list of possibilities. They studied the list and decided Fellows was their favorite. They gathered as much information as possible, contacted its headquarters, and obtained and mailed a Fellows application. They were excited when called in for a meeting with the manager. However, they were surprised to learn that the start-up cost was quite high and the fee was 8 percent of weekly sales.

After thinking about it for a few days, they decided that because the franchise business had a great reputation, it could not fail. There was no need to check with other franchisors. The business soon opened and customers were plentiful. While both were concerned about how much they had to pay the headquarters each week, they were surprised when they learned that a new Fellows franchise had recently been granted and would soon open less than two miles away. What would happen to their profits? They contacted a few other Fellows franchisees from other towns and learned that the franchisor often put other outlets too near to one another. Emi and Rosa were upset, as were other Fellows franchisees, but what could they do?

Think Critically:

1. Did Emi and Rosa make any mistakes in how they made their decision to select Fellows? Give reasons for your answer. (With directions from your instructor, you may prefer to form groups of three to five students. Half the groups should argue that Emi and Rosa made the right decision, while the others should argue that they made the wrong decision. Each group should then provide reasons for the decisions.)
2. If you believe it is unfair for the franchisor to cause reduced profits because outlets are located too near to one another, which of the following choices should the franchisor select: lower the weekly royalty percentage fee of 8 percent and reduce its profits; place outlets farther apart and make lower profits; or keep things the way they are? Provide a reason for your answer.
3. What action might the franchisees take to protect their interests in their franchise outlets?
4. What advice would you give others who want to open a franchised business?

PROJECT: MY BUSINESS, INC.

Throughout this course, you will participate in a continuing project in which you will plan your own business—a juice bar. This project will require you to gather and analyze information and make decisions about your new business. The section called "Project: My Business, Inc." at the end of each chapter will guide you through the next step in business planning, as you apply what you learned in the chapter to a realistic new business venture. Develop written answers to each of the Data Collection and Analysis activities identified by your teacher, using a computer if possible. After you have completed each chapter's activities, save your work in the notebook you have prepared.

Juice bars are a part of two industries—fast food and health foods. While juice bars are popular today, you will want your business to be successful in the future. It is not practical to start a business that may not be needed in a few years. In this chapter you will be asked to study information to help you determine the future of your business and to make the first specific decisions about your business.

DATA COLLECTION

1. Review newspapers, magazines, and other publications to gather information about the size and growth of the health and fitness market as well as the fast food industry.
2. In your city or neighborhood, identify the types of businesses that exist in the areas of fast food and health foods. (Try to include the very small businesses that operate as a part of a larger business such as a supermarket or health club.) Develop a list that includes the name of each business, a brief description of the business, the type of products offered, and the business location.
3. Find information that identifies the failure rate of new fast food businesses and of health and fitness businesses.

4. Using the Internet and the library or by visiting businesses in your area, identify the common types of products offered by juice bar businesses.

ANALYSIS

1. What factors have led to the growth of juice bars?
2. Is there any evidence that this type of business may not be as successful in the future?
3. What are the advantages and disadvantages of starting a small juice bar business in your community?
4. Create a name for your business. A good business name should be short and easy to remember. It should relate to the type of business being operated, should be appealing to prospective customers, and different from other similar businesses. You may want to create an interesting design for your business name that could be used on signs and in promotion.
5. Develop an initial business concept. The business concept is a one- to two-paragraph statement that describes the business and a possible location, the most likely customers, and the primary products and services that could be offered.

SOCIAL AND ETHICAL ENVIRONMENT OF BUSINESS

OBJECTIVES

2-1 Describe the changing nature of the population, the labor force, and their impact on businesses.

2-2 Discuss how the values of Americans have changed and how business has adapted to those changed values.

2-3 Debate the dilemma posed by the need for business to grow and the need to protect the natural environment.

2-4 Suggest ways in which businesses can be socially responsible.

2-5 Predict how changes in society and business will affect employment in the future.

THE SUPERVISOR'S SECRET

Tyler Eastman picked up the file folder and walked to his supervisor's office. He had finally saved enough money for the down payment and closing costs for a small stone house on the lake that he had long wanted. He now needed his supervisor's signature on several documents that the bank required in order to approve the loan money.

The Quest Company, where Tyler worked, was the main employer in this small Ohio town. Because the firm paid high wages, the town had nice stores and good restaurants. Taxes paid by the company supported the police and fire departments, the public school, and the recreation center.

Recently, however, Quest had fallen on hard times. Sales declined and unsold goods piled up. Some employees were let go. To survive, Quest had to cut costs. Rather than continue operations in Ohio, Quest decided to relocate to Georgia, where costs for taxes, wages, utilities, and raw materials were lower.

Only yesterday, Tyler's supervisor, Rayshawn Clark, had been informed that the town's factory would shut down over the next 12 months. He was being promoted but would move to the new Georgia plant. Many workers, like Tyler, would lose their jobs.

Therefore, when Tyler excitedly asked Rayshawn to sign the bank papers for his new home, Rayshawn was disturbed. Should he sign the loan papers when he knew Tyler's job would barely last a year? If he didn't sign, everyone would soon find out why. Morale among the employees would drop, and they would look for jobs elsewhere. It was important to keep the plant closure decision a secret as long as possible. The town would be devastated when it learned that its main employer would be relocating. Rayshawn pondered the dilemma he was in.

Since its establishment more than 225 years ago, the United States has become the world's leading economic, technical, and political power. The country has the world's largest economy and relies on highly sophisticated and modern means of production, transportation, and communication. Americans enjoy a very high standard of living. All these achievements can be attributed to the enormous resources that the country possesses, the ingenuity of its people, a democratic form of government, a social system that rewards individual initiative, and public policies that encourage innovation.

Despite the many successes, problems persist with regard to discrimination, crime and violence, environmental protection, ethical conduct, and social responsibility. Since businesses are a part of the total society in which they operate, social changes affect how they operate. Similarly, businesses affect society in different ways, as Tyler Eastman will soon discover. Thus, one cannot study business principles and management without also having an understanding of the social forces that shape business.

HUMAN RESOURCE ISSUES

People are a firm's most important resource. A recent study of top managers found that finding and retaining qualified workers was more important than finance, technology, product innovation, or international business. The workers help businesses achieve their organizational goals. The challenges faced by businesses are closely interwoven with those experienced by the workers. In particular, such issues as those caused by changes in population and lifestyles have a direct bearing on business operations and on the well being of the nation.

POPULATION

The gross domestic product (GDP) of a country cannot increase unless there are enough people to provide the necessary labor and to purchase the goods and services produced. Population statistics enable businesses to plan how much and what kinds of goods and services to offer. However, the GDP of a country must grow at a faster rate than its population in order to improve living standards. Both the size and the characteristics of the population are important in business planning. Information about the size and characteristics of the American population can be found at the website of the U.S. Census Bureau at www.census.gov.

GROWING POPULATION The population of the United States has grown steadily over the years, as shown in Figure 2-1. The growth rate is largely determined by the birth rate, the death rate, and the level of immigration into the country. Generally, as the standard of living increases, the birth rate falls, and this has been the case in the United States. At the same time, because of better health care and an improved public health system, people are living much longer.

Much of the population increase takes place through immigration. The United States annually accepts more legal immigrants than any other country in the world, with large numbers coming from Asian and Latin American nations. Many immigrants also enter the country illegally to seek a better life.

CHANGING POPULATION The nature of the population has been changing, too. Currently, more than 80 percent of Americans can be racially classified as white. Because of higher birth rates among non-white Hispanics and African-Americans, and recent immigration, their proportions in the population have been growing. This growing diversity of the workforce increases the need for better cross-cultural communication and sensitivity to the interests and concerns of various groups.

Changes in the birth rate have caused shifts in the number of people in different age groups. For example, because of the high birth rate during 1945-1965, there are more people in the 35–55 age group. Because of this **baby boom,** the number of people who are aged 55

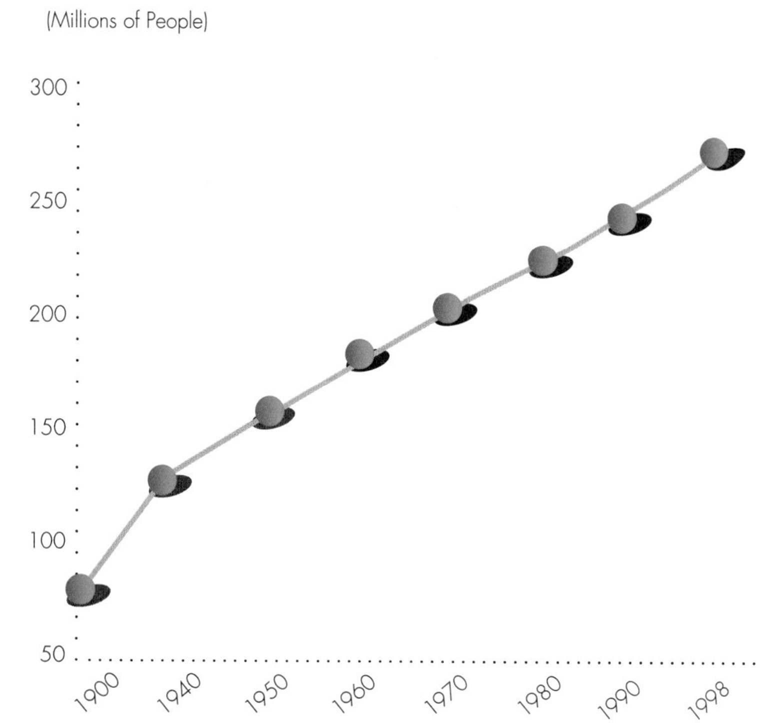

Source: *U.S. Census Bureau*

FIGURE 2-1

Size of Population in the United States

and over today has increased substantially. The low birth rate period that followed the boomer period is called the **baby bust** period. The baby bust period has created a shortage of young workers, called "busters." This shortage will continue to create serious problems, especially when the boomers retire in large numbers.

Businesses must be prepared to offer the kinds of goods and services needed by people of different age and racial groups. For instance,

ILLUSTRATION 2-1

How has the "baby bust" period affected the supply of young workers in business?

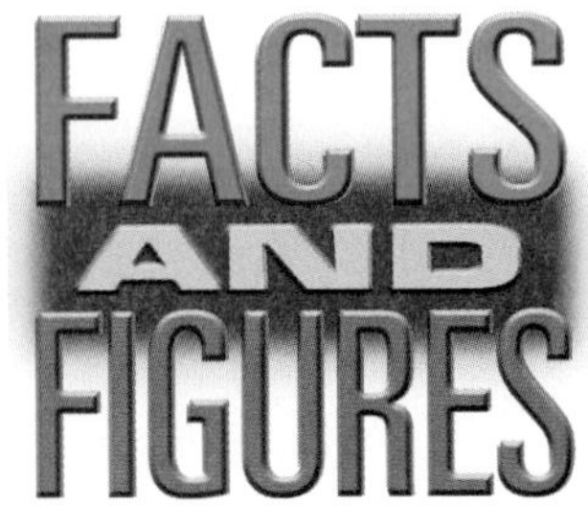

In 1998, Hispanic purchasing power in the U.S. was approximately $348 billion; by 2010, it is estimated to be $965 billion. By the year 2050, the Hispanic population will reach nearly 100 million, representing almost 25 percent of the U.S. population.

because of the increase of Spanish-speaking people, some newspapers and magazines publish Spanish language editions. As people live longer, food companies continue to develop special foods and products for the elderly.

MOVING POPULATION Americans are people on the move. Every year, on average, one out of five Americans changes his or her address. People move short distances, often from cities to suburbs. They also move long distances, such as from the **Frost Belt,** the colder northern half of the country, to the **Sun Belt,** the warmer southern half of the nation. As businesses relocate to where customers are located, they affect where other people move to in order to find jobs. For example, factories have relocated to the southeastern states, where wage rates are lower than in the **Rust Belt**—the north central and northeastern states where the major manufacturing firms once dominated. As illustrated at the beginning of this chapter, the Quest Company decided to move from Ohio to Georgia to lower its labor and other costs.

The continuing movement of people from the city to the suburbs, and from the north to the south, has led to many unintended consequences. When families and businesses leave cities in large numbers, the cities lose the financial ability to provide high-quality services. As a result, crime and poverty have increased in some large cities. Many southern states such as Georgia and Florida have experienced rapid economic and industrial growth. When businesses move from the Rust Belt, they leave behind unemployed workers, closed factories, decaying towns, and homeless people. However, in recent years, political and business leaders have taken bold steps to revitalize cities and communities in the northern states.

LABOR FORCE

As the population grows, so does the labor force. The **labor force** includes most people aged 16 or over who are available for work, whether employed or unemployed. Of course, many of the people in the labor force may be available for work but are not actively seeking employment, such as students and full-time homemakers. In a recent year, the Bureau of Labor Statistics reported that the size of the American labor force was almost 140 million. Figure 2-2 shows the growth of the labor force.

The **labor participation rate** is the percentage of the labor force that is either employed or actively seeking employment. In the last three decades, the labor participation rate increased primarily because many more women took jobs outside the home. In 1970, around 58 percent of women worked outside the home. By 1999, the figure had risen to nearly 80 percent. Some reasons for the increase are that women have been choosing not to marry, to delay marriage, or to marry and pursue careers before or while raising children. Figure 2-3 shows the trend in the labor

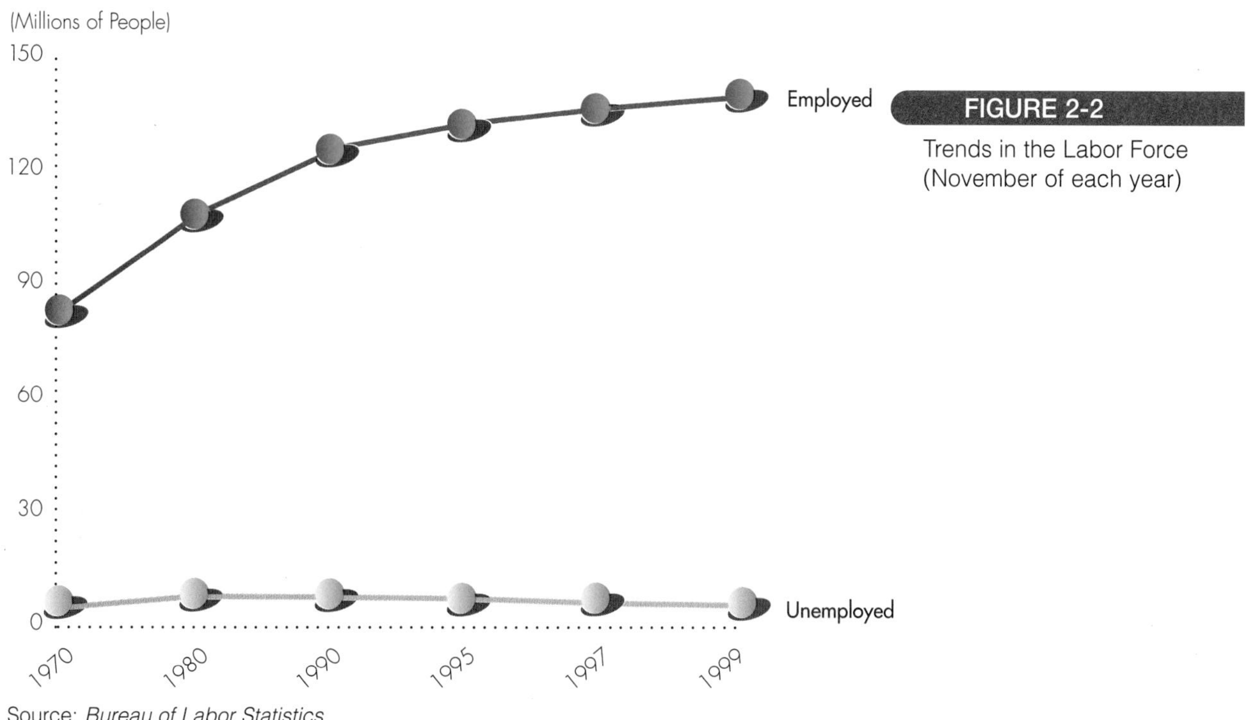

FIGURE 2-2

Trends in the Labor Force (November of each year)

Source: *Bureau of Labor Statistics*

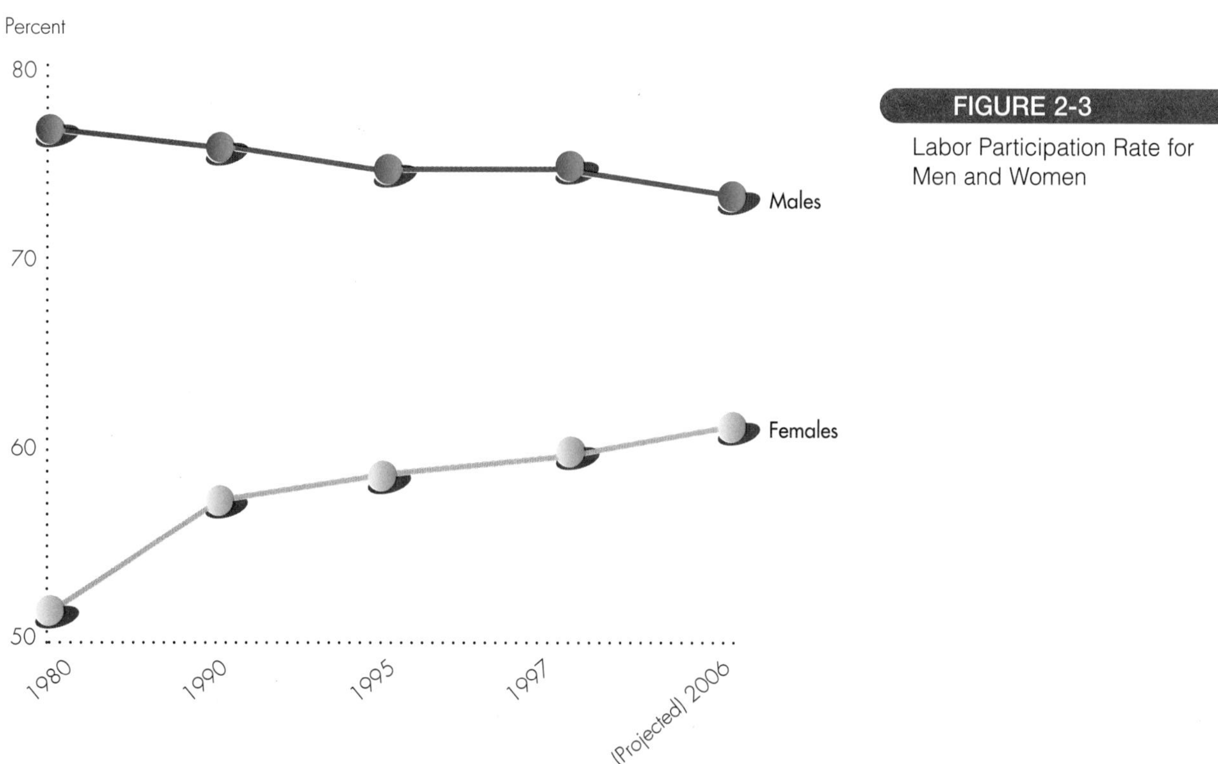

FIGURE 2-3

Labor Participation Rate for Men and Women

Source: *Statistical Abstract of the United States, 1998*

participation rates for males and females. The expansion of the economy through much of the 1990s coaxed many people, such as retirees, people with disabilities, and homemakers, to enter the labor force.

The growth of the economy, changes in the population and where people live, and technological advances have created a variety of new jobs. One of the great strengths of the American economy has been its ability to create new jobs. Most new jobs are in the service industries, such as computer programming, banking and insurance, leisure, food services, and health care. The growing use of computers has created a large number of technical jobs in areas such as computer applications and programming. The Internet has influenced how firms conduct business, and e-commerce is rapidly emerging as a new way to sell and buy goods and services. The rapid growth in the computer industry has led to a shortage of qualified workers and, in turn, has led to high wages for those with the necessary education and skills. To meet the demand for such high-tech workers, the government allows firms to hire workers from foreign countries.

Many of the new jobs require more skills, which means workers have to be educated. As a result, more people are going to college or acquiring training in new skills. As technology changes and old jobs disappear, many workers need retraining. At the same time, technology has simplified jobs, such as short-order cooks or bank tellers. These jobs now require little training and therefore pay low wages. Some jobs, such as telephone operators, have been eliminated since the work has been automated. A large number of workers are in dead-end jobs and are not earning an adequate income to maintain a reasonable standard of living.

For various reasons, including lack of financial resources, public schools in many areas are failing to provide the quality of education historically expected of high school graduates. High school graduates are particularly deficient in math, computer, social, and communication skills. Businesses are sometimes forced to provide remedial education in basic skills for newly hired workers.

POVERTY

The prosperity of Americans is not equally distributed among the population. According to the U.S. Bureau of the Census, between 12 and 15 percent of the population in any given year live in poverty. This means that these people are poorly housed, clothed, and fed. Many of these people live in inner-city slums or in rural areas. Statistics suggest that the richest 20 percent of American families have continued to earn more over the past 30 years, while the income of the lowest fifth has remained about the same. Thus, the gap between the rich and poor widens.

Due to such programs as Social Security, poverty among elderly people is much lower today than previously. However, many children live in poverty because they reside in households where one or more parents do not have the education and skills to hold high-paying jobs. Many parents cannot participate fully in the labor force because they don't have access to good-quality, affordable child care.

The government has several programs to reduce poverty. Minimum wage rates, unemployment benefits, financial or food aid, and subsidized medical care provide a basic safety net to the economically disadvantaged. Businesses increasingly offer training programs to provide skills that enable people to find and hold jobs.

EQUAL EMPLOYMENT

Equality for all is one of the basic principles on which the United States was founded. Yet, some groups of Americans have found it difficult to obtain jobs or be promoted on an equal basis. Several laws have been passed to outlaw discrimination on the basis of race, gender, national origin, color, religion, age, handicap, and other characteristics.

In many occupations, the numbers of women and racial minorities are few. Even when they find jobs, people in these groups may encounter difficulties in being promoted above a certain level. This has come to be known as the **glass ceiling**—an invisible barrier to job advancement. The barriers are often difficult to detect. For example, a white male's discomfort with having a female or black supervisor may make promotion of women and blacks less likely. Employers are now legally obligated to provide equal employment opportunities for all.

ILLUSTRATION 2-2

Women and minorities may hit the "glass ceiling" as they attempt to move to higher-level jobs. What obligations do employers have in such situations?

Many women and members of racial minority groups are employed in entry-level positions with little hope for career advancement. These are low-paying jobs requiring little skill and education, such as restaurant servers, salesclerks, or nurse's aides. The inability of these workers to move up from these jobs is referred to as the **sticky floor syndrome.** Higher education and redesigning the jobs offer the best opportunities for workers to escape from this predicament.

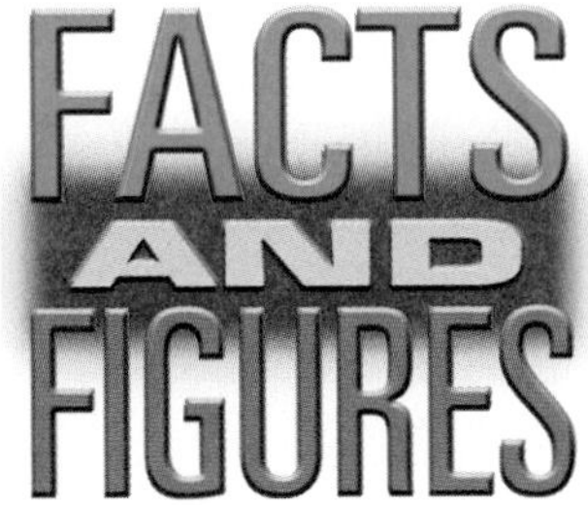

In 1966, women earned 58 cents for every dollar earned by men. That gap has closed by an average of half a penny each year since then. In 1996, women earned 74 cents for every dollar earned by men. Nearly every year the difference in earnings narrows somewhat.

COMPARABLE WORTH

Studies show that men tend to earn more than women do. It is not clear if this difference is due to discrimination against women or is because of the nature of jobs women do. There are a few professions in which women predominate. Wages tend to be lower in jobs that employ lots of women than in jobs held primarily by men. For instance, most dental hygienists are women, whereas most airline pilots are men. However, pilots tend to earn more money than dental hygienists.

But what happens when the jobs are not the same but require similar levels of training and responsibility? **Comparable worth** means paying workers equally for jobs with similar but not identical job requirements. The concept is also called "equal pay for comparable work." Jobs compared may be distinctly different, such as comparing legal secretaries and carpenters. However, if it can be determined that the two jobs require about the same level of training and responsibility, the pay scale for the two jobs should be the same. That is, legal secretaries should be paid more than what they currently earn to bring their pay up to that of carpenters. To determine whether work is of equal value, analysts compare factors such as special skills, physical strength, job dangers, responsibility, and education.

However, it is not easy to determine the specific factors that measure the worth of jobs. Should physical strength, for instance, be used to compare the worth of a legal secretary to a carpenter? And if few applicants are available for the carpenter's position and many are available for legal secretaries, is it fair to pay legal secretaries more than carpenters? These and other factors make it difficult for employers to design and implement comparable worth plans. But businesses are trying. Many states have passed laws that promote using comparable worth for determining wages in government jobs.

SOCIETAL VALUES

Change is constant in our society. We produce a steady stream of new products, new ideas, new ways of doing things, and new attitudes. In recent decades, societal values have been undergoing change at a fast pace.

An especially striking development has been the transformation of the family. The number of children living with both parents continues to fall, because of rising divorce rates and children born to single mothers. The birth rate, too, has declined, as women delay marriage and pursue careers outside the home. The traditional definition of "family" consisting of a working husband, a homemaker wife, two children, and a dog is now the exception. Less than one fourth of America's families fit this picture. Often, both parents work to support the family, as must single parents. Businesses have responded to the needs of today's fast-paced family life with a whole array of time-saving products and services from fast food of every description to dry cleaning delivery services to day care.

Because of increased competition in the economy, businesses are striving to produce more while keeping costs low. Employers have increased their demands on employees. Many employees find the pace and demands of work stressful. For dual-career couples and especially those with children, the quality of home life often suffers. Job insecurity discourages workers from taking vacations or time off, and instead they work longer hours to meet their job requirements. Factors such as these have strained the employer/employee relationship. Workers from the post-baby-boom generation, called **Generation X,** feel less loyal to a particular employer than did earlier generations. They expect to change jobs many times during their careers, as does the **Net Generation**—those born between 1977 and 1997. Also, competent women, stopped by the glass ceiling, often quit their jobs to start their own businesses. Women now operate a majority of new small businesses.

With so many men and women working side by side, workplace romance has blossomed, but so have incidents of sexual harassment. As the number of single adults and working couples has grown, dining at home is being replaced by dining out. American consumers spend more on restaurant meals than on groceries. People are placing more emphasis on safety and active lifestyles. This is reflected in airbags in cars, larger cars, and sporty vehicles.

A disturbing aspect of contemporary American society is the incidence of unpredictable and unprovoked violence through the use of guns, often by young people. Workplaces, schools, churches,

CYBER COMMUNICATION

Electronic mail—or *e-mail*—is the basic Internet tool for sending messages to other users. It's a method to create and send messages electronically to one or more individuals. The messages are stored in the destination mailbox until the receiver can read them. E-mail users don't have to be on the same network or using the same type of computer.

As more and more computers appear in schools, homes, and businesses, e-mail is becoming ingrained in our culture. It's fast, easy, and often free of charge for millions of Internet users. E-mail combines the low cost and efficiency of memos with the speed and conversational nature of phone calls. You can send and receive messages any time of the day or night, any day of the year. You can send one message to several people, and they can easily reply to, print, edit, file, or forward your message.

Activity Think about these forms of communication: e-mail, the telephone, and the regular mail system. What are the differences? Are there any similarities? What do you think the future holds for each of these communication modes? Write a one-page report about your ideas. If you have e-mail access, send the report to a friend or classmate.

and transportation systems are all susceptible to random gunfire killing and injuring of innocent people. This concern over violent crime has led to an expanding personal security business in the form of personal and home protective gadgets, guns, guards, gated communities, and prison construction.

The U.S. also has the dubious distinction of being lawsuit-happy. Individuals, groups, and organizations are quick to file lawsuits. Damage awards can run into millions of dollars. To avoid such expensive legal liabilities, businesses try to be very careful with respect to the safety of their products and the impact of their operations on employees, customers, and the overall society.

EMPLOYER PRACTICES

A changing society affects individuals as well as organizations. Many social issues transfer to work settings. Employees leave home each workday thinking about personal problems. Responsibilities may be enormous for workers with preschool children, aging parents, family illnesses, and financial burdens. Concerns such as these follow employees to their work sites and affect their job performance. To attract and retain competent workers, employers have responded to these social changes by taking action to improve the way work is done, to assure healthier and safer working conditions, and to help workers deal with some personal problems.

REDESIGNING JOBS As you will learn in other chapters, when jobs consist of mainly repetitive tasks, workers get bored, productivity drops, and morale declines. Many workers come late to work, call in sick, or even quit their jobs to find more interesting jobs elsewhere. Thus, to retain workers, employers redesign jobs to make them varied and challenging. In some cases, employees learn a variety of jobs and regularly switch jobs within the same organization. Such job rotation increases workers' interest in their jobs and enables employees to fill in for co-workers who may be absent.

Workers now often participate in job decisions, provide suggestions, and serve on committees that look for ways to improve work quality. Today's employees often work in teams. Work teams can improve morale as well as the quality of work. Businesses also try to improve job satisfaction through empowering workers to make important decisions.

IMPROVING HEALTH AND SAFETY In response to concerns over health and safety, businesses operate wellness and fitness programs. A physically unfit employee is absent more and is less productive than a fit employee. Many businesses encourage a healthy lifestyle by providing incentives to smokers to quit, membership to health clubs, counseling services where workers can receive support for stress or emotional problems, and payment for treatment of drug, alcohol, and other forms of addiction. Employers thereby reduce medical and insurance costs.

FAMILY-FRIENDLY PRACTICES Given the changes in the family structure, employers are making efforts to address this aspect of their employees' lives. By law, employers provide unpaid leave to employees to take care of their sick children or parents, or to give birth to, adopt, or take care of newborn children. Many progressive businesses provide day-care facilities for the young children of employees. Some employers provide flexible scheduling so that workers can avoid commuting to and from work during hectic rush hour traffic as well as accommodate their family needs and lifestyle. Advances in communication technology in the form of the Internet, e-mail, mobile phones, and fax have led many businesses to allow workers to **telecommute.** Telecommuters work from home or on the road, staying in contact with their employers electronically.

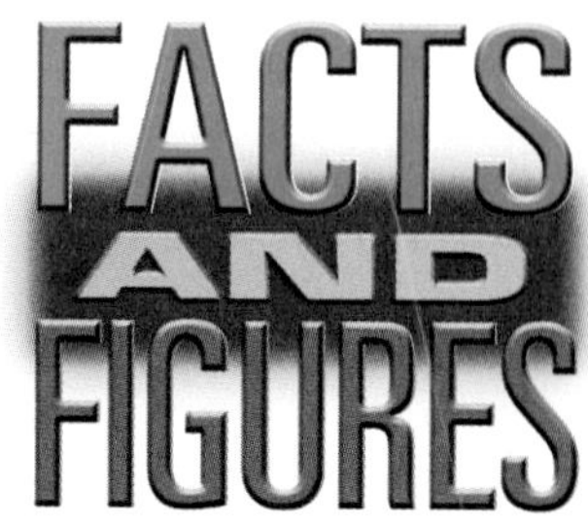

In 1999, more than 19.6 million Americans reported working as telecommuters. Increasing numbers of employees are conditioning their acceptance of new jobs on approval from the employer to telework.

NATURAL RESOURCE ISSUES

A growing population means more people to buy more things. More purchases mean more packaging, boxes, and worn-out products to throw away. Discarded plastic, chemical, and metal products take many years to break down in landfills. Moreover, some products (such as medical waste) may be harmful if not disposed of properly. The increasing demand for products places great pressure on natural resources, such as land, water, air, minerals, and forests. It also affects the habitats of wild animals and the lives of native peoples. Both business and society have to address these resource issues.

MANAGING THE ENVIRONMENT

Preserving the natural environment and properly disposing of consumer and industrial waste have become major concerns in our society. As landfills become full, we have shifted our focus to reducing the growth of waste and to **recycling**—reusing products and packaging whenever possible. We are trying to conserve non-renewable resources, such as oil, natural gas, and iron ore. At the same time, we are using more renewable resources, such as electricity generated from the sun (solar power), from water, and from wind.

At times, pollution-control goals, such as improvement of air quality, may be at odds with energy conservation goals. For example, the use of coal, which is currently in great supply, generally pollutes air more than natural gas, which is in short supply. A business changing from coal to natural gas meets environmental goals but violates conservation goals. In contrast, a business changing from natural gas to coal conserves natural gas but creates pollution. In time, scientists may discover ways to use coal without creating a great deal of pollution. Until then, people have to decide how best to conserve natural resources and protect the environment.

ILLUSTRATION 2-3

How can pollution-control goals be at odds with energy conservation goals?

Pollution dangers have become more and more apparent. Large cities are often covered by smog that contains pollutants from motor vehicles. As a result, many residents suffer from breathing problems. In numerous rivers and lakes, pollutants have killed fish and other marine life. Chemical products used to destroy insects and plant life have especially endangered waterways and farmlands, and in some places entered the food chain.

CONTROLLING ENVIRONMENTAL POLLUTION

Many groups have pressured governments and employers to tighten pollution standards and to conserve natural resources. The federal government created the Environmental Protection Agency (EPA) in 1974 to help control and reduce pollution in the basic areas of air, water, solid waste, pesticides, noise, and radiation. The EPA enforces such laws as the Clean Air Act, Clean Water Act, Resource Recovery Act, Federal Water Pollution Control Act, Federal Environmental Pesticide Control Act, Noise Control Act, and Resource Conservation and Recovery Act. For instance, laws have been passed that require engines in cars to be both fuel-efficient and less polluting.

New waste disposal rules, especially for hazardous materials like medical and nuclear waste, are very strictly enforced and often costly to carry out. These high costs also encourage illegal dumping in bodies of water or on remote land areas. To conserve resources and to protect the environment, more and more companies are using recycled materials in their production processes.

In the aftermath of the Exxon Valdez accident, which spilled oil along coastal Alaska in 1989 and killed large numbers of marine life, environmentalists and socially minded groups formed the Coalition of Environmentally Responsible Economies to encourage companies to behave responsibly. The Coalition developed a list of ten environmental guidelines, named the CERES Principles. The Coalition asks organizations to follow the principles voluntarily; they are not legally required to do so.

Sun Oil Company (Sunoco) was the first major company that promised to follow the CERES Principles listed in Figure 2-4.

Laws against pollution and demands for conserving natural resources are costly to businesses. An issue arises when foreign countries have weaker laws, law enforcement is lax, or public concern over pollution and conservation is not as strong as in the U.S. As a result, companies in these foreign countries can make goods more cheaply than products made in America. One of the objections to increasing trade with Mexico, for example, is that pollution laws in Mexico are much weaker than in the U.S.

ETHICAL ISSUES

Laws provide a minimum standard of behavior for people and businesses to follow. However, many behaviors are neither allowed nor disallowed by law. The guide that then comes into play is ethics. **Ethics**

FIGURE 2-4
The CERES Principles

1. **Protect the environment from the release of pollutants, especially hazardous substances that may damage the environment.**
2. **Conserve nonrenewable natural resources through efficient use and careful planning.**
3. **Minimize the creation of waste, especially hazardous waste, and dispose of such materials in a safe, responsible manner.**
4. **Make every effort to use environmentally safe and sustainable energy sources to meet organizational needs.**
5. **Reduce environmental, health, and safety risks to employees and surrounding communities.**
6. **Sell products that cause as little damage to the environment as possible and are safe to use.**
7. **Accept responsibility for any harm the company causes to the environment; correct damages made to the environment, and compensate injured parties.**
8. **Keep the public informed of incidents relating to operations that harm the environment or pose health or safety hazards.**
9. **Appoint one person to represent environmental interests to serve on the highest-level decision-making committee that represents owner interests.**
10. **Produce and publicize a yearly self-evaluation of progress toward implementing these principles and meeting all applicable laws worldwide.**

Source: *www.ceres.org. Adapted from CERES: 1990. The 1990 CERES Guide to the Valdez Principles, The Social Investment Forum, Boston, MA.*

refers to standards of moral conduct that individuals and groups set for themselves, defining what behavior they value as right or wrong.

Ethical behavior is closely linked to personal values—underlying beliefs and attitudes that individuals or groups possess. To decide whether a particular action is ethical or not, we have to ask questions such as: Is the action right or is it wrong, regardless of what the laws state? Therefore, ethical conduct goes beyond state and federal laws.

BUSINESS ETHICS

A collection of principles and rules that define what is right and wrong conduct for an organization is called **business ethics.** Any action that does not conform to these moral principles is unethical behavior. All firms do not have the same rules of ethical conduct, however. Notions of what are right and wrong vary from manager to manager, business to business, and country to country. Generally, moral conduct that is favorable to the largest number of people is considered ethically desirable.

Many businesses have created codes of ethics to guide managers and workers in their behavior. A **code of ethics** is a formal, published collection of values and rules that reflect the firm's philosophy and goals. Having such a code removes or reduces opportunities for unethical conduct. These codes deal with such issues as accepting business gifts, bribing government officials, respecting the privacy and dignity of employees, and using company property for personal use.

Ethical codes are communicated to employees through memos, newsletters, posters, and employee manuals. Organizations establish procedures to handle situations that arise when employees violate the codes. To be effective, codes of ethics must have the full support of the organization's top-level managers. Codes are ineffective if they are not enforced.

ETHICAL DILEMMAS

The issue of ethics often arises when it is not clear whether a particular action is legal or illegal. As the opening story illustrated, the supervisor, Rayshawn Clark, is caught in the dilemma of revealing the future plans of the company versus ensuring business as usual. Philosophers have debated the issue of right and wrong for centuries. One well-known approach is to ask the question: What is the value or worth of a specific behavior for society as a whole? The best behavior is that which does the most good for the most people. For example, assume a company employed 200 people and it eliminated 50 people so that it could continue to operate. While 50 people were left jobless, 150 benefited by retaining their jobs.

Businesses are constantly faced with ethical dilemmas of various kinds. Should a lumber company cut down a forest if doing so would endanger a rare species of bird that nests there? Should oil drilling be permitted off a coast, thus destroying its natural beauty? Should a

ETHICAL ISSUES

ON A WAGE OF A DOLLAR A DAY

Nike, Inc., based in Beaverton, Oregon, is one of the most famous names in sports shoes. Sports shoes of all kinds carrying the famous swoosh logo are sold throughout the world, often at prices above $100. But how much does it cost to make these shoes?

Nike does not manufacture any of its shoes. Instead, it has them made by private contractors in countries such as Indonesia and Vietnam. Nike provides design and quality specifications and places orders for millions of pairs of shoes. Indonesia and Vietnam are poor countries where there are lots of unemployed people, and government laws and regulations are weak and unenforced.

Various non-governmental organizations have alleged that Nike's shoes are made under unacceptable working conditions. Workers as young as 14 working over 60 hours a week receive wages of about $1 a day. Safety and health standards are minimal. The cost of labor was estimated at less than 4 percent of the price that the consumer paid for a pair of shoes. Thus, shoes sold for $100 have a labor cost of less than $4. Even after paying the manufacturers and the distributors, Nike makes a profit of $15 on the pair.

Nike argued that its profits are comparable to those made by Reebok, Adidas, and others in the industry. It also claimed that the company had little control over the manufacturers, though Nike tried to ensure that these companies followed the employment laws of the respective countries with regard to minimum wages, hours of work, and the like.

Labor unions and human rights groups in the U.S. began a campaign to draw attention to the harsh conditions in which Nike's shoes were made. Pressure mounted on Nike's shareholders, bankers, retailers, and other stakeholders to force Nike to make changes in the working conditions at the foreign factories.

Nike reacted to the demand for change by establishing an office to monitor working conditions in the foreign factories. The critics demanded that independent monitoring groups in which they would be represented must be allowed to visit and inspect the factories abroad.

All this negative publicity led to sharp declines in sales and profits. Nike argued that it was incorrect to compare working conditions in the U.S. with those in less prosperous countries. The company pointed out that not too long ago, working conditions in the U.S. were also harsh, and only economic growth had led to the enlightened work conditions prevalent today.

THINK CRITICALLY

1. Suggest how Nike can successfully deal with the protests against it.
2. What is the motivation of the protestors against Nike? Why can't Nike ignore them?
3. Are Nike and its suppliers reacting in socially responsible ways? Why or why not?
4. Should one society force its work standards and wage rates on another? Why or why not?

ILLUSTRATION 2-4

Answers to ethical dilemmas are not clear-cut. How can managers reconcile conflicting goals?

manager accept a request of a foreign official to arrange for his daughter's admission to an American university if the company wants to land a contract? Should a business hire a woman to win support from women's groups? How businesses handle these issues determine whether they are acting in an ethical manner. Notions of what is right or wrong change over time. Answers often are not clear-cut.

Because values also differ among nations, problems sometimes arise for firms involved in international business. Firms have to choose between the ethical practices of the foreign country or of their home country. For instance, it is an accepted business practice in Japan for employees to give expensive gifts to their bosses. Such behavior in the U.S. is generally discouraged. Should an American company behave in Japan as it does in the U.S., or should it follow the Japanese practice? Answers to such questions are not readily apparent, and managers have to find ways to reconcile conflicting goals.

SOCIAL RESPONSIBILITY OF BUSINESS

A question often raised is: What is business's responsibility to help solve society's problems? The answer is not simple, because the profit motive of the business often collides with what is good for society. Should businesses accept lower profit, for instance, in order to keep jobs in a declining community? In such cases, businesses must decide for themselves what is right and wrong.

The primary goal of business is to make a profit for the owners. Businesses cannot survive for long if their owners are not rewarded for their investment. Although profit plays a key role in our business system, businesses today also emphasize another business goal—social responsibility. **Social responsibility** refers to the duty of a business to contribute to the well being of society. Because businesses depend

ILLUSTRATION 2-5

The primary goal of a business is to make a profit. But does a business have a duty to contribute to society's well being?

on society for resources, opportunities, and rights, they have an obligation to the communities in which they operate.

Stakeholders are any individuals or groups that are affected by the firm's actions, such as owners, customers, suppliers, employees, creditors, government, and the public. Stakeholders expect a business to be responsible and responsive to their interests. Such responsibility may mean a variety of things. Examples include donating money to flood victims, sponsoring an exhibition on Hindu art at a local museum, providing scholarships to colleges for needy students, training gang members in job-related skills, and setting up day-care centers for employees' children.

Thus, a business's social responsibility means accepting a duty to contribute to the well being of its stakeholders. Stakeholders usually believe that a business has the resources to contribute to a community's well being. Also, good deeds translate into favorable publicity for the business, which, in turn, means more sales and profits. The founders of Ben and Jerry's, the ice cream makers, for example, commit themselves to buying expensive milk from hormone-free Vermont dairy farms and giving 7 percent of pre-tax profits to charity. Such actions endear them to the residents of Vermont, where their operations are based.

Milton Friedman, a renowned economist, once said that "the business of business is business." People who follow his view believe that if a business uses some of its profits for social causes rather than using all profits to grow the business, the company will not remain very profitable. Thus, workers will get lower wages, customers will pay higher prices, and the owners will make less profit. Questions are also raised about the ability of a business to solve social problems. Does a manager know how to solve drug abuse? Should a business be responsible for promoting sporting events in the community? Are these not roles for the government or others to perform?

Despite these serious concerns, it is now widely recognized that business has an important responsibility to its stakeholders. Business has also realized that by getting involved socially, it advances its own interests. Enhancing goodwill in the community reduces government's desire to regulate the business.

Some businesses review their social programs regularly. The reviews show what the business is doing to fulfill its social responsibilities, its success in accomplishing its goals, and its plans for pursuing future activities.

The conduct of businesses is being increasingly and closely examined by various independent groups known as **non-governmental organizations (NGOs).** Examples of such organizations are the American Civil Liberties Union and the Sierra Club. They specialize in particular issues, such as workplace discrimination or environmental protection. NGOs influence businesses through lobbying, publicity, and pressure tactics to alter their activities.

THE FUTURE

Given the fast pace of change in the world today, society and business will face different issues in the future. While it is difficult to predict the future, current trends provide hints of what may be in store in the years to come.

Various economic and social data provide an in-depth picture of changes occurring in American society. The racial and ethnic mix of the labor force will continue to change. The Internet is dramatically altering how people communicate and businesses operate. Computer-related jobs are multiplying, as entrepreneurs establish Internet companies to find new applications of this new technology.

Businesses are apt to become more and more involved in providing social services to the community that, in the past, had been provided by families, funded by the government, or purchased by individuals. The general public has become more conscious of environmental and human rights issues, and there is growing concern over balancing family and work life. Businesses have to ensure that their activities do not harm the natural environment and that they respect the individual rights of a rapidly diversifying workforce. As societal values change, each business will continue to shape and be shaped by the society in which it functions.

CHAPTER CONCEPTS

- The U.S. population has been growing largely because of immigration and because Americans are living longer. It is also becoming more diverse. The trend has been for people and businesses to locate to the southern part of the country.
- American society and its values are in constant change and this affects how businesses function. Changes include the growth in the number of women in the workforce, changes in the nature of the family, increasing job insecurity, stress, and violence. Poverty and discrimination persist. Businesses are becoming more environmentally conscious.
- Businesses are responding to employee needs by redesigning jobs, improving workplace health and safety, and providing flexible scheduling and family-friendly benefits.
- Ethical conduct by businesses requires doing more than the law prescribes. Businesses establish codes of ethics to identify right and wrong behavior for employees. Managers are often confronted by situations in which ethical solutions are not clear-cut.
- The goal of business extends beyond merely making profits to being socially responsible to their various stakeholders.

BUILD VOCABULARY POWER

Define the following terms and concepts.

1. baby boom
2. baby bust
3. Frost Belt
4. Sun Belt
5. Rust Belt
6. labor force
7. labor participation rate
8. glass ceiling
9. sticky floor syndrome
10. comparable worth
11. Generation X
12. Net Generation
13. telecommute
14. recycling
15. ethics
16. business ethics
17. code of ethics
18. social responsibility
19. stakeholders
20. non-governmental organizations

REVIEW FACTS

1. What factors are contributing to the growth of the population in the U.S.?
2. What has caused the decline in the number of young workers in recent years?
3. Why is the age and ethnic make-up of the population important to business?
4. How has the movement of people from the cities to the suburbs and from the Frost Belt to the Sun Belt affected the cities and businesses?

5. Why has there been an increase in the labor participation rate for women?
6. Why are many women and minorities unable to advance in their organization?
7. Why is it difficult for employers to design and implement comparable worth plans?
8. Give two examples of how values have changed in the U.S. in the past 20 years and how these changes have affected businesses.
9. Why do forward-looking firms provide wellness and fitness programs and child-care facilities for their employees?
10. What actions has the federal government taken to protect the environment?
11. If a firm agrees to abide by the CERES Principles, what impact will it have on how it organizes and operates its business?
12. How does ethics differ from laws?
13. Give two reasons why businesses should not get involved in socially responsible projects.
14. Give two reasons why businesses should be socially responsible.
15. In the coming decade, (a) what types of occupations will have the greatest growth potential and (b) what types of occupations will have the least growth potential?

DISCUSS IDEAS

1. Why should anyone who studies American business principles and management also study the social problems of the U.S.?
2. If present trends in the composition of the population continue, what types of businesses will be most affected in the future?
3. Employers cannot always find people to fill some of the new jobs that have been created. Discuss what employers, the education system, businesses, and governments can do to address this problem.
4. List and discuss the factors that contribute to poverty.
5. Most city bus drivers are male, but nearly all nurses are female. Bus drivers often earn more money than nurses. (a) Does the idea of comparable worth apply to both jobs? (b) How might you argue that nurses should be paid the same, more, or less than bus drivers?
6. How are changes in technology, primarily the Internet, affecting relationships between individuals and businesses?
7. Identify a list of employer practices that have enhanced the quality of work life for employees.
8. Give two examples of how environmental goals can be at odds with energy conservation goals.
9. Since businesses are established for making profits, the only way to ensure that they behave ethically is to have strong laws that require them to do so. Do you agree with this statement? Justify your answer.

10. On prom night at your school, your town's Taxicab Association announced that it would provide free drop-off and pick-up services to all students participating in the event. Give three reasons why the Taxicab Association is providing this service.
11. Since values differ from country to country, how should a manager address ethical issues? Should she (a) apply American values abroad, (b) follow the value system of the foreign country, or (c) develop a universal value system that can be applied in any country?
12. How can a business ensure that its code of ethics will be effective?

ANALYZE INFORMATION

1. Use the Internet to obtain data on where immigrants to the United States come from today and from where they came in the 1960s. Explain why and how they have changed. Data can be obtained from the U.S. Census Bureau.
2. Refer to Figure 2-3, which provides information about the labor force participation rate for males and females, and answer these questions:
   a. What is the trend in the labor force participation rate for females?
   b. What is the trend in the labor force participation rate for males?
   c. What are the explanations for these trends?
   d. Do you think participation rates can reach 100 percent? Why or why not?
3. Assume that the total population of the United States is 290 million, of which 220 million are 16 years of age and above. Of this 220 million, 35 million are full-time homemakers, 45 million are full-time students, and 20 million are retirees. Six million are unemployed but looking for work. The rest are employed. With this information, answer the following questions:
   a. What is the size of the labor force?
   b. Calculate the labor force participation rate.
   c. Which groups are not considered part of the labor force?
   d. What would happen to the labor force participation rate if the number of people unemployed increased?
4. Consider any business with which you are familiar. It might be a gas station, a supermarket, a restaurant, or a bank. Assume that your business has agreed to follow the CERES Principles. Develop a list of specific activities the business must perform if it is to live up to the Principles.
5. A recent study on ethics of over 2,000 office employees tried to determine whether people who attend religious services weekly are more ethical than those who attend rarely. The following

results were reported in percents. Answer the questions that follow the reported results.

Do you . . .	*Attend Religious Services* Weekly	Rarely
Twist rules when dealing with others	22	33
Bend the truth a bit in what you tell others	21	31
Use office equipment for personal projects	22	37
Take time off from work when you should not have	8	19
Feel somewhat less than completely honest when filing tax returns	8	6

a. Do those who attend religious services weekly or rarely act in unethical ways?

b. For which question is there the greatest percentage difference between those who attend religious services weekly and rarely?

c. Why might the people who attend religious services weekly be more unethical than those who attend rarely in regard to filing tax returns?

d. In one sentence, what conclusion can you reach from this study?

SOLVE BUSINESS PROBLEMS

CASE 2-1

Greengrocers, a major food company in the United States, stores cans and bottles of packaged foods such as vegetables, fruits, cereal, and meats in its warehouses. The quality of the food in the packages declines over time. Therefore, an expiration date is stamped on the packages, after which the product cannot be sold, even though the food in the packages is not spoiled and is still edible. Were it not for strict rules laid down by the government, the expiration date could easily be pushed to the future and the food would still be fit for human consumption.

Packages with expired dates are returned to Greengrocers, where they are destroyed. Recently an opportunity appeared for Greengrocers to use the expired food packages. A hurricane had devastated parts of Mexico, leaving people homeless and without food. Greengrocers decided to make a generous donation of free packaged food to the destitute Mexicans, and this was announced with great fanfare. The U.S. military transported the food on one of its relief flights. The donation was reported in the national media, and Greengrocers received favorable publicity as a socially responsible firm stepping in to lessen human misery in the highest tradition of American generosity.

The donated packages, of course, had expired dates. Mexico's laws on selling food products with expired dates were very weak and rarely enforced. Greengrocers' managers assumed that starving people would rather have food with expired dates than no food. In any case, the food was still edible. In addition, Greengrocers could claim a charitable contribution tax deduction in the United States.

Once the relief flight arrived in Mexico, the donated food was turned over to a relief organization, Save the Children Fund, for distribution to the hungry. While several young American volunteers unpacked the boxes, they noticed that the packages had expired dates. A huge group of starving Mexicans was waiting for the packages while the correspondent of a television network waited to broadcast the event in the United States. What was broadcast instead was news about the expired dates on the donated food.

Think Critically:

1. Since Mexico has weak laws on food dates and the food was still edible, do you think Greengrocers acted in a socially responsible manner? Explain.
2. If you were the president of Greengrocers, how would you explain your conduct now that the details of the donation were revealed?
3. Suggest some ways by which Greengrocers can discourage unethical conduct by its employees in the future.

CASE 2-2

Cigarettes are a lawful product in the U.S. Many farmers grow tobacco, and big companies such as Phillip Morris process the leaves into cigarettes. Thousands of people are employed in the industry, and local, state, and federal governments earn billions of dollars in taxes on the sale of tobacco products.

Although the Surgeon General of the United States has long required that cigarette packages carry a warning stating that smoking is injurious to health, it was only in the 1990s that a concerted campaign was mounted to discourage smoking and to punish tobacco companies. After denying it for decades, senior managers of the tobacco companies admitted that smoking was addictive and dangerous to human health. Lawsuits were filed against the company by state governments that claimed compensation for the extra medical costs that had to be incurred for treating people suffering from smoking-related illnesses. Individuals who had become ill from smoking sued the tobacco firms for being unwittingly seduced into the habit through aggressive advertising. Groups such as flight attendants claimed that they were subjected to second-hand smoke from passengers and thus needed to be compensated for their suffering. In addition, the government drew up plans to ban advertising of tobacco products and ultimately to ban the product itself.

Faced with such opposition, the tobacco companies agreed to pay the government billions of dollars, reduce their active advertising of the product, and accept stringent laws on how the product would be described and distributed. Phillip Morris recognized that the U.S. was no longer going to be a viable market for its cigarettes. The cost of doing business was only going to rise as individual Americans began filing lawsuits. The company instead turned its attention to countries in Asia, such as China, Thailand, and Turkey. In those countries, health concerns over smoking were not yet fully recognized, and the governments earned lots of money through taxing tobacco products. The quality of locally produced cigarettes was not high, and American cigarettes were highly valued. Through creative advertising, American cigarettes had acquired an image of success, glamour, and independence, all of which made a strong mark on young Asian consumers, whose numbers were very large. Phillip Morris agreed to build cigarette factories in the foreign countries to create jobs, and foreign governments welcomed that. Sales of Phillip Morris in foreign countries rose sharply while they stagnated in the United States.

Think Critically:

1. Is the behavior of Phillip Morris to aggressively sell cigarettes abroad socially responsible? Explain.
2. Should the foreign governments be as concerned over tobacco smoking as the American government is?
3. Should individual Americans sue tobacco companies because they smoke, although they have been warned through labels that smoking is harmful?
4. Should Phillip Morris have disclosed to the public that cigarette smoking was addictive as soon as it found out?

PROJECT: MY BUSINESS, INC.

The way people in a community view a business can often determine whether it will be successful or not. A business owner must consider changes in population, income, attitudes, and values. In this chapter, you will study the social environment in which your business will operate and the importance of socially responsible and ethical operations to business success.

DATA COLLECTION

INTERNET

1. Collect newspaper and magazine articles or information from the Internet that describes social and environmental changes that could affect your business. Try to identify issues that have national/international implications as well as those that are currently important to your own community.

2. Interview five people of various ages and backgrounds. Ask them to describe their positive and negative feelings about fast-food businesses. Then ask them the same questions about the health and fitness industry. Create a table that compares the positive and negative responses for each type of business.
3. Discuss the importance of ethics in business with a business person. (Use your business mentor if you have one for the continuing project.) Ask the person to identify the areas of business operations where he or she believes ethics is most important.

4. Contact government agencies in your community to identify local recycling regulations that will affect your type of business as well as health laws that your business must observe. (Many local and state governments have a Web site that provides information for businesses. Try to locate a government Web site that helps you gather the needed information.)

ANALYSIS

1. Using information from the Internet or business publications, try to describe the typical customers for health and fitness products. Develop charts that illustrate the information you gathered, including age, gender, education level, ethnicity/race, and any other important descriptive characteristics.
2. Develop a set of at least four operating rules and procedures for your business that will demonstrate to the citizens of the community that you are concerned about their feelings, will operate ethically, and have a sense of social responsibility. Examples include the use of resources, pollution, product quality, and employment practices.
3. Review the information collected from your interviews with the five people completed for #2 of the Data Collection activities. Indicate what you can do within the operation of your business to take advantage of the positive factors and to overcome the negative factors you identified.
4. A concern expressed about some juice bar businesses is the addition of supplements (vitamins, minerals, energy boosters, etc.) at an additional charge. One concern is the health impact of the supplements—can some actually be unhealthy for many people? Another concern is that the price charged for the supplements is very high compared to their cost to the business. Each of these is an ethical dilemma for a business owner. Select either the health dilemma or the pricing dilemma. Complete an analysis of the dilemma, describing both sides of the issue. Make a specific decision about how you would respond to the dilemma as the business owner.

ECONOMIC ENVIRONMENT OF BUSINESS

OBJECTIVES

- 3-1 Describe economic concepts that apply to satisfying economic wants.
- 3-2 Discuss three economic systems and three economic-political systems.
- 3-3 Summarize five fundamental elements of capitalism.
- 3-4 Explain how economic growth can be promoted and measured.
- 3-5 List basic economic problems that exist and state what government can do to correct the problems.

HARD WORK PAYS OFF

Juan Gonzales grew up in a small Mexican village. His parents were "dirt-poor shopkeepers," as he would often say, but Juan's dad was intent on going to America. And that's what the family did when Juan was 19. They moved to a large village in the state of New Mexico.

Upon arrival his parents bought a small neighborhood grocery store that had a large back yard. Juan entered a technical college where he learned about agricultural methods. One day after graduation his father said, "Join me in running the store, Juan. Maybe together we can expand with this growing neighborhood." Juan smiled and told his dad he would use the large back yard and his new knowledge to experiment with raising and selling vegetables. Within a year, customers from other neighborhoods were stopping by the Gonzales store to buy Juan's fresh produce.

By the second year, the family decided to expand the store and move to a nearby shopping area. Juan's dad had already bought a farm to expand the popular vegetable department and to add a homegrown fruit department as well. The store would now be called the Gonzales Fruit and Vegetable Market. Within a short time, the store was prospering. Like so many people before them, another family of motivated and hard-working immigrants had succeeded in a country known for its prosperous economic system. The Gonzales family had become an active part of the country's growing economy.

All societies face the problem of trying to satisfy the wants of their citizens for goods and services. Although all societies share this problem, different societies developed different systems for producing and using goods and services. The body of knowledge that relates to producing and using goods and services that satisfy human wants is called **economics**.

At the beginning of this chapter, you will study the concepts that are essential to understanding any economic system. You will then learn about the world's economic systems, along with economic-political systems. The chapter concludes with fundamentals of capitalism and factors related to economic growth.

SATISFYING OUR ECONOMIC WANTS

Businesses help to make the economic system work by producing and distributing the particular goods and services that people want. A good place to begin the study of economics is with the two broad categories of wants found throughout an economic system: economic wants and non-economic wants.

People have many wants. The economic system, however, operates on the basis of **economic wants**—the desire for scarce material goods and services. People want material goods, such as clothing, housing, and cars. They also want services, such as hair care, medical attention,

ILLUSTRATION 3-1

Everyone has wants for scarce goods and services, and not all wants can be satisfied. What do you want most that you cannot afford? And what are the greatest wants of your closest friend or your parents?

and public transportation. Items such as these are scarce because no economic system has the resources to satisfy all the wants of all people for all material goods and services. People also have non-economic wants. **Non-economic wants** are desires for non-material things that are not scarce, such as air, sunshine, friendship, and happiness.

The goods and services that people want have to be produced. Clothes must be made. Homes must be built. Personal services must be supplied. And as you learned in the opening scenario, the Gonzales family expects their customers to want fruit, vegetables, and other basic foods.

UTILITY

Utility is the ability of a good or a service to satisfy a want. In other words, a good or a service that has utility is a useful good or service. Something is not useful, however, unless it is available for use in the right form and place and at the right time. As a result, four common types of utility exist: form, place, time, and possession. Definitions of the four types of utility, with examples, appear in Figure 3-1.

Anyone who creates utility is a **producer.** Producers are entitled to a reward for the usefulness that they add to a good or service. Hair stylists are entitled to a reward for the usefulness of their services. The price you pay for a pen includes a reward for the manufacturer who made the pen, the shipping company that delivered it to the merchant, and the retailer who made it possible for you to buy the pen at the time you wanted it.

Types of Economic Utility

FORM UTILITY

Created by changes in the form or shape of a product to make it useful. (Form utility usually applies only to goods and not to services.) Example: Is the swimsuit you desire to buy available in a particular fabric and style?

PLACE UTILITY

Created by having a good or service at the place where it is needed or wanted. Example: Is the swimsuit you desire available in a nearby store where it can be purchased?

TIME UTILITY

Created when a product or service is available when it is needed or wanted. Example: Is the store open when you are ready to buy and use your swimsuit?

POSSESSION UTILITY

Created when ownership of a good or service is transferred from one person to another, but may also occur through renting and borrowing. Example: Is the swimsuit available at a price you can afford and are willing to pay?

FIGURE 3-1

Satisfying wants involves four common types of utility.

FACTORS OF PRODUCTION

In creating useful goods and services, a producer uses four basic resources. These resources, called **factors of production,** are land (natural resources), labor, capital goods, and entrepreneurship.

NATURAL RESOURCES The extent to which a country is able to produce goods and services is, in part, determined by its natural resources that its land provides. **Natural resources** are anything provided by nature that affects the productive ability of a country. The productive ability of the United States, for example, depends on its fertile soil, minerals, water and timber resources, and mild climate.

LABOR **Labor** is the human effort, either physical or mental, that goes into the production of goods and services. In today's world of technology and special equipment such as computers, physical effort is much less important than mental effort—knowing what tasks to complete and how to complete them. A part of labor is **human capital,** the accumulated knowledge and skills of human beings—the total value of each person's education and acquired skills. In a highly technological world, the need for human capital has increased significantly. Juan's expertise at growing fruit and vegetables and his father's knowledge and skill needed to operate a store are examples of labor and human capital.

CAPITAL GOODS To produce goods that people want, producers need capital goods. **Capital goods** are buildings, tools, machines, and other equipment used to produce other goods but do not directly satisfy human wants. A robot on a car assembly line is an example of a capital good. The robot does not directly satisfy human wants. Instead, it helps make the cars that do satisfy human wants. Capital goods allow the production of goods in large quantities which, in turn, should decrease production costs and increase the productivity of labor.

ENTREPRENEURSHIP For the production of goods, more is needed than the mere availability of natural resources, labor, and capital goods. Someone, or some group, must take the risks involved in starting a business and plan and manage the production of the final product. Entrepreneurship, the fourth factor of production, brings together the other three factors—land (natural resources), labor, and capital. By starting and managing a business, Juan and his father are acting as entrepreneurs. You will learn more about the many aspects of management in Unit 4.

Because government provides many services that are essential to the operation of a business, economists often list it as a fifth factor of production. Some of the essential services provided by government are streets and highways, police and fire protection, and courts that settle disputes.

CAPITAL FORMATION

The production of capital goods is called **capital formation.** Capital goods, such as buildings and equipment, are needed to produce consumer goods and services. The Ford truck that Juan uses to deliver farm products to the store is a capital good. Unlike capital goods, **consumer goods and services** are goods and services that directly satisfy people's economic wants. The foods that Juan's father sells customers are consumer goods.

A country is capable of producing a fixed quantity of goods and services at any one time. As a result, total production is divided between capital goods and consumer goods and services. When the production of consumer goods and services increases, the production of capital goods decreases. On the other hand, when the production of consumer goods and services decreases, the production of capital goods increases. New capital goods must be made—capital formation—in order to add to the total supply and to replace worn-out capital goods. Capital formation takes place, for example, when steel is used to produce the tools and machinery (capital goods) needed to make cars rather than to produce the cars themselves (consumer goods).

When productive resources are used for capital formation, it becomes possible to produce more consumer goods. For example, when robots and other tools and machinery are produced for making trucks, it is then possible to increase the production of trucks.

However, using steel, labor, and management to produce tools and machinery (capital goods) means that these same resources cannot also be used for automobiles (consumer goods). The immediate result is that consumers have fewer automobiles to buy. But, because the tools and machinery were made, consumers will have more automobiles to buy in the future. China and other developing countries are examples of nations that use a large portion of their productive resources in capital formation rather than in the production of consumer goods and services. Developing nations must take this first step before they can satisfy consumers with consumer products.

ECONOMIC SYSTEMS

Remember that no country has enough resources to satisfy all the wants of all people for material goods and services. Because productive resources are scarce, difficult decisions must be made about how to use these limited resources. For example, somehow countries must decide whether to produce more capital goods and fewer consumer goods or more consumer goods and fewer capital goods.

All countries have an economic system. An **economic system** is an organized way for a country to decide how to use its productive resources; that is, to decide what, how, and for whom goods and services will be produced. While there are many countries in the world, all economies operate under some form of three basic economic systems, described below.

TYPES OF ECONOMIC SYSTEMS

The primary types of economic systems are a market economy, a command economy, and a mixed economy. All countries' economic systems have characteristics of these basic three types.

A **market economy** is an economic system in which individual buying decisions in the marketplace together determine what, how, and for whom goods and services will be produced. For example, if more consumers choose to buy whole-grain bread than white bread, their buying decisions will influence bread producers to use their productive resources to produce more whole-grain and less white bread. Thus, individual consumers, making their own decisions about what to buy, collectively determine how the society's productive resources will be used. In a market economy, individual citizens, rather than the government, own most of the factors of production, such as land and manufacturing facilities. The free enterprise system found in the United States is the best example of a market economy.

A **command economy** is an economic system in which a central planning authority, under the control of the country's government, owns most of the factors of production and determines what, how, and for whom goods and services will be produced. Countries that adopt a command economy are often dictatorships. The government, rather than consumers, decides how the factors of production will be used.

Forms of command economies exist in some Asian countries—North Korea, Cambodia, and Vietnam—and in other small countries, such as Cuba.

A **mixed economy** is an economic system that uses aspects of a market and a command economy to make decisions about what, how, and for whom goods and services will be produced. In a mixed economy, the national government makes production decisions for certain goods and services. For example, the post office, telephone system, schools, health care facilities, and public utilities are often owned and operated by governments.

No country has a pure market economy or command economy. All have mixed economies, although some have more elements of a market economy and others have more elements of a command economy. In the United States and Canada, for example, the government plays a smaller role in the economy than it does in the more command-oriented economies of Cuba and Sweden. Even countries of the former Soviet Union, once a predominately command economy, now allow some privately owned businesses to operate freely and make their own economic decisions, such as what to offer for sale and at what prices. China and Iraq do as well.

Today most countries are moving more toward market economies. For example, England, France, Sweden, Mexico, and Eastern European countries have restricted the number of goods and services owned and controlled by national governments. China also has been making major attempts to move more toward a market economy.

Privatization is the transfer of authority to provide a good or service from a government to individuals or privately owned businesses.

ILLUSTRATION 3-2

Each nation decides whether to have a market, command, or mixed economic system. These same nations may change economic systems from time to time. Can you name any countries that have changed their economic systems in recent years?

Some governments of former Soviet countries have sold telephone and transportation services to private firms. Some states and cities in this country have privatized by paying businesses to operate jails, collect trash, run cafeterias in government buildings, and perform data processing activities. The governments' incentive is to reduce costs for the taxpayers and to increase efficiency.

TYPES OF ECONOMIC-POLITICAL SYSTEMS

Each country has an economic system and a political system. The political system nearly always determines the economic system. Because the two systems cannot be separated, we refer to them as an economic-political system.

The importance of the individual citizen has always been emphasized in the United States. Therefore, the U.S. developed an economic-political system that permits a great deal of individual freedom. History tells us that there is a relationship between political and economic freedom; that is, political freedom usually is found in countries where individuals and businesses have economic freedom. And political freedom is quite limited in countries that do not give people and organizations much economic freedom.

All economic-political systems are forms of three basic types: capitalism, socialism, and communism. As you read about these three economic-political systems, compare their features as shown in Figure 3-2.

CAPITALISM The economic-political system in the United States is called *capitalism,* or the *free enterprise system,* which operates in a democracy. **Capitalism** is an economic-political system in which private citizens are free to go into business for themselves, to produce whatever they choose to produce, and to distribute what they produce. Also included is the right to own property.

This strict definition of capitalism would have accurately described our economic system during much of the nineteenth century and the early part of the twentieth century. In recent decades, however, government has assumed an important economic role in the United States. As the economy developed without controls by government, certain abuses took place. For example, some people began to interfere with the economic freedom of others. Some large businesses began to exploit small businesses. In addition, manufacturing firms did not take into account the cost of pollution. In essence, these costs were passed on to the public. For example, assume a firm produced a new type of pesticide and sold it to farmers and gardeners. Several years after some pesticide had washed into streams and lakes, it was found to kill fish and harm swimmers. Neither the producer nor the buyers of the pesticide were required to pay for damages. The public ultimately pays in the form of poor health and medical costs as well as in the inability to safely swim in lakes. To protect the public and to correct such abuses,

Comparison of Economic-Political Systems

FIGURE 3-2

Three main economic-political systems exist throughout the world.

	CAPITALISM	SOCIALISM	COMMUNISM
	Market/ Mixed Economy	Mixed Economy	Command/ Mixed Economy
Who may own natural resources and capital goods?	Businesses and individuals	Government for some, but not all	Government for most
How are resources allocated?	By customers based on competition	By government for some and customers for others	By government only
To what extent does government attempt to control business decisions?	Limited	Extensive over the allocation of some resources, but little over distribution	Extensive
How are marketing decisions made?	By market conditions	By market conditions	By government
What one country is a good example of this economic system?	United States	Sweden	North Korea

Congress passed laws, many of which require producers to avoid harm to the public or reduce the costs to the public of the producers' operations.

SOCIALISM **Socialism** is an economic-political system in which the government controls the use of the country's factors of production. How scarce resources are used to satisfy the many wants of people is decided, in part, by the government.

Socialists do not agree as to how much of the productive resources government should own. The most extreme socialists want government to own all natural resources and capital goods. Middle-of-the-road socialists believe that planning production for the whole economy can be achieved if government owns certain key industries, but they also believe that other productive resources should be owned by individuals and businesses. As a result, socialism is often associated with mixed economies.

Socialism is generally disliked in the United States because it limits the right of the individual to own property for productive purposes. The right to own property, however, exists in socialistic economies in different degrees, depending upon the amount of government ownership and control. Socialism in its different forms exists in many countries, particularly in the Western European countries of Sweden and Italy.

COMMUNISM **Communism** is extreme socialism, in which all or almost all of a nation's factors of production are owned by the government. Decisions regarding what to produce, how much to produce, and how to divide the results of production among the citizens are made by government agencies on the basis of a government plan. Government measures how well producers perform on the basis of volume of goods and services produced, without much regard for the quality of or demand for the goods or services. A command economy is most often practiced by communist countries.

Consumer goods are often in short supply in communist countries such as Cuba and North Korea, because the government channels a large proportion of the factors of production toward capital formation. Even Chinese leaders have recognized the shortcomings of the system when it comes to meeting the needs of consumers. As a result, they are making adjustments that introduce market economy principles. Two such adjustments are judging the performance of producers by the demand for their products and permitting consumer demand to influence production.

Workers in a communist system cannot move easily from one job to another. And managers of businesses do not decide what is to be produced. A communist country's central planning agency makes most such decisions. Capitalism relies, instead, on consumers and managers to make these decisions. People in a communist society do not own property. All economic decisions are made by government leaders. These leaders decide how scarce resources will be used. The members of a communist country have few of the economic freedoms that Americans believe are important.

In general, communist countries that try to move toward capitalism face both political and economic problems in the short run, as Russia and China are now experiencing. The process of transition is difficult because the economic and social infrastructure needed for a market economy is not in place. For example, in the command economy of the Soviet Union, the government directed what was to be done and there essentially was no legal system governing contracts.

FUNDAMENTALS OF CAPITALISM

As you learned earlier, some economic-political systems either do not permit ownership of property (communism) or may impose limitations on ownership (socialism). One of the basic features of capitalism is the right to private property. Others include the right of each business to make a profit, to set its own prices, to compete, and to determine the wages paid to workers.

PRIVATE PROPERTY

The principle of private property is essential to our capitalistic system. **Private property** consists of items of value that individuals have the right to own, use, and sell. Thus, individuals can control productive resources. They can own land, hire labor, and own capital goods. They can use these resources to produce goods and services. Also, individuals own the products made from their use of land, labor, and capital goods. Thus, the company that produces furniture owns the furniture it makes. The furniture company may sell its furniture, and it owns the money received from the buyer. The Gonzales family owns its store, the farm it purchased, and the food it produces and buys before selling it. And the family is entitled to make and keep its profits.

PROFIT

In a capitalistic system, the incentive as well as the reward for producing goods and services is **profit,** which is computed by subtracting the total costs of producing the products from the total received from customers who buy them. The company making furniture, for example, has costs for land, labor, capital goods, and materials. Profit is what the furniture company has left after subtracting these costs from the amount received from selling its furniture.

ILLUSTRATION 3-3

One of the basic features of capitalism is the right to private property. How is property ownership handled in socialist and communist systems?

The profit earned by a business is often overestimated by society. The average profit is about 5 percent of total receipts while the remainder, 95 percent, represents costs. Consider a motel with yearly receipts of \$500,000. If the profit amounts to 5 percent, then the owner earns \$25,000; that is, \$500,000 times .05. Costs for the year are .95 times \$500,000, or \$475,000. Some types of businesses have higher average profit percentages, but many have lower ones or even losses. Owners, of course, try to earn a profit percentage that is better than average.

Being in business does not guarantee that a company will make a profit. Among other things, to be successful a company must produce goods or services that people want at a price they are willing to pay. Other fundamental features of capitalism covered next deal with competition and the distribution of income.

PRICE SETTING

Demand for a product refers to the number of products that will be bought at a given time at a given price. Thus, demand is not the same as want. Wanting an expensive luxury car without having the money to buy one does not represent demand. Demand for a Mercedes Benz is represented by the people who want it, have the money to buy it, and are willing to spend the money for it.

There is a relationship between price and demand. With increased demand, prices generally rise in the short run. Later, when demand decreases, prices generally fall. For example, if a new large-screen TV suddenly becomes popular, its price may rise. However, when the TV is no longer in high demand, its price will likely drop.

The supply of a product also influences its price. **Supply** of a product refers to the number of like products that will be offered for sale at a particular time and at a certain price. If there is a current shortage in the supply of a product, its price will usually rise as consumers bid against one another to obtain the product. For example, if bad weather damages an apple crop and apples are in short supply, the price of apples will go up. When apples become more abundant, their price will go down. Thus, price changes are the result of changes in both the demand for and the supply of a product.

Generally, changes in prices determine what is produced and how much is produced in our economy. Price changes indicate to businesses what is profitable or not profitable to produce. If consumers want more sports shoes than are being produced, they will bid up the price of

CYBER COMMUNICATION

There are several advantages to using e-mail. It is usually very fast. In many cases, messages can be delivered to the recipient either immediately or up to a few minutes later. It can also be very efficient, since the process is electronic and no paper is necessary. With certain software applications, you can copy material from other documents and insert it as part of the message, or you can attach files for the recipient to use.

E-mail is also very convenient. As long as your keyboarding skills are adequate, you can easily prepare a message and send it off any time you need to communicate with someone. Messages can be sent and received without the opposite party being available at that time.

ACTIVITY Despite all the advantages of using e-mail, there are definite disadvantages. Divide into teams with your classmates and prepare a list of at least five possible disadvantages. Then present your list to the rest of the class. If you are an e-mail user, give some examples of problems you have personally encountered.

sports shoes. The increase in the price of the shoes makes it more profitable to make them and provides the incentive for manufacturers to increase the production of sports shoes. As the supply of the shoes increases to satisfy the demand for more shoes, the price of the shoes will fall. Since it is now less profitable to make sports shoes, manufacturers will decrease their production of them.

Prices, then, are determined by the forces of supply and demand; that is, prices are the result of the decisions of individual consumers to buy products and of individual producers to make and sell products. Therefore, consumers help decide what will be produced and how much will be produced.

Here is how supply and demand work in setting prices. Refer to Figure 3-3 as you study this example of a producer planning to sell a sweatshirt. In Figure 3-3, the market price for the sweatshirt, $30, is shown where the supply line crosses the demand line. The market price is the price at which the producer can meet costs and make a reasonable profit. It is also the price at which consumers will buy enough of the product for the producer to make a reasonable profit.

If demand drops, profit drops; but if demand increases, the producer's profits will increase. If the profit gets quite large, other producers will enter into production with similar sweatshirts, which will then increase the total supply and lower the price. If the supply and demand lines never cross, the producer will not make the goods, because not enough consumers will want the product at the offered price and the profit reward disappears. If Juan Gonzales grows a new type of apple but only a small number of people buy them, he will lose money and stop growing those apples.

ILLUSTRATION 3-4

Prices for many products and services are determined by the forces of supply and demand. What causes the price of gasoline to change from time to time?

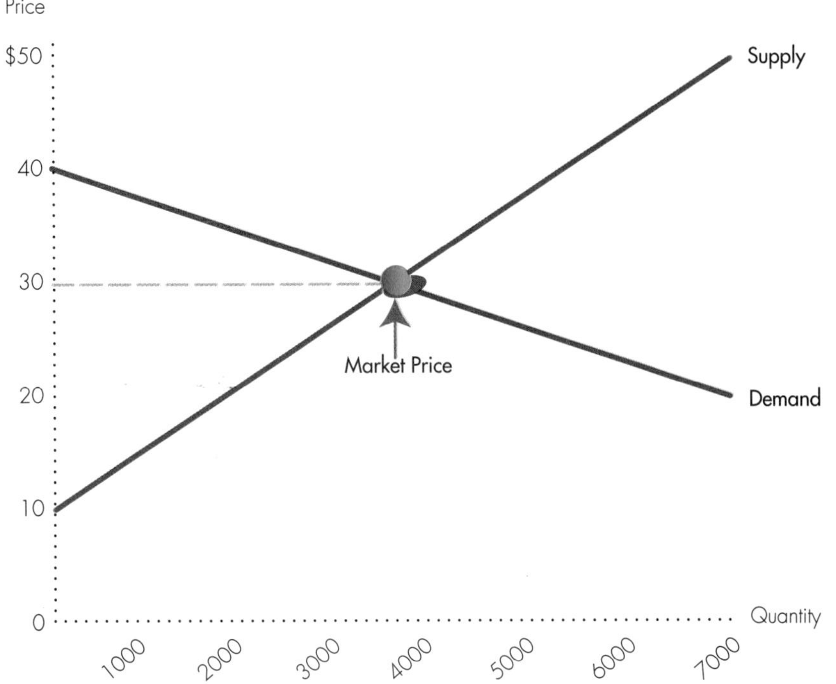

FIGURE 3-3

Supply and demand for a producer's sweatshirt determines market price.

COMPETITION

In our free enterprise system, sellers try to make a profit and buyers try to buy quality goods at the lowest possible prices. This conflict of interest between buyers and sellers is settled to the benefit of society by competition. **Competition** is the rivalry among sellers for consumers' dollars.

Competition in a free enterprise system benefits society in many ways. To attract customers away from other sellers, a business must improve the quality of its products, develop new products, and operate efficiently in order to keep its prices down. Thus, competition serves to ensure that consumers will get the quality products they want at fair prices.

In addition to benefiting consumers, competition benefits the country because it tends to make all businesses use our scarce productive resources efficiently. If a firm does not operate efficiently, it will fail because customers will buy lower-priced or higher-quality products from a firm that is operating efficiently. Often these competing firms are from foreign countries. Competition in our economic system also provides the chance for people to go into business for themselves and to share in the profits being made by those already in business.

One aspect of competition is price competition. Price competition occurs when a firm takes business away from its competitors by lowering prices for identical goods. Today, however, more and more competition takes place in the form of non-price competition. For example, a company attracts customers away from other sellers by providing

GLOBAL PERSPECTIVE

INDIA—YOUTHS CHANGE THE ECONOMY AND THE CULTURE

India's population numbers around one billion, and about 40 percent are under 25 years of age. By the year 2015, about 55 percent will be in this same age group. While the national average income per person is only $450, this youth group will shift the old India to a new India for themselves, their families, and their country. As a dominantly socialist country, India is moving toward capitalism as the young open new businesses and modify how business is conducted. How? The answer is the electronic age.

Computers and the Internet are already fast modifying the culture of India. Unlike their parents, children are buying computers, cellular phones, and other electronic gear. They are mingling among the world's citizens through television and the Internet. New technological devices make it easy for them to communicate with relatives and friends and to chat with people from other lands. It is not uncommon for India's youth to buy cellular phones and charge fees when villagers without phones wish to make calls, such as to distant family members. The money these entrepreneurs make often provides income for their families and causes them to stay closer to home rather than leave for one of the large, crowded cities. This helps to provide a better life for millions of village people. Most youth have a strong pride about their country and are helping families improve their standards of living.

Computers are a primary tool enabling India's youth to become a powerful force in producing rapid economic advances. The youth attend computer schools and have a strong desire to start and run their own Internet-type firms. They also admire young people from other countries who have started their own computer companies, such as Bill Gates of Microsoft Corporation. They are profit-motivated while at the same time respect their cultural ways. Much to the surprise of their elders, young women are also using computers, starting businesses, and shedding or modifying past cultural practices that are honored by their parents. For these reasons, many adults are both concerned about and proud of their children. India's youth are in the process of changing India's view of itself to the rest of the world.

THINK CRITICALLY

1. If India has one billion people now, how many people are now under 40 years of age? If by the year 2015 the population is 1.2 billion, how many people will be under 25 years of age?
2. From your knowledge of economic-political systems, what key factors probably exist in India that make it currently a socialist country?
3. How will India's youth contribute to making the country more capitalistic than it currently is?
4. From the library or the Internet, find out more about the general nature of the country. Such information can be found in an up-to-date encyclopedia in print or online, such as at www.encarta.msn.com/.

products that have better quality or by adding features to the product that competitors do not have. Or, a company may attract customers away from competitors by unusual and colorful product packaging. Another company may conduct an extensive advertising campaign to convince the public that its product is better than all other brands. All these are effective devices used in non-price competition.

Competition is the opposite of monopoly. *Monopoly* is the existence of only one seller of a product. With no competition, a monopolist can charge unreasonably high prices and make extraordinary profits. For example, if a seller does not have to compete with other sellers for consumer dollars, it can usually increase profit by raising the price. Consumers have no choice. If they want that product, they must pay whatever price the monopolist sets. As you will learn in Chapter 7, legislation exists that encourages competition and discourages monopolistic practices.

INCOME DISTRIBUTION

Not only must all countries decide how scarce productive resources are to be used, but they must also decide how the goods produced will be divided among the people in the society. In a free enterprise economy, the share of goods produced that an individual receives is determined by the amount of money that person has to purchase goods and services.

People receive income—wages and salaries—by contributing their labor to the production of goods and services. People also receive income as interest on money that they lend to others, as rent for land or buildings that they own, and as profit if they are owners of businesses.

The amount of money an individual receives in wages or salary is determined by many factors, including personal traits and abilities. The same factors that determine the prices of goods are also important factors in determining wages and salaries; that is, the amount of wages paid for a particular kind of labor is affected by the supply of and demand for that kind of labor. The demand is low and the supply is high for unskilled workers. Thus, the price (income) of unskilled workers is low. On the other hand, the demand for brain surgeons is high in terms of the supply of brain surgeons and the services they provide; therefore, their price (income) is high.

MANAGING THE ECONOMY

The strength of a nation depends upon its economic growth. Economic growth is measured by an annual increase in the gross domestic product, increased employment opportunities, and the continuous development of new and improved goods and services. However, growth cannot always be at the most desired rate. As you will soon learn, when the economy grows too fast or too slow, businesses and consumers suffer. Of concern to everyone is the promotion and measurement of such growth along with the identification and control of growth problems.

PROMOTING ECONOMIC GROWTH

Economic growth occurs when a country's output exceeds its population growth. As a result, more goods and services are available for each person. Growth has occurred and must continue if a nation is to remain economically strong.

The following are basic ways to increase the production of goods and services in order to encourage economic growth:

1. Increase the number of people in the workforce.
2. Increase the productivity of the workforce by means of improving human capital through education and job training.
3. Increase the supply of capital goods, such as more tools and machines, in order to increase production and sales.
4. Improve technology by inventing new and better machines and better methods for producing goods and services.
5. Redesign work processes in factories and offices to improve efficiency.
6. Increase the sale of goods and services to foreign countries.
7. Decrease the purchase of goods and services from foreign countries.

For economic growth to occur, more is required than just increasing the production of goods and services. More goods and services must also be consumed. The incentive for producing goods and services in a free enterprise economy is profit. If the goods and services produced are in demand and are profitable, business has the incentive to increase production.

Economic growth is basic to a healthy economy. Through such growth more and better products become available, such as a new drug that cures a disease, a battery that runs a small computer for months, and new ways to make fuel-efficient cars. More and better services also become available, such as those provided by hospitals, travel agencies, and banks. But more importantly, economic growth is needed to provide jobs for those who wish to work.

MEASURING ECONOMIC GROWTH

To know whether the economy is growing at a desirable rate, statistics must be gathered. The federal government collects vast amounts of information and uses a variety of figures to keep track of the economy. The gross domestic product (GDP) that was discussed in Chapter 1 is an extremely valuable statistic. Another is the Consumer Price Index.

The **Consumer Price Index (CPI)** indicates what is happening in general to prices in the country. It is a measure of the average change in prices of consumer goods and services typically purchased by people living in urban areas. To calculate the CPI, the government tracks price changes for hundreds of items, including food, gasoline, housing, and even cellular phones. With the CPI, comparisons can be made in the cost of living from month to month or from year to year, as shown in Figure 3-4.

Some commonly used indicators for tracking the economy are shown in Figure 3-5. Government economists and business leaders examine the CPI, GDP, and other statistics each month to evaluate the condition of the economy. If the growth rate appears to be undesirable, the government can take corrective action.

IDENTIFYING ECONOMIC PROBLEMS

Problems occur with the economy when the growth rate jumps ahead or drops back too quickly. One problem that occurs is a **recession,** which is a decline in the GDP that continues for six months or more. A recession occurs when demand for the total goods and services available is less than the supply. Sales drop, production of goods and services declines, and unemployment occurs during recessions. In most recessions, the rate of increase in prices is reduced greatly, and in some cases prices may actually decline slightly.

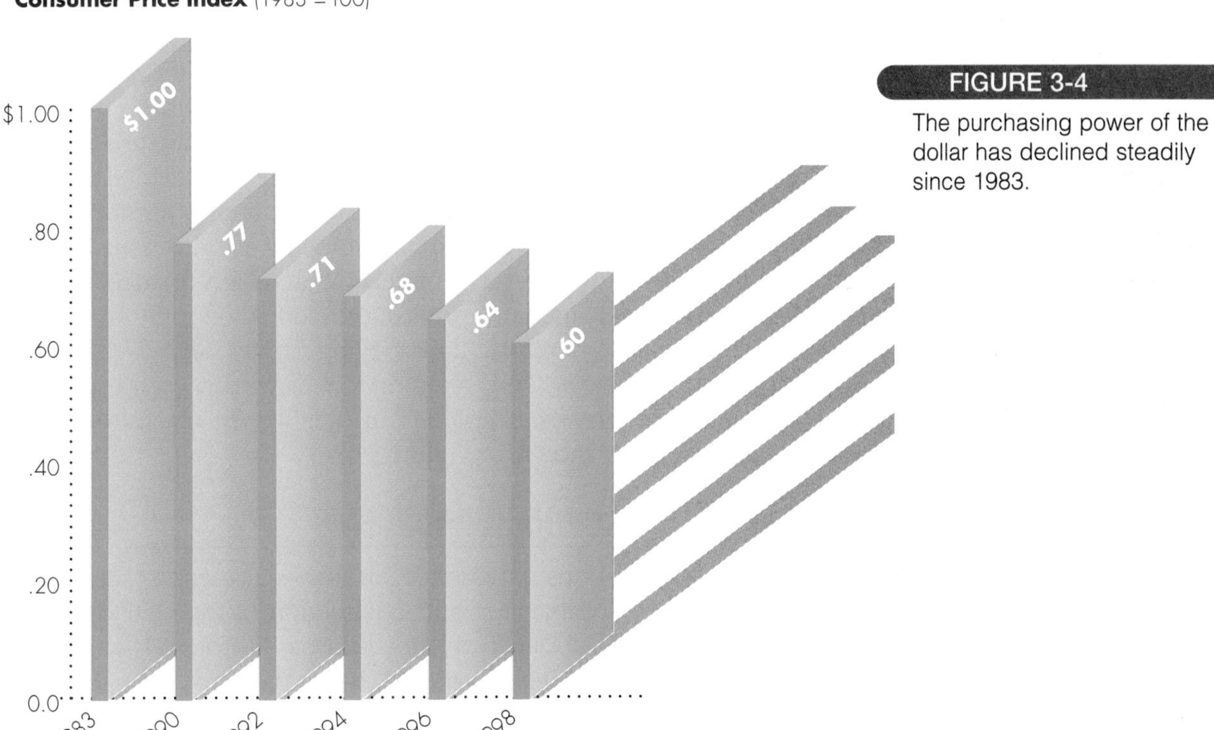

FIGURE 3-4

The purchasing power of the dollar has declined steadily since 1983.

FIGURE 3-5

The federal government issues many statistics each year to help determine whether the economy is growing or declining.

A Sample of Major Economic Reports Released Regularly by the U.S. Government

GROSS DOMESTIC PRODUCT

Measures the total goods and services produced. Released quarterly by the Commerce Department.

CONSUMER PRICE INDEX

Measures inflation at the retail level. Released monthly by the Department of Labor.

INDEX OF LEADING ECONOMIC INDICATORS

Measures the economy's strength for the next six to nine months using a variety of foward-looking indicators. Released monthly by the Commerce Department.

EMPLOYMENT

Measures the jobless rate and the number of jobs available. Released monthly by the Department of Labor.

RETAIL SALES

Measures consumer spending. Released monthly by the Commerce Department.

PERSONAL INCOME CONSUMPTION

Measures growth in personal income and consumer spending. Released monthly by the Commerce Department.

Another problem arises when consumers want to buy goods and services that are not readily available. As revealed in the Consumer Price Index, this increased demand causes prices for existing goods and services to rise. **Inflation** is the rapid rise in prices caused by an inadequate supply of goods and services. In other words, total demand exceeds supply. Inflation results in a decline in purchasing power of money; that is, a dollar does not buy as much as it did before inflation. Retired people and those with fixed incomes are financially hurt the most, because their incomes don't increase fast enough to keep up with rising prices. Therefore, their buying power decreases faster during inflation than does the buying power of workers who receive raises from their employers. The effect of inflation on the purchasing power of the dollar is shown in Figure 3-6.

CORRECTING ECONOMIC PROBLEMS

Most industrialized nations experience **business cycles,** a pattern of irregular but repeated expansion and contraction of the GDP. Business cycles, on average, last about five years, and pass through four phases, as shown in Figure 3-7. These four phases—expansion, peak, contraction, and trough—can vary in length and in intensity, with many lasting only a few years. Some, however, can be severe. When statistics

Dollars Needed to Buy an Item Costing $100 in 1983 (1983–1998)

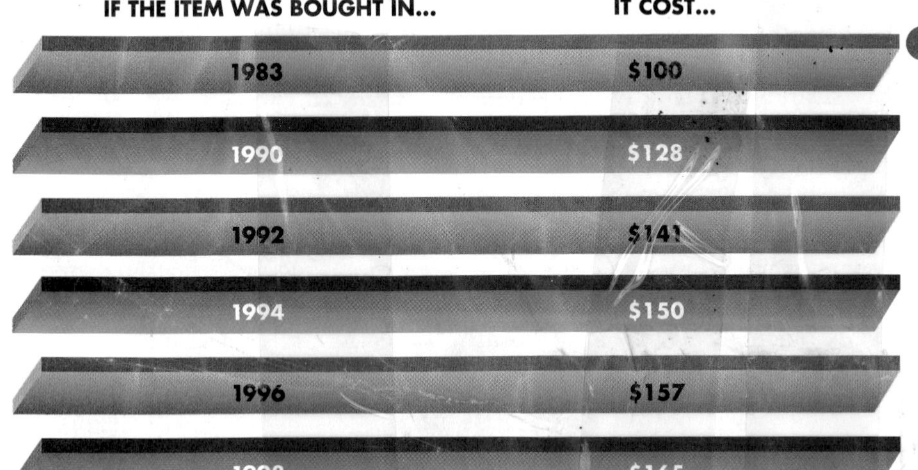

Source: *Statistical Abstract of the United States, 1998*

FIGURE 3-6

Inflation reduces the purchasing power of the dollar.

show that the economy may be about to enter a recessionary period (a contraction) or an inflationary period (an expansion), the government can take certain actions. Several specific devices used include controlling taxes, regulating government expenditures, and adjusting interest rates.

One way to control economic growth is to raise or lower taxes. Taxes are raised to slow growth and lowered to encourage growth. When taxes are raised, there is less money to spend, which discourages

Business Cycle Phases

PHASE	EXPLANATION	POPULAR NAME
Expansion	Modest rise in GDP, profits, and employment	Low inflation
Peak	Growth reaches its highest level, as do profit and employment	Modest to runaway inflation
Contraction	Growth begins to decline, as does employment	Modest inflation
Trough	Lowest point in the cycle, with increased unemployment	No growth, recession, or depression

FIGURE 3-7

Business cycles are irregular in length and in severity.

economic growth. When taxes are lowered, people and businesses have more money to spend, which encourages economic growth.

Government expenditures also influence economic growth. The federal government operates by spending billions of dollars each year to pay salaries and to buy equipment. Government can increase its spending to stimulate a slow economy or reduce spending to slow economic growth.

In addition, economic growth is regulated through interest rates, the money paid to borrow money. Borrowing by businesses and consumers generates spending. Spending stimulates economic growth. When interest rates are lowered, businesses are encouraged to borrow. This stimulates business activity and, in turn, the economy. When interest rates are raised to discourage borrowing, a slowdown occurs.

Through interest rates, government spending, taxes, and other devices, the rate of economic growth can be controlled somewhat. Control, however, is usually kept to a minimum in a free enterprise system. Furthermore, in a complex economic system the results of such controls are not always clearly visible in the short run. Economists do not always know exactly when control devices should be used, for how long they should be applied, or how effective they may be. While the nature of controls can be debated, some control is needed to prevent a destructive runaway inflationary period or a **depression**—a long and severe drop in the GDP. Such conditions affect not only U.S. citizens but also the economic climate of foreign countries.

Because most nations engage in international trade and because of the impact of global competition on nations, a major recession or depression in one country usually impacts negatively on other countries. For example, during the first half of the 1990s the United States experienced a period of recession and slow growth. Japan, Germany, France, England, and other major nations also faced similar circumstances shortly thereafter. Economic aspects of international trade will be discussed in the next chapter.

FACTS AND FIGURES

The Great Depression of the 1930s resulted in tremendous economic difficulties around the world. In the United States, the prices of stock fell 40 percent; 9,000 banks went out of business; 9 million savings accounts were wiped out; 86,000 businesses failed; and wages were decreased by an average of 60 percent. The unemployment rate went from 9 percent to 25 percent—about 15 million jobless people.

ILLUSTRATION 3-5

Unemployment grows during a recession or a depression, which means people are less able to buy goods and services. How can the rate of economic growth be controlled somewhat?

CHAPTER 3 REVIEW

ECONOMIC ENVIRONMENT OF BUSINESS

CHAPTER CONCEPTS

- To produce useful goods and services, businesses use land (natural resources), labor, capital goods, and entrepreneurship. Because a nation does not have enough resources to satisfy everyone's wants, an economic system must decide what goods or services will be produced, how they will be produced, and who will get them.
- All countries use some form of three economic systems—market, mixed, and command economies—to decide what, how, and for whom goods and services will be produced. A market system in a capitalistic society makes these decisions through the forces of supply and demand. In a command economy, generally in a communistic society, government makes these decisions. A mixed system is one that has characteristics of both market and command economies. Pure market and pure command economies don't exist. All are mixed, though aspects of one or the other predominate in different countries.
- Many formerly communistic and socialistic countries are shifting their political-economic systems toward market economies.
- Capitalism is founded on basic principles: the right for individuals and businesses to (1) own private property and produce goods and services; (2) compete with other producers, set prices, and earn a profit; and (3) buy whatever goods or services they like.
- In all political-economic systems, governments reserve the right to control unfair competition and to correct undesirable inflation and recession problems that occur in business cycles.

BUILD VOCABULARY POWER

Define the following terms and concepts.

1. economics
2. economic wants
3. non-economic wants
4. utility
5. producer
6. factors of production
7. natural resources
8. labor
9. human capital
10. capital goods
11. capital formation
12. consumer goods and services
13. economic system
14. market economy
15. command economy
16. mixed economy
17. privatization
18. capitalism
19. socialism
20. communism
21. private property
22. profit
23. demand
24. supply
25. competition
26. economic growth
27. Consumer Price Index (CPI)
28. recession
29. inflation
30. business cycles
31. depression

REVIEW FACTS

1. How does an economic want differ from a non-economic want? Give an example of each.
2. List the four most common types of utility and the four basic factors of production.
3. What is the difference between capital goods and consumer goods?
4. In relation to capital formation, what is one cause for the scarcity of consumer goods in North Korea?
5. How is a market economy different from a command economy?
6. Compare capitalism, socialism, and communism as to (a) how each allocates scarce resources among alternative wants and (b) the existence of private property.
7. Is the profit earned by business usually overestimated or underestimated?
8. What special feature of a free enterprise system helps keep the prices of goods and services down?
9. How might a business attract customers from other sellers?
10. List three examples of non-price competition.
11. Is the demand high and the supply low for unskilled workers?
12. Other than increasing the production of goods and services, what other element is required for economic growth?
13. List two ways that the government measures economic growth.
14. List three problems that can occur within an economy when the growth rate is too fast or too slow.
15. List three devices used by the government to control economic growth.

DISCUSS IDEAS

1. Discuss form, place, and time utility as they might apply to a small fast food pizza business that just opened in your community. See Figure 3-1.
2. How is capital formation important to the creation of consumer goods?
3. Explain the immediate and long-range effects that the production of capital goods has on consumer goods.
4. Discuss why the following statement might be true: "Economic decisions in a capitalistic country are influenced by the federal government about 10 percent of the time; in a socialist country, about 50 percent of the time; and in a communist country, about 90 percent of the time."
5. A person who works for a local business made the following statement: "The company took in $500,000 last year. It's doing great." Is the firm necessarily doing great? If it were an average firm, estimate its profit.

6. Explain how supply and demand help determine the price for goods and services.
7. How do businesses know what products to make and how many to produce?
8. Your friend said, "The company I work for had a 10 percent increase in demand for its goods but the supply went up by 15 percent. Management should have raised prices if it wanted to make a bigger profit." Is your friend correct? Explain.
9. Discuss how economic growth that is too fast can cause people who are retired to be hurt financially.
10. If you were an economist working for the federal government, what would you do if you discovered the GDP and CPI were dropping at too fast a rate? Explain.

ANALYZE INFORMATION

1. Use the Consumer Price Index information provided in Figure 3-4 to determine the following:
   - **a.** By what percent did the CPI change between 1983 and 1998?
   - **b.** If the CPI dropped by 10 percent between 1996 and 1998, what would the CPI be in 1998?
2. Use the following yearly gross domestic product figures to determine answers to the questions below:

Year	*GDP*
1989	$5.5 trillion
1995	$7.4 trillion
1999	$9.3 trillion

   - **a.** What was the percentage of increase between 1989 and 1995?
   - **b.** What was the percentage of increase between 1989 and 1999?
   - **c.** If the percentage of increase between 1989 and 1999 remains the same between 2000 and 2010, what will the GDP be in 2010?
3. Between 1996 and 1997, average yearly consumer prices rose for these countries as follows: United States, 2.3 percent; Brazil, 6.9 percent; Mexico, 20.6 percent; Israel, 9.0 percent; and Switzerland, 0.5 percent.
   - **a.** If you were retired on a fixed income, in which country would you fare the best? Worst?
   - **b.** Over a five-year period, by what percent would prices rise in the United States if consumer prices rose by the same percentage?
   - **c.** Which country was suffering from the greatest amount of inflation? By what percent would prices have increased in this country over a five-year period, assuming the rate stayed the same?

4. From Figure 3-5, select one of the economic indicators other than the GDP or CPI, and collect statistics from a library or from the Internet for the past five full years. Then calculate the rate of change between the first and second year and the first and fifth year. Prepare a report for your class.

5. Which two indexes shown in Figure 3-5 would be considered the *most* valuable and *least* valuable for deciding during the next year whether to expand the Gonzales family business described at the start of the chapter? Gather information from the library or Internet before preparing a report explaining your answers. Your instructor may decide to divide the class into groups to discuss and agree upon answers before reporting team results to the class.

6. Ask an older relative whose age you know what he or she paid for three or more of the following items when he or she was about your age: movie ticket, sweatshirt, ballpoint pen, shoes, candy bar, athletic or concert ticket. Search the Internet for a CPI calculator, such as the one at *www.westegg.com/inflation/,* and use it to find what these items would cost today. Also, insert today's price of each item, and find what it would have cost 25 years ago. Share your results with the class.

SOLVE BUSINESS PROBLEMS

CASE 3-1

Marsha and Carlos sat on the bench outside the entrance to the local mall chatting before going inside to their separate clerking jobs. The conversation turned to front-page headlines that stared at them from an abandoned newspaper left at the end of the bench. "Castro Experiments with Capitalism," one headline read, while another shouted, "Headwinds in China's Nudge to Market Economy." "Brazil's Inflation Out of Control," read still another. Lower on the page could be seen "CPI Inches Downward."

Silence ensued as Marsha and Carlos read. They were thinking about whether these stories had any bearing on their jobs and their lives. Finally, Carlos broke the silence and the following conversation occurred.

Carlos: *Now I know why I never liked reading newspapers. The headlines don't make any sense—nothing in common. The same stuff appears on the Internet. They jump all over the place, and most of the news is bad. And half of it isn't understandable. Then we have to hear it again on TV and on the radio.*

Marsha: *I try to read some of the articles, but many are unclear. For example, yesterday I saw "County Privatizes Trash Collection." The headlines aren't always clear, but fortunately things usually are explained in the stories. By reading each day, you learn more than you think you can, especially about economics.*

Carlos: *The sports pages are what I read. You get the "stats" like team won/lost records and learn about how much the superstars are paid in contracts. Some of them make as much in one year as you and I will make in a lifetime. You don't have to worry about inflation when you make $2 million.*

Marsha: *Today's headlines deal with economics, and you're talking economics when you deal with how much people are paid. If you like "stats," you'll like looking at the economic indicators. You have a contract with your employer, Carlos. Some day when you have more knowledge and skills to sell, your "contracts" will get larger, too.*

Carlos: *Maybe I'll take this paper and read some of those headline details later . . . after I find out who won last night's big game between the Cowboys and the Bears. See you after work.*

Think Critically:

1. Is the headline that reads "CPI Inches Downward" good news or bad news? Explain your answer.
2. What did all the headlines have in common?
3. Explain to Marsha what the county did when it "privatized" the trash service.
4. Bring the business section of a newspaper to class. Determine what economic ideas presented in this chapter are directly or indirectly revealed in one or more of the headlines. If your instructor decides to divide the class into groups, pick the two best stories in your group that cover the most important chapter ideas.

CASE 3-2

Mei-ling and Yi Cheng and their four children live on a farm in China located near the large city of Shanghai. Life on the farm today is unlike it was when they were younger. Less than ten years ago, the family was quite poor and lived in a run-down small home with no plumbing. There were seldom good times. Raising enough food to eat and to sell barely made ends meet, and the economy was not at all like today with the GDP growing so rapidly.

Many people have moved to the city in order to earn more money and to learn new skills while working in new or growing businesses. Some of the factories are foreign firms such as those from Germany, Japan, and the United States. Yi travels to the city each day to work in one of the new plants, while Mei-ling runs the farm with her oldest son and other children when they are not in school. The family cannot afford to live in the city.

During the last few years the Chengs have made improvements to their small home, added indoor plumbing, a telephone, and a small television. Yi even has a cell phone that he uses with pride when bicycling the seven miles to and from work. The days are long, but life is getting easier. If things continue to improve, Yi may consider buying a motor scooter. The children want a computer but even a used one is an unaffordable luxury for now. The Chengs have learned that good times do not last forever. They must save for bad times, for the children's education, and for retirement. There is no social security system to depend upon when Yi retires. And if someone becomes ill or injured, the government can provide only limited help. Yi is also concerned that his foreign employer might leave China because of government regulations that are often unfair to foreign competitors. For now, the happy times continue for the Chengs, who consider themselves somewhat well off for a rural family.

Think Critically:

1. How does the current life of the Chengs compare with the average American family? And by American standards, would they be classified at the poverty level? Explain your answer.
2. Do the Chengs live more under a capitalistic or a communistic system? Explain your answer.

3. By using the library or the Internet, find out whether the Chinese people who live in large cities have a better quality of life than do people like the Chengs who live in rural areas. Report your findings to the class.
4. What conditions exist or could occur that would cause Yi's employer to leave China? Obtain information from your library or the Internet to make a report to the class.

PROJECT: MY BUSINESS, INC.

As a new business owner, you must be aware of the type of competition the business will face and the strengths and weaknesses of that competition. Also, you must determine customer demand for the business's products. Competition affects the prices you can charge for your products. You will study these factors in this segment of your project.

DATA COLLECTION

1. Identify five businesses in your area that could be considered competitors for your juice bar. Review the information from your work in Chapter 1 to help you. Rate each business on the basis of variety of products, location, prices, service, and image. Use a

1–5 scale, with 1 meaning the most competitive and 5 meaning the least competitive.

2. Identify five products that would typically be offered on the menus of juice bars. Visit businesses in your area and determine the highest and lowest prices being charged for each of the products you identified.
3. Interview ten people to determine how price affects their purchase decisions. Ask the following questions and summarize the responses:
   a. How much would you usually expect to pay for a freshly prepared frozen juice drink?
   b. How important is the price when you decide to purchase that drink?
   c. What factors would cause you to pay a higher-than-normal price for a fresh juice drink?

ANALYSIS

1. A business must be able to satisfy consumer needs in order to be successful. Describe how your new business will provide the four basic utilities discussed in the textbook: form, place, time, and possession.
2. Identify four specific ways you can reduce the level of competition or increase the customer demand for your products.
3. How important do you think prices of your products will be to the success of your business? What is the evidence to support your decision? What non-price factors do you believe will be important in attracting and keeping customers?
4. Identify five products you plan to offer at your juice bar. The products may be five varieties of juice drinks or other food products such as muffins and bagels. Make initial pricing decisions for each of your products. (You may decide to change the prices later.) If you will serve different sizes of drinks, make sure to price each size. Justify why you selected those prices.

INTERNATIONAL ENVIRONMENT OF BUSINESS

OBJECTIVES

- **4-1** Describe the nature, growth, and importance of international trade and investment.
- **4-2** Distinguish between the different forms through which international business is conducted.
- **4-3** Identify common barriers to international business and reasons for growth.
- **4-4** Explain two theories of international trade.
- **4-5** Discuss the concepts of balance of trade and balance of payments.
- **4-6** Consider career opportunities in international business and understand the factors related to being sent abroad on assignment.

NOT MADE IN AMERICA

Jake Applegate owned a fish bait and tackle shop in Ely in northern Minnesota, just outside a region famous for fly fishing. During the long summer season, anglers—professional and amateur—from all over the country stopped by Jake's shop to stock up on lures, baits, and other supplies en route to their favorite fishing spots. Jake carried a full line of fishing-related products. They were good quality, American-made products. Sales were usually quite brisk. By late September, when he boarded up his business each year for the cold season, he usually had made enough to sustain himself and his family until April, when he would reopen.

This summer, Jake noticed that fewer tourists were stopping by his store. His sales were falling. It was not as if people had given up fishing. In fact, it was becoming more popular as more women took up the sport. Jake was very concerned.

Jake soon found out what was happening. A Wal-Mart department store had opened just outside Ely, and it carried a complete range of fishing gear including many new varieties of colorful and inexpensive lures. Checking out the prices, Jake found that they were all cheaper than comparable products that he carried. A close look at the packaging and boxes of the products told the story. In small print were the words "Made in Thailand."

International business is not new. People around the world have been trading since the beginning of history. Phoenician and Greek merchants were sailing the seas to sell and buy products in Africa and Europe long before recorded history. In 1600, the British East India Company was formed in order to establish branches and trade with countries in Asia. As Europeans discovered sea routes around the world, trade flourished among the nations of Europe and countries such as China, India, and Indonesia. American colonial traders began operating in a similar way.

Similarly, people throughout the world were investing in businesses abroad. An early example of successful American investment abroad was a factory built in Scotland by the Singer Sewing Machine Company in 1868. By 1880, Singer had become a worldwide organization with several sales offices and factories in other countries. During the 18th and 19th centuries, a great economic expansion occurred in the United States. Largely financed by foreign money, businesses laid railway lines, opened mines to extract coal and iron ore, and built factories.

IMPORTANCE OF INTERNATIONAL BUSINESS

International business typically means business activities that occur between two or more countries. Every country has its own laws and rules, its own currency, and its own traditions of doing business. When a restaurant in New Jersey buys lobsters from Maine, everyone understands the rules of business, because they are similar from state to state. When the restaurant buys salmon caught by Chilean fishermen, the rules of business are not as clear, because they differ from country to country.

Only since the end of World War II in 1945 has international business become a dominant aspect of economic life. Foreign trade has flourished. Companies have grown rapidly and operate on a global scale. Countries have become highly interdependent, so that events in one place have an impact in another place. Almost every business and individual is affected directly or indirectly by international business. As you saw in the opening vignette, although Jake was not directly involved in international business, his business was being hurt by the availability of cheaper products from Thailand.

EXTENT OF INTERNATIONAL TRADE

Look around and you will see names you are sure are foreign: Honda cars, Sony tapes, Benetton clothes, and Chanel perfume. But what about names such as Cadbury chocolates, Shell gasoline, 7-Eleven Stores, and Magnavox television? They are the brand names of products of foreign companies. See Figure 4-1 for a list of other common foreign brands. Also, think of familiar American companies such as MacDonald's, General Motors, IBM, Coca-Cola, and Eastman Kodak. A growing portion of their total sales occurs in foreign countries.

As we start the new millenium, it is clear that business activities are no longer confined to one country. Foreigners buy American products (computers, wheat, airplanes) and services (banking, insurance, data processing) just as Americans buy foreign products (petroleum, cars, clothes) and services (vacations, shipping, construction). American firms

ILLUSTRATION 4-1

Although international trade and investment have existed for centuries, they did not become major topics of study and interest until fairly recently. What are some reasons for this?

BRAND NAME	PRODUCT	COMPANY	COUNTRY
Acer	Computers	Acer	Taiwan
Adidas	Footwear	Adidas	Germany
Burger King	Fast food	Diageo	United Kingdom
Close-up	Toothpaste	Lever Brothers	United Kingdom
Michelin	Tires	Michelin	France
Novotel	Hotels	Accor	France
Nescafe	Coffee	Nestle	Switzerland
Panasonic	Television	Matsushita	Japan
Walkman	Personal stereo	Sony	Japan

FIGURE 4-1

Selected Products That Are Foreign-Owned

make many products in factories in foreign countries just as foreign companies make products in the U.S. In a recent year, world trade in goods exceeded $5.2 trillion.

Most of the world's trade takes place among the developed countries of North America, Western Europe, and Japan. Over the past thirty years, countries on the western edge of the Pacific Ocean—referred to as the **Pacific Rim**—have emerged as big trading nations. These countries include South Korea, Taiwan, China, Hong Kong, and Singapore, as shown in Figure 4-2. A list of the major countries with which the U.S. trades is shown in Figure 4-3.

Trade patterns have shifted from goods to services. While goods remain dominant, service industries now represent more than one-fifth of international trade. When service industries emerged as an important segment of the American economy, more and more trade and investments occurred in businesses such as tourism, banking, accounting, advertising, and computer services.

TRADE, INVESTMENT, AND THE ECONOMY

As with trade, most investments are made within and by the world's most industrialized economies. Annual foreign investment by businesses in these countries exceeded $300 billion. In recent years, though, China has become a major recipient of foreign investment, mostly from Taiwan, Japan, and the United States. Foreign investment occurs when firms of one country build new plants and facilities or buy existing businesses in another country. An example of such investment would be Daimler-Benz of Germany acquiring Chrysler of the U.S. in 1998.

Japanese officials want to launch a national campaign to establish English as Japan's second official language. Too few Japanese speak the language of the Internet and international finance—which is English. Some Japanese see this as a serious competitive disadvantage that undermines Japan's global influence, particularly in the areas of technology, commercial exploitation of the Internet, and finance, where English proficiency is critical.

FIGURE 4-2

Countries of the Pacific Rim and European Union

Pacific Rim

European Union

AUSTRIA
BELGIUM
DENMARK
FINLAND
FRANCE
GERMANY
GREAT BRITAIN
GREECE
IRELAND
ITALY
LUXEMBOURG
NETHERLANDS
PORTUGAL
SPAIN
SWEDEN

International trade and investment are a big and growing part of the American economy. In a recent year, America sold over $670 billion of its products to foreign customers. Almost 10 percent of all jobs depend on foreign trade, and nearly 5 percent of workers are employed by foreign companies operating in the U.S. Foreign firms have invested nearly $700 billion in the U.S. Total American investment abroad exceeds $860 billion. Figure 4-4 shows the top countries that have invested in the U.S. and the top countries where American businesses have invested.

FORMS OF INTERNATIONAL BUSINESS

International business takes place in many forms. Usually, when a firm decides to enter into international business, it starts by selling its products or services to buyers in another country. This is known as **exporting.** For example, Boeing makes airplanes in the U.S. and sells some of them to Qantas, an Australian airline. **Importing** refers to buying goods or services made in a foreign country. When Americans buy Darjeeling tea, they are buying goods imported from India. Exporting and importing are usually the simplest forms of international business. Both can be done with limited resources and relatively risk free.

Source: *U.S. Census Bureau (www.census.gov/foreign-trade/)*

FIGURE 4-3

The Top Ten Countries with Which the U.S. Trades, 1999

International business also takes place through licensing. **International licensing** occurs when one company allows a company in another country to make and sell products according to certain specifications. Thus, when an American pharmaceutical company allows a German firm to make and sell in Germany a medicine the American company has invented, this is licensing. The American company receives a royalty from the German company for any medicines the latter sells. Licensing and its related concept, franchising, are relatively more costly and risky methods of expanding abroad, compared to exporting.

Source: *Survey of Current Business, July 1999 (www.bea.doc.gov)*

FIGURE 4-4

Leading Investment Countries

ILLUSTRATION 4-2

What factors make exporting and importing the simplest forms of international business?

Firms may set up businesses in foreign countries by forming joint ventures with other companies. In **joint ventures,** two or more firms share the costs of doing business and also share the profits. When the firm sets up a business abroad on its own without any partners, it is known as a **wholly-owned subsidiary.** These are more expensive to set up and also more risky should the business fail.

In recent years, many competitors have entered into strategic alliances with each other. Under **strategic alliances,** firms agree to cooperate on certain aspects of business while remaining competitors on other aspects. Thus, because of the high cost of developing new medicines for curing cancer, two pharmaceutical companies may agree to share research information and costs while competing with each other in selling other medicines.

MULTINATIONAL FIRMS

The expansion of international business has created multinational firms. A **multinational firm** is a firm that owns or controls production or service facilities in more than one country. The country in which the business has its headquarters is referred to as the **home country.** The foreign location where it has facilities is referred to as the **host country.** Company headquarters is called the **parent firm;** and the foreign branches, if registered as independent legal entities, are referred to as **subsidiaries.** Most of the world's largest businesses are multinational firms. However, many small firms, too, are multinational businesses.

INTERNATIONAL TRADE CHALLENGES

Trade and investment in the international environment have some unique complications. Businesses must consider government policies toward foreign firms and products, the value of foreign currencies, and the contrast of cultures when doing business abroad.

GOVERNMENT POLICIES

Because international business takes place between two or more countries, the policies, rules, and laws of more than one national government affect trade and investment. Although economists consider free trade desirable for a society, on occasion governments impose **tariffs.** These are taxes on foreign goods to protect domestic industries and to earn revenue. For instance, assume that the U.S. government sets a tariff of 10 percent on a pair of jeans made in Colombia, South America. If the jeans are valued at $30, the American customs department will collect a tax of $3 ($30 x .10), and the price per pair will rise to $33.

Governments also impose tariffs when a foreign supplier is guilty of "dumping" its products. **Dumping** refers to the practice of selling goods in a foreign market at a price that is below cost or below what it charges in its home country. When a company dumps, it is trying to win more customers by driving domestic producers out of the market. The government prevents dumping by setting tariffs that increase the price of goods being dumped. For example, if Brazilian firms tried dumping steel in the U.S., a tariff might be levied to sufficiently raise the price of that steel to permit domestic producers to compete successfully.

Another way by which governments restrict the availability of foreign goods is to create quotas. A **quota** limits the quantity or value of units permitted to enter a country. For instance, the U.S. government may allow only 10,000 tons of salmon to enter the country annually from Chile, although much more salmon could be sold. Alternatively, the government could allow salmon worth up to $100 million into the U.S. from Chile annually. In either case, quotas limit the number or dollar value of foreign goods that can be sold in a country. Quotas are designed to protect the market share

CAREER CONNECTION

CUSTOMS INSPECTOR

Would you enjoy a career that involves legal enforcement? Customs inspectors enforce laws governing imports and exports. Stationed in the United States and overseas at airports, seaports, and border crossing points, they examine, count, weigh, and measure cargoes entering and leaving the U.S. in order to determine whether the shipments are legal and what amount of duty must be paid. They inspect baggage to ensure that all merchandise is declared and that illegal items aren't present. They also determine whether people, ships, planes, and anything used to import or export cargo comply with all necessary regulations.

Requirements for the position include a combination of education, experience, and often a passing grade on a written examination. All inspectors are trained in relevant laws and procedures through classroom and on-the-job training. The employment of inspectors is seldom affected by economic conditions because federal, state, and local governments usually provide workers with job security.

For more career information about customs inspectors, check your library or the Internet for resources.

of domestic producers. However, both tariffs and quotas increase the price of foreign goods to consumers.

In addition to tariffs and quotas, it may be difficult to sell goods and services abroad because of **non-tariff barriers.** These are non-tax methods of discouraging trade. In many cases, such barriers do not target specific foreign companies or products, but have the practical effect of keeping them out. In other cases, barriers are deliberately created to protect domestic producers.

Almost all countries have non-tariff barriers of one sort or another. For example, in the U.S., steering wheels are on the left side of motor vehicles, while in Ireland, the steering wheel is on the right side. Thus, before an American company can sell cars in Ireland, it would have to make changes to the vehicle. Other examples of non-tariff barriers are a public campaign of "Be American, Buy American" or the advertisements by labor unions to "Look for the union label." Both situations are clearly designed to discourage the buying of foreign goods and services. Non-tariff barriers are difficult to remove because they are often part of a country's culture and tradition.

Governments may place restrictions on what goods and services can be exported or imported. The goals are again to protect domestic businesses, citizens, or cultures and to ensure national security. American firms need government licenses to sell high-technology or military products abroad. For political reasons, a government may bar companies from doing business with particular countries. Such a restriction is known as an **embargo.** For instance, the U.S. government has established an embargo that bars U.S. companies from conducting business with Cuba.

Sanctions are a milder form of embargo that bans specific business ties with a foreign country. For instance, it is illegal for an American company to sell nuclear technology to Pakistan, which tested atomic bombs in 1998.

Governments place restrictions on what domestic companies foreigners are allowed to buy or invest in. In the U.S., foreign firms are not allowed to have a majority control of airlines or television stations. The government fears that allowing that to happen might endanger national security. In extreme cases, a government may seize foreign firms with or without compensation, if such businesses are thought to be harmful to the national interests.

CURRENCY VALUES

International business involves dealing with money, or currency, of foreign countries. Currencies have different names, such as the dollar in the U.S., peso in Mexico, and yen in Japan, but more important, they differ in value. This is a key difference between doing business domestically and doing business internationally. The **exchange rate** is the value of one country's currency expressed in the currency of another

ILLUSTRATION 4-3

The value of a country's currency can change frequently. What are some factors that affect exchange rates?

country. For example, one U.S. dollar might be worth nine Mexican pesos right now. If you were traveling to Mexico and wanted some Mexican money, you would receive nine pesos for every dollar you turned in to the bank at this exchange rate. The value of each currency in terms of another can change every minute, depending on many factors, such as the demand for a particular currency, interest rates, inflation rates, and government policies. Major newspapers and several Web sites publish exchange rates for most currencies.

Managers must closely watch exchange rates, as they affect profits and investment decisions in a big way. For example, assume the value of one American dollar is equal to 125 Japanese yen. A camera made in Japan for 12,500 yen would be selling in the U.S. for $100 (12,500/125). If the exchange rate changes to 100 yen to the dollar, that same camera will now cost $125 (12,500/100). Thus, the Japanese camera becomes more expensive in the U.S. entirely because of exchange rate changes. To protect the firm against adverse changes in the exchange rates, international business managers use many techniques.

CULTURAL DIFFERENCES

International business also requires understanding and coping with cultural values and traits in foreign countries that are different from those of the home country. **Culture** refers to the customs, beliefs, values, and patterns of behavior of the people of a country or group. It also includes language; religion; attitudes toward work, authority, and family; practices regarding courtship, etiquette, gestures, and joking; and manners and traditions. In many countries, especially large ones like India,

Russia, and South Africa, numerous cultural differences exist within their own populations. Likewise, in the U.S., there are cultural differences, such as among various racial and ethnic groups.

Some cultures may be more familiar to Americans, such as those of Canada and Great Britain. Others seem very unfamiliar to Americans, such as those of India and Thailand. Business people who work in foreign countries need to be aware of cultural differences in order to be successful in their assignments. The greater the cultural gap, the more the business person will have to adjust.

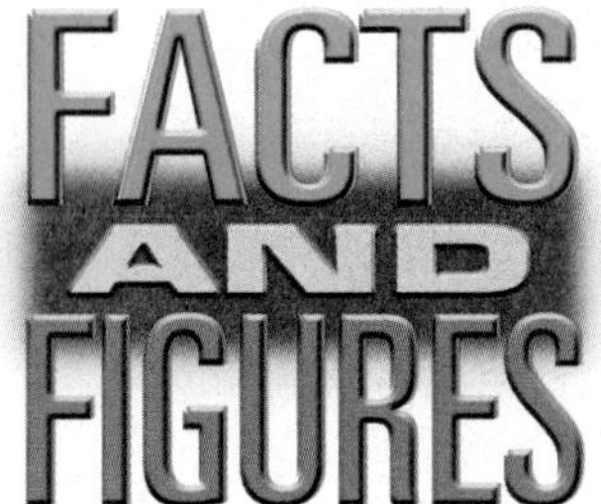

The Japanese find it hard to answer a definite "no" to either a question or a statement. They signal that they "don't know" or "don't understand" by waving their own hand in front of their face, with the palm outward.

Culture affects how people communicate in a country. In a **low-context culture** such as the U.S., people communicate directly and explicitly. A person is expected to come to the point directly and not beat around the bush. An American manager might say, "Do this task immediately." The receiver of this message is not expected to read between the lines. In contrast, in a **high-context culture** such as Japan, communication tends to occur through non-verbal signs and indirect suggestions. Ambiguity and indirect suggestions are expected and highly valued. A person is not supposed to come right out and say it. A Japanese manager might say, "This task is very important, and your attention to it will be greatly appreciated." The difference between high- and low-context cultures can cause communication misunderstandings.

Although English has become the language of international business, its usage and terminology varies across the world. As Figure 4-5 suggests, even though Australians speak English, Americans may not recognize some of their terms and phrases.

REASONS FOR GROWTH IN INTERNATIONAL BUSINESS

Why would McDonald's want to open a restaurant in Beijing, or Nokia sell mobile telephones in the U.S., or Volkswagen build its Beetle cars in Mexico? Or for that matter, why would Macy's buy the jeans it sells from a garment maker in Hong Kong? Firms usually enter international business for many good reasons.

The main reason is profit. Businesses may be able to earn more profit from selling abroad or may be able to charge higher prices abroad than at home, where competition could be more intense. When the cost of making goods is lower in foreign countries than at home, it then becomes cost effective for companies to buy goods made abroad or even set up their own factories abroad. The potential for sales abroad, when combined with the size of the domestic market, increases the overall size of the market. Using mass production techniques, production costs should drop and profits should rise.

In many cases, a company goes international in reaction to what other companies are doing or because of changes in the domestic market. If some firms are making large profits by selling abroad, other companies may be encouraged to do the same. When a large foreign market opens up, as in China in recent years, an American company may lose the market to firms from other countries if it does not act quickly.

Similarly, sales at home may be small, stagnant, or declining, while opportunities to sell abroad may be abundant. A company may have overproduced, and the only way to possibly dispose of its surplus goods profitably is to sell them abroad. It could also be that a company is physically close to foreign customers and markets. For example, Argentine firms can sell easily to Brazilian firms because they are neighbors.

Several factors help firms engage in international business. One key factor is treaties on trade and investment signed by different countries. The **World Trade Organization (WTO)** is an international organization that creates and enforces the rules governing trade among countries. Trade agreements negotiated under the authority of the WTO have led to huge cuts in tariffs. These cuts have boosted exports and imports among the 134 member countries.

FIGURE 4-5

Australian and American English

AUSTRALIAN ENGLISH	AMERICAN ENGLISH
Arvo	Afternoon
Biscuit	Cookie
Bloke	Man
Brolly	Umbrella
Cozzie	Bathing suit (also bathers or swimmers)
Crook	Sick
Entree	The appetizer, not the main course
Fair dinkum	The real thing
Footpath	Sidewalk
Jumbuck	Sheep
Jumper	Sweater
Lollies	Candy
Mate	Friend
Nought	Zero
Sandshoes	Sneakers
Serviette	Table napkin
Sweets	Dessert
Ta	Thank you
Takeaway food	Food to go
Taxi rank	Cab stand
Yank	An American

Source: *Destination-Australia, Australian Tourist Commission*

Development of trading blocs has also stimulated global trade and investment. A **trading bloc** is an agreement between two or more countries to remove all restrictions between them on the sales of goods and services, while imposing barriers on trade and investment from countries that are not part of the bloc.

There are many forms of trading blocs. The best example of an advanced form of trading bloc is the **European Union (EU).** The EU currently has 15 members—Austria, Belgium, Denmark, Finland, France, Germany, Great Britain, Greece, Ireland, Italy, Luxembourg, Netherlands, Portugal, Spain, and Sweden, as shown in Figure 4-2. Since it was formed in 1957 as the European Economic Community, the EU has gone beyond free trade among its members. It is trying to create a "United States of Europe," where there will also be free movement of capital and labor and where common economic and monetary policies would be followed. On January 1, 1999, 11 EU members took a major step toward integrating their economies by merging their national currencies into a single new currency called the **euro.** With a single currency, international firms can look at these European countries as a single market and do not have to worry about exchange rate changes.

In 1989, the U.S. signed a free trade agreement with Canada. In 1992, Canada and the U.S. signed a similar agreement with Mexico, called the **North American Free Trade Agreement (NAFTA),** which created the world's largest trading bloc by removing tariffs and other barriers to trade among the three nations. Many American firms have relocated to Mexico to take advantage of the lower costs of production in that country. Unlike the EU, under NAFTA there is no move yet to allow unrestricted movement of people among the three countries or to integrate the three economies with common monetary or economic policies.

International business is also facilitated by two major international institutions—the **International Monetary Fund (IMF)** and the **World Bank.** The IMF's main purpose is to help countries that are facing serious financial difficulties in paying for their imports or repaying loans. The World Bank provides low-cost, long-term loans to less-developed countries to develop basic industries and facilities, such as roads and electric power plants.

Another factor that has helped international business is the tremendous advances in communication and transportation. Telephone, fax, and the Internet have made it cheaper and quicker to obtain information from around the world and conduct business round the clock. The Internet and television broadcasts enable firms to advertise their products worldwide and create a global consumer culture. Faster and cheaper transportation has meant that firms can easily ship goods long distances. For example, thanks to air transport, tulips grown in the Netherlands are shipped daily to florists in New York City.

Since the early 1990s, the world has seen a move toward free enterprise practices. Many governments have reduced their control over the economy. Several types of businesses, such as telecommunications and airlines, that were strictly regulated by the government have now been opened up to competition. In many foreign countries, business

BUSINESS INNOVATION

THE INTERNET TRANSFORMS BUSINESS FOR HONG KONG COMPANY

When the Lee Hung Fat Garment Factory started 35 years ago, overseas orders usually came by messenger from one of the big Hong Kong trading houses. Today, customers send in specifications for denim jeans and leather jackets directly to a computer terminal on the desk of Mr. Eddy Wong Fun-Ming, the company's operations director. "What we do in one day used to take five weeks in the 1970s," says 39-year-old Mr. Wong.

This small Hong Kong company with annual sales of $40 million is using the Internet to completely change the way it does business. With the click of a mouse, Mr. Wong pulls up a customer's order on the screen. He can see all the details—from production at his factories in China and Bangladesh to shipping schedules to individual customers' accounts. So can many of his staff. Each order is simultaneously sent to any department involved in getting it filled.

Lee Hung Fat supplies apparel to about 60 companies in Europe. Many of these customers have gone online. So the decision to wire the company into the Internet was driven partly by customers wanting to do e-commerce, and partly by his own desire to cut costs.

Using the Internet to communicate has saved the company on phone bills. Before the company went online, fax and telephone calls to customers and factories overseas cost about $10,000 a month. With electronic mail, "you can have 50 messages to your buyer in a day and it doesn't really cost you anything," says Mr. Wong, who often checks his e-mails on the golf course using a mobile phone. He also applies over the Internet for required documents to ship his goods. Before, he had to send someone to the government office and apply for the export license in person.

The company saves money in other ways, too. Before, the company sent a mockup of a garment to buyers overseas by courier or by mail. Now, Mr. Wong holds the item in front of a camera mounted on his PC and flashes it over the Web. He can scan a picture of a sample and transmit that to the customers, who can play with the cloth pattern or the stitching and then zap back a new version. This means samples are approved three to four times faster. Even after paying for the costs of installing computers, Mr. Wong estimates he saves about 15 to 20 percent in costs.

THINK CRITICALLY

1. How does the Internet help Lee Hung Fat Garment Factory remain globally competitive?
2. Are there some aspects of the business that cannot be handled by the Internet?
3. What problems could the company encounter because of its heavy reliance on the Internet?

enterprises owned by the government have been sold to private owners—both domestic and foreign. All these changes have opened up new investment and trading opportunities for foreign firms.

THEORIES OF INTERNATIONAL TRADE AND INVESTMENT

Next you will learn about two well-known theories that explain why international trade and investment occur.

COMPARATIVE ADVANTAGE THEORY

The **comparative advantage theory** states that to gain a trade advantage, a country should specialize in products or services that it can provide more efficiently than can other countries. For instance, because of climate and soil conditions, Brazil is better able to grow coffee as compared to India, whose soil and climate favor the growing of tea. Each country could gain by specializing—Brazil in coffee and India in tea—and then trading with each other.

What if one country can produce both coffee and tea at a lower cost than another country? The comparative advantage theory says that the focus should be on comparing the cost of producing both products in each country. For example, it is possible that India may be able to produce more tea than coffee for the same cost, whereas Brazil may find that it can produce coffee at a lower cost than it can produce wine. In such a case, Brazilians should specialize in producing and selling coffee to the Indians and buying tea from India. Similarly, the Indians should produce tea and sell some to the Brazilians to pay for the coffee they need. This theory explains why the U.S. produces computers, Saudi Arabia extracts oil from the earth, and Indonesia makes athletic shoes.

PRODUCT LIFE CYCLE THEORY

The **product life cycle theory** provides another explanation for trade and investment. In a later chapter you will learn that a product or service goes through four stages: introduction, growth, maturity, and decline. Consider black-and-white televisions, for example. When they were first introduced in the 1940s and 1950s, they were the only televisions available. As more people in the country started buying TVs, their sales grew—the growth stage. When most households owned a TV, sales leveled off—the maturity stage. As color TVs started appearing, the sales of black-and-white sets started falling—the decline stage.

How does the product life cycle theory relate to trade and investment? When sales begin to slow in a country (the mature stage), Company A that makes the product starts selling it to foreign countries where the product may be in the introductory or growth stage. However, selling abroad is expensive because of transportation, tariffs, quotas, and other non-tariff barriers. Companies in the foreign country find it attractive to make and sell the product at lower prices. To counteract this action, Company A sets up a factory in the foreign country where it makes and sells the product. Company A may even sell some of the products back to the home country.

Many American companies move to foreign countries when sales at home start lagging. Examples are fast-food restaurants and soft-drink companies. Because of technological changes, the life cycle of new products is much shorter. New products are regularly introduced. Their sales grow, then flatten, and eventually decline. To prolong the life of the product, firms first ship their products abroad, and later build factories there.

BALANCE OF TRADE

Goods and services sold abroad by American companies bring money into the U.S. Money also comes from foreigners who buy American companies or set up new businesses in the U.S. or lend money to Americans. At the same time, money leaves the country when Americans buy foreign products, vacation abroad, invest in foreign businesses, or give aid to refugees in a troubled nation. National governments and international organizations such as the United Nations and WTO keep records of international transactions, and governments use these to develop economic policies.

All international transactions are recorded in an accounting statement called the **balance of payments.** The balance of payments statement has two parts: the current account and the capital account. The **current account** records the value of goods and services exported and those imported from foreigners, as well as other income and payments. The **capital account** records investment funds coming into and going out of a country. Investment funds include bank loans or deposits, purchase and sale of a business, and investing in a new business.

For several decades the U.S. has had a consistent deficit on its current account. Figure 4-6 shows how the deficit has ballooned over time. The balance of payments deficit means that Americans have been buying more goods and services made abroad than they have been selling to foreigners. How long can a country continue to buy more than it sells? Not indefinitely, of course. However, the U.S. has several advantages. Countries everywhere value its currency, the dollar, because the U.S. is a stable society, government policies are pro-business, and its economy is the world's largest and richest. Foreign banks and governments are willing to lend money to the U.S. to enable it to pay for the excess products it buys.

Not all countries are so fortunate. Countries with prolonged trade deficits may not be able to pay their bills or may have to limit international trade. In addition, their governments may have to place

FIGURE 4-6

U.S. Balance of Trade (in billions of $)

	1998	1980
1. Total exports of goods	670.2	224.3
2. Total exports of services	263.7	47.6
3. Other income from abroad (e.g., royalties)	258.3	72.6
4. TOTAL	1,192.2	344.5
5. Total imports of goods	917.2	249.8
6. Total exports of services	181.0	41.5
7. Other payments to foreigners	270.5	42.5
8. TOTAL	1,368.7	333.8
9. Balance on trade in merchandise (goods)	-247.0	-25.5
10. Balance on trade in services	82.7	6.1
11. Net balance on trade (9+10)	-164.3	-19.4
12. Current account balance (4-8)	-176.5	10.7

Source: *Statistical Abstract of the United States, 1999*

restrictions on the outward flow of money or on the activities of foreign businesses in their countries. At such times, they may obtain financial assistance and economic advice from the International Monetary Fund.

When deficits continue, it means that companies and individuals are demanding more foreign currency to buy the foreign goods. For instance, if Americans buy more Korean toys, the demand for the Korean currency—the won—goes up, because American toy companies will need won to pay the Koreans. When demand increases for won, more dollars are needed to buy won. Thus, the value of the dollar declines in relation to the won. In turn, Korean products become more expensive for Americans, while American products become less expensive for the Koreans. Theoretically, at this stage, higher prices discourage the sale of Korean products in America, and lower prices encourage the sale of American products abroad. In this way, the deficits can be reduced and eventually eliminated.

To illustrate this process, consider IBM computers made in the U.S. and sold in Korea. Assuming an exchange rate of 1 dollar = 1,000 won, a 1,200 dollar computer would sell in Korea for 1,200,000 won (1,200 x 1,000). As more Koreans buy IBM computers, they will need more and more U.S. dollars to pay for the computers. This will increase the demand for dollars and thus its price. In effect, more won will be needed to buy a dollar. Thus, if 1 dollar now becomes 1,200 won, the IBM computer will cost the Koreans 1,440,000 won (1,200 x 1,200).

With the computers costing more, Koreans will buy fewer of them and thus U.S. exports will decline.

Contrast this situation with what happens to a Korean product, say, a Samsung mobile phone costing 120,000 won. The phone will sell in the U.S. initially for $120 (120,000/1,000). When the exchange rate becomes 1 dollar = 1,200 won, the same phone will now cost the Americans less: 120,000/1,200, or $100. This decline in the price will lead Americans to buy more Samsung phones, which will lead to an increasing demand for won and raise the value of the won in terms of dollars. In turn, American goods will become less expensive to the Koreans, and they will buy more American products. Thus, the trade deficits work out over the long run.

ILLUSTRATION 4-4

Why has the United States usually had an advantage when it comes to the balance of trade?

CAREER OPPORTUNITIES IN INTERNATIONAL BUSINESS

The growth of international business has created many new types of jobs. In addition to those who work for foreign firms in the U.S., over 150,000 Americans work abroad for American or foreign firms.

Many people work in various aspects of international business, such as exporting and importing, teaching and translating languages, administering trade laws, managing offices and operations in foreign countries, and in banking and insurance firms. Others work in international trade organizations such as the WTO and the IMF, or in federal and state government agencies. As countries become economically interdependent, more and more jobs will require a knowledge of international business.

Most international companies hire at the entry level, but usually they send workers abroad who are very skilled, mature, and experienced. Studies show that the average salary in foreign companies located in the U.S. is higher than for similar jobs in American companies. As firms

ILLUSTRATION 4-5

Jobs in international business take many forms. What kinds of international careers appeal to you?

gain experience in doing business globally, they employ more and more people from various backgrounds and countries. However, while working several years overseas may promote workers' careers in many companies, it may hurt their careers in others. Workers abroad lose close contact with people and developments in the parent firm.

Today, both businesses and government agencies recruit extensively for jobs that require skills useful for international business. These include not only knowledge of business but also foreign language ability, familiarity with foreign countries, and being comfortable with and in a foreign culture. Many colleges and universities provide coursework and academic degrees in international business. Many offer programs that allow students to do part of their studies in a foreign country or even in a foreign company.

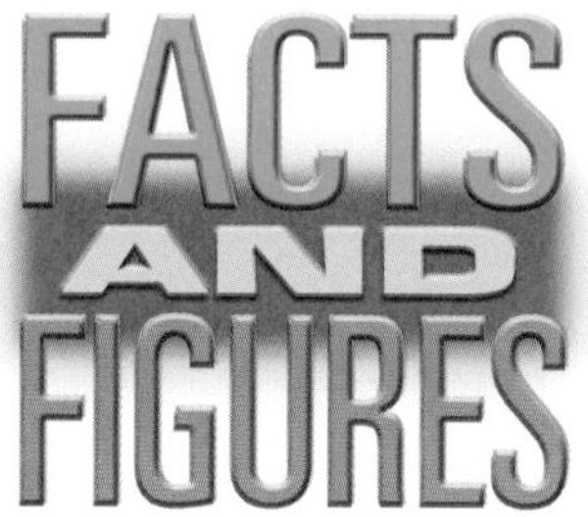

The Internet is an excellent resource for persons interested in obtaining international employment. Numerous job search agencies can be found on the World Wide Web. These agencies often feature online job centers, employer information, and the means by which applicants' resumes can be submitted online. However, as with any Internet resource, it pays to carefully read the "fine print" on the sites in order to determine any applicable restrictions, costs, and the like.

EMPLOYMENT OF INTERNATIONAL MANAGERS

Firms need managers who can work successfully in a wide variety of countries. Such managers adapt readily to people from other cultures and are competent, socially flexible, and receptive to new ideas. Managers benefit from knowing the foreign language and from having strong self-confidence, a motivation to live abroad, and an ability for innovative problem solving.

During the startup phase of foreign operations, firms tend to rely on managers sent from headquarters. However, most managers are citizens of the host country where the business is situated. Occasionally, businesses hire citizens of other countries (neither the home nor the host countries) because they are exceptionally qualified or because host country managers are not available. Sending managers abroad is expensive, because companies must provide extra benefits (such as housing, airfares for families, and cost-of-living allowances).

Managers sent to a country that is culturally different from their own may experience culture shock. Many firms provide cross-cultural training to managers before sending them abroad. The support of the entire family is often necessary for the manager to succeed in the foreign location. With more and more spouses of managers having careers of their own, many firms are finding it difficult to persuade managers to take long-term transfers to a foreign location. Instead, they are using frequent short business trips, bringing in host country managers to headquarters, and using teleconferencing and the Internet to manage their foreign operations.

CHAPTER 4 REVIEW

CHAPTER CONCEPTS

- International trade and investment have grown tremendously over the past fifty years, affecting businesses and individuals all over the world. International business occurs in various forms, such as exporting and importing, licensing, joint ventures, wholly owned subsidiaries, and strategic alliances. Multinational firms with operations in multiple countries have emerged.
- International business has some unique challenges, including the need to work within the rules set by more than one government, currency exchange rates, and cultural differences.
- Firms go into international business because of the potential for larger profits and limited opportunities in the home market. Removal of barriers to trade and investment, creation of trading blocs, and technological advances in communication and transportation have created a positive environment for conducting international business.
- Two theories explain international trade and investments. The theory of comparative advantage explains why a particular country specializes in producing a particular product or service. The product life cycle theory explains how a product's life stage encourages international business.
- Data on trade and investment are carefully collected and used to set business and economic policies. In particular, the balance of trade between countries is evidence of a nation's financial strength or weakness.
- Numerous opportunities exist for careers in international business. Colleges and universities offer programs for further study in this field. A multinational firm may fill its positions with managers from the home, host, or even third countries. It is generally very expensive to send managers overseas. Managers with working spouses are often reluctant to go abroad for long periods of time.

BUILD VOCABULARY POWER

Define the following terms and concepts.

1. international business
2. Pacific Rim
3. exporting
4. importing
5. international licensing
6. joint venture
7. wholly-owned subsidiary
8. strategic alliances
9. multinational firms
10. home country
11. host country
12. parent firm
13. subsidiary
14. tariff
15. dumping
16. quota
17. non-tariff barrier
18. embargo
19. sanctions
20. exchange rate
21. culture
22. low-context culture

23. high-context culture
24. World Trade Organization (WTO)
25. euro
26. trading bloc
27. European Union (EU)
28. North American Free Trade Agreement (NAFTA)
29. International Monetary Fund (IMF)
30. World Bank
31. comparative advantage theory
32. product life cycle theory
33. balance of payments
34. current account
35. capital account

REVIEW FACTS

1. What are some of the unique challenges of international business?
2. Why is it easier for a firm to export instead of setting up a wholly-owned foreign subsidiary?
3. What policies can a government adopt to protect domestic businesses from foreign competition?
4. Why are non-tariff barriers harder to remove than tariffs and quotas?
5. How do changes in currency exchange rates affect international business?
6. How do people communicate in low-context and high-context cultures?
7. Give four reasons why a firm may go into international business.
8. What countries are members of NAFTA and the EU?
9. Explain the purposes of the WTO, IMF, and the World Bank.
10. Explain how comparative advantage encourages international trade.
11. How does the product life cycle theory explain international trade and investment?
12. How is the U.S. able to have a deficit in its current account year after year?
13. What qualities do managers need to work in a foreign country?

DISCUSS IDEAS

1. Explain the reasons for the growing importance of international business.
2. The top five countries in which American firms have investments are the United Kingdom, Canada, Netherlands, Germany, and Bermuda. What explains this choice of countries?
3. If a firm sets up a Web page and sells products through the Internet to anyone in the world, is the firm engaged in international business?
4. Why might a company dump its products abroad?
5. Do you believe that some types of businesses in the U.S. should not be owned by foreign firms? Why or why not?
6. If the value of the Canadian dollar continues to rise in relation to the American dollar, what can a Canadian exporter do to keep the price of the goods it sells in the U.S. market competitive?

7. Identify a list of characteristics that you believe best describe the "American culture."
8. How can a person from a low-context culture communicate with a person from a high-context culture and avoid misunderstandings?
9. Develop a list of reasons why NAFTA is good for the American economy.
10. If a country regularly has a balance of trade surplus, what will happen to its international business?
11. Would you like to work in a foreign-owned firm? Why or why not?
12. Explain the situations under which a multinational firm will use home country, host country, and third country nationals in its foreign operations.

ANALYZE INFORMATION

1. The XYZ Electronic Corporation manufactures and sells microwave ovens. Since the product was introduced twenty years ago, nearly 90 percent of all American households have one such unit. Apply the product life cycle theory to answer the following questions.
   a. In what stage of the cycle are microwave ovens?
   b. What can XYZ do to increase sales and profits?
2. The current accounts of the imaginary nation of Utopia for the past three years are given below in millions of dollars.

	Year 1	***Year 2***	***Year 3***
Export of goods	$100	$120	$125
Import of goods	$175	$195	$205
Export of services	$ 80	$100	$150
Import of services	$ 40	$ 60	$ 80
Other income from abroad	$ 30	$ 25	$ 40
Other payments abroad	$ 50	$ 70	$ 70

   Given the above information, answer the following questions:
   a. Does Utopia have a deficit or surplus in its current account in Year 1, Year 2, and Year 3?
   b. Calculate the balance on merchandise trade for Year 1, Year 2, and Year 3.
   c. If you were the president of an American company, would you set up a business in Utopia? Why or why not?
   d. Suggest ways by which Utopia can reduce its deficit or surplus.
3. An Australian sheep farmer who sells much of his wool in the U.S. has seen the exchange rate for the Australian dollar (AUD) change from US $1 = AUD 1.20 to US $1 = AUD 1.45 over the past six months. Answer the following questions assuming the farmer sells 1000 AUDs' worth of wool:
   a. Will this change in currency rates help or hurt his sales in the U.S.?
   b. What may be some of the reasons for the change in the currency rates?

c. Do American consumers gain or suffer with the change in the currency rates?

4. You are planning to introduce your line of "SuperKids" comics in Thailand. In the U.S., the English-language comics, which are very popular with young girls, are sold mostly in supermarket checkout counters. You have just learned the following facts. Thais cannot read English. Books printed in color are very expensive. Thailand is not a wealthy country, but it is growing rapidly. Supermarkets are very few and far between in Thailand.
   a. Do you think your comics will be successful in Thailand? Why or why not?
   b. What modifications might you have to consider making for the Thai market?
   c. Given the information about Thailand, what do you think is the attraction for selling your comics in that country?

5. Using library or Internet resources, find out the value of U.S. exports and imports to Canada and Mexico since NAFTA was formed. What do the trends show?

SOLVE BUSINESS PROBLEMS

CASE 4-1

The premier of the Canadian province of Quebec announced that he was not ruling out the option of calling another referendum on whether Quebec should remain a part of Canada or become an independent country. Over the past ten years, two such referendums have been held. In the last one, the pro-independence supporters lost by only 50,000 votes.

Unlike the rest of Canada, the overwhelming majority of the residents of Quebec are of French ancestry. They fear that their cultural and linguistic identity is being swamped by the majority of Canadians, who are English-speaking. Independence would allow them to protect and advance their culture and society.

White Goods, Inc., an American firm that has a microwave oven manufacturing factory outside Montreal, was nervous when it heard the statement from the Quebec premier. The talk of separation created a great deal of uncertainty. Many foreign firms were passing over Montreal and establishing offices in another major Canadian city, Toronto. Many Canadian firms, too, were moving out of Quebec or postponing new investments in their Quebec operations. White Goods wondered whether the NAFTA agreement would remain in effect in Quebec if it became a separate country. There was also concern about other issues, such as being able to sell goods made in Quebec in other parts of Canada, whether there would be a new currency and what would be the exchange rates, if the political relationship with the U.S. would change, and many other matters.

The White Goods firm is doing well with sales growing rapidly. It has to decide soon whether to expand the Montreal plant or build a new one elsewhere in the U.S. or Canada.

Think Critically:

1. What should White Goods do? Why?
2. If Quebec became an independent country, how might this event affect White Goods' operations in that country?
3. If White Goods decides not to expand its factory in Montreal, how will that affect the company's relations with the Quebec provincial government?
4. Should White Goods get involved in Quebec politics and try to influence the outcome of the next referendum?

CASE 4-2

Despite intense lobbying by Mexican frozen-food companies against NAFTA, the Mexican government approved the treaty. Hidalgo Tortilla Company is a small firm based in Guadalajara, Mexico's second largest city. It makes frozen taco and enchilada products for Mexico's rapidly growing middle class. The company was against the trade treaty, because it feared that American competitors would come to Mexico and drive smaller Mexican firms like itself out of business. American food companies, such as Sara Lee and Swanson, are very large and resourceful. They have huge modern factories with low costs of production. Because the frozen-foods market is well developed in the U.S., the American companies produce a wide range of products and use sophisticated marketing techniques.

Once NAFTA became a reality, Hidalgo Tortilla Company turned its attention to how it could prepare for possible competition in Mexico from American frozen-food companies. It was clear to the company's managers that it could not go head-to-head in competition with larger and well-off American companies. However, the company's brand name is well known to Mexicans, and the company produces frozen food that appeals to the Mexican palate. One manager noted that there is a very large population of Mexicans in the American states just across the Mexican border.

Think Critically:

1. Does the fact that no tariffs and quotas will exist under NAFTA necessarily mean that American companies will be successful in Mexico? Explain.
2. Does NAFTA provide any opportunities for Hidalgo Tortilla Company to grow? Explain.
3. If Hidalgo proves to be a tough competitor to the American companies, what may the American companies do?
4. What should Hidalgo do to prepare itself for possible competition from American products?

PROJECT: MY BUSINESS, INC.

New small businesses seldom consider the impact of international business on their operations, yet almost all businesses today operate in an international business environment. Many suppliers of products and services purchased by small businesses are international or are owned by businesses located in other countries. A foreign market becomes less foreign as you learn more about it. As a business owner, you need to study those markets in order to understand potential foreign business opportunities. A small business that carefully researches a foreign market can be just as successful in international markets as a large business.

DATA COLLECTION

1. Fresh fruits are often imported from other countries. Using the Internet or the library, locate information that identifies the major international suppliers of fruits to the U.S. Prepare one or more pie charts that illustrate your findings.

2. Using the Internet or the library, collect information on recent trade agreements and legislation that deal with international business. Summarize what experts are predicting will be the effect of the agreements and laws on U.S. businesses.
3. If you have access to people who have lived in other countries, discuss the types of health and wellness businesses, including juice bars, they are familiar with in the country in which they lived. Identify similarities to and differences from the ways businesses operate in the U.S.

ANALYSIS

1. Identify three ways that international trade by U.S. businesses can have a positive effect on small businesses and three ways it can have a negative effect on those businesses.
2. Identify several food products popular in other countries and cultures that you would consider adding to your product line in the juice bar. Remember that the products should fit the image of health and fitness.
3. Assume that you have operated your business for 15 years, and it has been very successful in the U.S. You now have franchises in 30 states. You want to test the international market to see if the business will work in other countries. Identify at least two countries in which you would consider introducing your business and justify your choices. Base your justification on information you have collected from the Internet or the library about the countries you chose.

UNIT TWO

FORMS of BUSINESS OWNERSHIP and the LAW

CHAPTERS

"Recent changes in the economy have stimulated increased interest in being one's own boss. The downsizing of large corporations has displaced millions of workers and managers. Many of these employees have taken the trauma of being laid off and turned it into a self-employment opportunity, frequently financed in large part by severance pay or an early retirement bonus."

Stephen P. Robbins
Managing Today, 1997

PROPRIETORSHIPS AND PARTNERSHIPS

OBJECTIVES

- 5-1 Describe characteristics of successful entrepreneurs.
- 5-2 Outline responsibilities of owning your own business.
- 5-3 List advantages and disadvantages of proprietorships.
- 5-4 List advantages and disadvantages of partnerships.
- 5-5 Describe legal points to consider when selecting a name for a business.

ONE WAY TO START A BUSINESS

Nancy Watanabe wondered about the rest of her life as she sat in front of her computer. Was she too young to even consider starting her own business? Was the whole idea of opening a small computer rental business ridiculous for a nineteen-year-old? "My father would be proud if he knew my dream of investing the inherited money to start a business," she thought to herself. "If only he were here to show me what to do. Fortunately, the library and the Internet have plenty of information on how to get started."

Nancy continued thinking to herself. "I've learned plenty during the last several weeks, reading and talking with my neighbor who runs the local Taco Bell fast-food business. Working as a cashier and computer salesperson in the local computer store while in high school also gave me experience. Yet, there's so much I don't know. I never hired anyone or kept the books. But the idea is so exciting. Will people stop at . . . Nancy's Computer Rentals . . . for an extra computer during busy times or while they wait for their broken computer to be repaired?" Nancy turned back to her Web browser. "Did I just name my store?" she asked, smiling to herself.

Many people have dreamed about owning their own businesses. The idea may have crossed your mind, too. These dreams often start as simple ideas. Some of the dreamers with practical ideas do form businesses. That is how many well-known founders of large businesses got started. Hundreds of young entrepreneurs have started their own firms, including Dell Computer's Michael Dell, Microsoft's Bill Gates, and Amazon.com's Jeff Bezos.

Most businesses begin with one owner. But some firms start with two or more owners. One person, or a group of people, invests in a business with the hope of becoming successful owners. This chapter will examine the basic elements, advantages, and disadvantages of starting a business alone or with others.

CHARACTERISTICS OF ENTREPRENEURS

You learned earlier that an entrepreneur is a person who assumes the risk of starting, owning, and operating a business for the purpose of making a profit. Although individuals form businesses to earn a profit by providing consumers with a desired product or service, they often must invest months or even years of hard work before they earn a profit. About half of all new businesses end within the first five to six years. Businesses often fail for financial reasons, but many closings of young firms occur because the owners are not well suited to be entrepreneurs. But while successful entrepreneurs are all uniquely different, they also have some common personal characteristics.

Some people would rather work for others, while other people prefer to work for themselves. Entrepreneurs who prefer self-employment enjoy the freedom and independence that come from being their own bosses and from making their own decisions. Even when their businesses are not immediately successful, they do not give up. In fact, some entrepreneurs who are eventually successful often experience unsuccessful business start-ups. However, they learn from their mistakes and start over.

Entrepreneurs are self-starters who have plenty of energy and enjoy working on their own. They like to take charge of situations and usually work hard and for long periods in order to meet their goals. Entrepreneurs are also creative thinkers, often coming up with new ideas and new ways to solve problems. Most successful small business owners like people and people like them. As a result, they are often community leaders.

Prosperous entrepreneurs have other common characteristics. Generally, they obtain work experience in the types of businesses they launch. The person who starts a computer store, for example, will usually have taken some computer courses and will have worked for a business that makes, sells, or services computers. In addition to appropriate work experience, successful business owners are well informed about financial, marketing, and legal matters.

There is no magic age for starting a business. Teenagers, parents of teenagers, and retirees have all started successful firms. In recent years, increasing numbers of women, Asian-Americans, Hispanics, and African-Americans of all ages have opened their own firms. To start your own business, you need adequate funds, a general knowledge about business, some work experience, and a business opportunity.

One of the very first decisions a budding business owner must make is what legal form of ownership to adopt. The form of ownership

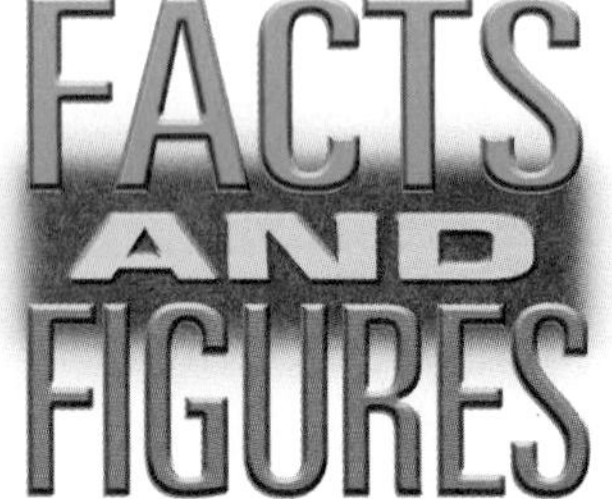

The U.S.economy is dominated by family businesses. According to some estimates, as many as 90 percent of all businesses, including the majority of small- and medium-sized companies, are owned by families.

ILLUSTRATION 5-1

An entrepreneur assumes the risk of starting and operating a business for the purpose of making a profit. What are some personal characteristics of entrepreneurs?

selected depends on several factors, such as the nature and size of the business, the capital needed, the tax laws, and the financial responsibility the owner is willing to assume. Two legal forms of business ownership—proprietorships and partnerships—are presented in this chapter. Also presented in this chapter is the selection of a legal name for a business. But first, let's investigate the challenging responsibilities that entrepreneurs face.

GETTING A BUSINESS STARTED

Starting a business entails many more responsibilities than simply being an employee. Assume, for example, that you are employed as a delivery person. Your duties include making pickups and deliveries. After obtaining several years of valuable work experience, you decide to start your own delivery service. You need to create a plan and to develop an awareness of your responsibilities as the owner of a business.

PREPARE A BUSINESS PLAN

Before starting a business, you need to prepare a business plan. A **business plan** is a written document that describes the nature of the business, the company's goals and objectives, and how they will be achieved. The business plan requires a great deal of careful thought. Most plans include those items shown in Figure 5-1.

Developing a business plan will help you see more clearly the risks and responsibilities involved in starting a business, and will help you decide whether you really want to do it. Writing down your strategies for achieving your goals can give you confidence that your business can succeed. Your plan can also inspire the confidence of others with whom you will deal. Bankers, for instance, will ask to see your plan if you wish to borrow startup funds. They will have greater assurance when they see how carefully you have considered potential problems and solutions before launching your new enterprise. Equally important will be your own conviction that your business will thrive. Too many people who enter business fail for three reasons: (1) they did not prepare a business plan, (2) their plan was unrealistic, or (3) they wrote the plan only because the moneylender, such as a bank, required it. To be successful, you need to start with a well-designed, realistic plan.

ASSUME THE RESPONSIBILITIES OF BUSINESS OWNERSHIP

By developing a workable business plan, entrepreneurs become aware of their risks. As a result, they may be able to anticipate problems and take preventive action. The business plan also causes the aspiring business owner to become more realistic about the responsibilities of ownership.

FIGURE 5-1

Elements of a Business Plan

NATURE OF THE BUSINESS

- Detailed description of products and/or services
- Estimation of risk based on analysis of the industry
- Size of business
- Location of business
- Background of entrepreneur(s)

GOALS AND OBJECTIVES

- Basic results expected in the short and long run
- Results expressed in terms of sales volume or profits

MARKETING PLAN

- Customers and their demand for the product or service
- Prices for the product or service
- Comparison of product or service with competitors

FINANCIAL PLAN

- Investment needed to start and maintain the business
- Projected income, expenses, and profit
- Cash start-up and cash flow needs

ORGANIZATIONAL PLAN

- Legal form of ownership
- Legal factors—licenses, leases, contracts
- Organization chart
- Job descriptions and employee skills needed
- Physical facilities—buildings, equipment, tools

As the owner of your new delivery service, you have duties that include not only pickups and deliveries but also many other responsibilities. Even if you run the business from your home, you will have added expenses for an office, a garage, a computer and printer, and communication devices such as a fax, cell phone, and answering machine. You must find customers, persuade those customers to pay a fair price for your services, and collect from those customers. Furthermore, you must assume responsibility for damage that may occur to your merchandise. You will have to pay fees for various licenses, taxes, insurance premiums, gasoline, van repairs, and other operating expenses. It may also be necessary to hire, train, and supervise employees.

Aspiring entrepreneurs should carefully consider the responsibilities of ownership before opening a business. These tasks are welcome challenges for some people, but may seem like overwhelming burdens to others. People who enjoy being leaders and enjoy making decisions find great satisfaction in owning a business. Ownership offers opportunities to make decisions and to experience other rewards. Some of these rewards will be identified in the section that follows.

PROPRIETORSHIP

The most common form of business organization is the proprietorship, of which there are over 16 million in this country. A business owned and managed by one person is known as a **sole proprietorship,** or a **proprietorship,** and the owner-manager is the **proprietor.** In addition to owning and managing the business, the proprietor often performs the day-to-day tasks that make a business successful, with the help of hired employees. Under the proprietorship form of organization, the owner furnishes expertise, money, and management. For assuming these responsibilities, the owner is entitled to all profits earned by the business.

Provided that no debts are owed, a proprietor has full claim to the *assets*—property owned by the business. If the proprietor has business debts, however, **creditors** (those to whom money is owed) have first claim against the assets. Figure 5-2 presents a simple financial statement of Jennifer York, who is the proprietor of a small retail grocery store and fruit market.

This simple financial statement, known as a *statement of financial position,* or *balance sheet,* shows that the assets of the business are valued at $218,400. Since York has *liabilities* (money owed by a business) amounting to $14,400, the balance sheet shows her capital as $204,000 ($218,400 minus $14,400). In accounting, the terms *capital, net worth,* and *equity* are interchangeable and are defined as assets less liabilities. If there are profits, York gets the total amount. She must also absorb losses. Since she owns the land and the building, she does not have to pay rent, although she must pay the cost of maintenance and taxes for the property.

ADVANTAGES OF PROPRIETORSHIPS

The fact that almost three out of four businesses are proprietorships indicates that this form of organization has definite advantages. Can you list any of the advantages before reading further?

ASSETS	
Cash	$ 17,760
Merchandise	31,680
Equipment	24,960
Land & Buildings	144 ,000
Total	$218,400

CLAIMS AGAINST ASSETS	
Accounts Payable (Liabilities)	$ 14,400
J. York, Capital	204,000
Total	$218,400

FIGURE 5-2

Jennifer York's Balance Sheet

OWNER IS BOSS There is a great deal of pride and satisfaction in being one's own boss and being responsible only to oneself. The proprietor can be inventive and creative in working out ideas to make the business a success.

OWNER RECEIVES ALL PROFITS Very closely related to this first advantage is the fact that all the profits belong to the sole proprietor. As a result, the owner is more likely to work overtime and to think continually of how the business can operate more efficiently.

OWNER PERSONALLY KNOWS EMPLOYEES AND CUSTOMERS Because most proprietorships are small, the proprietor and the employees know one another personally. This relationship can lead to mutual understanding and a feeling of "family" as employer and employees work side-by-side in daily business activities. Sole proprietors often develop close relationships with their customers as well.

OWNER CAN ACT QUICKLY IN DECISION MAKING Sole proprietors can make decisions without consulting others, so they can act promptly when the need arises. If an unusual opportunity to buy merchandise or equipment occurs, or if the owner wishes to change the location of the business or to sell on credit terms rather than on a cash basis, there are no dissenting partners to stop such action. Thus, the management of a proprietorship is flexible and can adjust rapidly to changing conditions.

OWNER IS FREE FROM RED TAPE A sole proprietor can usually begin or end business activities without legal formality. Sole proprietorships can be organized without a lot of legal documents or government red tape. In some types of businesses, however, such as a restaurant, it is necessary to obtain a license before operations can begin.

OWNER USUALLY PAYS LESS INCOME TAX THAN A CORPORATION In most sole proprietorships, the income tax is often less than in the corporation type of business, which is explained in the next chapter.

CAREER CONNECTION

ENTREPRENEUR

"Entrepreneur" is a long word that simply refers to someone who owns, operates, and takes the risk of a business venture. Today, millions of small businesses contribute billions of dollars to the United States economy. There are many opportunities for entrepreneurs in all types of businesses: manufacturing, wholesaling, retailing, and services.

Would entrepreneurship be right for you? Successful entrepreneurs are independent and self-confident; they have determination and perseverance; they are goal-oriented; they set high standards for themselves; they are creative; and they are able to act quickly.

Entrepreneurs are their own bosses and can choose a business that interests them. However, entrepreneurship is risky. Small businesses face the possibility of going out of business or losing money. In addition, entrepreneurs work long hours and face uncertain incomes. As you continue your study of business principles and management, think about whether you have what it takes to make it as an entrepreneur.

For more career information about entrepreneurs, check your library or the Internet for resources.

DISADVANTAGES OF PROPRIETORSHIPS

There are many advantages to owning your own business. However, there are also some disadvantages facing the sole proprietor.

OWNER MAY LACK NECESSARY SKILLS AND ABILITIES Each person has special skills and abilities. One person may excel at selling. Another person may be more talented at purchasing goods or keeping records. Still a third person may be superior at supervising employees. All of these activities are important to the success of a business, but the proprietor is likely to be weak in one or more areas. No one can do everything well. It is therefore easy to understand why some proprietorships end in failure within a short time.

OWNER MAY LACK FUNDS Additional funds (capital) are often needed for emergencies. Financial assistance on a large scale may be difficult to obtain by a single owner. Therefore, the expansion of the business may be slowed because of the owner's lack of capital.

OWNER BEARS ALL LOSSES Sole proprietors assume a great deal of risk. While sole owners receive all the profits of the business, they also bear all the losses if the business fails. If the business fails and the owner is unable to pay the debts of the business, the creditors have a claim against the owner's personal assets, not just the assets of the business. The sole entrepreneur may therefore lose not only the money invested in the enterprise but also personal possessions, such as a car or home.

ILLNESS OR DEATH MAY CLOSE THE BUSINESS The continuing operation of a sole proprietorship depends on the longevity of the proprietor. If the owner becomes unable to work because of illness or dies, the business would have to close.

BUSINESSES SUITED TO BEING PROPRIETORSHIPS

The kind of business that is primarily concerned with providing personal services is well suited to the proprietorship form of organization. Dentists, accountants, landscape gardeners, carpenters, painters, barbers, beauty salons, Web site developers, and computer *consultants* (experts) are examples of businesses frequently organized as proprietorships.

Another type of business that seems to be well adapted to the proprietorship form of business is the one that sells merchandise or services on a small scale. Newspaper and magazine stands, roadside markets, fast food and family restaurants, flower shops, gasoline stations, small grocery stores, fish markets, and many Web-based businesses that sell crafts, gourmet foods, or grocery delivery services are examples. In general, the type of business that can be operated suitably as a proprietorship is one that (1) is small enough to be managed by the proprietor or a few people hired by the proprietor and (2) does not require a large amount of capital.

ILLUSTRATION 5-2

The most common form of business ownership is the proprietorship. What are some advantages and disadvantages of proprietorships?

PARTNERSHIP

Jennifer York, who operates the proprietorship mentioned earlier, is faced with the problem of expanding her business. She has run the business successfully for over ten years. She sees new opportunities in the community for increasing her business, but she does not wish to assume full responsibility for the undertaking. She realizes that the expansion of the business will place on her considerable financial and managerial responsibilities. She also realizes that in order to expand she needs additional capital, but she does not want to borrow the money. Because of these reasons, she has decided that it will be wise to change her business from a proprietorship to a **partnership,** a business owned by two or more people.

Robert Burton operates an adjoining bakery, where he bakes fresh bread and pastries daily. He has proven to be honest and to have considerable business ability. Combining the two businesses could result in more customers for both groceries and fresh baked goods. Customers who have been coming to the bake shop may become grocery customers also. And those who have been buying at the grocery and fruit market may become customers of bakery products. A discussion between York and Burton leads to a tentative agreement to form a partnership if a third person can be found who will invest enough cash to remodel both stores to form one large store and to purchase additional equipment. The financial statement of Burton's business is shown in Figure 5-3.

The net worth of Burton's business is $153,600. In other words, after deducting the amount of his liabilities ($7,200) from the total value of his assets ($160,800), his business is worth $153,600. According to Jen-

ASSETS	
Cash	$ 10,560
Merchandise	3,600
Equipment	26,640
Land & Buildings	120,000
Total	$160,800

CLAIMS AGAINST ASSETS	
Accounts Payable (Liabilities)	$ 7,200
R. Burton, Capital	153,600
Total	$160,800

FIGURE 5-3

Balance Sheet for Robert Burton

nifer York's balance sheet in Figure 5-2, her business is worth $204,000. In order to have an equal investment in the partnership, Burton must invest an additional $50,400 in cash.

They find Lu Chan, a person with accounting experience, who has $144,000 and is able to borrow the remaining $60,000 to become an equal partner. The partnership agreement, shown in Figure 5-6, is then written and signed by York, Burton, and Chan.

Once the partnership is formed, a statement of financial position (balance sheet) must be prepared. This statement shows the total assets, liabilities, and capital of the owners at the start of the business. The partnership's balance sheet is shown in Figure 5-4. Each asset category on the combined balance sheet (merchandise, equipment, and land and buildings) as well as the accounts payable liability category are the totals of these categories from Burton's and York's businesses. The cash category combines the cash from both businesses plus Chan's cash investment of $204,000.

A key factor in the success of a partnership is for the partners to clearly agree upon each person's responsibilities. York, Burton, and Chan divide their duties: York supervises the grocery department, Burton supervises the bake shop and meat department, and Chan handles the finances, inventory, and records.

ASSETS	
Cash	$282,720
Merchandise	35,280
Equipment	51,600
Land & Buildings	264,000
Total	$633,600

CLAIMS AGAINST ASSETS	
Accounts Payable (Liabilities)	$ 21,600
J. York, Capital	204,000
R. Burton, Capital	204,000
L. Chan, Capital	204,000
Total	$633,600

FIGURE 5-4

Balance Sheet for York, Burton, and Chan at Startup

FIGURE 5-5

York, Burton, and Chan's Balance Sheet at Year's End

ASSETS		CLAIMS AGAINST ASSETS	
Cash	$ 240,000	Accounts Payable (Liabilities)	$ 74,900
Merchandise	60,000	J. York, Capital	221,700
Equipment	90,000	R. Burton, Capital	221,700
Land & Buildings	350,000	L. Chan, Capital	221,700
Total	$740,000	Total	$740,000

During the year the three partners combine the stores, remodel them, buy new equipment, and open for business. The financial statement at the end of the year, shown in Figure 5-5, shows the results of the new partnership.

Has the partnership had a successful year? Each partner has received a salary of $5,000 a month (according to the terms of the partnership agreement). In addition, the capital or net worth of each partner has increased from $204,000 to $221,700 as a result of profits made during the year. This increase in the total capital from $612,000 ($204,000 times 3) to $665,100 ($221,700 times 3) amounts to $53,100 and is an increase of nearly 8.7 percent. Chan, who borrowed some of the money for his investment, had to pay 7 percent interest to the lender. His investment in the partnership brought him a return that is more than the interest on his loan.

FACTS AND FIGURES

"Partners" can be classified in a variety of ways. For example, a silent partner may be known to the public as a partner, but takes no active part in management. A secret partner is not known to the public as a partner, yet participates in management. A dormant partner is neither known to the public as a partner nor active in management.

ADVANTAGES OF PARTNERSHIPS

Many businesses are organized as partnerships at the very beginning. Figure 5-6 shows a partnership agreement. There are nearly 1.6 million businesses operating as partnerships in the United States, which is small in comparison to sole proprietorships. While most partnerships have only two or three partners, there is no limit set on the number of partners. Some businesses have as many as ten or more partners. Some of the advantages of partnerships are discussed below.

SKILLS AND ABILITIES POOLED A partnership is likely to be operated more efficiently than a proprietorship, because a partnership can draw on the skills of two or more people, instead of just one. One partner may have special sales ability; another may have an aptitude for buying the right kind, quality, and quantity of merchandise. One partner may propose a change in the business; another partner may be able to point out disadvantages in the plan and suggest changes that were not initially apparent. In a sole proprietorship, the single owner must have skills in all key business areas or be able to hire people with the needed skills for the business to succeed.

Partnership Agreement

This contract, made and entered into on the first day of June, 20-- by and between Jennifer L. York, of Buffalo, New York, party of the first part, Robert R. Burton, of Buffalo, New York, party of the second part, Lu Chan of Niagara Falls, New York, party of the third part:

Witnesseth: That the said parties have this day formed a partnership for the purpose of engaging in and conducting a retail grocery-fruit-meat market and bakery under the following stipulations, which are made a part of the contract:

First: The said partnership is to continue for a term of ten years from date hereof.

Second: The business shall be conducted under the firm name of Y, B, & C Fine Foods, at 4467 Goodson Street, Buffalo, New York.

Third: The investments are as follows: Jennifer L. York: Cash, $17,760; Merchandise, $31,680; Equipment, $24,960; Land and Buildings, $144,000; Total Assets, $218,400; less Accounts Payable, $14,400, equals Net Investment, $204,000. Robert R. Burton: Cash, $10,560; Merchandise, $3,600; Equipment, $26,640; Land and Buildings, $120,000; Total Assets, $160,800, less Accounts Payable, $7,200, equals Net Investment, $153,000. Lu Chan: Cash, $204,000.

Fourth: All profits or losses arising from said business are to be shared equally.

Fifth: Each partner is to devote his or her entire time and attention to the business and to engage in no other business enterprise without the written consent of the others.

Sixth: Each partner is to have a salary of $5,000 a month, the same to be withdrawn at such time as he or she may elect. No partner is to withdraw from the business an amount in excess of his or her salary without the written consent of the others.

Seventh: The duties of each partner are defined as follows: Jennifer L. York is to supervise the grocery-fruit-vegetable departments. Robert R. Burton is to supervise the bakery and meat departments. Lu Chan is to manage finances, inventory, and records.

Eighth: No partner is to become surety for anyone without the written consent of the others.

Ninth: In case of the death, incapacity, or withdrawal of one partner, the business is to be conducted for the remainder of the fiscal year by the surviving partners, the profits for the year allocated to the withdrawing partner to be determined by the ratio of the time he or she was a partner during the year to the whole year.

Tenth: In case of dissolution the assets are to be divided in the ratio of the capital invested at the time of dissolution.

In Witness Whereof, the parties aforesaid have hereunto set their hands and affixed their seals on the day and year above written.

In the presence of: .... (Seal)

.... (Seal)

.... (Seal)

FIGURE 5-6

A clearly written and understood partnership agreement can prevent problems later.

SOURCES OF CAPITAL INCREASED A new business needs capital to buy the equipment, inventory, and office space needed to get started. Often two or more people can supply more capital than one person can. When the business needs to expand, generally several partners can obtain the additional capital needed for the expansion more easily than one person can.

ILLUSTRATION 5-3

A partnership is a business owned by two or more persons. Why might a partnership be operated more efficiently than a proprietorship?

CREDIT POSITION IMPROVED The partnership usually has a better credit reputation than the sole proprietorship. This is often true because more than one owner is responsible for the ownership and management of the business.

CONTRIBUTION OF GOODWILL Each partner is likely to have a large personal following. Some people will be more likely to do business with the newly formed partnership because they know one of the owners. This is known as *goodwill.*

INCREASED CONCERN IN BUSINESS MANAGEMENT Each owner of the business will have a greater interest in the firm as a partner than as an employee. Much of this is due to the greater financial responsibility each person has as a partner.

LESS TAX BURDEN THAN CORPORATIONS Partnerships usually have a tax advantage over corporations. You will learn more about this in Chapter 6. Partnerships prepare a federal income tax report but do not pay a tax on their profits, as do corporations. However, partners must pay a personal income tax on their individual share of the profit.

REDUCTION IN COMPETITION Two or more proprietors in the same line of business may become one organization by forming a partnership. This move may substantially decrease, or even eliminate, competition.

RETIREMENT FROM MANAGEMENT A sole proprietor may wish to retire. However, the proprietor may not want to close the business. In such a case, the owner may form a partnership and allow the new owner to manage the business.

OPERATING ECONOMIES It is often possible to operate more efficiently by combining two or more businesses. In such a case, certain operating expenses—such as advertising, supplies, equipment, fuel, and rent—can be reduced.

MANAGEMENT CLOSE-UP

BEN AND JERRY'S HOMEMADE, INC.

On May 5, 1978, Ben Cohen and Jerry Greenfield formed an ice cream parlor partnership in a renovated gas station in Burlington, Vermont. The two former seventh-grade buddies, who used top-quality ingredients, were delighted by their early success. Yet, to survive in those initial days they needed to improve sales to cover expenses.

The business grew rapidly, but they had early concerns about getting too large. When the business was small, they enjoyed working alongside employees while making and experimenting with new products and flavors. But as the business grew, they began to grow apart from their employees and started to feel as if they were losing the enjoyment experienced during the start-up days. Job fulfillment satisfied them more than profits.

They tried to resist further expansion but knew the business either had to grow or fade away. Jerry retired. Another entrepreneur, however, convinced Ben that he could serve employees and the public while continuing to expand. With a new focus, Jerry rejoined Ben. Together they modified the firm's goals to expand their product line and also improve the quality of life for employees and all of society.

Today, Ben and Jerry's has over 700 employees and produces enough flavors to satisfy millions of customers. The company makes, distributes, and sells super-premium ice cream, sorbet, and yogurt to supermarkets, restaurants, and over 140 franchised and company outlets in highly populated states and nine foreign countries. Sales exceed $200 million yearly.

Ben and Jerry remain committed to their employees. They achieved national recognition for developing a proud and productive workforce. The emphasis given workers was once reflected in their 7-to-1 rule that prevented any employee—including managers—from earning more than seven times what the lowest-paid employee earns. Recently the rule changed, however, because the pay scale for attracting excellent top executives was too low.

One important thing has not changed—Ben and Jerry's commitment to social responsibility. Each year a sizable percentage of profits goes to charities and social causes. Donations to charities, art, and public musical concerts are common. Ben and Jerry—an unusual pair of innovative partners—have created a unique style of doing business.

THINK CRITICALLY

1. At the outset, was Ben and Jerry's business typical for a new enterprise? Give reasons for your answer.
2. Why did Ben and Jerry want their company to remain small?
3. If the lowest-paid employee earned $15,000 a year, what would the maximum salary be for the highest-paid manager under the 7-to-1 rule? Why might this manager be unhappy with this rule?
4. Determine what the company is doing today to fulfill its social obligations and also find out about its new products, sales, and profits.

DISADVANTAGES OF PARTNERSHIPS

While there are many advantages of partnerships, there are also disadvantages, as described below.

UNLIMITED FINANCIAL LIABILITY According to law, each member of the partnership has an **unlimited financial liability** for all the debts of the business. If some of the partners are unable to pay their share, one partner may have to pay all the debts.

Suppose that the partnership of York, Burton, and Chan failed and that after all the business assets were changed into cash and used to pay business debts, the partnership still owed creditors $18,000. Legally, the partners must pay these debts from their own personal savings or sell personal property, such as their car or house, to obtain the cash to pay off the debts. In this case, each partner should contribute $6,000 ($18,000 divided by 3) from their personal assets. But if, say, Burton and Chan did not have the $6,000 in personal assets to pay their portions, York would be legally responsible for using her personal savings and property to pay the entire $18,000.

DISAGREEMENT AMONG PARTNERS There is always danger of disagreement among partners. The majority of the partners may want to change the nature of the business but are unable to do so because one partner refuses. For example, a partnership may have been formed to conduct a retail business selling audio equipment. After a while, the majority of the partners may think it wise to add cellular phones to their line of merchandise. The change may benefit the business. However, as long as one partner disagrees, the partnership cannot make the change. Furthermore, partners sometimes feel that they are not properly sharing in the management. This situation may cause disagreements that could hurt the business. Such a condition can be partly prevented if the partnership agreement states the duties of each partner.

EACH PARTNER BOUND BY CONTRACTS OF OTHERS Each partner is bound by the partnership contracts made by any partner if such contracts apply to the ordinary operations of the business. If one partner commits to a contract in the name of the partnership, all partners are legally bound by it, whether they think the contract is good for the business or not. Disagreements can eventually lead to partnership failure.

UNCERTAIN LIFE The life of a partnership is uncertain. Sometimes when partners draw up a partnership contract, they specify a definite length of time, such as ten years, for the existence of the business. Should one partner die, however, the partnership ends. The deceased partner may have been the principal manager; and, as a result of his or her death, the business may suffer. The heirs of the deceased partner may demand an unfair price from the surviving partners for the share of the deceased partner. Or the heirs may insist upon ending the partnership quickly to obtain the share belonging to the dead partner. In the latter case, the assets that are sold may not bring a fair price; and, as a result, all the partners suffer a loss. A partnership can carry insurance on the life of a partner to provide money to purchase the share of a partner who dies. Under the laws of most states, the bankruptcy of any partner or the admission of a new partner are other causes that may bring a sudden end to the partnership.

LIMITED SOURCES OF CAPITAL The contributions of the partners, the earnings of the business, and the money that can be borrowed limit the amount of funds that a partnership can obtain. It is difficult for a partnership to obtain enough capital to operate a large business unless each member of the partnership is wealthy or unless there are many partners. Too many partners, however, may cause inefficient operations.

UNSATISFACTORY DIVISION OF PROFITS Sometimes the partnership profits are not divided fairly according to the contributions of the individual partners. Partners should agree up front on how to divide profits according to the amount of labor, expertise, and capital each partner is expected to contribute. The partnership should then specify the agreed-upon division in the partnership agreement, such as 60 percent to one partner and 40 percent to another. If no provision is made in the agreement, the law requires an equal division of the profits. Then if, say, one partner contributes more time, expertise, or labor to the business than do the others, this partner may feel that he or she deserves more than an equal share of the profit.

DIFFICULTY IN WITHDRAWING FROM PARTNERSHIP If a partner wishes to sell his or her interest in the business, it may be difficult to do so. Even if a buyer is found, the buyer may not be acceptable to the other partners.

LIMITED PARTNERSHIPS

In an ordinary (general) partnership, each partner is personally liable for all the debts incurred by the partnership. The laws of some states, however, permit the formation of a **limited partnership,** which restricts the liability of a partner to the amount of the partner's investment. In a limited partnership, not all partners have unlimited financial liability for the partnership debts. However, at least one partner must be a general partner who has unlimited liability. In many states, the name of a limited partner may not be included in the firm name.

Under the Uniform Limited Partnership Act, the states have created similar regulations for controlling limited partnerships. For example, the law requires that a certificate of limited partnership be filed in a public office of record and that proper notice be given to each creditor with whom the limited partnership does business. If these requirements are not fulfilled, the limited partners have unlimited liability in the same manner as a general partner.

The limited partnership is a useful form of business organization in situations where one person wishes to invest in a business but does not have the time or interest to participate actively in its management. Any business that is formed as a proprietorship can usually be formed as a limited partnership.

BUSINESSES SUITED TO BEING PARTNERSHIPS

The partnership form of organization is common among businesses that furnish more than one kind of product or service. Each partner usually looks after a specialized phase of the business. For example, car dealers often have sales and service departments. One partner may handle the sale of new cars, and another partner may be in charge of servicing and repairing cars. Still another partner could be in charge of used car sales or of the accounting and financial side of the business. Similarly, if a business operates in more than one location, each partner can be in charge of a specific location. Businesses that operate longer than the usual eight hours a day, such as the retail food business advertised in Figure 5-7, find the partnership organization desirable. Each partner can be in charge for part of the day.

ILLUSTRATION 5-4

A limited partnership restricts the liability of a partner for the amount of the partner's investment. Why might a limited partnership be a useful form of business organization?

Partnerships are also common in the same types of businesses that are formed as proprietorships, particularly in selling goods and services to consumers. It is especially popular in professional services, such as lawyers, doctors, accountants, and financial consultants. Internet businesses have been formed as partnerships as well. Good faith, together with reasonable care in the exercise of management duties, is required of all partners in a business.

FIGURE 5-7

An Advertisement Used to Announce the Opening of the Y, B, and C Partnership

BUSINESS NAME

A proprietorship or a partnership may be conducted under the name or names of the owner or owners. In many states, the law prohibits the use of *and Company* or *& Co.* unless such identification indicates additional partners. For example, if there are only two partners, it is not permissible to use a firm name such as Jones, Smith & Co., because that name indicates at least three partners. The name or names included in the term "Company" must be identified by registration at a public recording office, usually the county clerk's office. Usually one can do business under a trade, or artificial name, such as The Superior Shoe Store or W-W Manufacturing Company. Likewise, proper registration is usually required so that creditors may know everyone who is responsible for the business. Operating under a trade name, therefore, does not reduce the owners' liability to creditors.

CHAPTER CONCEPTS

- Most small businesses begin with one or a few owners. These new entrepreneurs often possess certain characteristics that help assure their success, such as the strong need to be boss, to make their own decisions, and to take reasonable risks. To aid their success, however, they must prepare a carefully developed business plan.
- A sole proprietorship, or proprietorship, is a business owned and operated by one person. It is the most popular form of business ownership. Many small retail and service businesses are single-owner firms because they are the easiest to start. The proprietor has other advantages, such as the power to make all decisions and make them quickly if needed, receive all profits, pay less in taxes than corporations, and know employees and customers personally. A proprietor also has few legal obstacles in starting a business.
- Proprietorships have a few critical disadvantages, such as lacking skills or knowledge needed for performing all key business tasks, lacking funds for expansion, surviving when major financial losses occur, and closing should illness or death occur.
- A partnership is a business owned by two or more people. Partnerships have key advantages over sole proprietorships. For example, multiple owners can contribute more capital to start or expand and more skills to improve business efficiency. Also, more partners can obtain more credit from banks and other sources. Because partnerships are larger than proprietorships, they can compete better. Finally, a partnership need not close because of the retirement of an owner.
- Partnerships have several major disadvantages. Each partner has unlimited financial liability for all business debts. And each partner is responsible for the contracts made by other partners. Other problems can arise when breaking up a partnership, deciding how to divide profits, and lacking the capital needed to expand.
- Like proprietorships, small retail stores are often partnerships, as are professional service businesses, such as doctors, lawyers, and accountants. Some partnerships may have limited partners. A limited partner often does not participate in running a business and has limited liability. However, one or more of the members of a partnership must be an ordinary (general) partner with unlimited liability.

BUILD VOCABULARY POWER

Define the following terms and concepts.

1. business plan
2. sole proprietorship (proprietorship)
3. proprietor
4. creditors
5. partnership
6. unlimited financial liability
7. limited partnership

REVIEW FACTS

1. What are two common legal forms of business ownership?
2. How will a good business plan help someone successfully open a new business?
3. What types of people enjoy the responsibilities of business ownership?
4. List the major advantages of proprietorships.
5. List the major disadvantages of proprietorships.
6. Which kinds of businesses are most suited to the proprietorship form of business ownership?
7. List the major advantages of partnerships.
8. List the major disadvantages of partnerships.
9. Under what types of situations is a limited partnership useful?
10. Why is it necessary for proprietorships and partnerships to register their company names with local authorities?

DISCUSS IDEAS

1. Your friend followed your advice and made a business plan to create a new business called Cookies to Go. You noticed she did not include a marketing plan and you mention it. She then says, "Everyone likes cookies. My prices depend on how much it costs to make each type of cookie. And there isn't a cookie store within three blocks of where I plan to locate my business. How could I go wrong?" List questions that should be answered in the marketing plan that would make your friend give more thought to her decision.
2. You have been working part-time and summers at a local service station during your school years. You have performed just about every major task from pumping gas to repairing cars and even handling some of the bookkeeping. Discuss how your responsibilities as an employee will change if you become the owner of the station.
3. A sole proprietor has no partners to participate in making decisions. What disadvantages could result from not having partners help in the decision-making process?
4. If a proprietorship needs additional capital but the owner cannot furnish it from personal funds, from what sources might capital be obtained?
5. Why should a partnership agreement include a clause such as the fifth clause shown in Figure 5-6?
6. Why should a partnership agreement include a clause such as the seventh clause shown in Figure 5-6?
7. Why should a partnership agreement be in writing?
8. A partner signed a partnership contract for television advertising while the other two partners were on vacation. Upon returning,

the vacationing partners claimed that the partnership was not bound to the contract because both of them disapproved of television advertising. Was the partnership legally bound?

9. What effect is there on the life of a partnership when (a) a partner dies, (b) a partner quits, and (c) a new partner is added?
10. Why are proprietorships more common than partnerships?

ANALYZE INFORMATION

1. Assume you are planning to open a business of your own by using your home computer to prepare designs and slogans that can be printed and ironed on T-shirts. You already have the computer but need a few other items. However, you are not sure you really want to start such a business. To help you decide, make two columns on a sheet of paper or your word processor: Why I *Would* Like Running My Own Business and Why I *Would Not* Like Running My Own Business. Fill in all your reasons. When you finish, study the two lists and write a paragraph indicating whether you have the essential characteristics of a successful business owner.
2. Alvares invested $80,000 and Navarro invested $60,000 in their partnership business. They share profits and losses in proportion to their investments. What amount should each receive of the $33,600 profit earned last year?
3. Feng and Cooke had invested equal amounts in a partnership business. Later the business failed with $40,000 in liabilities (debts) and only $15,000 in assets (property). In addition to a share of the assets of the business, Cooke had $35,000 of other personal property at the time of the failure, but Feng had only $5,000 of additional personal property. Other than the partnership property, what amount will be required of each partner to pay the debts of the partnership? What would happen if Feng could not pay his or her share?
4. Lamar Johnson plans to go into business for himself. He wants to own a men's clothing store. He believes that he has adequate experience in this area, having managed a clothing department in a large local department store for several years. Lamar thinks that he has sufficient capital, but it may be a little tight financially getting through the first year of operation.

   Katasha Thomas, a long-time friend of Lamar's, is also planning to open a business. Her women's clothing store will be located next to Lamar's in the same busy shopping area. Although Katasha has almost no experience in the clothing business, she did work part-time one summer in a fashion shop. And now she has a degree in finance from the local university. Her uncle is willing to lend her the money needed to start the business.

   Both Katasha and Lamar have discussed their plans. The idea of forming a partnership has been mentioned, but they are not quite sure what to do. Form a committee of three to five students in order to (a) discuss the situation and then (b) prepare a summary of your committee's recommendations to the two people involved.

5. Assume that the balance sheet of the partnership of Tran and Nizami at the time they closed the business appeared as follows:

Assets	
Cash	$18,000
Merchandise	40,000
Fixtures and Equipment	24,000
Land and Building	108,000
Total	$190,000
Claims Against Assets	
Accounts Payable (Liabilities)	$10,000
N. S. Tran, Capital	90,000
A. J. Nizami, Capital	90,000
Total	$190,000

When selling the assets, the partners sold the merchandise for $32,000, the fixtures and equipment for $18,000, and the land and building for $110,000. After paying their debts, what amount of the remaining cash should each partner receive?

6. Assume you are considering forming a small business in your state. Search for information that will help you decide whether to open a sole proprietorship or a partnership. Use your school or public library to obtain information for writing a report on business plans, legal advice, and general state assistance. If you have access to the Internet, you can find information from a government Web site, such as the Small Business Administration (www.sba.gov), or from a magazine targeted to small businesses, such as www.blackenterprise.com, www.incmag.com, or www.entrepreneurmag.com. You could also try search engines such as www.askjeeves.com and www.alltheweb.com.

SOLVE BUSINESS PROBLEMS

CASE 5-1

Sharon Gillespie, John Jensen, and Laura Cho have been close friends for years. About two years ago they formed a partnership that builds Web pages for small entrepreneurs who want to expand their businesses. Sharon, John, and Laura are experts at what they do. However, their partnership has not been very successful and is not growing. John is in charge of finding and dealing with customers and handling necessary paperwork tasks. Both Sharon and Laura build the Web pages for their customers.

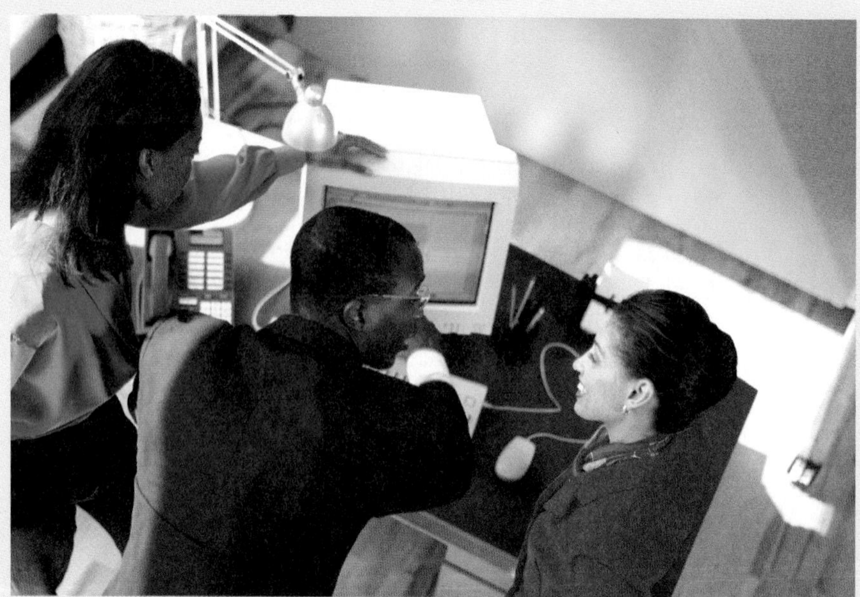

Recently, John confided to Laura that he is getting many complaints about Sharon's treatment of customers. "That may be the major reason why we aren't doing that well, but what can we do about it?" He continued, "Her customers don't often come back to us when they need to add new products or offer new services on their Web pages. Some have even jotted complaints about her on the bills I send them. Yesterday one customer said he'll take his business elsewhere if we don't replace her." The phone rang, and John excused himself to answer it.

After thinking about this for a while, Laura told John, "We have to get rid of her because she isn't going to change. If we want our business to survive and grow, let's ask her to leave. What else can we do?"

John paused and then said, "She owns one-third of our business. You can't fire a partner."

Laura asked, "Didn't our lawyer provide for this type of problem in our partnership agreement? Or maybe it's in our business plan."

"No, it's not in either place," John responded. "We have to work this out together."

Think Critically:

Your instructor may wish to place you into groups of three students each to answer the following questions and for each group to report their answers to the class.

1. What conditions existed before the partnership was formed that gave rise to this problem?
2. How important are the skills and personalities of the partners when considering the formation of a partnership?
3. Can Sharon's attitude toward customers somehow be changed? If yes, how?

4. What is the best solution for solving this problem? Carefully explain your answer.
5. Do you believe that John and Sharon would be better off trading jobs with each other?
6. How is this case situation different from that of student groups that attempt to solve other types of group problems?

CASE 5-2

John Willis, who is 27 and single, had just completed his fifth year of employment as a carpenter for a very small homebuilder. His boss, the sole owner of the company, is Tyrone Young. A few days ago, Tyrone asked John if he would like to become a partner, which he could do by contributing $70,000. In turn, John would receive 40 percent of all profits earned by the business. John had saved $30,000 and could borrow the balance needed from his grandmother at a low interest rate, but he would have to pay her back within 15 years.

John was undecided about becoming a partner. He liked the idea but he also knew there were risks and concerns. To help him make up his mind, he decided to talk to Tyrone at lunch. Here is how the conversation went.

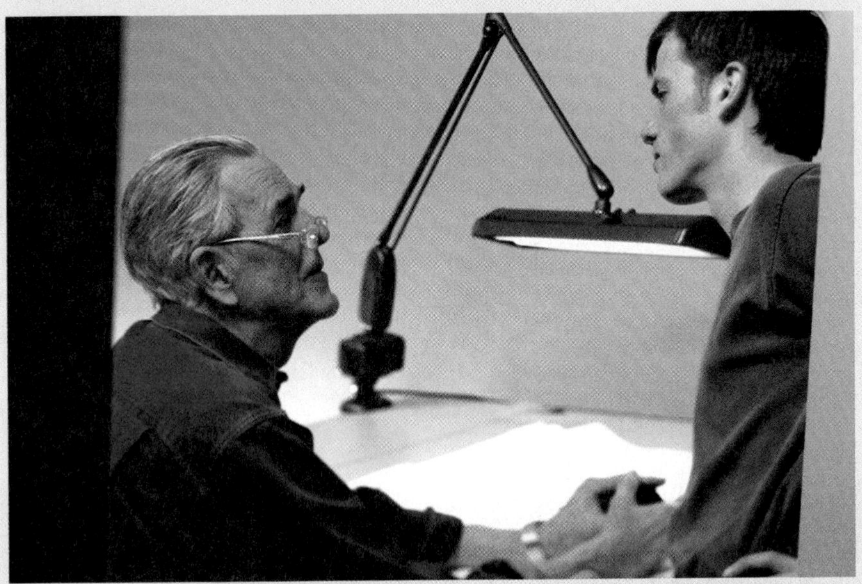

John: *I've been giving your offer a lot of thought, Tyrone. It's a tough decision, and I don't want to make the wrong one. So I'd like to chat with you about some of the problems involved in running a business.*

Tyrone: *Sure. I struggled with these issues about 15 years ago. When you own your own business, you're the boss. No one can tell you what to do or push you around. You can set up your own hours and make all the decisions. I enjoy the feeling of ownership.*

John: *I don't know if I'm ready to become part owner of a business. I'm still young and single, and I like working for you. I'm not sure I want all those responsibilities—getting customers, paying bills, and buying tools and lumber. You say you set your own hours, but I know you're already working when I arrive each morning, and you're still here when I leave in the evening. I know you spend some nights in the office, because I see the lights on when I drive by.*

Tyrone: *Well, I do put in many hours. That goes with the territory. But I don't mind all those hours because I like making decisions. And, when you join me as a partner, we'll share the work.*

John: *Then* I'll *be working longer hours. Both of us could go to work for that big new contracting firm on the other side of town. They could struggle with all the problems and decisions. Then we could work shorter hours and have more time to relax.*

Think Critically:

1. Do you think John is seriously ready to become a partner? Explain your answer.
2. If you were in John's position, how would you decide? Explain.
3. If John decides to accept Tyrone's offer, what action should be taken?

4. Find information from the library or Internet that might help John make a decision. One possible source is the Web site www.sba.gov/starting/indexstartup.html.

PROJECT: MY BUSINESS, INC.

New owners often start a business without carefully considering other possible forms of ownership. In this chapter, you will evaluate the advantages and disadvantages of the proprietorship and partnership forms of ownership for your new business.

DATA COLLECTION

1. Review copies of magazines written for entrepreneurs. Identify the current issues and problems faced by individual business own-

ers as well as the successful operating procedures described in the magazines.

2. Identify a person who currently is or has been a partner in a business. Ask the person to identify the advantages and disadvantages of operating a business as a partnership from his or her viewpoint.

3. Using the Internet, if possible, find a sample copy or an outline of a business plan. Speak with a banker or your business mentor about the importance of business plans for new businesses. Ask that person to describe the elements he or she feels are most important in a good business plan.

ANALYSIS

1. You have found a partner who wants to invest $6,000 and become involved in the operation of the business. You have already invested $12,000. Develop a simple partnership agreement for the business. After you have completed the agreement, ask your business mentor to review it with you.
2. Develop a chart that compares the proprietorship and partnership forms of business ownership for your business. Be certain to consider financial, personal, and management factors. When you have finished the analysis, decide whether you will remain a sole proprietor or form a partnership.
3. Develop an outline for a business plan for your new business. Begin to list the information that will go into each section of the plan. Identify the information you need to complete the business plan and the sources of that information. Continue to develop the business plan during the time you are working on this continuing project.

CORPORATE FORMS OF BUSINESS OWNERSHIP

OBJECTIVES

6-1 Explain the basic features of a corporation.

6-2 Describe how a corporation is formed and organized.

6-3 List some of the major advantages and disadvantages of the corporate form of business.

6-4 Describe several specialized forms of business organizations.

CORPORATE CONCEPT

Thanh Vu came to this country from Vietnam ten years ago and earned a college business degree. After graduation he worked as a manager in a small firm, where he learned a great deal. But after five years, the job became less challenging. He wondered about opening his own business with the money he had saved, but that seemed too risky.

Surely there was some way to be an entrepreneur without having to assume so much responsibility alone or with a partner. The partnership idea sounded acceptable, but fear of lawsuits from creditors if he didn't do well haunted him. Yet his fear of unlimited liability did not stop him from thinking about starting a business.

On his way home from work one day, Thanh stopped to get his hair styled. He overheard two other customers talking about changing their small partnership to a corporation. One said, "We would pay higher taxes." The other responded, "But our financial liability would be less than in our partnership." Thanh listened intently but said nothing until after the first person replied, "But we can't expand our successful business unless we can raise more money."

By now Thanh could no longer restrain himself. "Excuse me for listening, but I have an idea. I'm a manager and have a degree in business; but more important, I'm looking for an opportunity to become a business owner." The two men looked at each other and nodded. "Let's hear your idea," one said cautiously.

"There's a special type of corporation that permits you to be a corporation but allows you to pay taxes as if you were still a partnership," Thanh replied. "And if you're looking for another stockholder who can invest some money and help expand the business, I'd be very interested in talking with you."

After the introductions and handshakes, they scheduled a luncheon meeting for the next day.

In Chapter 5 you learned about proprietorships and partnerships as legal forms of organizing a business. This chapter will deal with the features and formation of corporations. In addition, you will learn about special organizational structures: limited liability companies, joint ventures, virtual corporations, nonprofit corporations, and cooperatives. If you were to join the three people in the opening story at their luncheon meeting tomorrow, you would need to understand the contents of this chapter.

CORPORATIONS

Corporations are towers on the business landscape. While proprietorships are many in number, they are generally small in size. In comparison, corporations are few in number, but generally large in size. Because corporations tend to be large, they play a powerful role in this country and in others. For example, corporations employ millions of people and provide consumers with many of the goods and services they need and want. In a recent year, corporate sales of goods and services were over 17 times more than sales from proprietorships, and over 16 times more than sales from partnerships in the United States.

Not all corporations are large. While corporations such as Ford, Compaq, and K-Mart are known to almost everyone, many small corporations also exist. Small corporations are popular for reasons you will discover later in this chapter.

Because the corporation plays a vital role in business, we need to understand its basic features as well as its advantages and disadvantages. To gain knowledge of the basic features of the corporation, we can follow York, Burton, and Chan as they consider incorporating their fast-growing food store partnership, which they launched in the last chapter.

BASIC FEATURES

Elena Morales, a lawyer, helped York, Burton, and Chan prepare the partnership agreement under which they now operate. The partners asked Elena to describe a corporation to them. She stated that a **corporation** is a business owned by a group of people and authorized by the state in which it is located to act as though it were a single person, separate from its owners. To get permission to form a corporation, organizers must obtain a charter. A **charter** (often called a **certificate of incorporation**) is the official document through which a state grants the power to operate as a corporation.

A corporation is, in a sense, an artificial person created by the laws of the state. A corporation can make contracts, borrow money, own property, and sue or be sued in its own name. Any act performed for the corporation by an authorized person, such as an employee, is done in the name of the business. For example, the treasurer of a corporation has the power to borrow money for the business. An unauthorized employee, such as a receptionist who was hired to answer the phone and greet visitors, could not borrow money for the corporation.

Morales further explained the important parts played by three key types of people in corporations: (1) stockholders, (2) directors, and (3) officers.

STOCKHOLDERS **Stockholders** (often called **shareholders**) are the owners of a corporation. Ownership is divided into equal parts called **shares.** A person who buys one share becomes a stockholder. Therefore, thousands of people can own a corporation. Each stockholder receives a certificate from the corporation, which shows the number of shares owned. Stockholders have a number of basic rights, including the following:

1. To transfer ownership to others.
2. To vote for members of the ruling body of the corporation and other special matters that may be brought before the stockholders.
3. To receive dividends. **Dividends** are profits that are distributed to stockholders on a per-share basis. The decision to distribute profits is made by the ruling body of the corporation.

4. To buy new shares of stock in proportion to one's present investment should the corporation issue more shares.
5. To share in the net proceeds (cash received from the sale of all assets less the payment of all debts) should the corporation go out of business.

A stockholder does not have the same financial responsibility as a partner; that is, there is no liability beyond the extent of the stockholder's ownership. If the corporation fails, a stockholder can lose only the money invested. Creditors cannot collect anything further from the stockholder.

DIRECTORS The **board of directors** (often shortened to **directors** or the **board**) is the ruling body of the corporation. Board members are elected by the stockholders. Directors develop plans and policies to guide the corporation as well as appoint officers to carry out the plans. If the corporation is performing successfully, its board is content to deal with policy issues and review the progress of the company. However, if the corporation's profits fall, or if it experiences other serious difficulties, the board often steps in and takes an active role in the operation of the business.

In large firms, boards generally consist of 10 to 25 directors. A few board members are top executives from within the corporation. The directors often are from outside the corporation and are usually executives from other businesses or people from nonprofit organizations, such as college professors. Often, directors are stockholders who hold many shares. But directors need not be stockholders. People who hold few or no shares are sometimes elected to the board because they have valuable knowledge needed by the board to make sound decisions. In some countries, such as Sweden, France, and China, an employee of the company is also a board member.

FACTS AND FIGURES

Business experts believe that in the 21st century, corporate boards will need to have one or more directors with expertise in the following areas: telecommunications and technology; marketing; international markets; top-level finance; restructuring; entrepreneurial skills; and service industries.

ILLUSTRATION 6-1

A person can become a stockholder in any one of hundreds of major corporations. In which corporations would you be interested in owning stock?

ETHICAL ISSUES

TROUBLE IN THE BOARDROOM

Experts agree that top management greatly influences the extent to which ethics are practiced in corporations by CEOs and boards of directors. Shareholders assume that their elected directors are ethical, but are they?

The relationships between shareholders, boards, and CEOs should be as harmonious as possible. In practice, however, CEOs sometimes manipulate boards. As a result, employees, retirees, customers, and shareholders often suffer.

For example, CEOs know that the boards who hire them can also fire them. As a result, CEOs want to build relationships with board members. CEOs in firms that are not doing well are often motivated to take defensive action. One such defense is to get elected as chairperson of the board. In this way, CEOs set meeting agendas and thereby control topics that are discussed. CEOs can also recommend friends as nominees to the board for stockholders to elect via proxy statements. Through such actions, CEOs build loyal followers.

On the other hand, directors who are elected by shareholders and who are loyal to CEOs may be disloyal to the stockholders they represent. A condition like this creates problems. For example, CEO salaries may be raised despite poor performance. A CEO's plans may be approved without adequate review. During tough competitive periods when a firm has difficulty making a profit, everyone is hurt. That's when employees get fired and stockholders lose money.

Employees get hurt in another way when employee pension funds are invested in corporations by the fund managers. Pension funds are pools of money set aside for employee retirement benefits. When corporations do poorly, managers of large pension funds try to see that changes are made within these companies. Changes made in recent years as the result of action taken by pension fund managers include these examples. First, boards now select more directors from outside firms who are more critical of poor CEO leadership. Second, more boards take greater care in selecting, evaluating, and paying CEOs.

Ethics in boardrooms have been improving gradually. Now good boards listen to stockholders and no longer permit CEOs to control them. Rather, good boards control CEOs. And good CEOs encourage frank discussions with their boards and stakeholders.

THINK CRITICALLY

1. What defensive actions have CEOs taken that might cause boards of directors to perform their jobs improperly?
2. What happens when boards and CEOs do not adequately represent stockholders?
3. Do you believe the ethics of corporations differ much from the ethics in nonprofit organizations, such as between the superintendent of a school system and the board of education? Explain your answer.
4. Using a library or the Internet, find a recent report that deals with a CEO being fired by a board. Determine the causes for dismissal.

OFFICERS

The **officers** of a corporation are the top executives who are hired to manage the business. The board of directors appoints them. The officers of a small corporation often consist of a president, a secretary, and a treasurer. In addition, large corporations may have vice presidents in charge of major areas, such as marketing, finance, and manufacturing. The titles of these officers are often shortened to letters. For example, the top officer is called a CEO (chief executive officer) and the head financial officer is the CFO (chief financial officer).

FORMATION OF CORPORATIONS

Over several months, York, Burton, and Chan asked their attorney, Elena Morales, many questions. Only after careful thought did the partners decide to form a corporation. Morales told them that there were basically three steps involved. First, a series of decisions had to be made about how the corporation would be organized. Second, the proper legal forms had to be prepared and sent to the state office that handles such matters. And third, the state would review the incorporation papers and issue a charter if it approved.

PREPARING THE CERTIFICATE OF INCORPORATION Each state has its own laws for forming corporations. No federal law exists. To incorporate a business, it is necessary in most states to file a certificate of incorporation with the appropriate state office. Morales prepared the certificate of incorporation for York, Burton, and Chan shown in Figure 6-1.

Notice the general type of information called for in the certificate of incorporation. In addition to the firm name, purpose, and capital stock, it requires information about the organizers.

Naming the Business. A business is usually required by law to have a name that indicates clearly that a corporation has been formed. Words or abbreviations such as *Corporation, Corp., Incorporated,* or *Inc.* are used; see Figure 6-2 for examples. The organizers have decided to name their corporation York, Burton, and Chan, Inc.

Stating the Purpose of the Business. A certificate of incorporation requires a corporation to describe its purpose clearly. In Figure 6-1, Article 3 precisely states the purpose of the corporation: "to operate a retail food business." It allows the corporation to expand into new food lines, but it does not allow the corporation to start non-food operations. For major changes in purpose, a new request must be submitted and approved by the state.

Investing in the Business. The certificate of incorporation could not be completed until York, Burton, and Chan decided how to invest their partnership holdings in the corporation. They agreed that the assets and

FIGURE 6-1

A certificate of incorporation includes information about the organizers of a corporation.

Certificate of Incorporation of
York, Burton, and Chan, Inc.

Pursuant to Article Two of the Stock Corporation Law.

State of New York
County of Cattaraugus } ss.

We, the undersigned, for the purpose of forming a Corporation pursuant to Article Two of the Stock Corporation Law of the State of New York, do hereby make, subscribe, acknowledge and file this certificate for that purpose as follows:

We, the undersigned, do hereby Certify

First.—That all the undersigned are full age, and all are citizens of the United States, and all residents of the State of New York.

Second.—That the name of said corporation is York, Burton, and Chan, Inc.

Third.—That the purpose for which said corporation is formed is to operate a retail food business.

Fourth.—That the amount of the Capital Stock of the said corporation is One Million Dollars ($ 1,000,000) to consist of Ten Thousand (10,000) shares of the par value of One Hundred dollars ($ 100) each.

Fifth.—That the office of said corporation is to be located in the City of Buffalo, County of Cattaraugus and State of New York.

Sixth.—That the duration of said corporation is to be perpetual.

Seventh.—That the number of Directors of said corporation is three.

Eighth.—That the names and post office addresses of the Directors until the first annual meeting are as follows:

Jennifer L. York 1868 Buffalo Street, Buffalo, NY 14760-1436
Robert R. Burton 1309 Main Street, Buffalo, NY 14760-1436
Lu Chan 4565 Erie Avenue, Niagara Falls, NY 14721-2348

Ninth.—That the names and post office addresses of the subscribers and the number of shares of stock which each agrees to take in said corporation are as follows:

Names	Post Office Addresses	No. of Shares
Jennifer L. York	1868 Buffalo Street	
	Buffalo, NY 14760-1436	2,217
Robert R. Burton	1309 Main Street	
	Buffalo, NY 14760-1436	2,217
Lu Chan	4565 Erie Avenue	
	Niagara Falls, NY 14721-2348	2,217

Tenth.—That the meetings of the Board of Directors shall be held only within the State of New York at Buffalo

In Witness Whereof, we have made, subscribed, and executed this certificate in duplicate the tenth day of September in the year Two thousand

Jennifer L. York
Robert R. Burton
Lu Chan

debts of the partnership should be taken over by the corporation. They further agreed that their capital (net worth or *equity*) of $221,700 each should be invested in the corporation. **Capital stock** (or simply **stock**) is the general term applied to the shares of ownership of a corporation.

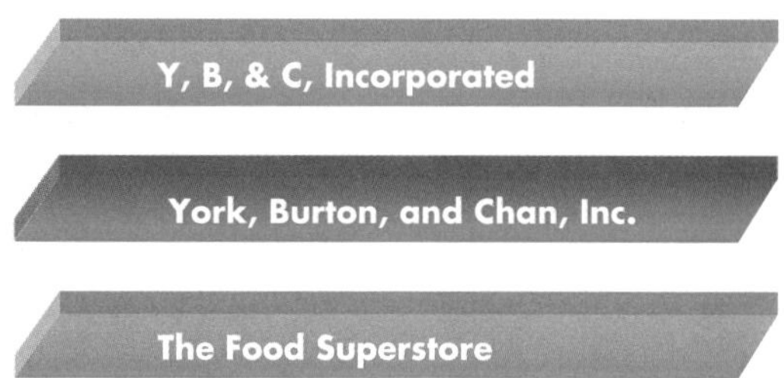

FIGURE 6-2

Organizers must select a name for the business to be recorded on the certificate of incorporation.

Here is how the details were worked out. The organizers requested authorization from the state to issue $1,000,000 in capital stock, as shown in Figure 6-1. Shares were valued at $100 each at the time of incorporation. There were 10,000 shares in all ($1,000,000 divided by $100 equals 10,000). York, Burton, and Chan each agreed to purchase 2,217 shares, as shown in Figure 6-3.

The 3,349 unissued shares (the difference between the 10,000 authorized shares and the 6,651 shares bought by the organizers) can be sold at a later date to raise more funds to expand the business.

Paying Incorporation Costs. Usually a new corporation must pay an organization tax, based on the amount of its capital stock. In addition, a new corporation usually pays a filing fee before the state will issue a charter entitling the business to operate as a corporation. In some states, the existence of the corporation begins when the application or certificate of incorporation has been filed with the Department of State.

OPERATING THE NEW CORPORATION York, Burton, and Chan, Inc., received approval to operate as a corporation. They turned their attention next to getting the business started.

Getting Organized. One of the first steps in getting the new corporation underway is to prepare a balance sheet or statement of financial position. The new corporation's balance sheet is shown in Figure 6-4.

The ownership of the corporation is in the same hands as was the ownership of the partnership. The ownership of the corporation, however, is evidenced by the issued capital stock. The former partners have each received a stock certificate indicating that each owns 2,217 shares of stock with a value of $100 a share.

York	2,217 shares x $100 per share =	$221,700
Burton	2,217 shares x $100 per share =	$221,700
Chan	2,217 shares x $100 per share =	$221,700
Total		$665,100

FIGURE 6-3

Division of shares held by York, Burton, and Chan, Inc.

FIGURE 6-4

Balance sheet of York, Burton, and Chan, Inc.

ASSETS	
Cash	$ 240,000
Merchandise	60,000
Equipment	90,000
Land & Buildings	350,000
Total	$740,000

CLAIMS AGAINST ASSETS	
Accounts Payable (Liabilities)	$ 74,900
Capital Stock	665,100
Total	$740,000

The three stockholders own the business and elect themselves directors. The new directors select officers. York is appointed president; Burton, vice president; and Chan, secretary and treasurer. An organization chart of the new corporation is shown in Figure 6-5.

Handling Voting Rights. The owners agreed that each owner will have 2,217 votes on matters arising in the meetings of the stockholders. Voting stockholders usually have one vote for each share owned. However, if Chan, for instance, sold 1,200 of his shares to Burton, Burton would own 3,417 shares, or more than 50 percent of the total 6,651 shares of stock that have been issued. Then Burton could control the corporation; that is, York and Chan would lose if Burton voted differently from them on an important issue. Burton would have more votes than York and Chan together.

Their lawyer told the officers of the corporation that they must send each stockholder notices of all stockholders' meetings to be held. Even stockholders with just one share must receive notices of meetings. If stockholders cannot attend the meetings personally, they can be represented through a proxy that can be submitted by Internet, phone, or mail. A **proxy** is a written authorization for someone to vote on behalf of the person signing the proxy. It is common practice for a proxy form to be enclosed with the letter that announces a stockholders' meeting. One example of a proxy that a corporation might use is shown in Figure 6-6.

CLOSE AND OPEN CORPORATIONS

A **close corporation** (also called a **closely held corporation**) is one that does not offer its shares of stock for public sale. Just a few stockholders own it; some of them may help run the business in the same manner as partners operate a business. York, Burton, and Chan, Inc., is an example of a close corporation. The three former partners own all the stock and operate the business as well.

In most states, a close corporation does not need to make its financial activities known to the public. Its stock is not offered for general sale. It must, however, prepare reports for the state from which it obtained its

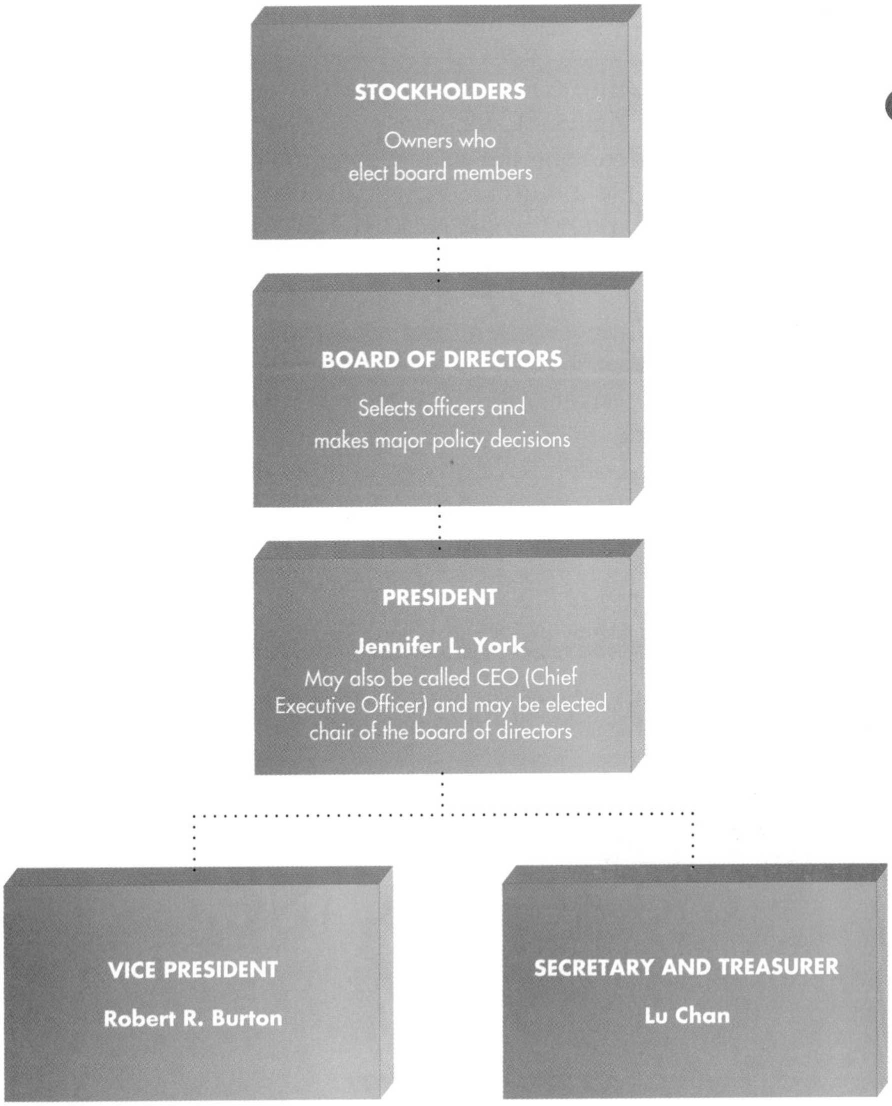

FIGURE 6-5

An organization chart of a corporation.

Brumway Eastmont Power Corporation – Proxy – Annual Meeting, Nov. 7, 20--

The undersigned hereby appoints Henry T. Brumleve III, Dean G. Rehme, D.A. Dromboski, and Donald F. Stark, and any of them, proxies of the undersigned, with power of substitution, to vote at the Annual Meeting of Stockholders of Brumway Eastmont Power Corporation, at Kenwood, Ohio, on November 7, 20--, at 11:00 a.m., and at any adjournments thereof.

This Proxy is Solicited by Management

(1) FOR ☒ or NOT FOR ☐ the election of a Board of Directors;

(2) FOR ☒ or AGAINST ☐ the proposal to increase the number of authorized shares of Common Stock; and

(3) for the transaction of any other business property brought before the meeting.

Dated *October 25, 20--*

Raymond L. Cooke

RAYMOND L COOKE
349 MIDPINES DRIVE
BUFFALO NY 14202-4449

Signature of Stockholder

If no preference is indicated, this proxy will be voted FOR items (1) & (2).

(Please give your full title when signing as attorney, trustee, executor, administrator, or guardian, etc.)

FIGURE 6-6

A proxy signed by a stockholder.

charter. And it must, for tax purposes, prepare reports for all states in which it operates.

An **open corporation** (also called a **publicly owned corporation**) is one that offers its shares of stock for public sale. Figure 6-7 shows a newspaper ad announcing the sale of common stock to the public. A corporation must file a registration statement with the Securities and Exchange Commission (SEC) containing extensive details about the corporation and the proposed issue of stock. A condensed version of this registration statement, called a prospectus, must be furnished to each prospective buyer of newly offered stocks (or bonds). A **prospectus** is a formal summary of the chief features of the business and its stock offering. Prospective buyers can find information in the prospectus that will help them decide whether or not to buy stock in the corporation.

Open corporations often have a large number of stockholders, perhaps hundreds of thousands or more. Many of the stockholders in large corporations own only a few shares. But because of the great number of stockholders, such a corporation has a large amount of capital. When

FIGURE 6-7

An open corporation must offer its shares for sale to the public.

This announcement is neither an offer to sell nor a solicitation of an offer to buy any of these Securities. The offer is made only by the Prospectus.

2,530,000 Shares

GALACTICA, INC.

Common Stock

Price $18 a Share

Copies of the Prospectus may be obtained in any State from only such of the undersigned as may legally offer these Securities in compliance with the securities laws of such State.

Morgan Stanley & Co. Incorporated	**Hambrecht & Quist** Incorporated
Goldman, Sachs & Co.	Cowen & Company
Donaldson, Lufkin & Jenrette Securities Corporation	Kidder, Peabody & Co. Incorporated
Merrill Lynch & Co.	Montgomery Securities

ILLUSTRATION 6-2

How are close corporations and open corporations different?

people buy stock, they are investing their capital (money) in the corporation. If the corporation fares well, stockholders will earn a return on their investment by receiving dividends and by selling their stock for more than they paid for it. If the corporation does not do well, stockholders may receive no dividends and may even have to sell their stock for less than they paid for it. If the corporation goes out of business, stockholders may lose their entire investment.

ADVANTAGES OF CORPORATIONS

The corporation has a number of advantages as compared with the proprietorship and partnership. Four such advantages are discussed below.

AVAILABLE SOURCES OF CAPITAL The corporation can obtain money from several sources. One of those sources is the sale of shares to stockholders. This special privilege helps to raise enough capital for running large-scale businesses. Because corporations are regulated closely, people usually invest more willingly than in proprietorships and partnerships. Also, corporations usually find borrowing large sums of money less of a problem than do proprietorships or partnerships.

LIMITED LIABILITY OF STOCKHOLDERS Except in a few situations, the owners (stockholders) are not legally liable for the debts of the corporation beyond their investments in the shares purchased. Thus, people—whether they have only a few dollars to invest or thousands of dollars—can invest in a corporation without the possibility of incurring a liability beyond their original investment.

PERMANENCY OF EXISTENCE The corporation is a more permanent type of organization than the proprietorship or the partnership. It can continue to operate indefinitely, or only as long as the term stated in the charter. The death or withdrawal of an owner (stockholder) does not affect its life.

EASE IN TRANSFERRING OWNERSHIP It is easy to transfer ownership in a corporation. A stockholder may sell stock to another person and transfer the stock certificate, which represents ownership, to the new owner. When shares are transferred, the transfer of ownership is indicated in the records of the corporation. A new certificate is issued in the name of the new stockholder. Millions of shares are bought and sold every day.

DISADVANTAGES OF CORPORATIONS

Although there are several distinct advantages to the corporation, there are also disadvantages. A discussion of some of the major disadvantages follows.

TAXATION The corporation is usually subject to more taxes than are imposed on the proprietorship and the partnership. Some taxes that are unique to the corporation are a filing fee, which is payable on application for a charter; an organization tax, which is based on the amount of authorized capital stock; an annual state tax, based on the profits; and a federal income tax.

Another tax disadvantage for corporations is that profits distributed to stockholders as dividends are taxed twice. This double taxation occurs in two steps. The corporation first pays taxes on its profits as just described. Then it distributes some of these profits to shareholders as dividends, and the shareholders pay taxes on the dividends they receive. Most other industrialized countries do not permit double taxation on corporate profits. (Small close corporations with few stockholders may avoid double taxation by changing their form of ownership, which you will learn about later in this chapter.)

GOVERNMENT REGULATIONS AND REPORTS A corporation cannot do business wherever it pleases. To form a corporation, an application for a charter must be submitted to the appropriate state official, usually the secretary of state. York, Burton, and Chan, Inc., has permission to conduct business only in the state of New York. Should it wish to conduct business in other states, each state will probably require the corporation to obtain a license and pay a fee to do business in that state. State incorporation fees are not very expensive. The attorney's fee accounts for the major costs of incorporating. Each state has different laws that govern the formation of corporations.

The regulation of corporations by states and by the federal government is extensive. A corporation must file special reports to the state from which it received its charter as well as in other states where it conducts business. The federal government requires firms whose stock is publicly traded to publish financial data. As a result, an increased need arises for detailed financial records and reports.

STOCKHOLDERS' RECORDS Corporations that have many stockholders have added problems—and expenses—in communicating with stockholders and in handling stockholders' records. By law, stockholders must be informed of corporate matters, notified of meetings, and given the right to vote on important matters. Letters and reports must be sent to stockholders on a regular basis. In addition, each time a share of stock is bought or sold and whenever a dividend is paid, detailed records must be kept. Keeping records for the thousands of stockholders of General Electric, for example, is a time-consuming and costly task.

CHARTER RESTRICTIONS A corporation is allowed to engage only in those activities that are stated in its charter. Should York, Burton, and Chan, Inc., wish to sell hardware, the organizers would have to go to the state to obtain a new charter or change the old one. As a partnership, they could have added the other line of merchandise without government approval.

BUSINESSES SUITED TO BEING CORPORATIONS

Even though the corporation has major disadvantages, a survey of business firms shows that almost every kind of business exists as a corporation, including Web-based firms. The corporate form of ownership is especially suited to the following types of businesses:

1. Businesses that require large amounts of capital, such as airlines and auto manufacturers. To start a 500-room hotel, for example, requires millions of dollars for buying land and for constructing and furnishing the hotel.
2. Businesses that may have uncertain futures, such as amusement parks, publishers of new magazines, and makers of novelty goods. The publisher of a new magazine, for example, takes a great risk in assuming that the magazine will be popular enough to make a profit. Organizers of firms with uncertain futures do not wish to assume the added financial risks that fall upon a proprietor or a partner in case the business fails.

Each form of business organization has special advantages to owners of different types of businesses. While the corporate form of organization is suited to firms that have uncertain futures or that require large amounts of capital, the partnership is especially suited to small, growing business firms. The proprietorship, in comparison, has great appeal to the person who wants to run a small business.

ILLUSTRATION 6-3

Why would the corporate form of ownership be suited to a mining company?

SPECIALIZED TYPES OF ORGANIZATIONS

In addition to sole proprietorships, partnerships, and corporations, organizations can be legally formed as joint ventures, virtual corporations, limited liability companies, nonprofit corporations, and cooperatives.

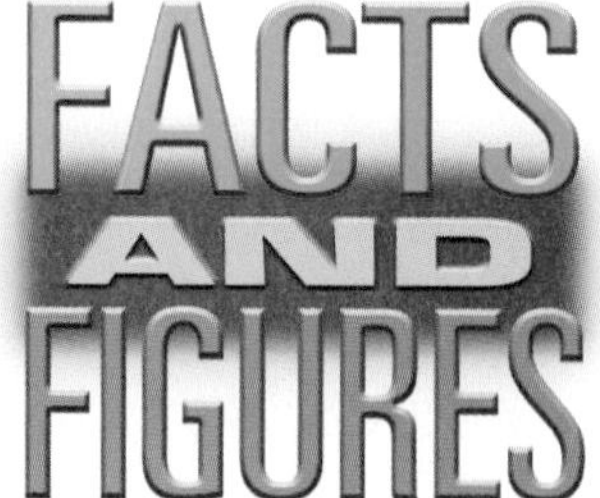

Joint ventures often include business partners from foreign countries. For example, Ford Motor Company produces cars in a joint venture with Mazda. Some multinational corporations have formed joint ventures with companies in once-communist countries. This helps the corporations expand into new markets. At the same time, the joint ventures serve as a way to help companies in the previously communist nations to learn about doing business in a free market economy.

JOINT VENTURES

At times businesses want to join forces in order to achieve an important objective. A **joint venture** is an agreement among two or more businesses to work together to provide a good or service. The legal formation of the business is not important. For example, a sole proprietorship and a corporation could agree to work together. Each partner in the joint venture is expected to bring management expertise and/or money to the venture. Many major corporations today have learned that alone they may not have all the expertise or capital needed.

An example of a joint venture might include an agreement between two major contractors to connect two cities by building a tunnel for cars under a river. A company working alone may not have the capital to build the tunnel, and each may lack special equipment or skills that the other firm has. By forming a joint venture, they can acquire the expertise to build the tunnel that they could not complete alone. There are thousands of joint ventures between and among many companies. Many Web-based companies rely extensively on joint ventures to build their businesses.

Because organizations must adapt quickly to compete effectively, a more fluid form of the joint venture, the virtual corporation, is evolving in the world of business. The **virtual corporation** is a network of companies that form alliances among themselves as needed to take advantage of fast-changing market conditions. Puma, the athletic shoe company, for example, is a virtual corporation. Puma markets its shoes in Germany. A small network of Asian companies purchases the materials to make the shoes. Other companies in China, Taiwan, Indonesia, and Korea manufacture the shoes. Then separate companies on all continents sell the shoes. In all, 80 companies worldwide participate in making and selling Puma shoes.

Virtual corporations tend to be more temporary relationships than are joint ventures. Several companies within the network may team up to take advantage of a market opportunity. These same companies may also work with a different combination of partners within the network, depending on the expertise needed to take advantage of a particular market opportunity at that time.

An example of a virtual corporation might include the following situation. Company A wishes to rush to market a new sophisticated computer but needs special parts that it does not produce. Company A learns that Company B produces one part and Company C produces the other needed part. Unfortunately, none of the three companies has customers who would likely have an interest in the new computer. After searching, the firms find that Company D sells computers to customers with special needs. Ultimately, all three companies agree to join with Company A to market the new computer. This virtual corporation situation, which is illustrated in Figure 6-8, makes it possible for all four companies to benefit when no one company could have made and marketed the new computer quickly on its own. Many companies involved in selling the goods of other firms, especially Web-based firms, are virtual corporations.

CYBER COMMUNICATION

Business memos are informal messages sent to persons within an organization. Sending a memo is a quick, easy way to communicate with a colleague or manager within your own department, in another department, or in another company office. The memo is a streamlined, efficient way to send a message to an internal audience.

In many businesses today, e-mail has taken over formal memo writing. E-mail memos are composed, transmitted, and usually read on a computer screen. They can be sent to more than one receiver; they take less time to format and key than letters; and they are less complex and time-consuming than meetings or conference calls.

Before you can organize an effective e-mail message, you must first plan your message. This requires asking yourself four questions: (1) What do I hope to accomplish in sending this message? (2) What do I want the receiver to do or to understand? (3) What does the receiver need to know about the main idea in order to respond to or understand the message? (4) What do I want the receiver to gain from the message?

ACTIVITY Assume that one of your classmates was out sick today. You have volunteered to send the classmate a brief memo describing what happened during the class session. Think about what you want to communicate in your message. Then write your answers to the four questions listed above.

LIMITED LIABILITY COMPANIES

Small, growing partnerships are especially attracted to the limited liability company (LLC) form of corporation, which was once called an "S-corporation." The **limited liability company (LLC)** is a special type of corporation that is taxed as if it were a sole proprietorship or

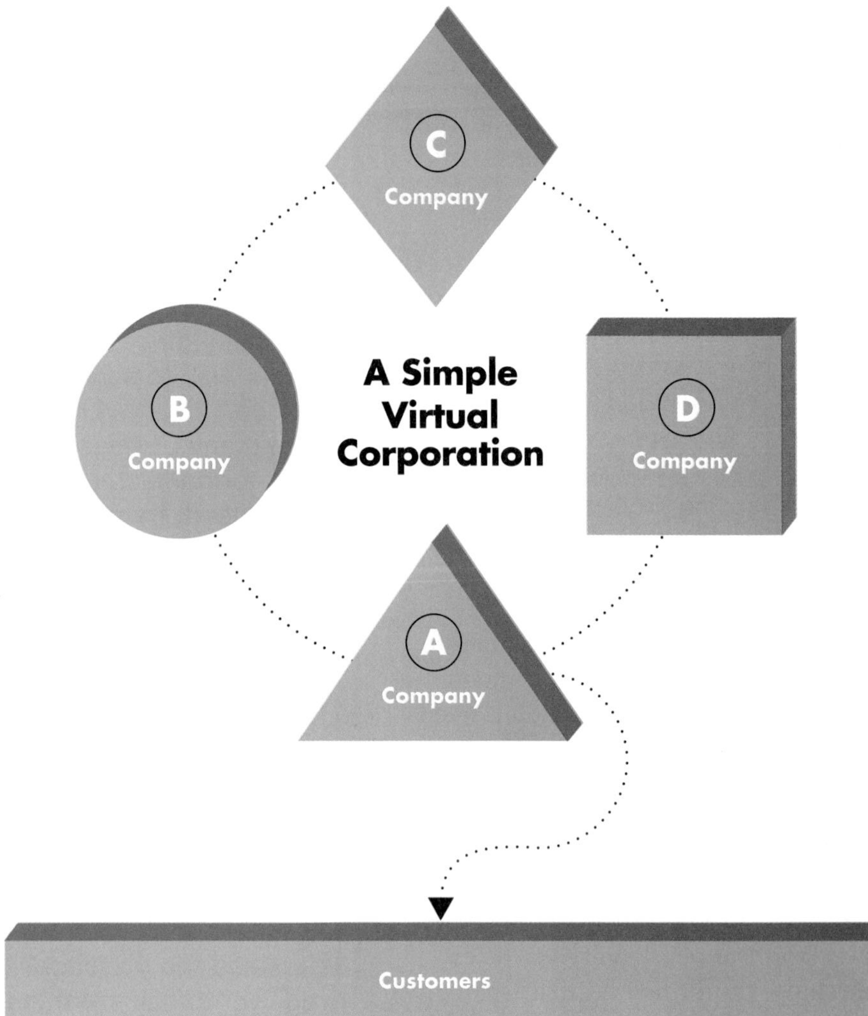

FIGURE 6-8

A virtual corporation is a network of companies that form alliances among themselves as needed to take advantage of fast-changing market conditions.

partnership. Two factors make LLCs popular. First, a major disadvantage of a partnership is unlimited liability, whereas a major advantage of a corporation is its limited liability. Second, a major advantage of a partnership is its lower income tax rate, whereas a disadvantage of a corporation is a higher income tax rate than that paid by partnerships. Stockholders also have to pay personal income taxes on dividends distributed by a corporation (double taxation). The LLC provides an ideal solution—lower taxes and limited liability. In addition, the profits from the corporation go directly to the stockholders, who then include the profits on their individual income tax returns. Double taxation is avoided. York, Burton, and Chan, Inc., would qualify for this special tax advantage. The LLC also may be the solution to the dilemma that Thanh Vu and his two acquaintances faced at the start of this chapter.

However, not all companies are eligible for LLC status. A few important rules determine eligibility. First, a firm must have no more than

35 stockholders. Second, the business cannot own 80 percent or more of the stock of another corporation. Third, not more than 25 percent of the income of the corporation can be from sources other than for the purpose(s) stated in the charter. And, fourth, all stockholders must be individuals who are permanent citizens or residents of this country. Large corporations and multinational firms do not meet these qualifications. Many partnerships, however, do qualify and find the LLC to be highly favorable.

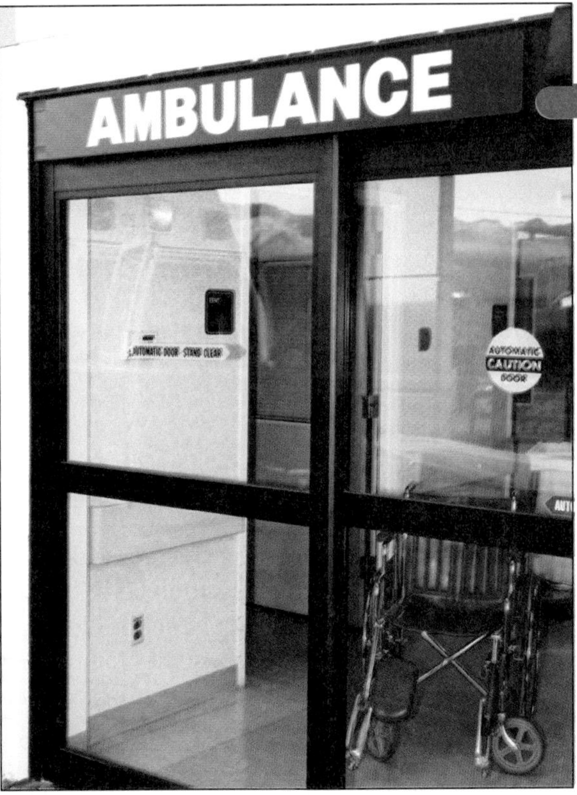

ILLUSTRATION 6-4

Nonprofit organizations do not make a profit for distribution to stockholders. Can you name some examples of nonprofit organizations in your community?

NONPROFIT CORPORATIONS

Close and open corporations, as discussed earlier, are businesses that operate mainly to make a profit for their owners. A **nonprofit corporation,** on the other hand, is an organization that does not pay taxes and does not exist to make a profit. Organizations that manage cities or operate schools are examples of nonprofit corporations. Because a nonprofit corporation is not established as a profit-making enterprise, it does not pay dividends to shareholders. Otherwise, it operates much like a close or open corporation. The Rotary Club, private schools and universities, United Way, and most local hospitals are other examples of nonprofit organizations. Even Educational Testing Service, the company that makes the Scholastic Aptitude Test (SAT), is a nonprofit organization.

In this country, nonprofit corporations provide nearly one-third of the GDP. However, in most other countries, nonprofit corporations contribute much more to the GDP. The principles of business and management provided in this text apply equally to managers who run profit-making as well as nonprofit corporations.

QUASI-PUBLIC CORPORATIONS

A business that is important to society, but lacks the profit potential to attract private investors, is often operated by local, state, or federal government. Government financial support (called a *subsidy*) may also be required. This type of business is usually described as a **quasi-public corporation.** Government imposes regulatory controls over quasi-public corporations.

The Tennessee Valley Authority, a rural electrification program started in the 1930s by the federal government, was one of the first quasi-public corporations. The organizations that run interstate highways, such as the Massachusetts and Pennsylvania turnpike authorities, are state-owned quasi-public corporations. At the local level, examples of quasi-public organizations include water and sewer systems, parking garages, and civic and cultural facilities. The Los Angeles County Museum of Art is a government-owned cultural organization.

COOPERATIVES

A **cooperative** is a business owned and operated by its user-members for the purpose of supplying themselves with goods and services. The members, who are much like stockholders in a corporation with the protection of limited liability, usually join a cooperative by buying shares of stock. The members elect a board of directors, which appoints officers to run the business. Much like a corporation, a cooperative must also obtain a charter from the state in which it is organized in order to operate. Some types of cooperatives need authorization from the federal government.

The purpose of cooperatives is to provide their members with cost and profit advantages that they do not otherwise have. For example, a group of blueberry growers believes that individually they can save money and make more profit by forming a cooperative for the purpose of selling their berries. Once the business is organized and operating, the members (owners) sell their berries through the cooperative. The cooperative markets the berries. In turn, the growers earn more than if they tried to market the berries on their own. In addition, as owners they share in the profits of the business.

With almost 19 million businesses in the United States, cooperatives represent only a small percentage of all businesses. This small number, however, does not reduce their importance. Cooperatives are popular in agriculture for buying and selling crops. And many employees belong to credit unions, where they can invest and borrow money at low interest rates. Many insurance firms are formed as cooperatives. Apartment buildings are often formed as cooperatives as well.

CHAPTER CONCEPTS

- A corporation is a form of ownership preferred by large and growing firms, but corporations are more difficult to form than are sole proprietorships or partnerships. A business must specify its purpose, identify its owners (stockholders), elect a board of directors, select officers, establish operating policies, and prepare a charter for approval by the state.
- A chief advantage of the corporate form of business is its limited liability feature, which limits the financial losses of stockholders to no more than their investments. Also, corporations can raise more capital for growth purposes than most other forms of business ownership. Stock can be bought and sold more easily than ownership shares in partnerships. And the life of the corporation does not end when owners sell their shares.
- The primary downside of corporations is higher tax rates. Also, stockholders must pay taxes on dividends received (double taxation). Record-keeping and government-required paperwork is usually more extensive for corporations than for proprietorships and partnerships.
- Joint ventures are alliances formed among companies to work together to produce a product or service that neither alone could provide efficiently. A virtual corporation is a type of joint venture in which a network of companies form temporary alliances among themselves as needed to take advantage of current market conditions. Companies within the network come together in different combinations, depending on the expertise needed to take advantage of a particular market opportunity at that time.
- The limited liability company (LLC) is a type of organization that avoids the double-taxation levied on corporations and the unlimited liability disadvantage of partnerships. Nonprofit corporations, such as charities, are organizations that do not pay taxes and do not exist to make a profit. Cooperatives, such as credit unions, are businesses owned and operated by their user-members for the purpose of supplying themselves with goods and services. Businesses that are important to society, but are government-run because they lack the profit potential to attract private investors, are quasi-public corporations. Your local waterworks is an example.

BUILD VOCABULARY POWER

Define the following terms and concepts.

1. corporation
2. charter (certificate of incorporation)
3. stockholders (shareholders)
4. shares
5. dividends
6. board of directors (directors or board)

7. officers
8. capital stock (stock)
9. proxy
10. close corporation (closely held corporation)
11. open corporation (publicly owned corporation)
12. prospectus
13. joint venture
14. virtual corporation
15. limited liability company (LLC)
16. nonprofit corporation
17. quasi-public corporation
18. cooperative

REVIEW FACTS

1. Which form of business is fewest in total number but highest in terms of total sales of goods and services?
2. What are five basic rights of stockholders?
3. How does someone become a stockholder in a corporation? A director? An officer?
4. What steps must be taken to form a corporation?
5. By what means can stockholders vote on matters affecting the corporation even when they cannot be present at meetings?
6. How does a close corporation differ from an open corporation?
7. Give four advantages of corporations.
8. Give three disadvantages of corporations.
9. Why would a business want to form a joint venture?
10. What is the purpose of cooperatives?

DISCUSS IDEAS

1. Why can a corporation be described as an artificial person?
2. Compare the financial responsibility of owners of a corporation with that of owners of a partnership.
3. Figure 6-6 shows a proxy. If the person receiving the proxy only signed the card but did not vote for or against the numbered items, would the proxy be valid?
4. In its certificate of incorporation, why would a corporation request more shares of capital stock than are needed to get started?
5. The following people own all the shares of stock in the same corporation: Brower, 100; Ramos, 70; Forcina, 30; and Stein, 10. If all have an interest in running for the board of directors, how could it be possible for someone other than the largest stockholder to get elected?
6. Under what conditions would you be able to buy stock in York, Burton, and Chan, Inc.?
7. Explain how a joint venture could be valuable in a situation in which Corporation A has expertise in one area and Corporation B has expertise in another.

8. What conditions should exist before York, Burton, and Chan, Inc., consider becoming a limited liability company (LLC)?
9. Discuss whether the Girl Scouts organization meets the qualifications for operating as a nonprofit corporation in light of the fact that it sells a large volume of cookies each year.
10. Why are cooperatives popular in agricultural regions?

ANALYZE INFORMATION

1. George Fernandez purchased stock in the Elite Manufacturing Co., Incorporated, for $76 a share. Last year he received quarterly dividends of $1, $1, $1, and $.80 on each share. His total dividends for the year amounted to what percentage of the price he paid for each share?
2. Three stockholders own all the issued shares of the Harris, Lopez, and Hall Corporation. Harris has 750 shares; Lopez, 260 shares; and Hall, 490.
   a. Is this a close or an open corporation? Why?
   b. What percentage of the shares does each partner own?
   c. Which partner, if any, has control over the results of any votes that are taken? Explain.
   d. If Hall wanted total control of the corporation, how many shares would she need to buy?
3. The board of directors of Melby Company, Inc., decided to distribute $40,950 as dividends to shareholders. There are 27,300 shares of stock held by stockholders.
   a. What is the amount of the dividend to be distributed on each share?
   b. John Taylor owns 240 shares. What amount will he receive in dividends?
4. On the statement of financial position of the Fenwick Company, the assets have a value of $117,000; the debts are listed as $37,000; and the capital stock as $80,000. The company decided to go out of business. The assets are converted into $97,000 cash. What amount of cash will the stockholders receive?
5. The net profit of a retail cooperative is $4,000, and the purchases made by members amount to $100,000. If the profit is divided in proportion to the purchases, how much should be given to a member who made purchases of $1,000?

6. Alone or in teams (as specified by your instructor), search the library or the Web to gather information about the basic features of a cooperative. Then report to your class on how cooperatives differ from typical corporations as to how they operate and how the investors share in the benefits. Use a search source such as www.altavista.com or www.yahoo. In particular, go to www.rurdev.usda.gov/rbs/pub/cir55/cir55rpt.htm.

SOLVE BUSINESS PROBLEMS

CASE 6-1

Takoda Koriyama, whose parents came from Japan, is interested in how corporations operate in Western countries, particularly the United States. In one of his business classes, he and two classmates—Marcus Jordan and Brianna Ashman—were assigned a team project to study the total pay of chief executive officers (CEOs) for ten companies. Takoda is the leader. Other class teams were assigned other firms. Their assignment was to determine the total pay that individual CEOs earn in American corporations in relation to how well their firms do for their stockholders.

All three members had gathered information. Before they could prepare a class report, they need to sort it all out. During their first meeting, the group shared information and created the chart below that summarizes their main points. CEO total pay is shown in thousands of dollars.

Corporations	*CEO Total Pay*	*Percent of Shareholder Return*
Walt Disney	$ 594,892	56
Citigroup	491,976	146
General Electric	151,179	199
Occidental Petroleum	110,670	−11
H. J. Heinz	104,678	86
Immunex	2,437	663
Microsoft	1,696	532
Costco	1,483	373
Capital One	1,312	393
Berkshire Hathaway	842	118

Source: *Business Week, April 19, 1999*

Think Critically:

1. Which five company CEOs benefited their shareholders the most? And which five company CEOs benefited their shareholders the least?
2. If you had purchased shares in Occidental Petroleum, what main point would you stress in your letter as a stockholder to the chairman of the board of directors?
3. What general statement can you make to Takoda and his team about the fairness of CEO pay and their contributions to their corporations?
4. If you were just elected to serve as a board member of Citigroup, what would you recommend to other board members about the CEO's future pay? Provide a reason for your answer.
5. Which CEO would most deserve a raise in pay? Justify your answer.

6. Alone or in teams, as specified by your instructor, gather information about CEO pay from *Business Week, Fortune,* or other magazines in your library or from the Internet. Prepare a report for your class that answers the question: Are CEOs overpaid, underpaid, or paid what they are worth? Also include proposals found on how to keep CEO pay fair and under control.

CASE 6-2

Alicia Fuentes owns 15 shares of stock in the Shale Oil Company, a large corporation that deals with oil and gas products. Hugh Jones, a friend of Alicia's, owns 20 shares. Today they both received an invitation to attend the annual stockholders' meeting in Chicago, which neither can attend. This conversation occurred during the evening when they were having dinner at a local restaurant:

Alicia: *Since I can't attend the meeting, I'm going to sign the proxy card and answer "for" regarding the two proposals that are to be voted upon. Of course, I don't know any of the board members who are up for election, but they must be OK. I wish they could distribute more dividends, though.*

Hugh: *You shouldn't just give your vote away to management, Alicia. You should elect one of the candidates to be an outside board member. That person could then shake things up a bit, get some changes made. You probably also don't know anything about the other item asking for approval to increase the number of shares of stock that can be sold.*

Alicia: *I don't have time to do homework on the company. Shale Oil Company always makes a profit; therefore, it deserves my vote.*

Hugh: *Too many stockholders don't do their homework on the company, and not many go to the meetings. So, management always has its own way. Why bother sending a proxy statement at all? I'm not going to waste time sending my proxy back.*

Alicia: *I'm still going to vote, Hugh. Besides, the company pays the postage.*

Hugh: *You're doing what everyone else does. Management always wins. But since you're going to vote, I will too. The difference is that I'm going to vote against the two items . . . no, on second thought, I'll just sign the proxy. That will really confuse them.*

Think Critically:

1. Whether they vote "for" or "against" the proposals listed on the proxy statement, how many votes can Alicia and Hugh cast?

2. If the proxy statement is like the one shown in Figure 6-6 and Hugh signs it but does not mark "for" or "against" the two proposals, how do you think the management will use the proxy?
3. If Hugh or Alicia wanted an important proposal to be made known and voted upon by the stockholders, how could they achieve their goal?
4. How should Alicia and Hugh have received information about each of the proposals from management that would enable them to vote with adequate information?
5. What might an outside board member do that an inside member might not do?

PROJECT: MY BUSINESS, INC.

Corporations are another form of business ownership. In addition to financial advantages, there are other reasons to organize a new business as a corporation. In this segment of the project, you will study some of those reasons as well as the procedures necessary to form a corporation in your state.

DATA COLLECTION

1. Make a list of the procedures you must follow in your state to organize a close corporation to operate your business. Obtain the information from a library, the Internet, or a government office.
2. Interview the owner of a small business that has been organized as a corporation. Ask the owner to identify the advantages and disadvantages of the corporate form of ownership for a small business.
3. Identify one other form of ownership that could be appropriate for your business other than a proprietorship, partnership, or corporation. Locate a business that is organized using that ownership form and study its operations.

ANALYSIS

1. Most new small businesses are formed as proprietorships and partnerships rather than corporations. However, new corporations have a higher success rate than other types of business organizations. What might be some reasons for that higher success rate?
2. Assume that your business is successful and expands during the next five years. Identify specific situations that could occur during that five-year period in which it would be beneficial to reor-

ganize the business as a corporation. Consider changing financial needs, management activities, business operations, and your own personal needs.

3. Assume you are going to organize your juice bar as a corporation. Collect and review the documents needed to register your corporation with the state and to complete the formation of the corporation.

LEGAL ASPECTS OF BUSINESS

OBJECTIVES

- **7-1** Explain how federal laws help control and promote competition.
- **7-2** Tell how patents, copyrights, and trademarks are beneficial to business.
- **7-3** Offer examples of how the government protects the public.
- **7-4** Provide three methods used by state and local governments to regulate business.
- **7-5** Discuss the nature of taxes and the fairness of progressive, proportional, and regressive taxes.
- **7-6** Identify and explain the most common types of taxes that affect business.

LEGAL LIMITS FOR A TAXI BUSINESS

Deion Banks, who owned a small taxi business in his hometown, was meeting for lunch with his lawyer, Laura Maddox. He needed to discuss several matters that had occurred during the past few weeks. While waiting for the server, Laura said, "You seem quite upset."

Deion sat back and replied, "I am, Laura. Here are the new tax forms that need to be filled out. And that's the easy part. Would you check with the town officials to see why they want to review my franchise before I buy another cab? Also, while you're at the Town Hall, see what you can do to prevent those officials from giving another taxi firm a license to operate. This town isn't big enough for two taxi companies. I'll get less business, and it will probably force down my fares. If there is a chance of going bankrupt, I should probably move my business across the river. The income tax rate in that state is much lower."

"Don't do anything drastic," said Laura. "Let me see what I can find out from our government officials. I'll get back to you in a few days with both your tax forms and the answers to your questions."

Deion Banks, like other business owners, must operate within the law. Laws that regulate business cover both products and services, and they govern general relationships of businesses with competitors, consumers, employees, and the public. Deion Banks's taxi business is no exception. He currently benefits from being the only taxi company in town, but he now feels threatened. The town may, indeed, allow someone else the right to open a competing firm. So what can Deion do?

In the following pages you will learn how government encourages free enterprise by controlling monopolies and promoting competition. You will also learn how the government protects the general public as well as business. Like Deion, you will learn about taxes and how taxes influence business decisions.

REGULATIONS MAINTAINING COMPETITION

Competition is the rivalry among companies for customers' dollars. Competition, however, does not always operate smoothly by itself. To provide for fair competition, government has passed laws and created regulations to enforce the laws. These laws and regulations grow out of a need to preserve competition, which is done, in part, by controlling monopolies and unfair business practices. Firms that cannot survive in a competitive atmosphere either go out of business or face bankruptcy.

CONTROLLING MONOPOLIES

A **monopoly** exists when only one company provides a product or service without competition from other companies. Without competitors, the one producer can control the supply and price of the product or service. By controlling the supply of an item, a single producer

LAWYER

Although the popular view of lawyers emphasizes sensational courtroom trials, many lawyers have jobs in government and in business firms, public utilities, banks, insurance companies, real estate agencies, manufacturing firms, and welfare organizations. But no matter what the situation, lawyers hold positions of great responsibility and must adhere to a strict code of ethics.

The more detailed aspects of lawyers' work have been greatly influenced by advances in technology. Software can be used to search legal literature and to organize and index material. Lawyers use the Internet, electronic filing, videoconferencing, and voice-recognition technology. These tools save time and reduce legal costs.

Formal educational requirements usually include a four-year college degree, followed by three years in law school. After that, states require that applicants pass a written bar examination. Persons interested in a particular aspect of law may find related courses useful. For example, tax lawyers must have a broad knowledge of accounting.

For more career information about lawyers, check your library or the Internet for resources.

can set a price that will generate the greatest profit. In a monopoly situation, such as Deion Banks's taxi company, the prices are generally very high. Without competitors to lure customers away with lower prices, the monopolistic company can raise its price as high as it wants. If customers want the product or service, they have no choice but to pay the monopolist's price.

In actual practice, however, few monopolies exist, because of the effectiveness of competition. To illustrate, assume a business offers a new product that no other business has. The product suddenly becomes quite popular. The prospect of profits to be made entices other companies to enter the market to help meet the demand. A temporary monopoly will exist until those competitors can produce and sell similar products. Usually, through competitive pricing, the more efficient companies will attract the greatest number of purchasers, while the less efficient may struggle for survival or go out of business. Even if some competitors fail, however, a monopoly will not exist as long as there are at least two or more producers.

In some situations, however, monopolies may be better for consumers than competition. These situations usually involve providing public services, such as public utilities, which have a fairly stable demand and which are costly to create. A natural gas company, for example, must build hundreds of miles of pipeline along streets and roads in order to deliver gas to homes and industries to fuel furnaces and stoves. If two or three gas companies incurred these same costs to sell gas to a relatively fixed number of customers, the price of gas would be higher than if only one company existed. Also, installing and maintaining so many pipelines would create nuisance problems along crowded streets and highways. In these types of situations, the government grants a monopoly to one company, regulates the prices that the company can charge, and influences other company policies.

Until recently, the federal government had approved of closely regulated monopolies, such as the postal system, utility companies, rail-

ILLUSTRATION 7-1

Deregulation of airlines and other industries has helped benefit consumers through lower prices and improved services. Are passenger fares on commercial airlines regulated?

roads, and communication firms. However, the trend has shifted from allowing monopolies to weakening or eliminating them in order to encourage competition. No longer, for example, are passenger fares on commercial airlines regulated. As a result, fares have generally dropped. Even telephone service, the trucking industry, and railroads have been deregulated. Today utilities are undergoing deregulation. Firms such as MCI WorldCom and Sprint offer communication services at competitive prices and compete fiercely with the once monopolistic AT&T. The result overall has been that consumers pay lower prices and have more services from which to select.

PROMOTING FAIR COMPETITION One way to promote competition is to limit the number of monopolies created and controlled by government. Monopoly conditions can also arise when businesses compete too harshly or unfairly. A large, powerful business can lower its prices deliberately to drive out competitors, thereby discouraging competition. Thus, the federal government supports business practices that encourage competition and discourage monopolies. To achieve this goal, government has passed important laws and created agencies to enforce the laws.

Sherman Act. The first major law promoting competition was the Sherman Antitrust Act of 1890. One of its primary purposes is to discourage monopolies by outlawing business agreements among competitors that might tend to promote monopolies. For example, agreements among competitors to set selling prices on goods are unlawful. If three sellers met and agreed to set the same selling price on the same product each sold, they would all be violating the Sherman Act.

Clayton Act. Like the Sherman Act, the Clayton Act of 1914 was aimed at discouraging monopolies. One part of the law forbids corporations from acquiring ownership rights in other corporations if the purpose is to create a monopoly or to discourage competition. Corporation A cannot, for example, buy over half the ownership rights of its main competitor, Corporation B, if the aim is to severely reduce or eliminate competition.

Another section of the Clayton Act forbids business contracts that require customers to purchase certain goods in order to get other goods. For example, a business that produces computers cannot require a buyer also to purchase supplies, such as paper and software, in order to get a computer. Microsoft Corporation was charged with such a violation. Microsoft required computer makers that wanted to buy its dominant Windows operating system to also accept its Internet Explorer browser. The result of this action was to severely damage the sales of Netscape's Navigator browser, which was Microsoft's dominant competitor.

Robinson-Patman Act. The Robinson-Patman Act of 1936 amended the portion of the Clayton Act dealing with the pricing of goods. The main purpose of the pricing provisions in both of these laws is to prevent **price discrimination**—setting different prices for different customers. For example, a seller cannot offer a price of $5 a unit to Buyer A and sell the same goods to Buyer B at $6 a unit. Different prices can be set, however, if the goods sold are different in quality or quantity. Buyer A is entitled to the $5 price if the quantity purchased is significantly greater or if the quality is lower. The same discounts must then be offered to all buyers purchasing the same quantity or quality as Buyer A.

Wheeler-Lea Act. In 1938, the Wheeler-Lea Act was passed to strengthen earlier laws outlawing unfair methods of competition. This law made unfair or deceptive acts or practices, including false advertising, unlawful. **False advertising** is advertising that is misleading in some important way, including the failure to reveal facts about possible results from using the advertised products. Under the Wheeler-Lea Act, it is unlawful for an advertiser to circulate false advertising that can lead to the purchase of foods, drugs, medical devices, or cosmetics, or to participate in any other unfair methods of competition.

FEDERAL TRADE COMMISSION The Federal Trade Commission (FTC) was created as the result of many businesses demanding protection from unfair methods of competition. The FTC administers most of the federal laws dealing with fair competition. Some of the unfair practices that the FTC protects businesses from are shown in Figure 7-1.

OTHER FEDERAL AGENCIES In addition to the FTC, the federal government has created other agencies to administer laws that regulate specialized areas of business, such as transportation and communication. Figure 7-2 lists some of the more important agencies.

PROVIDING BANKRUPTCY RELIEF

All firms face the risk of failure. The free enterprise system permits unsuccessful businesses to file for bankruptcy as a means of protect-

1. **Any act that restrains trade.**
2. **Any monopolies except those specifically authorized by law, such as public utilities.**
3. **Price fixing, such as agreements among competitors.**
4. **Agreements among competitors to divide territory, earnings, or profits.**
5. **Gaining control over the supply of any commodity in order to create an artificial scarcity.**
6. **False or misleading advertising.**
7. **Imitation of trademark or trade name.**
8. **Discrimination through prices or special deals.**
9. **Pretending to sell at a discount when there is no reduction in price.**
10. **Offering so-called free merchandise with a purchase when the price of the article sold has been raised to compensate for the free merchandise.**
11. **Misrepresentation about the quality, the composition, or the place of origin of a product.**
12. **Violation of one's guarantee of privacy of information on the Internet, including e-mail.**

FIGURE 7-1

Types of Practices Prohibited by the Federal Trade Commission

Some Federal Agencies That Regulate Business

AGENCY AND REGULATION

Federal Aviation Administration

Safety standards, airplane accidents, and take-offs and landings

Federal Communications Commission

Radio, television, telephone, telegraph, cable, and satellite communications

Food and Drug Administration

Foods, drugs, medical devices, cosmetics, and veterinary products

Nuclear Regulatory Commission

Nuclear power plants

Securities and Exchange Commission

Stocks and bonds

FIGURE 7-2

Laws promoting fair practices that benefit businesses and consumers are enforced by government agencies.

ILLUSTRATION 7-2

Various federal agencies have been created to administer laws that regulate specialized areas of business. Which federal agency regulates communications?

ing owners and others. **Bankruptcy** is a legal process that allows the selling of assets to pay off debts. Businesses as well as individuals can file for bankruptcy. If cash is not available to pay the debts after assets are sold, the law excuses the business or individual from paying the remaining unpaid debts. In such a case, all those to whom money was owed would very likely receive less than the full amount.

A bankruptcy judge can permit a company to survive bankruptcy proceedings if a survival plan can be developed that might enable the firm to recover. As a result, after starting bankruptcy proceedings, many firms do survive. However, bankruptcy carries serious consequences. The business will have a bad credit rating. A record of the unpaid debts will stay on file for ten years, and the business may not file for bankruptcy again for six years. As a result, the business will have difficulty obtaining credit.

In 1998, 44,367 U.S. businesses filed for bankruptcy. The state with the most business bankruptcy filings was California; the state with the least filings was North Dakota.

REGULATIONS PROTECTING BUSINESS AND THE PUBLIC

In the previous section, you learned about regulations that help to make the economic system work by establishing rules of fair competition. In this section, you will learn about regulations that protect those who create goods and services and those who use them.

PROTECTING BUSINESS

The federal government has passed laws to protect the rights of those who create uniquely different products and new ideas. Specifically, it grants intellectual property rights to inventors, authors, and creators of distinct symbols and names for goods and services (see Figure 7-3).

PATENTS A **patent** is an agreement in which the federal government gives an inventor the sole right for 20 years to make, use, and sell an invention or a process. No one is permitted to copy or use the invention without permission. This protection is a reward for the time and money invested to create the new product. An inventor may allow others to make or use a product by giving them a license to do so.

In a sense, through the Patent and Trademark Office, the government gives the inventor a monopoly on newly invented products, designs, and processes. This temporary monopoly provides a profit incentive that encourages manufacturers to spend the huge amounts of money required to research and develop new ideas. Research departments have produced many inventions. For example, Sony and other camera companies have developed digital cameras that allow users to see their pictures on a special display screen and even edit them before they ever leave the camera. Even synthetic tissue and altered vegetable plants are patentable. For example, insulin that diabetics need and a new rot-resistant tomato are products of biotechnology (biology plus technology) innovations.

New processes as well as new products can be patented, but process patenting can be undesirable at times. For example, Priceline.com, Inc., received a patent for its auction price bidding system on the Internet. If other companies used this simple process, they would be violating the owner's patent rights. However, the process is so fundamental to many Internet practices that competitors believe the patent is essentially unfair. Should doctors who develop a new method for healing people

Intellectual Property

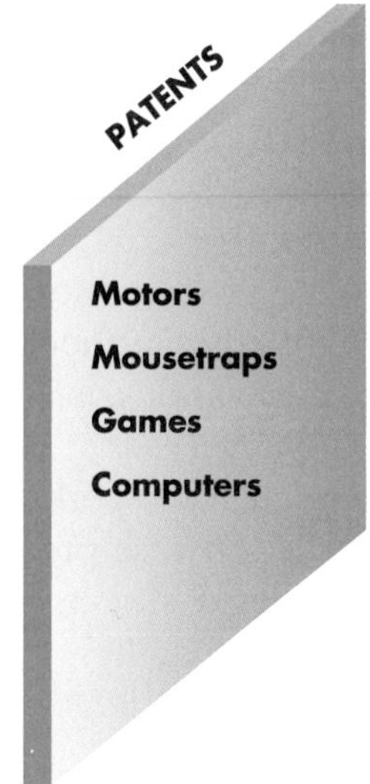

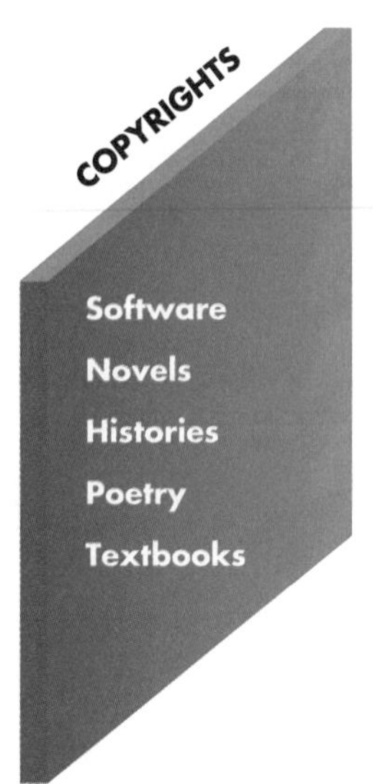

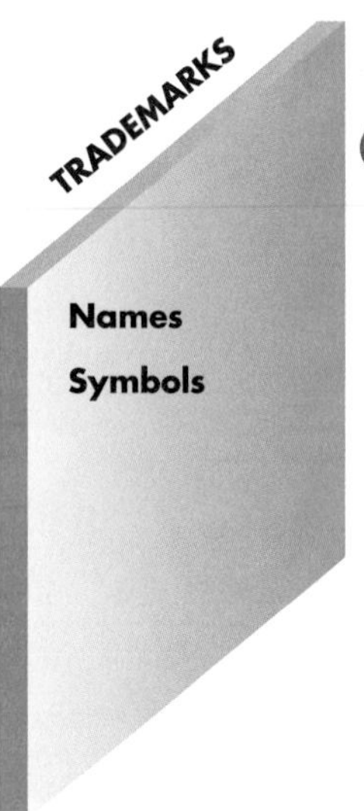

FIGURE 7-3

Federal, state, and local governments grant special property rights.

prohibit other doctors from using it or require them to pay a licensing fee? Occasionally the Patent and Trademark Office revokes or denies patents that discourage desirable competition.

Unfortunately, stealing patents is an acceptable practice in some countries that do not honor the U.S. patent law. As a result, American firms lose millions of dollars. By tightening trade agreements with these countries, this great loss to American firms may begin to decline. On the other hand, patent laws differ worldwide. For example, Japan's patents promote technology sharing, whereas U.S. patents protect inventors.

COPYRIGHTS A **copyright** is similar to a patent in that the federal government gives an author the sole right to reproduce, publish, and sell literary or artistic work for the life of the author, typically, plus 70 years. No one may publish or reproduce copyrighted work without permission of the copyright owner. However, the law permits occasional photocopying of copyrighted material. While a teacher could copy a magazine article to distribute to students, articles from the same magazine could not be copied and distributed weekly throughout the school year without obtaining permission.

Copyright laws also cover electronic methods for distributing creative work. Copyrights protect creators of CD games and music, video and audio tapes, and computer software programs, for example. Duplicating CDs, tapes, disks, and software programs for distribution to others is usually illegal. When an employee makes a personal copy of a computer software program for use on a home computer, the employee violates the copyright law. Furthermore, if a warning is not publicized that copying creative work such as a software program is illegal, the employer is also guilty.

ILLUSTRATION 7-3

What kinds of laws protect the duplication and distribution of computer software?

Copyrights are regulated by the federal

Copyright Office. Like a patent, a copyright is a special type of monopoly granted to authors, publishers, and other creators of original works. An example of a copyright notice appears on the back of the title page in the front of this book.

TRADEMARKS Trademarks are like patents because they are special types of monopolies. A **trademark** is a distinguishing name, symbol, or special mark placed on a good or service that is legally reserved for the sole use of the owner. Many nationally known products have trademarks that most people recognize. Some trademarks are symbols, such as the Nike "swoosh" or the McDonald's "golden arches." Others are company or product names, such as the Sony "Walkman" or Nintendo's "Game Boy." Trademarks, like patents, are regulated by the Patent and Trademark Office.

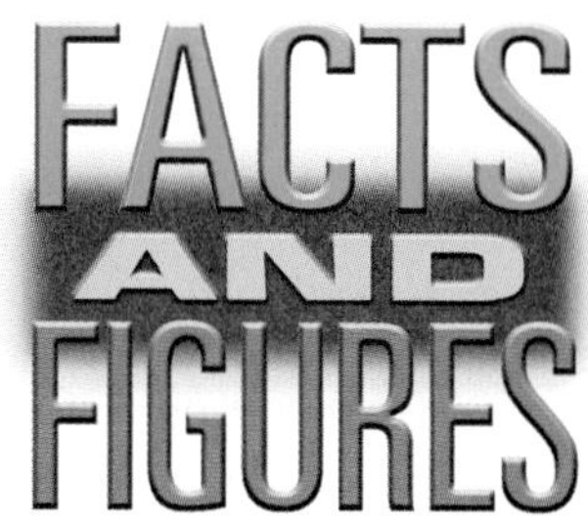

Trademark rights may continue indefinitely, as long as the mark is neither abandoned by the trademark owner nor loses its significance in the marketplace as a trademark by becoming a generic term. For example, the generic terms "escalator," "linoleum," and "zipper" were once trademarks.

PROTECTING THE PUBLIC

The federal government protects the legal rights of not only those who create new products and ideas but also those who consume goods and services. Two major goals of legislation are to ensure safe products for consumers and prevent the misuse of information.

FOOD AND DRUGS Products related to the human body are closely regulated. The Food and Drug Administration administers the Federal Food, Drug, and Cosmetic Act and related laws. These laws prohibit the sale of impure, improperly labeled, falsely guaranteed, and unhealthful foods, drugs, and cosmetics. Producers of cosmetics, for example, must show that their products will not harm users. Should a product cause harm, the Food and Drug Administration may require the producer to stop its sale or to notify the public of its possible danger.

NON-FOOD PRODUCTS Legislative activity dealing with the safety of nonfood products has increased in recent years. Laws now require labels on many products if possible danger exists from product use. A health warning message, for example, must appear on cigarette packages. The FTC forbids the sale of tobacco and smokeless tobacco to those under 18 because research shows that the majority of those who smoke when young die prematurely of smoking-related diseases. Also, auto and highway safety laws exist to reduce death and injury.

The Consumer Product Safety Act sets safety standards on many items. When products already sold are found to have a dangerous defect, businesses are legally required to recall, repair, or stop selling the products. Dangerous toys, for example, have been removed from the market. And recalls have occurred with such products as cars and sports utility vehicles. A federal Warranty Act requires sellers to specify what they will or will not do if their product is defective. Many product liability laws also exist at the state level.

ETHICAL ISSUES

ETHICS AND INTERNET ADVERTISING

The Internet is a popular place to browse for general information and to buy products or services. But as the Internet grows in popularity, buyers have become concerned about the privacy of their personal information and its possible misuse. Are buyers' fears justified?

DoubleClick, or DC, is a provider of advertising services to retailers who sell their wares to Internet shoppers. DC has over 2,300 business customers including Ford, Levi-Strauss, and NBC.

DC's clients want to target their Internet advertising to the people most likely to buy their products. DC can identify, for example, which potential customers might buy Ford cars online. The main way to identify these buyers is through "cookies"—files stored on customers' computers. The cookies collect information on what customers buy and where they go on the Web, revealing their preferences and buying habits.

DC manages the advertising for its client businesses, and from the customer information it connects online, it selects the customers that best match a firm's target audience. DC uses the customer information it collects to help its clients advertise effectively.

DC requires its business customers to collect information from customers when they make sales. DC itself claims not to collect personally identifiable information about people, such as names, addresses, and telephone numbers. It does collect non-personally identifiable information, such as whether people have responded to an advertisement and the type of computer system that they use. The non-personal information is used to measure advertisement effectiveness for DC's business clients. Internet customers have a choice of whether to forbid, restrict, or deny the use of information stored in cookies. Clear notice must be given customers, so that they can make their decisions.

DoubleClick is planning to merge with Abacus Direct, a company that has a massive collection of the catalog-buying habits of more than 80 million families, including names, addresses, and telephone numbers. This information can permit DC's business clients to target these people with e-mail advertising. Some consumer groups have objected strongly, claiming that this is an invasion of privacy that should be stopped. The Federal Trade Commission has initiated an investigation.

THINK CRITICALLY

1. Identify three people who have purchased an item on the Internet. Ask these people if they had read the privacy policy before purchasing and if they know what a "cookie" is. Report your findings to the class.
2. Do the selling methods of Internet advertisers invade your privacy any more than do companies who mail you advertising or call you at home to try to sell you their products? Defend your answer.
3. A very young person is often not concerned about what information he or she provides to others on the Internet. How could an unethical business capture and use this information in a way that could harm the family?

INFORMATION Businesses need information. This need has resulted in the heavy use of computers to manage data. Vast amounts of information from many sources are collected, processed, stored, and distributed by computer, especially on the Internet. As a result, individuals and businesses need protection from the wrongful use of private information.

Stores check credit card balances, banks check credit ratings, hospitals store patients' health records electronically, and the government collects income tax data on all taxpayers. Incorrect information in any of these sensitive records could be very damaging to the individual. Also, only authorized people should have access to such highly personal information.

Therefore, businesses that extensively use computer information must handle information carefully to protect the rights of individuals and organizations. Carelessly handled information can lead to **information liability**—the responsibility for physical or economic injury arising from incorrect data or wrongful use of data.

Information liability is similar to product liability. If a defective product injures someone, the injured party can sue the producer of the product. Similarly, if a person's credit rating suffers because an employee keys a social security number into a credit record incorrectly, the business is liable for creating the problem. Also, a company not directly involved in collecting or recording incorrect information may, however, be held liable for distributing it. For instance, if a store gives an incorrect credit balance to a bank that results in the refusal for a loan, the bank is as liable as the store that provided the incorrect information.

Occasionally, someone tampers with computerized data. The Electronic Communications Privacy Act and related laws make it a crime for any unauthorized person to access a major computer system and view, use, or change data. The laws deal with the interception and disclosure of electronic communications, including e-mail privacy. Privacy laws help protect the public from the wrongful use or misuse of information.

A debate continues over the electronic collection of information over the Internet. Web sites can place small files called "cookies" on the computers of site visitors without their knowledge. **Cookies** are files of information about the user that some Web sites create and store on the user's own computer. These cookies can, among other things, track where users go on the Net to gather information on interests and preferences for marketing purposes. Some people feel that such data gathering is an invasion of privacy. The companies argue that they are simply identifying what consumers want so they can better serve them.

STATE AND LOCAL REGULATIONS

The federal government regulates interstate commerce while the individual states regulate intrastate commerce. **Interstate commerce** is defined as business operations and transactions that cross state lines,

ILLUSTRATION 7-4

How could the concept of information liability affect the way in which a business handles computer information?

such as products that are produced in one state and sold in other states. **Intrastate commerce,** on the other hand, is defined as business transacted within a state. Most small service firms are involved mainly in intrastate commerce, since they usually sell to customers located within the same state. Because most large companies are likely to be involved in both interstate and intrastate commerce, they are subject to state and federal regulations.

Moreover, each state has a constitution that allows it to create other governing units, such as cities, towns, and counties. These units also regulate business transacted within them. Large businesses especially are subject to local, state, and federal laws.

Many state and local laws are related to federal laws. Most states, for instance, have laws that promote competition, protect consumers and the environment, safeguard the public's health, and improve employment conditions. In addition, however, state and local governments regulate business by issuing licenses, franchises, and building codes, and by passing zoning regulations.

LICENSING

State and local governments have used **licensing** as a way to limit and control those who plan to enter certain types of businesses. To start a business that requires a license, the owner must file an application. If the government believes there is a sufficient number of these kinds of businesses, the application can be refused.

Business is regulated not only by the granting of licenses but also by regular inspections by government officials to see that the company is operated according to the law. If it is not being properly operated, it can lose its license. For example, government agents inspect a licensed restaurant from time to time for cleanliness. If the restaurant fails inspection, the government may withdraw its license, and the restaurant would have to close.

Licensing laws vary from place to place. In some cities, businesses of all types must obtain licenses, while in other communities only certain types need licenses. It is particularly common to license restaurants, beauty salons, health and fitness centers, barber shops, and other types of service firms that may affect the health of customers. In most states and in many cities, licensing laws regulate the sale of such items as liquor and tobacco.

Businesses may also license the use of property. For example, a computer software company may give a business a license to use and copy a software program in return for a fee. Likewise, for a fee a business may license another firm to make a product using its patented device. Even firm names can be licensed. For example, Walt Disney Productions licenses its animal characters for use on clothing and other products.

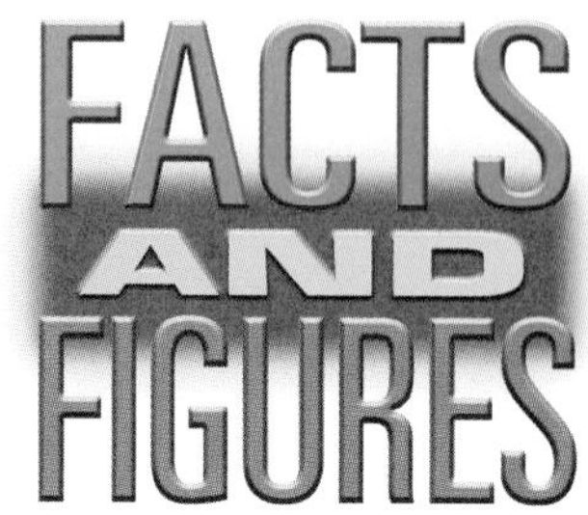

During the 1990s, Disney's licensing business became a victim of its own success. The strategy during the first half of the 1990s was geared around such animated hit films as "Beauty and the Beast," "Aladdin," and "The Lion King." Licensees reached a peak of more than 4,000. This became far too many relationships to manage. Disney eventually cut the number of licensees in half. By having broader relationships with fewer licensees, Disney was able to more effectively build new merchandise campaigns to strengthen established characters like Mickey Mouse and Winnie the Pooh.

PUBLIC FRANCHISING

Another way for state and local governments to control business is through public franchises. A **public franchise** is a contract that permits a person or organization to use public property for private profit. No individual member of society, however, has a right to use public property for profit except through a special grant by society. Cities often grant public franchises to companies to operate bus lines, or to install electric power or cable for television. For example, as presented in the story that started this chapter, Deion has a franchise from his community to operate his taxi company.

BUILDING CODES AND ZONING

Local governments regulate business through **building codes,** which control physical features of structures. Building codes may specify such things as the maximum height, minimum square feet of space, and the types of materials that can be used. Local governments also regulate the types of buildings and where they are built. **Zoning** regulations specify which land areas may be used for homes and which areas may be used for different types of businesses. A business must obey all local regulations relating to zoning and construction.

BUSINESS TAXES

While government uses many different ways to regulate business, no way is more important than taxes. The types and amounts of taxes influence business decisions that, in turn, can influence the total amount of business activity for a region and for the nation.

Both businesses and individuals pay many kinds of taxes to local, state, and federal governments. Taxes collected by the federal government account for about 56 percent of all taxes collected, while various state and local taxes account for the remaining 44 percent. Most corporations pay nearly one half of their profits in various kinds of taxes.

GENERAL NATURE OF TAXES

Government levies taxes for different reasons. When government decides to levy a particular type of tax, it must consider fairness to taxpayers.

REASONS FOR TAXES Governments use taxes mainly to raise revenue (money) to fund new and ongoing programs. Governments also use taxes to regulate business activity.

Governments set revenue goals that must be reached in order to provide the various services desired by the public. Examples of these services range from law enforcement and road building to providing for the military defense of the country. It is costly for government to provide the many services the public wants. To pay for these services, therefore, it must collect taxes.

ILLUSTRATION 7-5

For what purposes do governments use taxes?

Governments also use taxes to control business activity. They can speed up economic growth by lowering taxes and slow it by raising taxes. The federal government also taxes certain foreign goods that enter this country in order to encourage consumers to purchase American-made rather than foreign-made products. State and local governments also control business activity through taxation. For example, they often set high taxes on alcoholic beverages and tobacco, in part, to discourage customers from purchasing these products.

FAIRNESS OF TAXATION It is difficult for government to find ways to levy taxes fairly and still raise sufficient amounts of money to meet government expenses. The question of fairness has caused many debates. One problem is determining who will, in fact, pay the tax. For example, a firm may have to pay taxes on the goods it manufactures. But, since the tax is part of the cost of producing the product, this cost may be passed on to the customer. Another problem of fairness is whether those with the most assets or most income should pay at a higher rate than those who own or earn the least. Government tries to solve the fairness problem by adopting a proportional, progressive, or regressive tax policy.

Proportional Taxation. A **proportional tax**—sometimes called a **flat tax**—is one in which the tax rate remains the same regardless of the amount on which the tax is imposed. For example, in a given area the tax rate on real estate per $1,000 of property value is always the same, regardless of the amount of real estate the taxpayer owns. The total dollar amount of the tax paid by someone with a $400,000 home will differ from that paid by the person with a $175,000 home in the same area, but the rate of the tax is the same for both owners. A flat state tax of 6 percent on income is also proportional. Those with higher incomes pay more dollars than those with lower incomes. But the tax rate of 6 percent stays the same.

Progressive Taxation. A **progressive tax** is a tax based on the ability to pay. The policy of progressive taxation is a part of many state and federal income tax systems. As income increases, the tax rate increases. As a result, a lower-income person is taxed at a lower rate than a higher-income person is. In fact, the Tax Foundation found that in a recent year, 5 percent of the taxpayers that pay the most taxes contributed over half of all the federal individual income taxes collected.

Some local and state governments have combined the policies of proportional and progressive taxes. For example, a state may apply a flat tax of 5 percent to incomes up to $20,000 and 6 percent to all incomes over $20,000.

The current federal tax law is a combination of progressive and proportional taxation policy. A 15 percent tax applies to taxable income up to $43,050 for married couples filing joint returns. On taxable income from $43,050 and up to $104,050, the rate jumps to 28 percent. With still higher incomes, the rate jumps within brackets to 31 percent, 36 percent, and 39.6 percent, respectively. For single taxpayers, the rate is 15 percent up to $25,750. On taxable income from $25,750 to $62,450, the tax rate is 28 percent. Tax rates continue to rise within brackets to 31 percent, 36 percent, and then 39.6 percent, respectively, for people with higher taxable incomes. Because people with higher incomes pay more than those with lower incomes, most people consider the tax fair.

Regressive Taxation. The third type of tax policy is a **regressive tax.** With this type of tax, the actual tax rate decreases as the taxable amount increases. While general sales taxes are often thought to be proportional, they are actually regressive, because people with lower incomes pay a larger proportion of their incomes in taxes than those with higher incomes. Suppose, for example, that A and B live in a state with a 6 percent general sales tax. As shown in Figure 7-4, Person A with an annual take-home pay of $15,000 pays a 6 percent tax rate, while Person B with an annual take-home pay of $45,000 pays only a 5.7 percent tax rate. Because the sales tax applies to purchases rather than to income, the general sales tax is regressive. For a less regressive sales tax, some states exclude taxes on such purchases as food and clothing. These exclusions are usually items on which low-income families spend a high percentage of their income.

FIGURE 7-4

People with very high incomes often prefer regressive taxes.

	PERSON A	PERSON B
Take-Home Pay	$15,000	$45,000
State Sales Tax	6%	6%
Take-Home Pay Not Spent	0	$2,000
Take-Home Pay Spent	$15,000	$43,000
Tax Calculation	($15,000 x .06)	($43,000 x .06)
Tax	$900	$2,580
Tax Rate Calculation	($900 ÷ $15,000)	($2,580 ÷ $45,000)
Effective Tax Rate	6%	5.7%

KINDS OF TAXES

Taxation has become so complicated that the average businessperson spends a great deal of time filling out tax forms, computing taxes, and filing various reports. In many businesses, various taxes reduce a great percentage of their income. The three most common types of taxes affecting businesses and individuals are income taxes, sales taxes, and property taxes. Figure 7-5 gives examples of the types of taxes that a business operating in only one state may be required to pay.

INCOME TAX The federal government and most state governments use the income tax to raise revenues. An **income tax** is a tax on the profits of businesses and on earnings of individuals. For individuals, the tax is based on salaries and other income earned after certain deductions. For businesses, an income tax usually applies to net profits (receipts less expenses).

The income tax is the largest source of revenue for the federal government. While individuals pay about 70 percent of the total federal income taxes collected, businesses pay nearly all of the remaining 30 percent. Businesses share the cost of collecting individual income taxes. Every business is required to withhold income taxes from employees' earnings and turn it over to the government. Thus, business performs an important tax service for government. Individuals and businesses pay lower rates in the U.S. than in most other developed nations, as shown in Figure 7-6.

SALES TAX A **sales tax** is a tax levied on the retail price of goods and services at the time they are sold. A general sales tax usually applies to all goods or services sold by retailers. However, when a sales tax applies only to selected goods or services, such as cigarettes and gasoline, it is called an **excise tax.**

Sales taxes are the main source of revenue for most states and some cities and counties. Although state governments do not all administer sales taxes in the same way, in most cases the retail business collects

Assessments	Payroll taxes
Corporation taxes	Property tax—intangible property
Federal excise tax	Property tax—merchandise
Federal social security tax	Property tax—personal
Federal income tax	Property tax—real estate
Franchise tax	Sales tax
Gasoline tax	Severance tax
Licenses	State income tax
Local income tax	State unemployment tax
Motor truck licenses and taxes	State workers' insurance tax

FIGURE 7-5

The Most Common Business Taxes

FIGURE 7-6

U.S. tax rates are relatively low in comparison to those of other nations.

the tax from customers and turns this tax over to the state government. A business must be familiar with the sales tax law of the state in which it operates so that it can collect and report the tax properly.

From time to time, federal officials have considered charging a national sales tax. State officials, however, strongly oppose a national sales tax because that is their primary source of tax revenues. The question as to how and whether to tax Internet sales is also under debate between the states and the federal government. Both see this source of taxes as highly attractive. Traditional retailers, however, who pay sales taxes believe it is unfair for Internet sales not to be taxed.

PROPERTY TAX A **property tax** is a tax on material goods owned. While the sales tax is the primary source of revenue for most state governments, the property tax is the main source of revenue for most local governments. There may be a real property tax and a personal property tax. A **real property tax** is a tax on real estate, which is land and buildings. A **personal property tax** is a tax on possessions that are moveable, such as furniture, machinery, and equipment. Essentially, personal property is anything that is not real estate. In some states there is a special property tax on raw materials used to make goods and on finished goods available for sale.

A tax on property—whether it is real property or personal property—is stated in terms of dollars per hundred of assessed valuation.

Assessed valuation is the value of property determined by tax officials. Thus, a tax rate of $2.80 per $100 on property with an assessed valuation of $180,000 is $5,040 ($180,000/100 = $1,800; $1,800 X $2.80 = $5,040).

EFFECT OF TAXES ON BUSINESS DECISIONS

Businesses consider taxes in many of their major decisions. Taxes may influence the accounting method a business selects to calculate profits and the method used to pay managers. Often, taxes are used as a basis for deciding where to locate a new business or whether to move a business from one location to another.

For example, assume that a producer of garden tools is trying to decide in which of two cities to locate a new factory. City A is located in a state that has a low state income tax and low property taxes. City B is located in a state that has no state income tax but has high property taxes. After weighing all the factors, the producer has decided to locate in City A. City A, which has both an income tax and a property tax, has been selected mainly because the total tax cost each year is less than in City B.

CHAPTER 7 REVIEW

CHAPTER CONCEPTS

- The federal, state, and local governments regulate business activities to protect citizens and businesses. At the national level, the Federal Trade Commission administers federal laws that regulate commerce. Landmark laws such as the Sherman and Clayton Acts helped set the stage for defining fair competition. Other federal agencies regulate basic industries such as aviation, communications, and food and drugs.
- A primary activity of the Federal Trade Commission is to govern both publicly controlled monopolies such as utility companies and natural business monopolies. But the U.S. and other countries are moving more toward deregulation to reduce the number of public monopolies. Although the government promotes competition, there is a price to pay for business failures. A downside of free enterprise is that some firms go bankrupt, but bankruptcy laws allow businesses to recover or to exit business operations fairly. Also, when firms destroy major competitors to eliminate competition, they become monopolies and may be penalized in some way.
- The federal government protects individuals and firms from the theft or misuse of their inventions, publications, and other intellectual property by granting the owners patents, trademarks, or copyrights. Local and state governments also regulate business through licenses, zoning laws, and franchising regulations.
- Governments obtain revenues through taxes to pay for public services, such as police, schools, and other human services. The most common sources of revenue are income, sales, and property taxes.
- The fairness of taxes is based mostly on what is being taxed and who pays, but the meaning of fairness is subject to debate. A progressive tax such as an income tax is based on one's ability to pay, and levies a higher tax on those who earn more and than on those who earn less. A proportional tax such as a county's real estate tax is one in which the tax rate stays the same regardless of a property's current value. A regressive tax, such as a sales tax, is a tax that requires people who earn less to pay a greater portion of their income than do people who earn more. Arguments can be made for each of the three types of taxes.

BUILD VOCABULARY POWER

Define the following terms and concepts.

1. monopoly
2. price discrimination
3. false advertising
4. bankruptcy
5. patent
6. copyright
7. trademark
8. information liability
9. cookies
10. interstate commerce

11. intrastate commerce
12. licensing
13. public franchise
14. building codes
15. zoning
16. proportional tax (flat tax)
17. progressive tax
18. regressive tax
19. income tax
20. sales tax
21. excise tax
22. property tax
23. real property tax
24. personal property tax
25. assessed valuation

REVIEW FACTS

1. When does a monopoly exist?
2. What is the name of the first major law promoting competition and in what year was it passed?
3. Which federal law forbids corporations from acquiring ownership rights in other corporations if the purpose is to create a monopoly or to discourage competition?
4. What is the main purpose of the Robinson-Patman Act of 1936?
5. Which act makes it unlawful for an advertiser to circulate false advertising that can lead to the purchase of foods, drugs, medical devices, or cosmetics, or to participate in any other unfair methods of competition?
6. How is it possible for a business to continue operating even though it has filed for bankruptcy?
7. Name five federal agencies that regulate business activities.
8. What type of agreement gives an inventor the sole right for 20 years to make, use, and sell an invention?
9. How are patents and trademarks alike?
10. Name the federal agency that protects the consumer from dangerous food and non-food products.
11. How is product liability like information liability?
12. Give two reasons why governments impose taxes.
13. Would the federal income tax be considered a regressive tax? Why or why not?
14. In which tax policy does the actual rate of taxation decrease as the taxable amount increases?
15. What are the three most common types of business taxes?

DISCUSS IDEAS

1. Discuss how a business that has a monopoly on a good or service can keep its prices unreasonably high.
2. Why is it necessary for the federal government to pass laws promoting fair competition?
3. Determine whether the following situation violates one of the antitrust laws and, if it does, identify the law that it violates. Pinter, Inc., makes one type of flashlight and sells it mostly to large retail stores. For Stores A, B, and C it sells in about the same

quantity at the same price. It also sells to Store D in about the same quantity but at a much lower price because it has been doing business with Store D longer.

4. Name at least three different practices that are prohibited under the laws administered by the Federal Trade Commission.
5. Explain how a computer software program might be both copyrighted and licensed.
6. What must a business do to protect itself from possible lawsuits if many of its employees have personal computers at home?
7. Sundial Products placed an advertisement in the local newspaper stating that its latest suntan lotion would give a deep suntan within 24 hours, without any danger to the user's health. Within a week, ten people were badly burned by the product.
   a. In what unfair practice did Sundial engage?
   b. Discuss how the federal government might control this company and its new product.
8. Monica Lopez wants to start a sewing business in her home where she can alter clothes and sell sewing supplies. Discuss whether the local zoning law that forbids her from using her home as a business is fair or unfair.
9. Which do you think is the fairest kind of tax—a proportional tax, a progressive tax, or a regressive tax? Support your answer.
10. Discuss how a local community can attract or discourage new businesses through property taxes and/or controls.
11. Amazon.com received a patent in 1999 for its "one click" shopping cart technology that simplifies buying a series of items on the Internet. Barnes and Noble bookstore and other companies have copied this technology without approval from Amazon.com. Using newspapers, magazines, or the Internet, investigate this problem and report on what may be happening or has happened with any lawsuits that may have been filed against the "copy cats."

ANALYZE INFORMATION

1. Three manufacturers that sell nationally discuss prices of a product that they all manufacture but which has become unprofitable to each. They believe that it is foolish to sell at a loss. They all agree to raise prices, but they do not agree on how much each will charge. Do you consider this action illegal? Explain.
2. Two of your friends were working in the school's computer lab one day. Because they received a failing grade on a major test, they figured out how to break into the school's computer containing student grades. Your friends were about to raise their grades and then asked you which grades you wanted changed.
   a. Discuss the ethics of changing grades.
   b. Discuss the legality of changing grades.

c. If someone got into the system and lowered a student's grades, causing the student to be rejected by a specific college, how might a judge decide if the student sued the school?
d. Can the school sue the students who changed the records? And what law might be used?

3. You live in a state that has the following tax schedule:

Taxable Income	*Rate*
$0-$6,999	no tax
7,000-14,999	5%
15,000-24,999	6%
25,000 and over	7%

Your state permits everyone to have $2,000 of exemptions from total income to arrive at taxable income. Your taxable income this year is only $12,000 because of work lost due to illness. Your friend's income is $19,000.

a. What is your tax this year? What is your friend's tax?
b. What is the actual tax rate you and your friend paid this year based on your total incomes?

4. If the real estate tax rate is $3.40 per $100 of assessed valuation:
   a. What is the tax per $1,000 of valuation?
   b. What is the tax on real estate valued at $150,000?
   c. Using your local tax rate, compute the real estate tax on real estate valued at $150,000.
5. A married couple filed a joint return and had a taxable income of $45,000 after taking allowable deductions.
   a. Under the federal income tax law described in this chapter, calculate their tax.
   b. Calculate their tax rate if their total annual income before deductions had been $50,000.

SOLVE BUSINESS PROBLEMS

CASE 7-1

Hitesh Nazami owns and operates a hardware store in a community of 50,000 people. The nearest town is at least 25 miles away, but there are two competitors in the area, one of which is a large Home Depot. All usually run weekly advertisements.

Today, a customer he had never seen before came into the store. "I certainly hope you carry Weaver tools," the customer said. "The other stores in town don't carry the Weaver brand."

"Sure, we carry Weaver," answered Hitesh. "It's one of my best lines."

The customer looked happy and relieved, and went to his truck to get the old tool he wanted to replace. While the customer was outside, Hitesh had a chance to think about what the customer had said. Now Hitesh knew why the Weaver brand was so popular in his store. As a result, he decided to raise prices on Weaver tools by tomorrow morning. Also, he could promote Weaver tools in next week's advertisements. A smile crossed Hitesh's face as the customer returned.

"Here's the tool," said the customer. "I hope you can replace it. As you can see, it's quite different from the other brands."

"I can see that it's different," Hitesh responded. "You're lucky to get it at this low price. The price will be going up in the very near future."

Think Critically:

1. Does Hitesh have a monopoly on Weaver tools in his community?
2. If Hitesh raises his price by very much, what might happen?
3. Is raising the price suddenly (and for the reason given) an unfair business practice? Discuss.

CASE 7-2

Barbara Turner worked at the Dyme Corporation, where she negotiated sales terms and coordinated all large contracts. Jeff Collins had also worked for Dyme, but last Monday he just started working at a new company, Destiny, Inc. Barbara and Jeff had been good friends for some time.

His new company hired Jeff because he was an excellent computer person and they believed he would be valuable to the firm. During the second week, Jeff's boss informed him that the company was competing against a major rival for a rather large contract. Jeff was not told the name of the competing firm. His boss wondered whether Jeff could find out more about such contract proposals from his former employer. "The sooner the better," he said. "Any information would be extremely helpful."

That evening Jeff decided to e-mail Barbara from his home computer and ask a few questions. After an exchange of a few messages, Barbara said that recently she had been helping others develop new proposals. "In fact, we're working on a new one now and it's for a large amount." She was sure that Jeff's small company would not be making an offer of this size. "I'll receive the final details from our people by e-mail tomorrow, check them over, and then mail it to our client tomorrow morning. I can share that with you, Jeff, but I can't provide price information. In a few days I'll send the document along."

Jeff replied, "Thanks, Barbara," and closed down his computer.

The next morning Jeff's impatient boss asked him what he had learned. Jeff answered, "Give me a little more time, and I'll try to forward the information to you." A little later he tapped into Barbara's e-mail messages, found the actual proposal—with prices—and without examining it, forwarded it immediately to his boss. The boss's impatience and Jeff's desire to serve the firm well caused him to disregard Barbara's statement about prices. Later, his boss thanked Jeff

immensely and commented that the firm would not forget him when bonus time came. Later the next day Barbara sent Jeff the proposal without prices. A week later Jeff's boss gleefully announced that "we got that big contract with the Crown Hill Company." Somewhat shocked by the news, Jeff now worried about what had occurred, because the proposal he got from Barbara was also for Crown Hill. "What have I done?" he asked himself.

Think Critically:

1. Assume the CEO of Dyme Corporation found out about what happened and he decided to sue Destiny, Inc. If you were Dyme's lawyer, what law would you use?
2. Who was the most unethical person, Jeff or Jeff's boss? Explain.
3. Assume Jeff calls Barbara and asks to have lunch with her to explain what happened and to fix the situation. If you were Jeff, what would you say? Also, if you were Barbara, how would you respond to Jeff's explanation?

4. How should Barbara and Jeff have handled this situation if they could do it over?
5. Use your library or the Internet to find information related to the theft of e-mail information or deliberate misuse of data found in electronic files. Report your findings to the class.

PROJECT: MY BUSINESS, INC.

Every business, even a very small one, is regulated and taxed by government. Regulations and taxes harm business people most often when they are not aware of them or do not understand them. In this chapter, you will study the effects of local, state, and federal laws on your business.

DATA COLLECTION

1. Identify the city/county office you will need to contact about:
   a. local zoning regulations
   b. licenses and permits
   c. taxes and fees

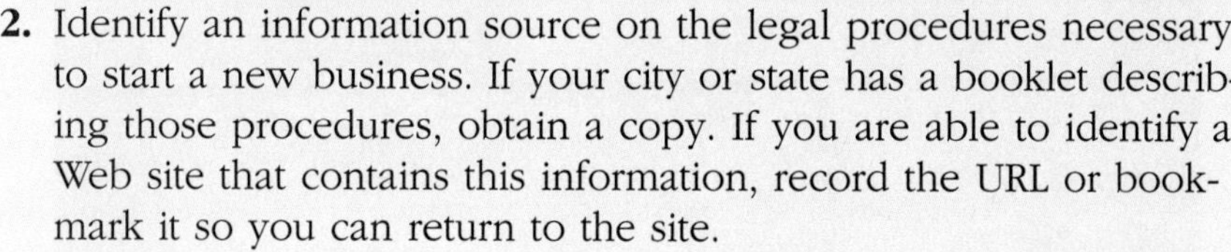

2. Identify an information source on the legal procedures necessary to start a new business. If your city or state has a booklet describing those procedures, obtain a copy. If you are able to identify a Web site that contains this information, record the URL or bookmark it so you can return to the site.

ANALYSIS

1. The legislature in your state has just increased the sales tax from 4 percent to 6 percent of total sales. This will cause you problems because of the way you have priced your products. In order to make prices easier to remember and to simplify making change, you priced your products as shown below to include the 4 percent tax. (Do not be concerned if these are not the same products or prices you have previously identified for your juice bar.)

Large one-variety juice/yogurt mix	$3.75
Small 3-juice combo	$2.50
Vitamin/mineral supplement	$ .60
Turkey sandwich	$5.25
Bagel with cream cheese	$1.25
Nutrition bar	$1.90

   It will be difficult to collect the additional 2 percent for sales tax and keep your pricing method. How will the sales tax increase affect your business? Evaluate several methods for dealing with the tax increase. Define your new pricing structure.

2. To reduce your startup costs and to find a business location with a large number of potential customers, you have decided to rent a mobile cart in a large local mall in which to start your juice bar. Many fast-food business owners in your city are concerned that if mobile carts are allowed to operate, they will take business away from the other restaurants. They have approached the city council to pass a zoning regulation to prevent food from being sold from mobile carts, suggesting that it might be a health hazard. What actions can you and the owners of other similar businesses take to prevent the zoning law from being adopted by the city council? If the law is passed, how will it affect your business?
3. Most businesses develop a unique name with a design or symbol to clearly identify the business for customers. They can then apply for a copyright or trademark to protect its use. Use a computer graphics program, if possible, to develop the name and symbol you will use for your business.

UNIT THREE

INFORMATION and COMMUNICATION SYSTEMS

CHAPTERS

"Already, the Web work style is changing business processes at Microsoft and other companies. Replacing paper processes with collaborative digital processes has cut weeks out of our budgeting and other operational processes. Groups of people are using electronic tools to act together almost as fast as a single person could act, but with the insights of the entire team. Highly motivated teams are getting the benefit of everyone's thinking. With faster access to information about our sales, our partner activities, and most important, our customers, we are able to react faster to problems and opportunities."

Bill Gates
Business@ the Speed of Thought, 2000

TECHNOLOGY AND INFORMATION MANAGEMENT

OBJECTIVES

- **8-1** Describe basic elements of computers and the Internet.
- **8-2** Explain the chief information officer's role in managing an organization's computer systems and its electronic networks.
- **8-3** Describe information systems that managers use to aid in their decision making.
- **8-4** Discuss types of problems that employees face when working in today's high-technology organizations.
- **8-5** Describe technology's present and future impact on today's businesses.

BRAVE NEW BUSINESS WORLD

After Mia Herrera rose, dressed, and hopped into her car, she used her voice-activated cell phone to call several customers who had e-mailed her late last evening. Before entering her favorite coffee shop, she reached into her pocket for her handheld computer and jotted a few brief messages that were then e-mailed to her regional sales manager. After enjoying breakfast and returning to the car, Mia opened her briefcase and was soon dictating a message on her computer that was sent wirelessly via the Internet to her office assistant. Before starting the engine, she checked her car's global positioning system for the most direct but timesaving route to her new client.

At the next two stoplights, she read a few e-mails and found a favorite Web site to check yesterday's closing stock price for Egloff and Fox, Inc. Her first client that morning was the E&F purchasing manager. After reaching the parking lot, Mia quickly reviewed E&F's background and database files from the small wireless computer kept in her briefcase. Now she felt ready to face the business day ahead.

Through the ages, discoveries and inventions have had major impacts on society. No inventions in recent years have had a greater impact than the computer, Internet, World Wide Web, and wireless communications. These new tools have profoundly affected the personal work lives of Mia Herrera and millions of other workers. New technologies have made dizzying changes in the way we live and work, and the pace of change is not likely slow in the years ahead.

The traditional business office that once operated with filing cabinets, typewriters, and secretaries was labor intensive when compared to today's electronic office. Simple business transactions that once took weeks of paper handling are now processed in minutes. Now workers create and store most documents electronically.

Whether an office is in a bank, factory, or day-care center, it must still collect, process, store, retrieve, and distribute data. The modern electronic office is an information center operated by **knowledge workers**—people who work with information. Clerks,

ILLUSTRATION 8-1

How have new technologies changed the traditional business office?

FACTS AND FIGURES

In 1997, the Census Bureau surveyed the U.S. population to assess ownership and use of computers. Among the findings: More than one in three American households had computers. Almost three quarters of children used a computer at home or at school. Nearly half of American adults used a computer at home, work, or school. One in five Americans used the Internet.

supervisors, and managers at all levels are knowledge workers who handle data and information. **Data** are the original facts and figures that businesses generate, while **information** is data that have been processed in some meaningful way that is useful to decision makers.

In this chapter you will learn how technology has changed the way businesses handle data and information. You will also learn how computers and the Internet affect organizations, people, and jobs. Finally, you will learn how information systems help managers make sound decisions by getting the right information in the right form at the right time to the right people.

ELECTRONIC TECHNOLOGY FUNDAMENTALS

The current electronic revolution started with the creation of the computer over 50 years ago. More recently the Internet developed into a tool that people and businesses could use to communicate with each other. The computer and the Internet plus additional electronic devices set the stage for reconstructing how businesses operate.

COMPUTERS

A **computer** is a machine that processes and stores data according to instructions stored in it. The machine parts and anything attached to it are called **hardware.** The instructions that tell the computer what to do are called **software**.

As illustrated in Figure 8-1, computers have three basic elements: a way to enter data, a central processing unit to act on the data, and a way to output the results. Users can enter data through such devices as keyboards, voice-recognition systems, and scanners. The central processing unit receives and processes the data as directed by the software stored permanently or temporarily in the computer. Users can view data entered and processed on monitors or can print or store the data on disks, such as hard drives, floppy disks, CDs (compact disks), and DVDs (digital video disks).

TYPES OF COMPUTERS Computers come in different sizes and serve different purposes. Companies use large computers (mainframes) to store and retrieve vast amounts of data for the entire company. Major divisions of the company may use medium-sized computers. The typical office computer that most workers use is a desktop or personal computer (PC). Workers can carry smaller computers (laptops or notebooks), such as those used by Mia Herrera in the opening story, in briefcases and backpacks.

In addition to desktops and laptops, smaller handheld devices also serve specific purposes. A **personal digital assistant (PDA)** is a computer-like device that can be carried in a pocket and used to, among other things, send and receive messages wirelessly. PDAs may also be built into cell phones. PDAs usually contain a calculator, an address

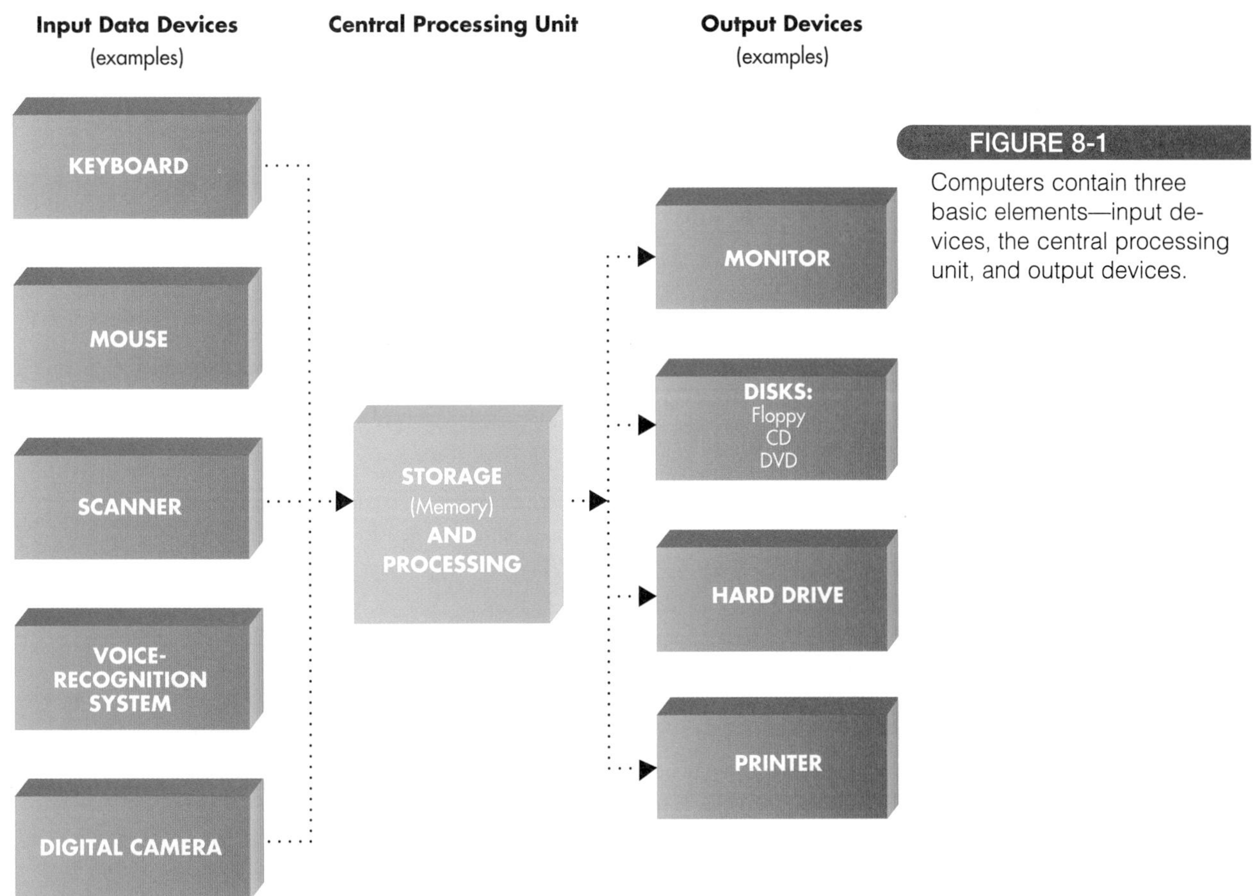

FIGURE 8-1
Computers contain three basic elements—input devices, the central processing unit, and output devices.

book, a notepad for keeping "to do" lists, and a fax modem. PDAs come with features to meet a variety of needs. Such devices will become standard voice-messaging equipment built into vehicles. Because wireless computing is rapidly developing, new products will continue to pour into the marketplace.

TYPES OF SOFTWARE All computers need two types software: operating system software and application software. **Operating system software** is a master control program that manages the computer's internal functions and file system. Operating system software directs and channels application software instructions and data for processing. Examples of operating system software include Microsoft Windows, MacOS, Unix, and Linux.

Application software refers to programs that perform specific tasks. The most common examples of application software are word processing for creating written documents, a spreadsheet for performing calculations on rows and columns of data, a database for storing related information for later retrieval, and software for creating graphics. A description of common business application software appears in Figure 8-2. Figure 8-3 shows an example of a spreadsheet. Many other types

FIGURE 8-2
Other Common Types of Software Application Programs

TYPE AND APPLICATION

ACCOUNTING

Maintain general and specific accounting records such as accounts receivable, accounts payable, and general ledger.

COMMUNICATIONS

Send and receive information from other computers, including fax, e-mail, and surfing the Web.

DESKTOP PUBLISHING

Create high-quality newsletters, brochures, manuals, advertising, and other special documents combining text, photographs, and graphics.

FORMS

Provide standard business forms such as invoices and purchase orders but allow for the modification of forms and the creation of entirely new forms.

GRAPHICS

Prepare diagrams, organization charts, line and bar graphs, pie charts, and other kinds of illustrations.

TRAINING

Teach employees about various topics, including how to use computers, how to supervise workers, and how to prepare a talk.

UTILITIES

Aid other software to work more effectively, such as providing a variety of type styles and font sizes, recovering lost files, and finding and correcting computer system errors.

FIGURE 8-3
Spreadsheets are used to prepare financial statements and other documents.

Cartright Corporation Comparative Income Statements

	Year 1	Year 2	Percent of Change
Sales	$58,000,000	$59,000,000	1.7
Cost of Goods Sold	30,000,000	32,000,000	6.7
Gross Profit on Sales	28,000,000	27,000,000	-3.6
Operating Expenses	12,000,000	11,000,000	-8.3
Administrative Expenses	10,000,000	9,000,000	-1.0
Net Profit Before Taxes	6,000,000	7,000,000	16.7

of popular software are available to perform specialized tasks. Companies, for example, produce sophisticated software packages that help businesses manage complex tasks, such as customer and supplier relationships.

MOORE'S LAW Advances in computer technology occur at an ever-increasing rate. An engineer named Gordon Moore of Intel Corporation predicted that the amount of data that could be processed by a computer chip would double about every 18 months. **Moore's Law,** as this prediction has become known, has proven to be rather accurate. Figure 8-4 shows this accelerating pace of change over the past two decades. According to Moore's Law, a computer bought only one to two years ago will be obsolete this year. As processing speed increases, high-tech companies are constantly producing new and better software to take advantage of the technology's capabilities.

But new technologies make old equipment obsolete. Buying and installing new equipment and software, as well as re-training employees, are costly business expenditures.

THE INTERNET

Advances in computer technology invited the entrance of another electronic wonder—the Internet. The **Internet,** or **Net,** is a worldwide network of linked computers that allows users to transfer data and information from one computer to another anywhere in the world. People can use the Net to send e-mail, visit Web sites, and participate in discussion groups.

The Internet permits businesses to work together electronically and for employees to communicate with other employees at any distance. Even consumers can buy online from businesses or sell personal products. Two individuals with common interests can chat or join a discussion group, seek information from electronic libraries, or compare

The Development of Microprocessors

MICROPROCESSOR	TRANSISTORS	TOP SPEED	YEAR
8086	29,000	10 Megahertz	1978
80386DX	275,000	16 Megahertz	1985
Pentium	1,200,000	25 Megahertz	1993
Pentium III	9,500,000	733 Megahertz	1999

Source: *Modified from Business Week, November 15, 1999*

FIGURE 8-4

Microprocessors composed of chips on integrated circuits are constantly being developed by Intel Corporation and other firms to process data at faster speeds.

CAREER CONNECTION

WEBMASTER

Webmasters are called the "guardians of cyberspace." They are the people who create, organize, and manage Web sites for schools, businesses, and governmental organizations. There are two kinds of Webmasters: those who focus on hardware, software, and communication protocols (such as "http"), and those who focus on the site's content.

Every Webmaster needs to know the basics of the hardware that links computers to the Internet, the software the Internet uses, and the specialized languages and programming commands required to make the World Wide Web function, such as HTML, Java, JavaScript, and VRML. Thus, Webmasters spend their time in a highly technical environment that is constantly changing.

Webmasters often have access to many kinds of sensitive information and restricted files. On some sites, the Webmaster may also maintain the e-mail system. Therefore, issues of ethics and confidentiality may frequently arise.

Qualified Webmasters for major companies can demand large salaries, but working hours are often long. Much of the work may have to be done at night, when users are less likely to be using their computers.

For more career information about Webmasters, check your library or the Internet for resources.

products. The Internet is also used as a substitute for phoning and to download music and update computer software. Internet uses are virtually unlimited.

WORLD WIDE WEB Creation of the **World Wide Web, WWW,** or **Web** made the Internet accessible to the average person. Previously, the Internet allowed computer users to share only printed text and required sophisticated technical knowledge to use. Therefore, at first, researchers and the military were the main users. Now the Web permits text plus photographs, videos, and sound to be transmitted over the Net, all with just a minimal amount of computer savvy. This Internet access tool for the general public enabled the Net to grow rapidly during the last decade. Now, for most of us, the Web is synonymous with the Internet.

The Web uses links, called hyperlinks, for navigating easily among its pages. A **hyperlink** is a Web page address embedded in a word, phrase, or graphic that, when clicked, transports users to that address. Web pages usually contain hyperlinks to other sites on the Web that contain information of interest to site visitors. Hyperlinks often appear as colored, underscored words, but addresses can be embedded just about anywhere on the Web page. As you move your mouse pointer around a Web page, you will know when you encounter a hyperlink, because the pointer will turn to a hand with a pointing index finger.

Many companies, large and small, have Web sites. Their addresses usually contain the company name or initials. For example, the General Electric site address is http://www.ge.com. All addresses begin with "http://" for "hypertext transport protocol," which is a code that helps computers connect to each other on the Web. Your browser will assume that all addresses begin with this, so you need not type it. The next part of the address, www, stands for "World Wide Web." Many Web addresses begin this way, but not all. The company name or abbreviation usually appears next. The three letters at the end identify the type of organization. The ".com" following "ge" indicates a commercial or profit-making organization. A government office is ".gov," a school is ".edu," and a not-for-profit organization is ".org." Saying "dot.com" is a way advertisers and others may refer to Web sites in general.

ILLUSTRATION 8-2

The creation of the World Wide Web has made the Internet accessible to the average person. What effect has it had on the transaction of business?

The line under the GE Web address shown above indicates a hyperlink. If you were reading this page on the Internet and you wanted to visit GE's home page, you could immediately jump there by clicking the mouse on the hyperlink. You may want to know what products GE sells or what jobs are available. You could find out about GE's products by following hyperlinks on the company's site to different product pages.

Much business is transacted on the Internet. The use of the letter "e" before a name means "electronic." For example, "e-commerce" refers to businesses that buy and sell to other businesses as well as to businesses that sell to consumers. "E-business" means businesses that buy and sell only to other businesses. Retailers that sell to customers on the Web are known as "e-tailers." Anyone who sends messages to others is using "e-mail." And "e-appliances" are consumer appliances, such as refrigerators and microwave ovens, that contain chips allowing people to use e-mail to obtain data such as cooking, freezing, and maintenance information that can be stored in the e-appliance. New "e" words are likely to evolve. You will learn more about e-commerce in Chapter 9.

USING THE INTERNET To get onto the Internet, you need a **modem,** an electronic device inside or outside the computer that enables it to send data over phone lines or cable. You also need an **Internet Service Provider,** or **ISP,** a service that provides access to the Internet through its large computers. Examples of ISPs include AOL, Mindspring, and AT&T WorldNet. ISPs usually charge a monthly fee, but you can get free Internet access through Web-based services such as Juno and NetZero. Advertising pays for these services.

To use the Web, you also need a **browser.** This is a program that permits you to navigate and view Web pages. Most computers come

BUSINESS INNOVATION

THE NET'S BOOSTER ROCKET—THE WEB

The purpose of the first crude Internet was as an emergency communication system for the military in case an enemy attack knocked out more conventional means of communication. Soon after this important goal was achieved, experts began using the slow, unreliable, and troublesome military Internet to share research findings. At the same time, improvements were being made, but the system's clumsiness and the need for technical knowledge limited its growth. However, the stage was set for the next breakthrough.

In 1989, Tim Berners-Lee, an English physicist who had been working at the European Particle Physics Laboratory, created the World Wide Web. This relatively unknown Web inventor developed a means for using the Internet to send more than just typed material to any computer in the world. Needed was a global Internet-based hypermedia means for sharing global information. His new system permitted multimedia—graphics, videos, animations, and sounds—to be sent over the Internet. The Net's popularity began growing by leaps and bounds as further refinements were made. This laboratory also created the first Web browser, leading to navigation through hyperlinks. The marriage of the Internet and the Web led to rapid global acceptance during the 20th century's last decade.

Tim Berners-Lee believes the Web is a powerful force for social and economic change and that it has already modified how we conduct business, entertain ourselves, find information, and swap ideas. His goal is to keep the Web wide open and free to everyone, but he expects the Web will continue to alter our lives. He resisted efforts by major corporations to own and operate parts of the Web, because that would lead to charging user fees, which would not make it free. As the director of the World Wide Web Consortium, Berners-Lee discusses Web refinements with other consortium members worldwide. The group also oversees and recommends solutions to a variety of problems.

Tim Berners-Lee could have easily become very rich if he had personally built his own Web business or worked closely with a major computer firm to exploit it. He chooses to guide his creation to most benefit humankind. *Time* magazine named him one of the greatest geniuses of the 20th century. Yet, he is not a household name like Albert Einstein. But unlike many other famous people before him, he has a Web site.

THINK CRITICALLY

1. Why was the first Internet created? And why didn't the early version of the Internet catch on with everyone?
2. How did the addition of the WWW increase use of the Internet?
3. Do you think Tim Berners-Lee would be happier being the CEO of a highly successful firm making millions than he is now as an employee in nonprofit organizations?
4. Using a library or the Internet, find out more about Tim Berners-Lee and write a report for the class.

already equipped with a browser, or your ISP will provide one. The two most popular browsers are Microsoft Internet Explorer and Netscape Navigator.

Once you are on the Net, you can go directly to a Web address or you may have to search for information. A **search engine** is a program that assists in locating information on the Net. After you type in one or more key words, the search engine will display a list of sites that contain information matching those key words. Some of these sites may have the information you want, while others may be way off target. A mouse click will take you to the Web sites that look promising. For example, assume you wish to buy a notebook computer. To use a search engine such as Excite (www.excite.com), key in "notebook computer" and wait for Excite to provide a list of Web sites that you could visit.

MANAGING TECHNOLOGY

As computers became a dominant force throughout the world, organizations had to manage the computer systems as well as the computer specialists. In major organizations, the top computer executive is the **chief information officer,** or **CIO.** The CIO reports to the CEO (chief executive officer). The CIO not only must have knowledge about electronic equipment but must also possess expert management skills.

CIOs must keep up with new technologies and know what types of equipment to purchase to meet an organization's specific needs. Because many workers use computers, keeping employees trained and productive is equally important. CIOs make it possible for all people who need information to get it easily and quickly from anywhere it exists. CIOs also protect information from being improperly used or getting to people who should not have it.

DISTRIBUTING INFORMATION

Employees are constantly using their computers to record, process, send, store, and retrieve information. The company's computer system must make these tasks easy and fast to perform. **Telecommunications (data communications)** is the movement of information from one location to another location electronically. The means used for this movement may be telephone lines, cable, or satellite. Telecommunications companies sell different systems for transmitting information within firms and to business partners and customers. Customers can even have training programs and sports events appear on a portion of their computer monitors, thanks to telecommunication providers.

Workers need an electronic means for sharing information. A **local area network (LAN)** is a network of linked computers that serves users in a single building or building complex. In a LAN, a computer that stores data and application software for all PC workstations is called a **file server,** or, more commonly, a **server.**

Firms with multiple locations have to send information to employees who are geographically dispersed. A **wide area network (WAN)** is a network of linked computers that covers a wide geographic area, such as a state or country. The LANs and the WANs and their servers are connected to a mainframe computer. The servers are also channels through which individual workers can use their computers to communicate with others inside and outside the organization.

INTRANETS AND EXTRANETS

An **intranet** is a private company network that allows employees to share resources no matter where they are located. An intranet works like the Internet. Users access information through a browser, navigate with hyperlinks, and send e-mail through the intranet. Usually the intranet even connects to the Internet, but it is sealed off from the general public to protect company information.

Intranets enable employees to accomplish many electronic tasks. Groups of employees working on the same project can discuss, share, plan, and implement ideas without having to leave their desks. These same employees can use company records stored electronically to aid in performing their tasks. Workers may use their computers to check employer-sponsored events, such as new training programs, or see choices of health care benefits and the balance in their retirement plan. The easy accessibility of information on an intranet reduces the time spent finding and thumbing through paper documents.

Another type of network that operates similar to the Internet is an extranet. An **extranet** is a private network that companies use to share certain information with selected people outside the organization, such as suppliers and major customers. A supplier of raw materials for a manufacturer or merchandise for a national retailer, for instance, could serve the company better by tracking the company's daily inventory balance. When inventory gets low, the supplier could deliver its goods just when the company needs them. An extranet can enable the supplier to see the company's inventory records without allowing access to other company data.

INFORMATION SECURITY

One of the major concerns of chief information officers is information security. The CIO must do whatever is necessary to make certain that hackers cannot steal, destroy, or alter information. The penalty for not controlling information may well be lawsuits by employees, customers, suppliers, and the public, as well as the loss of critical company records.

Organizations also may violate business ethics when they gather, and sometimes sell, information about people who use the Internet to browse or buy merchandise. Programs launched from Web sites can track your travels from Web site to Web site. Where you go frequently on the Web reveals your general interests and what you buy. After collecting this information, some firms may sell it to businesses that sell goods related to your interests. For example, if you frequently look at Web sites related to MP3 music or games, firms that sell these goods will contact you and try to sell you their products.

When you buy goods on the Net, you must provide basic information, such as name, address, telephone number, and e-mail address. Often Web sites store this information in your computer as a "cookie" file that the sites can retrieve when you visit again. This can be helpful when you buy from the business again. But the seller can also sell this personal information to other businesses without your knowledge.

The Federal Trade Commission and good business practice require that businesses notify buyers of their rights and how personal information will be used. However, some businesses may not properly inform buyers of their rights or continue to sell their confidential information. These actions are unethical and illegal in some states. Many computer users would buy on the Internet if they did not fear invasion of their privacy.

Companies must also take defensive strategies to protect electronic information. Such strategies often include requiring user passwords to access data, saving information as backup files, and scrambling information to make it unreadable to others.

Firms often use firewall systems to protect information from outsiders who try to break into their networks. A **firewall** uses special software that screens people who enter and/or exit a network by requesting specific information such as passwords. Passwords should change frequently. But even firewalls are not totally hacker proof. Other systems are either available or being developed. For example, fingerprints, voice verifica-

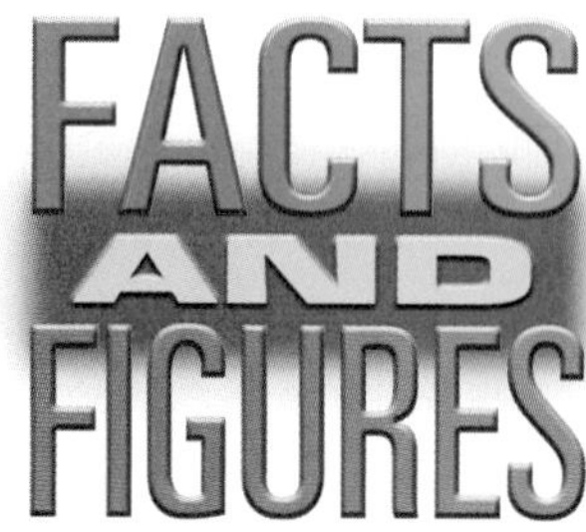

Businesses involved in e-commerce are advised to have a privacy policy, post it on their Web site, and make it well known. Companies should: give notice about what personal information is collected and how it is used; give consumers the choice about whether and how their information can be used; establish adequate security measures to provide data protection; and allow consumers to access the data about them, so they can attest to its accuracy and make changes if necessary.

ILLUSTRATION 8-3

Why is information security such a critical issue? What are some ways in which information can be protected?

tion, retina scanning, and other methods are being tested to safeguard organizational information.

INFORMATION SYSTEMS

Organizations are experiencing an information explosion. New computerized methods can gather and store more information quickly than could traditional methods. As a result, many managers suffer from information overload, the existence of more data than anyone can attend to. Information overload leads to needless costs and inefficiencies, as managers try to sort through all the available information to find what they really need to make decisions. Thus, organizations need effective means for managing information.

Employees generate business data constantly. They record sales transactions, collect customer information, and track inventory. When employees key such data into their computers, the data become part of the company's database. A **database** is a collection of data organized in a way that makes the data easy to find, update, and manage.

But a collection of data is not useful until it is processed into a form that decision makers can use. A computer system that processes data into meaningful information is called an **information system.** Three key types of information systems are management information systems, decision support systems, and executive information systems.

MANAGEMENT INFORMATION SYSTEM

A **management information system (MIS)** is an information system that integrates data from various departments to make it available to help managers with day-to-day business operations. An MIS deals with specific and highly structured data. Different departments collect and process the data. Employees enter daily transactions into the system as they occur, such as when they prepare purchase orders and record sales. From this gathered and stored information, managers can request reports to help them make daily operating decisions. For example, a sales report can show a manager where sales are slow. From this information, the manager might decide to do a special promotion for customers in this area.

DECISION SUPPORT SYSTEM

A **decision support system (DSS)** is a system that helps managers consider alternatives in making specific decisions. For example, a DSS can help a manager determine the most efficient routes for the company's delivery trucks. The ability to analyze "what if?" scenarios is a key capability of a DSS. *What if* we continue our current strategy? Would that work? *What if* we try something else? What are the likely consequences of that action? The company's management information system provides much of the information for its decision support system.

EXECUTIVE INFORMATION SYSTEM

An **executive information system (EIS)** combines and summarizes ongoing transactions within the company to provide top-level executives with information needed to make decisions affecting the present and future goals and direction of an organization. Information used in executive information systems is gathered from the MIS and DSS. An EIS collects data from both internal and external sources to help executives make decisions. For example, executives might use the EIS to collect outside information that affects the company, such as information regarding competitors, the state of the economy, and government policies. With information from inside and outside the organization, top managers make long-term decisions that help a business survive and grow.

THE EFFECTS OF TECHNOLOGY ON WORK AND WORKERS

Computers, the Internet, and other forms of electronic technology have affected our lives as consumers and as workers. The work of employees has changed because of new technological devices and because firms have restructured the ways in which they operate. Over the last several decades, computers have changed the way individuals perform work tasks, which in turn has caused anxieties in people about job security, about their ability to cope with new technology, and about electronic devices that may affect their health.

HEALTH PROBLEMS

Certain complaints arise among workers who spend most of their work time using computers and other automated equipment. Employees may complain about eyestrain, cancer-causing radiation, backaches, and hand-muscle problems. Eyestrain is likely to occur when computer operators view monitors (computer screens) for long periods. Usually, eyestrain can be reduced or eliminated by adjusting light intensity on screens, shading screens from glare, wearing glare-reducing glasses, and taking work breaks every few hours. Sitting in uncomfortable chairs for long periods can cause back problems. Hand problems are often the result of improper keyboard or chair heights. Proper chair design with good back support helps, as do special exercise routines and breaks from being seated for long periods.

Employees may also be concerned about radiation. Many types of electronic equipment such as cell phones, televisions, and computers give off modest amounts of radiation. Some studies have shown that the amount of radiation is small and therefore does not affect health. However, other studies claim computer radiation is harmful. Pregnant women are especially concerned. Many businesses assign women to non-computer jobs during pregnancy to avoid possible harm from radiation.

ILLUSTRATION 8-4

What health problems can occur when computers are used frequently? What steps can a business take to reduce such problems?

The science of adapting equipment to the work and health needs of people is called **ergonomics.** Ergonomic experts study the relationships between people and machines. For example, they work with engineers to design more comfortable chairs and to produce lighting that reduces eyestrain. In recent years, ergonomic experts have been spending much time making computer hardware, software, furniture, and lights adjustable, practical, and comfortable.

CHANGED JOBS

A major role of today's managers is to manage change. The rapid rate at which changes occur can be disruptive. To survive, businesses must be adaptable and employees must change to meet the needs of employers.

Nearly all jobs have been restructured, and new jobs are evolving. Large numbers of employees need to use computers. In turn, job tasks once done manually, such as using shorthand and typewriters, are now done on computers. Bosses who key their own messages have greatly modified the role of the secretary. For example, most secretaries have had title changes, with many becoming administrative assistants performing a variety of higher-level tasks. Many are assigned leadership roles, serve as project managers and members of work teams, and train employees on how to use electronic equipment. Similarly, other jobs have been greatly modified, with workers having far more responsibilities than during the pre-computer age.

Often employees are retrained for new jobs, but others are let go. This downsizing action creates anxiety among workers. While many firms help employees get retrained, some firms help employees find new jobs with other firms. Each new major technological change, however, creates employee anxiety. Managers must be ready to deal with this problem, because these employees may become less productive, leave, or create problems.

THE NEW JOB MARKET

Computerization has caused a reduction in the need for some skills and increased need for other skills. Today's employees must have technical skills as well as interpersonal skills. For example, employees who work at computer help desks give assistance to workers who have computer problems. Help desk employees must have "people skills," such as a friendly personality and a willingness to help others. They must also have a great deal of technical knowledge about computers and about solving software problems that employees encounter.

Other technically oriented jobs include programmer (one who creates and modifies software programs); network administrator; systems analyst (one who helps create and develop and maintain MIS, DSS, and EIS); software trainer; Web page designer; Webmaster (someone who manages and maintains a Web site); computer equipment salesperson; and computer repair person.

Telecommuters, as mentioned in Chapter 2, work at home using electronic equipment such as computers, scanners, and printers to complete their "at home" tasks. Still other individuals are entrepreneurs who start and run their own businesses from home using electronic equipment. Many of the popular Internet businesses were started from the homes of entrepreneurs.

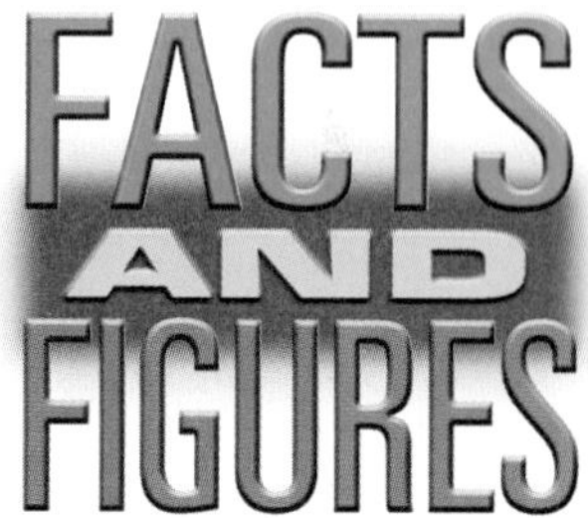

Computer scientists, computer engineers, and systems analysts are expected to be the three fastest growing occupations through the year 2006. The increase will be driven by the very rapid expansion in computer and data processing services, which is projected to be the fastest growing industry.

THE FUTURE

Computer technology is now an indispensable part of business throughout the world. Businesses either move with the technology or fade away. Well-managed firms do not stand still. How much additional change will occur during the next five to ten years? No one knows, because these are dynamic times. What is known, however, is that change is constant and is occurring at amazing speeds. Rapid change has been occurring in nearly every industry and in most countries. Slow-moving firms are attempting to catch up. Some of those are catching up by buying healthy firms or are creating joint ventures that will propel them into the 21st century.

The world is in the middle of a major shift in how to conduct business. Just as cars, planes, television, and telephones changed life during the last century, the computer is changing life in this century. It is transforming how we work and live. One of the biggest change agents in this age of transformation is the Internet. It has increased the intensity of worldwide competition. No longer can major businesses in any nation think of their markets or competitors being exclusively within their own boundaries.

The cost of producing goods and services in this electronic age has led to increased competition that has lowered prices. And computers and other electric marvels have cut paperwork, increased worker productivity, shed non-productive tasks, and maximized business efficiency. Consumers have been the beneficiaries. Even the nature of how businesses are organized and operated have been permanently affected. This Internet age, however, does not mean that all firms have closed their doors where customers might enter to see, touch, and even try before they purchase. You cannot go to a health club or a hairstylist on the Internet, but you can get advice there. You may prefer to go to the grocery store for the personal contact. But in this fast-paced world, you may prefer to buy your groceries on the Internet and have them delivered to you.

Many businesses will thrive by operating stores on Main Street and on the Internet. Like Mia Herrera in the opening story, we will have our personal digital assistants as we meet and talk with friends from our homes and cars, in restaurants, and at the mall.

CHAPTER CONCEPTS

- Computers come in all sizes, shapes, and configurations, and all need an operating system and application software to perform tasks. Advances in technology require computer systems and software to be updated often.
- The Internet is a worldwide network of linked computers that permits users to share data and information freely and quickly over phone lines or cable. The development of the World Wide Web made the Internet accessible to the non-technical general public through a Web browser and hyperlink navigation.
- The chief information officer is accountable for managing all of an organization's electronic information and supporting systems that help managers and other employees make timely and informed decisions. CIOs are responsible for keeping electronic systems up to date, safeguarding data, and making information available to managers in a form they can use to make decisions.
- Many businesses have management information systems (MIS), decision support systems (DSS), and executive information systems (ESS). An MIS integrates data from many departments, making it available to managers for day-to-day decisions. A DSS helps managers consider alternatives in making specific decisions by using "what if?" scenarios to predict results of different actions. An ESS combines and summarizes ongoing transactions within the company to help top-level managers make decisions affecting the future direction of the company.
- Computers have modified existing jobs and created new jobs. Employees have been affected in various ways, including new job and skill requirements, layoff fears, and health factors.
- The electronic world will continue to undergo vast changes. Business must adapt to technological advancements to survive.

BUILD VOCABULARY POWER

Define the following terms and concepts.

1. knowledge workers
2. data
3. information
4. computer
5. hardware
6. software
7. personal digital assistant (PDA)
8. operating system software
9. application software
10. Moore's law
11. Internet (Net)
12. World Wide Web (WWW or Web)
13. hyperlink
14. modem
15. internet service provider (ISP)
16. browser
17. search engine
18. chief information officer (CIO)
19. telecommunications (data communications)

20. local area network (LAN)
21. file server (server)
22. wide area network (WAN)
23. intranet
24. extranet
25. firewall
26. database
27. information system
28. management information system (MIS)
29. decision support system (DSS)
30. executive information system (EIS)
31. ergonomics

REVIEW FACTS

1. What are the three elements of a computer?
2. How does application software differ from operating system software?
3. What does Moore's Law predict about the computer equipment a company buys today?
4. How does the Internet differ from the World Wide Web?
5. What two things do you typically need in order to connect to the Internet?
6. What are the two main characteristics that a chief information officer must possess to be successful?
7. How does a LAN differ from a WAN?
8. Why does a CIO need to be concerned about information security?
9. What new ways are being tried to make sure that the wrong people do not gain entrance to information on a firm's computer system?
10. What kinds of data go into a management information system, and how do they get in the system?
11. How does a decision support system help managers make decisions?
12. Name three types of jobs that are available in the computer field.
13. From what kinds of electronic equipment might radiation cause damage to one's health?
14. Who have been the primary beneficiaries of the efficiencies that have resulted from the use of electronic technology by businesses?

DISCUSS IDEAS

1. How does an older type of business office differ from a computerized business office?
2. What type of employee would need a personal digital assistant at work?
3. What implications might Moore's Law have on the chief financial officer's job?
4. Assume you are exchanging ideas using e-mail with a friend. Your friend keyed "www.hp.com" and suggested it as a source of information for your next class report. What does the keyed-in information represent?

5. Using one or more search engines, find a master list of search engines. Make notes of your actions to locate the search engine list, and report your results to the class.
6. How has the development of the World Wide Web made the Internet accessible to the average person?
7. How does an intranet differ from an extranet, and how do these networks relate to the Internet?
8. Assume you work for a large business with lots of computerized equipment. It has branches in five American cities and seven foreign countries. The different branches need to share information. Discuss what you might require in terms of servers and information systems.
9. You have been made an ergonomics expert at your school. What changes would you propose that would be ergonomically sound and would most protect the health of students, teachers, and other employees?

ANALYZE INFORMATION

1. Deborah and Kenneth Parks obtained prices from the following companies for a desktop computer system with a modem for their new business.

	Computer House	*EZ-Electronics*
Computer	$1,200	$1,000
Monitor	500	550
Fax	300	275
Printer	400	350
Software programs	850	950

   a. Which company has the best total price and by how much?
   b. If the Parkses purchased each item from the company with the lowest price, what would their total cost be? How much would they pay each company?
2. The Parkses in the prior problem want to use the Internet to buy merchandise from suppliers and to set up a Web page for selling their goods. They checked the service reliability, quality, and monthly rates from three Internet service providers. Firm A charges $30, is nationally known, provides the first month of service free, and is disabled by hackers once or twice a month but is back up and running within an hour or two. Firm B charges $25 and is national but not well known. It offers no free-use time and is disabled infrequently for three to five hours; however, it offers outstanding assistance when users have questions or problems. Firm C charges $18, is much smaller, has never been disabled, offers no free-use time, and its help line is not especially good. What firm should the Parkses select? Give reasons for your answer.

3. The Onyx Corporation estimates it spends $50,000 annually to process data by using its traditional methods and equipment. A proposed computer system would cost $150,000 for equipment, software, and installation. In addition to depreciating the equipment at the rate of $30,000 per year, the company would spend $24,000 annually to process data.
   a. During the first year after installing the new computer, would it cost more or less to process data? By how much?
   b. How many years will it take to fully depreciate the equipment?
   c. What will it cost to operate the computer system during the sixth year?
   d. If the computer system is installed and lasts seven years, how much will Onyx spend in total for the computer system and how much will be saved or lost?
4. With instructions from your teacher, join other students to identify and analyze the types of computer problems your group has had. Include in your report any trouble group members have had with losing data and files from school or home computers on or off the Internet. Prepare a report to your class about the problems and indicate the security steps that should be taken to prevent or reduce these problems from happening.

5. Using a library or the Internet, find information about a specific ergonomic problem related to working with electronic equipment, such as one related to radiation from computer equipment, uncomfortable chairs, or poorly designed desks. Prepare a report of your findings.

SOLVE BUSINESS PROBLEMS

CASE 8-1

Carmen Alonso and Mary Ann Corsi were on their lunch break at work when a friend, Jan Bailey, joined them. In due time, each person expressed her concerns about trying to juggle home life with work, raising a family, and spending time with others. "It's a crazy world," Jan said. "No wonder everyone tries to keep up by being glued to cell phones." Carmen was concerned that cell phones cause accidents. Mary Ann added that she spent much time at home ordering things from the Internet. "There's almost no time for the mall or to grocery shop, let alone to spend quality time with the children." At that point, Jan launched the heated conversation that follows:

Jan: *The world has gone overboard with all this electronic technology. Yes, we use the phones and e-mail to chat with family and friends, but that's not the same as seeing people in person.*

Mary Ann: *That's better than not having cell phones or the Internet. I think these gadgets are aids, not obstacles. How else could we both work if we couldn't stay in touch, even if it's not in person?*

Carmen: *Communication is too impersonal these days, too cold. Everyone's rushing to get things done. Few people stop to have an old-fashioned conversation. I wish we could turn the calendars back 25 years when people just sat around and chatted.*

Mary Ann: *But you wouldn't have all the luxuries we have today. You'd be wasting time chatting. The Internet allows you to get so much more done. I'll bet my parents would have loved to have what we have.*

Carmen: *Mine refuse to learn to use the new technology. They're very happy without the gadgets.*

Jan: *I agree with Carmen's parents sometimes. We have new problems, like worrying about someone stealing our personal records, destroying our files, and crashing our computers. Those can be expensive problems in terms of time, money, and invasion of privacy.*

Think Critically:

1. Design a simple set of questions that you could ask people about the advantages and disadvantages of having much new technology to use away from work. Ask your parents, grandparents, or other similarly aged adults to answer your questions and to comment on life today versus the past, when computers may not have made much of an impact. Prepare a report for your class.
2. Do you tend to agree more with Jan, Mary Ann, or Carmen? Explain why you feel the way you do. Which person most likes and which most dislikes today's technological times?
3. Answer these questions about yourself:
   a. What electronic equipment such as cell phones, computers, access to the Internet, scanners, digital cameras, or other devices do you personally have readily available to you seven days a week?
   b. Which one piece of electronic equipment is *most* valuable and which is *least* valuable to you? Explain why.
   c. If you had the money to buy one additional new piece of electronic equipment, what would it be and how would it benefit you in terms of school or work?
4. Use your library or the Internet to find information that deals with the topic of how electronic equipment contributes to the possible depersonalization of everyday life. Report the results to your class.

CASE 8-2

Ai-ling Shen and Jack Compton are both employed at the Waterside Company, a small life insurance firm. Both Ai-ling and Jack have been with the business for over ten years but are now quite upset by recent events. The office manager announced yesterday that all employees must attend several all-day training sessions on two forthcoming changes. A new computer system is replacing the old one, and jobs are being restructured to improve processes that will lead to greater efficiencies and enhanced productivity.

Unlike past practice, the new plan will have each person in the office doing all of the tasks now done separately. The training will prepare them to do everyone else's work, but all work will be done on the computer. To even the workload, all ten standard insurance policies will be loaded in each computer, and employees and salespersons will be assigned specific customers on an alphabetic basis. Then, when a salesperson calls with questions, the designated office worker can find the answers immediately. With the old system, answers might take as long as two weeks to get to customers.

The new computerized system has been installed but will not be used until the employees are all trained. They have just returned from the first day's training session. The following conversation takes place:

Jack: *I don't know about you, Ai-ling, but this change is just like coming to an entirely new job. I don't know how all of this is going to work out.*

Ai-ling: *We should have at least been told about this in advance, rather than have it come as a complete surprise. We could easily get a job at another insurance company. Maybe we should quit. The company isn't willing to give us more money to learn all the new procedures, new software, and new computers. With our experience, we shouldn't have any trouble finding a new job.*

Jack: *Hold on, Ai-ling. We shouldn't be too hasty. We make good money here. I agree, however, that they should have told us about this so we could have been doing some reading and getting ourselves ready for the change. If the system works well, our jobs will be more secure. Most other insurance companies already operate the new way.*

Ai-ling: *From what we learned today, we could certainly make the company sorry that they didn't get our opinions before deciding to change computers and our jobs.*

Think Critically:

1. Describe what mistake the Waterside Company management made in replacing the computer system.
2. In what ways could Ai-ling make the company regret not involving the employees in the decision? Explain.
3. If the new computer system is to be successful, will it be because of restructuring the work, installing a new computer system, or both? Explain your answer.
4. If the new changes are successful, how will the salespeople and customers benefit?

PROJECT: MY BUSINESS, INC.

As the owner of a new business, you will spend a great deal of time dealing with information. Poorly organized business records would make it hard for you to find and use the information you need. Use the following activities to review information management systems for small businesses and make decisions about how technology will benefit your business.

DATA COLLECTION

1. Interview an owner of a small business. Discuss the type of information management system used in that business. Identify (a) the type of records and information maintained, (b) whether or not the system is computer based, (c) who is responsible for information management, and (d) how the system could be improved.
2. Visit a computer systems retailer and discuss the hardware and software the retailer recommends for new small businesses. Collect information on system prices, capabilities, and ease of operation.
3. Using the Yellow Pages or the Internet, identify businesses that offer information management services for businesses. Contact one company and determine the types of services offered and prices charged for those services.

ANALYSIS

1. The Internet can be a very valuable tool for small businesses. Identify and describe five specific types of information, accessible through the Internet, that can help you develop and manage your business. Then use an Internet search engine to identify one or more sites that supply each type of information you listed. Bookmark each location (use a diskette to store your bookmarks) so you can easily revisit the sites.
2. List three ways that e-commerce might have a negative effect on your business and three ways that you might use e-commerce to improve your new business.

E-COMMERCE

OBJECTIVES

- **9-1** Describe the recent growth of the Internet.
- **9-2** Discuss common business uses of the Internet besides selling products.
- **9-3** Describe the stages businesses commonly go through in developing an e-commerce business.
- **9-4** Identify successful e-commerce businesses and strategies.
- **9-5** Outline the steps for starting a new e-commerce business.

THE CASE FOR CYBER COMMERCE

Turan Ozmat sat in the Chamber of Commerce meeting only half-listening to the presentation. The speaker was talking about the use of the Internet by businesses. She had just made the statement that any business without a presence on the Web would be at a competitive disadvantage in the next few years.

Turan thought of his photography studio and believed the speaker couldn't be talking about that type of business. His business required personal contact between the photographer and the customer. Customers wanted to be able to come into the studio and see the quality of the portraits and photos as well as the settings and backgrounds that Turan used. Whether people were scheduling a wedding, family portraits, or students' graduation photos, Turan believed that face-to-face meetings always allowed him to understand the customer's needs and to develop the customer's trust and confidence. He didn't see how any of that could be possible with the Internet.

When Turan returned to his business that afternoon, he still was thinking about the speaker's comments. Even though he felt his business was different, he didn't want to miss an opportunity. He sat down at his computer, typed "photographer" into a search engine, and was amazed at the results. The search engine returned over 100,000 hits! Turan narrowed the search by typing in the name of his city. Immediately, three of his competitors' business names popped on the screen. Turan decided he would spend the weekend exploring how other photography businesses were using the Internet.

People are sitting down at their computers in ever-increasing numbers to use the Internet. Sometimes it is hard to believe that the Internet has a relatively short history. It developed from the first efforts to link computers less than 50 years ago. The introduction of the personal computer in the late 1970s began to expand computer access onto business desktops and into homes. Today, through low-cost or free connections to the Internet, millions of people throughout the world can instantly access information and communicate with each other.

The Internet has become a very important business tool. **E-commerce** means doing business online. It includes the use of the Internet to buy and sell products as well as exchange business-related information, such as transmitting purchase orders electronically or advertising online. E-commerce is now a multi-billion-dollar part of our economy.

The Internet has allowed many small businesses to compete with larger, established companies and to reach consumers all over the world. While currently less than 1 percent of all business sales are completed using the Internet, that figure is growing rapidly. Businesses need to plan for e-commerce.

THE GROWTH OF THE INTERNET

Since its infancy as a military and research tool in the 1950s, the Internet has grown impressively, as shown in Figure 9-1. Over 10,000,000 Web

ILLUSTRATION 9-1

Why is the Internet a very important tool to small businesses?

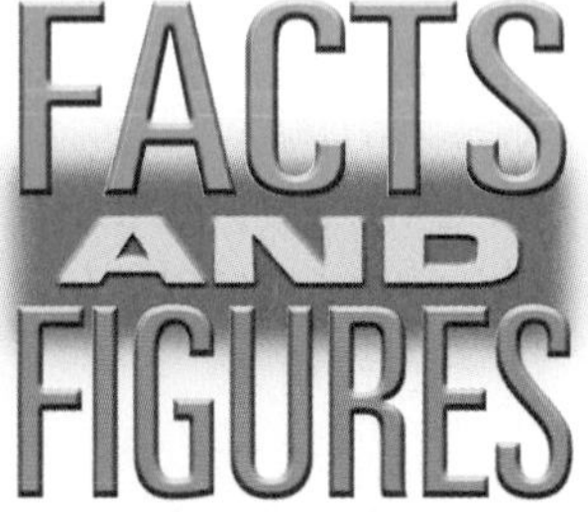

E-commerce experts believe that there is a tremendous amount of money to be made in online business-to-business selling. They attribute this to the fact that selling to businesses is more cost effective than to individual consumers; orders from businesses are, on the average, higher in dollar value; and businesses order larger quantities of an item.

sites were available at the end of the 1900s, with millions more being added each year. Since the invention of the World Wide Web in the late 1960s, access to the Internet has grown to an estimated 500 million people around the world. Almost 50 million homes in the U.S. had access to the Internet in 2000, up from just 13 million in 1995. The U.S. leads the world in Internet use, with approximately 40 percent of all users. However, Internet users are found all over the world, as shown in Figure 9-2.

Business use of the Internet is increasing rapidly as well. While there are many other business uses of the Internet, as we will discuss in the next section, an important measure of business Internet use is the sale of products and services. According to the U.S. Department of Commerce, U.S. Internet sales to consumers in 1998 totaled $8 billion. That seems like a very large figure, until it is compared to the business-to-business Internet sales in the same year. Business-to-business (B2B) sales totaled $45 billion. Still, there is a great deal of room for growth in the Internet sale of products and services. The total sales to consumers represent less than 1 percent of all consumer purchases. Internet sales worldwide are expected to reach two trillion dollars by 2005, with nearly 200 million regular Internet customers. Some experts say even that estimate is low.

FIGURE 9-1

The Growth of the Internet

Year	1970	1980	1990	2000
Estimated number of Web site providers	4	200	300,000	10,000,000

Source: *U.S. Department of Commerce*

RANK	COUNTRY	% OF USERS
1	United States	42.9%
2	Japan	6.9%
3	United Kingdom	5.4%
4	Canada	5.1%
5	Germany	4.7%
6	Australia	2.7%
7	Brazil	2.6%
8	China	2.4%
9	France	2.2%
10	South Korea	2.2%

Source: *Computer Industry Almanac*

FIGURE 9-2

Countries with the Most Internet Users in 2000

BUSINESS USES OF THE INTERNET

In the opening scenario, Turan didn't believe the Internet was useful for his photography business. Like many of us, he was considering only the ways he could sell his products using the Web and not the many other uses of the Internet. While the use of the Internet for selling products is important, businesses can benefit from this new tool in many other ways. Those uses include communications, information gathering, and improving business operations.

BUSINESS COMMUNICATIONS

Businesses use the Internet most for communication, both within and outside the company. Most internal communications on the Internet are completed using e-mail. But new tools are available to assist with communications, including videophones and software that allows several people to share application software and collaborate using text and graphics tools while sitting at their computers. Using the Internet, a company can post an employee newsletter online. This speeds the information to all employees while reducing the mailing and distribution costs. Employees can quickly send reports, memos,

ILLUSTRATION 9-2

For what purpose do businesses use the Internet most frequently?

and other information to co-workers.

Companies use the Internet to communicate with current and potential customers. The Internet has become an important way to provide information about the company and its products to customers. Remember in the chapter-opening story that when Turan was searching for information on photographers, he quickly located the Web sites of three of his local competitors. As customers try to locate specific products and businesses, they are increasingly turning to the Internet. Even those who use telephone directories to identify businesses often want more information than is typically included in a directory advertisement. By using the Internet, a customer can often obtain product descriptions, determine the days and hours a business is open, and even print a map showing the location of the business. Today, if a business has not posted information about its business, location, and products and services on the Internet, it will likely miss some customers.

Businesses also communicate with each other using the Internet. Business people send e-mail messages, exchange documents, and sell their company's products and services to other businesses. Common business-to-business services offered via the Internet include online training, financial planning and accounting, maintaining personnel records, and data processing.

INFORMATION GATHERING

A second business use of the Internet is for research. You have probably used the Internet to gather information for a project or report. Businesses also use the Internet to obtain information they need in order to make decisions. A great deal of information on the Internet is free and is provided by government agencies, colleges and universities, libraries, and even private businesses. Other information that businesses need can be purchased from companies specializing in research, from professional and trade associations, and from publishers. For example, Dun & Bradstreet provides specialized research reports, information, and publications for businesses.

Businesses can also gather information on current and prospective customers. When companies sell products, they often encourage purchasers to complete a product registration or warranty online. People who regularly use the Internet are more likely to complete a product registration if it is online than if they have to fill in a registration card by hand and mail it. The registration process allows the company to collect important information about the customer, including address, telephone number, and even an e-mail address. That information is valuable in future communications and promotional activities with customers. Also, the company can gather information on where the product was purchased, the price, reasons for purchasing the product, and other related products the consumer currently owns or plans to purchase.

Many Web sites include a place where prospective customers can request information, be placed on an e-mail or mailing list, or obtain answers to specific questions. That capability allows the company to develop a list of prospective customers and determine their specific interests. The information can be used for future communications and promotions.

Competitive information is easier to obtain using the Internet. A great deal of information is contained in many businesses' Web pages. It is relatively easy to learn about the competitors' products, prices, credit terms, distribution policies, and the types of customer services offered. Some Web sites provide information on product tests, offer comparisons and reviews of products, and even have places for consumers to discuss their experiences with a company and its products.

CYBER COMMUNICATION

Because of the simplicity involved in sending and receiving e-mail, many messages are brief and casual. However, in a business setting, e-mail should be used with care. Your managers and colleagues will use your messages to judge your on-the-job performance. Don't send messages just because you can.

In business, e-mail is generally used in the following ways:

- **To provide a record of certain events that have occurred or specific things that have been said.**
- **To advise supervisors or peers on particular topics or procedures.**
- **To direct others to do something specific.**
- **To state company policy and explain procedures.**
- **To pass on information.**
- **To promote goodwill.**

ACTIVITY **Look at the list above that shows how e-mail can be used in business circumstances. Select one of the situations, and describe—verbally or in writing—a possible scenario that would fit that situation. For example, as a supervisor, you might send an e-mail to an employee, directing that person to call a vendor about an undelivered shipment of merchandise.**

IMPROVING BUSINESS OPERATIONS

The Internet has become an important tool to improve business operations and control costs. Salespeople can log on to the company's Web site and determine whether a certain product is in inventory for delivery to a customer. When a product is sold, the order can immediately be entered into the computer from anywhere in the world to speed the processing and shipping of the order. A production manager can access the records of a transportation company to see when an expected shipment of raw materials will be delivered. An accountant in a branch office can download financial statements from the main computer to compare current financial performance with last year's information. Product designers from three countries can collaborate on a new design by examining a three-dimensional drawing online and making changes that each of them can see instantly.

Small businesses can benefit competitively from the use of the Internet due to the rapid exchange of information. For example, several small automotive parts retailers can consolidate their orders through an e-business wholesaler by submitting information on needed parts via the Internet. Then the wholesaler can place a very large order with the manufacturer and receive a significant price reduction for each of the retailers. This can be done almost instantly with online order processing. In addition to the lower costs, the needed parts get to the retailers quickly, rather than taking days and weeks under older purchasing methods.

The Internet has proven to be an important tool in reducing the cost of several business activities. A recent government report identified the following cost savings to businesses when customers used the Internet:

Ordering airline tickets	87% savings
Online banking	89% savings
Paying bills	67% savings
Distributing software	99% savings

STAGES OF E-COMMERCE DEVELOPMENT

A company that does almost all of its business activities through the Internet is often referred to as a **dot-com business.** The name "dot com" comes from the end of a commercial business's Web address: *.com*. While a growing number of dot-com companies have received a great deal of publicity (Amazon.com, Priceline.com, Ameritrade.com), most businesses use the Internet for only a portion of their activities. Businesses that complete most of their business activities at a physical location rather than through the Internet are referred to as **bricks-and-mortar businesses.** The name "bricks-and-mortar" suggests that the company conducts most of its business in an actual building.

Businesses generally progress through three stages as they develop their e-commerce presence on the Internet: (1) They begin by offering information only. (2) Then they progress to interactive capabilities and finally (3) to full integration of business transactions on the Web. Figure 9-3 summarizes these stages.

INFORMATION STAGE

Most existing businesses first begin using the Internet for e-commerce by developing a basic Web site. The site often is quite simple—only one or a very few pages. It provides basic information about the company that might typically be included in an advertisement or brochure. Customers can use the Web site when trying to locate information about where they can purchase specific products and to learn more about the

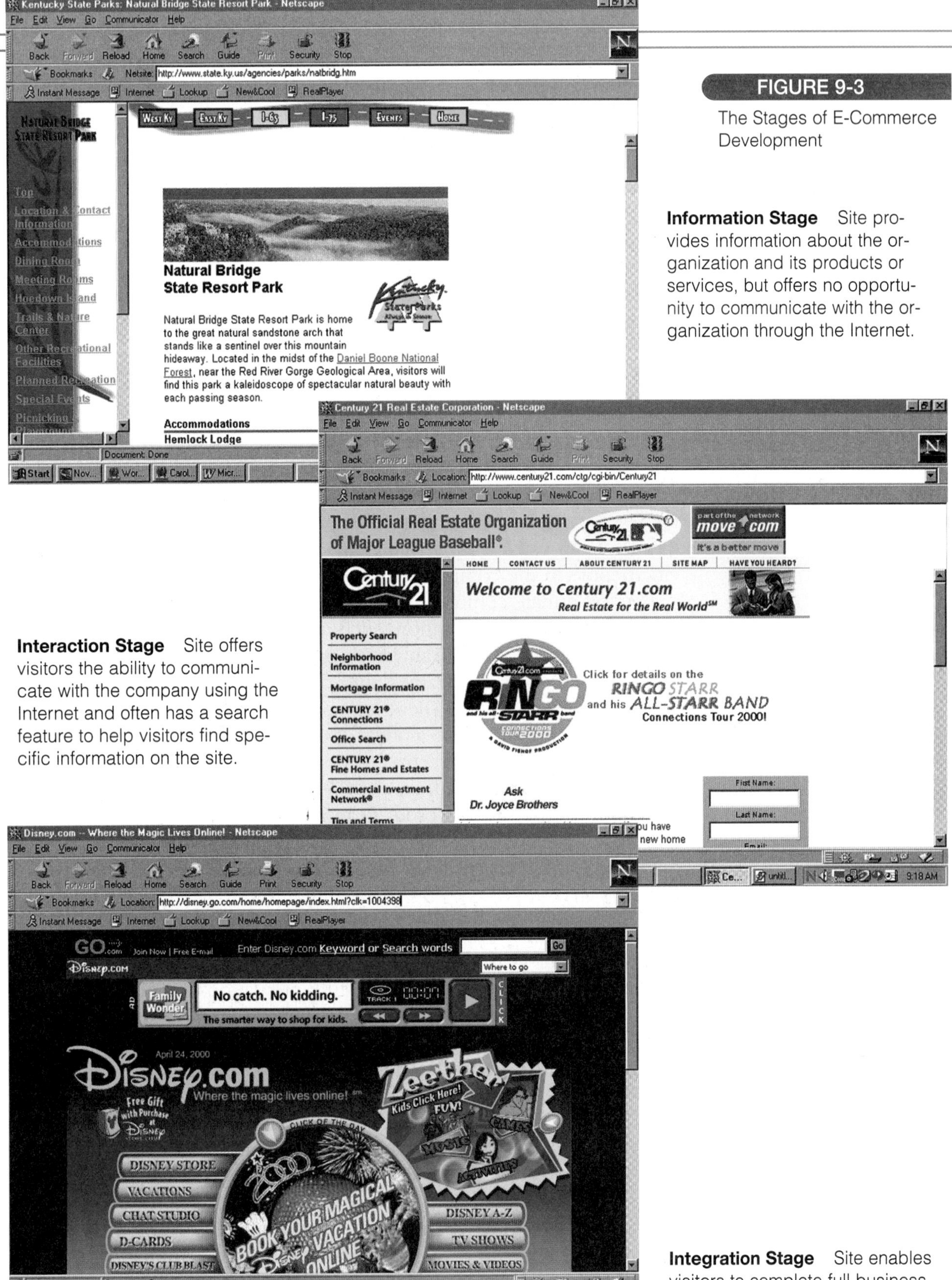

FIGURE 9-3

The Stages of E-Commerce Development

Information Stage Site provides information about the organization and its products or services, but offers no opportunity to communicate with the organization through the Internet.

Interaction Stage Site offers visitors the ability to communicate with the company using the Internet and often has a search feature to help visitors find specific information on the site.

Integration Stage Site enables visitors to complete full business transactions using the Internet.

company and its products. As the company gains more experience with the Internet, it will add additional information with *hyperlinks* (also called *links*) from the home page. The company might add complete product descriptions, information on payment methods, customer services, and even product manuals, updates, and procedures for obtaining product upgrades.

The limitation of the first stage of e-commerce development is that customers cannot use the Web site to interact with the business. They must still visit the business in person or use the telephone, mail, or other traditional methods to obtain information that is not on the Web site or to make a purchase.

INTERACTION STAGE

The second stage of e-commerce development is interaction. In addition to providing information, the site offers visitors the ability to interact with the company using the Web site. The first type of interaction is the use of e-mail. Site visitors click a link to bring up an e-mail form that they can use to request information, ask questions, or contact specific people in the company.

Beyond e-mail, companies can add a database, where customers can search for specific information, such as choices of brands, product features, and services. They can check product availability, calculate product costs and shipping charges, and determine how long it will take to have an order delivered. There may even be three-dimensional photos, short video clips, or simple models of products for customers to examine.

It is possible with interactive e-commerce for customers to place orders using information from the Web site, but not place the orders directly from the site. An order form may be included on the site along with a product catalog. Customers can complete, print, and then fax or mail the form to the company.

INTEGRATION STAGE

Companies that want to take full advantage of the Internet in their business move to full integration. With full integration, the entire customer transaction can be completed using the Internet. Customers can get necessary product, pricing, and shipping information. They can place an order and pay for the order, track their shipment until it is delivered, and obtain customer assistance following the sale—all using the Internet. Companies with integrated business activities do not have to be dot-com companies. Much of their business can still be accomplished through traditional methods. But customers will be able to complete their business transactions with the company using the Internet if they choose.

Consider how Turan Ozmot can begin to use the Internet in his photography business. Since competitors are already using the Internet, he should at least develop a Web page and advertise on the Web in order to make prospective customers aware of his business and the services he offers. He could include examples of his photos and portraits on the Web site. As Turan gains more experience with the Internet, he may find ways to build customer interaction into the site. Turan may choose not to have a fully integrated Web site, but he may be able to sell some types of products online, such as reprints of photos and related products such as frames and photo albums.

ILLUSTRATION 9-3

What does it mean if a company has a fully integrated e-commerce presence on the Internet?

SUCCESS WITH E-COMMERCE

Although e-commerce is still very young, it has already had a major impact on the way business is done. New types of businesses have appeared, offering products and services that did not exist prior to the Internet. Web design companies, Internet service providers (ISPs), and Web security businesses are some of these new types of businesses.

Web-based business activities have resulted in many new kinds of jobs as well. Today, you can become a Webmaster or Web applications developer, which wasn't possible just a few years ago. In 1999, over 2 million people worked in jobs directly related to the development and management of Internet operations in companies. Nearly 1 million more worked in positions that support companies' new e-commerce activities.

Companies such as Dell Computer Corporation and Charles Schwab investment brokerage company have emerged as industry leaders as a result of their moves into e-commerce. New companies including Amazon.com, eBay.com, and Buy.com have formed in order to take advantage of this new type of business activities.

LEADING INTERNET BUSINESSES

As you learned earlier, consumers currently purchase billions of dollars of products over the Internet each year. Customers are more likely to purchase certain types of products online than others. The top Internet retailers for 1999 are listed in Figure 9-4. As you can see, books, computer hardware and software, and music are the most frequently purchased items.

While most of the companies on the list sell computer hardware and software, several well-known bricks-and-mortar companies have moved

FIGURE 9-4

Top Internet Retailers in 1999

WEB SITE	TYPE OF BUSINESS	ESTIMATED ANNUAL SALES
Ebay.com	Online auctions	$1.3 billion
Amazon.com	Bookstore	1.1 billion
Dell.com	Computer manufacturer	600 million
Buy.com	Consumer electronics	400 million
OnSale.com	Computers & software	350 million
Gateway.com	Computer manufacturer	300 million
Egghead.com	Computers & software	200 million
Barnesandnoble.com	Books and CDs	175 million
CDNow.com	CDs and movies	175 million
AOL.com	Varied merchandise	150 million

Source: *Stores magazine*

into the top 20 of Internet retailers. They include The Gap, Lands' End, and Wal-Mart. Other rapidly growing product categories for consumer purchases on the Internet are travel, investing, insurance, and toys.

In business-to-business Internet sales, computers and electronics have the highest sales volume, as they do in consumer sales. The other top categories in business sales are utilities (electricity and gas), petroleum and chemicals, vehicles, office supplies, and shipping services.

Another rapidly growing area of Internet sales is advertising. In 1998, businesses spent less than 2 billion dollars to advertise their products and services on the Internet. By 2003, that figure is expected to grow to $15 billion or more. Among the top Internet advertisers are Microsoft, Amazon.com, Yahoo!, Barnes and Noble, and E*Trade. Some advertising costs are hidden, since many small Internet businesses use bartering to place their ads on another Web site. In return, they run advertisements for the cooperating businesses on their Web site. No money is exchanged between the companies to pay for the advertising.

You have probably noticed when you go online that the Internet is filled with advertisements. Since space on a Web page is limited, companies compete for the attention of Internet users. They will try to place their advertisements on pages that prospective customers are most likely to visit. They also use creative advertising designs. Varied sizes, colors, and placements of advertisements encourage Internet users to stop and read the company's information. Advertisements now include moving text and graphics plus links to more detailed information.

The Internet Advertising Bureau has established standards for the size and appearance of Internet advertisements. Internet advertising is measured in pixels. A **pixel,** short for PIX (picture) ELement, is one or more dots that act as the smallest unit on a video display screen. Some of the common sizes of Internet ads are illustrated in Figure 9-5.

MEETING CUSTOMER NEEDS

E-commerce is still a very new method of conducting business for both companies and consumers. As with anything new, only a small percentage of businesses and consumers are willing to try the Internet. From the successes and failures of the first e-commerce efforts, we can learn how to be more successful.

FIGURE 9-5

Sizes of Common Internet Advertisements

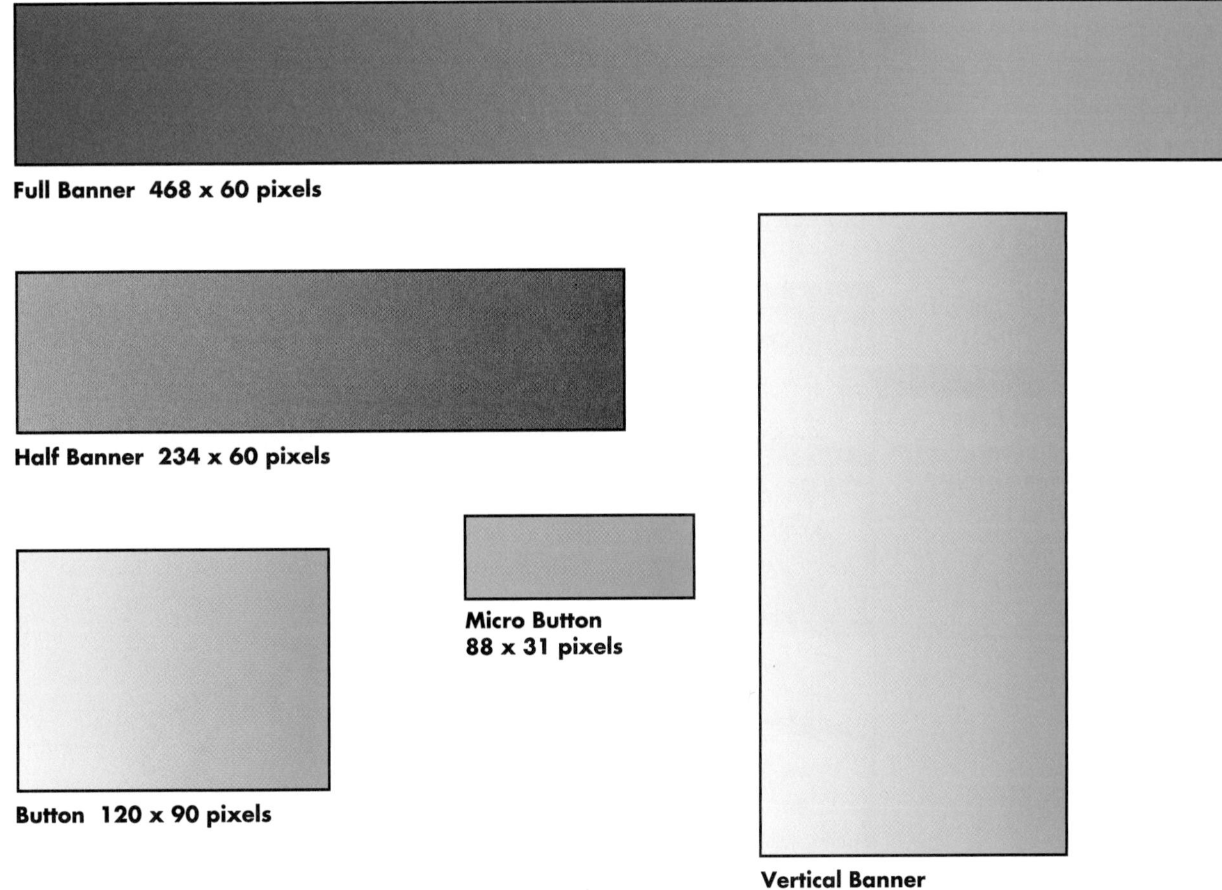

Most people today are not using the Internet to purchase products. In fact, only 2 percent of Internet users say they go online with the specific intention to make a purchase. Over 80 percent say their primary reason for going online is communication. If they are interested in purchasing products, consumers are more likely to use the Internet to gather information and to compare alternatives. Then many will go to a local business to make the purchase.

The primary reasons consumers report that they do not shop online are security concerns, difficulty in making purchases using the Internet, and a belief that they will receive poor customer service if there are problems with the order or the product. To be successful with e-commerce, businesses must create Web sites that move customers from information-gathering to making a purchase. Customers will need to have confidence that the shopping experience will be positive and trouble free.

Online shoppers are often very loyal to specific businesses and brands. They usually prefer to shop at the same businesses and buy the same brands that they have traditionally purchased. However, they will switch to other businesses and brands if the online shopping experience is not satisfactory. Consumers list the following factors as important in maintaining their loyalty to an e-commerce business:

1. An understandable, easy-to-use Web site
2. Getting products quickly after ordering them
3. Familiar businesses and brand names
4. Useful and accurate information

On the other hand, the factors that will cause customers to switch to another company for their online purchases are:

ILLUSTRATION 9-4

What are some reasons why consumers might be loyal to particular e-commerce businesses?

1. Out-of-date or limited information
2. Slow response time in answering questions, processing orders, and shipping merchandise
3. A Web site that is very slow or frequently does not work
4. Poor customer service

Advertising, careful pricing, and even online coupons are proving to be important in encouraging consumers to try online buying. Most important, however, is an inviting, easy-to-use Web site with effective customer service. If consumers have a bad experience with a company's online sales, it is very difficult to get them to come back. Consumers say that low prices and special offers will not influence them to use an online business again if they have had a bad shopping experience.

Because of the growth of the Internet and e-commerce, many organizations have begun to identify the best Web page designs and most effective online business sites. The Webby Awards were developed by the International Academy of Digital Arts and Sciences to recognize the best Web sites each year. This association presents awards in a large number of categories, including "commerce," which identifies the best business uses of the Web. Experts select one set of awards, and consumers vote on another set.

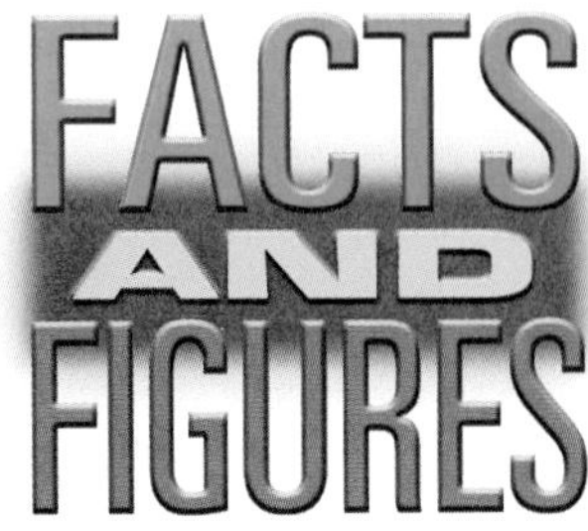

Sales copy on a business's Web site should be short and to the point. Paragraphs should be limited to fewer than 10 lines each. Use bulleted lists, indented paragraphs, bold or colored type, and other devices to break up copy.

ESTABLISHING AN E-COMMERCE BUSINESS

Developing an effective e-business requires careful planning. It is not easy to get people to buy from an online business, especially if it is a new business with which customers are not familiar. Large businesses invest millions of dollars in creating and managing their Internet operations. Small businesses can create attractive, professional-looking Web sites themselves for much less, using commercially available Web authoring software. Whether businesses create their sites themselves or hire professional Web designers to do it, they must still carefully plan the design and content of their site, and update it regularly to keep customers coming back.

If you own a small business and want to establish an e-commerce Web site, you should follow these steps to help insure its success:

1. Determine the purpose of your Web site.
2. Study your customers, their needs, and their Internet experience.
3. Plan your online business.
4. Obtain a Web server and domain name.
5. Develop order processing and customer service procedures.
6. Design the Web site.
7. Advertise your online business.
8. Open for business.

DETERMINE THE PURPOSE OF YOUR WEB SITE

You may want to have your entire business on the Internet or you may want to use it only to promote your bricks-and-mortar business and provide information to prospective customers. Some products and services are easier to sell over the Internet than others. Study the sites of similar businesses and talk to experts in e-commerce to determine whether to use the Internet for a limited set of business activities at first and progress gradually toward full integration, or limit your goals for your site to the informational or interactive stage.

STUDY YOUR CUSTOMERS

To develop an online business that your customers will use, you must first know who your customers are, what they want, and their interest in doing business online. You will want to know their experience with e-commerce and whether they use the Internet primarily for information or for shopping. What products do they typically buy online, and which are they more likely to buy from a bricks-and-mortar business? The ages of prospective customers are important as well. Younger consumers are often more comfortable with the use of computers, while older shoppers may be reluctant to purchase online. You need to understand your customers in order to design a Web site that is inviting to them and gives them confidence to purchase from your business.

PLAN YOUR ONLINE BUSINESS

Based on your study, you will determine what products and services to offer through your online business and whether you will have an information-only, interactive, or integrated Web site. If your entire business is not going to be online, you must determine where and how the bricks-and-mortar part of your business will operate.

Another decision is whether you will complete all activities yourself or use other businesses for some of them. For example, most e-commerce businesses use transportation companies such as FedEx or UPS to ship their merchandise. Others use banks or other financial institutions to process credit card transactions and collect payment from customers.

OBTAIN A SERVER AND DOMAIN NAME

An Internet business relies on computer technology for operations. In Chapter 8, you learned about servers—computers that contain the software and store the data for networks. A Web server is the backbone of an e-commerce business. In addition to the server, the Internet site must be easily accessible to a number of customers at one time, any time of the day. If customers cannot access the Web site whenever they want or if it has technical problems, they will not return to your online business.

Because many new and small businesses do not have adequate computer or network technology or do not have the needed technical skills to build and manage a Web site, they use a Web-hosting service. A **Web-hosting service** is a private business that maintains the Web sites of individuals and organizations on its computers for a fee. The Web-hosting service often provides design services, the hardware and software needed to maintain Web sites, and the technical personnel to make sure the Web sites operate effectively.

To open your Web business, you will need an Internet address to locate your site. A Web-site owner's unique Internet address is its **domain name.** Most Internet addresses for businesses use the following format—www.*businessname*.com. Before you can use a domain name, you must register it with one of several companies that maintain and approve all domain names used throughout the world. Registration currently costs $35 per year. Many possible domain names have already been registered, so you may not get your first choice. Also, individuals have registered many popular names and specific words related to products and services, hoping they can sell the domain name at a sizeable profit to a business wanting to use that name.

DEVELOP ORDER PROCESSING AND PROCEDURES

If your business will process orders and collect payments online, you will need specialized software. Many companies offer software that enables the use of **electronic shopping carts.** These are specialized programs that keep track of shoppers' selections as they shop, provide an order form for them to complete, and submit the form to the company through the Internet.

Also, you will need a secure server to accept credit card payments while protecting your customers' personal data from theft. Your business will need a process to quickly check the customers' credit and approve credit card purchases. You will also want to offer customers the alternative of paying by check if they are not comfortable with using a credit card online.

After the order has been accepted, you will need a process for quickly and accurately filling the order and delivering it to the customer. Also, customers will expect you to accept returns, replace products damaged in shipment, and offer other services to make sure their shopping experience is positive.

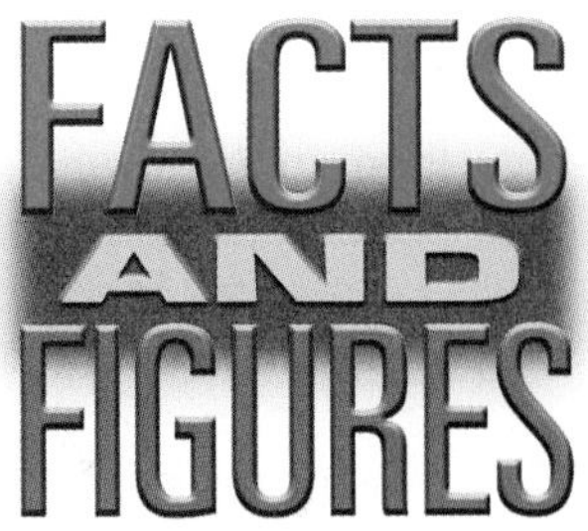

If consumers pay by credit or charge card online, their transactions are protected by the Fair Credit Billing Act. Under this law, consumers have the right to dispute charges under certain circumstances and temporarily withhold payment while the creditor is investigating them.

DESIGN THE WEB SITE

This step in developing an online business may seem to be out of order. Many people want to design their Web pages as the first step. However, until you plan the business completely, you will not know what needs to go on your Web site. Remember, to be successful, Web sites must be attractive and easy to use. If customers cannot find the information they need, if the site takes a long time to load, or if ordering instructions are confusing, prospective customers will leave your site and go to a competitor's business.

ETHICAL ISSUES

TAX FAIRNESS AND E-COMMERCE

Sales of products and services on the Internet have exceeded almost everyone's expectations. While e-commerce sales of both consumer products and business products are a very small percentage of the total sales of goods and services in the U.S., there is a mounting complaint from bricks-and-mortar retailers and from state and local government officials. The complaint—e-commerce companies are not currently required to collect sales taxes on the products they sell over the Internet, although some states require them to do so when they sell to customers within their home state.

Sales tax in most states is a small percentage of the cost of the purchase, usually 3-5 percent. So why should this tax matter to other businesses and to the government? Just look at the total amount of dollars spent on Internet purchases. When you total all of the purchases and apply the sales tax rate, it amounts to millions of dollars. State governments are missing out on those dollars that would help them balance their budgets.

Bricks-and-mortar businesses say it is unfair competition. Sales tax increases the price of products to customers. Traditional businesses believe that if e-commerce businesses don't have to collect sales tax from customers, they can sell their products for less, giving them an unfair advantage. Traditional businesses feel that if they must collect and pay the tax, e-commerce companies should as well.

On the other hand, e-commerce businesses say that customers already pay taxes for access to the Internet. Telephone companies and Internet Service Providers that provide connections to the Internet are required to collect federal and state taxes on their services. E-commerce companies also suggest that eliminating sales tax does not reduce the cost of products purchased online, since they charge shipping and handling costs that are much higher than the amount of the sales tax.

It would be very difficult for an Internet business to collect sales taxes imposed by each state and city. The tax rate would differ for each location and might change regularly. Each business would have to collect the correct amount of tax based on where the customer lives and then send the tax to the correct state or city.

THINK CRITICALLY

1. Currently in many states, some products (such as food and newspapers) are not subjected to sales tax while other products (such as automobiles and business equipment) have a lower sales tax rate. Do you agree that all businesses should be treated equally in the amount of taxes they are required to collect? Why or why not?
2. What effect, if any, do you believe it will have on Internet sales if e-businesses are required to collect sales taxes? Justify your answer.
3. Use the Internet to find recent information on the status of taxation of e-commerce sales by the federal government as well as by your state and city.

Web sites should use a basic design with easy-to-understand buttons and links. If customers can purchase products through the Web site, the shopping and ordering procedures should be very obvious and simple. Shoppers should be assured of security and customer service.

ILLUSTRATION 9-5

Why is designing a Web site not the first step in developing an online business?

ADVERTISE YOUR ONLINE BUSINESS

As with any new business, prospective customers will not know your online business exists without advertising and promotion. Two steps will help you promote your online business. First, register your business with the major search engines, such as Yahoo, Excite, AltaVista, and Infoseek. Each search engine has an electronic means for collecting site addresses and categorizing them by key words, so that Web visitors can find them. However, you can make sure the search engines include your site under appropriate key words by registering it with them directly. You can find registration information at the search engines sites.

The second step is to advertise and promote your e-commerce business. It is important to place advertising for your business in other Internet locations where prospective customers are likely to search for information related to the products and services you sell. You may want to sponsor sites that are popular with the people you would like to attract to your business. Make sure your Web address is included in all materials your business distributes and in all advertising you do.

FACTS AND FIGURES

Online entrepreneurs can ask themselves these questions when evaluating the shopping experience on their sites: Are there good pictures of all the products? Is ordering easy, and is the site navigation clear? Does the site look professional? Does the site offer something people can't get elsewhere?

OPEN FOR BUSINESS

After careful planning, you are now ready to open your Internet business. As with any business, you will have to maintain the Web site and update it regularly. You will want to keep in contact with customers to make sure they are pleased with your site and with their purchase experiences. Watch competitors to keep up-to-date with the products and services they are offering. Keep up with the latest technology and online business procedures to make sure your e-commerce business continues to be successful.

CHAPTER 9 REVIEW

CHAPTER CONCEPTS

- The Internet is growing rapidly, with over 500 million people worldwide who have access to the Internet and 10 million Web sites available at the end of the 1990s. Business is moving to the Internet as well. By 2000, online retail sales totaled over $8 billion dollars and business-to-business online sales topped $45 billion. Those figures are expected to increase dramatically each year.
- Buying and selling merchandise is not the primary use of the Internet for either consumers or businesses. Consumers use the Internet most frequently for communications and to gather information. Businesses use the Internet to communicate internally and externally, to gather information about prospective customers and other businesses, and to improve business operations.
- The growth of e-commerce has led to a number of new businesses and new jobs that would not exist without the Internet. Those jobs include the design and management of Web sites and the administration of Web security. Traditional businesses have also begun to use the Internet to advertise, to provide customer information, and even to buy and sell products and services.
- Online customers will be loyal to businesses that have easy-to-use Web sites, provide shopping security, and offer efficient delivery and customer service. However, if customers have problems with an online business, they are likely to switch to a competitor or use a bricks-and-mortar business.
- Planning your e-commerce business begins by determining how you want to use the Internet and studying your customers. With this information, you can then plan your online business. You will need special hardware and software to run your site and procedures for processing orders and delivering your products. Next, you must design and advertise your site. Finally, you are ready to open your e-commerce site for business.

BUILD VOCABULARY POWER

Define the following terms and concepts.

1. e-commerce
2. dot-com business
3. bricks-and-mortar business
4. pixel
5. Web-hosting service
6. domain name
7. electronic shopping carts

REVIEW FACTS

1. Was the approximate number of U.S. homes with access to the Internet in 2000 closer to 10 million or 50 million?
2. Are more consumer sales or business-to-business sales made using the Internet?
3. Are there more Internet users in the U.S. than in the rest of the world combined?

4. What other business activities are included in e-commerce besides buying and selling?
5. What are several common business-to-business services offered through the Internet?
6. How can businesses use the Internet to gather information on customers who have just purchased a product?
7. How did the name "dot-com" develop?
8. In which stage of e-commerce development do businesses make the least use of the Internet?
9. What are examples of types of businesses that did not exist prior to the development of the Internet?
10. Which types of products did consumers most frequently purchase using the Internet in 1999?
11. What are the names of several sizes of Internet advertisements?
12. What are the three primary reasons customers report that they do not shop online?
13. Why does an e-commerce business need a domain name?

DISCUSS IDEAS

1. Why does the Internet make it easier for small businesses to compete with larger businesses?
2. What are some possible reasons that the Internet sale of products and services is expected to grow very rapidly in the next several years?
3. Do you agree or disagree with the following statement: "Today, if a business has not posted information about its business, location, and products and services on the Internet, it will likely miss some customers." Justify your answer.
4. Why would private businesses choose to provide important information needed by other businesses free on the Internet rather than charging for it?
5. Why do you believe there are such large cost savings to businesses when they use the Internet to sell airline tickets, provide banking and bill-paying services, or distribute software?
6. What types of businesses do you believe are most likely to use the Internet only for information rather than developing interaction or integration? Why did you select those types of businesses?
7. What are some examples of effective and ineffective types of interaction you have seen on business Web sites?
8. Why do you believe most successful bricks-and-mortar companies are not among the top 20 Internet retailers?
9. Why do only a few Internet users go online to purchase products and services, while most go online to gather information and then purchase products from a local business?
10. If you owned a new e-commerce business that sold CDs and music videos, on what types of Internet sites would you advertise to make prospective customers aware of your business?

ANALYZE INFORMATION

1. A recent report showed the following past and projected growth in business-to-business Internet sales over a 5-year period:

Year	*Total Sales*
1998	$ 45 billion
1999	110 billion
2000	252 billion
2001	499 billion
2002	843 billion

   Using those figures, calculate the following amounts:
   a. the amount of increase in sales for each year
   b. the percentage of increase in sales for each year
   c. the total increase in sales for the 5-year period
   d. the total percentage of increase in sales for the 5-year period
   Using a computer graphing or spreadsheet program, prepare a bar graph illustrating the year-by-year growth in sales.

2. The use of the Internet varies, based on individuals' ethnic and racial background. The following chart illustrates the number of people in the U.S. based on major ethnic/racial classification and the percentage of that population that use the Internet.

Racial/Ethnic Classification	*U.S. Adult Population (in millions)*	*Percentage of Population Using the Internet*
African-Americans	4.9	28%
Hispanic	3.5	28%
All U.S. ethnic minorities	14.4	31%
Caucasian/White	52.8	37%

   a. Calculate the number of Internet users for each racial/ethnic classification listed. Then determine the total of the U.S. adult population, the total number of Internet users in the U.S. adult population, and the average percentage of the total population using the Internet.
   b. What are some possible reasons why the usage rate of the Internet varies, based on a person's racial/ethnic classification?

3. Go online and find at least three examples of businesses for each stage of e-commerce development: information, interaction, integration. If possible, print a copy of each company's home page. Using that home page, describe why the business fits the stage in which you classified it.

4. Go online and locate examples of advertisements that fit each of the types and sizes listed in Figure 9-5. Prepare an illustration of the advertisements you located by copying, saving, or printing the images or by drawing the ads on a sheet of paper. If you find other commonly used types and sizes of ads, add them to your

illustration. Your teacher may ask you and other class members to develop a visual display of all of the illustrations or to make an oral presentation of your illustration.

5. Form a team with other class members. As a team, develop a list of at least five factors that everyone agrees makes an effective e-commerce business. Then, using the Internet and your list of factors, find several e-commerce businesses and rate them using the list of factors. You may want to have each student rate each business and then combine your ratings into a total team rating. Using your results, identify the best and worst e-commerce business. Share your results in a discussion with other teams in your class. Compare the factors your team identified with those of other teams and compare each team's choice of best and worst e-commerce businesses.

SOLVE BUSINESS PROBLEMS

CASE 9-1

Jillian and Dontae were sitting in front of the computer, listening to music they had downloaded and looking at a Web site that identified the top e-tailers for the year.

Jillian: *I really like the idea of shopping on the Web. It seems like you get many more choices, probably lower prices, and it's so convenient.*

Dontae: *I'm not sure I'm convinced yet. Look at the names of some of the businesses on the list. I've never heard of many of them. Do you believe they're all legitimate?*

Jillian: *Well, some of our favorite stores are on the list, so you could start with buying from them.*

Dontae: *But why not just go to the mall and buy from the stores? I'd get the products faster and not have to pay shipping charges. Besides, I don't want to enter my credit card number online, even if it says it's safe.*

Jillian: *But you hand your credit card to a person in every store when you make a purchase. They process it through a telephone line to get the amount approved. Isn't that the same thing?*

Think Critically:

1. Many people do not trust businesses that sell products online, especially if they are not familiar with the company's name. Yet they will walk into a new business in their city and shop without a great deal of concern. What causes the difference in people's view of online businesses compared to traditional businesses?
2. Do you agree with Dontae that it is easier to shop in an actual store in a mall than shop from the same business online? Why or why not?

3. What is your opinion of Jillian's comparison between entering a credit card number online and handing the card to a clerk in a business, who checks it using a telephone line from the store to the credit card company?

CASE 9-2

Jimmy Lai Chee-Ying is taking on two giants in Hong Kong. According to a report from CNN.com/ASIANOW, his new business venture uses the Internet as well as telephones and fax to take orders for grocery products. The orders are filled in eight warehouses located throughout the city and are delivered in one of 220 vans to the customer's home. He is taking on giants, since two supermarket chains control over 60 percent of the grocery business in Hong Kong.

Lai believes his business can be successful for two reasons. He offers a very limited selection of products. He carefully studies customer needs and sells the products they buy frequently and in larger quantities, such as soda pop, juice, canned goods, and baby diapers. He also selects products that he can offer for prices as much as 40 percent lower than the big supermarkets. And, he also sells computers. Why? Every home needs a computer, and if they buy a computer, they are more likely to purchase over the Internet.

Some business experts say he cannot succeed. People aren't willing to buy most of their groceries in a store and then order a few online. Others feel the larger stores will cut their prices and drive Lai out of business. But Lai looks at it differently. All customers like to save money with the convenience of home delivery. As he becomes more successful online, he can add more products. Because the two chains are so large, they will hardly notice the lost business resulting from the new e-business.

Think Critically:

1. Do you believe it was a good idea for Jimmy Lai Chee-Ying to start a new business that competes with two very large businesses that control most of the grocery market in Hong Kong? Justify your answer.
2. Discuss the advantages and disadvantages of Lai's strategy of selling a very limited number of popular products. What do you think of his idea for selling computers?
3. Why is the new e-business able to sell products at a much lower price than the larger chains? Do you believe the large businesses will drop their prices on the products Lai sells? Why or why not?
4. Identify another new Internet business that is competing with much larger traditional businesses. What is the business doing to encourage customers to switch from the larger business to the new e-business?

PROJECT: MY BUSINESS, INC.

E-commerce presents unique opportunities for businesses and may allow new businesses to compete equally with larger, established businesses. Many businesses develop a simple Web site to provide information about the business, while others use the Internet more extensively. Some even complete all of their business online. In this project segment, you will consider how you can use the Internet in your business.

DATA COLLECTION

1. Use the Internet to identify:
   a. Information sources that will be helpful in completing your business planning.
   b. Examples of other juice and beverage businesses that are using the Internet.
   c. E-commerce businesses from which you could purchase products and services you will use in your business.
2. Identify at least two Web-hosting companies that work with small businesses. Collect information on the services they provide and the costs of their services.
3. Conduct a short survey of 10 or more people who you believe would be prospective customers of your business. Identify the following information:
   a. How regularly do they use the Internet and how much time per week do they spend online?
   b. Do they purchase products online? How regularly and what types of products?
   c. What are their positive and negative feelings about e-commerce and making purchases online?

ANALYSIS

1. Prepare a chart that compares the advantages and disadvantages of e-commerce for your business. Based on the chart, make a decision about whether you will use the Internet for your business: (a) right away, (b) after your business has operated for a few years, (c) probably not at all.
2. Outline the way you would use the Internet for your business if you used it for: (a) information, (b) interaction, and (c) integration.

3. Using three of the Internet advertisement formats shown in Figure 9-5, develop advertisements you would use to encourage consumers to visit your business's Web site. Then go to the Internet and identify three sites that accept advertising you believe would be good locations for your ads. List the URL address for each site and give a brief rationale for each choice.

ORGANIZATIONAL COMMUNICATIONS

OBJECTIVES

- **10-1** Describe the communication process and channels.
- **10-2** Identify communication barriers and means for overcoming them.
- **10-3** Explain how corporate culture influences formal and informal communication networks.
- **10-4** Describe how to handle conflicts and how to run productive meetings.
- **10-5** Explain the types of communication problems that can occur when conducting business in foreign countries.
- **10-6** Identify ways to improve communications in organizations.

MANY WAYS TO COMMUNICATE

Erica Komuro, one of many managers for an international book company, sat at her desk looking at tomorrow's schedule. In the morning, she would review the new organization chart for her department that would appear in the employees' manual. Later, she would meet with two other managers and her boss to resolve a conflict. She dreaded the shouting match that was sure to occur between two people who never agreed on anything.

The afternoon would include interviewing a new employee and giving her best worker instructions on how to perform a new assignment. Then Erica would write a few business letters and e-mail messages. She also had to finish her computerized monthly report for the division manager, which would be sent over the local area network. If the morning meeting did not drag on, Erica might also have time to return phone calls that came in while she was dealing with a customer relations problem. Perhaps she could also squeeze in a call to Sabrina in Accounting to learn more about a rumor regarding the sudden resignation of the vice president.

Just before leaving the office she flipped the calendar page ahead a few days. In large letters she saw: "Meet with Mr. Nozaki." She was not sure how to best deal with the major problems this manager had in running the Tokyo office. At least she could recall a few Japanese words from earlier days when her family lived in Kyoto.

As she closed the office door, she smiled and waved to the evening cleaning person arriving for duty. On the way to her car she thought, "Tomorrow will be a busy day."

Erica is a typical manager because much of her time is spent communicating—speaking, listening, writing, and reading. Managers communicate in person, by phone and fax, by e-mail, and by paper documents. They also communicate through other means, such as a smile, a frown, or a wave.

Communications are vital in running organizations. Communications provide a link between employees and customers and between employees and managers. In fact, it has been estimated that managers communicate more than two thirds of each workday, as shown in Figure 10-1.

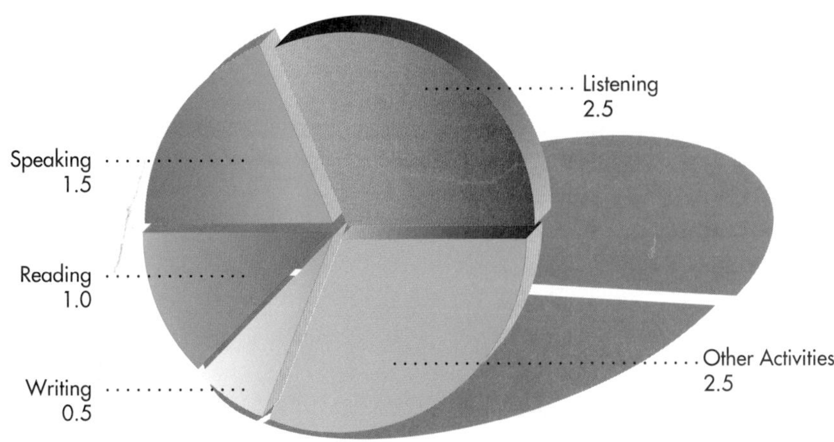

FIGURE 10-1

Managers spend most of their time communicating, especially listening and speaking.

In this chapter you will learn about the communication process, corporate communications, and communication problems. You will also learn what good businesses and managers do to improve communications.

THE COMMUNICATION PROCESS

Communication is the sharing of information, in which the receiver understands the meaning of the message in the way the sender intended. Communication includes more than passing along factual data. It includes sharing ideas, beliefs, and opinions. It is a *two-way process* between senders and receivers. The senders must put the information into clear words, and the receivers must try to understand the message as the senders intended. If the receivers do not fully understand the message or need more information, they should ask for clarification. Thus, feedback is critical to effective communication.

Feedback is a receiver's response to a sender's message. The response may be in the form of asking questions to clarify the meaning of a message. Or, receivers may restate the message in their own words, so that the senders can verify that the receivers understood the meaning as intended. The communication process and the role of feedback are illustrated in Figure 10-2.

COMMUNICATION BARRIERS

The meaning of communication is simple to understand. Yet, poor communication is one of the biggest problems managers face. Poor communication can lead to disagreements, faulty work, delayed performances, and major industrial accidents. Two major barriers that interfere with communication are distractions and distortions.

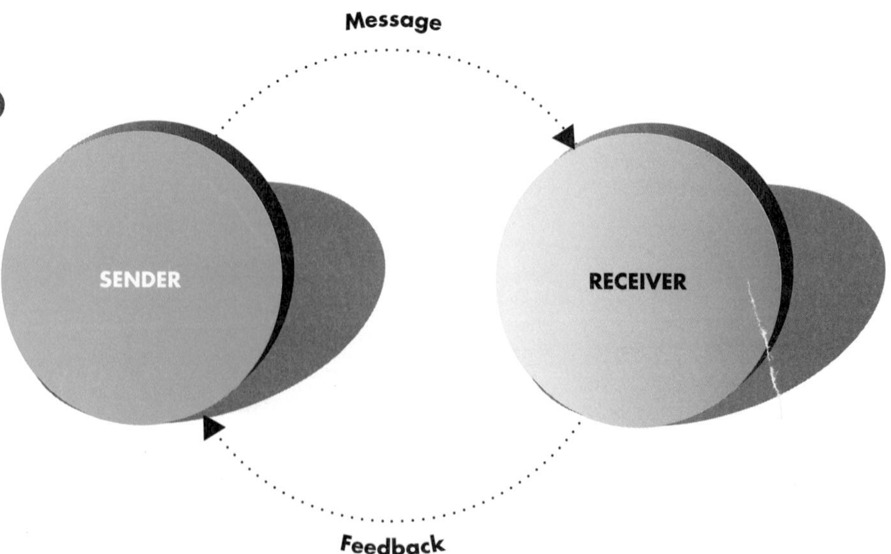

FIGURE 10-2

The communication process involves a sender, a message, and a receiver. Feedback helps the sender and receiver make sure that both understand the meaning in the same way.

ILLUSTRATION 10-1

What kinds of distractions can occur during a business meeting? How can these barriers to communication be overcome?

DISTRACTIONS Interruptions occur all too often while communicating. Anything that interferes with the sender's creating and delivering a message and the receiver's getting and interpreting a message is a **distraction.** Distractions are potential causes of communication problems. Two workers who whisper to each other during a meeting create a distraction that may cause a nearby worker to miss a point made by the manager. It may also cause the manager to forget to mention a point. Ringing phones, grammar errors in messages, and loud noises are other examples of barriers to communications.

Because distractions affect communication, some managers learn to work with various interruptions, while others try to keep interruptions to a minimum. For example, some managers place telephone calls or write messages during specific times of the day when interruptions are less likely to occur.

DISTORTIONS When senders create messages, they must select the information they want to include. They need not include every bit of data surrounding an idea, event, or situation. Senders select only the information that they think the receivers need in order to understand the message. Depending upon the information selected, though, the message can become distorted. **Distortion** refers to how people consciously or unconsciously change messages.

Distortion is usually not deliberate. People unconsciously pass along only information they feel others need. Often they leave out important data. Distortion may be deliberate, however, for self-enhancement or self-protection. For example, an employee may tell a supervisor about a machine breakdown but not admit that he or she did not oil the machine regularly. Or a manager may give an employee a very good rating because she likes him, even though the worker's performance may be only average.

Distortion can also occur because people often "hear" what they want to hear. We all bring our own perspectives to any communication situation. We filter messages we receive through our own system of beliefs and experience. Therefore, sometimes what we understand the sender to say was not at all what the sender meant. Receivers don't necessarily have to agree with the message, but they have a responsibility to use feedback to try to understand it as the sender intended.

CHANNELS OF COMMUNICATION

A **channel of communication** is the means by which the message is conveyed. The three major channels are oral, written, and non-verbal.

ORAL COMMUNICATION In the opening story we learned that Erica's schedule for the next business day is nearly filled with oral communications. Speaking with employees, attending meetings, and receiving and making phone calls consume a great deal of a manager's time. Day-to-day communications require frequent contact with people on a one-to-one basis. That contact may be formal, as when Erica interviews a potential employee, or it may be informal, as when she chats with another employee about the company picnic. Giving employees oral instructions is an especially common and significant task. How well managers communicate determines in great part how high they rise on the management ladder.

WRITTEN COMMUNICATION Written business communications take many forms. The most common are short memos, e-mails, formal reports, and letters. Figure 10-3 lists some common uses of business letters. Other written communications include manuals, invoices, telephone message reminders, and even notes. Written communications sent electronically include e-mails, faxes, and postings on electronic bulletin boards.

To communicate effectively in writing, senders should compose messages using precise, unambiguous word choice and proper grammar. The messages should also be concise. Long or unnecessary messages contribute to information overload. In turn, information overload slows decision making and becomes an obstacle to effective use of work time. Written messages may also include the use of psychology. For example, good news should appear early in a message, and bad news should appear later, after the explanation.

ELECTRONIC COMMUNICATION E-mail has changed the way we communicate. Yearly over a trillion e-mail messages replace what otherwise would be paper correspondence. Evidence of the growth of e-mail is the great decline in messages previously sent through the U.S. Postal System. Electronic mail is popular because it lowers communication costs, minimizes paper handling, speeds communications and decision-making, and improves office productivity. Because of its rapid growth and widespread use, businesses have adopted policies and practices that address e-mail use.

Some Uses for Business Letters

- request credit from suppliers
- give and refuse credit to customers
- collect overdue accounts from customers
- request product catalogs from suppliers
- order merchandise from suppliers
- send information customers requested
- acknowledge and fill orders from customers
- ask for and make adjustments in customers' orders
- refuse adjustments in customers' orders
- persuade others to take action
- convince others about an idea
- sell goods and services
- congratulate others
- thank people for tasks performed
- request information about job applicants
- request interviews with job applicants
- hire or reject job applicants

FIGURE 10-3

Business letters have many purposes.

E-Mail Policies. Some businesses establish e-mail policies to protect the organization, business partners, employees, and customers. Typically such policies state that employees should use e-mail only for job-related matters, with occasional exceptions. In fact, businesses can track all inbound and outbound messages and read them if they want. Employees should not use e-mail for personal purposes, such as contacting friends outside the organization or participating in chat groups. In general, employee communications cannot be considered private, because all employee actions represent the firm. Companies like General Electric remind employees as they log on that most Internet and e-mail use is solely for business tasks and all activity may be recorded and reviewed.

Also, e-mail should not be considered private, because outsiders can access it. For that reason, some organizations install software programs that can automatically self-destruct messages after a designated time, limit the number of times a message can be opened and read, and prevent the forwarding of messages.

Protecting the company from lawsuits is too critical to be left to chance. Jokes, off-color stories, and flame messages reflect negatively on the company image. A **flame** is an electronic message that contains abusive, threatening, or offensive content that may violate company policy or public law. Abusive sexual language, for example, can lead to a sexual harassment lawsuit by offended employees. Abusers are subject to dismissal and firms may be sued for permitting harassment situations to exist.

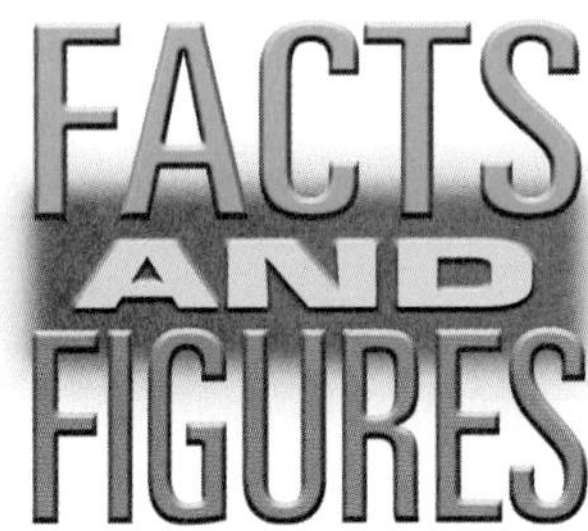

A recent survey of 900 employers by the American Management Association found that 35 percent do one or more of the following: monitor employee voice mail, phone calls, e-mail, and computer hard drives, and videotape employees at their jobs.

E-Mail Practices. E-mail volume can be quite heavy. Information overload is a common complaint of employees in information-intensive jobs. They need strategies for processing large amounts of mail efficiently. Different avenues are available for doing so. Important mail from superiors and co-workers deserves priority. Some mail need not be read at all, such as spam. **Spam** is unsolicited advertising that finds its way into e-mail boxes. Most common e-mail programs allow users to sort incoming messages by sender, subject line, or whatever they specify. Thus, users can have all messages from the boss grouped together, so they give these top priority. Spam from unknown senders can be grouped together for quick disposal. Productive employees set aside certain times of the day to send or read e-mail, so that this task does not interfere with other priority tasks.

Writing and responding to e-mail deserve the same courtesy that other written mail deserves. Good business writing requires that messages have a meaningful subject line as well as a pleasant but business-like tone that gets to the point quickly and ends graciously. Most messages should be short, but some may have attachments, such as a tables, charts, or diagrams. Users often write e-mail messages hurriedly, and do not carefully craft them. Furthermore, employees may not realize that e-mail, like letters, are written documents that can be used for legal purposes.

A possible weakness of e-mail, as opposed to phone or in-person conversations, is the lack of facial expressions and other gestures that show emotions. However, senders can express some common emotions through emoticons. **Emoticons** are facial expressions created with keyboard symbols and used to express feeling in an e-mail message. Figure 10-4 shows some common emoticons. To see the expressions, look at the emoticons sideways. Users should be careful not to overuse emoticons, especially in business correspondence. Too many emoticons can make the message seem unprofessional.

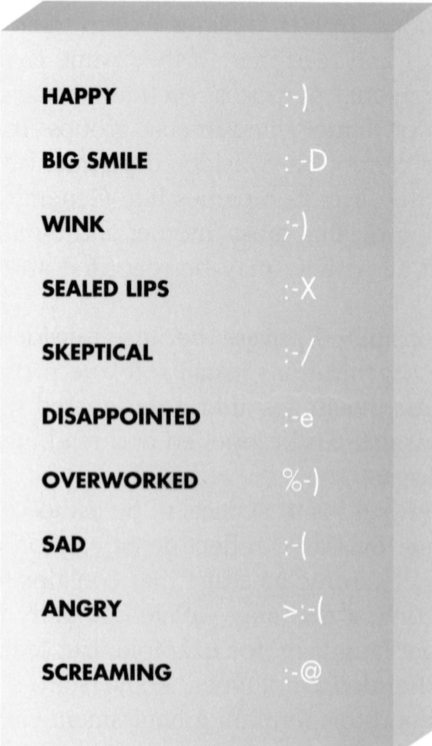

FIGURE 10-4

Emoticons provide e-mail users a way to convey feelings.

Each e-mail message should follow good

writing guidelines. Writers should construct sentences properly, without spelling errors. They should not include gossip or nasty comments. Carelessly prepared messages reflect negatively on the writer and the organization.

ILLUSTRATION 10-2

Body language may get the message across better than the spoken word. What message is this businesswoman sending?

NON-VERBAL COMMUNICATION

Delivering messages by means other than speaking or writing is called **non-verbal communications.** Flashing lights, stop signs, and sirens are examples of physical ways to communicate. Even colors, such as in traffic lights (green, yellow, and red), signal messages—go, caution, and stop. Non-verbal communication also appears in written documents in the form of charts, diagrams, and pictures. People also give non-verbal messages through body movements. "Body language," as this is sometimes called, may appear as frowns, smiles, posture, hand or body movements, or presence or absence of eye contact. Non-verbal messages convey meaning as much as verbal messages do.

Managers should be aware of the non-verbal messages they convey to others and that others convey to them. These messages are often given unconsciously. Sometimes a non-verbal message confirms or contradicts a verbal message. For example, what impression would Erica get if tomorrow's job applicant said, "I am extremely interested in the position," but came unprepared for the interview and wore jeans and a dirty T-shirt? If you were interviewing this person, which message would you believe—the verbal or non-verbal one? Actions often speak louder than words.

CORPORATE COMMUNICATIONS

Each business has its own internal atmosphere that influences the way formal and informal communications occur. In this section, you will learn how communication networks influence the communication process. You will also learn how to conduct effective meetings.

CORPORATE CULTURE

As you learned in Chapter 4, culture is shared values, beliefs, and behavior patterns of groups of people. The group may be a corporation, a nation, or any other organized group. An organization, such as a corporation, develops its own corporate culture or personality. Factors such as the type of business, personality of its leaders, and its operating procedures create this corporate culture, which members understand.

The culture of a corporation influences the communication climate. Cultures differ widely among firms. Cultures may be very closed, very open, or somewhere in between. A closed culture is one that relies on top-down decision making and adheres to numerous rules and strict disciplining for violating established procedures. Rigid rule-making and authoritarian leadership can breed distrust and secrecy while discouraging creativity and decision making at lower levels. In such organizations, communications tend to be quite formal. Experts refer to this type of organization as having a closed communication system.

When trust and confidence prevail in employees, an organization is said to have an open communication system. This type of culture encourages creativity and problem solving at all levels and supports communication and information sharing. Trust, supportiveness, risk taking, and decision making influence whether an employee will like or dislike working for a company. In turn, these factors help determine how productive employees will be.

Most organizations have neither a fully open nor closed culture. Sometimes a business may change its culture. A comfortable culture for one person, however, may not be comfortable for another. Some employees prefer a culture with primarily an open communication system, while others prefer a culture with primarily a closed communication system. Employees often change jobs in search of an organization that has a set of beliefs, values, and practices suited to their needs.

COMMUNICATION NETWORKS

A **communication network** is the structure through which information flows in a business. Communication networks can be formal or informal.

FORMAL NETWORKS A **formal communication network** is the system of official channels that carry organizationally approved messages. These channels generally follow the reporting relationships in the firm. Formal communication flows upward, downward, and across the organization in a prescribed manner. Typically, certain information, such as budget allocations, flows downward from top-level managers to lower-level managers. Other information, such as requests for budget expenditures, flows from the bottom to the top of the organization.

Upward communication includes oral and written reports from lower level to upper-level managers. Usually, upper-level managers rely on lower-level managers for information that deals with new or unusual problems, the quality of employee performance, and the way employees feel about their jobs and the company. Supervisors receive upward communication from their subordinates about such things as project status and suggestions for making a task more efficient.

Organizations with closed, rather than open, communications are less likely to benefit from upward communication. Upward communication is subject to distortion, especially in corporate cultures that are relatively closed. Supervisors, for example, might withhold or distort upward-flowing information when problems appear to reflect negatively on their performance. On the other hand, a supervisor might exaggerate information about successes. In a closed culture, employees often fear revealing negative information and avoid making honest criticisms.

Downward communication in organizations occurs mainly by memos, e-mails, reports, and manuals. To be effective, this information should be timely and clear. In organizations with closed communications, there is often no opportunity for feedback, because information does not flow upward easily. However, in open cultures, employees receive downward-flowing information at meetings and their feedback is welcome.

Lateral communication flows horizontally or across the organization. For example, the production manager in one plant might want to know what problems other production managers face. Perhaps common problems could be solved jointly. However, many organizations do not have easy and fast channels for such communications. In a business with an open corporate culture, lateral communications are more likely to exist. One communication expert has estimated that 80 percent of poor management decisions occur because of ineffective communications.

CAREER CONNECTION

COMPUTER SYSTEMS ANALYST

Computer systems analyst is expected to be one of the fastest-growing occupations in the first decade of the 2000s. The employment of computing professionals is expected to increase rapidly as technologies become more sophisticated and organizations continue to adopt and integrate them.

Systems analysts use their knowledge and skills to solve computer problems and enable computer technology to meet the individual needs of an organization. This may include planning and developing new computer systems or devising ways to apply existing systems' resources. Analysts work to help an organization realize the maximum benefit from its investment in equipment, personnel, and business processes. Most systems analysts generally work with a specific type of system, depending on the type of organization they work for—for example, business, accounting, or financial systems.

Given the technology available today, telecommuting is becoming more common for computer professionals. Often work can be done from remote locations using modems, laptops, e-mail, and through the Internet.

While there is no universally accepted way to prepare for a job as a computer professional because employers' preferences depend on the work to be done, a bachelor's degree is a prerequisite for most employers. Relevant work experience is also very important.

For more career information about systems analysts, check your library or the Internet for resources.

INFORMAL NETWORKS Like formal communication networks, informal networks exist in all organizations. **Informal communication networks** are the unofficial ways that employees share information in an organization. The most common informal networks include small informal groups and the grapevine. Informal networks rely heavily on interpersonal communications and e-mail.

A great deal of communicating occurs among small informal groups, especially among employees who get along well together. These employees may or may not have the same supervisors, but often they do. They share information about the organization, assist one another in solving work problems, and look after one another. Members may even support one another when conflicts arise with other employees. Most employees belong to a small informal group.

Managers should be aware of informal groups. Often informal groups have more influence than managers do over the behavior of individual workers. It is extremely important that informal groups support the efforts of the entire business. If they do not, informal groups can interfere with business goals and, in turn, hurt morale and decrease productivity. Managers often work closely with informal group leaders to obtain support and to test new ideas.

An extensive amount of organizational communications occurs in an unofficial way through interpersonal relationships. Employees working side by side, for example, generally talk about their jobs and about personal matters. These conversations are normal and usually do not interfere with work. Employees also talk together on breaks, in the hall, or around the drinking fountain.

The informal transmission of information among workers is called the **grapevine.** Informal messages travel quickly through the grapevine and can be distorted, because they are often based on unofficial, partial, or incorrect information. That is why grapevine messages are often labeled rumors. Very often, however, grapevines convey accurate messages. For example, when a formal memo announces that a manager has just retired for "health reasons," the grapevine may provide the actual reason. The manager may have been asked to quit but was given the opportunity to resign voluntarily. When Erica Komuro calls Sabrina in Accounting, she may also learn that the rumor about the vice president's resignation is true.

Generally, managers should not interfere with grapevines. Grapevines often fill the social needs of workers to communicate about their work lives. Only when a grapevine message is inaccurate and negatively affects company business should managers attempt to correct the situation.

CONDUCTING EFFECTIVE MEETINGS

Meetings are a common way for employees to share information, discuss problems, and make decisions. Managers often prefer meetings, because open communication encourages discussion and yields feed-

1. Have a good reason for calling a meeting.
2. Develop a specific agenda and stick to it.
3. Decide who should and who should not attend.
4. Schedule the meeting at a convenient time and place.
5. Start and stop the meeting on time.
6. Encourage communications by arranging the seating so that participants face one another.
7. Summarize the results at the end of the meeting.

FIGURE 10-5

Suggestions for Running Effective Meetings

back that helps in decision making. Employees doing the hands-on work often have good ideas about how to improve their work quality and efficiency. However, meetings also have disadvantages. The chief disadvantage is the excessive time meetings take. Good managers overcome this weakness by careful planning and by following suggestions such as those shown in Figure 10-5.

A second major problem with meetings occurs because of differences among those who attend the meetings. For example, an outspoken person may tend to dominate, while a quiet person may say nothing. Neither situation is desirable. The person who leads the meeting should encourage but control discussions, so that the group hears and discusses all ideas. Two methods used to encourage group thinking and problem solving are the nominal group technique and brainstorming.

NOMINAL GROUP TECHNIQUE The **nominal group technique (NGT)** is a group problem-solving method in which group members write down and evaluate ideas to be shared with the group. For example, assume a manager needs to solve a long-standing problem. The manager begins by stating the problem and then follows the steps described in Figure 10-6.

The NGT encourages each group member to think about the problem, and it gives the quiet person and the outspoken person equal

1. Present the problem to be resolved to group members.
2. Distribute blank cards and, without discussion, ask members to write possible solutions by using a different card for each solution.
3. Read solutions from the cards and display for all to see.
4. Discuss each solution listed.
5. Distribute blank cards and ask members to write their three best solutions on separate cards.
6. Tabulate and display results.
7. Select the solution receiving the most agreement and present it to the group leader.

FIGURE 10-6

Steps in Using the Nominal Group Technique

opportunity to be heard. Private voting encourages employees to choose the best solutions rather than spend time defending their own suggestions. As a result, this technique has been very effective.

BRAINSTORMING Problems arise in business for which prior solutions do not exist or are no longer acceptable. One technique for handling such situations is by brainstorming. **Brainstorming** is a group discussion technique used to generate as many ideas as possible for solving a problem. A group leader presents a problem and asks group members to offer any solution that comes to mind. Even wild and imaginative ideas are encouraged. The group should make no attempt to judge any ideas as good or bad while brainstorming is underway. Only after participants have identified all possible solutions should they begin to judge usefulness. Often, an idea that appeared to be impractical or unusual when first presented may become the best solution to the problem. Brainstorming is frequently used to deal with problems that need especially creative solutions, such as when generating new product ideas and creating advertisements.

COMMUNICATION PROBLEMS

Managers deal with a variety of communication problems. Some problems that challenge the communication skills of managers involve resolving conflicts and handling cross-cultural communications effectively.

DEALING WITH CONFLICT

At times, people disagree with each other. Most job-related disagreements are likely to be temporary and easy to settle. Disagreements become a concern to a business when they lead to conflict. **Conflict** is interference by one person with the achievement of another person's goals. Conflicts usually occur between two people, but they may also occur between an individual and a group, or between groups. Because conflicts are sometimes an obstacle to job performance, managers must deal with conflicts.

DESIRABLE CONFLICT A small amount of conflict is sometimes beneficial, because it may challenge employees and stimulate new ideas. For example, the advertising manager may decide to budget as little as possible to advertise a particular product, while the sales manager may have decided to try to boost sales for that particular product through increased advertising. At this point conflict exists because the goals set by each manager differ. However, this type of conflict can lead to a healthy discussion of how much to spend on advertising and how best to advertise to produce the highest sales at the lowest advertising cost. The result can lead to the achievement of a goal that is best for the business.

When employees discuss and resolve their conflicting goals, the organization can benefit. However, when conflicting goals are not resolved, long-term problems often result. If the sales and advertising managers went ahead with their individual plans, money would be wasted and sales would be lost.

ILLUSTRATION 10-3

If handled properly, conflicts can be beneficial and productive. How do you handle conflict with another person?

UNDESIRABLE CONFLICT While some conflict in organizations may be healthy, too much conflict can be harmful. Undesirable conflict results when the actions of any person or group interfere with the goals of the organization. If, in the preceding example, the sales manager became resentful of the advertising manager and undermined the company's budget goals by deliberately overspending the amount agreed upon for the product, undesirable conflict would result. Employees who dislike others and carry grudges often cause problems for an organization. Therefore, undesirable conflicts should be resolved as soon as possible.

RESOLVING CONFLICT Conflicts can be resolved in various ways. Since each situation differs, managers must decide which type of strategy will best resolve each conflict.

Avoidance Strategy. One strategy used to resolve conflict is to take a neutral position or to agree with another person's position even though it differs from your personal belief. This approach avoids the conflict. One manager may decide to accept the goal of another manager, or to avoid expressing an opposing opinion about the goal. When a conflict is relatively unimportant, the avoidance strategy may be the best approach. However, if a disagreement involves important issues, avoidance is not a good strategy. It can often lead to resentment.

Compromise Strategy. A second way to resolve conflict is to seek a compromise. Everyone involved in a conflict agrees to a mutually acceptable solution. Often, a compromise grows out of a thorough discussion of the goals and the best way to achieve those goals. This strategy is better than avoidance, because it usually leads to a workable solution, since everyone involved personally contributes to the decision.

FACTS AND FIGURES

Companies experiencing workplace violence report a dramatic increase in employee turnover and an equally dramatic drop in employee morale. Since most employees feel that it is the employer's duty to provide a safe work environment, workers feel betrayed when a violent incident occurs at work. The direct financial consequences of turnover and low morale are hiring and training expenses and decreased productivity.

Also, people are more likely to support a compromise solution that they have helped to develop.

Win/Lose Strategy. The most dangerous approach used to resolve conflict is a win/lose strategy. A win/lose strategy is one in which no one compromises, thereby resulting in one person winning and one losing. A win/lose strategy is never acceptable to everyone, although people often engage in such a strategy. Win/lose strategies interfere with the achievement of organizational goals because they often (1) take time and energy away from the main problems and issues, (2) delay decisions, (3) arouse anger that hurts human relationships, and (4) cause personal resentment, which can lead to other problems.

Because win/lose situations are destructive, managers should attempt to prevent them. Setting clear objectives that employees understand and agree on, stressing the need for cooperation in reaching objectives, and working for group decisions when special problems or disagreements arise are ways managers can avoid win/lose strategies.

CROSS-CULTURAL COMMUNICATION PROBLEMS

Cultures differ from country to country. A country's culture influences how its people communicate, just as corporate culture does within organizations. When doing business abroad, companies face communication barriers created by language, cultural, and non-verbal differences.

LANGUAGE DIFFERENCES Few American managers speak a foreign language fluently. However, doing so does not solve all problems when

ILLUSTRATION 10-4

What kinds of communication barriers might companies face when doing business abroad?

someone is transferred to another country. The people of most nations realize that learning a new language is difficult. But they are more than willing to help foreigners learn. They are especially impressed when someone who does not know their language makes a noble effort to learn. Many corporations now provide intensive language training for managers assigned to foreign branches. Knowledge of the social customs and education, legal, and political systems are included in the instructions.

Joint ventures between American and foreign firms often reveal language problems. A successful joint venture between Ford Motor Co. and the Japanese Mazda Motors Corp. provides an example of overcoming language difficulties. The president of Mazda estimates that 20 percent of the meaning of a conversation with Ford leaders is lost between him and the interpreters. Another 20 percent is lost between the interpreters and the Ford leaders. Working with only about two-thirds understanding, the Mazda president tries extra hard to make sure his message is getting through. He especially believes people should meet face-to-face and talk freely.

CULTURAL DIFFERENCES People from other countries place different values on such things as family, status, and power. Countries value families differently. In India, for example, providing jobs for male family members in a business is more important than earning a profit. Humor differs worldwide, too. In addition, accepted practices in one country may be impolite elsewhere. For example, American business people generally like to start and end meetings on time. In Japan and certain other countries, this practice would be considered rude rather than businesslike.

NON-VERBAL DIFFERENCES Great differences exist in the area of non-verbal communications, especially body language. For example, how close one stands when talking to someone else differs from one country to another. For most conversations, Americans stand two to three feet apart, whereas Middle Eastern people stand much closer. Even colors have different meanings. In Western countries, black is often associated with death, but in Latin American countries, death is represented by white and purple. A handshake also varies from place to place. In Spain, it should last from five to seven shakes, but the French prefer one single shake.

Because differences exist among nations, executives prefer to conduct extremely important business transactions in a formal manner. Usually, that means greater use of written reports and expert translators. For oral translation services by phone, long-distance telephone firms such as AT&T provide an 800-number to assist callers. However, for day-to-day international operations, managers must learn to understand the cultural and communication practices of other nations.

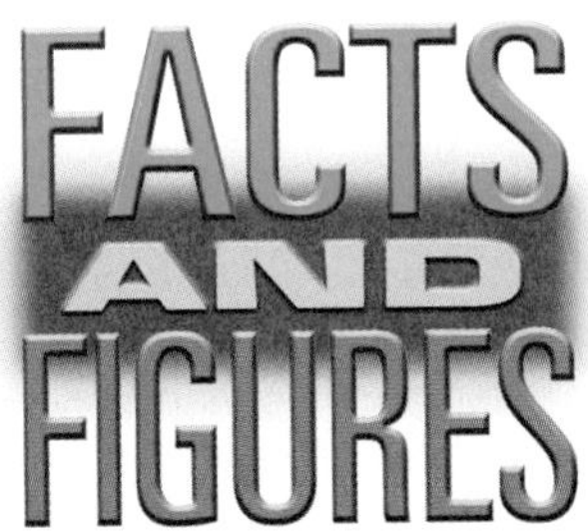

Listening is considered both a sign of politeness and a valuable skill in business negotiations in Japan. Japanese often think North Americans need to listen more attentively, not talk as much, and certainly not interrupt when someone else is speaking.

IMPROVING ORGANIZATIONAL COMMUNICATIONS

Good managers are usually good communicators. Some ways to improve communication are discussed next.

ENCOURAGE TWO-WAY COMMUNICATIONS

Small businesses provide for plenty of two-way communication between owners and employees. As companies get larger, however, a shift to one-way communications often occurs for efficiency purposes. When this happens, problems arise because valuable feedback from employees and customers is reduced. Good managers establish plans to obtain feedback even when they are extremely busy. Some managers, however, discourage two-way communications because they feel uncomfortable with it and because it is time-consuming. For example, one boss in a firm fired an employee by e-mail, even though the person's office was located next door. Organizations that encourage managers to consciously engage in two-way communications are often more successful than those that do not.

LISTEN ACTIVELY

Two-way communications assure feedback. Effective listening results in effective feedback. Frequently, employees have questions and encounter problems on the job. They need to talk to someone who listens carefully. Hearing and listening are not the same. Most people can hear when someone speaks, but they may not pay attention to the message. Listening involves hearing and understanding. Good listeners make

ILLUSTRATION 10-5

New managers often spend time listening to as many employee points of view as possible before making corporate changes. What kinds of questions would you ask employees before making such changes?

every effort to practice the rules of good listening shown in Figure 10-7 to make certain that they received the messages accurately.

FACILITATE UPWARD COMMUNICATION

In large organizations, upward communication is sometimes neglected. Managers may not want to hear complaints or deal with suggestions

FIGURE 10-7

Ten Rules for Good Listening

Rule and Reason Behind the Rule

1. Stop talking!

You cannot listen if you are talking.

2. Put the talker at ease.

Help a person feel free to talk; create a permissive environment.

3. Show a talker that you want to listen.

Look and act interested; listen to understand, not to oppose.

4. Remove distractions.

Don't doodle, tap, or shuffle papers; shut the door if necessary to acheive quiet.

5. Empathize with talkers.

Try to see the other person's point of view.

6. Be patient.

Allow plenty of time; do not interrupt; do not start for the door or walk away.

7. Hold your temper.

An angry person takes the wrong meaning from words.

8. Go easy on argument and criticism.

These put people on the defensive and may cause them to "clam up" or become angry. Do not argue—even if you win, you lose.

9. Ask questions.

This encourages a talker and shows that you are listening. It helps to develop points further.

10. Stop talking!

This is first and last, because all other guides depend on it. You cannot do an effective listening job while you are talking. Remember that:

- Nature gave people two ears but only one tongue, which is a gentle hint that they should listen more than they talk.
- Listening requires two ears, one for meaning and one for feeling.
- Decision makers who do not listen have less information for making sound decisions.

because they require time. To make certain that upward communications occur, some businesses ask managers to use specific techniques.

One technique is called "management by walking around." Managers leave their offices from time to time and make trips through the working areas. While doing this, they chat with employees about various problems and conditions.

Another practice is for managers to encourage employees to meet with them when they have concerns. To control the time this "open door policy" takes, some managers restrict the practice to one hour per week when employees can make appointments. Suggestion boxes have been used for many years and have great value in encouraging communications.

No technique is better than regular meetings with employees. Some firms select a certain number of employees from different departments and organizational levels to meet with top managers on a regular basis. The manager informs them about important company matters and invites questions and ideas. Studies have shown that employees who are informed about their companies have stronger positive feelings than those who are not. These top-level managers benefit by getting feedback from people throughout the company.

SELECT COMMUNICATION CHANNELS CAREFULLY

When managers want to communicate with others, they should carefully select an appropriate communication channel. Generally, when a manager must reprimand an employee or settle a dispute, the oral communication channel is best. The oral channel is needed to explain the reason for the reprimand or to work out an acceptable solution to a dispute.

The written communication channel is best when managers want to communicate information requiring future action or to communicate information of a general nature, such as a new policy or a revised operating procedure. Such matters should be put in writing for later reference. Managers should follow up on information provided in writing, because it serves as a reminder that the information is important and it provides an opportunity for the receiver to ask questions. E-mail is a good way to follow up because it is fast, easy, and provides immediate feedback. E-mail is not a good substitute for oral communication in situations that call for face-to-face discussion.

In some situations, two channels of communication work best—first oral and then written. Managers should use both channels when they want to (1) give an immediate order, (2) announce a new policy, (3) contact a supervisor about work problems, or (4) compliment an employee for excellent work. In most of these situations, the information is best delivered orally on a one-to-one basis, which personalizes it and allows for immediate feedback. The written channel then allows for reinforcement and creates a record of the event.

ETHICAL ISSUES

COMMUNICATING TO CHANGE ATTITUDES

Monsanto frequently ranks as one of America's two hundred largest firms. While the public may not recognize the name, many recognize at least one product—NutraSweet. NutraSweet is Monsanto's brand of the sugar substitute aspartame often used in diet foods and drinks. At any grocery store, read the "contents" portion of labels on canned and packaged foods, and you will see how popular aspartame has become.

Aspartame received bad press in its early days and still does in spite of the fact that the Food and Drug Administration, American Diabetes Association, and other groups declared it safe for public consumption. Research by organizations other than Monsanto have also found it safe. Critics, however, think aspartame is not safe. Some think it may lead to headaches, blindness, cancer, and other problems, though these assertions are not supported by scientific evidence. Yet, Monsanto continues to receive complaints in spite of its extensive communication efforts to convince the public otherwise.

Although American-made products must list sugar substitutes, that is not true in some countries. In Europe and Asia, for example, manufacturers are not required to list sugar substitutes. Simply listing "sweetener" is acceptable, whether it is sugar, aspartame, or something else. This practice arises for economic reasons. For example, aspartame is easier and cheaper to ship, is subjected to fewer trade barriers and tariffs, is easily available when there is a sugar shortage, and is cheaper when sugar prices are high.

Monsanto makes other controversial products that have also received public criticism. Those products involve biotechnology—the genetic altering of crops that we eat. Examples include modifying one or two genes in soybeans, potatoes, and corn to make them more resistant to insects and diseases. While scientific experts find biotechnology acceptable, critics reject genetic altering and want it stopped or tightly controlled. With a growing population worldwide, how can farmers increase crop output and be more productive? Biotechnology can increase crop yields. Again, Monsanto has spent millions of dollars persuading the public that its new products, which are approved by the Food and Drug Administration and the American Dietetic Association, are not injurious to human health.

THINK CRITICALLY

1. How does the public's resistance to Monsanto's NutraSweet differ from the resistance to its biotechnology products?
2. Is it unethical to exclude aspartame from the contents of prepared foods in other countries?
3. Would Americans find it acceptable if the contents of food and drink products simply listed "sweetener" rather than "sugar" or "aspartame"?
4. Investigate Monsanto's success with its public communications efforts. Obtain information from your library or visit Web sites such as www.monsanto. com. Make a report to your class.

CHAPTER 10 REVIEW

CHAPTER CONCEPTS

- Managers spend much of their time communicating by writing, speaking, and listening. Communication involves creating, sending, receiving, and interpreting messages with the knowledge that each step in the communication process includes potential barriers.
- Corporate culture involves the shared values, beliefs, and behavior of an organization. The culture is established by its CEO and managers, and it influences the way people communicate within the firm. Cultures may be (1) entirely open with extensive interactive communication among all organizational members, (2) entirely closed with dominantly downward communication, or (3) a combination of open and closed communication. An open culture exists more often in today's successful firms and is characterized by trust, support, and a positive outlook among employees.
- Communications in organizations follow both formal and informal networks. Formal communication networks are official company channels, such as between managers and their employees. Informal communication networks are communications that occur among informal groups or through the grapevine.
- Managers must deal with many types of problems that challenge their communication skills, such as conflicts and communication across cultures. They must also learn to run meetings effectively by using techniques such as the nominal group technique and brainstorming to arrive at solutions to business problems.
- Good managers are generally good communicators. They listen effectively, facilitate upward communications, and choose the appropriate communication channels for their messages.

BUILD VOCABULARY POWER

Define the following terms and concepts.

1. communication
2. feedback
3. distraction
4. distortion
5. channel of communication
6. flame
7. spam
8. emoticons
9. non-verbal communications
10. communication network
11. formal communication network
12. informal communication networks
13. grapevine
14. nominal group technique (NGT)
15. brainstorming
16. conflict

REVIEW FACTS

1. How much time do managers spend each day communicating?
2. Why is communication referred to as a two-way process?
3. Name three problems that can occur in a business when poor communications exist.

4. What are two major barriers to communications?
5. Name the major channels used in business for communicating.
6. How do emoticons overcome a weakness of e-mail as a means of communication?
7. What is "body language"?
8. What are some characteristics of a business that has a closed culture?
9. Are messages that flow through the grapevine often incorrect?
10. What three strategies can a manager use to resolve conflicts?
11. Give five suggestions for running an effective meeting.
12. Would the nominal group technique or brainstorming be more effective in generating a large number of creative ideas for solving a problem?
13. List three differences about which American managers must be aware when transacting business in other countries.
14. How is listening different from hearing?
15. In what types of situations should managers use both oral and written channels of communication?

DISCUSS IDEAS

1. Discuss the importance of feedback in two-way communications.
2. Explain how a grammar error in a memo might be considered a distraction and thus a barrier to communications.
3. Distortion is not always unconsciously done. Discuss how conscious distortion can be harmful if an employee regularly distorts information to a supervisor.
4. Describe the psychology behind why good news should be stated early in a written message and why bad news should be delayed somewhat.
5. A manager was enjoying giving a talk to a group of young people about business. An audience member asked the manager whether he believed in open communications. The manager looked uncomfortable with the question, snapped a fast "yes," and quickly asked, "Any other questions?" Compare the oral and non-verbal message of the manager.
6. Discuss the main factors that help to determine the culture of an organization.
7. Discuss what strategy you would use to help resolve a conflict situation between two employees who always disagree on how a task should be handled.
8. Ann and Susan became friends at work and often e-mailed each other during the day about personal matters. One day Susan sent a negative message about her manager, but it accidentally was sent to a higher-level manager, who asked Susan for an explanation. What would you do as that manager if Susan had violated company policy prohibiting such messages?

9. Although cultures differ from country to country, how can cultures differ within a country such as the United States?
10. How might busy managers follow a policy of encouraging effective listening?

ANALYZE INFORMATION

1. From Figure 10-1, determine the percentage of time managers spend each workday (a) listening, (b) speaking, (c) reading, and (d) writing. Also, determine the total percentage of time that they spend in communicating and in other activities.
2. One type of non-verbal communication involves the use of body language. When your teacher directs you, demonstrate five different messages by using only your hands and/or arms. Identify emoticons that match any of your five messages.
3. With the help of your teacher, complete the following activities that show communication breakdowns. Find a picture from a magazine that shows action, such as someone running, dancing, or playing a musical instrument. Then, ask for three, four, or five volunteers. Tell one volunteer to stay at the front of the class and ask the other volunteers to go beyond hearing and viewing distance. Now follow these steps:
   - **a.** Explain to the first volunteer that you will allow one minute to study the action picture, which the person must then describe to the second volunteer. (Show the picture for one minute to the volunteer and then conceal the picture.)
   - **b.** Call in the second volunteer, and ask the first volunteer to describe the picture in as much detail as possible. Two-way communications are acceptable.
   - **c.** Call the third volunteer and ask the second volunteer to relay the description just received. Continue this process until all volunteers have had a chance to listen to the description and repeat what they heard.
   - **d.** Show the picture to the volunteers and the class, and ask if the scene is what they thought was being described.
   - **e.** Summarize by a discussion or written report what you learned about the communication process and how communication breakdowns occur.
4. Assume that you are working for a business that has many new young part-time workers. Many of the workers are often late or absent. As a result, other employees must work longer hours and are often called in on weekends. The manager and the workers are concerned and want to solve this problem. Follow the directions of your teacher and use the nominal group technique to solve this problem. Present your best solution to your teacher, who will serve as the manager of the work group. When done, discuss how well the NGT worked.

5. LaToya put the following idea in her company's suggestion box: "Rather than hire a new full-time worker at $15.00 per hour to handle our increased business, hire two half-time workers at $10.00 per hour. Then if business slows later, we can cut back to one half-time worker or no workers."
   a. As the manager, write LaToya a note saying that her suggestion has been accepted and she will earn 20 percent of one year's saving for the idea.
   b. Assume one year went by and that one half-time employee worked 860 hours and the second worked 600 hours. A full-time employee would have worked 2,000 hours. How much will LaToya receive for her suggestion?

SOLVE BUSINESS PROBLEMS

CASE 10-1

Lauren Lemaster works at the headquarters office for a major Internet corporation that has offices in five countries. The company has a strict set of rules regarding the use of e-mail. Hackers often try to break into the operating system to damage it and that naturally hurts business.

The CEO sends all newly hired employees the following message: "Be careful what you say to others, especially when using e-mail with other employees. A year ago a hacker learned that we were planning to buy another business that would increase the value of the company. He found out about our intended purchase and took the idea to a competitor, so we lost 'big' on that failed operation. For reasons like this, we require you to sign the attached oath. The oath states that if an employee is responsible in any way for inside information getting to the outside, that employee will be released immediately." Without further thought, Lauren signed, but that was two years ago.

Yesterday, on her lunch hour Lauren sent a secret e-mail message to her best friend, Douglas, who likes to buy stock in Internet companies when they do something new and exciting. Lauren's message said: "Douglas, I learned that my company has its eye on Dawson and Donaldson, Inc. Keep it to yourself. Hopefully this will repay the favor you did to help me get this job. Trash this message after reading it. Lauren."

Douglas bought stock in the company and shared the message with several friends, who also bought stock. Then he destroyed the message. And within 24 hours, the stock doubled in price. However, Lauren's boss called her in and fired her on the spot for having violated company policy.

Think Critically:

1. Was the company's Internet policy too severe? Why or why not? Because Lauren wrote the e-mail on her lunch hour, is she actually in violation of company policy?
2. How did the company find out about Lauren's e-mail message?
3. Does Lauren have any privacy rights that would enable her to sue the company for the loss of her job? Explain.
4. Was Lauren as unethical as Douglas was? And what responsibility does Douglas have for Lauren's plight?
5. How would the ten rules for good listening apply when Lauren and Douglas meet to discuss what happened?

CASE 10-2

As a former regional manager for Graphix International, Seth McClaren was promoted and transferred to the Philadelphia headquarters several years ago. A close friend, Josh Berry, manages the company's regional office in Atlanta. Josh arrived in Philadelphia today, along with other regional managers. At tomorrow's meeting, the latest procedures for submitting monthly reports will be explained by the new top managers. Seth called Josh and invited him to dinner this evening to discuss concerns about changes going on. After dinner the following conversation occurs:

Seth: *Tomorrow's a big meeting. The new president and the two new vice presidents will be there to explain the new reporting procedures.*

Josh: *Was something wrong with the old method? It worked fine for my office. We do the reports according to the rules. We hear from headquarters only when something isn't done right.*

Seth: *The new managers are different. They like meetings and lots of contact with employees. They even stop by my office every few weeks to chat. They seem friendly . . . even invited me to stop by their offices if I have a problem. Nothing like the former managers! You never saw them and never heard from them unless something went wrong. Then threatening memos would come from all directions.*

Josh: *Is that why most of the regional managers kept clear of headquarters? The person I replaced warned me not to break any of the rules. "Just keep your nose clean," she said. "If you don't bother them, they won't bother you."*

Seth: *That's the main reason why the board of directors changed the top managers. The new managers expect good work, but they also seem to want the employees and managers to discuss problems. They even want us to suggest solutions. Imagine that! Some of us aren't sure whether to trust them yet. We're afraid if we make one mistake, we'll be fired.*

Josh: *They seem to be practicing what they preach, Seth. The Houston regional manager stuck her neck out and made a suggestion, and a vice president flew down to talk with her. The grapevine said he made a real big thing over the idea. Her picture is in the newsletter that just came out. The newsletter has plenty of information about the business and about her suggestion.*

Seth: *That's what I mean, Josh. The way these new people operate . . . it's different. I'm not sure I like it. The new monthly report even has a place in it where you can state complaints and make suggestions. They're going to get an earful when the next month's forms are returned. That's no way to run a business.*

Josh: *Let's give them a chance, Seth. At least they're willing to listen, which is more than you could say about the departed managers.*

Think Critically:

1. Did the corporate culture change between the old and new top management? Explain.
2. What evidence is there that the new top management will encourage or discourage upward communication?
3. Did the vice president who flew out to see the Houston regional manager regarding a suggestion for improvement use more than one channel of communication? If yes, how?
4. Did the old or the new top managers place more stress on two-way communications? Explain.
5. Will Seth be as comfortable as Josh with the new managers? Explain your answer.

PROJECT: MY BUSINESS, INC.

As a small business owner, you will be responsible for making sure communications flow smoothly within your business and with others outside your business. Unclear or poor communications can be very damaging to a new business as you work with employees, customers, other business people, and the public. You need to plan communications carefully and use effective communications whenever you interact with others.

DATA COLLECTION

INTERNET

1. Using newspapers, business magazines, and Internet news services, identify situations where businesses faced problems resulting from poor communications. Make a list of the types of communication problems you identify, using the following categories: communications problems with (a) employees, (b) customers, (c) other business people, (d) the public, (e) other.
2. Advertising is one method of communicating with customers. However, advertisements often do not communicate the same message to everyone. Locate three advertisements from small businesses. If possible, find advertisements from businesses similar to your juice bar business. Show the advertisements to five different people. Record their answers to the following questions:
   a What is the most important message you receive from the advertisement?
   b. In general, do you believe the advertisement is effective or ineffective?
   c. As a result of the advertisement, would you be more or less likely to be a customer of the business? Why?

ANALYSIS

1. Compose a letter that you would send to local health clubs and recreation centers. Use the letter to request that your juice bar be identified as the "exclusive source for juice drinks" for their facility. Make sure the letter is persuasive and offers some value or benefit to the businesses you will contact.
2. You have been asked by the local organization of retailers to make a brief presentation at their monthly luncheon meeting about your new business. Prepare a five-minute speech that describes the business and its operations and some of the challenges you believe that you will face. (You may want to use a computer to create some visual aids for your presentation.) Your teacher may allow you to videotape your presentation or give the presentation to the class.

UNIT FOUR

MANAGEMENT RESPONSIBILITIES

CHAPTERS

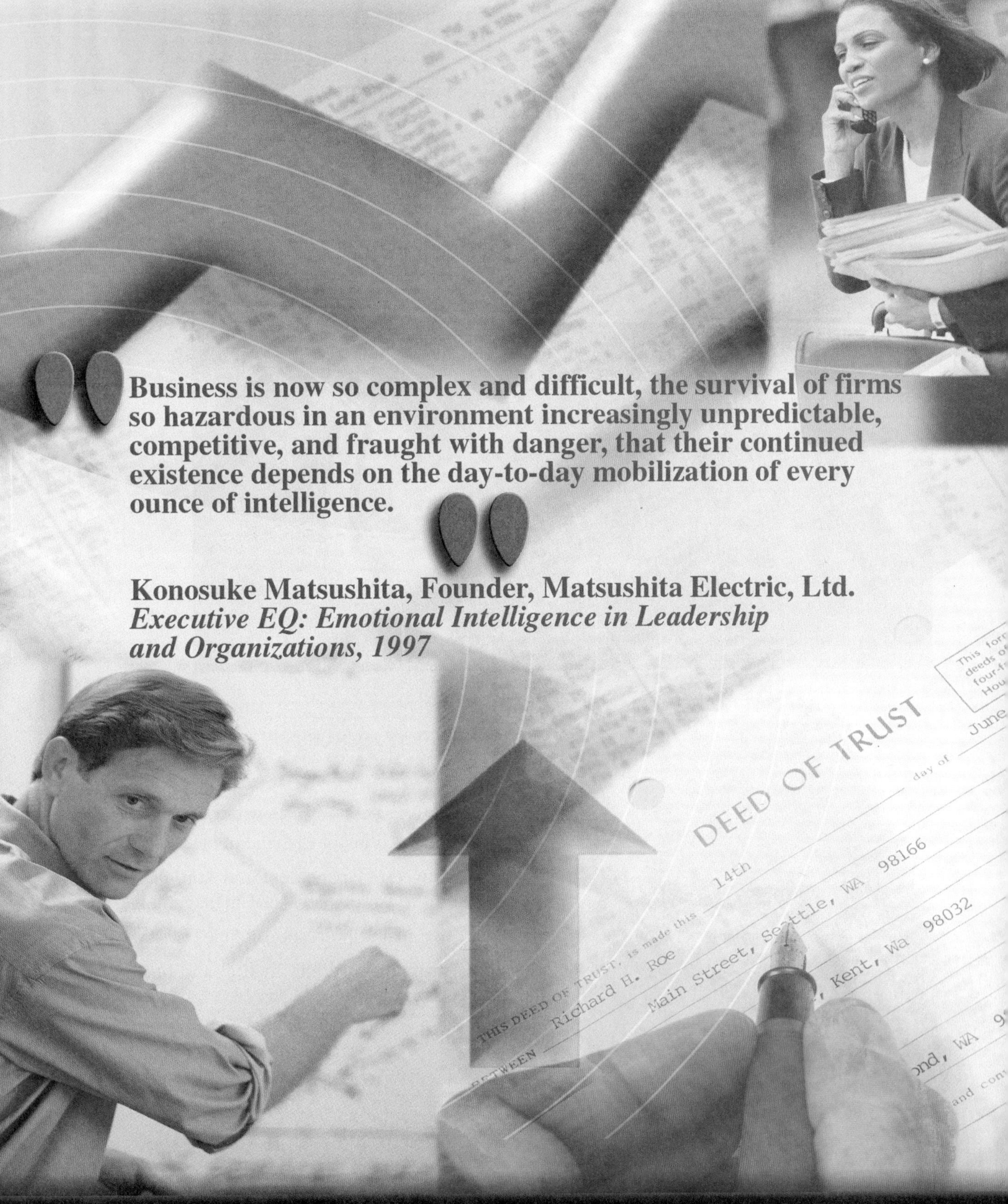

"Business is now so complex and difficult, the survival of firms so hazardous in an environment increasingly unpredictable, competitive, and fraught with danger, that their continued existence depends on the day-to-day mobilization of every ounce of intelligence."

Konosuke Matsushita, Founder, Matsushita Electric, Ltd.
Executive EQ: Emotional Intelligence in Leadership and Organizations, 1997

MANAGEMENT FUNCTIONS AND DECISION MAKING

OBJECTIVES

11-1 Define the four functions of management.

11-2 Differentiate between management and non-management employees and the various levels of management.

11-3 Describe the five major job responsibilities of supervisors.

11-4 Identify how managers use information and business research in their work.

11-5 Outline the steps in an effective decision-making process.

WHAT DO I REALLY WANT?

Erik Berman has worked for Freeden Web Technologies for five years. It was his first job since graduating from the local community college with a degree in Computer Network Systems. He enjoys his work as a network specialist, a position he has held for over two years now. The company recognized his ability, and he has moved up rapidly from his first job as networking assistant to his current position.

Erik is facing an important career decision. At the end of his last six-month performance evaluation conference, his manager told him that the supervisor who has responsibility for Erik's work team and three other teams would be promoted in three weeks. The manager wants Erik to consider applying for the supervisor's position.

The opportunity to move into a management position is exciting. The job would provide a higher salary and status as a manager. At the same time, Erik isn't sure he has the skills or the interest in being a supervisor. It seems to him that supervisors are constantly dealing with employee complaints or with concerns from their own bosses. He is used to working a lot of hours when big projects have to be completed. However, he knows that the company's supervisors work many extra hours each week to get all of their own work done while solving the problems that seemed to come up regularly.

Erik really enjoys his current work in network systems, and he knows that he won't do as much of that work as a supervisor. Yet, he isn't sure if he wants to do technical computer work for the rest of his career. He also knows that he likes working with and helping to train the new employees who are assigned to his work group. He really feels good when he sees them performing well and being recognized for their excellent work. His biggest concern, however, is that he really doesn't know very much about the supervisor's job, and he's concerned that he won't succeed. He already knows he's a good network specialist. Freeden does not provide any specific training for prospective supervisors, and Erik's only preparation was a management course he completed while attending the community college.

MOVING INTO MANAGEMENT

Erik's experience is similar to that of many employees. For people who want to become managers, their first management position will often be as a supervisor. However, they may not know very much about the work of managers. If they have worked for effective managers, it may appear that the job is quite easy. On the other hand, employees may have had experiences with poor managers who make their own jobs difficult and cause problems for their subordinates.

Many employees believe they would like to be managers and often think they can do a better job than the managers for whom they work. However, when presented with the decision of whether to move into management, they may find the decision difficult to make. If they like the work they do, moving into management will mean they can no longer do that work. Will they enjoy a management job as much? If they have been successful in their current job, a move into management can be very risky. What if they are not successful in the management position? It is not likely they will be able to move back into their previous jobs, and, indeed, they may be fired if they do not succeed as a manager.

Understanding management and the work of managers will make it easier for employees to choose a management career. If the company helps employees move into management with training programs, there will be less risk and a greater opportunity for employees to be successful. Some companies are now allowing employees an opportunity to work in a beginning management position for a short time before making a permanent decision. If they find the job is not what they expected or if the company decides these new managers are not performing at the level required, they can reach an agreement to move the employees back into the same type of job they held before.

Companies need good managers just as they need effective employees. Being able to identify managers from current employees allows a company to reward its employees with promotions and to have managers who understand company operations and policies. You can see why Erik would be a good candidate for a management position in Freeden Web Technologies. If you were Erik, what decision would you make?

NATURE OF MANAGEMENT

Managers make things happen in business. From the original idea for a business, through accumulating and determining the best ways to use the resources needed to operate the business, to managing people, managers are responsible for the success or failure of the company. The decisions managers make determine what a company will do and how well it will perform.

ILLUSTRATION 11-1

Management training is as important to business success as employee training. What topics do you believe should be included in a management training program?

MANAGEMENT ACTIVITIES

Because there are so many types of managers, it is difficult to identify exactly what they do. However, there are a number of activities that all managers must perform no matter what the type or size of the company or in what part of the business they work. The president of a large international corporation made up of several companies and thousands of employees is a manager, but so is the owner of a small service business with one location and only a few employees. The people who are responsible for human resource departments and for purchasing departments, for a company's salespeople, or for its information management activities are all managers. So are supervisors of people working on an assembly line, in a warehouse, or at data-entry terminals. While each of these jobs involves many unique activities, each is also concerned with management.

Management is the process of accomplishing the goals of an organization through the effective use of people and other resources. As you learned earlier, those resources include money, buildings, equipment, and materials. The primary work of all managers can be grouped within four functions: (1) planning, (2) organizing, (3) implementing, and (4) controlling.

Planning involves analyzing information and making decisions about what needs to be done. **Organizing** is concerned with determining how plans can be accomplished most effectively and arranging resources to complete work. A manager is **implementing** when carrying out the plans and helping employees to work effectively, and is **controlling** when evaluating results to determine if the company's objectives have been accomplished as planned.

Operating any business is a very complex process. Even managers of small businesses must make product, marketing, personnel, and finance decisions every day. If managers are not well prepared to

ILLUSTRATION 11-2

The manager of a large manufacturing company and the manager of a small service business complete many of the same activities. How are their jobs similar and different?

operate the business, problems will soon develop. The manager who knows how to plan, organize, implement, and control is prepared to make the decisions needed to operate a business successfully.

MANAGEMENT AND NON-MANAGEMENT EMPLOYEES

Many employees of a business complete activities that could be considered management activities. They might plan and organize their work or decide how to organize materials to complete work efficiently. An experienced employee may be given the responsibility to be the leader on a group project, and the group members may help the manager evaluate the project when it has been completed. The increasing use of teams in organizations is providing employees many more opportunities to participate in activities that previously have been the domain of managers.

In each of these examples, the employee is getting valuable experience. That experience will help the employee to understand the work of managers and to prepare for possible promotion to a management position. If the company in the earlier example had used these types of experiences to develop employees, Erik might have had a better idea of what it would be like to be a supervisor. Giving those types of responsibilities to employees can also be an effective motivating technique. However, even though employees perform some work that is similar to managers' responsibilities, the employees are not managers.

A **manager** completes all four management functions on a regular basis and has authority over other jobs and people. In each of the sit-

ILLUSTRATION 11-3

Giving employees responsibilities that include planning, organizing, implementing, and controlling helps to prepare them for management careers. What other benefits can result for the company and the employees?

uations above, where employees were completing what seemed to be management functions, they were doing those tasks infrequently, were not completing all of the management functions, or were completing them for their job only.

There is typically more than one level of management in most companies. Large companies may have five or six management classifications. However, today many companies are attempting to reduce the number of levels of management, making each level of management and each manager's work more important.

A manager whose main job is to direct the work of employees is called a supervisor. **Supervisors** are typically the first (or beginning) level of management in a company and often have many non-managerial activities to perform as well. An **executive** is a top-level manager who spends almost all of his or her time on management functions. Executives have other managers reporting to them. Between executives and supervisors in larger organizations, there will be one or more levels of mid-managers.

A **mid-manager** completes all of the management functions, but spends most of the time on one management function such as planning or controlling, or is responsible for a specific part of the company's operations. Figure 11-1 shows how the time spent on management functions changes for different levels of managers in a business.

You can see from the figure that as a manager moves up in the organization, responsibilities change. Supervisors work most directly with employees and are involved primarily in ensuring that the day-to-day work of the business is completed. Therefore, they devote most of their management time to implementing. Executives work with other managers and are responsible for the long-term direction of the business. They spend most of their time on planning and organizing.

Today, skilled managers, professionals, and technicians are in increasingly short supply. Finding and affording skilled professionals and technicians have been a problem for organizations for quite a while; but more recently, labor shortages have expanded into the ranks of skilled hourly wage-earners and even middle managers and supervisors.

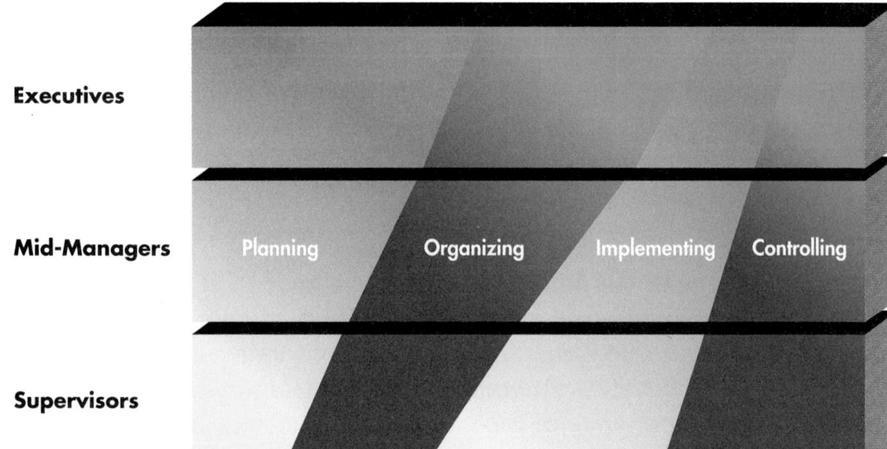

FIGURE 11-1

The amount of time spent on each function depends on the level of management.

SUPERVISION

Supervisors are critical to the success of a business. They work directly with employees and are responsible for translating the company's plan into action. One of their most important tasks is to create a work environment that motivates employees to do their best.

THE SUPERVISOR'S JOB

Supervisors are often promoted from the area where they work. Remember from the beginning of the chapter that Erik was a network specialist for Freeden. Usually, supervisors are selected from among the most experienced and most skilled workers. However, they may have little or no management training. As first-level managers, supervisors are responsible for the day-to-day activities of the company's employees. They need to understand and work with both employees and management. Supervisors must implement the decisions of management; at the same time, they must solve employee problems and present employee concerns to management.

The effectiveness of a supervisor's job is determined by three factors: (1) the quality of the work of the supervised employees, (2) the efficient use of the company's resources, and (3) the satisfaction of the supervisor's employees. If the employees are not doing the work well, management will not be pleased with the supervisor's performance. If they are not using resources efficiently, a company may not be able to make a profit. And if the employees are not happy with their work, they will not perform their jobs well for long and may decide to leave the company.

RESPONSIBILITIES OF SUPERVISORS

You learned earlier that supervisors often divide their time between management activities and other work. They are responsible for implementing the plans of executives by getting employees to perform effectively on a day-to-day basis. One supervisor's job may be very different from another's, especially from supervisors in other departments and companies. Employees have different levels of education, training, and experience. Some supervisors manage experienced employees, while others work with new employees. In spite of the differences in their jobs, however, supervisors still have a common set of responsibilities in all companies. Those responsibilities are summarized in Figure 11-2.

COMMUNICATE THE GOALS AND DIRECTIONS OF MANAGEMENT TO EMPLOYEES

In order for employees to complete work effectively, they must understand what needs to be done and why. Supervisors must be able to communicate effectively with employees. Good supervisors can show employees the importance of the company's goals and help them see how they can accomplish their own goals by helping the company to be successful.

Supervisor's Job Description

FIGURE 11-2
Common Responsibilities of Supervisors

EXPLAIN EMPLOYEE CONCERNS AND IDEAS TO MANAGEMENT Employees want to feel that they are a part of the company and that management considers their ideas and opinions. Therefore, supervisors must take the time to talk with the people they supervise in order to find out their concerns and ideas. Then they must communicate those concerns and ideas to management and follow up to find out what action was taken. Employees like to work for a supervisor who is interested in them and their ideas. They will work hard for a company that is concerned about them, involves employees in planning and decision making, and takes their ideas and suggestions seriously.

EVALUATE AND IMPROVE EMPLOYEE PERFORMANCE Supervisors get work done through individual employees and work teams. They need to be sure that each employee is performing as effectively as possible. Regular formal and informal performance reviews can reveal the employee's strengths and weaknesses. Supervisors must be both positive and objective when they complete evaluations of employees. Good supervisors discuss these evaluations with their employees in ways that contribute to effective understanding, not conflict. They provide rewards and recognition for employees who perform well. They also provide help for employees who are not performing well, so that their skills can be improved. This help might be in the form of advice and coaching, or it might involve informal and formal training. When serious problems occur, supervisors may be required to discipline employees or even recommend termination.

ENCOURAGE EMPLOYEES TO DO THEIR BEST WORK How employees feel about their jobs affects their performance. If they are unsure about what they are doing or if the work environment is one of constant conflict, employees will not be able to perform well. Supervisors need to create a pleasant atmosphere in which employees can enjoy their work and do a good job. Employees want to feel accepted and comfortable. They want to know that they can get help if they have problems.

Keeping the best and brightest employees may be the wisest decision an organization can make. Many companies strive to give employees valid reasons to stay and minimize their reasons for leaving. Lack of recognition is a common feeling among disenchanted employees; secondary reasons include low wages, lack of opportunities, outdated skills, and lack of creative input. Entrepreneurial employees who believe that their companies won't accept their innovative ideas are likely to leave—to join the competition or to start new (and perhaps competing) companies of their own.

They want others to realize that what they do is important and that they will be recognized for good work.

USE RESOURCES EFFICIENTLY Companies won't operate long if they are unable to make a profit. An important part of earning a profit is controlling the costs of the business. Since supervisors are responsible for the day-to-day activities of a business, they have a great deal of control over whether a company makes a profit or a loss. Good supervisors continually look for ways to operate more efficiently and to use resources more effectively. They seek advice from employees and make suggestions to managers on how activities can be improved.

DAY-TO-DAY MANAGEMENT

Supervisors are essential to a business, because they are responsible for the work of employees in the business. Each employee gets direction from a supervisor, and the supervisor is responsible for the work of each employee. Supervisors must be able to manage their own work effectively as well as the work of the employees for whom they are responsible. Supervisors are responsible for planning, organizing, implementing, and controlling the daily work of their units. Several management activities are important for day-to-day management. Those activities and some common tools used to complete those activities are shown in Figure 11-3.

Supervisors complete daily planning through the use of work schedules. Schedules identify the tasks to be done and the timeframe for completion of each task. Supervisors may be responsible for both full-time and part-time employees. The business may operate 7 days a week and 24 hours a day. Supervisors will have to decide what days

ILLUSTRATION 11-4

Supervisors are sometimes called the most important managers in a business. Do you agree or disagree with that statement? Why?

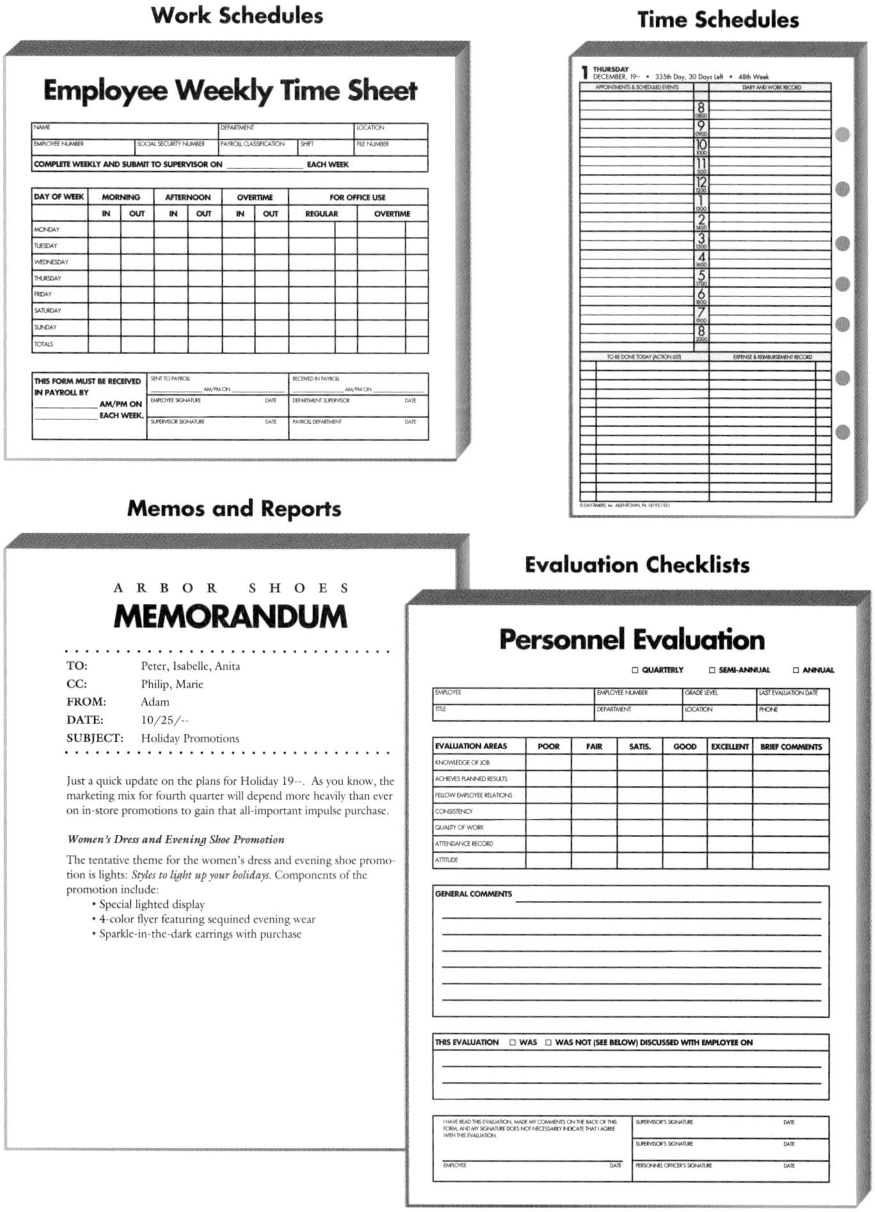

Work Schedules

Employee Weekly Time Sheet

NAME		DEPARTMENT		LOCATION
EMPLOYEE NUMBER	SOCIAL SECURITY NUMBER	PAYROLL CLASSIFICATION	SHIFT	FILE NUMBER
COMPLETE WEEKLY AND SUBMIT TO SUPERVISOR ON ____________ EACH WEEK				

DAY OF WEEK	MORNING		AFTERNOON		OVERTIME		FOR OFFICE USE	
	IN	OUT	IN	OUT	IN	OUT	REGULAR	OVERTIME
MONDAY								
TUESDAY								
WEDNESDAY								
THURSDAY								
FRIDAY								
SATURDAY								
SUNDAY								
TOTALS								

THIS FORM MUST BE RECEIVED IN PAYROLL BY ____________ AM/PM ON ____________ EACH WEEK.	SENT TO PAYROLL ______ AM/PM ON ______	RECEIVED IN PAYROLL ______ AM/PM ON ______
	EMPLOYEE SIGNATURE — DATE	DEPARTMENT SUPERVISOR — DATE
	SUPERVISOR SIGNATURE — DATE	PAYROLL DEPARTMENT — DATE

Time Schedules

1 THURSDAY DECEMBER, 19-- • 335th Day, 30 Days Left • 48th Week

APPOINTMENTS & SCHEDULED EVENTS		DIARY AND WORK RECORD
	8	
	9	
	10	
	11	
	12	
	1	
	2	
	3	
	4	
	5	
	6	
	7	
	8	

TO BE DONE TODAY (ACTION LIST)	EXPENSE & REIMBURSEMENT RECORD

© DAY-TIMERS, Inc. ALLENTOWN, PA 18195-1551

Memos and Reports

A R B O R   S H O E S

MEMORANDUM

TO: Peter, Isabelle, Anita
CC: Philip, Marie
FROM: Adam
DATE: 10/25/--
SUBJECT: Holiday Promotions

Just a quick update on the plans for Holiday 19--. As you know, the marketing mix for fourth quarter will depend more heavily than ever on in-store promotions to gain that all-important impulse purchase.

Women's Dress and Evening Shoe Promotion

The tentative theme for the women's dress and evening shoe promotion is lights: *Styles to light up your holidays.* Components of the promotion include:

- Special lighted display
- 4-color flyer featuring sequined evening wear
- Sparkle-in-the-dark earrings with purchase

Evaluation Checklists

Personnel Evaluation

☐ QUARTERLY ☐ SEMI-ANNUAL ☐ ANNUAL

EMPLOYEE	EMPLOYEE NUMBER	GRADE LEVEL	LAST EVALUATION DATE
TITLE	DEPARTMENT	LOCATION	PHONE

EVALUATION AREAS	POOR	FAIR	SATIS.	GOOD	EXCELLENT	BRIEF COMMENTS
KNOWLEDGE OF JOB						
ACHIEVES PLANNED RESULTS						
FELLOW EMPLOYEE RELATIONS						
CONSISTENCY						
QUALITY OF WORK						
ATTENDANCE RECORD						
ATTITUDE						

GENERAL COMMENTS

THIS EVALUATION ☐ WAS ☐ WAS NOT (SEE BELOW) DISCUSSED WITH EMPLOYEE ON

I HAVE READ THIS EVALUATION, MADE MY COMMENTS ON THE BACK OF THIS FORM, AND MY SIGNATURE DOES NOT NECESSARILY INDICATE THAT I AGREE WITH THIS EVALUATION.	SUPERVISOR'S SIGNATURE — DATE
	SUPERVISOR'S SIGNATURE — DATE
EMPLOYEE — DATE	PERSONNEL OFFICER'S SIGNATURE — DATE

FIGURE 11-3

Common Tools Used by Supervisors for Day-to-Day Management

of the week employees will work and which projects each person will complete. If they schedule too few people, the work will not get done. If they schedule too many employees, costs will increase. Projects may be assigned to individuals or to groups. The people assigned must have the skills to complete the work as well as the motivation to do it and must work well together if they are part of a work team.

Time management is an important management skill for supervisors. A great deal of work must be done in a short time. Supervisors must be able to determine the work to be done, set priorities for the most important work, and ensure that it is completed properly and on time.

BUSINESS INNOVATION

IMPROVING QUALITY AND PROFITS THROUGH TQM

For much of the 20th century, the approach to business management did not change. Managers believed the best way to be successful was to operate the business as efficiently as possible. To achieve that goal, managers tried to get more and more work out of employees, make as few changes in products as possible, and find ways to reduce costs even if it meant lowering the quality of the products.

In the early 1950s, Dr. W. Edwards Deming developed 14 guiding principles for managers that taught them to view their role as leaders rather than managers. He suggested that a long-term commitment to quality, customer satisfaction, and employee morale would lead to success. His process was called Total Quality Management (TQM).

- TQM emphasizes increasing quality and developing an effective organization.
- TQM is concerned about customer satisfaction and employee motivation.
- TQM relies on leadership and cooperation versus the traditional management focus on closely supervising employee behavior.
- TQM businesses constantly look for new and improved ways to complete their work to increase effectiveness and quality.
- TQM emphasizes teamwork, and employee involvement in decision making.
- Finally, TQM businesses view employees as valuable contributors to success and use training and education to improve employee effectiveness and motivation.

A set of tools has been developed to help businesses implement Total Quality Management. A few examples of the tools are:

- *Flow charts.* These identify each step in a procedure and how the steps are related to each other. They can be used to compare how work is being done to how it is supposed to be done in order to reduce errors.
- *Cause and effect analysis.* Employee and management teams brainstorm about problems to find solutions. They develop a diagram that lists problems and possible causes and link them together until they discover and agree on the basic problem. Then they can develop solutions.
- *Scatter diagrams.* Data from two different factors are visually plotted on a chart and analyzed to discover relationships. For example, the number of employee absences over a six-month period is compared to the number of product defects to see if the use of temporary employees is related to a reduction in product quality.

Today, quality, customer satisfaction, teamwork, and process improvement are making a difference in business competitiveness.

THINK CRITICALLY

1. Why do U.S. companies find it so difficult to change from traditional approaches to TQM?
2. Many schools are now implementing TQM and teaching students to use its tools. What types of procedures in schools could benefit from TQM?
3. If a school was facing a problem with students being tardy from classes, how could the school use one of the TQM tools to help solve that problem?

They must not only use their time effectively, but also help their employees determine how to use their time most effectively each day.

Supervisors communicate every day with their employees. While much of the communication between supervisors and employees is oral, they communicate in writing as well. Supervisors and employees today often communicate using technology such as e-mail and other computer communications.

Whether oral or written, communications must be specific and clear. Supervisors need to plan the content of their communications and determine the best method, place, and time to communicate the information. Supervisors should follow up on communications and ask for feedback to make sure the receivers understood the messages. Listening is an important communication skill for supervisors.

The final daily management skill for supervisors is quality control. In some companies, employees spend a great deal of time correcting errors and redoing work that was not done well the first time. Supervisors can reduce those problems by planning work carefully, developing quality standards, and regularly checking the quality of the work being done. Also, supervisors can help employees recognize the importance of quality work, so the employees will take responsibility for reducing errors and controlling costs.

IMPROVING SUPERVISORY SKILLS

One of the most difficult problems facing new supervisors is to accept the fact that they must spend less time on the non-managerial activities and more time on management functions. Because supervisors are usually skilled employees, they often want to continue to do the work they were doing before being promoted. At times, they may think that their employees are not doing the job as well as it can be done. Therefore, new supervisors are often tempted to step in and do the job themselves. That will cause employees to believe the supervisor does not have confidence in their work. Both the quality and quantity of the employees' work will suffer. Supervisors must rely on their employees to get the work done, so they can concentrate on management activities and use the talents of the people with whom they work.

Today, more companies are helping supervisors develop and improve their management skills. Many companies provide formal training programs for new supervisors. They might, for instance, participate in management classes full-time for a few weeks and then continue training through a series of meetings and short training sessions. Or, they might study training materials, such as books and audio or videotapes, for several months after they begin their supervisory duties. Other companies help supervisors develop their skills by paying for them to attend management classes at a nearby college or sending them to management development programs offered by companies specializing in training and development. A newer method of helping supervisors is to provide an experienced supervisor or another manager to serve as a coach for the new supervisor.

If companies do not provide training, the new supervisor needs to develop management skills individually by enrolling in classes, attending meetings, reading management books and magazines, participating in professional associations for managers, and other similar activities. There are now computer-based training programs as well as training available on the Internet to help supervisors continue their development using technology. Talking with and observing the work of experienced supervisors is another way to improve management skills.

USING MANAGEMENT INFORMATION

To do a good job of planning, organizing, implementing, and controlling, managers must have a great deal of information available. They need records on production and sales, personnel, expenses, and profit or loss to make decisions. Data must be collected, organized, and made available to managers so they can make decisions quickly and efficiently.

Even in very small businesses, managers cannot remember all of the information needed to make decisions. In large companies with many managers and hundreds of employees, it is impossible to operate without a systematic way to gather information for managers to use in decision making.

MANAGEMENT INFORMATION SYSTEMS

Management information systems were described in detail earlier in the book. Every company needs such a system as an important management tool. Computers help managers control business operations.

ILLUSTRATION 11-5

Managers have much more information available today than ever before. How can too much information actually decrease a manager's effectiveness?

Managers can use information systems to reduce the amount of time spent on controlling activities. If managers took the time to review all of the information collected on business operations, they would have little time for other activities. Computers can be used to monitor the performance of activities in a company. If activities are performed as planned and standards are met, no management attention is needed. Managers should become involved only when activities do not occur as planned or results do not meet standards.

BUSINESS RESEARCH

Managers must be careful not to make decisions without sufficient information about the problem or possible solutions. When they need more information to make a good decision, they may need to conduct research.

Business research is conducted in many areas to aid in decision making. Marketing research and product development research are two common areas. A manager may want to determine why certain groups of customers are purchasing a product while others are not. A proposed new product should not be developed unless research shows that the product can be produced at a profit and that customers will be likely to purchase it.

Human resource studies are conducted on such topics as the supply and demand of labor, employee motivation, and training techniques. Financial executives need the results of research that deals with borrowing and investing money. Managers also need research results regarding economic factors, such as the expected economic performance of specific companies or for the industry in which a company operates. The research described as well as other types of research helps executives make important decisions relative to the growth and development of their companies.

Much of the needed business research is done by the business itself. Most large companies have research departments that complete research related to the specific problems of the company. But since research departments are expensive to maintain, small companies must depend to a considerable degree on professional research organizations.

Research centers and faculty members in universities conduct studies that are often helpful to businesses. Various divisions of the federal government undertake extensive research, and much of this information is available to and useful for business. Trade and professional associations conduct research studies that are useful to the particular industries they serve. Companies may also employ research organizations or individual consultants to gather and analyze information to solve problems or improve decision making.

DECISION MAKING

In the process of planning, organizing, implementing, and controlling, managers encounter problems that require them to make decisions. Top-level managers make some of the decisions, such as new products to be developed or new markets that the business will enter. Mid-managers make other decisions, which may result in new ways of organizing work, the use of new technology, or improved procedures for completing work. First-level managers, such as department heads and supervisors, make decisions about the daily operations of their units. It is important to the overall success of any business that the decisions be made as carefully as possible at every level of management.

PROBLEMS AND DECISION MAKING

Generally, a **problem** is a difficult situation requiring a solution. Problems usually do not have single solutions. Instead, they have a series of possible solutions. There may be several good solutions, but there may also be several poor solutions. For example, the problem may be to find the most effective and efficient method to ship products from a manufacturing plant in Texas to customers in Montreal, Canada. Possible solutions are to ship by airplane, ship, train, or truck. Depending on the circumstances, any one of the shipping methods could be the best or the worst solution. To find the best solution, managers should follow a systematic approach to solving problems. That procedure is outlined in Figure 11-4.

STEPS IN PROBLEM SOLVING

Most problems can be analyzed by completing a series of steps. You may have learned this problem-solving process already in other classes, such as a science class. The procedure works as well in business as it does in scientific problem solving. The four steps in problem solving are (1) identify the problem, (2) list possible solutions, (3) carefully analyze the possible solutions, and (4) select the best solution using the results of the analysis.

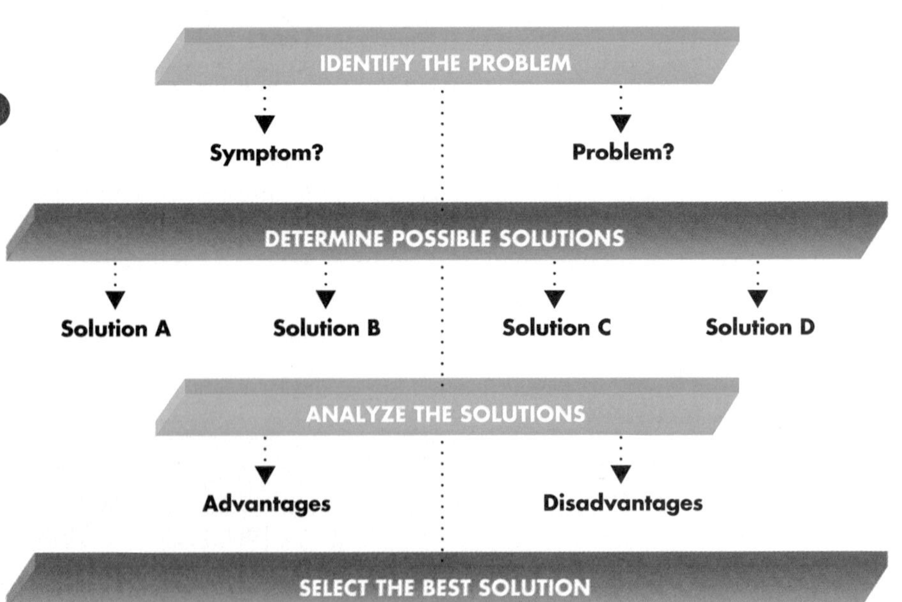

FIGURE 11-4

Developing an effective solution to a problem requires a step-by-step process.

IDENTIFY THE PROBLEM Before a manager can make a decision to solve a problem, the problem must first be located and identified. Often, a manager may not even be aware that a problem exists. For example, employees may be unhappy about a co-worker. The manager may not know about the problem unless employees communicate this concern or it begins to affect their work.

A manager must also be careful not to identify a symptom as the problem. A **symptom** is a sign or indication of something that appears to be the problem. When a patient complains of a headache, the headache may be a symptom. The problem could be high blood pressure, a cold, or another illness. Falling sales of a line of appliances for a retailer is a symptom. The problem could be ineffective advertising, a bad product location in the store, untrained salespeople, quality problems in the products, poor service, and so on. Therefore, it will be difficult to change the symptom until the problem can be correctly identified and corrected.

What are some reasons that sales are declining? Are fewer customers entering the business? Are customers shopping but not buying? Are customers buying but then returning the products because they are not performing as expected? Or are customers now beginning to use the Internet to purchase products rather than buying from the store? Managers can often identify the problem by asking questions and gathering information. They can use the symptom to gather information that can isolate the problem.

Sometimes managers are unaware that problems exist until it is too late. They need to review plans and performance regularly to determine if operations are proceeding as planned. When any evidence appears that suggests a problem, they should study the evidence carefully rather than ignore it. It is better to review symptoms and determine that there is no problem than to wait until problems are so big that they are difficult to correct.

LIST POSSIBLE SOLUTIONS Once they identify a problem, managers should begin to list all possible solutions. For example, if the problem is ineffective advertising, they should list all possible ways to change the advertising. The list might include more informative advertisements, a change in the advertising media used, the frequency and timing of advertising, as well as many other possibilities. Every problem has at least two or more possible solutions, and managers should not overlook any reasonable solution at this point in the problem-solving process.

There are many ways to identify possible solutions. Brainstorming, discussed in Chapter 10, is one method of developing a long list for later analysis. Managers should review solutions that have been used in the past or that were considered for solving related problems. Discussing the problems with other managers or with outside experts helps to identify solutions. Reading and studying can keep managers aware

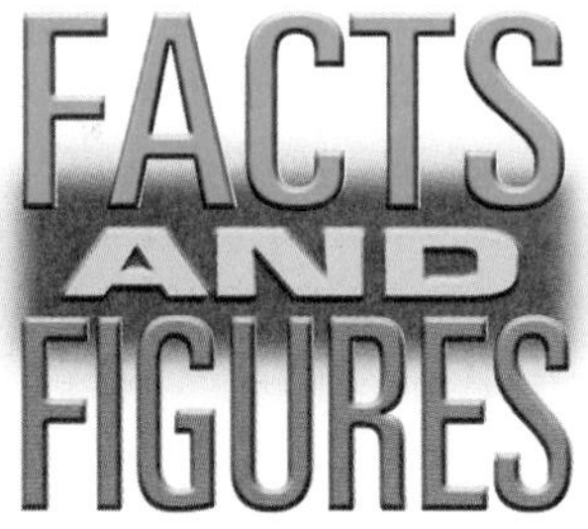

Experts in creative problem solving recommend the use of "incubation," which is a "time-out" stage to let the mind wander, without forcing it to think about any particular aspect of the problem or solution. This stage could be as simple as a lunch break or a good night's sleep. Some of the world's most creative thinkers depend on moments of solitude for their best ideas.

CYBER COMMUNICATION

Electronic-mail software generally provides a memo format for composing messages, with boxes to fill in the name and/or e-mail address of each receiver, a subject line, and the text of the message.

The header is the first part of an e-mail message, which gives information such as who sent the e-mail, to whom it was sent, who should receive copies, and the subject of the message. The subject line provides a place for the sender to supply a brief description of the message contents. The subject line is very important, because it is one of the first things the recipient sees in his or her inbox. Be sure that the subject line is concise and summarizes the topic adequately. When business people receive a lot of e-mail, informative subject lines let them know how important or useful the message will be to the receiver.

The message's text should be written in short paragraphs of only a few sentences each. This helps the reader follow your train of thought while scrolling through the message. Remember to proofread your message and think twice about its appropriateness and tone.

It's wise to sign your name at the end of the message, particularly if your mailbox address doesn't show your real name.

ACTIVITY If you have e-mail access, prepare a short message about a hobby that interests you. Be sure to fill out the header, including a relevant subject line, and the body of the message. Send the message to a friend or classmate. If you don't have e-mail access, write the appropriate information on a sheet of paper.

of new types of solutions. Many managers recognize that employees and customers are sources of possible solutions.

ANALYZE THE SOLUTIONS The third step in problem solving is to analyze the solutions. Managers do this by studying each possible solution separately, comparing the solutions, and reducing the number of solutions to the best two or three. To study each solution thoroughly and objectively, managers may need information from business records, trade associations, libraries, consultants, government sources, or the Internet. The use of management information systems and business research is an important part of this step.

After collecting all of the necessary information, managers should examine the strengths and weaknesses of each solution one by one. Then they should compare solutions and classify them in some way, such as extremely desirable, somewhat desirable, and least desirable. Some solutions may be too costly or impractical, while others may be inexpensive or very practical. For example, in a list of solutions comparing advertising media the business is considering, managers may find that the cost of television advertising is more than is available in the budget, while newspaper advertising is affordable. Managers need to compare the solutions on how effectively they will solve the problem, not just the symptom. After all the analyses have been completed, only two or three solutions may appear to effectively solve the problem.

For very important decisions, managers may want to conduct an experiment to test one or more solutions. A likely solution is often tested in one part of the organization to see how it works. The results are then compared with other tests to determine which was more effective in solving the problem before using it throughout the business. Managers then analyze the results of the experiment to eliminate some solutions and to identify those that seem to be effective.

SELECT THE BEST SOLUTION The last step in problem solving is to make the final decision from among the remaining solutions. Some problems have to be solved quickly, but for very important decisions, managers take several days or more before selecting the solution. Only after careful thought do they make the final decision and put it into action. For certain problems, managers may be able to make the decision and implement the solution. For others, managers may need to seek the approval or cooperation of other managers first.

After selecting a solution, the managers must determine the best way to implement it and who will be part of the implementation. As implementation proceeds, the managers must gather information to determine if the solution is solving the problem or if they need additional efforts or even another solution.

The problem is not solved just because the solution has been selected and implemented. The managers will want to carefully study the results and be prepared to make changes if the problem is not corrected. Once again, management information systems will be very helpful in monitoring the implementation of the solution and the results obtained. Studying and evaluating the results of solutions to problems is a part of the controlling function for managers.

At the beginning of the chapter, Erik Berman was trying to decide if he wanted to move into management as a supervisor. He knows that most of his time will be spent on management activities—planning, organizing, implementing, and controlling. As a supervisor, he will be the link between the employees he supervises and the company's management. Because of his work with computers, he may be familiar with management information systems, but he will have to become skilled at using information to make decisions. He needs to follow a careful decision-making process to identify and solve problems. If Erik finds that type of work challenging and interesting and is willing to develop the needed skills, he can become an effective supervisor for Freeden.

CHAPTER 11 REVIEW

CHAPTER CONCEPTS

- Managers make things happen in a business. They are responsible for planning, organizing, implementing, and controlling activities in order to accomplish the goals of the business. All managers complete the four management responsibilities, although higher-level managers emphasize planning and organizing while lower-level managers emphasize implementing and controlling.
- Supervisors are the first level of management and are responsible for directing the work of employees. The primary activities of supervisors are to communicate the goals and directions of management to employees, explain employee concerns and ideas to management, evaluate and improve employee performance, encourage employees to do their best work, and use resources efficiently.
- Managers need information to make good decisions and operate their businesses successfully. Management information systems are designed using computers to collect, store, and summarize information for managers. Managers need to be aware when performance is not meeting expectations, so they can quickly identify and correct problems. Managers use business research when they encounter unique problems or when needed information is not available.
- A careful, systematic process should be used to solve problems and make decisions in a business. A commonly used process involves four steps: (1) identify the problem, (2) list possible solutions, (3) carefully analyze the possible solutions, and (4) select the best solution using the results of the analysis.

BUILD VOCABULARY POWER

Define the following terms and concepts.

1. management
2. planning
3. organizing
4. implementing
5. controlling
6. manager
7. supervisor
8. executive
9. mid-manager
10. problem
11. symptom

REVIEW FACTS

1. Do managers in both small and large companies perform similar types of activities?
2. Would a person who is responsible for planning and organizing the work for one job be considered a manager?
3. Which of the four management functions do supervisors perform most often?
4. What employee qualifications are often used to select new supervisors?

5. What two factors are used to determine the effectiveness of a supervisor's performance?
6. Do supervisors have responsibility for employee evaluation? Why or why not?
7. What can new supervisors do to improve their management skills if the company does not have a training program?
8. Why is it important for data to be collected, organized, and made available for managers?
9. Why is business research important for managers?
10. What are some areas in which managers use business research?
11. How is a problem different from a symptom?
12. Why should managers identify more than one possible solution to a problem?
13. What are some ways to identify possible solutions to a problem?
14. What does a manager do after selecting a solution?

DISCUSS IDEAS

1. How could an employee perform all four of the management functions and still not be a manager?
2. Why would large companies need mid-managers who spend most of their time on one management function, such as controlling?
3. List the advantages and disadvantages that Erik Berman should consider when deciding whether to apply for the supervisor's position at Freeden Web Technologies.
4. What are some reasons why the best employee in a job may not make the best supervisor for other people in that job?
5. Why are most supervisors required to divide their time between supervisory responsibilities and other work?
6. Of the five areas of responsibility listed in Figure 11-2, which do you believe is the most important to the success of the company, and why?
7. What are some ways that supervisors can help employees manage their time better?
8. What skills do supervisors and other managers need in order to manage business information effectively?
9. Should all managers be involved in problem solving, or should that be a responsibility of experienced managers and executives?
10. Should managers involve employees and customers in problem solving? Provide an example of how employees and customers could be helpful in identifying and solving the problem facing the appliance retailer discussed on page 287.

ANALYZE INFORMATION

1. Assume that your class has decided to hold an auction to raise funds for a charity. The auction will sell used, but useful, items

that students and their families have in their homes but no longer need. Develop a chart with four headings: Planning, Organizing, Implementing, Controlling. Form a team with three other students and agree on which student will be responsible for each of the management functions. The assigned student should prepare a list of the activities that he/she believes will have to be completed for the auction to be successful. When each list is developed, the team should compare the lists and develop a final management plan of auction activities. Compare your team's list with those of the other teams in the class.

2. During one month, three managers recorded the number of hours they spent on each of the four management functions. Ms. Perez spent 42 hours on planning activities, 26 hours on organizing activities, 83 hours on implementing activities, and 57 hours on controlling activities. Mr. Pagliaro used 65 hours on planning, 24 hours on organizing, 36 hours on implementing, and 59 hours on controlling. Ms. Matsumi spent 18 hours planning, 40 hours organizing, 60 hours implementing, and 74 hours controlling. For each manager, determine the total hours worked during the month and the percentage of time devoted to each management function. Then determine the total percentage of time spent by the three managers on each of the functions. Develop a chart to illustrate the results. What conclusions would you draw from the information in the chart?
3. Keep a record of how you spend your time for two days. Record your activities for every half hour. After you have completed the list, review the use of your time. Identify the times when you believe you were using time effectively and the times when you believe you were not using time effectively. Then prepare a set of written recommendations on how you could more effectively manage your time in the future.
4. Identify an experienced supervisor whom you can interview. Discuss information management with the supervisor. Prepare a chart with the following headings to focus your discussion on information needed for decision making: Type of Information, Source of Information, Form of Information, Use of Information. After your interview, complete the chart describing the types of information the supervisor uses as a part of his or her job. Compare your chart with those prepared by the other members of your class.
5. A list of symptoms of business problems follows. For each symptom, write a question that could be used to help identify the actual problem.
   a. The number of products returned by customers has increased greatly in the last six months for an e-commerce company.
   b. Three employees who have worked for the company less than a month quit without giving notice.
   c. Advertising costs have increased by 10 percent this year.

d. The number of customers who have overdue credit accounts has doubled in the past six months.
e. Employees have been given the authority to stop the assembly line any time they notice a defective product. Since that decision was made, work stoppages have increased by four per week.

SOLVE BUSINESS PROBLEMS

CASE 11-1

Amber and Travis are both considering careers as managers. One day they were discussing their views of a manager's work. The following conversation took place:

Travis: *A manager's job is really very easy if the company hires good employees. All a manager has to do is make sure the work gets done.*

Amber: *Do you really think it's that easy? First, I don't think companies can always find employees who can do the work well. Also, a manager's job involves much more than working with employees.*

Travis: *I think a manager just has to be a good communicator. If a manager can explain clearly what needs to be done, good employees will take it from there.*

Amber: *But what about all of the things that can go wrong in a company that a manager can't plan for? Equipment can break down, new employees may not be well trained, or a big order may require everyone to work overtime.*

Travis: *I read that companies spend a large amount of their training budgets on management development. If you ask me, either you're a good manager or you aren't. I don't think taking classes on how to manage will do much good if you aren't the right type of person.*

Amber: *I might have agreed with you a few years ago, but today it seems that management is much more complicated. In fact I believe that the problems each manager faces are so different it would be difficult to develop training programs that would benefit all of the managers in a company.*

Think Critically:

1. Analyze the views of Amber and Travis toward management. With what do you agree or disagree?
2. Do you believe that managers spend most of their time working with employees? Justify your answer.
3. Do you believe companies should spend a large amount of their training budgets on management training? Why or why not? Can people be taught to be better managers?

4. What characteristics are common to all managers' jobs? What are the types of things that would be quite different from one manager's job to another?
5. If you were responsible for developing a training program for managers, what would you include?

6. Visit one of the many employment sites on the Internet where companies list job openings. An example is www.monsterboard.com. Find several management jobs that are listed and identify the common and unique categories of job duties.

CASE 11-2

A'yanna Lyons is the manager of the accounting department for the Hemmerle Supply Company, an office supplies wholesaler. The company established a standard that invoices would be prepared, printed, and mailed to customers within 24 hours after receiving the order. Recently, A'yanna learned that some invoices were not being mailed until three or four days after receiving the order. Upon checking further, she discovered that her department did not always receive the necessary information from the shipping department on schedule.

Think Critically:

1. What are some possible problems in this situation? Identify problems that could be occurring in the accounting department as well as in other departments of the company.
2. List the symptoms of the problems. Explain why you believe the things you listed are symptoms rather than problems.
3. What are some alternative solutions?
4. How would you suggest that A'yanna proceed in this situation?
5. How can a management information system contribute to resolving this situation?

PROJECT: MY BUSINESS, INC.

There is a very high failure rate for new small businesses. One of the major reasons for failure is that the owner does not practice effective management skills. As an owner, you must devote adequate time to management and complete all major management functions. In addition, you must be prepared to solve problems before they negatively affect the business.

DATA COLLECTION

1. Survey five managers of small businesses. Ask them to identify the types of activities they commonly perform during the day and estimate the amount of time they spend on each activity during the typical day. Use your own judgment to classify the activities

within the four management functions. You may also need a category for non-management activities. Prepare a chart to illustrate your findings on how small business managers spend their time.

2. Identify two problems you expect to face in operating your business. Complete the steps in problem solving to develop an appropriate solution. As you analyze possible solutions, identify several sources of useful information, including business research.

ANALYSIS

1. Develop a chart with four headings: Planning, Organizing, Implementing, and Controlling. Under each heading, list the activities you will need to complete to manage your juice bar effectively.
2. Under the list of activities developed above, estimate (a) how much time you will need to devote to each activity and (b) when you will need to complete each activity during a typical month. Then develop a sample monthly calendar on which you schedule management activities.
3. For each problem identified in the data collection section above, select the solution you believe is likely to be most effective. Then develop a written set of procedures to follow to accomplish each solution and prevent the problem from occurring.

THE MANAGER AS LEADER

OBJECTIVES

12-1 Define the concept of leadership and important characteristics of leaders.

12-2 Identify five important human relations skills needed by managers.

12-3 Discuss two viewpoints of managers about employees' attitudes toward work.

12-4 Compare three different leadership styles and determine when each is most effective.

12-5 Describe the importance of work rules in a business and the procedures managers should follow in enforcing them.

IS POLITICS A POPULARITY CONTEST?

Brittany and Foster walked to the bus stop to return home after attending a political debate. Since the election for the city's mayor and council members was only three weeks away, their government and economics class decided to attend the debate and then discuss the candidates the next day in class. Each student was asked to identify the characteristics they believed were most important for the office of mayor and be prepared to discuss each candidate using those characteristics.

Brittany: *Our city is growing rapidly and has a lot of problems. We need a mayor who's a problem-solver and willing to make tough decisions. I don't know if any of the candidates showed me they were willing to do that.*

Foster: *I think as politicians they want people to like them. They all seem to be effective communicators but don't want to say anything that will upset voters. Do you really think they can do what has to be done for the city without making some people upset with them?*

Brittany: *Running a city is just like managing a large company. If you're a good manager and the business is successful, people will be satisfied.*

Foster: *I'm not sure. Being mayor of a city and manager of a large business may be similar in some ways. But a manager can make decisions that are best for the business and still have dissatisfied employees and customers. I don't think a mayor can risk upsetting voters even if a decision seems to be best for the city's future.*

Brittany: *I think we both agree that it's not easy to lead a large organization, whether it's a city or a business. It's hard to decide what the most important characteristics of an effective manager or mayor should be.*

Anyone who holds a responsible position in an organization must have a number of qualities to meet his or her responsibilities successfully. One of the key qualities for managers at any level is to be an effective leader. If you plan a career in business, you need to develop your leadership skills.

THE IMPORTANCE OF LEADERSHIP

Many years ago, managers were totally responsible for all decisions in a business. The goal of management was to get the work of the business done. Therefore, managers just told employees what to do and expected them to do it.

Today, we recognize that management is not that simple. To get work done effectively, employees must understand why the work is important and must want to do the work. Employees want to be an important part of the business and want managers to value their ideas as well as their work. A manager who earns the respect and cooperation of employees to effectively accomplish the work of the organization is known as a **leader.**

FACTS AND FIGURES

Today's business leaders must cope with a unique set of challenges. Some of these include: a changing workforce; daily innovations in technology; geographic shifts in economic power; information overload; changing expectations of a more educated workforce; and globalization of business, leading to greater travel demands and cross-cultural expertise.

Leadership is the ability to influence individuals and groups to cooperatively achieve organizational goals. Leaders have excellent human relations skills. **Human relations** refers to how well people get along with each other when working together. A group of people who respect each other and work well together will likely do better work than groups characterized by negative feelings, misunderstandings, hostility, and a lack of respect for each other. In a negative group atmosphere, individuals—and often the entire group—will do things that interfere with the group's success rather than contributing to it. You can probably think of groups that do not work well together. How do the members treat each other? How do they spend their time when the group is together? Usually it is not enjoyable to be part of a group with poor human relations.

A manager can contribute to effective or ineffective human relations. All managers have a responsibility for getting work done through others, so relationships are important. Not everyone is currently an effective leader, but leadership skills can be developed. Because leadership is so important in business, most management training programs today emphasize leadership and effective human relations

LEADERSHIP CHARACTERISTICS

Although managers have many responsibilities, one of the most important is creating an atmosphere that encourages employees to do their best work to make the business successful. Individual employees, however, have their own goals and needs. Employees will be most productive when the work meets their needs as well as those of the company. Managers must work to satisfy important needs of each employee while

ILLUSTRATION 12-1

An effective manager must be concerned about human relations within the work group. What should a manager do when it appears that a conflict is developing between two employees?

also meeting the goals of the business. Success in this task requires leadership.

Because leadership has been shown to be directly related to the success of an organization, it is important that managers possess certain leadership characteristics. Leaders help employees get work done correctly and willingly. A poor manager may be able to get employees to perform the necessary tasks, but the work may be done poorly and inefficiently. A good manager, on the other hand, creates a work environment in which employees enjoy their work and want to do a good job.

In the past several years, many leaders have been studied to identify the characteristics that make them successful. The common characteristics that effective leaders possess are shown in Figure 12-1. Having those characteristics does not ensure that a person will be a good manager. Leaders must also understand the work to be done, and the business in which they work must be well organized. In addition, as you learned in the last chapter, managers must be able to plan, organize, implement, and control work.

Leadership characteristics are personal qualities rather than specific ways that managers behave. Each company, each job, and each situation is different. Leadership characteristics prepare managers to be flexible and adjust to changes. Two managers who possess the same leadership qualities will probably respond in different ways to specific situations but will be able to work well with people to get the necessary work accomplished.

INFLUENCING PEOPLE

Managers influence people to accomplish the work of the organization. However, there are both negative and positive ways to influence others. Just because managers can get others to do what they want does not mean that the managers are effective leaders.

Managers can influence employees because of their power. **Power** is the ability to control behavior. There are several ways that managers obtain power. The type of power will determine how employees respond to managers. Four types of power available to managers and the source of each type are summarized in Figure 12-2.

Position power comes from the position the manager holds in the organization. If a manager is an employee's boss, the manager has the power to give directions and expect the employee to complete that work. If the manager does not directly supervise the employee, the manager's directions are more requests than orders. The manager does not have the position power to tell that employee what to do.

Reward power is power based on the ability to control rewards and punishments. If a manager can determine who receives new equipment, preferred work schedules, or pay increases, or can penalize people for poor work or inappropriate performance, employees are likely to respond to that manager's requests.

FIGURE 12-1

Effective leaders possess most of these characteristics.

Basic Leadership Traits

INTELLIGENCE

A certain amount of intelligence is needed to direct others. Leaders use their intelligence to study, learn, and improve their management skills. They also help the people they work with to learn and develop new skills. Leaders must use their intelligence effectively.

JUDGMENT

Leaders must make many decisions. They consider all facts carefully; apply knowledge, experience, and new information; and use good judgment.

OBJECTIVITY

Leaders must be able to look at all sides of a problem and not make biased judgments or statements. They gather information and do not rush into actions before considering the possible results. They value individual differences, not stereotypes or first impressions.

INITIATIVE

Leaders have ambition and persistence in reaching goals. They are self-starters who plan what they want to do and then do it. They have drive and are highly motivated. They encourage others to take actions and make decisions when appropriate.

DEPENDABILITY

Those who lead are consistent in their actions, and others can rely on them. They do not make promises that cannot be fulfilled. When they make a commitment, they follow through, and expect others to do the same. The people they work with can count on leaders to help them.

COOPERATION

Leaders understand the importance of other people and enjoy being with them. Thus, they work well with others. They understand that people working together can accomplish more than the same people working alone. They work to develop cooperative relations.

HONESTY

Leaders are honest and have high standards of personal integrity. They are ethical in decisions and their treatment of others.

COURAGE

Leaders possess the courage to make unpopular decisions and try new approaches in solving problems. They are willing to take risks to support others.

CONFIDENCE

Leaders have a great deal of self-confidence. They attempt to make the best decisions possible and trust their own judgment. They respect others and expect quality work.

STABILITY

Leaders are not highly emotional. You can depend on their reactions. They can help others to solve problems and reduce conflicts.

UNDERSTANDING

Leaders recognize that the feelings and ideas of others are important. They try to understand the people they work with. They encourage others to share their ideas, experiences, and opinions and show that each person is a valuable member of the organization.

TYPE OF POWER	RESULTS FROM
Position	The manager's position in the organization
Reward	The manager's control of rewards/punishments
Expert	The manager's knowledge and skill
Identity	The employee's perception of the manager

FIGURE 12-2

Managers use power to influence the behavior of employees.

Expert power is power given to people because of their superior knowledge about the work. When workers are unsure of how to perform a task or need information to solve a problem, they may turn to an expert. That person will be able to influence behavior because of the knowledge and skill he or she has.

Identity power is power given to people because others identify with and want to be accepted by them. If an employee respects a manager and wants positive recognition from that person, the employee will likely do what the manager requests. Experienced or well-liked employees often have identity power. Those people can influence the work of others in the organization.

An analysis of the types of power shows that managers can influence their employees because of position or because of the rewards and punishments they control. However, those types of power are not related to leadership characteristics. Employees do not grant those types of power to managers. Position and reward power come from the manager's position in the company. If a manager has only position and reward power, employees may do the requested work but may not do it willingly or well.

However, expert and identity power come from employees, not position in the company. Employees grant these kinds of power to managers they consider worthy of it. If employees consider the manager to be an expert, they will seek the manager's advice and help. If employees want the approval or positive recognition of the manager, they will work cooperatively and support the requests of the manager. Both expert and identity power are related to effective leadership characteristics.

Sometimes people other than managers have power in an organization. Other employees can influence people's behavior because they can control rewards and punishments, they are considered experts, or other employees identify with them and want their approval. If those powerful employees support the work of the organization, they can have a positive influence on other employees. On the other hand, employees with power can be disruptive if their needs and goals differ from those of the organization. Employees may choose to be influenced by those people rather than by their managers.

DEVELOPING LEADERSHIP SKILLS

For the most part, people are not "born" leaders. Through training and personal development, individuals can improve their leadership qualities. People can learn to be dependable, to take initiative, to cooperate with others, and so on. Training and experience can improve a manager's judgment in making business decisions. Most people can become effective leaders with preparation and practice.

Managers are not the only people in an organization who need leadership skills. Many businesses are using employee teams to plan work and make decisions. The team may include a manager, although many do not. Even when a manager is a part of the team, the leader of the group will not always be the manager. As the team completes various projects, individual team members may assume leadership for specific activities. If the team is well organized, the leaders will have expert and identity power to get individual projects completed. The entire team may be given position and reward power that they can use to manage team activities and to achieve the team goals.

Today, companies frequently evaluate applicants' leadership abilities before hiring them. Companies often prefer to hire workers who have already developed many leadership characteristics and have had leadership experience. Training programs for employees emphasize team building and leadership development. Some companies allow employees to volunteer for leadership training, while others expect everyone to be involved. Companies recognize that employees with leadership skills can make valuable contributions to a business's success. It is important to take advantage of leadership development opportunities whenever they occur.

HUMAN RELATIONS

Managers are continually in contact with employees, other managers, customers, and others who have interest in the work of the business. Because of these contacts, managers need human relations skills. They must be able to work well with others both inside and outside the business and help employees work well together.

ILLUSTRATION 12-2

Selection procedures for managers often emphasize leadership characteristics. What are some ways in which a person's leadership ability could be evaluated in an employment interview?

Human relations involve several skills. Those skills may be just as important to the success of a business as the ability to make decisions or operate a complicated piece of equipment. Important human relations skills are (1) self-understanding, (2) understanding of others, (3) communication, (4) team building, and (5) developing job satisfaction.

SELF-UNDERSTANDING

In order to work well with others, managers must have self-understanding. Self-understanding involves an awareness of your attitudes and opinions, your leadership style, your decision-making style, and your relationships with other people.

Employees look to managers for information and direction. They want managers to be able to make decisions, solve problems, and communicate expectations. If managers understand themselves and what other people expect of them, they can decide on the best way to work with people and the leadership style to use. They can use the understanding of their strengths, weaknesses, and how others perceive them to improve their skills as managers.

UNDERSTANDING OTHERS

Every individual is different. Each person has a different background as well as different attitudes, skills, and needs. A manager cannot treat everyone the same way. Some people want a great deal of support and regular communication from their supervisor; others do not. Some employees want managers to consult them when making important decisions, while others do not care to be involved in decision making. Some people work harder when praised; others expect managers to tell them when their work needs improvement.

ILLUSTRATION 12-3

Many human relations problems occur when managers fail to recognize the unique qualities and differences among employees. Should all employees be treated the same by a manager? Why or why not?

Managers need to know the best way to work with each employee. They need to be able to satisfy individual workers' needs and, at the same time, accomplish the goals of the company. The leader who works hard to get to know each person and his or her needs will be a better manager.

COMMUNICATION

In Chapter 10, you learned the importance of communication in business. Managers spend much of their time communicating. When communication breakdowns occur, human relations problems will likely develop.

Managers must understand what information needs to be communicated and what methods to use. They need to know when too much communication is occurring and when there is not enough. Managers must have skill in using official communications channels and in understanding informal channels.

Managers do not just provide information, although they must be skilled in both written and oral communications. Listening is an important communication skill as well. By listening to employee concerns, managers can identify problems, determine needs, and respond to them more effectively.

The language used in communications is very important. Managers must communicate with employees in language they can understand and through their communication channels. When employees have concerns or are involved in planning and decision making, managers must convey their information to upper management.

Some management experts believe that women's management style, which centers around communication and positive working relationships, may be better suited than men's to the team-oriented leadership of today's business. Women are seen as better at managing a diverse workforce, better at motivating others, and better at using influencing skills rather than authority. Nevertheless, women hold only 13% of management positions and only 7% of executive positions.

TEAM BUILDING

People need to feel that they are a part of a team, that they are important, and that they can count on other team members for help. Team building means getting people to believe in the goals of the company and work well together to accomplish them. Teams that take responsibility for work and pride in the results reduce the amount of time managers must spend in monitoring the team's work.

DEVELOPING JOB SATISFACTION

Most people who work at a job for a reasonable length of time are not totally satisfied or dissatisfied with their jobs. However, some people enjoy their work much more than others. An employee's feelings about work may be very different from one day to the next. There are many reasons for these differences in job satisfaction. It can be influenced by factors such as the personal characteristics of employees and managers, the needs of the individuals, the people with whom the employees work, and the actual work itself.

Managers must be aware of the differences among their employees to help them maintain a high level of job satisfaction. For example, when two people with different backgrounds, values, and needs must work together, they may have trouble relating to each other. Managers must consider those differences when making job assignments to keep personal differences from interfering with the work. Managers may offer training and development opportunities to improve the human relations skills of employees to decrease the number of job problems.

ILLUSTRATION 12-4

Employees are willing to work hard when they are satisfied with their jobs. Do employees as well as managers have a responsibility for increasing job satisfaction?

People should be carefully matched with the kind of work they perform, because personal characteristics can affect job performance. A shy person, or one who enjoys working alone, might perform better as a computer data entry operator than as a salesperson. A person who does not pay close attention to details may not be an effective quality inspector on a production line. Human resources departments often test new employees or those seeking a promotion in order to match people with appropriate jobs. Whenever possible, managers should match the job tasks with the needs and interests of the employees and watch people when they begin new tasks to identify possible problems.

MANAGEMENT VIEWPOINTS ABOUT EMPLOYEES

While management jobs include the same basic functions, the way individual managers deal with employees may be very different. Each manager has attitudes about people and work that affect the way they do their jobs and treat the people they supervise. Good managers adjust their style of management to the characteristics of the people they supervise and to the situation.

EMPLOYEES NEED TO BE CLOSELY MANAGED

Some managers believe that employees will not complete work well unless they are closely managed. This attitude results from a feeling that employees are lazy and work only because they get paid. With this attitude, managers are likely to assume that workers will not work any harder than necessary and will try to avoid responsibility. These managers expect that they will have to find ways to force employees to put forth the effort necessary for the organization to achieve its goals. They do not assume that employees will take individual initiative or be concerned about the quality of their work. Managers with these beliefs closely supervise and control employees and make all important decisions. They are likely to use rewards and penalties regularly to try to influence worker performance.

EMPLOYEES PERFORM WELL WITH LIMITED MANAGEMENT

Managers who believe employees generally enjoy their work will relate to people in a very different way. These managers believe that employees like to work and that the job meets many of their personal needs. Employees who enjoy their work obtain satisfaction from doing a job well. With this set of beliefs, managers assume that employees like responsibility and will take the initiative to solve problems, help others, and complete their work. Employees with those characteristics do not need close supervision and control. Managers with this set of beliefs ask people for their ideas on how to complete the work. They allow employees a great deal of control over their own work and do not apply immediate punishments or rewards. These managers spend more time on other management activities and less on employee supervision.

A FLEXIBLE VIEWPOINT

Studies have found that neither of these management views is correct for all employees and all jobs. Although many managers tend to favor one viewpoint over the other, managers who adjust their approach as circumstances change are likely to be the more effective managers. For example, for a job that workers strongly dislike, supervisors may have to supervise more closely. When employees are doing work they enjoy, supervisors may not need to supervise as closely. Flexibility in managers' viewpoints toward employees permits flexibility in their treatment. Employees tend to prefer managers who are flexible enough to increase or decrease the amount of supervision when needed.

Managers can help to influence whether employees like or dislike their work. Newly hired employees are usually excited about the work and want to do a good job. Only if they decide that the work is not something they enjoy or they believe their manager does not trust them will they begin to require additional management attention.

If the employees do not seem to enjoy the work they are doing, managers can do some things to change their attitudes. Managers can work with the employees to determine the reasons for their attitudes and to find out what they like and dislike about that type of work. The managers can find opportunities to involve employees, encourage and respect their ideas, and give them opportunities to do more of the type of work they enjoy. In that way, managers may begin to change employees' attitudes and gradually reduce the amount of supervision and control required.

LEADERSHIP STYLE

The general way a manager treats and supervises employees is called **leadership style.** It includes the way a manager gives directions, handles problems, and makes decisions. Leadership style is influenced by many factors, including the manager's preparation, experience, and beliefs about whether employees like or dislike work. Because numerous factors influence leadership style, each manager has a slightly different style from all other managers. However, leadership styles fall into three general categories. Those categories are (1) autocratic, (2) democratic, and (3) open leadership.

AUTOCRATIC LEADERSHIP

The **autocratic leader** is one who gives direct, clear, and precise orders with detailed instructions as to what, when, and how work is to be done. With an autocratic leader, employees usually do not make decisions about the work they perform. When questions or problems arise, employees look to the manager to handle them. The autocratic manager seldom consults with employees about what should be done or the decisions to be made.

Efficiency is one of the reasons for using the autocratic style. The employees are supposed to do the work exactly the way the manager says—no surprises. Employees generally know what the manager expects. If they are in doubt about what to do or how to do it, they consult the manager. The autocratic leader believes that managers are in the best position to determine how to achieve the goals of the organization. They also assume that workers cannot or do not want to make decisions about their work.

While some workers prefer leaders with autocratic styles, many do not. A major disadvantage of the autocratic style is that it discourages employees from thinking about better ways of doing their work. As a result, some employees become bored. This type of leadership may lead to employee dissatisfaction and a decline in their work performance. Human relations problems arise, especially between managers and employees, when managers use an autocratic leadership style extensively. Finally, the autocratic style does not prepare employees for

CAREER CONNECTION

WORKER SUPERVISOR

For the millions of workers who assemble manufactured goods, service electronic equipment, work in construction, load trucks, or perform thousands of other activities, a worker supervisor is the boss. Such supervisors go by many different titles, which usually vary according to the industry. The most common titles are first-line supervisor or foreman/forewoman.

Although the responsibilities of worker supervisors are as varied as the titles they hold, their primary task is to ensure that workers, equipment, and materials are used properly to maximize productivity. Supervisors create work schedules, keep production and employee records, monitor employees, and ensure that work is done correctly and one time. In addition, they organize workers' activities, train new workers, and ensure the existence of a safe work environment. Supervisors now use computers to schedule work flow, monitor the quality of workers' output, keep track of materials used, and update inventory control systems.

Two out of every five worker supervisors are employed in manufacturing. Other industries include wholesale and retail trade, public utilities, repair shops, transportation, construction, and government.

Although many worker supervisors rise through the ranks with high school diplomas, employers increasingly seek applicants with post-secondary technical degrees. Employers generally look for experience, job knowledge, organizational skills, and leadership qualities.

For more career information about worker supervisors, check your library or the Internet for resources.

leadership opportunities or promotion, since they do not gain experience in decision making or problem solving.

The autocratic style is effective in some situations. For example, it is often the best style to use in emergencies. Getting out a large rush order, for example, may not allow time for a supervisor to discuss the necessary procedures with employees. It is much more efficient for a supervisor to give specific orders and expect a rapid response. Managers may also need to use an autocratic style with temporary employees, such as part-time workers hired for short periods of time. The effective leader is one who knows when a situation calls for an autocratic style of leadership and uses it only until that situation is over.

DEMOCRATIC LEADERSHIP

The **democratic leader** is one who encourages workers to share in making decisions about their work and work-related problems. When using the democratic style, managers communicate openly with employees and discuss problems and solutions with them rather than merely announcing decisions. The manager may still make the final decision but only after discussing possible solutions with employees and seeking their advice. Even when a decision is not involved, the democratic manager provides workers with assistance or encouragement and offers reasons about why certain work changes must occur. The principal characteristic of the democratic style, however, is that it encourages employees to participate in planning work, solving work problems, and making decisions.

Many people say they prefer a manager who uses a democratic style of leadership. Involvement in planning and decision making helps employees feel like active members of a team striving to reach common goals, rather than just workers putting in their time. They are more likely to carry out plans and decisions that they helped to create. Employees who see that managers have confidence in them are often highly motivated and, as a result, need not be as closely supervised.

As good as the democratic style may sound, however, it has limitations. Not all people like to participate in decisions. Some prefer to just do the work for which they were hired. Also, the democratic style is time consuming, because planning and discussing problems takes time. Furthermore, many jobs are fairly routine with little opportunity for sharing in decision making. Employees will certainly be upset if managers ask them to help make only unimportant decisions or if they don't see management carefully considering their ideas.

The democratic leadership style is effective in many situations, especially when employees are committed to their jobs and are looking for more responsibility. It is also effective with experienced, well-trained workers who are very knowledgeable about the company and their work. When special problems arise and the manager wants to gather as many helpful ideas as possible, the democratic style is effective.

OPEN LEADERSHIP

The **open leader** is a manager who gives little or no direction to employees. Employees understand the work that needs to be accomplished, but methods, details, and decisions are left to individual employees or teams. In the open style, any employee may become the leader when certain decisions must be made. Generally, employees concentrate on specific tasks and are not often involved in the tasks of others.

The open style works best with experienced workers and in businesses where few major changes occur. If people have their own specialized jobs and are experts at them, the manager might use this style of leadership. If people work in many different locations, such as salespeople or home-based employees, the open style may work well. Managers will not be able to closely control employees' work because of their location, and getting together to make decisions may not be feasible.

Managers should be careful when using the open style of leadership with inexperienced employees or employees who are not used to making their own decisions. When employees are not confident in their abilities or do not trust that managers will let them make their own decisions, they are likely to be ineffective with the open style. When effective teamwork is required without training in team responsibilities, the open style can lead to confusion and lack of direction. Open leadership should be used very carefully and only after ensuring that employees are prepared for it and comfortable with the individual responsibility.

SITUATIONAL LEADERSHIP

We have seen in our discussion of management and leadership that effective management is very difficult. It requires understanding of the four management functions, development of leadership characteristics, and skill in selecting and using the most appropriate management style. The most effective manager is one who uses situational leadership. A **situational leader** is one who understands employees and job requirements and matches his or her actions and decisions to the circumstances. For example, if the situational leader forms a team of very experienced employees to work on a task, the leader will use an open style. If that team had been composed of new employees, the leader might be more involved and provide greater direction for the team.

Employees have very different expectations of managers and want to work for an effective manager who understands them and their needs. The qualities employees would like to see in their managers are shown in Figure 12-3.

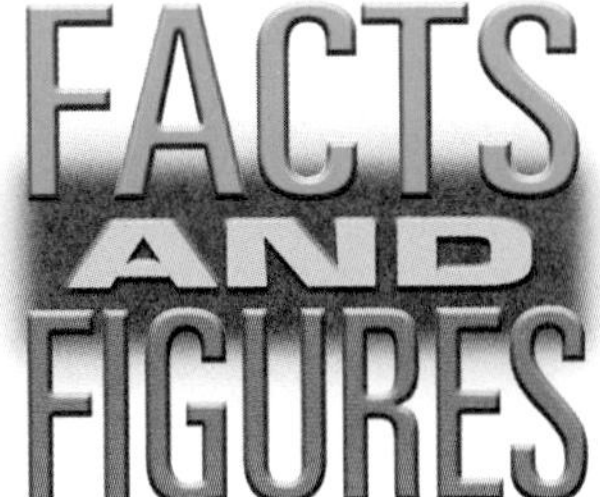

Recent studies have shown that rates of illicit drug and heavy alcohol use were higher among workers age 18-25 than among older workers, and higher among males than females. Rates were also higher among white, non-Hispanics than among black, non-Hispanics or Hispanics. In addition, rates were higher among those with less than a high school education than among those with a high school diploma or more education.

HANDLING EMPLOYEE PROBLEMS

Sometimes employees face personal problems that affect their work. In most cases, the employee is able to resolve the problem, and the manager doesn't have to take any action. At other times, a manager just needs to be sympathetic by listening to employees and showing an understanding of their situation. These situations occur infrequently, such as an employee who has an ill child or is late to work because of a transportation problem. Many businesses develop procedures that allow employees to deal with those types of problems.

In some situations, however, personal problems may be more serious and more disruptive. Problems such as drug or alcohol abuse, conflicts in personal relationships, or serious financial difficulties may result in employees being unable to perform their jobs well. Managers need to be aware of employees who are having difficulty on the job and try

Employees prefer a manager who:

1. Encourages employee participation and suggestions.
2. Keeps employees informed and shares employee ideas with upper management.
3. Works to build and maintain morale.
4. Is available to employees and easy to talk to.
5. Supports employee training and development.
6. Communicates effectively with employees.
7. Is considerate of the ideas and feelings of others.
8. Makes changes when needed rather than relying on past practices.
9. Supports employees who are doing their best even when mistakes are made.
10. Shows appreciation and provides recognition for good work.

FIGURE 12-3

Employees prefer managers who possess these leadership qualities.

ILLUSTRATION 12-5

Many businesses offer professional counseling and other services to help employees with personal problems. What role should managers play in dealing with such problems?

to determine the reasons for it. Then they need to work with the employee to get the necessary help to resolve the problem.

Most managers are not trained to solve difficult personal problems, and they should not attempt to do so. But they should not ignore the problem either. Many businesses offer professional counseling and other services to help employees with personal problems. Managers need to make employees aware of those services and the importance of solving personal problems before they affect job performance. Managers should encourage employees to use the services available in the company when the problem first occurs. Then the manager should support the employee's decision to seek help. That usually means treating the problem confidentially and providing some accommodation for the employee's schedule while he or she works to solve the problem.

One difficult management responsibility is dealing with employees who violate work rules. **Work rules** are regulations created to maintain an effective working environment in a business. Employees must meet certain expectations if a business is to operate effectively. Those expectations might deal with hours of work, care of equipment, worker safety, and relationships among employees and between employees and management.

Many companies have developed work rules that apply to all employees. Other companies have unique sets of rules for workers in different divisions or for employees with different job classifications. For businesses with negotiated agreements between the business and a labor union, the union contract specifies most work rules and the procedures for handling violations. Procedures sometimes include an oral warning for the first violation, a written warning entered into the personnel file for the second violation, a short suspension, and finally

ETHICAL ISSUES

EMPLOYEE MANAGEMENT

EndCore is a packaging manufacturer. The third unit produces cardboard boxes. EndCore led the industry in total box sales for 20 years. However, during the past five years, it fell to fifth place in sales. Competing businesses had improved the quality of their products and were able to undercut EndCore in product prices.

EndCore employees were trained for specific production jobs that had changed little over time. The management structure was very autocratic with managers responsible for all decisions.

Because of the declining performance, EndCore management decided to implement a new democratic management philosophy. Employee work teams would be developed, and they would share in decision making with management. The company made a commitment to the new philosophy, the teams were formed, and training was provided to prepare the company for the new structure.

Now the unit three team had to find ways to reduce production costs so the company could price its boxes closer to the competition. The team developed several methods to change the way work was done, and boxes were assembled for a cost savings of about 4 percent. This left the company's costs just slightly higher than those of competitors.

Then the team learned of a new automatic glue machine that was coming on the market. EndCore always hand-glued its boxes because the quality of the seals was much better. Gluing was a major part of the process, with over 15 percent of the employees used as box gluers. The new machine completely automated the gluing process and increased the speed with which boxes could be assembled. It had a 98 percent reliability rating—equal to the hand-gluing method. The cost of the machines was just under $1 million. However, the cost would be recovered in three years because production could be increased by 5 percent with a reduction in labor costs of 12 percent. Using the gluing machines would put them below competitors' costs by more than 2 percent.

The employee team had found the solution needed by the company to make it competitive. However, implementing that solution would mean that at least 30 employees would lose their jobs.

THINK CRITICALLY

1. What are the advantages and disadvantages of the two solutions identified by the employee team: (a) from management's viewpoint and (b) from employees' viewpoint?
2. What responsibility does the employee team have to management and to other employees in making a recommendation?
3. What recommendation do you believe the employee team should make? Why?
4. Do you believe that under the traditional autocratic management philosophy, the same decision would be made? Why or why not?

termination if the problem continues. Penalties are usually more severe for serious violations of work rules. Also, there are normally protections for employees in the procedures that include hearings, appeals of penalties, and union representation for the employee.

If a business does not have a formal set of work rules, each manager needs to develop procedures and policies that tell employees what the manager expects of them and how the manager will resolve problems if they occur. If managers do not communicate expectations to employees and do not handle problems in a reasonable and equitable way, they soon lose the respect of the employees. Managers who involve employees in developing rules and procedures usually find greater support for those rules and fewer problems when penalties need to be applied for rules violations. Guidelines for managers to follow in enforcing work rules are listed in Figure 12-4.

It is not easy for new managers to handle difficult employee situations, especially if they must reprimand or punish an employee. Managers do not want employees to dislike them or perceive their actions negatively. However, it is important that managers deal with those situations in a direct way rather than postponing or ignoring them. The result of not dealing with an obvious rule violation or other employee problem is that employees will not have clear expectations and will not know whether the manager intends to enforce the rules or not. Often if a manager ignores a problem created by an employee, the manager will remember the situation and wait for the employee to make another

Management Guidelines for Enforcing Work Rules

1. **Explain work rules and provide written copies of the rules to all employees.**
2. **Acquaint employees with penalties for work rule violations and make sure they understand the penalties as well as when and how they will be applied.**
3. **Investigate any violation thoroughly before taking action.**
4. **Consider any special circumstances before determining the violation and the penalty.**
5. **Act as soon as possible after investigating a violation and deciding on the action to be taken.**
6. **Inform the employee who violated a work rule of the rule that was violated, the penalty that will be applied, and the reason for the penalty.**
7. **Treat similar violations consistently.**
8. **Punish in private and praise in public.**
9. **Encourage employees to follow work rules by rewarding those who consistently follow the rules.**

FIGURE 12-4

Managers must be objective, fair, and consistent when enforcing established work rules.

mistake. If that happens, even for a minor problem, the memory of the earlier employee problem will cause the manager to overreact to the new situation and confront the employee for both problems.

Reacting immediately, objectively, and firmly to rules violations is sometimes referred to as the "hot stove principle." We may remember as small children that if we touched a hot stove we got immediate feedback in the form of a burn and probably an immediate reprimand from an adult. Because of that feedback, we learned not to touch the hot stove again. In the same way, if employees get an immediate reprimand from a manager for a violation of the rule, the employee will pay more careful attention to the rules in the future.

Effective leaders handle many types of work-related problems confidently. The successful leader understands human behavior and applies good management and human relations principles in working with people. They also continue to study and learn to improve their management skills. When conflicts and problems occur, leaders work to solve them before they create larger problems. They understand that they must help employees satisfy their own needs while also accomplishing the goals of the business.

CHAPTER CONCEPTS

- To be effective, managers must be able to do more than just perform the four management functions. They must also be good leaders. A leader earns the respect and cooperation of employees to effectively accomplish the work of the organization. Leaders share a number of personal qualities that can be developed through training and experience.
- Managers get work done through people because of the power they hold. Their position in the organization gives them position and reward power. But employees grant expert and identity power to managers and co-workers.
- Effective human relations skills are important in successful management. Managers need self-understanding, understanding of others, communication skills, team-building skills, and the ability to develop employee job satisfaction.
- A manager's view of employees will affect the amount of supervision he or she provides. A manager may use a more autocratic, democratic, or open style of leadership. Situational leadership is effective because the manager changes the type of management to fit the situation and the employees.
- Employees sometimes have personal problems that affect their work performance. When the problems are more serious than simply listening will solve, managers must know where to direct employees to get help.
- Organizations develop work rules to communicate expectations and specify guidelines for managers to follow in dealing with rule violations.

BUILD VOCABULARY POWER

Define the following terms and concepts.

1. leader
2. leadership
3. human relations
4. power
5. position power
6. reward power
7. expert power
8. identity power
9. leadership style
10. autocratic leader
11. democratic leader
12. open leader
13. situational leader
14. work rules

REVIEW FACTS

1. When a manager exercises total authority over employees, how will the manager assign work?
2. What are some characteristics of good human relations?
3. In addition to leadership characteristics, what is necessary for a person to be a good leader in business?

4. What are the characteristics of effective leaders?
5. What are examples of rewards managers can provide to employees?
6. What types of power do employees give to managers?
7. Why do employees need leadership skills?
8. What important human relations skills do managers need?
9. What are the two general viewpoints that managers may have about workers?
10. What is involved in a manager's leadership style?
11. What type of leadership style is most effective for emergencies?
12. For what type of employees does the open leadership style typically work best?
13. How should managers deal with serious personal problems of employees that disrupt the work?
14. What should a manager do in a business that does not have a formal set of work rules?

DISCUSS IDEAS

1. Why does a management approach that involves employees in decision making work better than the old approach in which managers tell employees what to do and expect them to do it?
2. Is the leadership provided by the top executives of a company different from the leadership provided by supervisors?
3. Which are the most important leadership characteristics and why? Are there other characteristics of leaders not on the list that you believe are important?
4. What happens if managers use position and reward power but do not use the other two types?
5. What are some ways you can develop leadership skills while still in school?
6. It has been said that good leaders are born, not made. What evidence can you provide that the statement is not true?
7. Why do some managers continue to hold to the opinion that employees do not enjoy work even when it often leads to distrust and conflicts between employees and managers?
8. Why might a manager decide to use both autocratic and democratic leadership styles at different times with the same group of employees?
9. Do you believe that the characteristics that employees like to see in managers (Figure 12-3) have changed over the years?
10. What types of procedures could companies develop to help employees deal with personal problems such as the illness of children, automobile trouble, dentist appointments, etc.? How would the procedures affect the profitability of the business?

ANALYZE INFORMATION

1. Identify ten people who are different in age, education, and work experience. In an interview with each, ask them to define the term "leadership." Then show them the list of characteristics in Figure 12-1. Ask them to identify the top five from the list. Prepare a written report of the results of your interviews, including one bar graph. Compare the results of your research with those of your classmates.
2. Form a team of at least three classmates or join a team assigned by your teacher. Select one of the five human relations skills discussed in the chapter or use the skill assigned to you by your teacher. Think of a situation that could occur in a business that demonstrates the effective or ineffective use of that skill. Then prepare a short script of dialogue between a manager and one or more employees that illustrates the situation. Your scripts should contain at least four statements by each of the participants. Prepare to role-play the situation for your classmates using the script. Students from other teams should attempt to determine which human relations skill you are demonstrating and whether the role play demonstrates a positive or negative example of the skill.
3. Identify someone you believe is a good manager. Interview the person to determine his or her beliefs about (a) the use of power by a manager, (b) whether people need close or limited supervision, and (c) leadership style. Using a computer, prepare three or more charts that list the major points on these topics from the textbook and compare these points with the viewpoints of the manager you interviewed. Share your findings in an oral report with your class, using a computer graphics presentation program if possible.
4. With a group of your class members, brainstorm things supervisors can do to increase the job satisfaction of workers. Identify the things that would have a direct cost to the business and those that could be provided with no real cost to the business. Compare the list developed by your group with other groups in your class. Try to reach agreement among the groups on the top five factors that your class feels would work for teenage employees. Then see if you can agree on five factors that the class believes would be most effective for employees over 30 years of age. Discuss reasons for any differences among the two lists.
5. Compare the list of management guidelines for enforcing work rules in Figure 12-4 with the procedures used by administrators and teachers to enforce the rules in your school. What are the similarities and differences? Why do you believe those similarities and differences exist?

SOLVE BUSINESS PROBLEMS

CASE 12-1

Laniece Mayes had been a supervisor for five research specialists in her company's marketing department for nearly two years. The workers thought a great deal of Laniece. In fact, many of them said she was the best supervisor they had ever had. Laniece's manager, Cristina Suarez, was most impressed with the good human relations among the employees and with the excellent work Laniece's department did. The manager was so impressed that she transferred Laniece to manage ten office assistants in the accounting department. Since Laniece had prior accounting training and experience working as a bookkeeper, Cristina thought she would be perfect in the new job.

After only two months, however, human relations in the accounting department had gone down and work output had declined. "What's happening, Laniece?" Cristina asked. "Why isn't it working out?"

Laniece responded, "I don't know. In the marketing department, I always discussed problems with the workers, and as a group we worked out solutions acceptable to everyone. In the accounting department, no one wants to discuss problems and solutions. They want me to solve all of the problems for them. That's just not my style."

Think Critically:

1. Is it possible that a person might be an effective leader in one situation but not in another? Explain.
2. What type of leadership style does Laniece practice?
3. What do you recommend that Cristina and Laniece should do to improve the situation in the accounting department?

4. If you could talk to Laniece before she moved from marketing to accounting, what recommendations would you make to help her avoid the problem she encountered?

CASE 12-2

Mikayla Fletcher was very upset because she had just suspended one of the employees she supervised, Dylan Holcomb. While he was a good worker, he had begun to develop a problem with coming to work on time. Once and sometimes twice a week, he was 5 to 10 minutes late.

The company had a policy on employee tardiness: a half-hour of pay was deducted for any part of 15 minutes the employee was late. If the employee was late more than 30 minutes, a verbal warning was given the first time, a written warning was given the second time, and the employee would be suspended for one week without pay for the third time.

Dylan didn't seem to mind losing the money when he was late. Mikayla had talked with him recently about the problem, and he simply said he would try to do better. He had not been late for several weeks. Then two weeks ago, he was late 35 minutes on Tuesday. Last Thursday he was late by 50 minutes. Following company policy, Mikayla had given him both a verbal and written warning.

Yesterday, the city was hit by a heavy snowstorm. Because roads in the area were very slippery early in the morning, the company decided that employees who were late for work would not be penalized. Mikayla was surprised when Dylan showed up on time. He said that he had used his new four-wheel drive vehicle and had fun driving to work through the snow.

Today, Mikayla was furious when Dylan walked in 40 minutes late. She confronted him and told him he was suspended. Dylan accused Mikayla of being unfair. He said the battery on his new vehicle had failed; otherwise, he would have been on time. Besides, the company hadn't penalized employees for tardiness yesterday when he had been on time. Because of that, he didn't feel he should be penalized today.

Think Critically:

1. What are the advantages and disadvantages of a policy such as the one described in the case?
2. Do you believe Mikayla should have suspended Dylan under the circumstances? Why or why not?
3. Do you believe Dylan was justified in his claim that Mikayla was being unfair? Support your answer.
4. What do you think Mikayla should do after Dylan returns from his suspension?

PROJECT: MY BUSINESS, INC.

If your business is successful, it will likely grow either by adding more employees to your current location or by opening additional locations. As you add more employees, you will need to provide effective leadership to ensure that they will do a good job. The activities below allow you to study your leadership style and to develop necessary work rules for your expanding business.

DATA COLLECTION

1. Write brief descriptions of each of the three leadership styles on a piece of paper. Give the sheet of paper to several of your family members, teachers, or close friends. Ask them to identify the description that best describes the way you work with people. Summarize their responses to see if you have a clear-cut leadership style.
2. Contact the owner or manager of a restaurant or fast-food business. Ask to review the company's employee handbook. Identify the work rules in the handbook. Discuss the rules with the owner or manager to determine how effective the rules are in helping the person manage the business.

ANALYSIS

1. Using the information you collected on your leadership style in the Data Collection section above, do you agree or disagree with the responses of others? If you disagree, why do you believe others' view of your style differs from your own view of it? Develop

a written statement of what you can do during this school year to increase your leadership skills.

2. Identify three situations that are likely to occur in your business in which you will need to provide leadership with employees. One situation should require an autocratic leadership style, another a democratic style, and the third an open style. Describe why each situation requires the specific leadership style you identified.
3. Develop a list of work rules for the employees of your business. Be certain to consider rules on attendance, hours of work, grooming, care of equipment, safety, and the handling of cash as well as other important areas of employee responsibility.

PLANNING AND ORGANIZING

OBJECTIVES

- 13-1 Justify the value of planning for a business.
- 13-2 Differentiate between the two levels of planning.
- 13-3 Provide examples of seven planning tools used by managers.
- 13-4 Identify four characteristics of a good organization.
- 13-5 Define two traditional types and two newer types of organization structure.

NOT SO FAST!

Eldron Huntley was excited after attending a seminar titled "Moving Your Business to the Internet." His catering business had been successful for the past ten years. Now, based on the seminar, he felt he had discovered a whole new business idea.

People told Eldron that he offered menu items they could not find anywhere else. In addition, they could always count on the quality and taste of the meals. Customers who had moved from the area frequently called his business to purchase their favorite meals. In fact, about one-third of the company's orders were now coming from out-of-town customers. Eldron had been looking for ways to expand that part of the business.

At the seminar Eldron attended, the speaker explained the growth of Internet commerce and suggested any business that had a successful product should consider using the World Wide Web to expand its market. That was just the idea Eldron was looking for. Most of his out-of-town business currently came from the word-of-mouth recommendations of satisfied customers. He knew he couldn't afford national advertising, but the Internet provided a way to affordably get his business name and menu to people all over the country.

Eldron estimated it would take about $80,000 for the computer hardware and software for reliable Internet service; an additional $200,000 to expand his food preparation and shipping facilities; and probably $50,000 to pay the expenses of additional personnel for several months until adequate sales were generated to meet the payroll costs. However, he also believed the increased sales would easily pay for the additional expenses, and he could make a nice profit on the new business. He scheduled a meeting with his banker so he could request a loan to pay for the Internet expansion.

The banker was not quite as excited as Eldron was. The banker explained, "Everyone seems to want to use the Internet for their business. I agree it has a great deal of potential, but there are no guarantees that you'll be successful. Before I can loan you the money you want, I'll need to see a business plan that demonstrates how you'll be able to repay the loan. Who will be your customers and your competitors? How much will each customer buy and what will they be willing to pay? Will this new business affect your ability to serve your current customers? What will it cost to ship the food to customers so that it arrives in perfect condition? When do you expect the new part of your business to start making a profit?" Eldron recognized that the answers to those questions were important but had not thought about preparing a written plan.

New businesses are started every day, and existing businesses regularly look for opportunities to expand. At the same time, many new and existing businesses fail. Most often that failure can be blamed to a large extent on a failure to adequately plan. Owners and managers who can effectively plan for a business's future are much more likely to be successful than those who concentrate only on day-to-day operations. In this chapter, you will study the procedures and tools managers use to plan and the ways they organize businesses for effective operations.

THE PLANNING FUNCTION

Eldron's banker reminded him that he had to plan carefully in order to make the best decisions about starting and managing the Internet business. Poor planning could result in huge losses and the possible failure of his existing business. However, the correct decision could result in a much larger business, higher profits, and a great deal of personal satisfaction.

In Chapter 5 you learned that a *business plan* is a written description of the nature of the business, its goals and objectives, and how they will be achieved. Review the elements of a business plan listed in Figure 5-1 on page 116. Planning how to achieve objectives includes an analysis of the opportunities and risks the business faces. The business plan is an important tool for any business that is planning a major change. The business plan sets goals for the business and outlines the activities that need to be completed to achieve the goals. It includes a detailed financial analysis showing the potential profitability that should result from the planned operations.

If Eldron Huntley develops an effective business plan, he will have long-range goals and directions for the business as well as specific plans for operations, marketing, financial management, and human resource decisions. His banker will have the information needed to determine if granting the requested loan is a wise business decision.

IMPORTANCE OF PLANNING

Not all managers are responsible for preparing a business plan. However, all managers are involved in planning in some way. Their decisions may be bigger or smaller than Eldron Huntley's. Some managers make complex and expensive decisions, such as whether to build a new

ILLUSTRATION 13-1

Managers are involved in planning that is as specific as approving a vacation schedule or as broad as acquiring a new factory. How do you think the procedures used for planning would be different in each of those situations?

$20 million factory or to expand operations into another country. Other managers develop very short-term plans, such as preparing an employee work schedule for the next week.

Planning is probably the most important management activity. It sets the direction for the business and establishes specific goals. Plans serve as guides for making decisions. Managers also use their plans to determine whether the business is making progress. Planning also helps managers communicate with each other and with their employees and coordinate the activities of the business. Careful planning encourages managers to be more specific and objective in their decisions.

LEVELS OF PLANNING

Managers plan on two levels—strategic planning and operational planning. **Strategic planning** is long term and provides broad goals and direction for the entire business. **Operational planning** is short term and identifies specific activities for each area of the business.

STRATEGIC PLANNING Many important changes in a business require planning over a long period of time. Developing and producing a new product line can take more than a year. Building a new factory in another country may require several years for planning and completing the construction. A manufacturer that decides to take over responsibility for transporting products to major retailers rather than using wholesalers will likely need a long time to obtain the needed buildings and equipment, get appropriate approvals and licenses from state and local governments, and hire and train employees.

When Eldron Huntley prepares his business plan, he will be involved in strategic planning. The banker was telling him that he should not make the decision to expand his business quickly without carefully considering how to do it. Managers need a great deal of information to determine if a particular decision will be profitable. Strategic planning provides the needed information and procedures for making effective decisions. Figure 13-1 describes the steps in strategic planning.

The internal and external analyses (Steps 1 and 2 of Figure 13-1) are often referred to as SWOT analysis. **SWOT analysis** is the examination of the organization's internal ***S***trengths and ***W***eaknesses as well as the ***O***pportunities and ***T***hreats from its external environment. In Step 1 of the analysis, managers identify any opportunities for expanding and improving the business and any threats the company faces from competition, changes in the economy, new laws and regulations, and other factors outside the company. For example, Eldron Huntley identified an opportunity when he noticed that customers from outside his operating area wanted to have his meals shipped to them. In Step 2, managers evaluate the organization's own capabilities and weaknesses. For example, Huntley identified his company's strengths as having unique menu items and dependable quality and taste. Managers want to build on the company's strengths and reduce its weaknesses whenever possible.

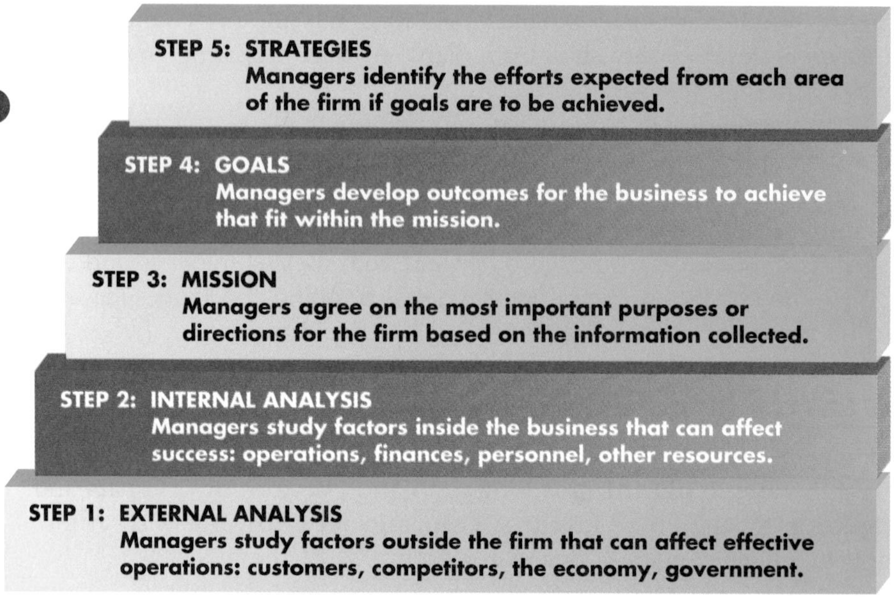

FIGURE 13-1

Strategic planning consists of a series of steps that set the direction for a business.

STEP 5: STRATEGIES
Managers identify the efforts expected from each area of the firm if goals are to be achieved.

STEP 4: GOALS
Managers develop outcomes for the business to achieve that fit within the mission.

STEP 3: MISSION
Managers agree on the most important purposes or directions for the firm based on the information collected.

STEP 2: INTERNAL ANALYSIS
Managers study factors inside the business that can affect success: operations, finances, personnel, other resources.

STEP 1: EXTERNAL ANALYSIS
Managers study factors outside the firm that can affect effective operations: customers, competitors, the economy, government.

In Step 3, managers develop the mission of the business. A **mission statement** is a short, specific statement of the purpose and direction of the business. For example, the mission for Huntley's business could be "to prepare special meals to satisfy the tastes of our customers when and where they want them." Steps 4 and 5 then use the planning information and the mission to set specific goals for the company and descriptions of activities and resources needed to achieve the goals.

The top executives in a business are responsible for strategic planning. They use information collected from lower-level managers, from the company's employees, and from other sources. Large companies may have a special department to collect and analyze information and to develop proposals for executives to consider. Smaller companies may hire research firms or consultants to help with strategic planning. New and small businesses may be able to obtain planning assistance from state and federal government agencies or from the business departments of area colleges and universities.

OPERATIONAL PLANNING A good strategic plan tells managers where the business is going. The managers must then take action to move the business toward those goals. Operational planning determines how work will be done, who will do it, and what resources will be needed to get the work done in a specific area of the business.

Operational plans in a factory could include developing department budgets, planning inventory levels and purchases of raw materials, setting production levels for each month, and preparing employee work schedules. Operational planning in a marketing department might include the development of promotional plans, identifying training needed by salespeople, deciding how to support retailers who will handle the product, and selecting pricing methods. A great deal of the operational planning in a business is the responsibility of middle-level managers and supervisors and even some experienced employees.

PLANNING TOOLS

All managers must develop skills in planning. There are a number of tools that can help in developing effective plans. Those tools are discussed next.

GOALS It has been said that you will never know when you have arrived if you don't know where you are going. Goals provide that direction for a business. A **goal** is a specific statement of a result the business expects to achieve. All types and sizes of businesses and all parts of a business need to develop goals. Goals keep the business focused on where it wants to be in the future and the results it expects to accomplish. Managers and employees may overreact to short-term problems or the actions of competitors if goals are not clearly stated and communicated. Managers in large companies may take actions that conflict with those of other managers if they are not aware of goals. Here are several characteristics of effective goals:

1. *Goals must be specific and meaningful.* The goal "to make a profit" is vague. However, the goal "to increase sales by $25,000 in the next six months" is much more specific. Goals should relate to the activities and operations of the business so that employees see how their work relates to the goals.

   Managers must be careful in setting goals and must consider such factors as (1) the general economic conditions facing the business, (2) past sales and profits, (3) the demand for products and services,

ILLUSTRATION 13-2

Goals provide direction for a business. Should the manager of a new business be as careful in setting goals as the manager of an established business?

(4) the reactions of current and prospective customers, (5) the resources of the business, (6) the actions of competitors, and (7) any other factors that can influence the achievement of the goals.

2. *Goals must be achievable.* While it is important that goals move the company forward, they must also be realistic. It is not useful to set a goal "to increase unit sales by 5 percent" if the company does not have the capability of manufacturing that many more units. If telemarketing salespeople are already completing many more calls each day than the industry average, it may not be realistic to set a higher goal for completing calls without increasing the number of salespeople.
3. *Goals should be clearly communicated.* Company and departmental goals should be communicated to all employees, because they will be responsible for accomplishing those goals. Communicating the company's goals will help employees understand that they are part of a team effort working together for a common purpose. Usually, they will work harder to achieve goals they understand.
4. *Goals should be consistent with each other and with overall company goals.* Each department within a business has its own specific goals, but the goals must be coordinated with those of other departments. Assume, for example, that the sales manager sets a goal of increasing sales in a specific area of the country. The advertising manager, however, sets a goal of reducing expenditures in the same area to use the money for a new product introduction that will occur in another part of the country. If advertising is needed to support the sales efforts, the managers have conflicting goals. Managers must work together so that their goals will complement each other and support the overall company goals.

BUDGETS The most widely used planning tool is the budget. A *budget* is a specific financial plan. Financial budgets assist managers in determining the best way to use available money to reach goals. As a part of Eldron Huntley's business plan, his banker will require him to develop a budget for the new Internet business. This budget will help both Eldron and the banker see how much money he will need as well as if and when the new part of the business can be profitable. When department managers complete operational planning, they will prepare budgets for their departments. In addition to the financial budget, the managers often prepare budgets for personnel expenses, production costs, advertising, inventories of materials and supplies, and many others. You will learn more about budgets in Chapter 15.

SCHEDULES Just as budgets help in financial planning, schedules are valuable in planning for the most effective use of time. For most business purposes, a **schedule** is a time plan for reaching objectives. Schedules identify the tasks to be completed by a department or individual and the approximate time required to complete each task. A supervisor may develop a schedule to organize the work done by each employee

WORK SCHEDULE FOR JULY 23		SPECIAL ORDER DEPARTMENT	
Employee	Order 532	Order 533	Order 534
Shenker, M.	X		
Duffy, P.		X	
Gaston, S.			X
Robinson, J.			X
Kingston, C.		X	

FIGURE 13-2

Schedules are important planning tools. A work schedule is one example.

for a day or a week (see Figure 13-2). Production managers use schedules to plan the completion and shipment of orders. Salespeople use schedules to plan their sales calls efficiently, and advertising people use schedules to make sure the ads appear at the correct time and in the proper media. Office managers need to schedule the preparation and printing of mailings and reports to make sure they are completed on time.

STANDARDS Another planning tool for managers is the use of standards. A **standard** is a specific measure against which something is judged. Businesses set quality standards for the goods and services they produce. Managers then compare the products against the standards to judge whether or not the quality is acceptable. Companies also set standards for the amount of time that tasks should take. For example, a fast-food restaurant may set a standard that customers will receive their food within three minutes of placing their orders. If managers see that customers are getting their food five minutes after ordering, then the service time is not meeting company standards and is therefore not acceptable. Companies may also set standards for the number of defective products allowed on an assembly line or the number of calls a salesperson must make during a day.

Managers are responsible for setting realistic standards and for using those standards to judge performance. They also must know when to revise outdated standards. In Chapter 14, you will learn how standards are used to control work as well as to plan.

POLICIES As part of planning, managers frequently establish policies. **Policies** are guidelines used in making decisions regarding specific, recurring situations. A policy is often a general rule to be followed by the entire business or by specific departments. Remember the discussion of work rules in Chapter 12? Work rules are examples of business policies.

A broad policy may state that the performance of each employee must be evaluated at least twice a year using the company's performance review procedures. Because of that policy, even an employee who has been with the company for ten years must be evaluated. Policies help to reduce misunderstandings and encourage consistent decisions for similar conditions by all managers and employees.

PROCEDURES A **procedure** is a list of steps to be followed for performing certain work. In order to implement the policy described in the previous paragraph, the company must develop specific performance review procedures. For routine tasks, procedures improve business efficiency and are of special help to employees who are learning a new job. The procedure shown in Figure 13-3 would be a great help to a new employee in the catalog order department for the Johnson Company. Experienced employees can help managers design new procedures and improve old ones.

RESEARCH To do a good job of planning, managers need a great deal of information. To develop budgets, they need to know how money

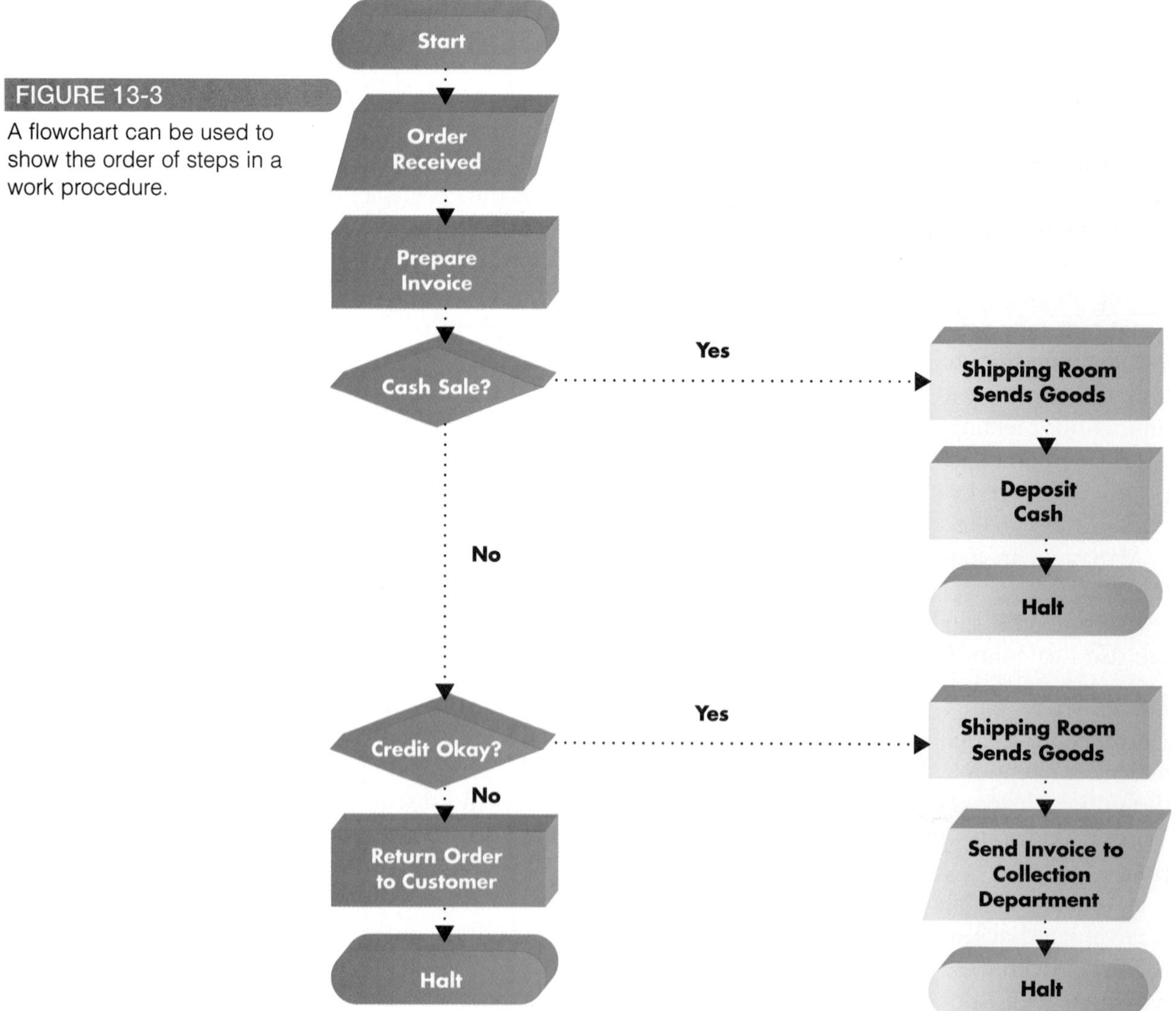

FIGURE 13-3

A flowchart can be used to show the order of steps in a work procedure.

was spent in past years, what certain tasks will cost, and how competitors are spending their money. Managers can improve schedules if they know how long certain jobs take to complete. They can establish better standards and procedures by analyzing carefully collected information on the way jobs are performed. Research is used to collect data for managers and to provide the information needed to improve their planning decisions. Businesses need to complete research and provide the results of research to managers to improve planning.

THE ORGANIZING FUNCTION

Before a plan can be put into operation, the company must be organized to carry out the plans and complete work effectively. In Chapter 11, you learned that *organizing* is concerned with determining how plans can be accomplished most effectively and arranging resources to complete work. More specifically, it involves arranging resources and relationships between departments and employees and defining the responsibility each has for accomplishing work. For example, when the plan is to start manufacturing a new product, managers must determine who is involved in accomplishing each part of the job. Making a new product would probably involve these departments: research, manufacturing, human resources, sales, advertising, and finance. Department managers would then determine the responsibilities of the people within their departments.

ROLE OF ORGANIZATION CHARTS

An **organization chart** is a drawing that shows the structure of an organization, major job classifications, and the reporting relation-

ILLUSTRATION 13-3

Work is done more efficiently if it is organized well. What are some ways that businesses can help employees to be more effective at organizing their work?

ships among the organization's personnel. Figure 13-4 shows an example of an organization chart. The purposes of the organization chart are to (1) show the departments that make up the business, (2) indicate each employee's department and to whom each reports, and (3) identify lines of authority and formal communication within the organization.

Large organizations usually give new employees information in an employee handbook or on the company's Web site that explains the organization of the business and shows an organization chart. By understanding an organization chart, employees have some idea of where and how they fit into the company and what promotional opportunities they might have. The organization chart can easily become outdated, however. The chart must be revised when changes occur in the organizational structure.

ELEMENTS OF ORGANIZATION

The manager of a new business has the complicated task of organizing the entire structure of the business. A manager for an ongoing business cannot ignore the organization function either. Organization may need to change, for example, when goals are revised or when the business expands. Using the example from the beginning of the chapter, if Eldron Huntley is successful in developing the new Internet business, he will have a very different organization than before the expansion. He will need to carefully organize the business to complete the new activities efficiently while maintaining the existing business activities. Whether the focus is on a new or existing department, division, or firm, the process of organizing involves three elements:

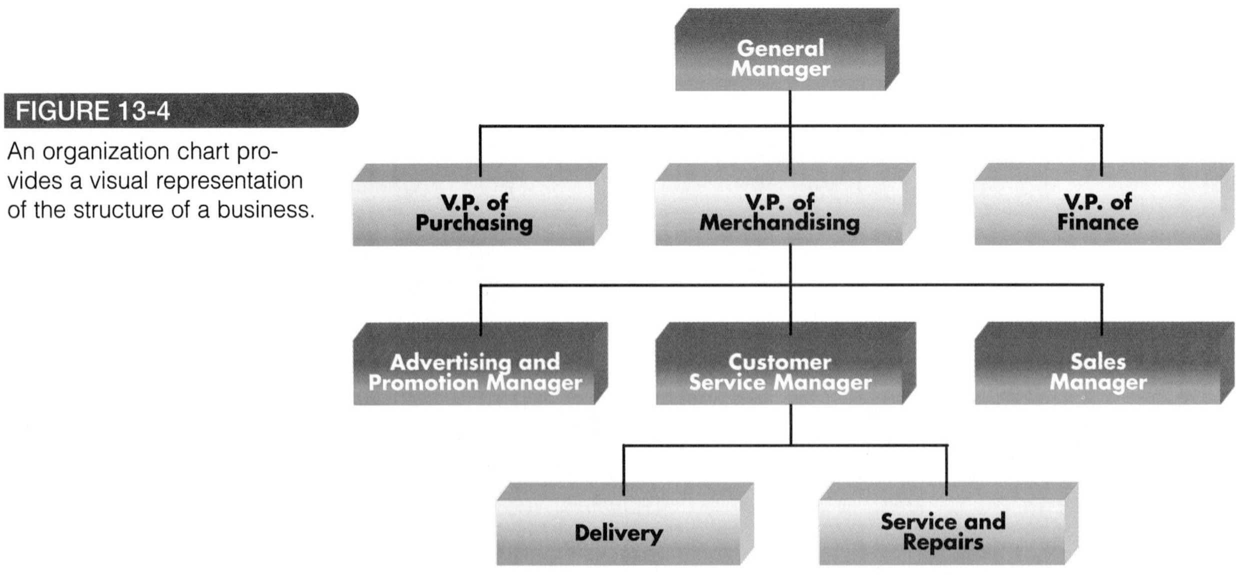

FIGURE 13-4

An organization chart provides a visual representation of the structure of a business.

(1) the division of work, (2) the facilities and working conditions, and (3) the employees.

DIVISION OF WORK In establishing an organization structure, the total work to be done must be divided into units, such as departments. The first consideration is the grouping of activities into broad, natural divisions, such as buying and selling. For small businesses, these may be the only divisions needed to separate the work into manageable units. For large businesses with many employees and activities, the major divisions may need to be further divided into departments or work units of reasonable size. Departments should be composed of related tasks, work should flow smoothly within and among departments, and all tasks should have employees assigned to complete them.

Major divisions of work vary with the type of industry and business. A small retailer may be divided into purchasing, merchandising, and operations. A manufacturer may organize work within production, marketing, and finance divisions. Most businesses have an administrative unit and a human resources unit. An information management unit is also quite common. You can see that the work of even small businesses may require many units in its organization structure.

As a business grows, the number of major divisions must be increased or new units must be added to existing divisions. When the small retailer expands, the basic selling division may be subdivided. A larger marketing division may be established and subdivided into advertising and promotion, personal selling, and customer service. Determining how to divide work into efficient units is based on (1) the type of work to be done in each business and (2) the amount of work to be done. The organization charts shown in Figures 13-5, 13-6, and 13-7 point out how a business may grow from a one-person enterprise into a partnership with specialized duties, and then expand as additional employees assume certain responsibilities.

A small business as well as a large business needs good organization. For example, the owner of a retail store that sells and services home appliances has

CYBER COMMUNICATION

Writing clear, concise e-mail messages becomes easier with practice. Consider the following guidelines:

- Restrict your message to one main idea. This will simplify and help ensure the recipient's understanding.
- Compose a short, clear subject line, which reflects the main idea.
- Use tables or visual aids, if appropriate. With many e-mail systems, such separate files can be included as attachments to the main message.
- Use headings in long messages, to guide the reader.
- Number items in a list.
- Proofread your message, because errors and typos interfere with clear communication.

ACTIVITY Review the letters-to-the-editor section of a recent newspaper, and select a topic that interests you. Prepare an e-mail message, giving your opinion of the topic and using the guidelines shown above. If you have e-mail access and the newspaper has an e-mail address, get your instructor's approval to send the message. If you don't have e-mail access, write the appropriate information on a sheet of paper.

FIGURE 13-5

The owner of a small proprietorship might perform all the work.

Mr. Ingram
Purchasing
Inventory
Advertising
Credit and Collections
Pricing
Sales
Accounting and Finance

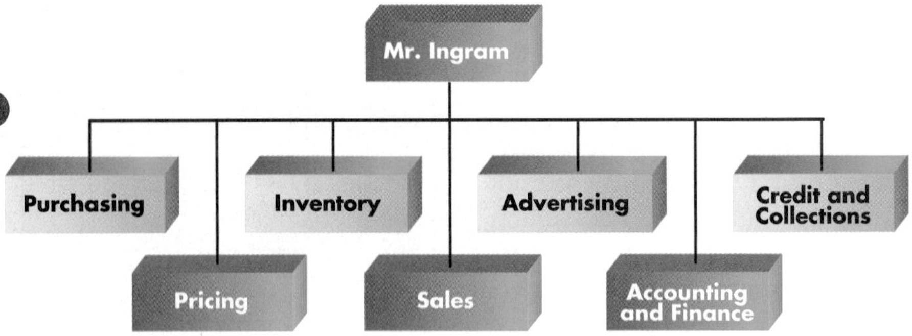

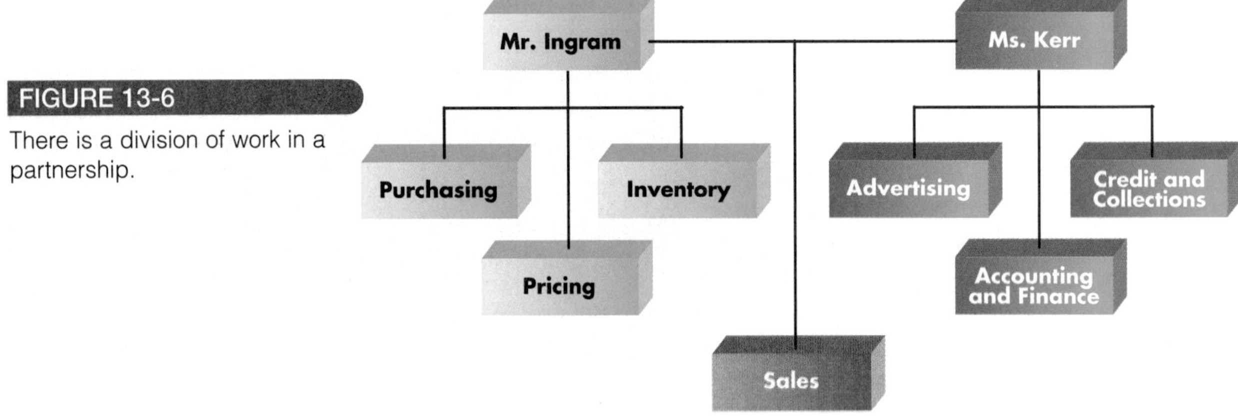

FIGURE 13-6

There is a division of work in a partnership.

Mr. Ingram
Ms. Kerr
Purchasing
Inventory
Advertising
Credit and Collections
Pricing
Accounting and Finance
Sales

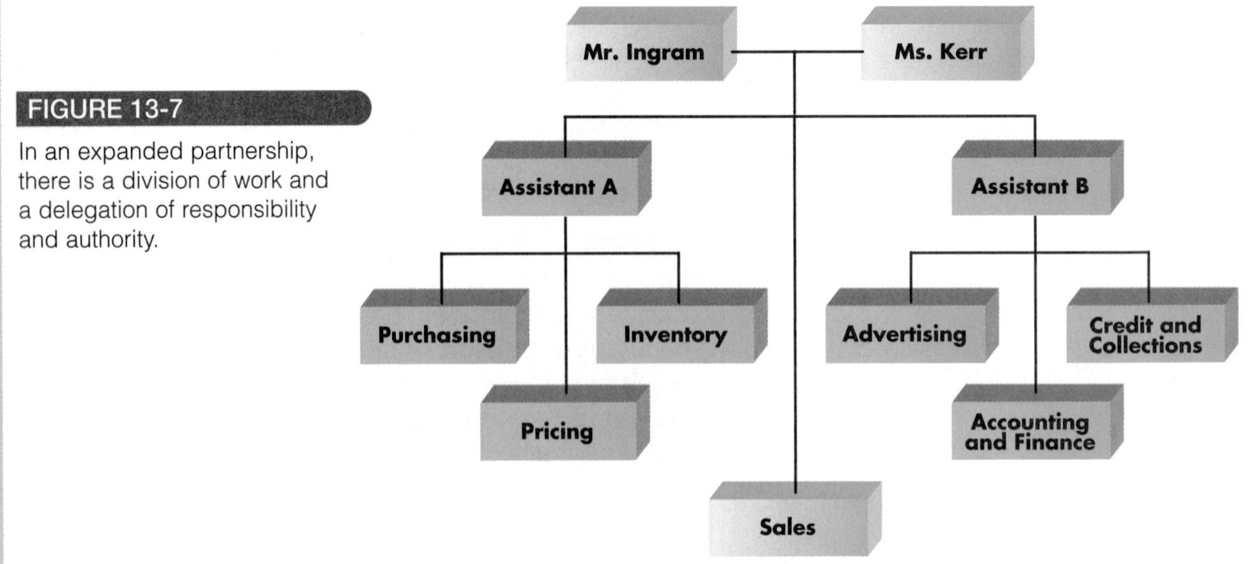

FIGURE 13-7

In an expanded partnership, there is a division of work and a delegation of responsibility and authority.

Mr. Ingram
Ms. Kerr
Assistant A
Assistant B
Purchasing
Inventory
Advertising
Credit and Collections
Pricing
Accounting and Finance
Sales

hired two employees—A and B. The owner is responsible for management of the business and is involved in both selling and service as time permits. Employee A is in charge of appliance sales and is responsible for relationships with the businesses from which the company purchases appliances. Employee A is also in charge of the business when the owner is absent. Employee B is in charge of appliance service and repair and has the authority to make decisions related to customer relationships. These organizational decisions clearly identify the work to be done and the relationships among each of the people involved. The example illustrates how even very small organizations can assign responsibility and delegate authority.

FACILITIES AND WORKING CONDITIONS While divisions of work are being established, the physical aspects of organizing must also be considered. These aspects include providing necessary equipment and materials for employees to be able to complete their work, and arranging the layout of the facilities so that all work flows smoothly and provides the best working conditions possible.

Work should move through the business as efficiently as possible. Employees should not have to waste time, and the work of one group should not delay the work of others. A mechanic repairing an automobile, for example, should have ready access to the needed tools and parts close to the work area. If special parts are needed, a system to quickly order and obtain the parts should be in place so the repairs are not delayed. Most auto repair companies have computer systems that can quickly locate auto parts from area suppliers and an express pick-up and delivery service to immediately obtain the needed parts.

ILLUSTRATION 13-4

The flow of work through a factory is an important consideration when designing a building. What examples can you identify from school, home, or a business in which the design of a building makes working there easier or more difficult?

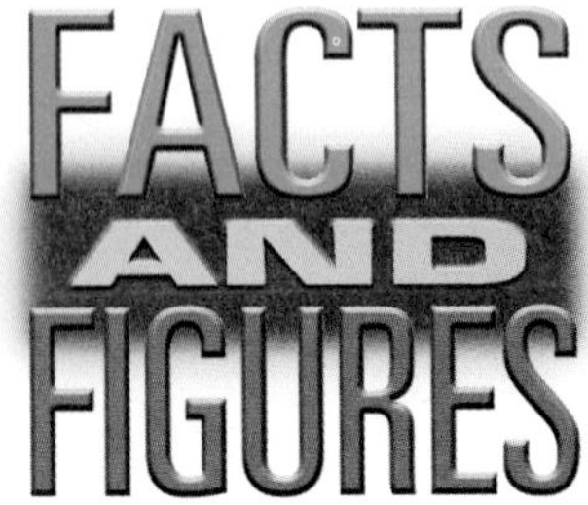

Committed employees gain satisfaction from having a say in what affects their careers. One expert suggests asking these questions to determine how much power employees have in their organization: What kind of access does the employee have to organization decision makers? How does the organization encourage employee participation? What systems are in place for acting on employee ideas? Do employees feel they can innovate and take risks?

Physical working conditions also have an effect on the morale of workers. Job satisfaction is influenced by lighting, temperature, ventilation, and cleanliness of the work areas, as well as the quality and maintenance of tools and equipment. Even facilities outside the work area should be carefully planned, such as convenient and safe parking facilities and easy access to cafeterias and break rooms.

EMPLOYEES Dividing the work into manageable units and providing adequate equipment and facilities must be done with employees in mind. In fact, organizing involves establishing good relationships among the employees, the work to be performed, and the facilities needed, so that productivity will be high. In part, organization is a successful matching of the employee and the employee's materials and work. Employees should be matched to work that they are prepared to do. That means that they have the necessary preparation and skill to complete the assigned tasks. If employees are members of work teams, the total skills of the team should match the work requirements.

In addition, employees should be assigned to work that they enjoy. If employees are dissatisfied with their work assignment, problems with the quality and quantity of work of those employees will result. While not all work is enjoyable, managers should look for opportunities to make the best work assignments possible; to spread less desirable assignments among employees so a few people do not have to spend all of their time doing that work; and to work closely with employees to establish a positive working environment.

CHARACTERISTICS OF GOOD ORGANIZATION

When one person operates a business, there is little need for an organization chart—that person performs all the work. The need for organization increases when two or more people work together. When people engage in any kind of cooperative activity, whether as members of an athletic team or as construction workers building a house, they can accomplish better results if the overall task is planned and organized, so that each person knows what is expected and how to perform the necessary work. Several characteristics of good organization apply to the management of work.

RESPONSIBILITY AND AUTHORITY **Responsibility** is the obligation to do an assigned task. In a good organization, the assigned tasks are clearly identified, so that all employees know exactly the work for which they are responsible. **Authority** is the right to make decisions about assigned work and to make assignments to others concerning that work. Authority is delegated from the top of the organization to others at lower levels.

One of the greatest mistakes in business is to assign responsibilities to employees without giving them sufficient authority to carry out those responsibilities. Consider the situation of an employee at an auto rental counter. The employee is responsible for providing a car to a customer standing at the counter who has a reservation, but that type of car is currently unavailable. The employee must have the authority to rent another car that will meet the customer's needs, or the customer will be very upset. Each employee and each manager should know specifically (1) the description and duties of each job, (2) what authority accompanies the job, (3) the manager in charge, (4) who reports to the manager, and (5) what is considered satisfactory performance.

A growing practice in many organizations today is employee empowerment. **Empowerment** is the authority given to individual employees to solve problems they encounter on their jobs with the resources available to them. Empowered employees need to be well trained and be effective problem-solvers. They need to have the confidence that their managers will support the decisions they make. Some companies are reluctant to use employee empowerment, believing that managers will lose control of the organization. However, experience has shown that empowerment increases employee morale, produces more satisfied customers and fewer reported problems, and increases work efficiency.

Unless employees know their specific responsibilities, duties, and authority, they are likely to be unsure about the work they are to do. Furthermore, conflicts may occur due to misunderstandings about what needs to be done and who makes decisions about work assignments and satisfactory performance. When employees understand responsibility and authority, overlapping duties can be eliminated easily. Effective organization is helpful in eliminating conflicts between individuals and between departments and in increasing cooperation and collaboration.

ACCOUNTABILITY **Accountability** is the obligation to accept responsibility for the outcomes of assigned tasks. When any manager assigns responsibility and delegates authority to an employee, the manager does not give away the responsibility for ensuring that the work is completed and for evaluating the quality of that employee's performance. While the manager is ultimately responsible for the work, the employee is accountable to the manager for performing the assigned work properly, including the quality, quantity, and completion time. The manager, in turn, is accountable to his or her boss for the outcomes of all work done in the unit. Figure 13-8

FACTS AND FIGURES

Empowerment is appropriate when the following situations exist in the work environment: technology is complex; processes are changing rapidly; employees need motivating; close supervision is impossible; employees are ready to accept responsibility; and the manager is supportive and a good coach.

ILLUSTRATION 13-5

Experienced employees are often given responsibility for helping new employees learn their jobs. What can happen if an experienced employee assigns responsibilities to a new employee without the necessary authority or accountability?

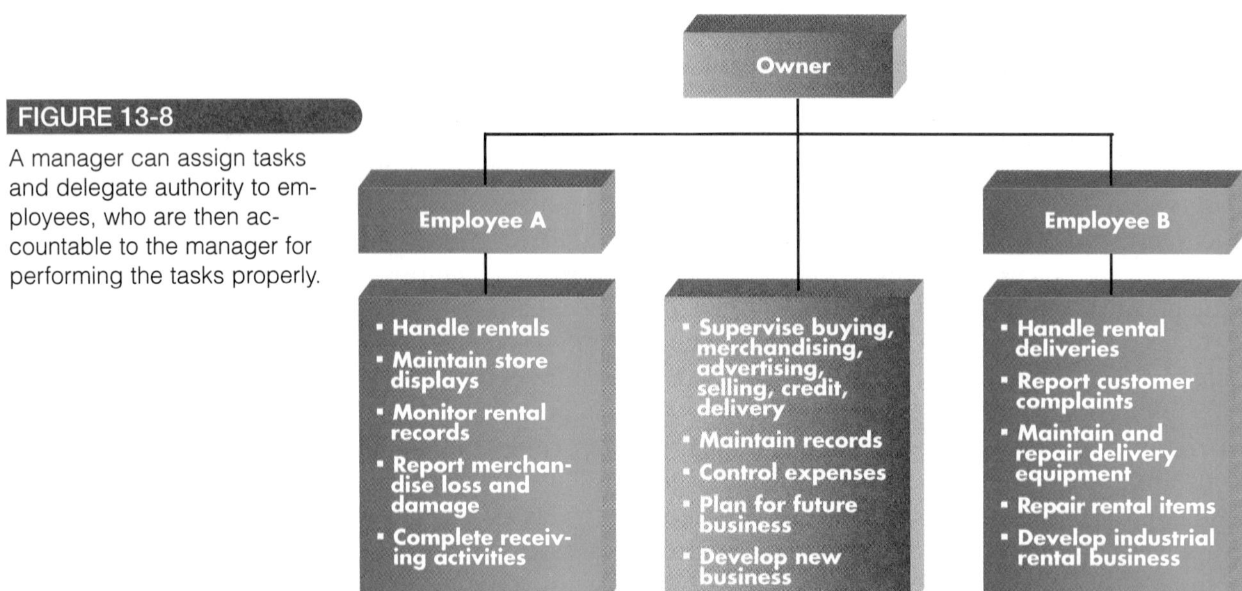

FIGURE 13-8

A manager can assign tasks and delegate authority to employees, who are then accountable to the manager for performing the tasks properly.

shows how a small rental business might assign responsibilities and delegate authority. Use the figure to identify the accountability of each person for the work of the organization.

Managers evaluate employees' work by comparing it to the established goals and work standards. For the assigned work, each employee is accountable for achieving the quality and quantity defined by the goals and standards. Managers need to communicate the goals and expected standards when assigning work and then use those same goals and standards when evaluating the employee's work.

UNITY OF COMMAND A traditional principle of good organization is unity of command. **Unity of command** means that no employee reports to more than one supervisor at a time. Confusion and poor work relations result when a person has work assigned by and is accountable to more than one supervisor. The person may not know which assignment to perform first or may receive conflicting instructions regarding the same work assignment. With the increasing use of teams, problems with unity of command can occur. Teams must practice the same careful organization of work as more traditional structures. Teams need clear assignments of responsibility and authority for their tasks, and all team members need to be aware of who is in charge of each activity.

SPAN OF CONTROL **Span of control** is the number of employees that any one manager supervises directly. Organizations must establish a reasonable span of control for each manager. The manager who supervises too many people is overworked and unable to perform all duties effectively. On the other hand, valuable time is wasted if a manager has too few people to supervise. That manager may supervise each person too closely or spend too much time in non-management work. In general, the span of control is larger at the lower levels of an organization than at the higher levels. For example, the head nurse in charge of a floor unit in a hospital may supervise 15 or more employees, while only three vice-presidents report to the chief executive of the hospital.

Companies that use work teams and encourage employees to be more involved in planning and decision making have found that they can increase the span of control. Well-trained and motivated employees do not require as much direct supervision as those who must rely on managers for direction. These companies have been able to reduce the numbers of managers required or have been able to increase the size of their workforces without hiring additional managers.

TYPES OF ORGANIZATIONAL STRUCTURE

The type of organizational structure identifies the relationships among departments and personnel and indicates the lines of communication and decision making. Two principal types of organizational structures are (1) line and (2) line-and-staff organizations. Two newer structures in companies today are matrix and team organizations.

LINE ORGANIZATION In a **line organization,** all authority and responsibility can be traced in a direct line from the top executive down to the lowest employee level in the organization. A line organization is shown in Figure 13-9 (sales is the only area for which the complete organization is shown). The lines joining the individual boxes indicate the lines of authority. The lines show, for example, that the president has authority over the sales manager, the sales manager has authority over the assistant sales manager, the assistant sales manager has authority over

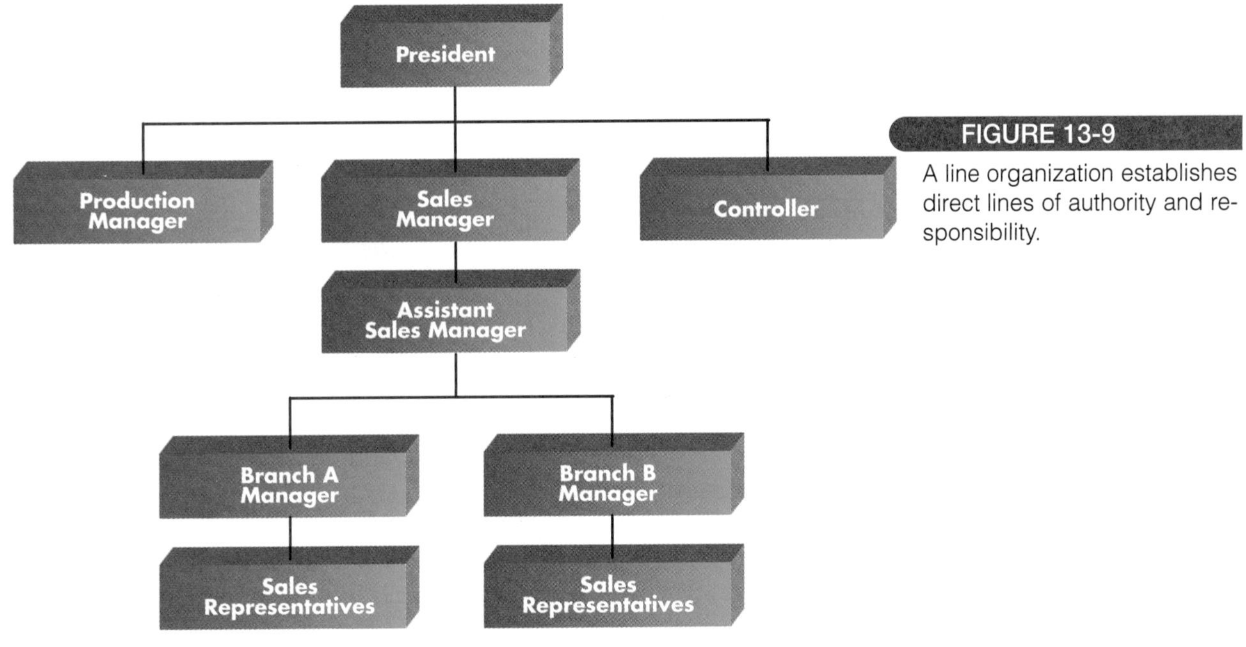

FIGURE 13-9

A line organization establishes direct lines of authority and responsibility.

the branch managers, and the branch managers have authority over the sales representatives. In addition, the lines describe how formal communications are expected to flow up and down the organization.

In a line organization, the president has direct control over all units of the business, but responsibility, authority, and accountability are passed along from one person to another, down to the lowest level. Under this form of organization, each person is responsible to only one manager who, in turn, is responsible to someone else. This type of organization can be very efficient, since new plans and ideas can be put into effect immediately in one area of the business without involvement from other areas. However, it often leads to many layers of management and isolation or lack of communication between departments and divisions.

LINE-AND-STAFF ORGANIZATION Large and complex businesses need a great deal of expertise to operate well. Managers have greater difficulty mastering the knowledge and skills they need in all of their areas of responsibility. In the **line-and-staff organization**, managers have direct control over the units and employees they supervise but have access to staff specialists for assistance. Specifically, the line-and-staff organization adds staff specialists to a line organization. It is designed to solve the problem of complexity and still retain the advantages of direct and definite lines of authority. Staff specialists give advice and assistance to line personnel. Staff personnel have no authority over line personnel; that is, staff personnel cannot require anyone in the line organization to perform any task. They are there to help with specialized jobs. Thus, line personnel are still responsible to only one supervisor.

The line-and-staff organization in Figure 13-10 is like the line organization in Figure 13-9 except for the addition of the advertising specialist and the marketing research specialist. Their responsibility is to give specialized advice and assistance to the sales organization of the business. This relationship is indicated in the organization chart by the broken lines. Other examples of staff positions in some organizations are legal, information management, strategic planning, and human resources specialists.

MATRIX ORGANIZATION A newer, more flexible structure is the matrix organization, which is sometimes called a *project organization*. A **matrix organization** combines workers into temporary work teams to complete specific projects. Employees report to a project manager with authority and responsibility for the project. When a new project must be done, employees with the needed skills are assigned to work on the project team. They work for that manager until the project is finished. Then they are assigned to a new project and another project manager.

In the matrix organization, there is no permanent organizational structure in which an employee continues to report to the same manager and works in only one functional area. It is difficult to develop an organizational chart for this type of organization because it changes regularly. Typically, the company prepares an organization chart for each

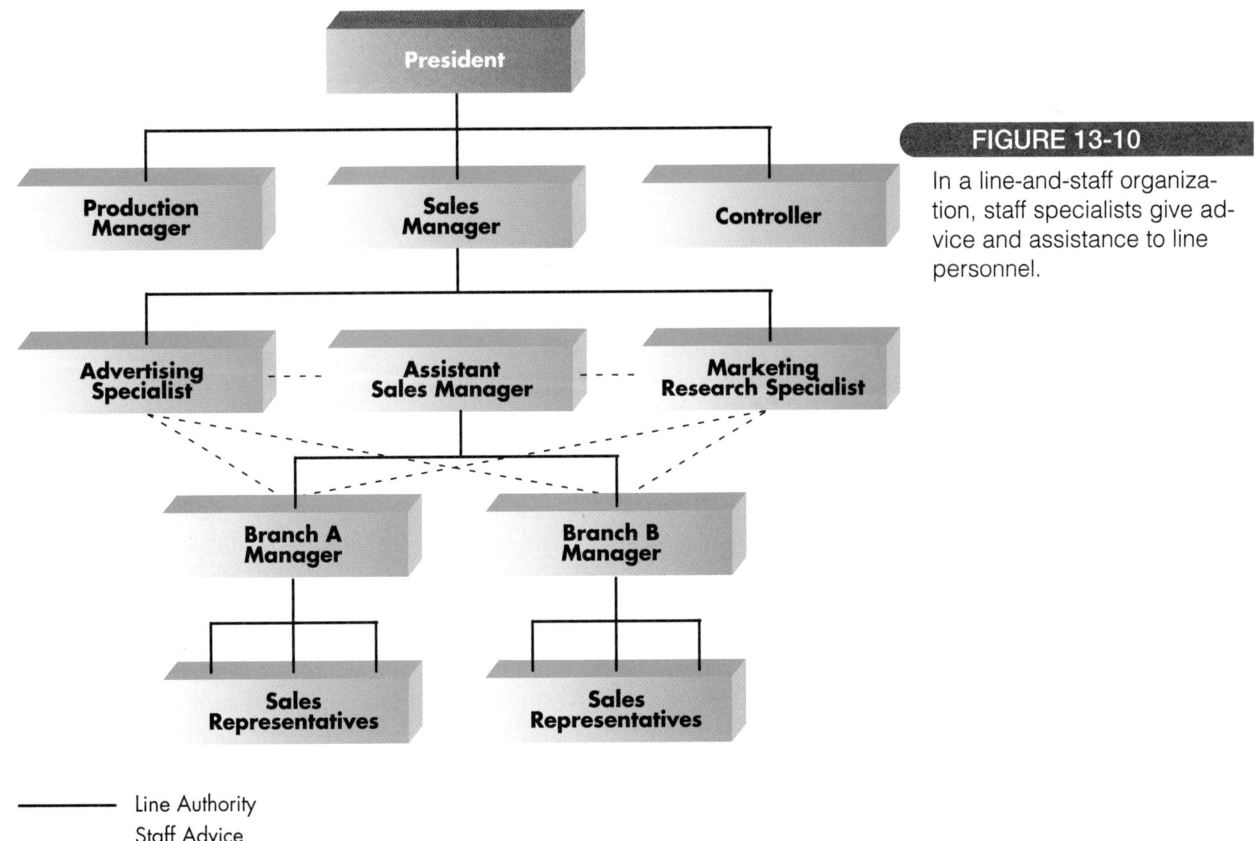

FIGURE 13-10

In a line-and-staff organization, staff specialists give advice and assistance to line personnel.

project, so that employees know the current project structure and the management and employee relationships. The company prepares a new chart when that project ends and a new one begins.

The matrix organization is used successfully in research firms, advertising agencies, and construction companies, but it is being considered by other types of businesses as well because it provides flexibility and allows for rapid change. This structure uses the specific skills of managers and employees as effectively as possible by bringing together people with the right skills for each project. When employees are given new project assignments, managers must be careful to define authority and responsibility, so as not to violate unity of command.

TEAM ORGANIZATION The newest type of organization structure is known as a team organization. A **team organization** divides employees into permanent work teams. The teams have responsibility and authority for important business activities with limited management control over their daily work. Teams often have team leaders. Team leaders replace the traditional position of supervisor and act as facilitators more than as traditional managers. Rather than solve most problems themselves, team leaders help their teams identify problems and work with them to solve the problems as a group. Team members report to the team leader, and the team leader makes some management decisions for the team.

MANAGEMENT CLOSE-UP

THE TEAM TAKES THE CHECKERED FLAG

If you are in the stands at a NASCAR race, it is easy to forget that each car and driver represents a complex business. (NASCAR stands for National Association for Stock Car Auto Racing.) In recent years, one name stands out from all of the drivers—Jeff Gordon. Named Rookie of the Year in 1993, Gordon has been one of the top drivers ever since.

Jeff drives the same model car as many other drivers, and NASCAR rules keep the technology similar for all cars in a race. So what makes the difference that allows one racing team to finish at the top? The leader of the racing team, Ray Evernham, and the team of people who are behind the scenes—the mechanics and the pit crew. Without people who view themselves as responsible for victory or defeat and who work to perfect the jobs they do, Jeff Gordon would just be another racecar driver.

Here are a few of the things they do differently from other racing crews:

- People are hired to work on the team because of their motivation and intelligence. They may not have any previous experience on a racing crew. Ray believes that people who want to be a part of a winning team can learn how to do their job, but it is hard to develop the desire to be the best.
- Teams are developed for specific tasks. While many other racing teams use the same people to be mechanics before the race and the pit crew during the race, Jeff's team members are specialists. In that way, they can learn as much as possible about their jobs in order to improve their work and spend more time perfecting their skills.
- The pit crew trains and practices as a team. They have a coach who concentrates on team skills so each person is committed to the entire process, not just one task. The team believes that together they are better than each individual alone.

The team is totally involved in decisions. If a problem occurs during a race, anyone may suggest a possible solution.

Everybody shares in success. When Jeff wins a race, the prize money is divided among the team members.

Jeff Gordon's success has caused other racing teams and other businesses to look at his team's secrets for success. It involves assembling a good team, developing effective teamwork, committing to success, and constantly looking for ways to improve.

THINK CRITICALLY

1. Why should a racing team be considered a business? What characteristics does it share with other types of businesses?
2. What does Ray Evernham do that makes him a manager? What types of planning and organizing activities do you believe he completes?
3. Which of the team success factors listed do you think is the most important? What other factors would you add that might make a team successful?

Source: *Adapted from Fast Company, October, 1998, p. 175*

Sometimes teams are organized without a permanently designated team leader. These are **self-directed work teams,** in which team members together are responsible for the work assigned to the team. Self-directed work teams have a manager to whom they can turn with unusual or very difficult problems, but most of the time they work together to establish goals and to plan and organize their work. Often members take turns as team leader or facilitator. A self-directed team has full authority over planning, performing, and evaluating its work. For feedback, the team may talk to other departments and customers who receive its work. In addition, the team is expected to talk to providers of raw materials or services to get feedback from inside or outside the firm.

In self-directed work teams, the team decides who will do which types of work and how they will do it. Each worker must be able to perform the tasks of most other team members to cover for absent members. Team members train other team members, hire and fire workers, evaluate performance, and handle most of the management tasks. The role of the manager is to serve as the team's consultant and to concentrate on higher-level management tasks. Some differences between self-directed work teams and traditional work teams are shown in Figure 13-11.

Effective work teams, whether self-directed or not, can increase productivity. To support their team, individuals work hard to improve the quality and quantity of work. Companies that have developed effective team structures have a better record of keeping customers happy, reducing absenteeism, reducing turnover, and keeping motivation high.

A study of customer service workers in the telecommunications industry showed that work groups organized into self-managing teams produced more sales volume and better customer service. Teams gained a 26 percent sales increase and a 6 percent customer service quality increase over work groups using the Total Quality Management and mass production work organization approaches.

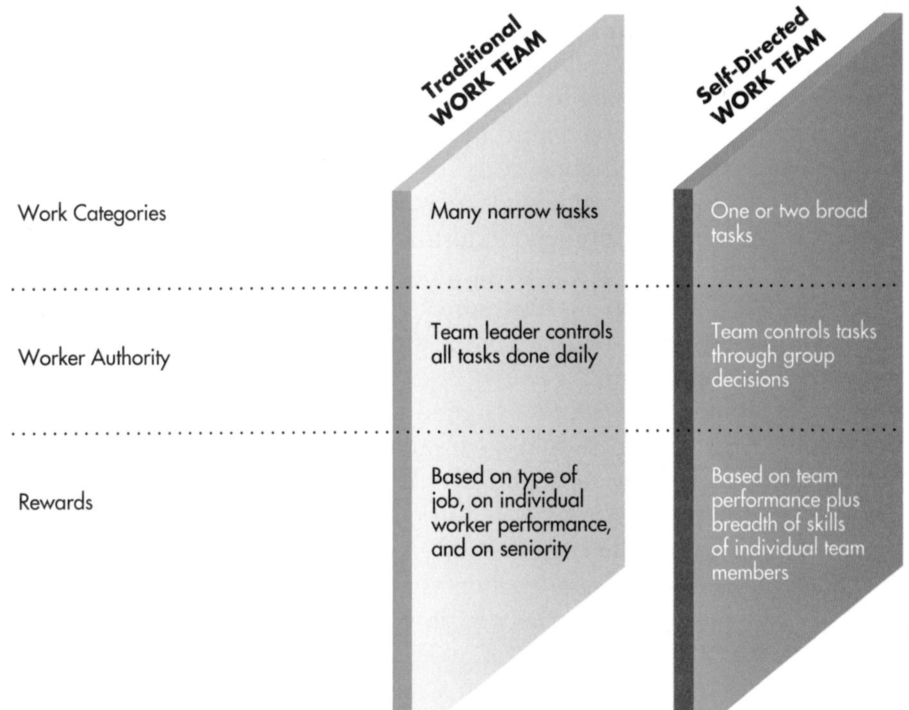

FIGURE 13-11

Differences Between Traditional Work Teams and Self-Directed Work Teams

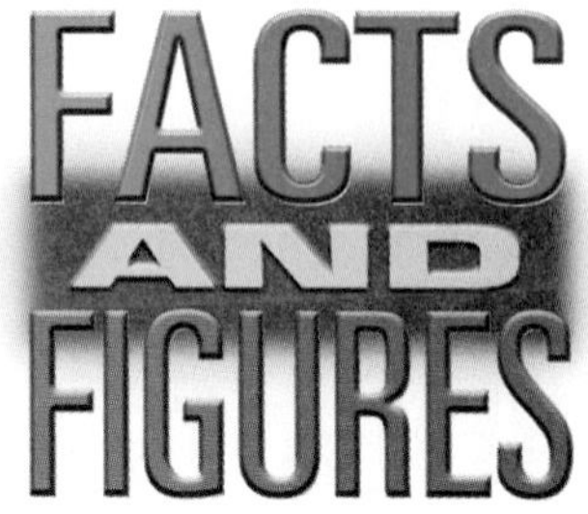

Most teams go through stages before coming together as a unit to achieve team goals. The difficulty in team development is breaking the habits established in the traditional system and developing new habits required by the team-based system. All members need training to learn how to operate as a team.

Teams require certain ingredients for success. Managers must support the idea and assist the teams as needed. Team members must become competent in three areas:

1. Technical job skills
2. Interpersonal skills, such as writing, speaking, discussing, and negotiating
3. Administrative skills, such as leading meetings, thinking analytically, and maintaining records

Teams need top-management support as well as skills in these three areas to do well. Often, teams take two to five years to mature to their full potential.

IMPROVING BUSINESS ORGANIZATION

Traditionally, businesses have used a **centralized organization,** in which a few top managers do all major planning and decision making. Recent studies of business organization have discovered that centralized organizations cause problems in some companies. Large companies often develop very complex centralized organizational structures. Those structures may cause communication problems and the need for many policies and rules to control the organization. Individual managers and employees then begin to feel like unimportant parts of the business. They get frustrated when rules keep them from doing things they consider important or when it takes a long time to get decisions made.

To overcome these types of problems, companies are moving to a **decentralized organization.** In this structure, a very large business is divided into smaller operating units, and unit managers have almost total responsibility and authority for the operation of their units. In many ways, the units operate as if they were independent companies. For example, a large computer manufacturer could be decentralized into work units by categories of products (mainframes, personal computers, accessory equipment) or by types of customers (industrial, government, international).

Another major type of reorganization occurring in businesses today is known as "flattening." A **flattened organization** is one with fewer levels of management than traditional structures. To achieve a flattened organization, the remaining managers and employees assume many of the responsibilities previously assigned to other levels of management. A flattened organization should have improved communication, because information has to flow through fewer levels of the organization. There should also be more coordination and cooperation because there is less specialization within the organization. As competition increases and customers expect businesses to increase quality and service, the organization of a business becomes very important. A complex organizational structure that requires a great deal of time for making decisions and for communicating information will not be as competitive as one that is more flexible and responsive.

CHAPTER CONCEPTS

- Planning is probably the most important management activity, because it establishes the goals and directions for the business on which all other management activities are based.
- Managers plan on two levels—strategic planning and operational planning. Long-term strategic planning develops goals and direction for the entire business. Short-term operational planning is based on the strategic plans and identifies specific activities for each area of the business. Planning tools used by managers include goals, budgets, schedules, standards, policies, procedures, and research.
- The process of organizing involves three elements: the division of work, the facilities and working conditions, and the employees. The total work to be done must be divided into units, such as departments. The company must provide equipment and materials employees need in order to complete their work and must arrange the layout of the facilities so that all work flows smoothly and provides the best working conditions possible. High productivity depends on good relationships among the employees and well-organized work tasks and facilities.
- For organizations to be effective, managers must assign authority, responsibility, and accountability appropriately. Also, the organization should not violate unity of command, and managers' span of control must not be too large or small. Businesses typically use line, line-and-staff, matrix, or team organization. Today's business organizations are becoming more decentralized and flatter to increase productivity and meet customer needs.

BUILD VOCABULARY POWER

Define the following terms and concepts.

1. strategic planning
2. operational planning
3. SWOT analysis
4. mission statement
5. goal
6. schedule
7. standard
8. policies
9. procedure
10. organization chart
11. responsibility
12. authority
13. empowerment
14. accountability
15. unity of command
16. span of control
17. line organization
18. line-and-staff organization
19. matrix organization
20. team organization
21. self-directed work team
22. centralized organization
23. decentralized organization
24. flattened organization

REVIEW FACTS

1. Why is a business plan so important for a business considering a major change?

2. What are the two levels of planning done in a business?
3. What level of management is responsible for strategic planning?
4. What are the four characteristics of an effective goal?
5. Explain how a manager might use a schedule to plan.
6. Why are written procedures valuable for a new employee?
7. List three purposes of an organization chart.
8. What factors should be considered when establishing a division of work within a company?
9. How can you determine if authority and responsibility have been assigned properly?
10. Why should an employee report to only one supervisor?
11. How is span of control different at lower than upper levels of an organization?
12. What do broken lines in an organization chart mean?
13. What are two newer forms of organization in businesses today?
14. What types of problems often result within centralized organizations?
15. Why are companies moving to decentralized and flattened organizations?

DISCUSS IDEAS

1. In addition to providing financial information, what other benefits does a business owner get from a business plan? What are the non-financial benefits to the business's banker?
2. If the business environment is changing rapidly, why should businesses spend time on long-range planning?
3. Why is strategic planning done before operational planning?
4. How is your schedule of classes related to a business schedule?
5. Explain how the flowchart in Figure 13-3 can help a new employee in the catalog order department.
6. What are several things you can learn about a company by studying its organizational chart?
7. What problems are likely to result when a manager assigns responsibilities to an employee but does not give that employee the authority to carry out the assigned responsibilities?
8. Identify the potential problems that might occur if a manager's span of control is too big or too small.
9. Why should an employee report to only one boss?
10. What problems are likely to occur when a company decentralizes or flattens its organizational structure? How should that change benefit the company?

ANALYZE INFORMATION

1. Using the Internet, search for information on developing a business plan. Using the information you find, develop an outline of the information you believe should be included in a business

plan. Provide a brief statement for each topic you include, justifying its importance.

2. A local business owner has asked you to prepare an organization chart that illustrates the business's operations and management. The owner provides you with the following information. Draw a chart that reflects the information provided. If possible, use a graphics or drawing program on a computer to prepare the organization chart.
   a. The owner of the business is J. M. Gray.
   b. The business consists of a service station, a used-car sales department, a repair department, and a parts department.
   c. Mr. Gray's daughter, Joan, acts as his assistant but also manages the parts department and supervises to a certain extent all of the other functions.
   d. B. L. O'Hara and three assistants operate the repair department.
   e. O. P. Thompson is in charge of the used-car sales, but an employee by the name of Linda Williams spends most of her time selling the cars.
   f. Gray's nephew, Jim Blake, takes care of the service station with the assistance of two part-time employees, Bo Jakes and Rundell Brown.
3. Gather a small team of classmates or join a team formed by your teacher. Working together in your team, identify 15 school- and work-related activities that your team members must complete during the next three weeks. Make sure the list includes some activities that must be completed by the entire team, some by a few but not all of the team members, and some that must be completed by only one team member. Then develop a schedule that illustrates how team members will complete the activities by the end of the three weeks.
4. Review the information from the beginning of the chapter about Eldron Huntley's idea to expand his catering business using the Internet. Identify two planning activities and two organizing activities Mr. Huntley will need to complete if he goes forward with the business idea. Write two goals that Mr. Huntley could set for the business—one that should be achieved in three months and one that should be achieved by the end of the first year. Write the goals to include the four characteristics of an effective goal.
5. Your class has been given three projects: (a) to organize and write several sections of the school's student handbook, (b) to work with a local organization to collect food from the community for needy families, and (c) to operate a Saturday-morning recreation program for elementary students. Work with your entire class to develop a team organizational plan for the projects. (Your teacher may choose to divide the class into smaller groups to complete this assignment.) For each project, prepare a project organization

chart with a manager and at least five positions to complete the work. Develop a list of activities for each position. Then assign specific class members to the positions in each project, based on the activities to be completed and the person's interests and skills.

SOLVE BUSINESS PROBLEMS

CASE 13-1

The ToyTime Company makes and sells a line of children's toys. In six months, retail stores will begin buying the company's products in large quantities in preparation for the holiday shopping season. The marketing manager is confident that sales will be higher this year than last. Thus, several new salespeople have been hired and are being trained for the upcoming rush period. Increased advertising has also been planned.

The production manager, on the other hand, has been running into difficulties getting raw materials from the firm's only supplier. Production has been cut by 20 percent during the last two months, and the inventory of finished goods is less than planned. The production manager, not having received word to the contrary, has planned to keep the finished goods inventory at last year's level. There is no indication as to when the raw material problem will be solved. In addition, the labor contract with the union expires in three months, and there has been discussion of a possible strike.

Think Critically:

1. What management problems are apparent in the ToyTime Company?
2. Why have these problems occurred?
3. Using the management tools discussed in the chapter, give examples of how each of the problems could be solved.

CASE 13-2

Hector Fuego had just been hired by the board of directors to become the new CEO of You Build, Inc. You Build is a 50-year-old building supply company that operates in the southwestern United States. The company has a very successful history that has seen expansion to 50 stores in 23 cities. However, in the past three years, operations have been much less successful because the largest retailer in the industry, Home Warehouse, began to expand into the areas served by You Build. Home Warehouse builds larger stores in very convenient locations with a broader set of products and low prices. As the new CEO, Mr. Fuego had to find ways to meet the competition and maintain the success of You Build, Inc.

Because of its history, You Build had developed a very traditional line organizational structure. All strategic planning and major decisions were made by the CEO and a team of three vice presidents. There were two more levels of management at the corporate level; four regional offices with managers that reported to the corporate level; a management team in every city that had three or more stores; and a store management team. Most of the managers had many years of experience with You Build and had worked their way up through the system. Mr. Fuego believed most of the managers were very good at their jobs and worked very hard to make the company successful. However, it seemed that the current organizational structure made decision-making very slow, and the many employees at the store level who worked with customers had very little input into store operations.

Hector Fuego wanted to change the organizational structure of You Build, Inc. He believed the business would be more effective with a flattened organization and by replacing the line organization with a team organization. The city management positions would be eliminated, and each store would develop teams of employees to make decisions for the store's departments. He knew the change would not be easy since the company had used the traditional organizational structure for 50 years.

Think Critically:

1. What are the advantages and disadvantages of the change in organizational structure Hector Fuego is planning?
2. How do you believe the You Build, Inc., managers will feel about the change? How do you believe the employees will feel about the change?
3. What steps do you recommend that Mr. Fuego follow to prepare managers for the change? What should he do to prepare employees for their new role in the organization?

PROJECT: MY BUSINESS, INC.

As a new business owner, you will spend the majority of time on planning and organizing activities. Starting with a business plan, you must develop goals, budgets, schedules, policies, and procedures. As you add employees, you will have to make decisions on how to organize and divide work so that it will be completed effectively. In the project activities for this chapter, you will plan and organize your business.

DATA COLLECTION

1. Meet with your business mentor and discuss the importance of planning, how the business person plans for the business, and the types of planning tools he or she used.
2. Using the Internet or your library, find and read several articles on ways that businesses are reorganizing work for more effective operations. Summarize the key points from those articles that you believe are useful to small businesses.

ANALYSIS

1. Divide a sheet of paper or word processing document into two columns. Label one column "strategic planning" and the other "operational planning." List as many areas as you can under each label that need to be completed for your business.
2. For each of the planning tools discussed in this chapter, identify how and when you will use the tool in your business. Prepare a

one-month planning schedule where you list when you will use each tool.

3. Assume you have hired two full-time and four part-time employees to help you operate your business. Consider the operations and activities that must be completed in your business. Then prepare an organizational chart for the business in which you list job titles and duties for each employee. Identify whether the type of organizational structure is line, line-and-staff, or some other type. Why do you believe that structure will be most effective?

IMPLEMENTING AND CONTROLLING

OBJECTIVES

- **14-1** Identify the major management tasks involved in implementing the work of an organization.
- **14-2** Explain the differences among three theories of employee motivation.
- **14-3** Discuss the steps in an effective change process.
- **14-4** Describe the controlling process and four types of business standards.
- **14-5** Recognize control methods businesses use for inventory, credit, theft, and health and safety.

OUT OF CONTROL

Jasmine Marsh had been hired as the manager of the new telemarketing department of an office supply company. The department was fully automated with computerized telephone and order processing systems. Jasmine was given a large budget to retrain current employees who had volunteered, as well as to hire and train new employees for telephone sales. She had three months to organize the work and prepare the employees for their new tasks.

A strategy was developed to sell office supplies through catalogs and telephone sales. A catalog was prepared and mailed to all businesses in the city. Follow-up telephone calls were made, introducing the service and promoting the delivery guarantee. The promise to customers was that any order placed by 10 p.m. would be delivered by 10 a.m. the next day.

Things got off to a good start. There was a real excitement among the employees when they made the sales calls to introduce the new service, and the orders began to come in to the office. The employees seemed to enjoy using the new computer equipment, and the training made them comfortable with their work. However, problems began to appear after the first month of operation.

The first problem occurred when Jasmine established sales quotas for each employee. With sales growing rapidly, it didn't seem difficult for most employees to make their quotas. However, some people had high sales volumes and others had few sales. Jasmine believed the quotas would encourage everyone to emphasize selling rather than just waiting for customers to call in orders from the catalog. Several employees complained that the quotas emphasized selling too much and didn't allow them adequate time to answer customer questions and solve their problems.

The department began to experience some computer difficulties. When a high volume of calls came in, the computers would slow down. Employees would have to wait to get information on their screens, and occasionally all of the information entered would be lost before the order could be processed. Also, it appeared that the company sometimes was not able to meet its goal of overnight delivery. The telemarketing employees were starting to receive customer complaints, which they were not prepared to handle.

The most serious problem was a rapid increase in employee dissatisfaction and turnover. The growing sales volume was putting pressure on Jasmine's department. While she was hiring and training new employees, it seemed there never were enough employees to handle the growing amount of business. To get new employees on the job faster, training time was reduced. That seemed to result in more errors in the orders they processed. Veteran employees were being asked to work overtime to meet the demand. Experienced employees, especially ones who had worked for the company before the change, were quitting or asking for transfers because of the pressure they were facing on the job.

Jasmine knew that her department was essential to the success of the company. If the department was not able to maintain and increase the level of sales and process orders efficiently, the new business strategy would fail. As the manager, she needed to figure out ways to solve the growing number of problems.

Jasmine is discovering what many experienced managers have learned. Plans are not effective unless they are implemented well. Changing conditions in a business create problems in the way work is accomplished.

As you learned in Chapter 11, implementing involves carrying out the plans and helping employees to work effectively. The controlling function involves evaluating results to determine if the company's objectives have been accomplished as planned. The majority of managers, especially supervisors and middle-level managers, spend a great deal of their time on implementing and controlling activities. In this chapter, you will learn about these two important management activities.

THE IMPLEMENTING FUNCTION

Implementing involves guiding employee work toward achieving the company's goals. For example, a manager may communicate important goals to an employee team, provide leadership to help them determine how to complete the necessary work, and make sure that rewards and recognition are provided to everyone involved when their work achieves the goals. You will remember from the scenario at the beginning of the chapter that Jasmine had many activities for which she was responsible in the new department. She was spending a great deal of time implementing the company's plans.

IMPLEMENTING ACTIVITIES

To implement successfully, managers must complete a number of activities designed to channel employee efforts in the right direction to achieve the goals. These activities include effective communications, motivating employees, developing effective work teams, and operations management.

EFFECTIVE COMMUNICATIONS Communication is an essential part of implementing work in a business. Managers must be able to communicate plans and directions, gather feedback from employees, and iden-

ILLUSTRATION 14-1

Supervisors must be able to implement the plans that have been developed. What types of information are available in business plans to help supervisors to direct employees?

tify and resolve communication problems. Both personal and organizational communications are important. Managing communication technology has become an important responsibility.

Communication is much more than telling employees what to do. In fact, if employees believe managers are being too directive, they will likely be dissatisfied and not work as hard or effectively as they could. An important communication skill for managers is to listen to employees and involve them in deciding how work should be done. A manager should use both formal and informal communications. Encouraging employees to contribute their ideas and involving them in deciding the best way to do the work will help gain their commitment to achieving the goals.

EMPLOYEE MOTIVATION **Motivation** is a set of factors that influence an individual's actions toward accomplishing a goal. Employees may be motivated to achieve company goals, or they may be motivated to pursue other goals that do not benefit the company. Managers don't actually "motivate" employees, but they can use rewards and punishments to encourage employees to motivate themselves toward pursuing company objectives. A key to motivation is to know what employees value and give them these things for achieving company goals. A reward is not motivating unless it is something the employee values. The reward need not be money. People also value things like praise, respect, an interesting job assignment, or an extra day off.

Motivation comes from influences both inside and outside the individual. Internal motivation arises from a person's beliefs, feelings, and attitudes that influence the person's actions. For example, many workers are motivated to do a good job because they get an internal sense of satisfaction from a job well done. External motivation comes from rewards and punishments supplied by other people. For example, doing a good job may result in a pay raise, admiration from co-workers, or praise from the boss.

Sometimes the internal factors have the most influence on behavior. If an employee believes that the work is boring, she will not be motivated to do a good job. At other times, external factors have the strongest influence on performance. An employee who values praise would likely be motivated to greater performance when he sees his name posted on the bulletin board as "employee of the week." Simply repainting the work area can serve as a motivating reward for employees who value a pleasing work environment.

All people have their own needs, and they will choose to do things that will satisfy their needs and avoid doing things that don't. Managers can influence employee performance by understanding individual needs and providing rewards that satisfy those needs when employees accomplish work goals. Psychologists have studied behavior to try to understand what motivates people to do what they do. Several theories of motivation will be reviewed in the next section.

Human resources experts say that managers can motivate employees without spending money. They suggest the following: provide lots of encouragement; tolerate learning errors by avoiding harsh criticism; add some fun and variety to routine work; promote job ownership; encourage responsibility and leadership opportunities; provide employees with input and choice in their tasks; and promote social interaction and teamwork between employees.

WORK TEAMS Seldom do people complete all of their work alone. Most people are part of a work group and rely on cooperation from others to perform their work. It has been said that groups can accomplish more than the same number of people working independently. Managers need to be able to develop effective work teams. A **work team** is a group of individuals who cooperate to achieve a common goal.

Effective work teams have several characteristics, as shown in Figure 14-1. First, the members of the group understand and support its purpose. They clearly understand the activities to be completed, know which activities they must perform, and have the knowledge and skills necessary to complete the activities. Group members are committed to helping the group succeed and meeting the expectations of others in the group. Finally, group members communicate well with each other and work to resolve problems within the group.

Just because several people work together does not guarantee that they will be an effective work team. In fact, there are many reasons why they may not be an effective team. They may not know each other well and do not trust each other. They may have biases or stereotypes about other group members. They may not be prepared to cooperate in completing a task or know how to make effective team decisions.

Managers can play an important role in developing team effectiveness. To develop effective teams, they must understand the character-

FIGURE 14-1

Characteristics of Effective Work Teams

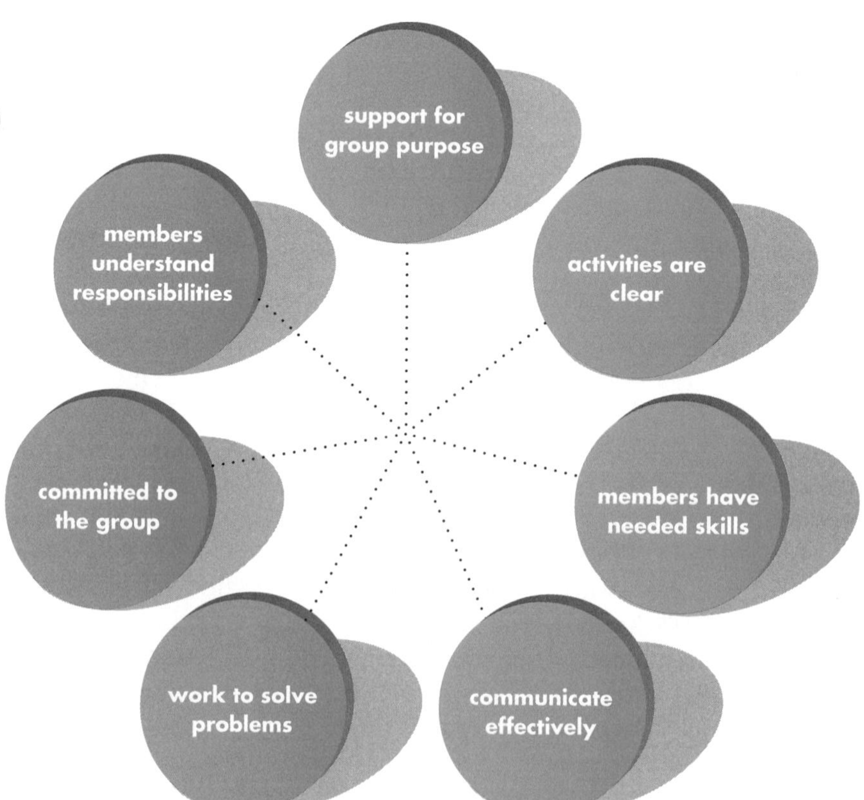

MANAGEMENT CLOSE-UP

GE TEAMS UP FOR SUCCESS

You can't make a mistake when building airplane engines. The jet engines produced by the General Electric Aircraft Engines plant in Durham, North Carolina, have over 10,000 parts. When completely assembled, they weigh over 8 tons. Yet a bolt not tightened, a tool left inside the engine, or a safety procedure not followed can cost hundreds of lives.

Approximately 200 people assemble the huge engines. Yet there is only one boss, the plant manager, and only one direction. Employees are told what date each engine needs to be finished. They make every decision on how the work will be completed. They have a record of delivering every engine ordered on schedule for over three years. During that time, they were able to reduce the cost of producing the engine by nearly one third.

How does this GE plant achieve its amazing record with only one manager? Here are some unique characteristics of the organization:

- Employees are organized into nine teams that make almost all decisions. Everyone is on a team, and team meetings are scheduled when all employees are available.
- There are three pay levels for employees, and pay is based on the amount of skill an employee has.
- There is no time clock. If someone has a doctor's appointment or needs to go to their children's school activities, they work with team members to be able to leave.
- Everyone learns how to do many of the assembly tasks so they can help each other.
- Teams are responsible for hiring new team members. They do the interviewing, and they have to agree on the people they will hire.
- Teams solve problems and often come up with unique but simple solutions.

The team environment in Durham works. The plant has the lowest turnover rate and the lowest production costs of any of the other General Electric engine assembly plants. The unique type of organization shows that when employees are given the chance to work together to manage their work, they do it better than anyone could have imagined.

THINK CRITICALLY

1. Why do you believe employees are willing to spend time in team meetings to solve problems and discuss issues that are usually handled by managers?
2. How do you believe the pay plan affects employee motivation? What are the advantages and disadvantages of that plan?
3. Discuss reasons why the team problem-solving process seems to come up with unique but effective solutions. Are there reasons why solutions developed by employees are likely to be more successful than if the same solution was developed by a manager without the input of employees?
4. Use the Internet to find examples of other companies that have successfully used teams in their business. Identify the type of company and how the team was used.

istics that make groups effective, help to organize the team and develop needed team skills, create a work environment that supports teamwork, and help the group resolve problems when they occur.

OPERATIONS MANAGEMENT Operations are the major ongoing activities of a business. When completing the implementing function, managers are ensuring that employees are performing business activities as planned. Several activities are part of operations management. Facilities, equipment, materials, and supplies must be available and in good operating condition, so employees can perform their work. Employees must have the knowledge and skills needed to complete their work. Managers must make sure that employees complete their tasks on schedule, and work to resolve problems that could interfere with the successful completion of the job. Refer back to the beginning of the chapter and try to identify the operations issues that Jasmine was facing.

Effective planning and organizing are important parts of operations management. Planning helps employees know what to do. In the same way, well-organized work space and procedures for completing work tasks help operations run smoothly. If problems occur in the operations of a business, managers should examine the planning and organizing of the work.

Managers must be prepared to implement the activities assigned to their area of responsibility. Some activities are common to most management areas. For example, most managers must hire new employees, monitor work schedules, and communicate policies and procedures. However, most departments are organized to perform specialized operations. For example, the manager of the marketing department may be responsible for advertising and sales. The information systems manager must ensure that computer systems are operational, the company's Internet sites are up-to-date, and that software is problem-free. Man-

ILLUSTRATION 14-2

Ensuring effective operations is an important management responsibility. What are examples of operations that occur in a company with which you are familiar?

agers need to understand the unique work of their departments in order to help employees complete that work.

In the past several years, organizations have paid a great deal of attention to improving the way work is done. Due to increasing competition, companies must operate efficiently to keep costs low, so that they can compete successfully. Customers are demanding improved quality, so the company must produce products free of defects. The efforts to increase the effectiveness and efficiency of specific business operations are known as **process improvement**.

MOTIVATION THEORIES

Think of the days when you are excited to get up and go to school or work. You enjoy the day and work hard. Time seems to move faster than usual. Compare that to the days when it is impossible to get up and you dread going to work or school. The day seems to go on forever, and you don't seem to be able to get anything done.

In the same way, you probably can identify teachers, coaches, or business people for whom you enjoy working and who seem to be able to encourage your best work. You also know others whom you would prefer to avoid and for whom it is a struggle to perform well. What causes the differences?

You learned earlier that internal and external factors motivate people to act in certain ways. Psychologists have developed theories about what factors motivate people to behave as they do. Figure 14-2 summarizes these theories. Managers can influence employees to behave in ways that help achieve company goals by influencing these motivational factors.

MASLOW'S HIERARCHY OF NEEDS Abraham Maslow described motivation in terms of a *hierarchy of needs*. The lowest level is physiological needs, followed by security, social, esteem, and self-actualization needs. Physiological needs are things required to sustain life, such as food and shelter. Security needs involve making sure you and those you care about are safe and free from harm. Social needs include the need to belong, to interact with others, to have friends, and to love and be loved. The need for esteem includes the need for recognition and respect from others. Finally, self-actualization is the need to grow, to be creative, and to achieve your full potential.

According to the theory, people seek to satisfy these needs in order, from lowest to highest. Not until they fulfill the lowest needs on the hierarchy will the next level of needs motivate their behavior. For example, starving people will be more motivated to find food than to find friends. But once people have satisfied their physiological and security needs, then the need for social interaction will motivate their behavior. Applying Maslow's hierarchy, managers can influence employee behavior by recognizing the levels of the hierarchy that are motivating

FIGURE 14-2
Important Theories of Employee Motivation

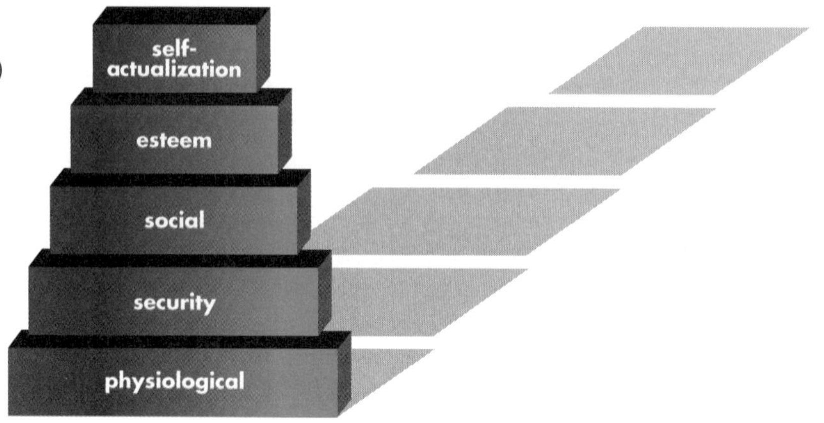

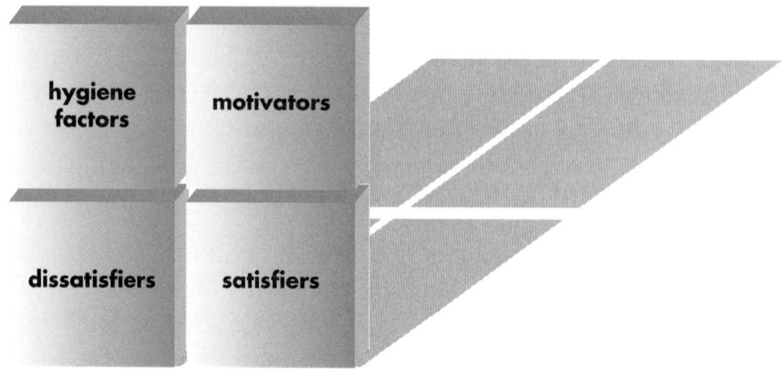

employee behavior at that time and then try to use things such as job assignments, compensation, and reinforcement to meet those employee needs.

McCLELLAND'S ACHIEVEMENT MOTIVATION While Maslow's theory is based on a set of needs common to all people, David McClelland believed that people are influenced most strongly by one of three specific needs. He identified the major needs as the need for achievement, the need for affiliation, and the need for power.

McClelland suggested that people with a high **achievement need** take personal responsibility for their own work, set personal goals, and want immediate feedback on their work. People with a strong **affiliation need** are concerned about their relationships with others and work to get along well and fit in with a group. Finally, those with a strong **power need** want to influence and control others and to be responsible for a group's activities. You can probably think of people who fit into each of these three need classifications.

Managers who believe in McClelland's theory recognize that various jobs provide better or worse opportunities for achievement, affiliation, or power. Managers working with individuals with a high achievement need should provide opportunities for them to make decisions and control their own work. When managers see a high affiliation need in their employees, they should assign the employees to group projects and teams. These employees will respond well if socializing opportunities are built into the work environment. Finally, people with a high need for power will work best when given the opportunity to be a project leader or to be involved in planning and decision-making. McClelland's theory suggests that the strength of the three needs can be changed over time with careful development.

HERZBERG'S TWO-FACTOR THEORY A third important motivation theory was developed by Frederick Herzberg. He conducted studies of employees to identify what satisfied and dissatisfied them in their work. His research resulted in the identification of two distinct groups of factors related to motivation. Therefore his theory is known as the *two-factor theory.*

Herzberg called one group hygiene factors. **Hygiene factors** are job factors that dissatisfy when absent but do not contribute to satisfaction when they are present. Examples of hygiene factors are the amount of pay and fringe benefits, working conditions, rules, and the amount and type of supervision. For example, a good company-sponsored healthcare plan will not motivate employees to do a better job. But the lack of a good health plan could cause employees to be dissatisfied with their jobs.

Herzberg called the second group motivators. **Motivators** are factors that increase job satisfaction. The people whom Herzberg studied were motivated by factors such as challenging work, recognition, achievement, accomplishment, increased responsibility, and personal development.

The interesting part of Herzberg's theory is that the two types of factors and their results are separate from each other. In other words, hygiene factors can create dissatisfaction but cannot improve satisfaction. For example, people can be dissatisfied with the level of their pay and fringe benefits, but pay increases will not increase satisfaction. So, providing hygiene factors, such as pay increases and better working conditions, will only prevent employees from being dissatisfied. It will not motivate employees to better performance.

On the other hand, motivators increase satisfaction. To stimulate workers to higher achievement, managers should provide motivators, such as opportunities for interesting work, greater individual control and responsibility, and recognition for good work.

Managers are often surprised by Herzberg's studies. It is easy to believe that a pay increase will motivate employees to perform better. However, people are often dissatisfied when they compare their pay to that of others, or they believe they are worth more than they are currently being paid. Factors such as fair pay, flexible work hours, and good fringe benefits can keep people from being dissatisfied but seldom are the major reason people are motivated to perform well.

FACTS AND FIGURES

In a recent survey of 350 human resources executives, nearly half reported that the retention of employees was a very serious issue in their companies. Retention was particularly difficult in the case of employees less than 30 years old. Companies with programs to retain employees said that educational and lifestyle incentives were more effective than monetary compensation. Technical training, employability training, and flexible work arrangements were seen as most valuable.

MANAGING CHANGE

The only thing that seems certain in business today is change. Reengineering, downsizing, mergers, and many other organizational changes affect workers and their jobs.

People are not always comfortable with change. Consider changes you have experienced. Examples could include moving, changing schools, relationships with family or friends, or an important decision you may be facing. How did you react to that change? When it appears that things will be different, those affected by the change are likely to be very concerned.

When people's jobs are threatened, when they are uncertain about how a change will affect them, or when they do not trust those responsible for planning the change, they will probably resist the change. To implement organizational change, managers must work to overcome that resistance and to make change as comfortable as possible for the employees affected.

The steps in an effective change process are shown in Figure 14-3. People resist change most when it occurs suddenly, when they are not prepared, or when they don't understand the reasons for the

ILLUSTRATION 14-3

Change occurs regularly in business today. What are some examples of recent changes that have occurred in businesses in your community?

1. Carefully plan for the change.
2. Communicate with people, so that change does not surprise them.
3. Involve people, so they feel a part of the change.
4. Educate people, so they understand the change.
5. Support people in their efforts to change.

FIGURE 14-3

Steps in Successfully Implementing Change

change. Careful planning will make the transition smoother, and the people affected will be more likely to support the change.

PLANNING Managers must be careful not to move too rapidly to make changes. They must be certain that change is needed and that the organization will be better off as a result of the change. Then they should follow a careful procedure to gather information, identify and study alternatives, and determine the consequences of change. A well-considered plan will help to assure the best results and will give confidence to those most affected by the change.

COMMUNICATING Sometimes managers believe it is best not to say anything to employees about possible changes until a final decision has been made and they are ready to take action. They believe that early information will create confusion and misunderstanding. People who study the change process recognize that it is almost impossible to conceal information about pending changes. Using informal communication and limited information, rumors and misinformation will spread. If people are surprised by a change or feel they have been misled, the result is usually more damaging to the organization than the result of early, direct communications from management.

Managers who have previously established open communications with employees will be in the best position to communicate with them about possible changes. Since change occurs frequently in business, employees who are used to regular communications with their managers will not be surprised by information about potential changes, even if the changes may appear to be negative. Open, two-way communications between managers and employees are a part of an effective change process.

INVOLVING It is frequently said that people support what they create. Managers must recognize that employees can be a good source of ideas on effective solutions and how to make changes. Most effective change processes involve the people who will be affected in gathering information, considering alternatives, and testing solutions. It is usually not possible to involve everyone in all parts of the change process or to use a majority vote to decide on a change. However, employees will be more supportive when they know their voices will be heard and that they have input into plans that result in change.

Managers must respect the input of employees. Sometimes managers say they want employees' ideas but then ignore that input. That will frustrate employees and make them reluctant to participate in the future. Managers must make it clear that every idea contributed by an employee cannot be implemented, but they will carefully consider each idea when planning the change.

EDUCATING Change in business does not just happen. New products, new technology, or redesigned jobs require people to prepare. Usually, that means information and training. As plans for change develop, managers must determine who will be affected and what new knowledge and skills those employees will need. Then managers should implement information meetings and training programs to prepare employees for the required changes.

Many companies have had to reduce the number of employees through downsizing. That type of change is very difficult for managers to implement and employees to accept. Some companies are trying to help the people who will no longer have jobs by offering training for other positions available in the company or to develop skills that will help them get jobs with another company.

SUPPORTING How willing are you to make a change if you are uncertain of the result? When people believe they will receive support from their organization, they are more willing to accept changes. All changes involve some amount of risk, and organizations cannot guarantee success. However, managers need to assure employees that there is support available to help them adjust to the change.

The support can take many forms. Part of the support is allowing time to adjust to change. Managers may provide more feedback on how employees are performing and be less critical of mistakes early in the process. Counseling, training, and additional information are other methods of support.

Sometimes changes have negative effects on employees that cannot be avoided. Employees may have to be terminated or undergo major job changes that can require reductions in pay, different working conditions, and so forth. Support is especially needed under those circumstances. Employees who lose their jobs need time to adjust. Companies may provide full or partial salary for several weeks or months while the people affected try to find new jobs. The companies may look for other positions in the organization and help employees retrain or relocate. They can also give preference to those employees when new positions open. Many companies now provide personal and career counseling, help with job-seeking skills, and even pay for employment services for employees who are terminated due to change.

THE CONTROLLING FUNCTION

"Employee absences have increased by 3 percent this year."

"Maintenance costs are down an average of $150 per vehicle."

"Salespeople in the southern district have increased new customer orders by 12.3 percent in a three-year period."

"An average of 16 additional employees per month are enrolling in the company's wellness program."

"The adjustments to the welding robot's computer program have reduced the variations in the seam to .0004 mm."

These statements provide very valuable information to managers. With the proper information, managers can tell how well activities are being performed. Reviewing performance is one part of the fourth management function—controlling. Managers must be able to determine if performance meets expectations. If problems are occurring, managers need problem-solving skills to develop good solutions. In the last part of this chapter, you will study the controlling function of management.

As you have learned, all managers perform four management functions. Planning involves setting goals and directions for the business. Organizing deals with obtaining and arranging resources so the goals can be met. Implementing is the responsibility for carrying out the work of the organization. Controlling is determining whether goals are being met and what actions to take if performance falls short of the goals.

While each of the functions includes a specific set of activities, they are all related. Planning improves if there is an effective organization to provide information to managers. Without effective planning, it is difficult to decide how to organize a business and what resources are needed. Implementation is impossible without plans and difficult with a poorly designed organization. Controlling cannot be completed unless the company has specific goals and plans. Figure 14-4 shows that management is a continuous process and that each function supports the others. Controlling is the final function and provides the information needed to improve the management process and business operations.

BASIC STEPS

Controlling involves three basic steps:

1. Establishing standards for each of the company's goals.
2. Measuring and comparing performance against the established standards to see if performance met the goals.
3. Taking corrective action when performance falls short of the standards.

The important activities in controlling are shown in the following example. A business has a goal to manufacture and deliver to a cus-

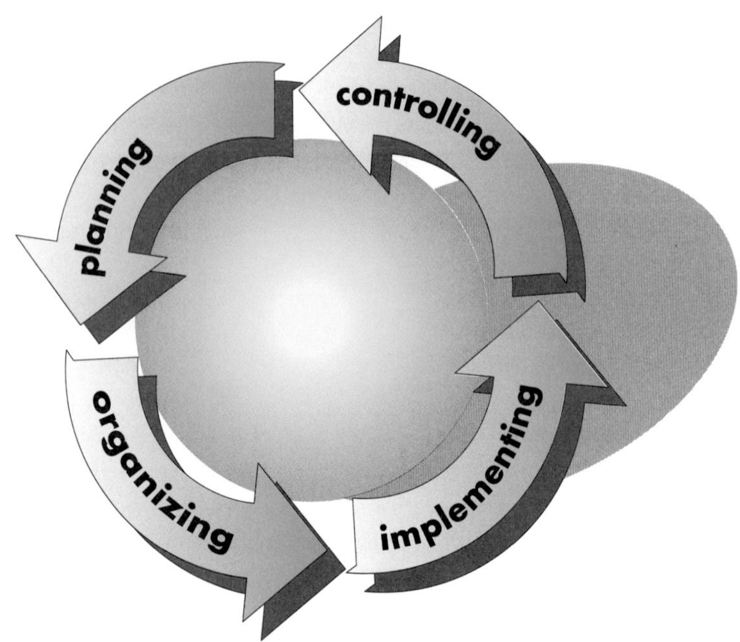

FIGURE 14-4

The four functions of management are directly related.

tomer 1,000 made-to-order blankets by a specific date. The standard is to produce 25 blankets each day for 40 consecutive days. During the first ten days, only 200 blankets are produced, or an average of 20 blankets a day. Because production is 50 blankets below the standard—250 blankets in ten days—the managers must take action to increase production during the remaining 30 days. The corrective action may include scheduling overtime work or assigning more workers to the task. Even as they take corrective action, the managers should carefully study the manufacturing process to see why the standard that was originally set could not be met.

As another example, the manager of a shoe store wants to make sure that new styles of shoes sell rapidly. The standard is that 30 percent of all shoes in a new style are sold within one month. If the store sells only 20 percent of a certain style in one month, the manager must take corrective action. The manager may choose to increase the advertising for the shoes, give salespeople a higher commission for selling that style, or mark down the price to sell more. The manager will also want to use this information when planning purchases in the future.

In each example, the managers had to set a standard based on the work to be accomplished. Then they compared performance against the standard to see if the company's goals could be met. Finally, if performance was not meeting the standard, the managers had to determine what to do to correct the problem.

Notice that in both examples the managers did not wait very long to begin measuring performance. Controlling activities should be completed before the problem is too big or too expensive to correct.

TYPES OF STANDARDS

Managers establish standards in the planning stage. They need to set high but achievable standards. Managers can determine reasonable standards by studying the job, past experience, industry information, and input from experienced workers. The standards become the means for judging success and for applying controls.

The standards used to control business operations depend on the type of business, the size of the business, and the activities being controlled. The major types of standards are quantity, quality, time, and cost standards.

QUANTITY STANDARDS Quantity standards take different forms, depending on the tasks. Production managers may specify the minimum number of units to be produced each hour, day, or month by individual workers or groups of workers. Sales managers may establish the number of prospective customers that sales representatives must contact daily or weekly. A manager of administrative services may establish a minimum number of forms that should be completed or the number of lines of information to be keyed in an hour by information processing personnel. The quotas Jasmine established for her employees in the telemarketing department described at the beginning of the chapter are examples of quantity standards.

QUALITY STANDARDS Quantity standards alone are often not enough to judge an employee, a product, or a service. A fast worker, for example, can be very careless, or a slow worker can be extremely careful. Thus, the quality of the work performed is often just as important as the quantity produced.

Perfection—having no errors—may be the only acceptable standard for some products and services. An automobile battery that does not work cannot be sold. An invoice with pricing errors cannot be sent to a customer. An accountant cannot calculate a client's taxes incorrectly. While perfection is the standard, it may not always be practical or cost effective to develop procedures to check every finished product. On an assembly line where thousands of products are produced every hour, sampling a few products each hour may be enough to identify when quality problems occur so corrective action can be taken.

TIME STANDARDS Time standards are closely related to quantity and quality standards. Most business activities can be measured by time. The amount of time it takes to complete an activity has an effect on costs, the quantity of work completed, and often on the quality of the work. Time standards are more important to some businesses than to others. Building contractors, bakeries, and newspaper publishers normally have very strict time schedules. If they do not meet the schedules, they suffer an immediate financial loss. If a building is not completed on time, the builder usually must pay a penalty fee. A baker

ILLUSTRATION 14-4

Most business activities can be measured by time. How are time standards closely related to quantity and quality standards?

who does not have doughnuts ready for the breakfast rush will lose a major portion of the day's sales. A day-old newspaper has almost no value to the reader. Other businesses may not see the immediate financial loss, but failure to maintain time standards will result in fewer products being produced, poor coordination of activities between departments, or other problems.

COST STANDARDS An important measure of the success or failure of a firm is financial profit or loss. Profit equals sales income (called "revenue") minus costs. Therefore, managers can increase profits by either (1) increasing sales revenue or (2) decreasing costs. Not all managers or employees are directly connected with work that increases sales. However, most employees and managers do influence costs. Wasting material or taking more time than necessary to perform a task adds to the cost of doing business. Increased costs, without a proportionate increase in sales dollars, decreases profit. Businesses must be cost conscious at all times.

Generally, businesses pay more attention to cost controls than to any other type of control. The control devices used, as a result, are numerous. One of the main purposes of the accounting department is to provide detailed cost information. This is why the head of an accounting department is often called a controller. Most managers, however, act as cost controllers in some way. Increasingly, employee work teams and individual employees are assigned responsibility for cost controls.

The most widely used controlling device is the budget. Budgets, like schedules and standards, are also planning devices. When a budget is prepared, it is a planning device; after that, it is a controlling device. Actual cost information is collected and compared with budgeted amounts. These comparisons permit judgments about the success of planning efforts and provide clues for making changes that will help the company reach its financial goals. Once again, managers should not wait too long to check on costs. They can take corrective action if they identify budget problems early. If they wait too long, the needed changes may cause serious problems in the business.

MEASURING AND COMPARING PERFORMANCE

Standards become the basis for determining effective performance. Managers gather information on all parts of business operations for which they are responsible. They compare that information against the standards to determine if performance is meeting the standards. A **variance** is a difference between current performance and the standard. A variance can be positive (performance exceeds standard) or negative (performance falls short of standard). Whenever a variance exists, managers must identify the reasons for the difference.

Actual performance exceeding the standard may seem to be an ideal situation that requires no corrective action. However, it is important to understand why the higher-than-expected performance occurred so that the performance can be repeated. Or, perhaps the positive performance in one area of the business is having a negative effect on another area. In addition, managers should review the process for developing standards to see why they set the standard lower than the possible performance.

The greatest concern occurs when performance is lower than the standard. That means that the company will probably not be able to perform at the expected level. It also says that there are problems between planning and implementing activities. Managers not only need to take corrective action as soon as possible to improve performance but must review procedures carefully to avoid the same problem in the future. Managers must be careful in the way they communicate the problem to employees and how they take corrective action. If employees believe the manager is blaming them for the poor performance, they may not be motivated to help solve the problem. On the other hand, if employees do not recognize the seriousness of the problem, they will continue the past level of performance, which will not result in improvement.

Monitoring all of the activities for which managers are responsible can take a great deal of time. Managers can use information systems to reduce the amount of time spent on controlling activities. Computers can monitor performance and compare it to the established standard. When the computer identifies a variance, it prepares a variance report for the manager. Through the use of computer monitoring and variance reports, managers can identify problems quickly.

TAKING CORRECTIVE ACTION

When managers discover that performance is not meeting standards, they can take three possible actions:

1. Take steps to improve performance.
2. Change policies and procedures.
3. Revise the standard.

If managers have planned carefully, they should be reluctant to change standards. In the blanket manufacturing business discussed earlier, managers should know from past experience whether produc-

ILLUSTRATION 14-5

Standards need to be revised when procedures are changed or new equipment is added. How can managers develop effective standards for procedures or equipment with which they are unfamiliar?

ing 25 blankets a day is reasonable. Only under unusual circumstances (major equipment breakdown, problems with suppliers, employee strikes, etc.) would the blanket managers reduce the standard. However, failure to meet the goal of 1,000 blankets by the specified date will not please the customer and may result in a loss of sales.

Most often, managers need to improve performance of activities when standards are not being met. This usually means making sure that the work is well organized, that supplies and materials are available when needed, that equipment is in good working order, and that employees are well trained and motivated.

Occasionally, standards are not met because activities cannot be accomplished as planned, or policies and procedures are not appropriate. This is likely to happen when a business begins a new procedure, starts to use new equipment, or has other major changes. In this situation, managers may need to change the policies or procedures that are not working in order to meet the standards. Process improvement discussed earlier usually results in policy or procedure changes.

Finally, when the managers have explored all possibilities to improve performance and it still does not meet the standards, they need to evaluate the standards themselves. Planning is usually not exact. Conditions can change from the time plans and standards are developed and the activities are performed. Managers cannot expect that all standards will be appropriate. Managers like to increase standards when they believe workers can achieve higher performance. It is difficult to make the decision to reduce standards, but that may be necessary from time to time. If a group of new employees is doing the task, performance standards may need to be reduced until the employees have had the necessary training and opportunity to perfect their skills.

When new planning procedures are used or new activities are implemented, planning is less likely to be accurate. Standards developed in those situations should be studied more carefully than the standards for ongoing activities or standards that have been developed in the same way for a long period of time.

Standards should be revised when it is clear they will not accurately reflect performance, and attempts to improve performance have not been successful. When standards are changed, the new standards and the reasons for the changes should be clearly communicated to the employees affected. Also, the procedures for setting standards should be revised to increase the likelihood that standards developed in the future will be more accurate.

CONTROLLING COSTS

All managers need to watch constantly for ways to reduce costs. Excessive costs reduce the company's profit. There are several areas in a business where managers can anticipate cost problems. They are inventory, credit, theft, and employee health and safety.

INVENTORY Manufacturers need to produce enough of each product to fill the orders they receive. They need enough raw materials to produce those products. Wholesalers and retailers must maintain inventories to meet their customers' needs. In all types of businesses, if inventories are too low, sales will be lost. If inventories are too high, costs of storage and handling will increase. There may be products in inventory that are never used or sold. In that situation, the company loses all of the money invested in those products.

Inventory control requires managers to walk a fine line. They must maintain sufficient inventory to meet their production and sales needs yet not so much that it is too costly to handle and store. They must select products to purchase that can be sold quickly at a profit. They must purchase products at the right time and in the correct quantities to minimize the company's inventory cost.

Many companies now use **just-in-time (JIT) inventory controls.** JIT is a method of inventory control in which the company maintains very small inventories and obtains materials just in time for use. To set up a JIT system, managers carefully study production time, sales activity, and purchasing requirements to determine the lowest possible inventory levels. They then place orders for materials so that they arrive just as they are needed for production or to fill sales orders. Production levels are set so the company has only enough products to fill orders as they are received. Effective inventory control methods can be very complicated.

CREDIT Most businesses must be able to extend credit to customers. Businesses also use credit when buying products from suppliers. If the company extends credit to customers who do not pay their bills, the company loses money. Also, businesses that use credit too often when making purchases spend a great deal of money for interest payments.

Businesses must develop credit policies to reduce the amount of losses. They must check customers' credit history carefully before giving them credit. They must develop billing and collection procedures that will collect most accounts on time. The age of an account is the number of days that payment is past due. Managers need to watch the

CAREER CONNECTION

ADMINISTRATIVE SERVICES MANAGER

Administrative services managers are employed throughout the American economy, and their range of duties is broad. They coordinate and direct support services, which may include: secretarial and reception; administration; payroll; conference planning and travel; information and data processing; facilities management; materials scheduling and distribution; records management; and telecommunications management.

In small organizations, a single administrative services manager may oversee all support services. In larger ones, however, first-line administrative services managers report to mid-level supervisors, who then report to top-level managers. First-line managers directly oversee a staff that performs various support services. Mid-level managers develop departmental plans, set goals and deadlines, develop procedures to improve productivity and customer service, and may hire or dismiss employees.

Educational requirements for these managers vary widely, depending on the size and complexity of the organization. In small businesses, experience may be the only requirement needed to enter a position as office manager. However, for managers of highly complex services, a bachelor's degree in business, human resources, or finance is often required. Ability to work under pressure and cope with deadlines is also important.

For more career information about administrative services managers, check your library or the Internet for resources.

age of accounts, because the longer an account goes unpaid, the greater the chance that the company will never collect the full payment.

Managers responsible for purchasing must control the amount of money the company owes to other businesses. It is easy to make too many purchases on credit. When this happens, the interest charges are very high, and the company may not have enough money to pay all of its debts on time. Companies should buy on credit when they will lose money if they don't make the purchase. Companies may also need credit to purchase expensive equipment or large orders of products and materials.

Managers must be sure bills are paid on time to protect the credit reputation of the business. If the supplier offers a discount for paying cash, managers should check to see if the company will benefit from taking advantage of the discount. Before using credit, managers should study the credit terms to see what the final cost will be. Credit can be a good business tool if used carefully but can harm the business if not controlled.

THEFT Businesses can lose a great deal of money if products are stolen. Thefts can occur in many parts of a business and can be done by employees as well as by customers and others. By establishing theft controls, businesses usually are able to reduce losses. Businesses can lose cash, merchandise, supplies, and other resources due to theft.

The theft of merchandise from warehouses and stores is a major business concern. Retail stores are the hardest hit by such losses. Retailers lose billions of dollars annually due to crime, much of which is from theft of merchandise. Shoplifting by customers and employees equals 6 percent or more of total sales each year for the typical retailer. Much of the loss occurs during the end-of-year holiday shopping season when stores are crowded and part-time workers are employed. Basic procedures followed by many retail businesses to reduce shoplifting are shown in Figure 14-5.

Many stores, warehouses, and trucks are burglarized during the night or when merchandise is being transported. Security guards or special equipment are frequently used to reduce the chances of such thefts. Many companies carry insurance against losses, but with high loss rates the cost of insurance is very expensive.

HEALTH AND SAFETY Even when employees are absent from work because of sickness or injury, the company must continue to operate. Other employees must be available to fill in for the absent employee or the work will go undone. Usually, the salary of both the absent employee and the substitute employee must be paid. A major share of health insurance costs are often paid by the company as well. Studies estimate that the annual costs to many businesses for employee absence and health costs now exceed 20 percent of the salary paid to each employee. An employee paid at the rate of $7.00 per hour requires an additional $1.40 each hour to pay those costs. A person earning $35,000 will add $7,000 or more to the costs of the business just for health expenses and employee absences.

Costs that result from health and safety problems can be reduced. Companies should provide safety training for all employees. Work areas and equipment should be inspected regularly to be sure they operate correctly and safely. Employees can be provided information on ways to improve health and wellness. Investments in fitness centers and exercise programs may result in lower costs for the business.

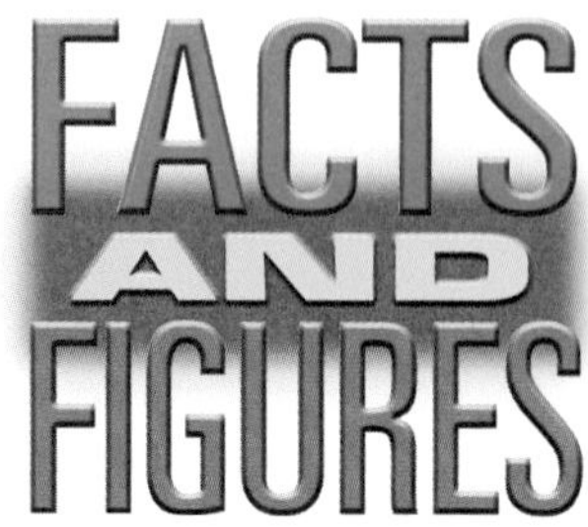

Employee theft costs employers over $1 billion a week and is the cause of one-third of the bankruptcies in the United States. It is estimated that three out of every ten employees engage in theft, and that 95 percent of businesses experience varying degrees of ongoing employee theft.

Common Methods for Controlling Shoplifting

1. Hire security guards (in uniform).
2. Hire store dectectives (not in uniform).
3. Install television cameras that scan entrances, exits, and checkout counters.
4. Place mirrors at key locations, which give views of various parts of the store.
5. Attach special inventory tags to products, which give a signal when products are taken from the store. (When an article is sold, the salesperson will remove the tag.)
6. Position station attendants at dressing rooms.
7. Keep unused checkout aisles closed.
8. Keep small, expensive items in locked display cases.
9. Post signs warning customers of the consequences of shoplifting.
10. Train employees on procedures to follow when they identify a shoplifter.

FIGURE 14-5

Businesses must protect themselves against loss from theft.

CHAPTER 14 REVIEW

CHAPTER CONCEPTS

- The implementing function for managers involves communicating effectively, motivating employees to do their best work, developing work teams, and managing operations in their area of responsibility.
- People choose to do things that will satisfy their needs and avoid doing things that don't. Managers can influence performance by providing rewards that satisfy employees' needs when they accomplish work goals. The theories of motivation developed by Maslow, McClelland, and Herzberg describe factors that influence employee behavior. To influence employees to higher performance, managers should apply rewards and punishments to these motivating factors.
- Change is a part of most organizations today and managers need to help employees accept change. The steps in an effective change process are planning, communicating, involving, educating, and supporting.
- The fourth management function, controlling, ensures that company operations meet expectations. Controlling involves three basic steps: (1) establishing standards for each company goal, (2) measuring and comparing performance against the established standards, and (3) taking corrective action when performance falls short of standards. Common types of standards are quantity, quality, time, and cost standards.
- To help the company make a profit, managers must control costs. Areas commonly monitored for cost control are inventory, credit, theft, and employee health and safety.

BUILD VOCABULARY POWER

Define the following terms and concepts.

1. motivation
2. work team
3. process improvement
4. achievement need
5. affiliation need
6. power need
7. hygiene factors
8. motivators
9. variance
10. just-in-time (JIT) inventory controls

REVIEW FACTS

1. Why do managers who have planned effectively sometimes still have problems?
2. What are the major implementing activities managers can use to channel employee efforts in the right direction to achieve the goals?
3. What are several ways that managers use communications as part of implementing work in a business?
4. What is the difference between internal and external motivation?

5. Why do managers need to develop effective work teams?
6. What are some examples of operations activities that are common to most managers in a business?
7. Why do managers attempt to understand motivation?
8. According to Abraham Maslow, how do people seek to satisfy their needs?
9. What are the three categories of needs identified by McClelland?
10. According to Herzberg, what types of factors are likely to cause employee dissatisfaction?
11. What are the steps in an effective change process?
12. What are the three basic steps that are part of the controlling function?
13. What are the major types of standards used in business?
14. What actions can managers take if performance does not meet standards?
15. What areas of business operations should managers monitor to control costs?

DISCUSS IDEAS

1. Can managers be effective with implementing if they do not have good working relationships with the employees they supervise?
2. Which do you believe is most effective in increasing employee effectiveness in the long run—internal motivation or external motivation?
3. Why are businesses paying much more attention to developing effective work teams today than in the past?
4. What differences in implementation activities, if any, would there be for a manager of a small business and a manager in a large business?
5. In your view, which of the three theories presented in the chapter best describes the way you believe employees are motivated?
6. What should a manager do if it is clear that many employees will view a planned change negatively?
7. Provide an example of a management activity that clearly demonstrates the three steps of the controlling process.
8. What can happen if managers delay controlling activities for a long time after implementing plans?
9. What are some examples of business activities where perfection is the only acceptable standard for performance?
10. Should managers delegate controlling activities to employees and employee teams? Why or why not?

ANALYZE INFORMATION

1. Many companies today are concerned about employee attitudes about their work environment. One company sends an e-mail

survey to every employee twice a year. The survey asks each employee to rate the effectiveness of his/her work group on seven characteristics. Each characteristic is rated on a five-point scale from 5 (very effective) to 1 (very ineffective). The average ratings of all employees are shown below for the e-mail responses received from the January 30 and June 30 surveys.

Characteristic	***Jan. 30 Rating***	***June 30 Rating***
Members support team purpose	3.5	3.8
Activities are clear	2.0	2.2
Members understand responsibilities	2.8	2.8
Members have needed skills	4.8	4.6
Members are committed to the group	3.5	4.0
Members communicate effectively	4.1	4.8
Team works to solve problems	4.0	3.6

a. Calculate the amount of change (increase or decrease) for each item during the six-month period and the average rating for each item when the two ratings are combined.

b. Prepare a rank-order listing of the characteristics based on the combined averages.

c. Calculate an average of the ratings for all characteristics for each of the ratings periods to determine an overall effectiveness rating for each period.

2. Form a team with three or four other students in your class to analyze motivation theories. As a team, develop a list of at least 15 things you believe motivate employees to perform well. After completing the list, prepare diagrams using a computer graphics program or on separate sheets of paper that illustrate each of the three motivation theories discussed in the chapter. Then add your team's motivating items in the appropriate locations on each of the three illustrations. Present your diagrams to the other teams and provide reasons for your decisions about the motivating items and the theories.

3. The following chart shows several items from a budget of a business. Column 1 shows the categories for which a budget amount has been determined. The budgeted amounts are shown in Column 2 and the actual amounts are shown in Column 3. Complete the chart by calculating the variance between the budgeted and actual amounts (Column 4) and the percentage increase or decrease (Column 5).

Budget Category	***Budget***	***Actual***	***Variance***	***% + or −***
Sales	$680,000	$720,000		
Merchandise Returns	11,000	12,500		
Cost of Goods	229,400	240,000		

(continued)

Budget Category	*Budget*	*Actual*	*Variance*	*% + or −*
Operating Expenses	52,000	46,500		
Administrative Costs	34,000	31,500		
Marketing Expenses	306,000	350,500		
Net Profit	47,600	39,000		

4. Write a sample quantity standard, quality standard, and time standard for each of the following situations:
 a. A computer manufacturer assembling laptop computers.
 b. A salesperson calling on customers in a new territory.
 c. An Internet service provider providing modem connections to the Internet for customers dialing from their homes.
 d. A data processor at a bank processing deposits and withdrawals for customers' accounts.
 e. An airline selling tickets for flights to ensure that the available seats for flights are filled with passengers.

5. Choose one of the following statements that best represents your beliefs. Develop a one-page paper, using a word processing program if possible, defending the statement and suggesting why the other statement is not correct in your opinion.
 a. The best way to develop management skills is to work for a company for several years and observe successful managers doing their work. You can't learn management from a book.
 b. Management in the 21st century is very different from management in the past. The best managers take classes to study management activities and motivation theories rather than relying on experience.

SOLVE BUSINESS PROBLEMS

CASE 14-1

Kane's Buy-Rite Used Cars had experienced its third straight year of declining profits. While a few more cars were sold each year, the profit per sale was down. Kane Shouk, the owner, had traditionally relied on a loyal group of customers who returned to buy a second and even third car, demonstrating their satisfaction with the company. Fewer customers were returning, however, and the company had to increase its promotional budget to attract new customers.

Kane believed two factors were contributing to the declining business. First, many new car dealers were now leasing many of their cars rather than selling them. This meant customers needed very low or no down payments and lower monthly payments. New car payments were now comparable to used car payments. Second, Kane's salespeople were getting more aggressive in order to sell cars. Because profits were down, more cars needed to be sold. Some customers were complaining they felt pressured by salespeople.

Kane decided the procedures used to sell automobiles had to change. He knew that several of the new autodealers had gone to a one-price, no-negotiation strategy where a low but fair price was put on each car. The car would be sold at that price so there would be no pressure from the salesperson regarding the price to be paid. Kane hoped the salespeople would help the customer select the best car rather than worrying about negotiating the best price.

Kane expected two problems in convincing the salespeople that the new sales strategy would be effective. First, it would require a different type of selling relationship with the customer, and some salespeople might have a hard time adjusting. Second, the salesperson would be paid a salary rather than a commission. Several of the top salespeople would not be able to make as much money as they could when sales were good, but all salespeople would make a decent salary.

Think Critically:

1. How should Kane work with the salespeople to introduce the change?
2. How can Kane motivate the salespeople now that commissions will not be paid on sales?
3. What controlling activities could Kane undertake to be able to specifically determine why profits have been declining?

CASE 14-2

The TieDown Company is planning a major change in the way it produces its belts and fasteners. In the past, most production has been handled by skilled machine operators who completed a three-year apprenticeship program before operating the manufacturing equipment. A new computerized manufacturing process will allow the production activities to be completed by people with fewer skills who require only a very short training period. That means that the company will reduce the number of machine operators by 20 percent and will cut the pay rate for machine operators by $3 per hour. However, the company will need a number of computer programmers and computer technicians for the new equipment. Those jobs will pay $5 per hour more than the average skilled machine operator is currently making. TieDown will encourage the current operators to switch jobs and will provide the needed training for the new high-paying computer jobs. It is expected that half of the current machine operators will be able to switch jobs if they choose to do so. The rest can be employed in the lower paying production jobs but will have to take the lower pay rate for the job. To make the change easier for those operators, TieDown will provide a one-time payment of $600 to help them with the adjustment to the new pay rate.

Think Critically:

1. What is your opinion of TieDown's plans for the change to the new production equipment?
2. What would you recommend that the company do, if anything, for the machine operators that are not hired for the computer positions and choose not to accept the pay reduction for the new production jobs?
3. Assume you are the manager of production for the TieDown Company and outline the procedure you would follow to implement the change described so that most employees will support the change.

PROJECT: MY BUSINESS, INC.

If you hire employees to work for you, they must be motivated to work well. Managers must develop a theory of motivation and translate that into effective policies and procedures. The final step in business management is to determine if decisions are working well or if changes must be made. To do this, you must establish standards, collect and study information, and take corrective action if needed.

DATA COLLECTION

1. Survey 10 people who are employed full- or part-time. Ask them to list the factors related to their work that motivate them to perform well and the factors that dissatisfy them. Using those factors, classify each person based on the three motivation theories discussed in this chapter that best describe their motivation.
2. Review sources of business information to identify where you can obtain information for your business on the following important areas of cost control for a small business: inventory, cash and credit management, theft, and personnel health and safety. Make a list of the resources you locate, along with a brief description of the information available from each resource.

ANALYSIS

1. Assume that you have several employees working for your business. Identify the factors you would use to motivate the employees to maintain effective performance. Estimate the cost of each of the motivation methods.
2. Develop a standard to evaluate each of the following activities in your business: (a) daily sales of each product, (b) amount of product spoilage and loss, and (c) customer satisfaction. Then describe the data collection and analysis procedure you would follow to determine if the standard is being met.

UNIT FIVE

FINANCIAL MANAGEMENT

CHAPTERS

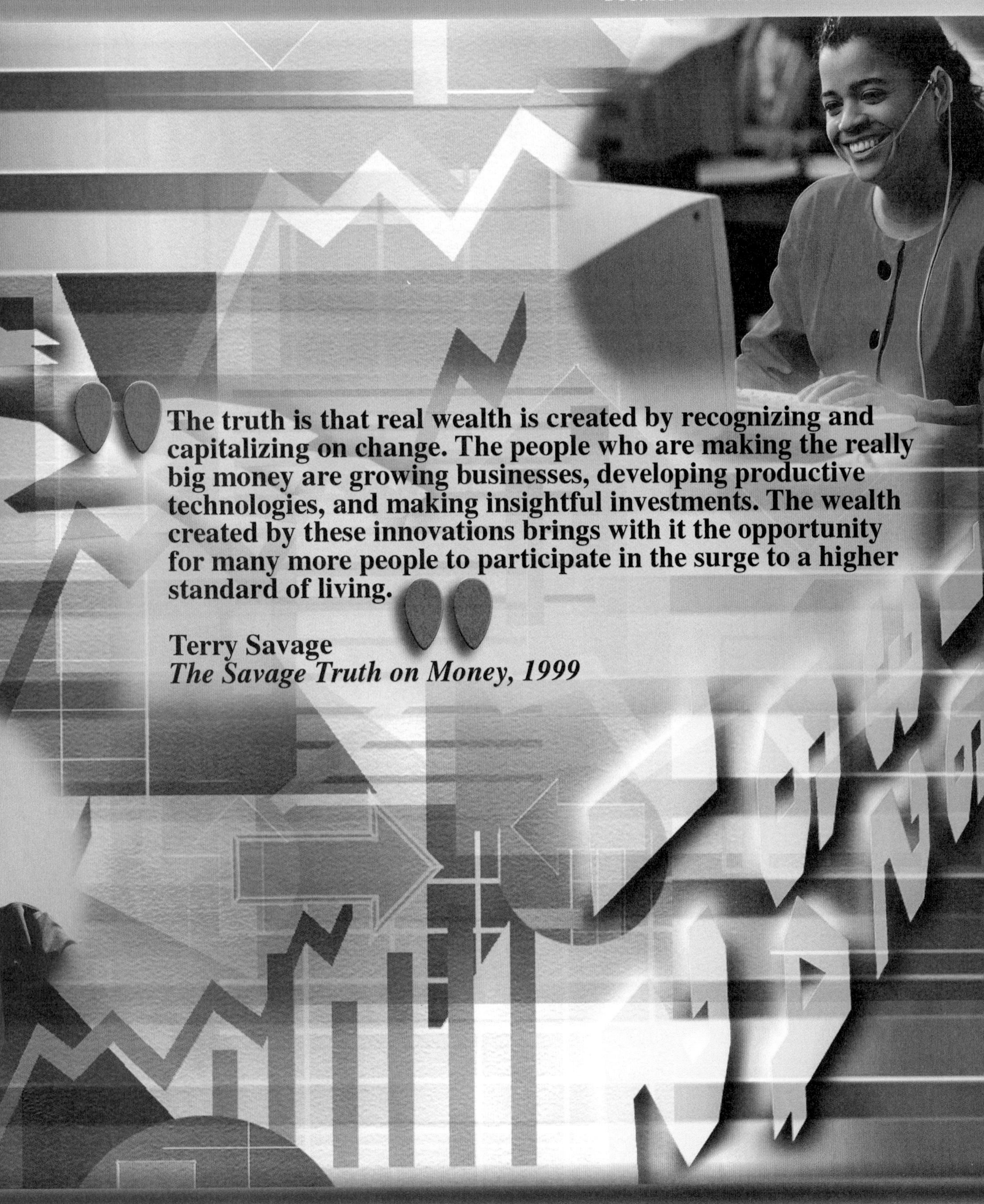
"The truth is that real wealth is created by recognizing and capitalizing on change. The people who are making the really big money are growing businesses, developing productive technologies, and making insightful investments. The wealth created by these innovations brings with it the opportunity for many more people to participate in the surge to a higher standard of living."
Terry Savage
The Savage Truth on Money, 1999

FINANCIAL RECORDS IN A BUSINESS

OBJECTIVES

- **15-1** Discuss record keeping systems needed in large and small businesses.
- **15-2** Identify and discuss types of records used in business.
- **15-3** Define depreciation, obsolescence, and other accounting terms.
- **15-4** Give two reasons why assets should be safeguarded against damage or loss.
- **15-5** Describe different types of business budgets.
- **15-6** Explain how businesses use budgets to help them run efficiently.

RECORD KEEPING—TIME CONSUMING BUT IMPORTANT

Clark walked the two blocks from his car rental business to the bank. He always liked taking his deposits to the bank, although he knew that he should be doing the paperwork instead of depending on the tellers to handle it.

Clark's business had done well this past week, and he felt a bit uneasy carrying today's large amount. While most of the deposit wasn't cash, he realized that he needed a better way to keep track of receipts and payments. As he walked into the bank, he recalled that his accountant had told him last month to keep better records.

Clark greeted the teller. "Good morning, Monica. I've got a stack for you today!"

Monica greeted Clark, but she looked unhappy. "Clark, that stack will take me forever to complete. Haven't you gotten someone to help you with your books?"

"Not really," Clark replied, "but I'm thinking about it."

Monica smiled. "You've been thinking about it for over a year. How do you know if you're really making any money? Last month you overdrew your account. And now you're overdrawn again. My boss wants to see you right away."

Clark knew he had to keep better records, but thought nothing could cloud his image of today's big deposit. Clearly, the most tangible reward that any business owner gets is profit.

All businesses—large and small—must keep records. Firms keep records mainly to determine whether they have made a profit or a loss. If a business is not making a profit, it may cease to exist. **Accounting records** are organized summaries of a business's financial activities. Common reasons for keeping records are to:

1. Identify the source of receipts.
2. Identify expenses paid or owed to others.
3. Determine the kinds and values of assets.
4. Prepare financial statements.
5. Prepare and support tax returns and other government reports.
6. Check on the progress of the business.
7. Plan the future direction of the business.

ILLUSTRATION 15-1

Businesses must keep accurate records. Why do you also need to keep records for your personal needs?

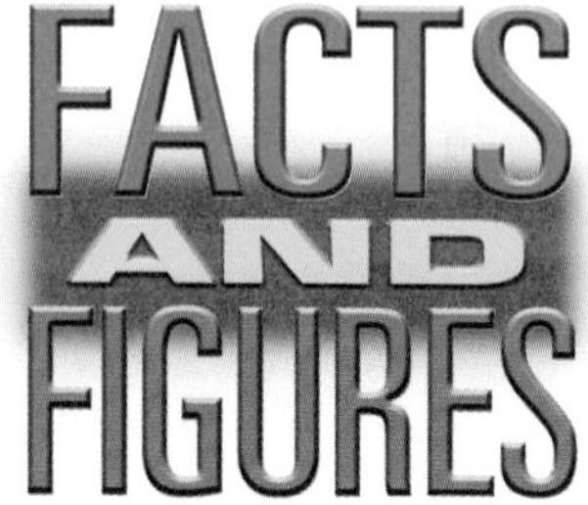

The earliest civilizations in Babylonia, Egypt, Peru, Greece, China, and Rome used record keeping much as we do today. Governments kept accurate records of receipts and payments, especially of tax collections. Wealthy people also demanded good record keeping in order to prove that those who took care of their property did the work properly.

The smallest business can determine how profitable it is by using a business checking account to record income deposited and by writing checks for all payments. The total receipts (deposits) less the total of all checks written tells the entrepreneur how well the business is doing. Most businesses, however, need far more records than a checkbook to satisfy their information needs. All companies must determine what records to keep, how to keep them, and who should prepare them. Once a records system has been developed, managers can then use the information to prepare budgets.

Businesses handle financial records in various ways. The business owner can keep the records personally, employ a full-time or part-time accountant, establish an accounting department, or use an accounting service organization. The record keeping system a business adopts determines, in part, the way it will handle its records.

RECORD SYSTEMS

Systems for keeping accounting records may be simple or complex, and they may require no equipment or be highly computerized. Regardless of the type of record system a company selects, the system must be easy to use and must be designed to provide timely and accurate information. Because the type of business determines in part the type of record system used, the systems for small and large businesses need to be examined.

SYSTEMS IN SMALL BUSINESSES

Manual record systems have existed for thousands of years. They are still popular today with very small firms that require limited records. Small firms can buy standardized forms at office supply stores, such as Staples and Office Max. Trade associations and franchisers usually supply their branch stores with standard forms.

ILLUSTRATION 15-2

Why might a small firm buy financial software programs, such as QuickBooks?

Many small firms rely primarily on their cash register to gather most of the information needed for their financial records. Figure 15-1 shows an example of a financial record that a small firm might keep. Cash register tapes show transaction details. This information can be transferred daily onto a standard form.

Many small and medium-sized firms buy software programs designed for small businesses. For example, QuickBooks® software from Intuit, Inc., can be tailored to the firm's needs. Options include deposits, checkbook payments, purchase orders, invoices, and payroll.

SYSTEMS IN LARGE BUSINESSES

Today most large firms and many small ones use accounting software programs to record, process, and store information. A desktop computer

DAILY BALANCE FORM

Store Name....04..... Prepared by..Hal Vogel.... Date Mar. 8, 20--

	RESET TOTALS OF REG. (SALES)	RESET TOTALS OF REG. (RETURNS AND VOIDS)	NET REGISTER TOTALS
DEPT. 1 Meat	7,020. 00	108. 00	6,912 00
DEPT. 2 Produce	2,106. 00	54. 00	2,052 00
DEPT. 3 Deli	1,404. 00	-0-	1,409 00
DEPT. 4 Grocery	21,060. 00	81. 00	20,979 00
DEPT. 5 Frozen food	2,808. 00	27. 00	2,781 00
DEPT. 6 Household	702. 00	13. 50	688 50
DEPT. 7			
TAX			
TOTAL			
CASH	35,100. 00	283. 50	34,816. 50
CHARGE	675. 00	-0-	675 00
TOTAL	35,775 00	283. 50	35,775 00
ACCT. NO.	CH0079		
REC'D ON ACCT.			
CASH			
TOTAL			
CASH RETURNS	(X Reed Cash Total) →		OTHER INCOME
ACCT. NO.			TOTAL
LAYAWAY PAYMENTS REFUND	(X Reed R. A/C) →		
TOTAL			
PAID OUTS		RETURNS AND VOIDS / MDSE. AND EXP.	( )
CASH TO BE ACCOUNTED FOR			34,816. 50
ACTUAL CASH			34,816. 50
CASH OVER OR SHORT			-0-

PAID OUTS TO DR. & CR	$ KEPT ON RET.	P.O. AMOUNT	D.R. CODE	ACCOUNTS RECEIVABLE CONTROL	
#1				BEGINNING ACCTS. RECEIVABLE	
#2				NET CHARGES TODAY	675. 00
#3				TOTAL	675. 00
#4				LESS: NET REC'D ON ACCT. TODAY	
#5					
#6				ENDING ACCTS. RECEIVABLE	675. 00
#7				• DATA PROCESSING NO.	
#8				• TODAY'S DATE	
#9				• CASH SHORT DR. ___ CR. ___	-0-
CREDIT CODE	CR MISC. INC.			• CASH OVER DR. ___ CR. ___	-0-
AUDITOR'S CREDIT •				•	
MARK DOWNS OR UNITS					
PURCHASES AT RETAIL OR SALES AT COST					
Register Totals					

FIGURE 15-1

The cash register (point of sale terminal) often provides the information shown on this daily balance form.

CYBER COMMUNICATION

Although one of the attractions of e-mail is the fact that we can easily and quickly communicate with people around the globe, we sometimes forget that messages can take anywhere from several minutes to several hours to be delivered. Sometimes e-mail servers can malfunction, leaving users without service until the problem is corrected.

Once you do receive and read a message, you have several options: you can delete it, save it, print it, forward it to other people, or reply to the original sender. When responding to a message, include enough information in your reply so your reader knows what it's about. Business people who receive many e-mails during the day may easily forget the specific topics of earlier messages.

E-mails can also be forwarded to other users. However, before doing so, be sure that the recipients actually have an interest in or a need to see the message.

ACTIVITY You have received an e-mail message that was sent to a group of recipients—not just to you. How would you decide whether your reply should go to just the original sender or to the entire group? What problems could result if your reply is sent to the entire group?

is adequate for most small companies, but larger firms need more complex equipment. Large corporations employ many bookkeepers and accountants. Some prefer to hire outside firms to perform some of their required record keeping.

Outsourcing is hiring an outside firm to perform specialized tasks for a business. A business outsources because the outsourcing firm has expertise that the business needs. Buying these expert services when needed may be less expensive than hiring someone into the business who has the expertise. One type of outsourcing firm is a **data processing center**, which is a business that uses computers to analyze and organize data for other businesses for a fee. A business delivers data to the data processing center periodically. The data processing center processes the data and prepares reports that the business needs. Many firms use a data processing center to outsource selected tasks, such as preparing bills for customers, keeping track of inventory, and preparing payroll records and checks. Banks and data processing firms like Automatic Data Processing and Electronic Data Processing, Inc., are popular for outsourcing. Data can be transmitted over the Internet and reports returned overnight, even when the data processing firms are located in foreign countries.

Large companies require advanced systems for keeping records. Accounting departments usually maintain these records, although the initial recording of transactions occurs throughout the organization. An accounting department is commonly divided into several sections. Each section is typically responsible for handling one or more phases of accounting, such as cash records, receipt and payment records, depreciation records, and tax and payroll records.

Most large stores with many branches use sophisticated cash registers connected to computers. Such a register is called a **point-of-sale terminal.** When cashiers use bar code scanners to record sales, for example, each item sold is subtracted from the inventory recorded in the computer. The computer calculates when the store needs to reorder merchandise (based on predetermined inventory needs) and provides other valuable information for management. With point-of-sale terminals, scanners electronically read product codes stamped on merchandise, thereby speeding the checkout service for customers and reducing manual paperwork and labor costs for the store.

TYPES OF RECORDS

Accounting records in all types of businesses have similar characteristics. The kinds of records that a business uses depend on the type and size of the business. A few of the most common records kept by all businesses are discussed next.

ACCOUNTING FOR CASH

Cash is constantly coming into a business from customers and other sources, and cash must go out of the business to pay for things purchased. Regardless of whether a business employs a bookkeeper or the owner keeps the records, businesses follow similar procedures in accounting for cash. Figure 15-2 lists several suggestions for the safe handling of cash.

In accounting for cash, a special problem arises when a business wants to make small payments quickly. For example, a store may need a small box of paper clips that can be purchased at a nearby store or to pay a delivery service to mail a package to a customer. Businesses usually make small payments in two ways. When the business uses a cash register and has no special petty cash fund, the usual practice is to take cash from the register and replace it with a petty cash voucher, such as the one shown in Figure 15-3, in the cash register drawer. When the business puts aside money (often in a special box or drawer)

ILLUSTRATION 15-3

A business should not wait until it has collected large sums before making a bank deposit. Why should money be deposited periodically at a banking institution?

FIGURE 15-2

Suggestions for the Safe Handling of Cash

1. A petty cash fund, adequate for small emergency payments, should be kept in a safe place with someone responsible for it. A written record of all money put into the fund and all money paid out must be kept. Receipts for payments should be obtained where possible, and the fund should be replenished by check to provide a further record.
2. If a cash register is used, small emergency payments can be made out of cash register funds instead of through a petty cash fund, but adequate records of payments must be made and receipts obtained.
3. If a cash register is used, there should be a daily change fund of a fixed amount, which is never deposited in the bank but is kept available to start each day's operations. This fund should be counted and verified daily.
4. All receipts should be deposited in a bank account.
5. Make payments by check for all items except small emergency payments.
6. Verify by a double check any cash overages or cash shortages in the daily transactions.
7. Do not keep any more cash in the office than is necessary and, if convenient, make more than one deposit in the bank daily.
8. Pay salaries by check instead of by cash.
9. Audit regularly the amounts received on account.
10. Audit regularly the receipts by comparing them with the bank deposits you have made.
11. Audit regularly the actual cash paid out by comparing the check stubs with bills paid.
12. Endorse all checks for deposit with a company rubber stamp or, when signing checks for endorsement, write "For deposit only."
13. Reconcile the monthly bank statement promptly and regularly as explained in Chapter 18.

FIGURE 15-3

A Petty Cash Voucher

PETTY CASH VOUCHER

NO. 6 DATE February 9, 20--

PAID TO United Parcel Service

FOR Goods Delivered AMOUNT 28 | 50

CHARGE TO Miscellaneous Expenses

PAYMENT RECEIVED: Helen Jones

REED AND MALLOCH

APPROVED BY George Ajax

for a petty cash fund, it keeps a petty cash record that shows the amount of cash used and the reason for the payment.

It is very important to watch a bank account carefully in accounting for cash. A bank normally provides a monthly statement that should be compared with the checkbook. If the checkbook balance does not agree with the bank's monthly statement balance, the reasons for the difference must be determined. You will learn about the reason for bringing the checkbook balance and bank statement balance into agreement in Chapter 18.

Harold Biddle Company
1672 E. [illegible] Street
Princeton, NJ 08540-1321

Sales Receipt

Date	Sale No.
2/17/2000	7382

Sold To
Barbara Linkerheimer Associate Main Street Princeton, NJ 08540-1245

Payment Method	Sold By	Mdse. Rcvd.
On Account	HJR	

Item	Description	Qty	Price	Amount
75-A	Chairs	4	450.00	1,800.00T
120-B	Table	1	2,500.00	2,500.00T

KEEP THIS SLIP FOR REFERENCE

Subtotal	$4,300.00
Sales Tax (6.0%)	$258.00
Total	$4,558.00

Source: *QuickBooks® by Intuit*

FIGURE 15-4

The information found in the accounts receivable record is obtained from sales slips like this one.

RECEIPT AND PAYMENT RECORDS

All businesses must deal with money that they receive as a result of the sale of goods or services to customers. Because many businesses sell on credit, they keep records showing what each customer owes and pays. This record is called an **accounts receivable record.** When a sale is made, the salesperson completes a sales slip, such as the one shown in Figure 15-4. The information on this form is transferred to the accounts receivable record. Money owed to the business and money received from customers are recorded on these records.

Businesses must also keep records showing money they owe and payments they make to purchase supplies and merchandise on credit. This kind of record is an **accounts payable record**.

DEPRECIATION RECORDS

An **asset** is anything of value owned. Businesses use assets, such as tools and computers, in their normal operations. The value of an asset decreases through use over time. This gradual loss of an asset's value due to age and wear is called **depreciation.** For example, a Jiffy Lube franchise owner buys a piece of equipment that costs $1,600.

The owner knows from experience that at the end of five years the equipment will not be worth any more than its value as junk, about \$100. The owner estimates, therefore, that the equipment will wear out or depreciate at the average rate of \$300 a year:

$$\$1{,}600 - \$100 = \$1{,}500 \text{ value lost}$$
$$\$1{,}500/5 \text{ years} = \$300 \text{ depreciation per year}$$

When this asset loses its usefulness, it must be replaced. Therefore, depreciation represents a cost to the business.

Fixed assets, or **plant assets,** are material assets that will last a long time—land, equipment, and buildings, for example. Except for land, fixed assets depreciate over time. A business records the value of fixed assets on its books when it purchases them. They become part of the property the business owns. As the assets wear out or become less valuable, the business is allowed by law to charge the loss in value each year as an operating expense.

Property may also decrease in value because of **obsolescence.** That is, the asset may become out of date or inadequate for a particular purpose. An older computer, for example, may not have the capacity to run new programs that the business needs. Even though the computer still functions, it is obsolete and no longer as valuable to the business. Therefore, obsolescence is a form of depreciation.

The loss due to depreciation is very real, although it usually cannot be computed with great accuracy. The depreciation of assets is part of the cost of doing business. Businesses need to consider depreciation in their planning, so they have money available to replace assets when they wear out.

SPECIAL ASSET RECORDS

Financial statements provide information on such items as insurance, fixed assets, and real property, but they do not provide detailed information about these assets. As a result, a business must keep special records. For example, a business should maintain a precise record of insurance policies, showing such details as type of policy, the company from which it was purchased, amount, premium, the purchase and expiration dates, and the amount to be charged each month as insurance expense. A business maintains detailed special records for all fixed assets, such as vans and forklifts. These records provide such information as asset description, date of purchase, cost, monthly depreciation expense, and asset book value. **Asset book value** is the original cost less accumulated depreciation. In the Jiffy Lube example above, the equipment depreciates at a rate of \$300 per year. At the end of the second year, the \$1,600 equipment will have an asset book value of \$1,000:

$$\$300 \text{ depreciation} \times 2 \text{ years} = \$600 \text{ accumulated depreciation}$$
$$\$1{,}600 - \$600 = \$1{,}000 \text{ asset book value at the end of year 2}$$

TAX RECORDS

The federal income tax law requires every business to keep satisfactory records, so that the business can report its income and expenses. Preparation of an income tax return for a small business is relatively simple. However, both small and large firms use the services of tax accountants. Tax reporting computer software is also readily available from computer supply stores.

The law requires employers to withhold a certain percentage of each employee's wages for federal income tax purposes. Each employee must fill out a W-4 form that provides information on family status. Using this information and a table furnished by the Internal Revenue Service, the employer can determine the amount to withhold from the employee's paycheck. Periodically, the employer must pay these withholdings to the Internal Revenue Service.

Most employers have to pay social security taxes for old-age benefits and pay for government-sponsored unemployment compensation insurance. The employer must also withhold taxes from each employee's wages for social security purposes. The business also must pay the federal government its own taxes and those withheld from employees.

PAYROLL RECORDS

To keep satisfactory payroll records for business information and tax purposes, businesses must keep complete records for each employee, showing the hours worked, regular wages, overtime wages, and all types of deductions from wages. From these records an employer makes regular reports. Payroll information generated using QuickBooks® software is shown in Figure 15-5.

Here are just some of the employment tax records that businesses are advised to keep: amounts and dates of all wages paid and tips reported; the fair market value of non-cash wages; the names, addresses, social security numbers, and job titles of all employees and the dates of their employment; the rate of pay of each employee; copies of Form W-4, showing each employee's withholding allowances; and canceled checks or check stubs for all wages and deposits paid.

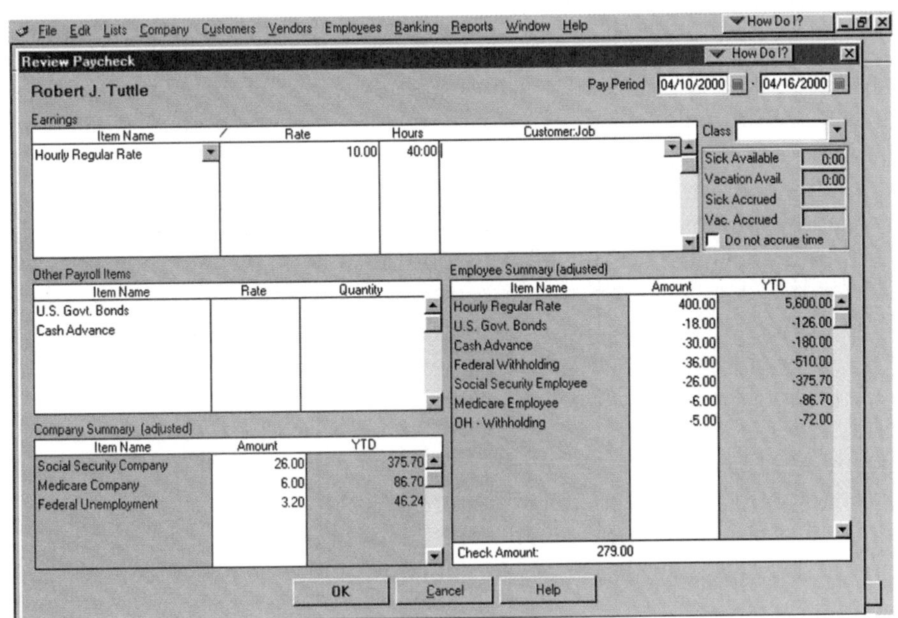

Source: *QuickBooks® by Intuit*

FIGURE 15-5

A Simplified Payroll Record

USING AND KEEPING RECORDS

Business records should be accurate and always up to date. A convenient filing system that permits quick storage and retrieval of financial records is essential, whether on paper or in computers. Office supply firms and filing equipment companies usually recommend appropriate filing systems for various kinds of businesses.

The financial records, including the accounts of customers and all other vital information, should be protected from such hazards as fire and theft. Every office, therefore, should have a fireproof safe or vault for such records. Fireproof filing cabinets are also needed for storing important and frequently used documents, but deeds, leases, contracts, and critical documents may be better placed in bank safe deposit boxes if there is no adequate protection in the office. As you learned in Chapter 8, companies protect their computer records by using such precautions as firewalls and passwords to keep out intruders. Companies may also store electronic records in an off-site computer or storage area. Service companies rent storage space on their computers or in their climate-controlled warehouses for safe record archiving.

BUDGET SYSTEMS

Budgeting is critical to financial success. A study conducted by the U.S. Department of Commerce reveals that stores that budget their financial operations are more successful than stores that do not. The stores that are most successful are those that (1) keep recommended accounting records, (2) have their accounts audited or checked by an experienced accountant, (3) take an inventory of merchandise more than once a year, and (4) operate under a financial budget. A new company's business plan should include a budget for the first year or two of operations. Unfortunately, a recent study of small businesses reveals that most do not have an annual budget in writing. Worse still, 60 percent of these small firms have no plans at all on paper, which is one reason why so many small businesses fail.

A **budget** is a financial plan extending usually for one year. It shows the business's estimated revenue and expenses over the time period. Based on these estimates, businesses can set financial goals. By comparing actual results with these goals throughout the year, managers can control operations and keep expenses in line with income. A realistic budget can prevent overbuying and plan for needed borrowing.

Actual budgeting procedures depend on the type of business. For a small business, the process is mostly one of budgeting sales, expenses, purchases, and cash. Figure 15-6 outlines the budgeting procedure for a large business.

1. The estimate of sales is based on past experience and future expectations. As will be explained later, there is more than one method of making this estimate.
2. The advertising budget is based on expected sales and on the amount that the company should spend to promote new products and open new territories.
3. The production plans should be based on the expected sales of the individual products. It is, therefore, necessary to take into consideration the production capacity of the business and the equipment needed.
4. The purchasing requirements are based on expected sales and production. Purchases must be made far enough in advance to allow time for delivery and production. It is, therefore, necessary to be familiar with the times of the year when sales are the greatest.
5. In a large manufacturing business, it is necessary to anticipate labor requirements. The labor budget must, therefore, be based on production requirements.
6. The budget of administrative costs, office costs, and costs of supplies must be based on all previously mentioned factors.
7. The complete budget is made up after all of the preceding budgets have been made.
8. The cash budget, which is explained later in this chapter, is a budget that shows the cash balance that can be expected at any particular time. Such a budget is necessary when a company anticipates borrowing.

FIGURE 15-6

Budgeting Procedure for a Manufacturing Business

TYPES OF BUDGETS

The final overall budget for a business is made up of several specific budgets, such as the sales, merchandising, advertising, cash, capital, and income statement budgets. Most specialized budgets are based on sales projections. However, in some types of businesses, either the production capacity or the financial capacity must be determined first. Sales and all other estimates are then based on the ability to produce. Small businesses mostly budget sales, purchases, expenses, and cash.

SALES BUDGET

The **sales budget** is a forecast of the sales revenue a company expects to receive for month, a quarter (three months), or a year. Estimated sales could be based on sales territories, sales representatives, branch offices, departments, or particular products or services. Sometimes, managers make independent estimates on all of these bases and, after some discussion, prepare a final sales budget. Sometimes, managers

ILLUSTRATION 15-4

Managers from all departments develop and discuss budgets. Because budgets are based on estimates or projections, should managers give them much attention?

prepare sales estimates with the idea of developing sales quotas or goals for sales representatives and territories. These estimates provide a goal for the sales department, as well as a basis for preparing the merchandising, purchasing, and other operating budgets.

Figure 15-7 shows sales estimates determined in two different ways for the same company. Since the two sets of estimated figures are not the same, someone must combine them into one satisfactory estimate that the sales department can follow.

Numerous factors influence sales estimates. General business conditions play an important part. Although one company may enjoy brisk sales, another—at the same time and under the same conditions—may suffer a decline in sales. If a good harvest and favorable prices for crops are anticipated in a certain geographic area, a company that sells farm machinery should have good prospects for sales in that area. A retail store located in such an area should expect increased sales. A flood or drought may affect certain businesses unfavorably but others favorably. These are examples of some of the influences that should guide a manager in making a sales estimate.

The following factors should be considered in preparing a sales budget:

1. Previous sales
2. Economic trends
3. Changes in competition
4. Factors such as weather
5. Population shifts
6. Sales force
7. Availability of merchandise
8. Buying habits
9. Season of the year

When starting a new business, entrepreneurs should investigate the experiences of other people in the same line of business. They should find out about business conditions from wholesalers, manufacturers, trade associations, and government agencies.

Budget Based on Analysis of Sales Representatives

SALES REPRESENTATIVE	YEAR 1 SALES (ACTUAL)	YEAR 2 SALES (ESTIMATE)
T. A. Nader	$ 356,720	$ 380,000
H. E. Loch	348,380	360,000
C. D. Heidel	471,240	440,000
J. H. Sharmon	442,940	440,000
C. F. Powell	426,980	440,000
J. G. Dunbar	408,360	400,000
Total	$2,454,620	$2,460,000

Budget Based on Analysis of Products

PRODUCT	YEAR 1 SALES (ACTUAL)	YEAR 2 SALES (ESTIMATE)
Washers	$ 642,840	$ 680,000
Dryers	202,320	200,000
Ranges	189,260	180,000
Lamps	209,360	200,000
Refrigerators	1,210,840	1,300,000
Total	$2,454,620	$2,560,000

FIGURE 15-7

Two Ways of Budgeting Sales

MERCHANDISING BUDGET

The **merchandising budget** is a forecast of the amount of merchandise the company expects to sell to customers over the specified time period. The company can use this budget to plan and control the supply of merchandise it has on hand. If it has too little merchandise to meet the demand, it will lose sales. On the other hand, if the business has too much merchandise, valuable cash may be tied up in inventory that could be better used elsewhere. Furthermore, excess merchandise has to be stored, protected, and insured. These expenses add to the cost of doing business. It is important, therefore, to manage properly the purchase of merchandise in relation to sales.

The business must determine the kinds of stock to have on hand at all times. Managers set the maximum and minimum inventory levels.

They plan purchases and give this information to the finance department, so that managers there can estimate cash needs. Managers check sources of supply and schedule delivery dates and relay delivery information to the receiving department. Careful procedures must be set so that all departments are fully aware of the merchandise needed, on hand, and ordered.

ADVERTISING BUDGET

The **advertising budget** is a plan for the amount of money a firm should spend for advertising, based on estimated sales. Advertising expenditures should be kept within reasonable bounds, for it is not true that sales will always be in direct proportion to advertising. In other words, if estimated sales have been steadily rising at a rate of 10 percent, it is unwise to spend more than an additional 10 percent for advertising. Such a plan may result in a loss. On the other hand, a special advertising campaign, properly planned, may increase the sales of a certain product, if only temporarily. As a result, the advertising budget will influence the sales budget. Merchandising and advertising budgets should, therefore, be planned together.

CASH BUDGET

During normal operations, companies receive cash from customers and from borrowing and make payments for things they buy. The **cash budget** is an estimate of the flow of cash into and out of the business over a specified time period. Companies budget cash to make certain that enough cash will be available at the right times to meet payments as they come due. Cash comes into the company from two primary sources: (1) cash receipts and/or (2) borrowing. When companies borrow money, they must eventually pay it back. Therefore, the cash budget shows borrowed money as cash flowing in and repayments as cash flowing out when each payment is due.

Figure 15-8 shows a cash budget for a small business. Cash budgets are important for all companies, no matter how successful they are. A company can be highly profitable yet not have enough cash on hand at the right times to pay its bills. This situation could cause the company to borrow unnecessarily.

CAPITAL BUDGET

Every business must plan for replacing worn-out or obsolete fixed assets. For instance, a company's van will have to be replaced at some future date. Also, if the business is highly successful, it may wish to buy a second van. The company must have a plan for replacing the old van or buying a new one.

A **capital budget** is a financial plan for replacing fixed assets or acquiring new ones. Capital budgeting is important because acquiring

Cash Budget—for Three Months Ending March 31, 20--

	JANUARY	FEBRUARY	MARCH
NET SALES	$ 80,000	$ 80,000	$ 80,000
Beginning cash balance	33,500	4,000	7,000
Collections from customers	70,000	70,000	80,000
Total cash available	$103,500	$74,000	$87,000
Payments			
Accounts to be paid	45,000	45,000	60,000
Labor	9,500	12,000	16,000
Salaries and administrative expense	7,000	7,000	7,000
Sales expense	15,000	15,000	15,000
Other operating expenses	13,000	18,000	24,000
Purchase of fixed assets		10,000	10,000
Repayment of bank loan	10,000		
Total cash payments	$ 99,500	$107,000	$132,000
Expected cash shortage		33,000	45,000
Bank loans needed		40,000	50,000
Ending cash balance	4,000	7,000	5,000
End-of-month situation:			
Materials purchased	$ 45,000	$ 60,000	$ 80,000
Accounts receivable	150,000	160,000	170,000
Accounts payable	45,000	60,000	80,000
Bank loans		40,000	90,000

FIGURE 15-8

A Cash Budget

assets ties up large sums of money for long periods of time. A wrong decision can be costly. For example, a decision to buy a new van that will last five years involves a large expenditure. The manager must plan well in advance if the money is to be available when the van is needed. Assume that the company buys the van based on a forecast that future sales will justify the need for the van. However, if sales do

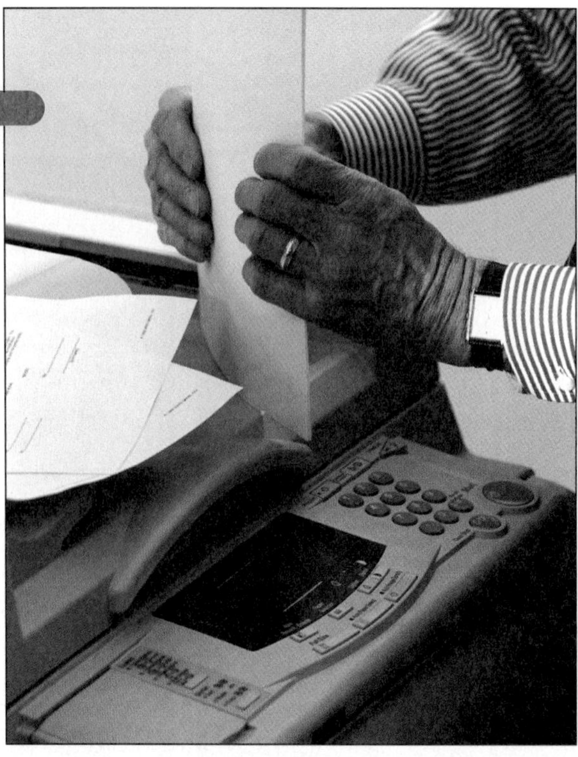

ILLUSTRATION 15-5

Replacing equipment can be very expensive. Such planned expenditures must be included in the capital budget. Should a small business include a new copier in next year's capital budget?

not increase as expected, profits will be lower as a result of the added costs related to the van.

INCOME STATEMENT BUDGET

An **income statement budget** is a plan showing projected sales, costs, expenses, and profits for a future period, such as for one month, three months, or a year. By subtracting its total projected costs and expenses from projected sales, a business can estimate its profit.

ADMINISTERING THE BUDGET

Because a budget is an estimate of what might happen, it usually cannot be followed exactly. Staying close to the amount budgeted is desirable. However, for various reasons beyond the control of managers, actual income and expenses may vary from the budgeted amounts. For that reason, managers of large organizations often prepare three budget estimates. The first estimate assumes that sales will be less than expected. The second estimate considers what most likely will occur. And the third estimate assumes sales will be better than expected.

The second estimate—the one most likely to occur—is used unless anticipated conditions change. If sales are less than expected, the business can shift immediately to the first (lower) set of budget figures. Should sales be better than expected, the business can shift to the third (higher) set of budget figures. Having more than one budget estimate allows for realistic flexibility during budget planning.

Whether a business is large or small or uses one or more budgets, managers must check the estimates against actual business conditions. The comparison determines whether the business is on, under, or over budget. If expenditures exceed budgeted amounts, managers want to know why, so they can make necessary changes. Some adjustments may be easy, while others may not be possible. For example, labor costs might exceed budget estimates because too many employees are poorly trained. A training program might help reduce the labor cost

MANAGEMENT CLOSE-UP

OFFICE DEPOT'S OFFSPRING: VIKING OFFICE PRODUCTS, INC.

Office Depot is America's largest seller of office supply products, with over 700 superstores in 45 states and 19 countries. Annual sales exceed $5 billion. Viking Office Products is one of its subdivisions and is a leading direct mail marketer of office products.

For decades, the traditional approach to buying office products such as paper and desks was to find a local office supply store. Today there are other choices. One is to find a large discount store such as Office Max and Staples. Another choice is to make purchases by phone, the Internet, or from a catalog.

Viking Office Products, Inc., sells computer supplies, office furniture, and a wide variety of general office supplies. Like Dell Direct, described in Chapter 1, Viking does not have retail stores. With an Internet address, an 800-telephone number, and a catalog of brand-name products, Viking has made its mark. Firms with fewer than 100 employees are its main customers. And cost and convenience are its strong selling weapons. In addition to discounted prices, Viking offers customers a one-year guarantee on all merchandise, free overnight nationwide delivery, and free return and pickup of any unwanted product. Its buzzwords are "quality, respect, courtesy, and assurance." Viking's reputation has added to the firm's popularity, which has produced plenty of repeat customers.

Success is further attributed to superior customer service that is achieved, in part, through efficient business operations. A sophisticated computer system keeps track of all of Viking's sales records. An analysis of customer purchases permits Viking to tailor-make special catalogs and to offer special sales that attract new customers and retain current customers.

Viking has made heavy investments in computer technology to further expand sales and to better serve buyers. Domestic and foreign expansion is a dominant topic when Viking managers plan next year's expansion efforts during budget-setting discussions. It continues to make Office Depot a proud parent.

THINK CRITICALLY

1. Why would an office supply business like Viking prefer to sell by direct marketing rather than through retail stores?
2. What features attract small and medium-size firms to buy office products from Viking?
3. Do you believe that preparing a budget that includes foreign sales would be easier, harder, or about the same as preparing a budget for just the American market? Give reasons for your answer.
4. Using one or two local office supply stores, or one local store and the Internet, compare prices for three office supply products such as a box of legal-sized envelopes, a ream of printer paper, and a petty cash book. Prepare a class report comparing such factors as price, quality, convenience, and customer service.

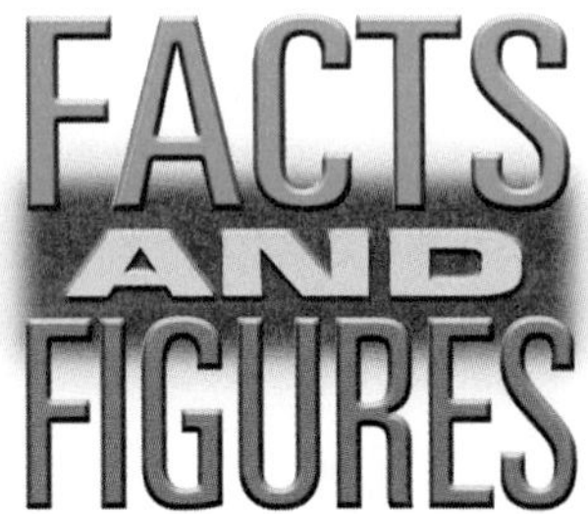

One business authority believes that a small business has an even greater need for budgeting than mid-sized or large businesses because a smaller operation often has limited resources and even more limited access to capital should an unforeseen problem occur.

during the rest of the budget period. However, if labor costs increase because of a recent pay raise given to all workers, little can be done to lower those costs. Comparing budgets with actual operating conditions provides a basis for making timely and knowledgeable management decisions, which, in turn, leads to efficient and profitable business operations.

Figure 15-9 shows a comparison of actual sales for the first quarter of a year with estimated sales for the same quarter. If a comparison of actual operating performance with the budget estimates reveals that the business will not make the expected profit or will have a loss, the manager must review the expenses to determine what can be done to reduce them. The business can save by budgeting inventories carefully to avoid buying unnecessary new merchandise and to reduce the quantity of old items in inventory. The difference between the budgeted and actual figures, which is called the *variance,* is generally considered acceptable if it is plus or minus 5 percent. If sales are considerably below the anticipated level, managers may have to make drastic adjustments, such as reducing delivery service, discharging workers, or canceling certain purchases.

The use of budgets and a budgeting system cannot guarantee the success of a business, but these management devices can help reduce losses or increase profits. The entire budgeting process is valuable in planning and controlling operations. But whether a business is a success or not can be determined only after the budget time periods have passed. As you will learn in the next chapter, a business measures past success by preparing and analyzing financial statements.

FIGURE 15-9

A Comparison of Estimated and Actual Sales

ITEMS	ESTIMATED SALES FIRST QUARTER	ACTUAL SALES FIRST QUARTER	VARIANCE	PERCENT OF CHANGE
Ranges	$27,300	$23,100	-$4,200	-15.4%
Refrigerators	$59,150	$60,350	+$1,200	+ 2.0%
Microwaves	$26,000	$26,200	+$ 200	+ 0.8%
Washers	$19,500	$24,000	+$4,500	+23.1%
Dryers	$31,200	$25,800	-$5,400	-17.3%

CHAPTER CONCEPTS

- All businesses—large and small—must keep records to determine how well they are performing financially and to use the generated information to plan for the future. Businesses keep records for items such as receipts from customers, payments for purchases, assets owned, expenses incurred in running the business, and tax returns. Records may be kept manually, but most firms use computers. An accountant, an accounting department, or an outsourcing firm may be hired to handle specialized record keeping tasks.
- Business records commonly deal with accounting for cash (incoming and outgoing), accounts receivable and payable, depreciation, fixed and other kinds of assets, taxes, and payroll. Records must be accurate, up to date, protected from damage or loss, and readily available for decision making.
- Budgets help businesses plan revenue and expenses over a specified time period, such as a year. Businesses often budget for sales, merchandising, advertising, cash, capital, and income. These specialized budgets depend upon sales forecasts and together make up the company's overall budget.
- Managers compare actual results against budget estimates throughout the year, so they can make adjustments if necessary.

BUILD VOCABULARY POWER

Define the following terms and concepts.

1. accounting records
2. outsourcing
3. data processing center
4. point-of-sale terminal
5. accounts receivable record
6. accounts payable record
7. asset
8. depreciation
9. fixed assets (plant assets)
10. obsolescence
11. asset book value
12. budget
13. sales budget
14. merchandising budget
15. advertising budget
16. cash budget
17. capital budget
18. income statement budget

REVIEW FACTS

1. Name at least five kinds of information that a manager or owner of a business should expect to obtain from the accounting records.
2. How can a business use a data processing center?
3. What do many small businesses use as a basis for obtaining most of the information for their financial records?
4. Use the daily balance form of a small retail business shown in Figure 15-1 and record the following information.
   a. What is the amount of cash sales?
   b. What is the amount of charge sales?

c. What is the cash register total?
d. What are the total cash returns?

5. Give at least three suggestions for the safe handling of cash.
6. Why is depreciation a cost of doing business?
7. What kind of information is shown in a fixed assets record?
8. Is an employer required by law to make income tax deductions from the wages of employees?
9. Name the types of information that must be recorded for social security and payroll tax purposes for each employee and for all employees as a group.
10. In most businesses, where does cash come from?
11. In what ways does a budget help a business?
12. List six types of budgets that are a part of the final overall budget for a business.
13. Name six areas on which sales estimates could be based.
14. Why can't budgets be followed exactly as prepared?
15. In a typical business, when would a manager want to determine the reasons why a budgeted expense turns out to cost far more than expected?

DISCUSS IDEAS

1. Regardless of the type of record system a company selects, what features should the system have?
2. Discuss why the safe handling of cash is so important to a business.
3. How could a truck be a fixed asset? Under what circumstances would land not be a fixed asset?
4. Could a piece of equipment, such as a computer, both depreciate and become obsolete? Explain.
5. What are some of the advantages of keeping an insurance policy record?
6. What problems would be created if a business had a fire and all customer records were destroyed?
7. Why must the production manager know the estimated sales budget?
8. Explain why the advertising and sales budgets should be prepared at the same time.
9. Why is the cash budget so important from the viewpoint of the owner of a small business or the director of a large business?
10. Why is it valuable for managers to compare budgeted amounts with actual amounts spent?

ANALYZE INFORMATION

1. Study the following petty cash form, which is defective. Identify (a) what is wrong with the items included on this form and (b) what items should be added.

PETTY CASH SLIP

Date: ______ Month ______ Day Amount: __________
Cash Given To: ______________________________
Employee Giving Cash (print)____________________

2. L. A. Hendricks has assets as follows: (a) a store building bought two years ago at a cost of $360,000, not including the value of the land; (b) store equipment that cost $54,000 and was installed when the building was bought; and (c) a used delivery truck bought two years ago for $12,000. Assume the following with regard to depreciation: (a) the building decreases in value at the estimated rate of 5 percent a year; (b) the store equipment decreases at the estimated rate of 10 percent a year; and (c) the truck will last one additional year and can be traded in then for $1,800. What is the asset book value of the assets now?

3. A list of certain items kept by the Fine Fabrics Shop, a small retail store, follows. Decide where each item should be kept for safekeeping. Make three columns across a sheet of paper and place these headings at the top: Office Safe, Fireproof Filing Cabinet, and Bank Safe Deposit Box. Write the items below in the column where they best belong.

a. Office lease
b. Petty cash
c. Customers' accounts
d. Contracts
e. Bills owed suppliers
f. Checks received from customers and not yet deposited
g. Insurance policies

4. The sales budget by product for the Gonzalez Supply Company for this year was estimated to be as follows:

Product A	$150,000
Product B	60,000
Product C	180,000
Product D	210,000

a. What are the estimated total sales?
b. If total sales the prior year were $480,000, what percentage of increase does the company expect this year over last year?
c. What percentage of this year's total sales will Product A provide?
d. The actual sales for this year for Products A, B, and D were as shown, but the sales for Product C were only 50 percent of the budgeted amount. What are the actual total sales for the year?

5. As the budget director, you presented the following realistic yearly expense budget to the manager of a service business for final approval. After studying the figures, the manager asked you to prepare a flexible set of budget estimates because certain conditions might cause a 15 percent increase in sales, while certain other conditions might cause a 5 percent decrease in sales. Assume, however, the amounts budgeted for rent and insurance will not change under any circumstances.

Sales Salaries	$300,000
Office Salaries	60,000
Supplies	80,000
Advertising	48,000
Rent	36,000
Insurance	8,000

a. Prepare a new flexible budget showing three columns of figures: 5 percent Decrease, Expected, and 15 percent Increase.
b. What is the total of each of the three budget columns?

SOLVE BUSINESS PROBLEMS

CASE 15-1

George Gorski operates his own restaurant, George's Place. His accountant, Rosalind Quinn, is quite concerned about the way George handles cash.

Each morning before opening the business, George counts all the money in the cash drawer that was taken in the day before. He then leaves all the coins in the cash drawer so there will be enough on most days for making change. On days when the change runs low, he sends a worker to the nearby bank to get some. All the paper money in the cash drawer is put in a file cabinet that can be locked. When he buys restaurant supplies. George uses the money in the file cabinet to pay cash for them. On Friday of each week, the money in the file drawer is deposited in the bank.

George cannot understand why Rosalind is upset with his cash practices. "It has been working fine for years," he says.

Think Critically:

1. Which of George's procedures are improper business practices? Why?
2. What methods should George follow to correct the improper business practices?

CASE 15-2

Karen Kline and Joe Kim are both accounting clerks in a medium-sized manufacturing firm called Electrical Home Products, Inc. The head accountant, Brooke Shenker, has just asked Karen to provide the sales budget for next month's annual budget meeting. Brooke asked Joe to construct the cash budget. Neither was happy about the request, though neither complained directly to the head accountant. Karen did, however, let her feelings be known to Joe.

Karen: *We spend weeks developing these budgets and all the budget committee does is argue for two days and change our estimates. It makes me wonder why they ask for our figures in the first place.*

Joe: *I agree. What's worse is that we never come in on target. Those credit sales projections are never right, and it makes me look bad because my cash budget is off. Last year they*

projected sales to be $350,000 for the first quarter, and they were only $335,000.

Karen: *Why don't they just agree to try to improve sales? The company should put a little more money in advertising expenses to help boost sales, and then hope for the best. I'm sure that would be just as good a way to plan and everyone would be happier. I hate all that arguing that goes on.*

Joe: *Last year they argued for three days and look what happened. They were so far off budget that I heard Brooke say a child could have done a better job forecasting. Budgeting is a waste of time.*

Karen: *I'll start on the sales budget tomorrow, but if I were smart my vacation would begin then, too!*

Think Critically:

1. If Karen and Joe prepared budget figures, why is it necessary for management to discuss them?
2. Do you agree with Joe that when budgeted amounts and actual figures do not agree, the budgeting process is not worthwhile? Explain your answer.
3. How serious is the variance between forecast and actual sales? And what might have thrown the sales budget forecast off? Explain your answers.
4. Do you agree with Karen that by increasing the advertising budget, sales will increase?

PROJECT: MY BUSINESS, INC.

Business people need a complete set of financial records to make management decisions. This is very important for new businesses, as financial resources are usually limited. As you complete this part of the Project, you will review the record systems needed for your business and the sources of record keeping assistance available.

DATA COLLECTION

1. Interview an accountant or review small business management materials. Use the interview or materials review to determine the types of financial records you will need for your business. Develop a list of all of the records you believe you will need to maintain as the business owner.
2. Obtain a copy of a small business financial planning software package for use on a desktop computer. Examine each of the forms and records included with the package and determine the type of information the business would need to acquire in order to complete each of the forms and records.

ANALYSIS

1. Develop a detailed set of procedures to be followed in your business for the safe handling of cash. Be certain to consider all situations in which cash will be handled.
2. Prepare a sample cash budget for your business. The budget should cover the first three months of business operations. The budget can be modeled after the example in Figure 15-8 in the chapter.

FINANCIAL ANALYSIS OF A BUSINESS

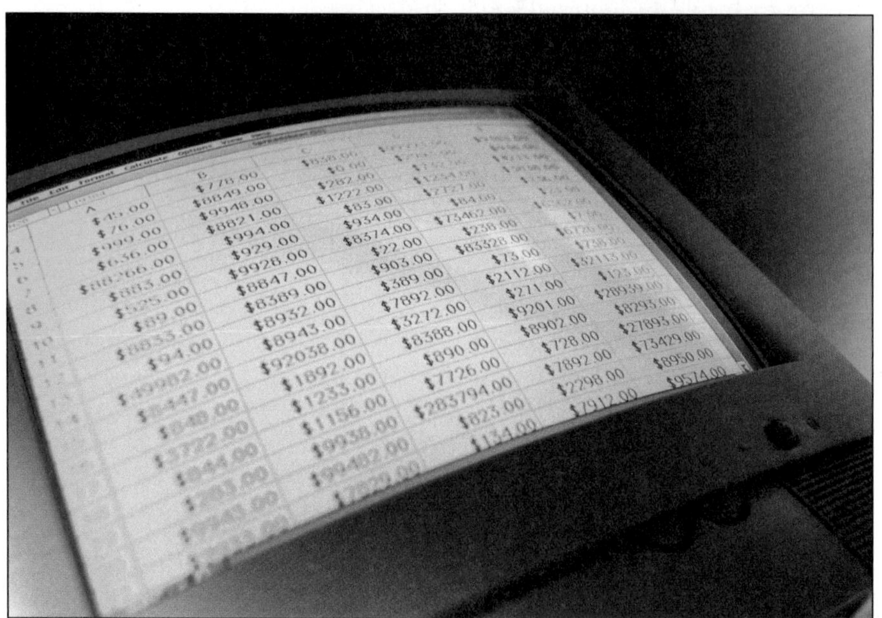

OBJECTIVES

- **16-1** Describe a balance sheet and explain how it can be useful to a business.
- **16-2** Point out the usefulness of the income statement in making business decisions.
- **16-3** Describe the importance of cash flow and working capital.
- **16-4** Explain several useful financial ratios.
- **16-5** Describe how various financial experts can assist business managers.

THE MYSTERIES OF ACCOUNTING

Austin Pratt never liked visiting his accountant. She always talked about his financial standing, ratios, and bottom line. Most of this made little sense to Austin, but he also knew understanding them was important to understanding his business.

"Either your current assets are too low or your current liabilities are too high," Brendalee Roper had said to him on his last visit. "If you want to get that bank loan, you have to improve your working capital. Your inventory turnover is also too low to impress your bank manager."

"I'm going to take an accounting course at the local community college," Austin thought. "It seems Brendalee talks to me in a foreign language, and I've got to learn what she means. That bank loan is just too important."

Like many other business owners, Austin Pratt never had an accounting course, even though he has great need for grasping the basics about his financial condition. A knowledge of accounting helps business owners make sound business decisions. Accounting is the language of business.

USES OF FINANCIAL REPORTS

Business activity is in large part measured in terms of money, and the amount of money a business earns is one way to judge its success. Because success is judged in dollar terms, every business must (1) keep thorough and accurate records, (2) prepare important financial reports regularly, (3) interpret the financial information in the reports, and (4) make decisions that will affect future financial results.

In this chapter you will learn about financial reports and how to use information they contain. The two financial reports businesses use most are the balance sheet and the income statement.

ILLUSTRATION 16-1

What uses do financial reports have in business?

Poor financial management is one of the leading reasons that businesses fail. In many cases, failure could have been avoided if the owners had applied sound financial principles to their decisions. Financial management is not something that owners can leave to bankers, financial planners, or accountants. Owners need to understand the basic principles and use them on a daily basis.

Financial reports have many uses in business. Executives use financial reports as a means to run an efficient, profitable business. Suppliers, lenders, unions, governments, and owners also use financial reports when making business decisions. Figure 16-1 lists some reasons why various users need financial information.

FINANCIAL STATEMENTS

Financial statements are reports that summarize financial data over a period of time, such as a month, three months, a year, or even the life of the business. We will focus on the two most used financial statements—the balance sheet and the income statement.

BALANCE SHEET

A **balance sheet,** or **statement of financial position,** is a financial statement that reports a business's assets, liabilities, and capital on a specific date. As you learned in the last chapter, *assets* are anything of

FIGURE 16-1

The financial reports of a business serve a variety of purposes.

USER	NEEDS FINANCIAL DATA TO...
Manager	make day-to-day decisions. review past results. plan for the future.
Owner	decide whether to increase or decrease ownership investment. decide whether to continue business operations.
Supplier	decide whether to extend credit. decide how much credit to extend.
Lender	decide whether to lend a business money. decide on the terms of a loan to a business (amount, time period, and interest rate).
Union	determine fair increases in wages, salaries, and fringe benefits.
Government	arrive at fair tax rates. detect fraudulent practices.

value owned, such as cash and buildings. **Liabilities** are claims against assets. In other words, liabilities are the business's debts. And **capital** (also called **net worth, owner's equity,** or **stockholders' equity**) is the amount an organization or individual is worth after subtracting liabilities from assets.

A balance sheet has two sides. Assets are listed and totaled on the left. Liabilities and capital are listed and totaled on the right. The two halves must always balance. That is, the total of all assets must equal the total of all liabilities plus capital. In fact, the basic **accounting equation** is expressed as:

$$\text{Assets} = \text{Liabilities} + \text{Capital}$$

You may think of the basic accounting formula as an old-fashioned scale, as shown in Figure 16-2. An actual balance sheet appears in Figure 16-3.

Each balance sheet has a heading that includes the name of the person or business, the title "Balance Sheet," and the date. The information in the balance sheet presents a picture of the financial position of a business on the date shown in the heading. Balance sheets are prepared at least once a year.

KINDS OF DATA An example of a balance sheet for a jewelry store, the Crown Corporation, is shown in Figure 16-3. On December 31, the accountants for the Crown Corporation prepared a balance sheet. The value of every asset the business owns is listed under Assets. As shown

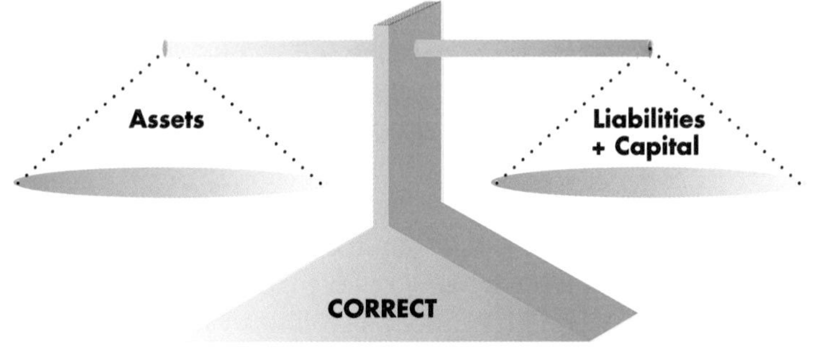

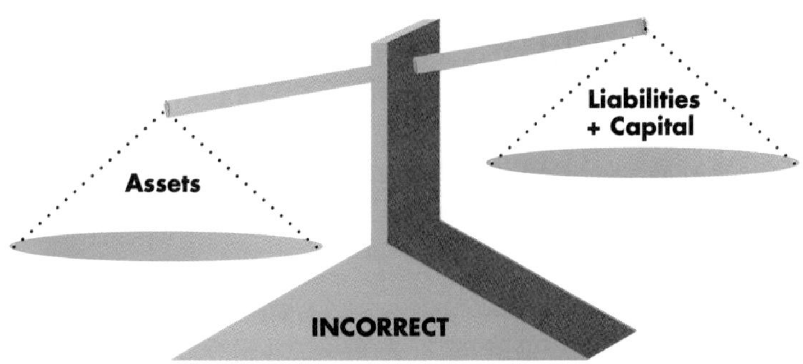

FIGURE 16-2

If assets do not equal liabilities plus capital, an accounting error exists in the balance sheet.

FIGURE 16-3

The balance sheet shows the financial position of a company on a given date.

Crown Corporation
Balance Sheet
December 31, 20--

ASSETS	
Cash	$ 24,000
Accounts Receivable	8,000
Merchandise Inventory	64,000
Equipment	80,000
Land and Building	360,000
Total Assets	$536,000

LIABILITIES AND CAPITAL	
Liabilities:	
Accounts Payable	$ 32,000
Mortgage Payable	104,000
Total Liabilities	$136,000
Capital:	
Stockholders' Net Worth	400,000
Total Liabilities and Capital	$536,000

in Figure 16-3, Crown's total assets are $536,000. The company debts—items purchased on credit and the mortgage still owed on the land and building—are listed under Liabilities, which total $136,000. The accountants subtracted total liabilities from total assets to calculate Crown's capital, $400,000.

Crown purchases jewelry from a manufacturer, displays the jewelry in its store, and then sells it to customers. Until the jewelry is sold, it is listed as an asset called merchandise inventory. **Merchandise inventory** is the value of goods purchased to sell to customers at a profit.

Crown Corporation sells merchandise on a cash or credit basis. For credit sales, the company allows customers to pay in 30, 60, or 90 days or use a credit card. The amount customers owe the business is an asset called **accounts receivable.** It is an asset because the business has a legal right to obtain cash for the goods sold and can sue customers who do not pay. The store will eventually collect cash from the customers.

The **accounts payable** item under Liabilities on the balance sheet is the amount the company owes for purchases it made on credit. In this example, the store bought jewelry worth $32,000 on credit from a manufacturer. Until the company pays the bill, the amount remains on the balance sheet as a liability, or debt.

VALUE OF DATA The balance sheet for the Crown Corporation provides a great deal of useful data. It lists specific types and amounts of assets and liabilities. The balance sheet also shows that the business owns assets of $536,000, owes $136,000, and is worth $400,000 on December 31. The total figures on the balance sheet agree with the basic accounting formula as follows:

$$\text{Assets} = \text{Liabilities} + \text{Capital}$$
$$\$536{,}000 = \$136{,}000 + \$400{,}000$$

A careful look at the specific items reveals other valuable information. For example, Crown cannot now pay the $32,000 that it owes under accounts payable because it has only $24,000 in cash available. Hopefully, the company will make enough cash sales and will collect cash from some of those customers listed under accounts receivable soon enough to pay its bills when due. Even though the money owed under accounts payable is not likely to become due all at once, the company could possibly have trouble meeting other day-to-day expenses. The company would be in trouble if a sudden emergency arose that called for much cash.

Crown may use its balance sheet to compare financial results with prior time periods or with other companies. Because companies prepare a yearly balance sheet, the business can review its financial progress by comparing this year's results with last year's results. It may find, for example, that the amount of capital increased over last year without an increase in liabilities. If Crown wished to do so, it could also compare some information on its balance sheet with that of other businesses of similar size and kind. Published information is available from several sources, such as trade associations. With comparative figures, the business can make judgments about its success and perhaps even find ways to improve its financial picture in the future.

INCOME STATEMENT

The **income statement,** or **profit and loss statement,** is a financial statement that reports total revenue and expenses for a specific period, such as a month or a year. Income statements have three major parts:

1. Revenue—income earned for the period, such as from the sale of goods and services.
2. Expenses—all costs incurred in operating the business, such as the cost of materials used to manufacture the company's products.
3. Profit or Loss—the difference between total revenue and total expenses.

When revenue is greater than expenses, the company has earned a profit. When expenses are greater than revenue, the company has incurred a loss. The income statement shows a picture of success or failure (profit or loss) for a specific period of a year or less. The balance sheet, on the other hand, shows the financial condition of a business at a particular point in time. Both types of financial statements serve useful but different purposes. An example of an income statement is shown in Figure 16-4. The period covered for the Crown Corporation is one year, as shown in the heading.

KINDS OF DATA The revenue for the Crown Corporation comes from one source—the sale of jewelry. Total revenue for the year was $800,000. If the company earned other income, such as from the repair of jewelry, the income from this source would be listed separately under Revenue.

FIGURE 16-4

The income statement shows profit or loss for a specified period of time.

Crown Corporation
Income Statement
For the Year Ending December 31, 20--

Revenue from Sales	$800,000	
Cost of Goods Sold	440,000	
Gross Profit		$360,000
Operating Expenses		
Salaries and Wages	$160,000	
Advertising and Promotion	48,000	
Depreciation	32,000	
Utilities	20,000	
Supplies Used	12,000	
Other	8,000	
Total Operating Expenses		280,000
Net Profit (before Taxes)		$ 80,000

In order to earn revenue, a retail business purchases merchandise from suppliers and sells it to customers at a profit. The amount the retailer paid the supplier for the merchandise it bought and sold is called *cost of goods sold.* In a manufacturing business, the cost of goods sold would include the amount the company paid for raw materials and parts to make its products.

Generally, the cost of goods sold is a rather large deduction from revenue. To make the cost of goods sold easy to identify on the income statement, it is listed separately from other deductions. *Gross profit* is the amount remaining after subtracting the cost of goods sold from revenue. *Net profit* is the amount remaining after subtracting all expenses from revenue, except taxes. Gross profit for the Crown Corporation is $360,000, which is calculated by subtracting the cost of goods sold ($440,000) from sales revenue ($800,000).

Expenses needed to operate the business during the year are listed next on the income statement. *Operating expenses* are all expenses that are not directly associated with creating or buying merchandise the business sells. For example, businesses spend money on advertising, supplies, and building maintenance. For Crown Corporation, operating expenses total $280,000. On the income statement, operating expenses are subtracted from gross profit, $360,000, to arrive at the net profit or "bottom line," $80,000.

The net result of the business activity reported in the form of revenue, cost of goods sold, expenses, and profit on the income statement will appear in one form or another on the balance sheet. For the Crown Corporation, the net profit of $80,000 will be added to its assets (left side of the balance sheet) and capital (right side of the balance sheet). Thus, the two sides of the balance sheet will still balance. The accounting equation will still show that assets equal liabilities plus capital.

VALUE OF DATA The manager of Crown Corporation can learn a great deal about the business from the income statement. Specifically, the total deductions from the $800,000 in revenue are $720,000, which consists of cost of goods sold ($440,000) and operating expenses ($280,000). The manager can also see that the net profit before taxes—$80,000—is a rather small part of the total revenue. Both of these observations might warn of a possible problem with high costs.

The Crown Corporation can improve its financial controlling and budget planning by doing an item-by-item analysis of the income statement, such as that shown in the first two columns of numbers in Figure 16-5. Each expenditure can be calculated as a percentage of total sales. Managers can then compare the percentages with similar figures from prior months and years to reveal trends.

For instance, the first and largest operating expense is $160,000 for salaries and wages. When $160,000 is divided by total sales, $800,000, and the answer is changed to a percentage, the result is 20 percent. If last year the total wages and salaries expense amounted to only 18 percent of sales, the business would know that this expense had increased in relation to total sales. If possible, the company can try to correct this 2 percent increase for the next year by trying to increase sales, raise prices, or get by with fewer employees. The same type of calculation and analysis can be made for each of the remaining expenses on the income statement. In addition, managers can determine the percentages of gross profit and net profit in relation to sales.

CAREER CONNECTION

BUDGET ANALYST

Budgets are financial plans used to estimate financial requirements and organize and allocate operating and capital resources effectively. The analysis of spending behavior and the planning of future operations are an important part of the decision-making process in most corporations and government agencies. Budget analysts play a critical role in this process.

A major responsibility of budget analysts is to provide advice and technical assistance in the preparation of annual budgets. Then, throughout the fiscal year, analysts monitor the budget by reviewing reports and accounting records to determine if allocated funds have been spent as specified. In private industry, a budget analyst examines, analyzes, and looks for new ways to improve efficiency and increase profits. Government budget analysts seek to find the most efficient distribution of funds and other resources among various departments and programs.

Federal, state, and local governments account for one third of budget analyst jobs. Other major employers are schools, hospitals, banks, and manufacturers. Budget analysts usually are required to have a bachelor's degree in an area such as accounting, finance, economics, planning, statistics, or social sciences. A master's degree may also be necessary in order to ensure adequate analytical and communication skills.

For more career information about budget analysts, check your library or the Internet for resources.

FIGURE 16-5

Income statement budgets can be prepared from income statements.

Crown Corporation
Budgeted Income Statement
for 12 Months Ending December 31, 20--

INCOME, EXPENSE, AND PROFIT	AMOUNTS FOR PAST 12 MONTHS	PERCENTAGE OF SALES	AMOUNTS BUDGETED FOR NEXT 12 MONTHS	ESTIMATED PERCENTAGE OF SALES
Sales	$800,000	100.0%	$960,000	100.0%
Cost of Goods Sold	440,000	55.0	528,000	55.0
Gross Profit	360,000	45.0	432,000	45.0
Operating Expenses				
Salaries and Wages	160,000	20.0	182,400	19.0
Advertising/Promotion	48,000	6.0	58,560	6.1
Depreciation	32,000	4.0	32,000	3.3
Utilities	20,000	2.5	28,800	3.0
Supplies Used	12,000	1.5	14,400	1.5
Other Expenses	8,000	1.0	9,600	1.0
Total Operating Expenses	280,000	35.0	325,760	33.9
Net Profit	80,000	10.0	106,240	11.1

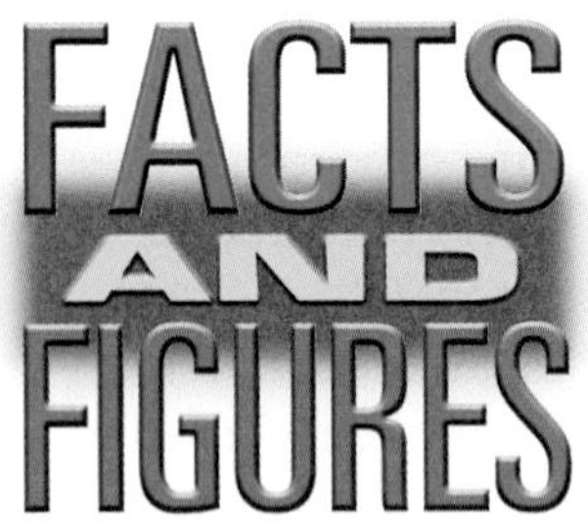

A cash flow budget is a good way of predicting a business's cash flow for the next month, six months, or even the next year. The budget predicts a business's ability to take in more cash than it pays out. This gives some indication of the business's ability to create the resources necessary for expansion or its ability to support the owners.

ANALYSIS OF FINANCIAL DATA

Managers use financial statements as well as other financial information to interpret the financial health of the business. They want to know such things as whether their cash flow and working capital are sufficient to pay the company's bills. They also analyze ratios calculated from financial statements to identify where financial problems lie.

CASH FLOW

Cash flow is the movement of cash into and out of a business. Money comes in immediately as a result of the sale of goods and services for cash and later from customers who buy on credit. Money goes out to pay for various costs and operating expenses. Because money does not always flow in at the same rate that it flows out, managers need to plan for the flow of cash.

Regardless of the size of a business, cash is both a short-term and a long-term concern. Businesses must have cash on hand to pay bills when they are due and to plan ahead for large cash payments, such as the purchase of equipment or the launching of a new product.

Figure 16-6 shows cash flow planning for a retail piano store. While the company sells some pianos for cash, it sells most on credit. The

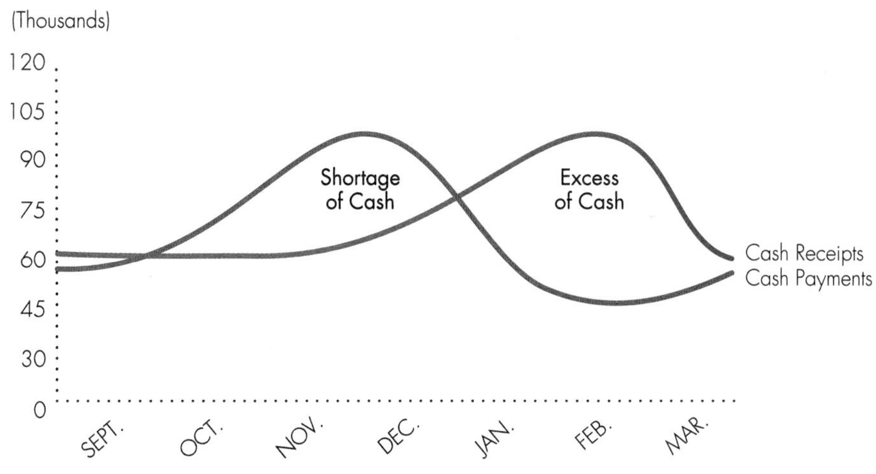

FIGURE 16-6

Cash flow changes each month. Businesses must plan their spending around their cash shortages and cash excesses.

bulk of piano sales occurs during the December holiday season. The need for cash is greatest during September, October, and November when the company buys its inventory of pianos to sell. It needs large sums of cash to pay for the pianos, for sales promotions such as advertising, and for regular operating expenses. The cash flowing out of the company from October through December is greater than the cash flowing in.

Large amounts of cash start to flow in during December from customers who pay cash for their purchases. Credit customers who purchased in December, however, will make cash payments in January, February, and March. During these three months, the flow of cash coming into the business will be greater than the cash going out. From this information, managers can plan for short-term borrowing during times of cash shortage. They can also plan when to make any needed large purchases, so that their payments will be due when they have cash available to pay them.

ILLUSTRATION 16-2

Some businesses have a cash flow problem when cash does not flow into and out of the business on a steady basis. Can you name some businesses that may have cash flow problems?

WORKING CAPITAL

Working capital is the difference between current assets and current liabilities. The word "current" refers to assets and liabilities that are expected to be exchanged for cash within one year or less, such as accounts receivable and payable. For example, companies expect most customers to pay for their credit purchases within a year. Therefore, accounts receivable are current assets. Similarly, companies expect to pay for their credit purchases in accounts payable within a year, so accounts payable are a current liability.

When current assets are much larger than current liabilities, businesses are better able to pay current liabilities. The amount of working capital is one indicator that a business can pay its short-term debts. Businesses with large amounts of working capital usually find it easier to borrow money, because lenders feel assured that these businesses will have the means to repay their loans. The working capital analysis for the Crown Corporation is shown in Figure 16-7. Notice that the numbers used in the analysis are the current assets and current liabilities drawn from the company's balance sheet shown in Figure 16-3.

FINANCIAL RATIOS

Managers use ratios to examine different areas of the business for possible financial problems. Figure 16-8 shows some important ratios and their uses. The data for these ratios come from Crown Corporation's financial statements: Figure 16-3 (balance sheet), Figure 16-4 (income statement), and Figure 16-7 (working capital). Managers can compare financial ratios with the same ratios from prior periods, with ratios from other firms, and with other types of ratios. Organizations such as Dun & Bradstreet publish a standard list of average ratios for various types of businesses. Companies can then compare their own ratios to

FIGURE 16-7

Working capital can be calculated from the balance sheet by subtracting current liabilities from current assets.

Crown Corporation
Working Capital
December 31, 20--

Current Assets:		
Cash	**$24,000**	
Accounts Receivable	**8,000**	
Merchandise Inventory	**64,000**	**$96,000**
Current Liabilities:		
Accounts Payable		**32,000**
Total Working Capital		**$64,000**

Frequently Used Financial Ratios

RATIO	CALCULATION	CROWN CORPORATION*	PURPOSE
Return on Sales	Net Profit / Sales	80,000 / 800,000 = 10.0%	Shows how profitable a firm was for a specified period of time.
Inventory Turnover	Cost of Goods Sold / Ave. Mdse. Inventory	440,000 / 64,000 = 6.88%	Shows whether the average monthly inventory might be too large or small.
Current Ratio	Current Assets / Current Liabilities	96,000 / 32,000 = 3.0%	Shows whether a firm can meet its current debts comfortably.
Return on Owners' Equity	Net Profit / Owners' Equity	80,000 / 400,000 = 20.0%	Shows whether the owners are making a fair return on their investment.
Return on Investment	Net Profit / Total Assets	80,000 / 536,000 = 14.9%	Shows rate of return on the total money invested by owners and others in a firm.

* See Fig. 16-3, 16-4, and 16-7 for sources of figures for calculations.

FIGURE 16-8

Financial ratios help evaluate the financial condition of a business.

these average ratios to get a sense of how they are doing in relation to other companies in their industry.

Lenders use ratios to decide whether the company is a good loan risk. Managers use ratios to identify possible problems needing corrective action. For example, if the company's return on investment is below average for its industry, then managers know that they may have to increase profits to attract new investors. If the company's current ratio keeps decreasing each period, then its liabilities are growing faster than its assets. This indicates that the company may be getting into debt trouble.

SOURCES OF FINANCIAL INFORMATION

If a business needs general advice or special help with a financial problem, it hires an expert. Types of experts available to businesses are accountants, bankers, consultants, and the federal government.

ETHICAL ISSUES

DUNLAP'S DISASTER AT SUNBEAM

Sunbeam Corporation had been experiencing financial difficulties before the Board of Directors hired CEO Al Dunlap to fix the company, which makes and sells brand name household appliances and camping equipment. Dunlap had successfully turned other companies around. Once Dunlap was on board, Sunbeam's stock started to climb. Within seven months, he had saved the company $225 million by such actions as firing 12,000 employees, closing 16 of 26 factories, and disposing of unwanted properties.

Employees learned early why others had nicknamed him "Chainsaw Al." The firm's culture changed quickly. Before Dunlap's arrival, the firm was in trouble, with few new products, weakening sales, and declining profits. His arrival sent Sunbeam's stock up within 18 months. The stockholders and investors were happy.

But soon after major cost-reduction steps were completed, sales and profits began to decline. Pressure was put on all product managers to do whatever was necessary to increase sales. Action was taken to make it appear as if sales were rising and expenses were falling. Many actions were unacceptable business practices. Dunlap eliminated the information technology department by outsourcing it. In the meantime, the computer system was replaced, but no backup files had been created. Chaos prevailed. Workers manually prepared inventories and invoices and handled hundreds of calls from upset customers and suppliers.

Dunlap pressured employees relentlessly to produce more. Morale dipped. Budget goals were unrealistic. To make it appear as though goals were being met without creating cash flow problems, some managers postponed paying bills and suppliers were asked to accept only partial payment to keep costs down temporarily. Credit terms to large stores were extended to make sales. And large discounts were given customers to encourage them to buy well in advance so as to make Sunbeam's income statement look good. The undesirable business practices led to high inventory levels, accounts receivable and payable both rose, and cash flow weakened. Sales were recorded for the current year that under accounting rules should have been postponed to the next year. Profit margins got thinner. The firm was in deep trouble.

The Board of Directors met and agreed it had made a serious error in hiring Al Dunlap. He was fired. The firm reorganized, but it will need time to improve the corporate culture, the financial condition, and its image.

THINK CRITICALLY

1. If you were offered a job at Sunbeam while Al Dunlap was CEO, would you accept if other jobs were also available? Give a reason for your answer.
2. Do you think there was a relationship between outsourcing the computer systems and replacing the computers, and the failure to back up records? If so, explain your answer.
3. If you were a Sunbeam accountant and you were asked to perform a task that was against good accounting practice, would you perform the task, quit, or become a whistleblower?
4. Find out more about the current financial condition of Sunbeam and report to your class.

ACCOUNTANTS

ILLUSTRATION 16-3

What would be the value in a firm's hiring a Certified Public Accountant?

Accountants establish systems for collecting, sorting, and summarizing all types of financial data. They prepare and explain in detail the many figures found on financial statements. Accountants also help managers interpret financial data and make suggestions for handling various financial aspects of a business. Large firms have full-time accountants, while small firms usually hire accountants on a part-time basis. A firm may hire a **Certified Public Accountant,** or **CPA,** a person who has met a state's education, experience, and examination requirements in accounting. Corporations that sell stock to the public must hire CPAs to approve their yearly financial records.

BANKERS

Bankers also assist businesses with financial decisions. Bankers are well informed about the financial condition of businesses, and they also provide advice on how and where to get loans. Since bankers frequently work with businesses, they are aware of businesses' problems and needs. In the opening story, Austin can get financial help from his banker when he is ready to request a loan.

CONSULTANTS

A **consultant** is an expert whom companies hire to help them solve problems within the consultant's area of expertise. Consultants are not employees. They are outside experts with specialized knowledge.

A financial consultant is valuable to people thinking about starting a business. For example, consultants provide advice on the amount of money needed to get started and on handling finances during the early years of operation. Professors of accounting, finance, and management at local colleges or universities often serve as consultants. Also, many consulting firms sell their services to other businesses.

ILLUSTRATION 16-4

If you are thinking of starting a business, why might you want to see a financial consultant?

SMALL BUSINESS ADMINISTRATION

The Small Business Administration (SBA) is an agency of the federal government that provides helpful literature on money matters and often free advice on many aspects of running a business. The SBA can assist small firms in getting loans under special conditions. The SBA can also recommend consultants to businesses.

FACTS AND FIGURES

The Small Business Administration Web site (www.sba.gov) is an excellent resource for business information. It includes advice on business plans, financing, and expansion, and it features an online library with publications and shareware. The SBA's online "classroom" even provides entrepreneurial training.

CHAPTER CONCEPTS

- Owners, managers, suppliers, employees, and the government need financial statements to make business decisions. The balance sheet reports a firm's assets, liabilities, and capital at a specific moment in time. The income statement covers a specific time period, such as a year, and reports revenue, expenses, and the bottom line—the net profit or net loss.
- Balance sheets show assets on one side and liabilities plus capital on the other. The totals on both sides must match, or "balance." Stated in the form of the basic accounting equation: Assets = Liabilities + Capital.
- Owners, managers, and lenders analyze key financial statements not only to determine a firm's profitability but also to make comparisons with prior periods and with other businesses. To identify possible problem areas within the business, they analyze data on cash flow, working capital, and financial ratio calculations.
- Accountants collect, sort, and summarize financial data. Accountants, bankers, consultants, and the Small Business Administration are experts that businesses can use to help them solve financial problems.

BUILD VOCABULARY POWER

Define the following terms and concepts.

1. financial statements
2. balance sheet (statement of financial position)
3. liabilities
4. capital (net worth, owner's equity, or stockholders' equity)
5. accounting equation
6. merchandise inventory
7. accounts receivable
8. accounts payable
9. income statement (profit and loss statement)
10. cash flow
11. working capital
12. Certified Public Accountant (CPA)
13. consultant

REVIEW FACTS

1. Explain how each of the following might use financial information: (a) managers, (b) owners, and (c) suppliers.
2. What are the two most common financial statements?
3. Name the three parts to a balance sheet.
4. Why are accounts receivable listed on the balance sheet as an asset when customers have not yet paid?
5. Give an example of what a business can learn by comparing one year's balance sheet figures with another year's.
6. Name the three major parts to an income statement.
7. Does the income statement show results for the same period of time as the balance sheet?

8. Is net profit likely to be larger than gross profit?
9. How can a percentage be calculated for an income statement expense?
10. Why is cash flow a concern for most businesses?
11. If current liabilities are larger than current assets, what does this mean about a business's ability to pay bills that are coming due soon?
12. How are ratios helpful to managers?
13. What do accountants do?
14. Why would a business want to use a consultant?
15. What is the SBA and what does it do?

DISCUSS IDEAS

1. Assume a business recently started and its balance sheet shows: Assets, $75,000; Liabilities, $30,000; and Capital, $45,000. However, the owner forgot to include a $3,500 computer purchased for cash. How would this affect the total assets, total liabilities, and capital?
2. If, in Figure 16-3, all the customers paid their bills (shown in accounts receivable), what effect would it have on the total assets, total liabilities, and the stockholders' net worth?
3. Discuss the accuracy of this statement: The balance sheet tells you whether you made a profit or a loss for the year.
4. A net loss of $5,000 appears on an income statement. How would this loss affect the Capital section of the balance sheet?
5. From Figure 16-5, which two operating expenses account for the decrease in total operating expenses from 35 percent to 33.9 percent?
6. If a business that previously sold on a cash basis now permits customers to buy on 30-day credit terms, how will the cash flow be affected during the first month of credit sales?
7. Discuss whether it would be possible for working capital to ever go below zero.
8. If the average return on sales for all jewelry stores reported by the trade association is 7 percent, how would you judge the success of the Crown Corporation? See Figure 16-8.
9. What experts would you contact for help if you were planning to open a gift shop, but you were having trouble deciding where to get financial help and how much to borrow?

ANALYZE INFORMATION

1. Use the following items to prepare a balance sheet dated today for the Starboard Corporation. Use Figure 16-3 as a model.

Cash	$ 5,000
Accounts Receivable	8,000
Merchandise Inventory	15,000
Land and Buildings	120,000
Accounts Payable	12,000
Mortgage Payable	90,000
Stockholders' Net Worth	46,000

2. Use the following items to prepare an annual income statement dated today for the Portside Corporation. Use Figure 16-4 as a model.

Revenue from Sales	$250,000
Cost of Goods Sold	80,000
Operating Expenses:	
Wages	$ 40,000
Advertising	13,000
Depreciation	10,000
Insurance	6,000
Supplies Used	3,000
Other	2,500

3. A friend asked you to help analyze her financial affairs. You agreed and obtained from her the following items and amounts:

Cash	$125
Clothing	450
VCR, Radio, & Tapes	600
Balance owed on charge accounts	700
Savings account balance	700
Checking account balance	200

a. Prepare a balance sheet.
b. Offer financial advice to your friend.

4. The following is a portion of an income statement for a local retail store. Calculate the percentage that each item represents of the total sales so that the manager can use the information to help prepare next year's budget.

Revenue from Sales	$500,000
Cost of Goods Sold	300,000
Gross Profit	$200,000
Operating Expenses:	
Wages and Salaries	$ 90,000
Advertising	15,000
Supplies Used	30,000
Other	20,000
Total Operating Expenses	$155,000
Net Profit	$ 45,000

5. Use the following information that was obtained from the balance sheet and income statement of the Waterwing Company to calculate the following financial ratios: (a) inventory turnover, (b) current ratio, (c) return on owners' equity, and (d) return on investment. See Figure 16-8.

Revenue from Sales	$600,000
Cost of Goods Sold	320,000
Net Profit	25,000
Current Assets	36,000
Total Assets	200,000
Current Liabilities	15,000
Owners' Equity	50,000
Average Merchandise Inventory	20,000

SOLVE BUSINESS PROBLEMS

CASE 16-1

Anneika Lafferty and her friend Bernie Williams started an Internet business 15 months ago selling affordable musical instruments for beginners. They named it A&B Musical Instruments. Because they live near each other, Bernie keeps the inventory in his garage and Anneika has the computer system, phones, and office space in her home. Business has not done as well as they expected, but they are still optimistic. They have learned from their mistakes and realize that their products are not as popular as expected. They would like to sell the business and create a different type of online business.

A larger Internet music company wants to buy them but the $50,000 offered is not nearly what Anneika and Bernie expected, based upon the potential for the company. They quickly rejected the offer. The offer was based on last year's balance sheet (shown below) and the income statement that showed $175,000 in sales and $110,000 in expenses. Many of the expenditures were to get the business started.

A & B Musical Instruments
Balance Sheet
December 31, 20—

Assets		**Liabilities and Capital**	
Cash	$ 9,000	Liabilities:	
Accounts Receivable	8,000	Accounts Payable	$ 31,000
Inventory	37,000		
Equipment	25,000	Total Liabilities	31,000
		Capital:	
		A. Lafferty	24,000
		B. Williams	24,000
Total Assets	$79,000	Total Liabilities & Capital	$79,000

Think Critically:

1. On what basis did the potential buyer probably make the $50,000 offer? And what did the buyer learn from the sellers' rejection?
2. How might the working capital, current ratio, and return on sales have affected the offering price? Prepare the necessary calculations before answering.
3. Assume you wish to buy the company. What additional information would you want to gather from the sellers?

CASE 16-2

For several years, Delia and Lorenzo Garcia have been making leather items, such as belts, purses, and wallets, in their home as a hobby. They have sold many items to friends and neighbors. Because Lorenzo has just lost his regular job, he and Delia have decided to go into business full time making leathercraft items. The items will be sold to retailers and, perhaps later, to wholesalers. They will need a large amount of money, some of which they have saved. Both agree that they know a great deal about how to make leather items but very little about financial matters.

Delia believes they should hire a consultant before they do anything else to start the business. Lorenzo, on the other hand, believes they should go to a bank to borrow as much as they can and then start the business. Lorenzo thinks that they can hire an accountant after they have gotten the business started. He does not believe the consultant will know enough about the leather business to give advice. "Besides," he adds, "consultants are too expensive."

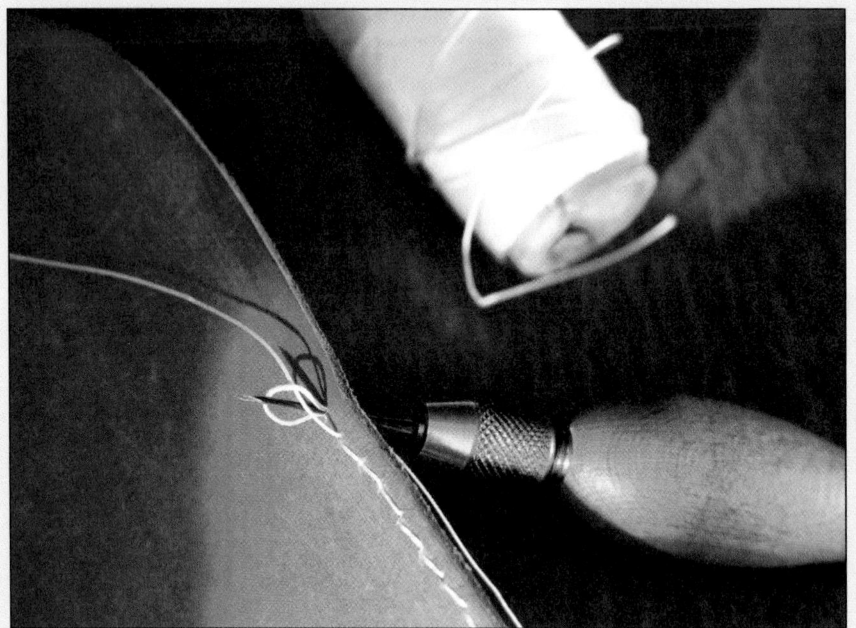

Think Critically:

1. Do you agree with Delia or Lorenzo about whether they need a consultant? Explain.
2. How could a consultant help them?
3. Could the Small Business Administration be of help? How?

PROJECT: MY BUSINESS, INC.

As a new business owner, you must be able to assess the financial needs of your business realistically. You will need this information to obtain financing and make operating decisions.

DATA COLLECTION

1. Locate a source that provides sample financial information for small retail businesses (especially fast-food or specialty-food businesses). You should be able to find average figures for balance sheets and income statements as well as average financial ratios. The Internet as well as most libraries have the needed information.
2. Obtain copies of a balance sheet and an income statement for a small business. These statements are often available in small business management textbooks, in financial magazines, or from the Small Business Administration (www.sba.gov). Review the

type of information included and think about how a business owner might use each of the forms.

ANALYSIS

1. Prepare a beginning estimated balance sheet for your new business. It should show the planned financial position of your business for its first day of operation.
2. Prepare an estimated income statement for the first three months of the operation of your business. Be realistic in your estimates. You may not show a profit.

FINANCING A BUSINESS

OBJECTIVES

- **17-1** Distinguish between equity (owner) capital, retained earnings, and debt (creditor) capital.
- **17-2** Explain the differences between common and preferred stock, and discuss three ways to value stock.
- **17-3** Discuss ways that companies can obtain short-term and long-term debt capital.
- **17-4** Describe important factors companies consider in deciding how to obtain the capital they need.
- **17-5** Discuss common sources of outside capital for companies.

SHOW ME THE MONEY!

The Video Shoppe opened for business in a popular mall a few years ago. Eva Diaz, its owner, used her entire savings to launch "The Shoppe," as she called it. After losing money the first year, she nearly closed down. But through hard work and creative marketing, Eva has made The Shoppe quite successful. Furthermore, she left all the profits in the business except for a modest amount of cash for personal living expenses.

Today, Caleb Wegman, her accountant and friend, was in the back room balancing the books. As Caleb finished his work, Eva excitedly asked, "Can I open another shop with my current earnings?"

Caleb's shocked response was fast. "No. Your earnings are good, but your balance sheet needs more muscle."

"But Caleb, my business sense tells me I could open other shops and begin making healthy profits right away. Don't tell me no. Tell me how. And let's not think of opening one shop. My idea is to have a chain of shops within the next two years."

Caleb, somewhat startled by Eva's bold plan, was momentarily speechless. "But how would you finance a chain?" Caleb asked.

"I was hoping you could give me some ideas," Eva replied. "For starters, I have an aunt who might be able to lend me some money. Perhaps my bank would provide a loan. Maybe my brother. . . ."

"Your family might help some," Caleb interrupted, "but you'll need 'big' dollars. Right now, I have to see my next client. Until I return next week, think about forming a partnership with someone or a corporation so you could sell stock to others."

After Caleb left, Eva sat wondering how she could raise the money to expand her business. "Strike now while the market is hot," again entered her mind as three steady customers walked in.

Eva faces the same problem most successful business owners face—how to get financial backing. On a balance sheet, capital is a business's assets minus its liabilities. Capital also refers to the money required to start or expand a business. Businesses need capital to acquire assets.

Capital comes from many sources. Owners can provide it from their own savings. They can also obtain capital by borrowing, by buying business necessities on credit, or by making profits and leaving those profits in the business.

In this chapter, you will learn about various methods for raising capital and about important considerations when deciding upon sources of capital. In addition, you will learn how stocks and bonds are marketed to the public.

METHODS OF OBTAINING CAPITAL

Business owners have several options for obtaining the capital they need to start and operate their business. One way is to contribute their own money to the business. Business owners' personal contributions

ILLUSTRATION 17-1

When successful entrepreneurs want to enlarge their businesses, they often face the problem of raising large sums of capital. Other than from friends and family, where can a small business obtain money to enlarge or open branch stores?

to the business are called **equity capital** or **owner capital.** This capital may come from personal funds, such as from accumulated savings, or from funds the owners borrow using their homes or other personal property as security for the loan. Eva Diaz can consider such sources for expanding The Video Shoppe. As shown in Figure 17-1, small businesses rely heavily on equity capital.

A second way to obtain capital is through retained earnings. **Retained earnings** are the profits that the owners do not take out of the business but instead save for use by the business. Retained earnings are a type of equity capital, since profits belong to the owners of the business.

A third way of financing a business is through **debt capital,** or **creditor capital**—capital that others loan to a business. Banks and other types of lending institutions usually will not lend money to a business unless the equity capital exceeds the debt capital. As a result, businesses in financial difficulty often have trouble getting debt capital. McGraw's Pet Shop, as shown in Figure 17-2, might be able to get an additional loan from the bank because its liabilities, or debt, are much less than its equity capital. However, if its liabilities were $240,000 and its equity capital were $160,000, the Pet Shop probably would not get the loan.

EQUITY CAPITAL

To finance a business by acquiring equity capital, the proprietor has several alternatives. The owner can sell personal assets, borrow from an individual, or mortgage personal property.

The sole owner of a business can also obtain additional funds by (1) forming a partnership and requiring the new partner to invest money in the business or by (2) forming a corporation and bringing in owners by selling stock. A business that expands in one of these ways might increase its sales and profits, but the profits must be shared among more owners. In the short run, the result may be less profitable for

Percentage of Businesses

Sources	Percentage of Businesses
Personal Savings	79%
Banks	50%
Friends and Relatives	25%
Investors	10%
Suppliers	8%
Other	6%

Sources

FIGURE 17-1

Sources of Capital to Start a New Business

Source: *New Business in America, The NFIB Foundation*

McGraw's Pet Shop
Balance Sheet
July 31, 20--

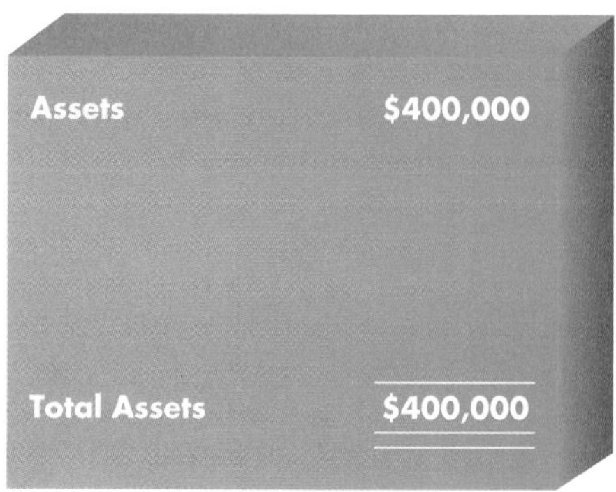

Liabilities:	
Creditor Capital	
Debt Capital Obtained from Bank	**$160,000**
Capital:	
Proprietary Capital	
Equity Capital Invested by Owner	**$240,000**
Total	**$400,000**

FIGURE 17-2

Relationship Between Debt and Equity Capital as Shown in a Balance Sheet

each owner. To raise capital, therefore, the business owner must estimate whether it will be more profitable to remain a sole owner or form a partnership or a corporation. Eva Diaz must deal with this question if she wishes to expand her Video Shoppe.

Assume that the proprietor decides to secure additional equity capital by incorporating and selling shares of stock. **Stock** (or a *share*) is a

ILLUSTRATION 17-2

Corporations obtain capital by selling stock. Can sole proprietorships and partnerships sell stock? Where would you go to buy a share of stock?

share of ownership in a corporation. Stocks, as well as bonds, are known as **securities.** Corporations issue two kinds of stock: common stock and preferred stock.

COMMON STOCK **Common stock** is stock that gives holders the right to share in the corporation's profits and to participate in managing the business by voting on basic issues. When the corporation makes a profit, stockholders share in the profit by receiving dividends. Typically, both Class A and Class B stockholders are entitled to dividends, but only Class A stockholders may vote. No common stockholders, however, receive dividends until all other investors have been paid. Furthermore, the dividend rate on common stock can vary over time. For young firms, there may be no dividends for a number of years.

PREFERRED STOCK **Preferred stock** is stock that gives holders first claim on corporate dividends and other assets after debts have been paid, but holders have no voting rights. A corporation must use its earnings first to pay its debts. Then some portion of the remaining profits may be distributed to stockholders as dividends. Preferred stockholders receive a fixed dividend based on a percentage of the stock's face value. The corporation must pay this dividend to preferred stockholders before common stockholders get anything. If any profits remain, the corporation can then pay dividends to common stockholders.

For example, suppose that a corporation issues $100,000 of 7 percent preferred stock and $100,000 of common stock. Further assume that profits for the year are $10,000. The preferred stockholders would receive 7 percent of $100,000, or $7,000. Only $3,000 would be left for the holders of common stock. Their return on $100,000 would yield only 3 percent ($3,000/$100,000).

But what would happen if the same corporation earns $31,000 in profits during the following year? In this case, the preferred stockholders would be paid their fixed rate of dividends (7 percent of $100,000), or $7,000, and $24,000 would be left to distribute to the common stockholders. If the entire amount were distributed, subject to approval of the board of directors, the holders of the common stock would receive a dividend of 24 percent ($24,000/$100,000).

Normally, a good policy for a firm is not to distribute all of its profits. It is better to hold some of its profits in reserve (retained earnings) for use in the business. If the corporation distributes all of its profits as dividends to stockholders, it may later need to borrow money to carry on its operations. As illustrated in Figure 17-3, corporations usually distribute some of their profits as dividends and keep some in the business as retained earnings. In addition, if the corporation earns no profit during a particular period, it can use retained earnings to pay dividends that period. If the corporation pays out all of its profits to stockholders, it has no retained earnings to fall back on during tough times.

Preferred stockholders have priority over common stockholders with regard to not only dividends but also assets. For instance, if the corporation ceases operations, its assets belong to its owners, the stockholders. The assets are first distributed to preferred stockholders. If any remain, they go to common stockholders.

What would happen if a corporation with $500,000 of outstanding common stock and $500,000 of outstanding preferred stock ceased operating? Assume that after selling all of the assets for cash and after paying all of its creditors, $800,000 in cash remains. The sum of $500,000 (the face value of the preferred stock) must be paid to the preferred stockholders, because their stock has asset priority. As a result, the common stockholders would receive only $300,000, which is 60 percent of the full face value of their stock ($300,000/$500,000). If no one had priority in receiving assets, both common and preferred stockholders would have shared equally, with each group receiving $400,000.

When a corporation ceases operations, preferred and common stockholders seldom get much money from the assets. The assets that are sold often do not raise enough cash to pay the creditors, who must be paid before either preferred or common stockholders are paid.

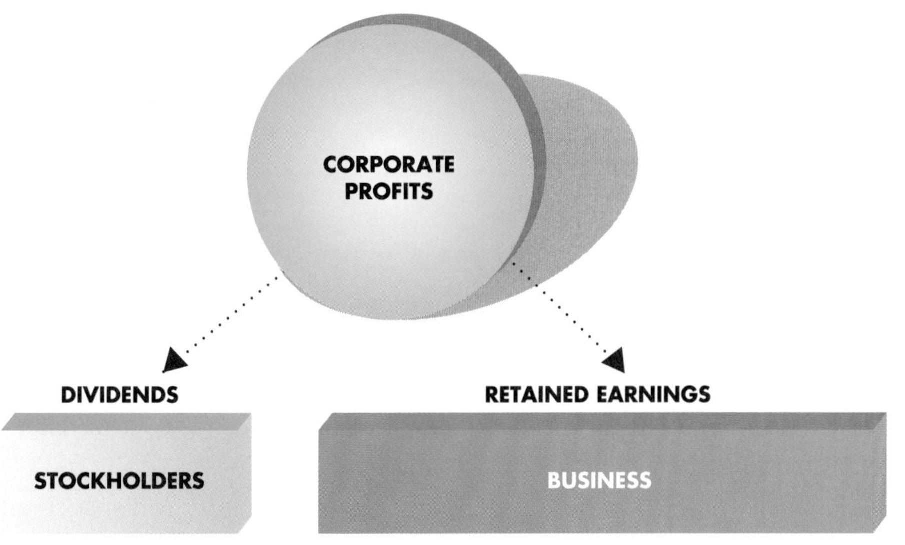

FIGURE 17-3

A corporation distributes some profits to stockholders and retains the rest.

VALUE OF STOCK There are three ways to look at the value of stock: its (1) market value, (2) par or stated value, and (3) book value. Its **market value** is the price investors pay for the stock on any given day. The dollar value printed on the stock certificate is its **par value** or **stated value.** This is an arbitrarily assigned amount that is used for bookkeeping purposes. This arbitrary amount, such as $1, has little practical value, because it does not indicate the current worth of the stock. A company whose stock shows a par value of $1, for example, may have a market value of over $100, depending upon how well it has performed financially. The real value of stock is not the par value but the amount buyers are willing to pay for it.

The **book value** of a share of stock is found by dividing the corporation's net worth (assets minus liabilities) by the total number of shares outstanding. Thus, if the corporation's net worth is $75,000,000 and the number of shares of stock outstanding is 1,000,000, the book value of each share is $75 ($75,000,000/1,000,000), regardless of the stock's par value or market value. Book value is used in special situations, such as to help determine the value of an entire business that is about to be sold. Book value may also be used, in part, to estimate the amount of money to distribute to shareholders when a corporation is dissolved.

KIND OF STOCK TO ISSUE Corporations must determine the kind of stock to issue. The certificate of incorporation states whether all authorized stock is common stock or whether part is common and part preferred. Corporations can issue no other stock unless they receive authorization from the government.

It is usually a good practice to issue only common stock when starting a business. Even though the new corporation may earn profits from the very beginning, it is often wise to use those profits to expand the business, rather than to distribute the profits as dividends. Although a corporation often pays dividends to holders of common stock, it is not required to do so. When the corporation issues preferred stock, however, it is obligated to pay the specified dividend from its profits. If it issues only common initially and it later wants to expand, it may then issue preferred stock in order to encourage others to invest in the business.

RETAINED EARNINGS

Rather than distribute all profits earned as dividends, a business should reserve some of its earnings to reinvest in the business. This is called "plowing back" earnings. A business plows back earnings for some or all of the following reasons:

1. Replacement of buildings and equipment as the result of depreciation (wearing out).
2. Replacement of equipment as a result of obsolescence (out of date).
3. Addition of new facilities for expanding the business.
4. Financial protection during periods of low sales and profits, such as recessions and tough competitive times.

ILLUSTRATION 17-3

Businesses may choose to pay for expansion with retained earnings rather than through borrowing. How does a business obtain retained earnings?

Even when the business is not making a profit, it should plan to replace assets that decrease in value because of depreciation or obsolescence. For instance, a car rental company may start operations with new cars. The company may not make a profit, but it may have considerable cash available each month. If the owners of the business remove the retained earnings, funds will not be available with which to buy new cars when the present ones wear out.

Retained earnings are not kept in the form of cash only. Retained earnings may be tied up in such current assets as inventories and accounts receivable, which are later converted to cash. Since retained earnings are a part of owner's equity, the earnings can be used for investment purposes and for future expansion.

DEBT CAPITAL

Regardless of size, businesses often borrow capital to pay expenses, replace their merchandise inventory, buy supplies, or purchase equipment. Much of this capital is made available from the savings of individuals. Millions of people deposit their savings in banks and in other financial institutions that lend these funds to businesses. Since a business can borrow for as few as 30 days or for several years or longer, debt capital is of two types: short term and long term.

SHORT-TERM CAPITAL **Short-term capital** is debt capital that must be repaid with interest within a year, and often in 30, 60, or 90 days. Short-term capital may be obtained from a bank or other lending institution.

Obtaining Funds from Banks. Before lending, banks want to be fairly certain that the borrowers will repay their loans. Figure 17-4 lists some of the questions that banks may ask borrowers. If they receive satis-

Questions That May Be Asked About a Borrower

FIGURE 17-4

Lenders ask borrowers many questions before lending them money.

1. **Is the borrower of good character?**
2. **Is the borrower putting up enough cash?**
3. **What experience has the borrower had in this business?**
4. **Will the loan be secured properly? Will payments on debts be made from profits only?**
5. **Will financing be sound? (Lender will want to see the net worth to debt and the cash-to-cash needs ratios; also the debt payments to income ratio.)**
6. **Is enough cash being raised to supply needs:**
   for repairs on buildings and equipment?
   for modernization, new equipment?
   to build up accounts receivable?
   for build-up of inventory expansion?
7. **How good is the estimate of salaries, wages, utilities, advertising, supplies, taxes, insurance, and other expenses?**
8. **What are the terms of the lease or mortgage? What amount must be paid in taxes?**
9. **Does the borrower have good accounting knowledge?**
10. **Does the borrower keep proper accounting records?**

factory answers to these questions, banks may grant a loan or an open line of credit. An **open line of credit** is the authorization to borrow up to a specified amount for a specified period of time. For example, a business may be allowed a line of credit up to $50,000 for a year. Whenever it needs to borrow, it may do so up to the $50,000 limit. Should the business borrow $10,000, it could still borrow an additional $40,000 during the year. Another form of debt equity is a small business credit card, which has a somewhat lower interest rate than personal credit cards.

When a business wants to borrow money from a lending institution, whether the business has a line of credit or not, it must sign a promissory note. A **promissory note** (see Figure 17-5) is an unconditional written promise to pay to the lender a certain sum of money at a particular time or on demand.

If the bank has some doubt about the ability of the firm to repay a loan, it may require the business to pledge its accounts receivable or merchandise inventory as security for the loan. If the loan is not repaid, the bank can claim the money collected from the accounts of customers or can reclaim the merchandise and sell it.

Obtaining Funds from Other Sources. Depending upon the type of business, it may have access to other sources of short-term capital. Owners with life insurance policies can borrow from the insurance com-

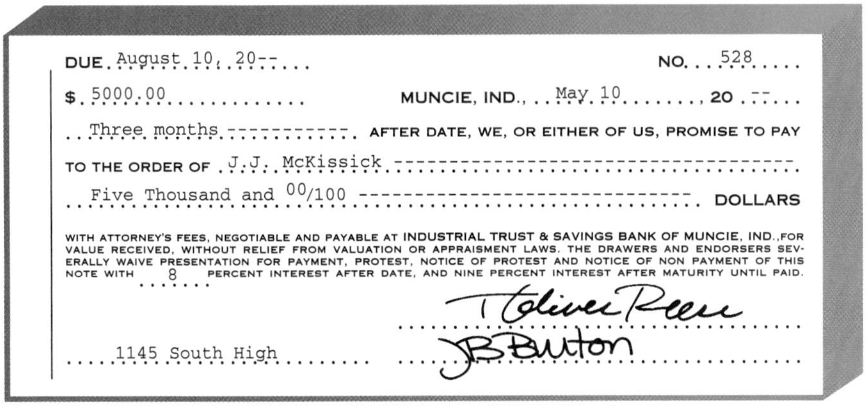

DUE August 10, 20-- NO. 528

$ 5000.00 MUNCIE, IND., May 10 20 --

Three months AFTER DATE, WE, OR EITHER OF US, PROMISE TO PAY

TO THE ORDER OF J.J. McKissick

Five Thousand and 00/100 DOLLARS

WITH ATTORNEY'S FEES, NEGOTIABLE AND PAYABLE AT INDUSTRIAL TRUST & SAVINGS BANK OF MUNCIE, IND., FOR VALUE RECEIVED, WITHOUT RELIEF FROM VALUATION OR APPRAISMENT LAWS. THE DRAWERS AND ENDORSERS SEVERALLY WAIVE PRESENTATION FOR PAYMENT, PROTEST, NOTICE OF PROTEST AND NOTICE OF NON PAYMENT OF THIS NOTE WITH 8 PERCENT INTEREST AFTER DATE, AND NINE PERCENT INTEREST AFTER MATURITY UNTIL PAID.

1145 South High

FIGURE 17-5

A Promissory Note

pany, using the current cash value of their policy as security for the loan. Credit unions (described in the next chapter) are also a source of debt financing. Federal agencies can assist small business owners in borrowing funds. Some states, cities, counties, and towns offer loans at favorable rates to encourage businesses to locate in a particular area or to encourage businesses not to leave.

A **factor** is a firm that specializes in lending money to businesses based on the business's accounts receivable. The usual practice, however, is that the factor purchases the company's accounts receivable at a discount and then collects the full amount when customers pay their bills. In a similar manner, a **sales finance company** purchases installment sales contracts at a discount from businesses that need cash or that do not care to handle collections. A sales finance company may also lend money to a business and use the business's installment contracts as security for the loan.

LONG-TERM CAPITAL **Long-term capital** is capital borrowed for longer than a year. A business usually obtains such debt capital by issuing long-term notes and bonds.

Notes. Notes are a significant source of capital in modern business. Written for periods of 1 to 15 years, they are often called **long-term notes** or **term loans.** Because term loans extend for a long period, lending institutions require the principal and interest to be repaid on a regular basis over the life of the note.

Long-term notes are often used to purchase equipment. Rather than borrow large sums of money to buy an expensive piece of equipment, however, a company may prefer to lease it. A **lease** is a contract that allows the use of an asset for a fee paid on a schedule, such as monthly. Leasing is a practical substitute for long-term financing, especially if capital is difficult to obtain. For example, like a business, you may wish to lease rather than buy cars, because they are costly, constantly changing, and soon obsolete. Even though you would not legally own the car, you would have full use of it for the life of the lease. The maintenance of the asset, your leased car, may be included in the leasing agreement.

CYBER COMMUNICATION

With the rise of e-mail usage in both personal and business situations, some abuses have become widespread. These abuses reflect negatively upon the e-mail sender. Observe a few common-sense rules of etiquette—or "netiquette"—when you use e-mail.

- Avoid hostile or thoughtless statements that invite similar responses in return. Consider your comments and responses carefully before communicating something you'll regret later. Think about the tone and feeling of your message—as well as the words. Remember that a message you send can always be forwarded to someone else—whom you may not want to read it!
- Use ordinary capitalization. Using all caps is considering "shouting."
- Watch for spelling, punctuation, and grammar errors, which are easy to commit when keying quickly.
- Read your mail as soon as possible. Let the sender know if your response must be delayed. Allowing unread messages to sit in your mailbox defeats the purpose of e-mail.
- Send copies of messages to the smallest number of people necessary. Most users are busy and don't want to read messages that aren't relevant to them.

ACTIVITY Assume that you are a supervisor in a business, and you discover that one of your employees sends e-mail messages that violate "netiquette." Write what you would say to the employee about the importance of using effective e-mail techniques in a business situation.

Bonds. A **bond** is a long-term written promise to pay a definite sum of money at a specified time. The issuer must pay the bondholder the amount borrowed—called the *principal* or *par value*—at the bond's maturity or due date. Bonds also include an agreement to pay interest at a specified rate at certain intervals. Bonds are usually issued in units of $1,000—for example, $1,000, $5,000, or $10,000.

Bonds are debt equity and do not represent a share of ownership in a corporation. Rather, they are debts the corporation owes to bondholders. People buy bonds as investments, as they do stocks. But bondholders are creditors, not owners, so they have a priority claim against the earnings of a corporation. Bondholders must be paid before stockholders share in the earnings.

There are two general types of bonds: debenture and mortgage bonds. **Debentures** are unsecured bonds. No specific assets are pledged as security. Debentures are backed by the faith and credit of the corporation that issues them. Public corporations, such as city, state, and federal governments, usually issue debentures when they need to borrow money. Reputable, successful corporations usually find it relatively easy to sell debentures. However, relatively unknown and financially weak firms usually find it easier to attract investors with secured bonds. **Mortgage bonds** are bonds secured by specific assets pledged as a guarantee that the principal and interest will be paid according to the terms specified on the bond certificate. Property often used as security includes real estate, equipment, stocks and bonds held in other companies, and life insurance policies. If the company does not pay the principal and interest when due, creditors can take legal action to collect the value of the debt. Creditors can force the company to sell the pledged property to recover the amount of the outstanding debt. Often, however, property cannot be sold for the amount of the loan. In some cases, a bond contract may have a provision that allows bondholders to claim assets other than the assets originally used as security.

Businesses issue debentures and mortgage bonds when they need funds for an extended period. Special features may be attached to these bonds to attract investors. For example, a mortgage bond can have a convertible feature to make it appealing to bond buyers. A **convertible bond** permits a bondholder to exchange bonds for a prescribed number of shares of common stock.

SELECTING A METHOD OF OBTAINING CAPITAL

Companies consider three important factors when deciding how to get the capital they need: (1) the original cost of obtaining the capital, (2) the interest rate, and (3) the power that the contributors of capital will have to influence business operations.

COST OF CAPITAL

It can be costly for a business to obtain capital by selling bonds, long-term notes, and new stock issues. For example, to launch a new bond issue, the business must file forms, obtain approvals from government authorities, make agreements, print bonds, find buyers, and keep careful records. These costs are usually so high that only large or highly successful firms even consider obtaining capital by issuing new stocks or bonds. It is far less costly to obtain capital from a simple mortgage or a note.

INTEREST RATES

As suggested in Figure 17-6, interest rates can vary from week to week and from month to month. Borrowing when rates are low will cost less than borrowing when rates are high. If a business needs money when interest rates are high, it will usually borrow for a short time with the hope that rates will drop. If rates drop, it can then issue long-term obligations, such as bonds, and use a portion of the capital obtained to pay off short-term obligations. In this way, a company has to pay high interest rates for only a short time. In following this plan, however, a business exposes itself to possible difficulty in obtaining funds when short-term obligations fall due, and to the possibility that interest rates may rise even higher.

POWER OF CONTRIBUTORS

If short-term creditors contribute capital, they usually have no control over the affairs of the business. If the obligations are not paid, creditors can take legal action to recover the amount due. Otherwise, owners of the business are relatively unrestricted by short-term creditors.

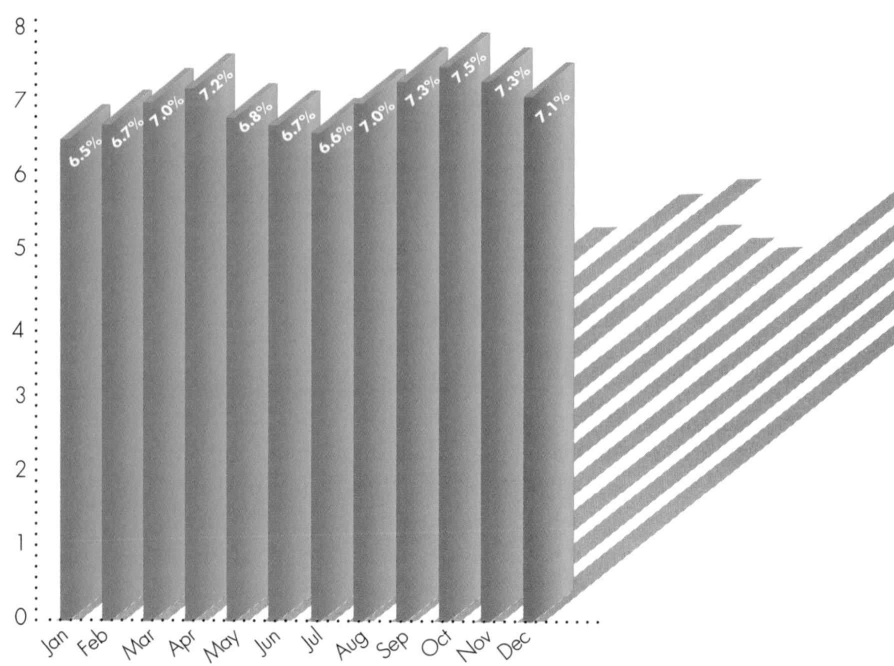

FIGURE 17-6

Because interest rates change frequently, the cost of borrowing also changes.

If the company obtains capital from mortgage bonds, however, the holders usually have a lien (claim) on at least part of the assets of the company. This lien may impose limitations on the use of these assets, and the agreement under which the mortgage bonds were issued may limit the use of the income of the company.

If new stockholders or new partners contribute equity capital, they gain a voice in the management of the business. In most states, stock can be issued that does not have voting rights, but such stock may be difficult to sell. Of course, if existing stockholders or partners provide the additional funds, the control of the company will not be affected as long as the existing stockholders contribute in proportion to past holdings.

If the company increases the number of shares of stock by selling new shares to stockholders, it must share earnings with an increased number of shareholders. For example, when the number of shareholders increases from 2,000 to 2,500, the distribution of $130,000 in dividends changes from $65 per share ($130,000/2,000) to $52 per share ($130,000/2,500). The original owners may not wish to give up any of their profits or voice in management unless it is profitable to do so. An increase in shareholders would need to be offset by an increase in earnings.

SOURCES OF OUTSIDE CAPITAL

When a business decides to obtain capital, it must find sources. Some common sources of capital are shown in Figure 17-7. The particular

Sources of Capital

1. Banks and related financial firms (the most popular source of outside capital)
2. Small loan companies (firms that lend money to individuals and businesses that may involve more risk than other lenders might accept)
3. Venture capital firms (companies that lend large sums of money to promising new or growing businesses)
4. Commercial credit companies (companies that lend money on current assets, such as accounts receivable and notes receivable)
5. Sales finance companies (used primarily when installment sales are involved; these firms purchase installment sales contracts)
6. Insurance companies (portions of funds collected from policyholders may be loaned to firms)
7. Individual investors and investment groups
8. Pension funds (retirement funds collected from employees may be loaned to firms)
9. Investment banking organizations (firms that specialize in selling new security issues to the public)
10. Equipment manufacturers (firms that do not actually lend money, but will sell needed equipment on an extended-time payment plan)

FIGURE 17-7

Businesses can get capital from many sources.

source a business selects depends, in part, on such factors as the amount of capital needed and the risk involved. Companies with a poor performance record find it hard to sell stocks or bonds to potential investors. A newly formed company has similar difficulties in securing a loan. Many banks avoid doing business with these types of organizations because of the added risk. When they do assist such firms, interest rates and other charges will be much higher than for successful firms.

ILLUSTRATION 17-4

When a business decides to obtain capital, sources must be found. How could a business decide which source to use?

INVESTMENT BANKS

Typical community banks do not generally become involved in helping large organizations raise capital by selling stocks and bonds. For these services, a corporation may turn to an **investment bank**—an organization that helps a business raise large sums of capital through the sales of stocks and bonds. Investment banks can also assist a rapidly growing small company through an **initial public offering,** or **IPO.** An IPO is the first time that a company sells stock to the public. It is also known as "going public." In recent years, many fast-growing Internet firms have raised money through IPOs.

The process of selling securities is simple but expensive. Assume a corporation wishes to raise $50 million by selling bonds. It first finds a willing investment bank. The bank offers advice, buys the bonds at a price below the expected market value, and then sells the bonds to the investing public through its marketing channels. The bank's profit would be the difference between what it paid the corporation for the bonds and the selling price it receives from the bond purchasers.

STOCK RIGHTS OPTIONS

Some corporations, on the other hand, may wish to sell only a small number of additional shares of stock. In such cases, a corporation can handle the sale itself. The sale of additional shares can be made attractive to current stockholders by offering stock rights options. A **stock rights option** is a contract that allows stockholders to buy additional shares for less than the market price for a specified period of time. These options give current stockholders the opportunity to buy enough stock at a bargain price to maintain the same percentage of ownership in the company as they had before the new stock was issued. The

ILLUSTRATION 17-5

Venture capitalists provide large sums of money to people who want to start new companies. What do you think would most influence a venture capitalist's loan decision?

MANAGEMENT CLOSE-UP

UNITED PARCEL SERVICE

Almost daily, most Americans see UPS brown vans driven by people in brown uniforms delivering packages to businesses and consumers. The United Parcel Service also flies brown airplanes to make deliveries in many other countries. Since 1927, much of the company's owners equity is held by the original owners and by those who participate in the firm's popular employee stock option plan. UPS is a financially healthy company with plenty of assets and retained earnings. So why did it need to sell shares of stock to the public? Here's the story.

UPS launched an IPO (Initial Public Offering) that at the time was the largest in Wall Street history. With its sound financial position and growth strategy, it must still compete with its arch rival, Federal Express. The real reason it sold the stock was to benefit its current owners, the men and women who wear or once wore those brown uniforms. Its purpose was not the same as the typical fast-growing firm that wants additional equity capital to gain large sums for expansion. Rather, UPS wanted the stock sale to obtain cash to buy back stock held by current managers and workers plus retirees and the families of company founders if they wish. Up to this time, the firm has been a closely held corporation, not a publicly held corporation. As explained in Chapter 6, a closely held corporation cannot sell its shares on any public stock exchange.

The IPO's main investment bank was Morgan Stanley Dean Witter, which raised what was then a record-setting $5.27 billion minus investment bank costs and issued 109.4 million shares of Class B stock. The firm's employees own Class A stock but could not easily sell shares to others as a closely held corporation. The IPO now permits the public and UPS employees as well as retirees and other investors to buy and sell UPS stock conveniently. In fact, soon after the IPO was completed, the firm offered to buy the stock from its shareholders at a price higher than the market price. All shareholders—insiders and outsiders—were pleased.

THINK CRITICALLY

1. Why would UPS sell Class A stock rather than Class B stock?
2. Assume you are considering buying ten shares of Class B stock in UPS. Do you think you would have to pay more, less, or the same as the people who buy Class A stock? Give reasons.
3. If you were retired or nearing retirement at UPS, how would you benefit from both the IPO and the firm's offer to buy stock from its shareholders? If you were an investor but not a present or past employee, how would you benefit from UPS's actions?
4. Using your library or the Internet, decide whether today you would prefer to become an owner of stock in UPS or Federal Express. Offer reasons for your answer.

lower price may attract more funds to the corporation without the additional expense of selling through an investment banker. If stockholders do not wish to take advantage of their stock rights, they can sell their options to others within a stated period at a small gain. Employers sometimes offer employees stock rights options as part of an employee stock ownership plan (ESOP).

VENTURE CAPITALISTS

A **venture capitalist** is an investor or investment group that lends large sums of money to promising new or expanding small companies. These investors expect some of the businesses to fail, but they accept the risks in the expectation that enough will succeed to more than offset losses. These investors demand a carefully developed business plan (see Chapter 5 for details) that shows high potential for success. Venture capitalists, many of whom are former entrepreneurs, have helped many small firms become large successful firms.

CHAPTER CONCEPTS

- Businesses can obtain capital in three ways: sell ownership shares in the company (equity or owner capital), keep profits in the company (retained earnings), and borrow (debt capital).
- Equity capital is the investment owners have in a business. For corporations, common and preferred stock are shares of ownership. Retained earnings are profits that have not been distributed to stockholders but may be used to help firms survive hard times as well as to expand.
- Debt capital is either short- or long-term loans, such as notes and bonds, which must be paid back with interest to the lenders. Types of debt financing include loans obtained through banks, business credit cards, open lines of credit, and factors.
- When equity financing is used to raise capital, owners give up some ownership rights regarding decision making and sharing of profits. Debt financing creates a legal obligation to pay back the lenders, usually on a fixed schedule. The lenders have priority rights to be paid before the business owners.
- Large sums of outside capital can be obtained through initial public offerings (IPOs) and from venture capitalists. Firms desiring rapid growth often use these sources. The costs for raising such capital can be high, especially for companies selling bonds and raising funds through IPOs. Large firms hire investment bankers with special expertise to assist in obtaining such capital.

BUILD VOCABULARY POWER

Define the following terms and concepts.

1. equity capital (owner capital)
2. retained earnings
3. debt capital (creditor capital)
4. stock
5. securities
6. common stock
7. preferred stock
8. market value
9. par value (stated value)
10. book value
11. short-term capital
12. open line of credit
13. promissory note
14. factor
15. sales finance company
16. long-term capital
17. long-term notes (term loans)
18. lease
19. bond
20. debentures
21. mortgage bond
22. convertible bond
23. investment bank
24. initial public offering (IPO)
25. stock rights option
26. venture capitalist

REVIEW FACTS

1. On a balance sheet, what is the meaning of capital?
2. What are three methods of obtaining capital?

3. What is the difference between equity capital and debt capital?
4. Are holders of common stock the first investors to get dividends?
5. Are preferred stockholders guaranteed a fixed dividend?
6. Do preferred stockholders ordinarily have voting privileges in the management of the business?
7. When a corporation goes out of business, are both preferred and common stockholders likely to get much money from the assets?
8. What is the relationship between the par value of stock and its market value?
9. How is the book value of a share of stock calculated?
10. List two situations in which book value might be used.
11. What are some questions that a borrower must be prepared to answer when applying for a loan?
12. List three ways that a corporation obtains long-term debt capital.
13. What is the principal difference between mortgage bonds and debentures?
14. What three factors should companies consider when deciding how to get the capital they need?
15. What is the major service provided by investment banks?

DISCUSS IDEAS

1. Distinguish between types of equity capital and debt capital.
2. Why do you think that a corporation's preferred stock would probably cost more per share than its common stock?
3. Why should a business retain some of its profits as a reserve?
4. Why might a bank require a business to pledge its accounts receivable or merchandise inventory as security for a loan?
5. When might a business lease, rather than purchase, equipment?
6. Explain the importance of an investor's owning secured debt as opposed to unsecured debt in the event a company is forced to go out of business.
7. Assume interest rates are high but a corporation needs to borrow money. Give an advantage and a disadvantage of borrowing capital for a short time rather than for a long period.
8. Why would a corporation wishing to raise $75 million by selling bonds hire an investment bank rather than handle the matter itself?
9. How can venture capitalists make a profit, even though they often invest in firms that eventually fail?
10. Assume that you are starting a new business. What do you think your greatest obstacles will be in obtaining funds for the new venture? Why?

ANALYZE INFORMATION

1. The assets of the Rosemont Corporation are $750,000; the accounts payable, $45,000; bonds payable, $100,000; common stock, $350,000; and preferred stock, $150,000. Does the corporation have a surplus or a deficit? By what amount?
2. Refer to The Barker-Trowe Corporation balance sheet provided and answer these questions:
   a. If the par value of both common and preferred stock is $10 a share, how many shares of each kind are outstanding?
   b. If the preferred and common stock shares have equal claims, what is the book value of each share?
   c. If the directors decide to distribute $9,600 as dividends, how much will be paid to preferred stockholders and how much to common stockholders?
   d. If a stockholder owns 10 shares of preferred stock and 10 shares of common stock, how much of the dividends in (c) should the stockholder receive?

The Barker-Trowe Corporation
Balance Sheet
December 31, 20--

ASSETS		
Cash		$ 37,000
Notes Receivable		1,000
Accounts Receivable		15,000
Merchandise		70,000
Equipment		16,000
Real Estate		96,000
Total Assets:		$235,000
LIABILITIES AND CAPITAL		
Notes Payable		$ 2,000
Accounts Payable		7,000
6% Bonds Payable		50,000
Common Stock:		
Authorized	$100,000	
Unissued	20,000	
Outstanding		80,000
7% Preferred Stock:		
Authorized	100,000	
Unissued	20,000	
Outstanding		80,000
Retained Earnings		16,000
Total Liabilities and Capital:		$235,000

3. The net profit of the Ajax Corporation has averaged $60,000 a year. There are 12,000 shares of common stock authorized, but only 6,000 are issued and outstanding. More capital is needed, and the owners might sell the additional 6,000 shares at $100 a share. It is estimated that the new capital will make it possible to increase the net profit to $90,000.
   a. What is the net profit per share now?
   b. What is the expected net profit per share if 6,000 new shares are sold?
   c. Does it appear to be a good action to take? Why or why not?
4. Don Cobb and Sandy Sanyal each own 2,000 shares of stock, representing all of the common stock outstanding in their own rural bottled gas company, a product that customers buy to heat their dwellings. They need $20,000, and they must decide whether to borrow the money, sell common stock, or sell preferred stock. They can: (a) borrow $20,000 for a period of three months—April, May, and June—and again for a period of three months—October, November, and December—at a yearly interest rate of 9 percent; (b) sell 2,000 additional shares of common stock at $10 each to raise a total of $20,000 for permanent working capital; or (c) sell 2,000 shares of preferred stock at $10 a share with a dividend rate of 11 percent. Assume that the profit of the company is $36,000 a year without anticipating any interest charges.
   a. How will the interest on the borrowed money affect Don and Sandy's profits if they borrow $20,000 as indicated?
   b. How will their profits be affected if they sell 2,000 shares of common stock?
   c. How will their profits be affected if they sell 2,000 shares of preferred stock?
5. A venture capitalist company invested in five new businesses during the past year. The results at the end of the year were as follows:

Business A: Loss	$ 500,000
Business B: Loss	900,000
Business C: Loss	250,000
Business D: Loss	50,000
Business E: Profit	2,500,000

   a. What was the total loss for the year?
   b. What was the net gain or loss for the year?
   c. Might investments in Businesses A, B, C, and D all be good? If yes, why?

SOLVE BUSINESS PROBLEMS

CASE 17-1

The Kyle Camping Company sells camping equipment and supplies and is located between a major state park and a national park in

New York State's Adirondack Mountains. Over the last two years the pace of business has doubled. Kyle used his personal savings to start the business and has saved $70,000 from his business earnings.

Kyle now wishes to expand his summer business to include supplies that boat owners might need on the area's lakes. He doesn't have enough capital to make an addition to his store, build a dock on the nearby lake for boating customers, and to build an inventory. To enable him to stay open year round, he also has a plan to sell hunting rifles and ammunition. Deer hunting is a popular sport in this area as is ice fishing. He also wants to create a Web site through which he could sell his merchandise plus provide hunting and fishing information.

Kyle is interested only in debt financing but is willing to consider equity financing as a last resort. A small community five miles away has a commercial bank where he has had good relations since starting his business five years ago. His credit rating is acceptable but not great; it is marred only by several late loan payments during the first two years of business. Kyle has calculated that he will need to find $75,000 to add a dock and fishing supplies this year and $30,000 additional capital next year to carry out all of his plans.

Think Critically:

1. If you were the local bank's loan officer, what type of general business and financial advice would you recommend to Kyle about his request?
2. Other than from his bank, what debt equity financial sources might Kyle consider, given his financial situation and his plans?
3. Why might Kyle wish to consider debt financing rather than equity financing?

CASE 17-2

Reiko Mori is a member of a four-person car pool. Morning conversations on the way to work often deal with what people did the night before. Reiko started the discussion today because she had attended a lecture last evening on investing in stocks and bonds. Selected parts of the conversation by car pool members follow:

Lou: *What did you learn that we don't already know, Reiko?*

Reiko: *I learned that there are all kinds of stocks and bonds. There's something to meet everyone's needs. But it's all quite confusing.*

Pablo: *My broker suggested I buy some new debentures, but I didn't understand what he was talking about. Did the lecturer explain these things?*

Reiko: *Not really. The lecturer spent nearly all the time talking about stocks. Maybe next week's lecture will cover bonds.*

Keisha: *My uncle gave Larry and me a mortgage bond for a wedding gift. We're going to keep it because the company has been doing great. I wish I had some stock in this company, too, but we can't afford it right now.*

Reiko: *Keisha, can you have lunch with me today? I did learn something about mortgage bonds that might be helpful.*

Think Critically:

1. Explain debentures to Pablo.
2. If you were having lunch with Keisha, what would you tell her about the mortgage bond she owns?

PROJECT: MY BUSINESS, INC.

A very important step in financial planning for a new business is to determine the amount of capital needed and the sources of that capital. Most new businesses fail because they do not have adequate capital to operate the business until it becomes profitable. Since you have already estimated your financial needs in the Chapter 16 activities, you now need to develop a plan to obtain the capital.

DATA COLLECTION

1. Identify three sources of long-term financing for your business. For each source, determine the (a) amount of capital available, (b) interest rate, (c) amount and type of security needed, and (d) procedures for obtaining financing.
2. Ask several small business owners how they obtained the initial financing for their businesses. Have them identify problems they have faced in financing continuing operations and any expansions.

ANALYSIS

1. Based on the amount of capital you will need to start your business and operate it for six months, determine:
   - **a.** The amount of money you can personally invest.
   - **b.** Capital available from family and friends. How you can obtain and repay the money?
   - **c.** Sources for the remaining capital needs, interest rates, and procedures for obtaining the capital.

2. Develop a written request for funds that can be presented to prospective investors. It must contain enough specific information to encourage them to invest money in your business. Develop the request on a computer so it has a professional look when printed. Provide supporting data including the appropriate financial statements and graphs or charts showing the source and amount of each type of capital.

FINANCIAL SERVICES

OBJECTIVES

- **18-1** Distinguish between banks and non-banks and the services they provide.
- **18-2** Describe common banking services, such as checking accounts and loans.
- **18-3** Explain why banks have added computer-related services, such as direct deposit, automatic teller machines, and electronic banking.
- **18-4** Describe investment instruments and the importance of liquidity, safety, and growth in investment planning.
- **18-5** Discuss basic concepts related to buying securities through stock markets.
- **18-6** Identify past and present governmental regulations that have changed the financial world.

WHAT SHOULD WE DO WITH THE MONEY?

Among his other duties, Andrew Jones is newly in charge of office and financial matters for the small but growing firm of Kilgore Appliances, distributor for all types of kitchen gadgets. During the morning break, he planned to discuss the large balance in Kilgore's checking account with Julie Vernon, the accountant. As they entered the nearby deli, Julie expressed her frustration in balancing this month's checking account.

"You know, Julie," Andrew commented, "we should start thinking of other places to park the excess amount of cash building up in that account. That's money not working for us."

"I agree, Andrew," Julie said. "We make no money in a regular checking account. And during the next three months, I don't see any heavy payment drains. Why don't we put some into short-term investments?"

Andrew paused and then remarked, "But we need answers to some questions first. Where can we put the money and earn the most on it? Is one bank any different from another? What investment opportunities exist for short and long time periods?"

"Andrew, let's work together on this," Julie replied. "Can you find time by lunch tomorrow to do some financial shopping? Then we can sort out our information and perhaps be ready to make a decision."

"Sounds like the right move to make, Julie. I'll try the savings and loan association down the street and our own commercial bank. Do you want to contact the new mutual savings bank near your home and perhaps the investment company that has been running ads in the local paper?"

Julie nodded her approval and then added, "See you at lunch tomorrow."

All businesses rely on the services of financial institutions. A business like Kilgore Appliances must deposit cash, make payments, invest excess funds, and borrow money. Knowledge of the available types of financial institutions and the services they provide help managers like Andrew and Julie operate businesses efficiently.

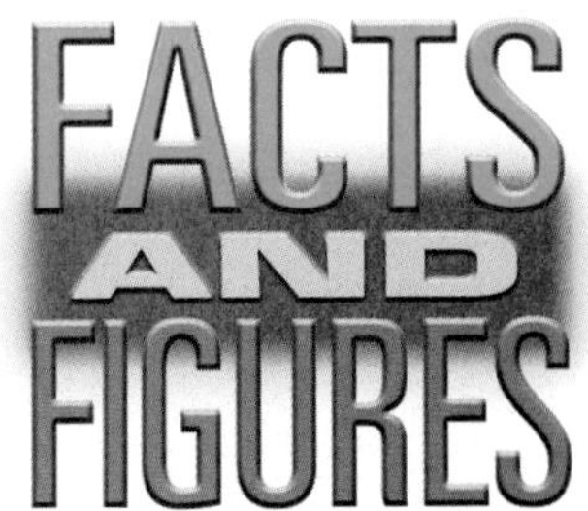

The banking industry has been consolidating sharply. In the mid-1970s, there were around 14,000 banks. By the year 2000, this number had decreased to 10,000.

FINANCIAL INSTITUTIONS

Financial institutions handle transactions that deal primarily with money and securities. While banks provide many of the needed services, other financial institutions also provide essential services. In fact, each year it is getting more and more difficult to distinguish among the services provided by various financial institutions.

In recent years, financial institutions have rapidly expanded the services they offer. Deregulation of banking, borrowing and investing online, and competitive pressures among institutions have affected much of our financial life. Computer technology and the Internet have contributed much to changing how the world conducts its financial affairs.

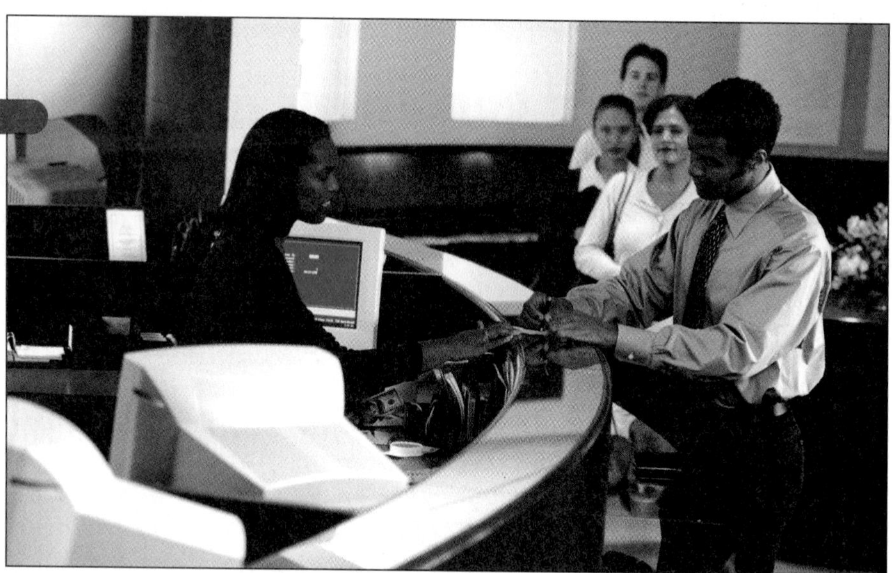

ILLUSTRATION 18-1

Competition among financial institutions has grown as the services offered become more similar. Can you name three financial institutions in your community from which you might obtain financial services?

DIFFERENCES AMONG BANKS

To be considered a **bank,** a financial institution must include among its services both demand deposits and commercial loans. A **demand deposit** is money put into a financial institution that the depositors can withdraw at any time without penalty. A checking account is a demand deposit account. Banks usually offer both commercial and consumer loans. A **commercial loan** is a loan made to a business, whereas a **consumer loan** is a loan made to an individual. If an institution offers either demand deposits or commercial loans, but not both, it is called a **non-bank financial institution,** or **non-bank.** As you will discover, the distinction between banks and non-banks is fading fast.

In the past, federal banking laws regulated banks more than non-banks. As a result, non-banks gained a competitive advantage over banks. To avoid regulation, some banks become non-banks by dropping commercial loans or demand deposits. To avoid intensive federal regulations, many corporations, such as American Express and General Motors, have added non-banks to their operations to provide customers with credit card, lending, and other financial services.

BANKING INSTITUTIONS

In spite of the changes that have occurred in the financial world, financial services have improved greatly in recent decades. The common types of banking institutions and their services are shown and briefly described in Figure 18-1.

Today, the majority of banking institutions provide a host of services. None, however, offers a more complete line of services that are more valuable to small businesses than the commercial bank. A **commercial bank** is a bank that offers a wide variety of financial services,

Common Banking Institutions

COMMERCIAL BANK

Handles time and demand deposits, commercial and consumer loans, and many other special services.

MUTUAL SAVINGS BANK OR SAVINGS BANK

Specializes in handling savings accounts and loans, particularly long-term loans such as mortgages.

TRUST COMPANY

Manages property such as securities, real estate, and cash as directed by its customers. May be a separate institution or a department within a commercial or savings bank.

SAVINGS AND LOAN ASSOCIATION

Specializes in savings accounts and home mortgage loans. Also known as S&L.

FIGURE 18-1

Financial institutions are available in most communities.

including savings and checking accounts and commercial and consumer loans. Commercial banks also rent safe deposit boxes and provide financial advice. They may even offer legal and tax advice, along with bill-paying and payroll-preparation services. Commercial banks can collect promissory notes and sell insurance. Many also sell stocks and mutual funds. Because commercial banks provide a variety of services, they are referred to as "full-service banks." Commercial banks outnumber all other types of banks.

NON-BANK FINANCIAL INSTITUTIONS

Non-bank financial institutions have grown rapidly because of the many valuable financial services they offer. One reason for growth is that they gradually overcame the demand-deposit disadvantage and may now offer check-writing services. Non-banks exist in many forms. Stock brokerage firms, for example, not only buy and sell stocks and bonds, but also offer checking privileges and even credit card services. The stock brokerage firm of Merrill Lynch, for example, also provides mortgages, insurance policies, and credit-card services for customers. On the other hand, banks may sell stocks and bonds if they wish. Fierce banking competition has benefited consumers through better and more abundant services at lower cost.

Credit unions are non-bank financial institutions created for employees in some large organizations. They provide many of the services available at banks but for members only. Insurance companies and business pension funds are also non-banks that offer long-term loans in large amounts to eligible businesses. Non-banks also include investment companies such as mortgage, insurance, and finance businesses as well as investment firms.

COMMON BANKING SERVICES

Two of the most common banking services are checking accounts and loans. Nearly all businesses need these services.

CHECKING ACCOUNTS

Checking accounts enable depositors to write checks rather than pay bills in cash. A **check** is a written order requiring the financial institution to pay previously deposited money to a third party on demand. Businesses use checks to pay for purchases, such as office furniture and inventory. When customers pay by check, the business must take precautions, such as requesting identification to make sure the check is not stolen or forged.

To cash or deposit a check, the person to whom the check is written—the *payee*—must endorse the check. An **endorsement** is the payee's signature on the back of the check. A properly written check and three types of endorsements are shown in Figures 18-2 and 18-3.

Banks send customers a monthly statement showing their deposits, their checks that payees have cashed, and bank service fees. Customers should compare the bank statement to their own record of deposits and checks written and reconcile any differences.

LOANS

Banks make many business loans. Before making a loan, banks require the business to clearly state the purpose of the loan and provide financial evidence to show that it can repay the loan. Most loans are for short time periods, usually less than one year. A business may need

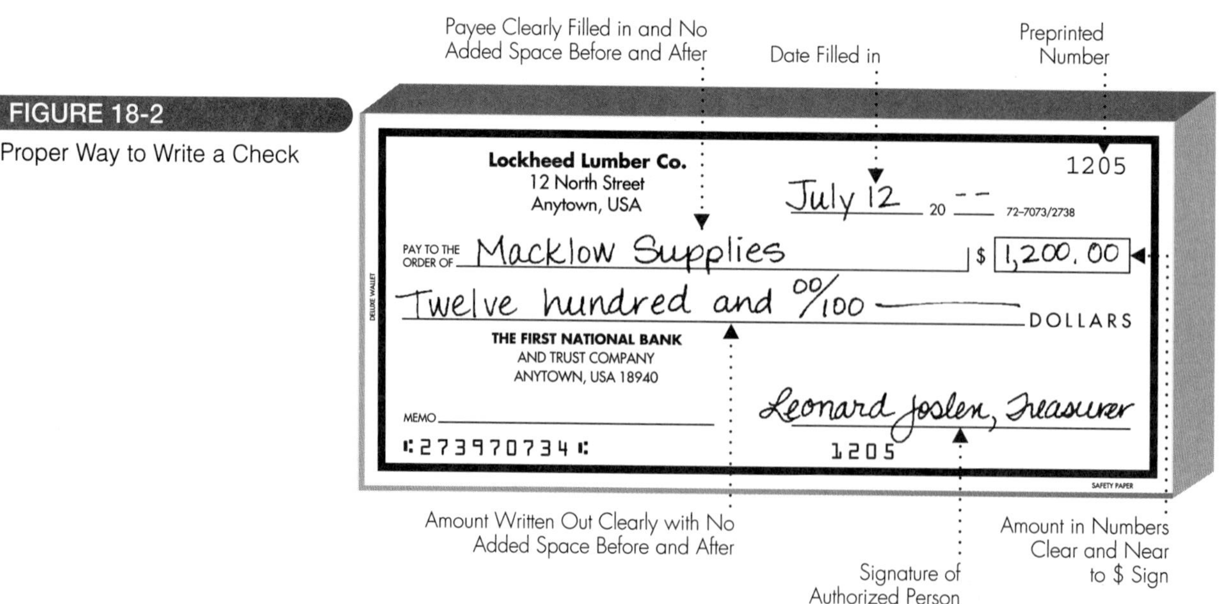

FIGURE 18-2

Proper Way to Write a Check

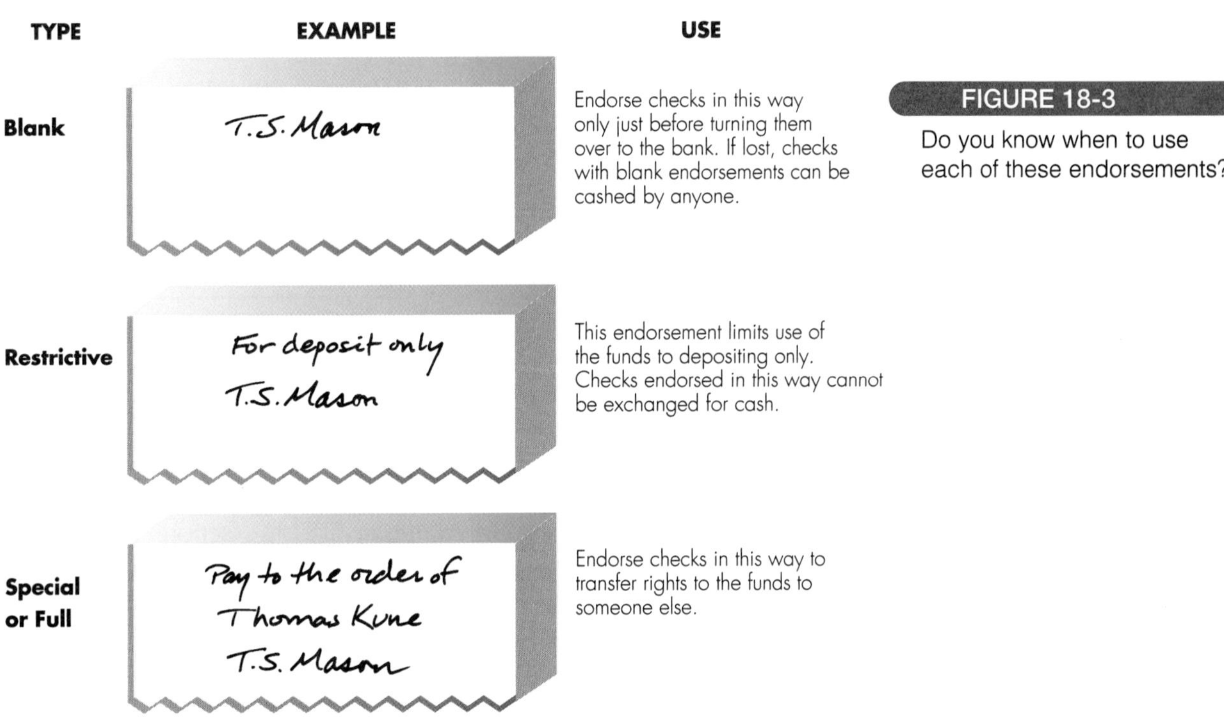

FIGURE 18-3

Do you know when to use each of these endorsements?

funds to cover operating expenses at certain times, such as when it needs new equipment or when sales are temporarily slow.

Collateral is property a borrower pledges to assure repayment of a loan. If the borrower does not repay the loan, the lender has the right to use the pledged property for repayment. An **unsecured loan** is a loan that is not backed by collateral. Usually only successful long-standing businesses can obtain unsecured loans. For new or less successful businesses, a bank may require a secured loan. A **secured loan,** also called a **collateral loan,** is a loan backed by something of value pledged to ensure repayment. For example, if an entrepreneur owned a fleet of cars for the business's salespeople and wanted to borrow $10,000, the fleet could become acceptable collateral. In case of failure to repay the loan, the bank could sell enough of the cars in the fleet to collect the money loaned. Often the loan is for an amount substantially less than the actual value of the collateral.

INTEREST RATES

Banks earn income when loaning money by charging interest for the life of the loan. Interest rates are based on the supply of and demand for money at any given time. As a result, the rate of interest can change daily, based upon general business conditions. The lowest rate is the **prime rate,** which is the rate at which large banks lend large sums to the best-qualified borrowers. Small loans and loans to less-qualified customers are made at rates higher than the prime rate. Borrowers and lenders must establish a specific repayment plan, so that the deal benefits both parties. Borrowers may be forced into bankruptcy and the lenders may be hurt financially when loans are not repaid. To help prevent losses, repaying a loan at intervals is safer than paying one lump sum at the end of the time period. Borrowers can then include the monthly payments in their budget plan.

COMPUTERS AND BANKING

Remarkable changes have occurred in banking practices over the last decade, thanks to the rapid development of computers. Much of the work once done by clerks, such as processing checks, recording deposits and withdrawals, and keeping customer accounts up to date, is now done electronically. **Electronic funds transfer (EFT),** transferring money by computer rather than by check, has enabled financial institutions to provide faster, improved services. For example, EFT transactions reduce the need for checks. Direct deposits, automatic teller machine transactions, and Internet banking are three common uses of EFTs. Debit cards, discussed in the next chapter, are another use of EFTs.

DIRECT DEPOSITS

A **direct deposit** is the electronic transfer of a paycheck directly from the employer's bank account into the employee's bank account. The use of direct-deposit banking has increased in popularity. Employees who select this service receive immediate use of their earnings. They no longer have to wait in line to cash checks or make deposits. For each pay period, the employer must provide the employee with a record listing gross pay and all deductions. The Social Security Administration and the Internal Revenue Service both prefer that individuals receiving checks from them use direct deposit. In this way, checks do not get lost or stolen.

Although the use of computers has created a revolution in banking, some persons fear that one result may be a "de-personalization" of service. One large bank charges its customers $3.00 to speak with a live teller.

AUTOMATIC TELLER MACHINES

An **automatic teller machine (ATM)** is a computer terminal that enables bank customers to deposit, withdraw, or transfer funds by using a bank-provided plastic card. ATMs are located at banks and at other convenient places, such as outside banks and inside malls. ATMs are also found in many foreign countries. ATMs are quick and convenient to use and are especially valuable for people who do not wish to carry large sums of money or who want to make transactions when banks are closed. In addition to attracting more customers with ATMs, banks lower operating costs by reducing the need for human tellers and increase income from service fees each time a customer withdraws cash. Furthermore, banks with ATMs need fewer branch offices to serve their customers.

Financial institutions try to reduce ATM-related crime by locating ATMs in well-lighted areas. Some have installed hidden cameras that may help police identify thieves. Along with crime, ATM customers are concerned about high withdrawal fees and having to pay an additional fee when withdrawing funds from another bank's ATM. For example, if your bank's ATM fee to withdraw $50 is $1.50, and you withdraw the money from a competitor's ATM that charges $2.50, you would pay $4 to obtain $50. Many customers object to paying both banks a high fee. Yet, with so much banking competition, ATM fees are another means for small banks to survive.

ILLUSTRATION 18-2

Why do consumers find it so appealing to use automatic teller machines?

ELECTRONIC BANKING

Electronic banking speeds business activities and serves customers more conveniently. Through computers, modems, and the Internet, banking without leaving the office or home has become common. Electronic banking makes it possible to obtain loans, pay bills, and transfer funds from one bank account to another. Of course, most banks charge fees for these services.

ILLUSTRATION 18-3

What kinds of activities can take place through the use of electronic banking?

The Internet is a new way for banks and nonbanks to survive, with many having Web sites publicizing their services. Customers can search the Internet for the best interest rates for loans, the best savings account rates, and best checking account terms. Loan and credit-card application forms can be processed and approved quickly online. Internet banks have advantages over traditional banks. Not only can they perform most of the same services traditional banks offer, but they can also do it at lower cost. An Internet bank does not need large expensive downtown buildings with numerous branches from which to conduct business. It can operate from a single, low-rent building 24 hours a day, seven days a week (often expressed as 24/7) to reach worldwide customers. For many customers, online banking can satisfy most day-to-day banking needs. Breaking old banking habits, however, may not be easy to do for many people.

One study found that a single banking transaction costs a traditional bank $1.07, whereas an Internet bank's cost is 2 cents. That cost difference is one reason why many large banks are quickly adding Internet banking departments. Figure 18-4 lists some typical banking services offered online.

INVESTMENT INSTRUMENTS AND DECISIONS

As cash flows into a business from its daily operations, it can choose to invest the money in the business or in financial instruments, from which it can earn additional income. To make good investment decisions, managers and individual investors need to know about basic investment instruments and how to decide upon their investment goals.

FIGURE 18-4

Examples of Banking Services Available Online

Source: *People's Bank Commercial Services at http://www.peoples.com/commercial/*

INVESTMENT INSTRUMENTS

Financial institutions are constantly seeking new and better ways to serve customers. They offer a wide variety of financial instruments from which customers can select those that best fit their investment needs. Figure 18-5 lists a few of the most common financial instruments.

INTEREST-BEARING CHECKING ACCOUNTS Many checking accounts pay interest under certain conditions, such as keeping account balances to a certain minimum. If a balance falls below the minimum, the bank may charge service fees or lower or eliminate the interest. Investors with small sums of money find interest-bearing checking accounts a convenient way to save and use funds to pay for items purchased. Because checking accounts are not primarily designed as savings instruments, however, they serve that purpose only to a limited extent. The interest rate earned is relatively small in comparison to most other investments, including savings accounts.

SAVINGS ACCOUNTS A **savings account** is an account that allows customers to make deposits, earn interest, and make withdrawals at any time without financial penalties. Customers can deposit small amounts, but they will usually earn low interest rates compared with other investment instruments. The bank may charge a service fee if the amount on deposit falls below the minimum balance required.

CERTIFICATES OF DEPOSIT A **certificate of deposit (CD)** is a savings account that requires an investor to deposit a minimum specified sum for a fixed period at a fixed interest rate. Banks offer CDs for $500 or more and for periods ranging from three months to five years. Typically, the longer the term of the CD, the higher the interest rate earned. For example, the interest rate on a six-month CD will normally be less than on a two-year CD. Although CDs usually pay a higher rate of interest than do savings accounts without restrictions, a CD cannot be withdrawn before its stated time without penalty—a substantial loss of earned interest.

MONEY MARKET ACCOUNTS A **money market account** is a type of savings account in which the deposits are invested in short-term, government-backed securities. The interest rate on the account is not fixed. It goes up and down as interest rates in the economy change. Financial institutions often grant check-writing privileges on money

Interest-Bearing Checking Accounts	Treasury Bills
Regular Savings Accounts	Treasury Notes
Certificates of Deposit (CDs)	Treasury Bonds
Money Market Funds	Corporate Stocks
Mutual Funds	Corporate Bonds

FIGURE 18-5

Financial institutions provide many types of investment instruments.

market accounts, but require a minimum size for the checks. For example, they may permit depositors to write checks for no less than $200.

Unlike CDs, there is no minimum time the money must remain in the account. Depositors can withdraw their money at any time. Also, initial deposits may be as low as $500. Businesses often invest in money market accounts when they will need the money soon or when they want to earn some interest while waiting for a more profitable investment opportunity. Because government-backed securities are not very risky, the interest paid on money market accounts is generally lower than for other stock or bond investment options. However, this account generally pays a bit higher interest than does a typical savings account.

MUTUAL FUNDS An **investment company** specializes in the sale of stocks, bonds, and other securities. Fidelity Investments and The Vanguard Group are two popular examples of investment companies, each of which handles various types of mutual funds. A **mutual fund** pools the money of many investors primarily for the purchase of stocks and bonds. Investors who do not have the time or expertise to select individual stocks and bonds usually make mutual fund investments. Professional fund managers carefully evaluate and select a variety of securities in which to invest the fund's money.

Mutual fund investors can choose from among many types of funds, depending on their investment goals. Growth funds, for example, focus on stocks that show potential for rapid growth. Some investment companies specialize in small, medium, or large companies. Some funds invest in international stock. Still others aim to generate a steady income for investors. Investors may easily transfer funds from one fund to another, but check writing is generally not permitted.

ILLUSTRATION 18-4

What kinds of investment instruments are backed by the United States Treasury Department?

TREASURY BILLS The U.S. government borrows money from investors by selling bills, notes, and bonds backed by the U.S. Treasury. A **Treasury bill**, or **T-bill**, is a short-term security sold to finance the cost of running the government. T-bills are sold in $10,000 to $1 million amounts and mature in 3 to 12 months. Like other government securities, they are one of the safest of all short-term investments.

TREASURY NOTES AND BONDS A **Treasury note** is a U.S. government interest-bearing security that is available in amounts of $1,000 up to $5,000 and generally mature in one to ten years. A **Treasury bond** is an interest-bearing U.S. government security that is available in $1,000 to $1 million amounts with maturities ranging from 10 to 30 years. Businesses frequently invest in these securities because they are practically risk free and are easy to buy and sell.

INVESTMENT GOALS

Inexperienced investors frequently give too little thought to determining their investment goals before selecting a specific investment. They may even put all of their funds into one investment. To make good choices, investors must set their investment goals based on the amount of liquidity, safety, and growth that is right for them.

Liquidity refers to the ease of turning an investment into cash without significant loss. For example, checking accounts are very liquid. Depositors can withdraw their deposit as cash whenever they want without penalty. Certificates of deposit are less liquid. If depositors withdraw their money from a CD before the end of its term, they will have to pay a substantial penalty. If a small company, like Kilgore Appliances in the chapter-opening story, needs cash regularly, it should choose more liquid investments. Kilgore's owners might choose to invest in money market accounts rather than mutual funds, so they can get cash when they need it without much risk of financial loss. On the other hand, an established, profitable firm may have a steady source of cash from its operations. Instead of needing cash soon, it may need to replace costly equipment in about five years, so it may choose to invest in less liquid but more profitable investments. Certificates of deposit or Treasury notes and bills might be appropriate choices for this firm. The different objectives of these two firms will determine, in part, the investments they select.

A second investment goal is the degree of safety desired. In general, riskier investments have higher earning potential than do less risky investments. However, risky investments are more likely to lose all or part of the investment. Some investors want maximum safety—they do not want to risk losing any of their money. To achieve a high degree of safety, they will likely have to accept smaller earnings on the investment. Investment in savings accounts, money market accounts, and government bonds should appeal to them, because these are low-risk investments. Other investors like to take some risks for the opportunity to earn more money. These investors might prefer to buy stock in a new corporation, in a developing country, or in a new Internet firm.

FACTS AND FIGURES

Ethical or socially responsible investment is becoming popular around the globe. This is defined as "putting your money where your morals are," or investing according to your beliefs. Ethical investments tend to avoid companies involved in areas such as environmentally damaging practices, unsafe products and services, and countries with poor human rights records.

The third investment goal involves the tradeoff between investment growth and income (dividends) from the investment. Investors who do not need a steady income from investments and are willing to invest for long periods of time will choose to invest in growth-oriented corporations. They hope to see their investments grow faster than inflation. Investors who want high dividends invest in stocks or mutual funds with a history of paying high dividends.

Most experienced investors also suggest another rule that pertains to safety: "Don't put all your eggs in one basket." Investors should *diversify,* that is, spread their risk by placing money in different categories of investments, never in one alone. For example, a diversified investment plan might be to put one-third of one's investment money into bonds, one-third into stocks, and one-third into money market accounts. To follow this rule further, not all investments in bonds should be in one company, nor should all stock investments be in one corporation. Diversification greatly reduces the risk factor.

INVESTMENT TRADING

Buyers and sellers trade all types of securities through special channels called *stock markets.* For help in making investments, individuals and businesses often use stockbrokers. A **stockbroker,** or **broker,** is a professional who buys and sells corporate securities for customers through a stock brokerage firm and gives investment advice. Examples

ILLUSTRATION 18-5

Why is it wise for investors to diversify?

of brokerage firms available from the telephone directory or Internet are PaineWebber and Prudential Securities. Investors ask their brokers to buy or sell certain securities. The broker then processes the request through a stock exchange that connects buyers and sellers. Although there are a number of such exchanges, the two largest are the New York Stock Exchange and the National Association of Securities Dealers' NASDAQ exchange.

Corporations that want to sell their stock to investors must be listed on a stock exchange. Technology firms, such as Microsoft, Intel, and Cisco Systems, are listed on NASDAQ, which is the nation's first electronic stock market. The much older New York Stock Exchange (NYSE) trades on Wall Street with floor traders buying and selling securities face-to-face with other traders on the floor of the exchange. The NYSE attracts more traditional companies like Eastman Kodak, General Motors, and Motorola. Most stock exchanges handle stocks, bonds, and other types of investments. Mergers and partnerships among stock exchanges continue to evolve, as electronic trading grows worldwide.

A **stock index** is a kind of average of the prices of selected stocks considered to be representative of a certain class of stocks or of the economy in general. Investors watch the movement of the indexes to get a sense of stock market trends for those types of stocks and for the overall growth of the economy. The most famous indexes are the Dow Jones Industrial Average Index, NASDAQ Market Index, and Standard and Poor's 500 Index. When compared over time, each index provides investors with a picture of what is happening in this nation's and the world's financial markets. An index trend of rising share prices may influence investors to buy more shares, and a downward trend may prompt them to sell some shares. Unfortunately, predicting when the market will reach its low and high points is nearly impossible, even for the most skilled investors.

CAREER CONNECTION

LOAN OFFICER

Companies and individuals who apply for loans and credit from banks and other financial institutions are usually seen first by loan officers. These employees prepare, analyze, and verify loan applications, make decisions regarding the extension of credit, and help borrowers fill out loan applications.

Loan officers usually specialize in commercial, consumer, or mortgage loans. Commercial or business loans help companies pay for new equipment or expand operations. Consumer loans include home equity, automobile, and personal loans. Mortgage loans are made to purchase real estate or to refinance an existing mortgage.

About three out of five loan officers are employed by commercial banks, savings institutions, and credit unions. Others are employed by non-bank financial institutions, such as mortgage brokerage firms and personal credit firms.

Loan officer positions generally require a bachelor's degree in finance, economics, or a related field. Applicants should also be familiar with computers and their applications in banking. Loan officers should be confident in their abilities, highly motivated, and capable of developing effective working relationships with others.

For more career information about loan officers, check your library or the Internet for resources.

GLOBAL PERSPECTIVE

THE WORLD SERIES OF BANKING

In the World Series of banking games soon to be played in New York, London, Paris, and other major international cities, plenty of teams are strengthening their clubs.

This comparison of international banking to a baseball contest may be more real than imagined. Today many banks are eyeing the world as their market; and financial barriers are fast disappearing in the Internet age. Bankers in Europe, for example, are now buying, merging, or partnering with other bank players within the European Union and beyond. Some banks are also joining organizations unrelated to banking. For example, Spain's Banco Bilbao Vizcaya Argentaria recently announced an e-commerce partnership with the major local "telecom," a nickname given to a telecommunication company, giant Telefonica. Soon after, the stock value of both firms zoomed upward.

Why would a bank and a telephone company team up to play in the banking World Series? One prediction is that telephones may become a primary means for customers to gain immediate access to money. Cell phones, many with Internet capabilities, are very popular in Europe, and their use is growing quickly elsewhere. These phones may become a primary means for delivering banking services. Phone companies possess cable lines and have excellent computer systems as well. The delivery of banking services through phones is expected to occur sometime soon. Banks provide banking services to current and future customers, while the phone companies deliver the services electronically to them through wireless and Internet channels.

Other banks are also seeking phone company players. Germany's Deutsche Bank, for example, plans to develop an all-Europe e-commerce bank by linking up with mobile telephone provider Mannesmann. The Bank of Scotland and England's Halifax bank have both teamed up with telecom provider BT Cellnet. The league of nations playing banking e-commerce will get larger every year.

Source: *Business Week, March 13, 2000*

THINK CRITICALLY

1. If you owned stock in Citigroup, a large New York–based bank, and it made a partnership agreement with AT&T to compete with large European banks, it might affect you. Specifically, would it cause you to sell your stock, take a wait-and-see attitude, or buy more stock? Give reasons for your answer.
2. What might go wrong with the plans being made by these joint foreign bank and telephone company deals, especially if telephone companies know little about the banking business? And what do they have to gain by seeking such partnerships?
3. Investigate a branch of a local bank to determine the extent to which it engages in international business. Prepare a written or oral report of your findings to the class.

THE CHANGING NATURE OF FINANCIAL INSTITUTIONS

The financial world has undergone dramatic changes during the last several decades as a result of legislation aimed at deregulating the banking industry. Legislation has led to extensive competition among banks and non-banks.

In 1980, Congress passed the Depository Institutions Deregulation and Monetary Act. A major aim of the law was to increase competition among financial institutions. Prior to this law, many state and federal laws tightly controlled what financial institutions could and could not do.

The 1980 law and a 1982 law allowed savings banks, savings and loan associations, and credit unions the right to offer services previously reserved for commercial banks. It also gave more freedom to financial institutions regarding interest rates set on savings accounts, certificates of deposit, and mortgages. Further, the laws allowed non-bank institutions to extend the geographic area served.

Changes in laws have created competition among banks (commercial banks and savings banks, for example) and among non-banks (stock brokerage firms like Merrill Lynch and mutual funds like The Vanguard Group funds). Competition has also increased between banks and non-banks, such as stock brokerage firms and savings and loan associations. While competition proved beneficial to customers, it in turn created competitive problems that drove many savings and loan associations into bankruptcy.

The lessons learned were that deregulation encourages competition, and the old banking regulations are no longer appropriate. The laws discussed above started a major shift toward banks operating nationally, not just locally. The Financial Services Act, proposed in 1999 and still pending in 2000, would break the barriers that would permit greater integration among banks, insurance companies, and investment firms. Estimates are that customers of financial institutions might save as much as $15 million annually. Increased competition would give customers greater choice and convenience at lower cost. The passage of this law, or a similar law, would likely lead to changes such as mergers among banks, insurance companies, and brokerage firms. The new law would point to the need for federal regulators to assure the soundness, safety, and stability of all our financial institutions. Open competition with reasonable regulatory controls can lead to still more and better financial services.

CHAPTER 18 REVIEW

CHAPTER CONCEPTS

- To be considered a bank, a financial institution must include among its services both demand deposits and commercial loans. Non-banks may do one or the other but not both. The most common banking institutions are commercial banks, savings banks, trust companies, and savings and loan associations. The distinction between banks and non-banks is fast disappearing.
- Commercial banks offer a wide range of savings and checking options, loans, and other services. Checks are orders requiring the bank to pay the specified amount to the payee. To cash a check, the payee must sign or endorse the back of the check.
- Secured loans are loans backed by some property of value as collateral. An unsecured loan is backed only by the borrower's reputation, not by collateral.
- Many banking transactions can be done electronically. Customers can transfer funds electronically through direct deposits, ATMs (automated teller machines), and Internet banking.
- Certificates of deposit are savings accounts that require investors to deposit a minimum specified sum for a fixed period at a fixed interest rate. Early withdrawal will result in a substantial penalty. Money market accounts are deposits invested primarily in government-backed securities. Mutual funds pool the money of many investors, primarily for the purchase of stocks and bonds.
- Treasury bills, Treasury notes, and Treasury bonds are securities with built-in safety, because they are backed by the U.S. government.
- Investors need to clarify their investment goals as to liquidity, safety, and growth before making investment choices. Actual investments may be made through banks, non-banks, and brokers.
- Deregulation of banking is increasing competition among financial institutions by eliminating many of the restrictions that prevented different types of financial institutions from offering the same services.

BUILD VOCABULARY POWER

Define the following terms and concepts.

1. bank
2. demand deposit
3. commercial loan
4. consumer loan
5. non-bank financial institution (non-bank)
6. commercial bank
7. check
8. endorsement
9. collateral
10. unsecured loan
11. secured loan (collateral loan)
12. prime rate
13. electronic funds transfer (EFT)
14. direct deposit
15. automated teller machine (ATM)
16. savings account
17. certificate of deposit (CD)

18. money market account
19. investment company
20. mutual fund
21. Treasury bill (T-bill)
22. Treasury note
23. Treasury bond
24. liquidity
25. stockbroker (broker)
26. stock index

REVIEW FACTS

1. If Joanne Day borrowed funds from a bank in order to buy a new cash register for her business, would she apply for a commercial or consumer loan?
2. If Joanne Day went to a financial institution that handled checking accounts and commercial loans only, did she go to a bank or a non-bank financial institution?
3. What type of bank would provide the greatest number of useful services to a business?
4. Give three examples of non-bank institutions.
5. How could examining a driver's license help protect a business when accepting payment from a customer by check?
6. Why would a bank prefer to make a collateral loan rather than an unsecured loan?
7. What effect does the prime rate have on those who apply for bank loans?
8. What are some advantages of direct deposit?
9. Do ATMs increase, decrease, or have no effect on the bank's costs?
10. How has the Internet improved banking services?
11. How is an interest-bearing checking account similar to a money market account?
12. What are the advantages and disadvantages of certificates of deposit over savings accounts?
13. What most attracts people to buying Treasury bills?
14. If you were to buy Dell Computer Corporation stock, which stock exchange would your broker need to use?
15. What effects have recent banking deregulation laws had on financial institutions?

DISCUSS IDEAS

1. A financial institution handles CDs, money market accounts, personal car loans, home insurance, and home mortgage loans. Is this institution a bank or a non-bank? Explain your answer.
2. Assume you own a five-year-old car that you believe is worth $10,000. You want to borrow $8,600 to buy equipment to open your second laundromat. If you were a bank lender, would you accept the car as collateral? Why or why not?
3. Discuss the disadvantages of the use of direct deposit for employees and retirees.

4. Why do ATM users complain about paying a bank fee twice when using another bank's ATM? What action might banks take to minimize their complaints?
5. This chapter opened with Kilgore Appliances' problem of handling the "excess cash" currently building up in its checking account. Assume the excess cash amounts to $10,000 and the company will continue to use its regular checking account to pay bills. What two investments would be safe as well as earn the highest rate of interest for a six-month period?
6. How are money market accounts and mutual funds alike and how do they differ?
7. How are the following financial instruments alike and how are they different: Treasury bills, Treasury notes, and Treasury bonds?
8. Assume you are an investment adviser. One of your clients is a 35-year-old single female who is making $60,000 a year with excellent computer skills and is employed by a fast-growing firm. She wants her current savings of $25,000 to be 80 percent liquid and the balance in short-term bonds. Would you advise her to reconsider her goals? Give reasons for your answer.
9. A new business has $15,000 to invest for 6-12 months, and it wants a safe investment that makes as much money as possible. Suggest an investment instrument or instruments to the owner and give reasons for your answer.
10. When a traditional stock brokerage firm buys a share of stock listed on the New York Stock Exchange for an investor, it charges a fee. Might an online brokerage firm charge a lower fee to buy stock listed on the NASDAQ stock exchange? Give a reason for your answer.

ANALYZE INFORMATION

1. Draw three rectangles about the shape of an average check. These will be used to represent the backs of actual checks. Use Figure 18-3 to guide your endorsement selection for each of the situations below. Give a reason for each endorsement that you select.
   a. You walk up to the idle bank teller's window to cash your unendorsed paycheck.
   b. You received a check in the mail and want to mail it to your bank for deposit along with other checks received.
   c. You received a check for $15 for mowing a lawn. Since you owe your sister $15, you decided to pay her back by signing your check over to her.
2. Assume that you have an invoice for $1,153. The terms permit you to deduct 2 percent if you pay within 10 days; otherwise, the total is due in 30 days. You wish to take the discount, but to do so, you would have to borrow money at 8 percent until the

end of 30 days to pay the invoice. Because you have $153, you will need to borrow only $1,000. How much money will you save by borrowing the money for 20 days to obtain the discount?

3. The Clemson Company has $30,000 to invest for a two-year period. The company has asked you to select the investments, but it specified that one third of the investment should always be available every six months without paying a penalty. Also, the earned interest should be paid to the company in cash rather than invested. You have decided to invest in CDs. The annual interest rates from three financial institutions appear below. Use the following formula and example for calculating the interest earned.

Interest = Principal x Rate x Time

Example for a three-month $10,000 CD paying 12% interest:

Interest = $10,000 x 12% x 3/12

	Months and Rates		
	6	***12***	***24***
Capitol State Bank	3.8%	4.5%	5.7%
First Savings & Loan	4.4%	4.9%	5.2%
Merchants Bank & Trust	4.6%	4.8%	5.4%

a. Select First Savings & Loan in which to make all investments and develop an investment plan.
b. Use the investment plan developed in (a) above and determine the total interest you would have earned for the company if the interest rates did not change.
c. Could you invest in more than just one company and earn more interest? Explain your answer.

4. Using the daily newspaper or the Internet, select a company that is listed on the NASDAQ exchange and keep a record of its daily price for five days. For the same five days, record the NASDAQ Composite Index number. At the same time, select a company that is listed on the New York Stock Exchange and keep a record of its daily price for the same five days as the first stock. Also record the Dow Jones Industrial Average Index for the matching five days. (The stock market is closed on weekends and holidays.)
a. During the five-day period, did the prices of each stock rise, fall, or remain somewhat stable? Can you give a reason for why the stock may have changed in value?
b. Comparing each stock against the matching index, did the stock move in the same direction as the index overall for the week?
c. Did the second stock's index move in the same direction as the first index? If it did not, what might the reason be?
d. What overall conclusion can you make about the direction of the economy for the five days and for your two companies?

e. Calculate your total gain or loss between day one and day five for the two stocks.

5. Using the library or the Internet, investigate the current state of federal banking regulations. Make a report to your class about any significant developments within the last two or three years.

SOLVE BUSINESS PROBLEMS

CASE 18-1

Jun Wang, owner of a delicatessen in a shopping center, often chats outside his business with Cassidy Hall, who owns the bakery next door. One weekday morning when business was slow, Jun mentioned that he needed to go to his bank to put cash in his savings account. Jun was not that familiar with the American financial system. Cassidy asked Jun how much money he had in his savings account. Jun said he had a regular practice of putting 10 percent of his profits in the account each month. Jun was now concerned that perhaps he should start an account with another bank because the sum was getting quite large. The rest of the conversation follows:

Cassidy: *You're losing money, Jun, by putting that much of your savings in a savings account.*

Jun: *What do you mean? I've always believed that a savings bank was the best place to save money. Now you tell me I'm losing money.*

Cassidy: *It's a way to save money, but the interest you're making right now is 2-1/2 percent less than what you could make elsewhere. In fact, you should buy CDs and T-bills, or even put some of your money in a money market account. You should shop at non-bank financial institutions as well as at banks.*

Jun: *Wait. I don't understand these words you are using. But I do know that I don't want to lose my hard-earned profits in any risky investments.*

Think Critically:

1. Could Jun invest his money in other savings instruments at his savings bank? Explain.
2. Are T-bills and CDs considered risky investments? Explain your answer.
3. How much more could Jun earn if he withdrew the $100,000 he had in his savings account and invested it instead in Treasury notes earning 2-1/2 percent more interest?

CASE 18-2

Doria Russell had just sold a half-acre lot on one side of her prosperous Tile and Wallpaper Shop. The empty lot on the other side will be used for enlarging the store as part of her business expansion plan that includes selling shades, drapes, and other window accessories in addition to tiles and wallpaper. She needs the remaining empty lot to enlarge her current building and parking lot.

Doria will need $500,000 to reach her growth goal, but not all at once. She needs time to find and hire an architect, obtain a building permit, and start construction. Once the building is enlarged, she will then order inventory items, train a new salesperson, hire another installer, and plan a promotional campaign. Each step will take time, and overlooked tasks might require additional time and money.

Her financial plan is to invest the current funds in such a way that cash will be available when needed, but she will also earn as much as possible on the investments until the expansion is completed. Doria believes the total plan will take from 18 to 36 months to complete once it starts six months from now.

Doria received $200,000 for the half-acre lot she sold and will use this money to enlarge the current store, buy equipment, and add to the current inventory. Her business currently has $40,000 available in a savings account and $80,000 in a mutual fund. She does not want to use any of her personal savings to finance the business's new venture. Doria is willing to take some risk but needs to be somewhat conservative in her investments. She accepts the possibility that she might need a short-term loan during this time on at least one occasion, but only if necessary.

Think Critically:

1. What is the total amount of money Doria has available to invest?
2. As Doria's investment adviser, suggest an overall financial plan for investing available funds that will enable her to reach her goals. Provide reasons for your investment advice.
3. If Doria needs a short-term loan, what type of loan would you recommend she seek and from what type of financial institution?
4. Assume a year has passed and that Doria's plan is on schedule, but she needs a $75,000 loan. Find out where she can get a six-month loan at the lowest interest rate. Compare your best loan terms with others in your class.

PROJECT: MY BUSINESS, INC.

A good working relationship with a financial institution is important for a small business. Income received through cash, checks, and credit cards must be invested and protected, since they can be important sources of interest income. You must select the correct types of accounts and manage them carefully, so that your account balance is neither too large nor too small to meet your business's financial needs. You may need short-term loans to solve cash-flow problems. Other banking services may help you make the best financial decisions for your business.

DATA COLLECTION

1. Identify at least two bank and two non-bank financial institutions in your community that offer services for individuals and businesses. Gather information on the types of accounts and services each offers. If possible, identify the interest rates they offer on checking and savings accounts as well as the interests rates

charged for common types of loans. Prepare a chart comparing each of the businesses on the information you collected.

2. Use the Internet to identify:
   a. Financial institutions that offer banking services via the Internet.
   b. Sources of financial information to aid small business owners, such as information on loans, interest rate comparisons, and advice on investments.

ANALYSIS

1. Assume that you will need a four-year loan for $15,000 to start your business. You estimate that you will need a $2,000 line of credit for the first year of operation. With the information collected in Data Collection #1 above, which financial institution would you use to obtain the necessary financing? Justify your answer. What do you feel the greatest personal obstacles will be in obtaining a line of credit for your new business? Why?
2. Obtain a loan application form from a local bank and fill in the necessary information as if you were requesting the $2,000 line of credit.
3. Answer the following questions:
   a. What financial institution will you use for regular business activities? Why?
   b. What type of checking account will you open?
   c. What minimum and maximum balances will you attempt to maintain in the checking account? What will you do with any excess funds beyond the maximum checking account balance?
   d. What will you do with your deposits of daily receipts? When will you do it?

CREDIT AND INSURANCE

OBJECTIVES

- **19-1** Explain how businesses establish credit card operations.
- **19-2** Discuss the different kinds of credit cards and how legislation might influence credit decisions.
- **19-3** Describe the factors that determine credit ratings and the role of credit agencies.
- **19-4** Describe sound credit and collection policies and ways companies can analyze their credit sales.
- **19-5** Identify the purpose of insurance and how businesses manage risks with and without insurance.
- **19-6** Identify types of insurance developed for specific business activities.
- **19-7** Offer examples of non-insurable business risks and discuss how businesses can reduce those risks.

SETBACKS FOR SANDRA

Sandra Gilbert started her jewelry business six months ago on a cash-only basis. She reasoned that her large inventory took much of her capital as well as the time needed to manage it. "Besides, customers don't like waiting for credit sales to be processed."

Contrary to her expectations, her business did not seem to hurt the nearest competitor. And Sandra was making only a small profit. By word of mouth, she learned that some customers were not returning because the nearest competitor offered credit terms. She wondered whether she had made a mistake. She quickly approached a bank, which established a credit service for her business, even though it was quite expensive.

The credit seemed to increase sales, but within a few weeks she was faced with an even more serious problem. An employee left a storage area unlocked. Someone took a great deal of her merchandise, including several large customer orders that were being held until final payments were made. While she had purchased an insurance policy that protected her merchandise against damage from fire and burglary, her insurance policy didn't cover this type of theft. Without adequate insurance coverage, she could not replace her merchandise and was sure to lose the customers whose orders could not be filled. Her only alternative seemed to be to file for bankruptcy.

The human body is a system with subsystems. The body's subsystems, like the heart, lungs, and brain, work together. If your heart is defective, it affects other parts of the body. Taking good care of yourself will most likely result in your being healthy. A business is also a system composed of many subsystems, such as production, marketing, and finance. When your business system and subsystems are all performing well, your business will also be healthy. This chapter deals with two business subsystems—credit and insurance.

CREDIT PRINCIPLES AND PRACTICES

When establishing a system for credit sales, entrepreneurs need to understand various types of credit plans, the relationship with the credit card company and bank, the kinds of cards available, and guidelines for establishing general credit policies. They must also be familiar with sources of credit information, credit laws, and basic practices for managing customers who do not pay on time. Businesses offer credit if they believe it will increase sales and profits while satisfying customer needs. Consumers approach credit from the point of view of convenience, and they buy from businesses that satisfy that need.

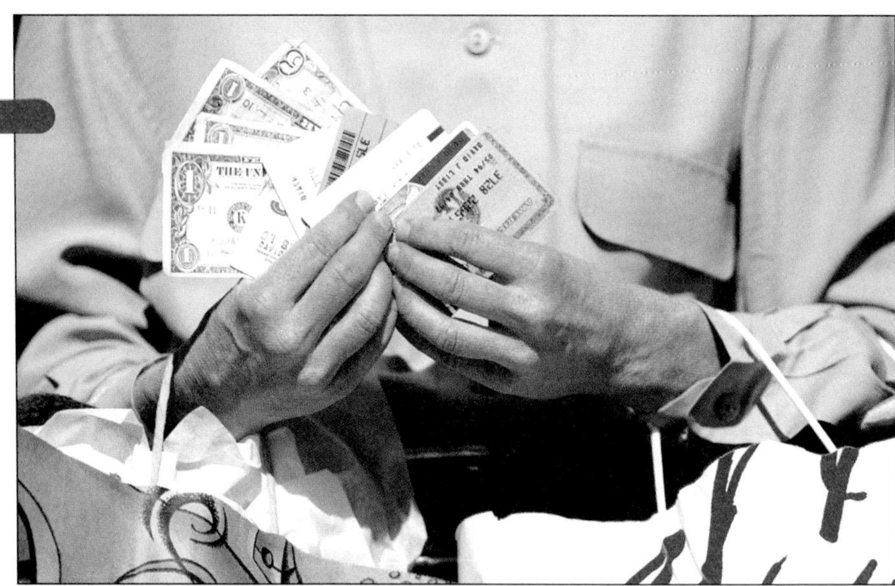

ILLUSTRATION 19-1

Why might a consumer want to pay using a credit card rather than with cash?

ESTABLISHING A CREDIT SYSTEM

Businesses that wish to start selling on credit have several choices to make: (1) They can choose to work with a national credit card company. (2) They can offer their own store credit card. (3) Or, they can offer consumers other credit plans.

CREATING A BUSINESS CREDIT CARD OPERATION Starting a credit operation involves a series of actions. The most common approach is to establish a relationship with a bank that has an agreement with a credit card company, such as Visa, MasterCard, or American Express. If you are not yet a bank business customer, the bank will want to know a great deal about you and your firm. The bank and the credit card company will need a business description, including the number of years your company has been in business. They will also want bankruptcy and credit reports, financial statements, and evidence of your creditworthiness. They will even examine your personal credit history. Banks need to be cautious, because too many businesses fail to handle credit operations well. If you have been a reliable business customer in the past, the bank will find it easier to accept your request for credit card services.

If the bank has approved your business application, you must obtain credit card equipment. If your business is not computerized, you will need a small non-electronic device. A salesperson places the customer's credit card in the device and mechanically imprints the card information on the sales slip. The customer then signs the sales slip. Your business delivers a copy of all the sales slips to the bank daily for reimbursement. The bank then forwards the slips to the credit card company. This process may take weeks to complete. Upon receipt of the sales slips, the credit card company informs the bank, and the bank then credits your bank account. Some businesses may call the credit card company to verify the acceptability of a customer's payment before completing the sale.

Computerized equipment is costlier but much faster and more efficient. The customer's credit card is swiped through an electronic device that records the sale and prints a sales slip for the customer's signature. The bank and credit card company receive the sales slip information electronically at the same time. The electronic system also checks to make certain the customer's card was not stolen. For security purposes, many businesses also require their salespeople to compare the signature on the credit card with the signature written by the customer on the purchase sales slip. Of course, sales made by phone or over the Internet don't require signatures, but the business must be cautious when selling to first-time customers.

Once your business makes a credit sale, the credit card firm sends your bank the amount of the sale electronically, and your bank credits the payment to your account. The credit card company then collects the payment from your customer. If the customer returns the merchandise, a similar process occurs, and your bank deducts the amount from your account.

DEALING WITH THE BANK AND CREDIT CARD COMPANY When you consider a credit card operation for your business, it pays to shop around. You should carefully examine the contractual agreements that you will need to sign and compare the cost for services. Credit card company and bank agreements are not all the same. Business owners should compare the operating rules to make certain they are acceptable and establish policies that will ensure those rules are met. Equally important is the cost business owners must pay for credit sales. The bank and the credit card company both provide a service for which they receive a fee. Those fees often vary between 2.5 and 5.5 percent of credit sales. The rate usually depends upon the total of the monthly credit sales and the average size of each sale. The greater your sales volume, the lower the percentage rate will be.

You may also be charged fees if the number of errors you make on credit sales exceeds a reasonable limit. For example, if your salespeople are careless and do not obtain customer signatures as required or process the same sale twice, you have created unnecessary work for the bank and credit card company. You will also pay a fee if you accept expired credit cards too often or cause frequent customer disputes, such as by giving customers the wrong merchandise that they need to return. Laxness in credit practices can be costly.

CREATING A STORE CREDIT CARD SYSTEM Large local and national retail stores, in particular, often create their own store cards in addition to using a national credit card system. Running your own credit system requires your business to establish a credit department that must perform the tasks that a bank and credit card company would do. You would have to hire a credit manager to seek credit card applicants, check whether the applicants qualify for credit, and issue cards. The major advantage to a store credit card is the opportunity to provide mail advertising to cardholders and to offer special promotions that appeal to loyal customers. One major disadvantage to the business issuing its own card is the cost and inconvenience of operating the credit system. To customers, the major disadvantage is that they must obtain a separate credit card from each business where they make credit purchases. The large majority of consumers prefer cards that they can use whether they shop in Boston, Bombay, or Beijing.

CONSUMER CREDIT PLANS In addition to credit cards, businesses may extend credit to customers under many types of plans. For sizable purchases, businesses often offer an **installment credit plan.** Under this plan, customers agree to make a stated number of payments over a fixed period of time and at a specified interest rate. Consumers often buy cars, furniture, and major home appliances on an installment plan. For example, if you bought a car on an installment plan, you would pay a fixed monthly amount for perhaps five years until you gain full title to the car.

The most popular type of installment credit is revolving credit, such as that provided by Visa, MasterCard, and American Express. This plan combines the features of a store credit card and installment credit. A **revolving credit plan** allows customers to make credit purchases on the account at any time up to a specified dollar limit. Under most revolving plans, customers may pay off the full amount by the end of the billing period without a finance charge. However, customers who do not wish to pay in full have the option of making partial payments each month. The minimum amount of a partial payment depends on the amount of the unpaid balance in the account. A finance charge, stated as an interest rate, is added each month to the unpaid amount. Figure 19-1 shows an example of a revolving credit plan agreement.

TYPES OF CREDIT CARDS

Consumers often view credit cards as plastic money. Over the years, purchases with "plastic" have grown steadily. Most people have two or more credit cards. The major credit card firms compete intensely in most industrialized nations.

BANK AND NON-BANK CREDIT CARDS Banks and non-banks provide credit cards. Visa and MasterCard are bank cards, but they do not differ much from non-bank cards, such as American Express and Discover. However, these major credit cards are different from individual store cards. They overcome the weaknesses of the typical store credit card. Rather than each firm establishing and maintaining its own system, a large credit card firm operates the credit system. Customers can apply for a major credit card in many locations, including online. Customers

Credit Card Bank of Philadelphia
Key Terms of Agreement

This application is for residents of AK, AL, AR, AZ, CA, CO, DC, DE, FL, GA, HI, IA, ID, IL, IN, KS, LA, MD, ME, MI, MN, MO, MS, MT, NC, ND, NE, NJ, NM, NV, NY, OH, OK, OR, RI, SC, SD, TN, TX, UT, WA, WI, WV, WY. If you live in another state, please call 1-800-555-0000 for a credit application.

Annual Percentage Rate (APR for Purchases)	**Minimum Finance Charge**
Standard Accounts – 21% Starter Accounts – 23.9% All Accounts – Delinquency Rate – 24.99%*	50¢
Grace Period for the Repayment of the Balance for Purchases – 25 days if no previous balance or full payment is made; otherwise, none.	
Method of Computing the Balance for Purchases – Average Daily Balance (including New Purchases)	
Late Payment Fee - $25 ($15 in IA). If your New Balance is less than $50, the Late Payment Fee is $10.	

***Finance Charge – Delinquency Rate** – The Delinquency Rate will apply if the required minimum payment is past due twice in any six consecutive billing periods. Once in effect, if you are not late with any required minimum payment for six consecutive billing periods, the rate will return to the higher of the rate applicable to your Account before the Delinquency Rate was imposed or 21%.

The information about the costs of the card described above is accurate as of November 2000. This information may have changed after that date. To find out what may have changed, write us at P.O. Box 25, Philadelphia, PA 17054.

By signing this application, I ask that Credit Card Bank of Philadelphia ("you") issue me a credit card. I understand that if I qualify for a credit card, you may open an account for me depending on my creditworthiness as determined by you. I affirm that the information I have submitted is complete and truthful and that my account will be used only for personal, family, and household purposes. I authorize you to make inquiries you consider necessary (including requesting reports from consumer reporting agencies and other sources) in evaluating my application, and subsequently, for purposes of reviewing, maintaining or collecting my account. Upon my request, you will advise me of the name and address of each consumer reporting agency from which you obtained a report. I also understand that the credit card agreement will govern my account, the terms of which are hereby incorporated by reference into and made a part of this application and that my signature on this application represents my signature on the Agreement. I understand that there is no agreement between us until you approve my application, and that if approved, our Agreement will be deemed to have been made in Pennsylvania. I understand that I may apply for my own Account regardless of my marital status. I ALSO UNDERSTAND THAT THE AGREEMENT CONTAINS AN ARBITRATION PROVISION WHICH MAY SUBSTANTIALLY LIMIT MY RIGHTS IN THE EVENT OF A DISPUTE, INCLUDING MY RIGHT TO LITIGATE IN COURT OR HAVE A JURY TRIAL, DISCOVERY AND APPEAL RIGHTS, AND THE RIGHT TO PARTICIPATE AS A REPRESENTATIVE OR MEMBER OF A CLASS ACTION. I MAY REQUEST THE CODE OF PROCEDURE, RULES AND FORMS OF THE ARBITRATION ASSOCIATION I SELECT BY CALLING THE TOLL-FREE NUMBERS LISTED IN THE AGREEMENT.

Information About You and Your Account – I acknowledge that the terms of the agreement and the applicable law provide that certain information about me or my account may be shared with third parties. By requesting a credit card, I am agreeing to this sharing of information, subject to my right described in the Agreement to be excluded from certain information sharing, and from certain marketing lists. In addition, I agree that you may provide information from this application to Dawn's Department Store (and its affiliates) to enable Dawn's Department Store to create its customer records for me, and in connection with the offering or products and services to me, among other purposes.

FIGURE 19-1

A revolving credit plan requires the customer to follow all terms in the agreement.

benefit by making one monthly payment, even though they may purchase at many different stores. And the business benefits by selling on credit without needing to operate its own credit system.

Many credit card companies have different cards for different types of customers. For example, American Express offers cards with services that range from few to many. The blue, green, gold, platinum, and optima cards meet the needs of different consumers and businesses.

FACTS AND FIGURES

Visa cards are the world's most widely used and accepted form of "plastic" payment. In 1998, nearly $1.4 trillion in products and services were purchased using Visa cards. Visa-branded cards are accepted at more than 16 million locations in 300 countries.

So-called "prestige cards," such as the platinum card, often charge higher fees for added services but can be free of annual fees for good credit customers.

DEBIT CARDS Debit cards resemble credit cards in appearance but are very different. A credit card is like a short-term loan, whereas a debit card is more like cash or a check. A **debit card** transfers funds electronically from the customer's checking account to the store's account to pay for a purchase. Using a debit card, customers can withdraw cash from their checking accounts using ATMs, pay bills by phone from their checking account, and pay for purchases on-site at stores. Instead of the customer using cash or a check, the debit card is swiped through the store's scanner. Computers automatically withdraw money from the cardholder's bank account and deposit it in the store's bank account.

A debit card saves retailers the trouble of sending sales slips to the bank, and the bank doesn't have to bill and collect from customers. The bank, however, sends monthly summaries of transactions to retailers and customers. The bank charges fees, of course, for debit card services. The use of debit cards and credit cards reduces the amount of cash and the number of checks handled in the economy.

Prepaid debit cards have become popular for telephone calls and for use by students. The card can be used to pay for a variety of low-cost goods and services, such as school supplies, snack-bar foods, and even laundry machines. The price of prepaid debit cards includes a profit margin for retailers that sell them. These cards can be purchased at convenience stores and on the Internet. Customers who buy them find less need to carry cash, but they have no protection against lost or stolen cards.

SMART CARDS A **smart card** is a plastic card the size of a credit card that contains a memory microchip, like those in computers, that can process different kinds of information. The information on these cards can be tailored to specific purposes, and it can be changed and updated. For example, financial institutions can have a smart card that serves as a credit, debit, and ATM card. Healthcare professionals can record medical information on each patient's smart card. A city bus company can use this card to collect bus fares from passengers and to pay tolls on highways. Students at universities can use them for student identification, library book checkout, parking lot meters, copy machines, and campus computer labs.

Unlike credit cards that contain limited space on a magnetic stripe, smart cards hold several pages of information. They also have the potential to replace debit, credit, and ATM cards for several reasons. First, because the card provides up-to-the-minute account balances after every transaction, it can reduce bad debts. Second, because lost or stolen cards cannot be used without knowing the cardholder's personal identification number, the cards can reduce fraud. Uses of smart cards are expected to expand in the future, including use as online security protection when buying on the Internet.

DETERMINING CREDIT STANDING

A business needs a policy and a system for approving credit for customers. **Creditworthiness** is a measure of a person's ability and willingness to repay a loan. Two methods commonly used for checking applicants' creditworthiness are (1) the four Cs of credit and (2) the point system.

THE FOUR Cs OF CREDIT To determine the creditworthiness of people or organizations, businesses often apply the "four Cs" of credit: character, capacity, capital, and conditions. The C factors help to determine the answers to two basic questions: (1) Can the customer pay? and (2) Will the customer pay?

Character is a measure of a person's financial responsibility or sense of moral obligation to pay debts. It includes honesty, integrity, morality, and attitude toward indebtedness. Credit-granting businesses check an applicant's credit reputation, payment habits, and job stability to judge the person's character. The applicant who is always late in making payments or who frequently changes jobs will not likely be approved for credit. Character is considered the most important factor in approving credit. New Internet businesses started by young, inexperienced entrepreneurs often experience losses from credit sales to people who steal credit cards and use them to buy on the Internet. More experienced credit managers can often identify buyers such as these who lack character.

Capacity is a measure of earning power and reflects the person's potential to pay, based on current income. To judge capacity for consumer credit, businesses look at the credit applicant's history of steady employment, income, and credit obligations. For business credit, they look for technical know-how, management skill, and a sound performance record as reflected in financial statements.

Capital, the third "C," is a measure of the credit applicant's current financial worth, or ability to pay based on assets. For an individual, "capital" means having assets such as savings, a car, or a home. For a business, "capital" means a healthy balance sheet—far more assets than liabilities. Capital is especially important when people lose their jobs or when businesses suffer losses. With capital, individuals or businesses can still pay for credit purchases. Assets can also be used as collateral.

Conditions, the last of the four Cs of credit, are an assessment of the economic environment, such as the economic health of a community or nation and the extent of business competition that affects credit decisions. The local economy, for example, may be depressed. As a result, many people would be unemployed. Inflation, wars, and recessions also affect credit decisions. These types of conditions influence a business's willingness to grant credit.

POINT SYSTEM Businesses often use a point system for making credit decisions. They assign points to each of the four C factors. Credit applicants provide information about these factors by answering questions on credit applications. Answers are assigned a specific number of points. To receive credit, an applicant must earn a predetermined score. Some factors that are rated and assigned points include the type of job, the length of time the applicant has held the job, and the applicant's income, savings, and total debts. The higher the person's income, for example, the higher the number of points assigned. No points will be assigned if the applicant's income is too small to cover the loan payments.

Credit experts agree that the best single measure of whether to grant credit is the applicant's past credit-paying record. For that reason alone, credit applicants need to build and maintain excellent credit records.

SOURCES OF CREDIT INFORMATION

After selecting a method for making decisions about credit applicants, businesses must collect information about them. They can obtain much of the information directly from the applicants and from credit agencies.

APPLICANTS Retail businesses that operate credit departments obtain information directly from applicants who complete credit application forms, such as the one shown in Figure 19-2. The application requests basic information, such as name, address, phone, date of birth, social security number, bank accounts, and employer's name and phone number. After the retailer reviews the credit application, it either rejects or approves the applicant temporarily for a limited amount of credit. At this point, the retailer seeks additional information from one or more consumer credit agencies.

CREDIT AGENCIES In general, there are two types of credit agencies—one that provides credit information about individual consumers and another that provides credit information about businesses. Private credit agencies, or bureaus, regularly collect data from businesses and publish confidential reports for their subscribers, who are usually retailers. While there are hundreds of credit agencies, most local credit bureaus are associated with the top three national credit reporting firms: Experian (formerly TRW), Equifax, and Trans Union. Each national agency shares with its local agencies vast amounts of computerized data about millions of customers. A business subscriber, therefore, can get information quickly for making credit decisions. Without credit agencies, credit decision making would be a slow process indeed.

Businesses that sell on credit to other businesses need different types of credit information than do retailers that sell to consumers. An important source of information on the credit standing of retailers, wholesalers, and manufacturers is Dun & Bradstreet (D&B). As a service to subscribers, D&B regularly publishes and sells credit ratings nationwide. In addition, a subscriber can obtain a special report on any business or professional person from any part of the country.

DAWN'S DEPARTMENT STORE CREDIT APPLICATION
APPLICANT INFORMATION

A married applicant may apply for a separate account. **PLEASE PRINT IN BLUE OR BLACK INK**

Your First Name	Middle Initial	Last Name		Social Security Number		
Laura	B.	Cooper		000-00-000		
Street Address		City		State	ZIP	
1400 Walnut Street		Philadelphia		PA	17054	
Years at Address	Number of Dependent Children	Home Phone with Area Code		Business Phone with Area Code		Date/Birth
Yrs. 2 Mos 3	2	215-555-2337		215-555-6870		5/8/72
Do You Own ☐	Rent ☑	Own Mobile Home ☐	Live with Parents ☐	Other ☐	Monthly Rent/Mortgage $850.00	
Monthly Income – Total from All Sources*	Employer	Years on Job		Occupation		
$4,200	Wanamaker's	Yrs. 2 Mos. 6		Assistant Buyer		

*You need not furnish alimony, child support, or separate maintenance income information if you do not want us to consider it in evaluating your application. Include co-applicant income if applicable.

CREDIT INFORMATION

Checking/Savings	Checking	Savings	Bank Loan	MasterCard/Visa	Discover	AMX/Diners	Dept. Store	Other
☑	☐	☑	☐	☑	☐	☐	☑	☐

CO-APPLICANT ☐ Also Responsible For Account **AUTHORIZED BUYER** ☐ Allows Person to Purchase on Account **SPOUSE** Yes ☐ No ☐

Name (First, Middle Initial, last)	Occupation	Business Phone With Area Code	Years on Job Yrs. Mos.

NOTICE TO APPLICANT(S): A) Do not sign before you read the agreement or if the agreement contains any blank spaces. B) You are entitled to a completely filled in copy of the agreement. C) You may at any time pay off the full unpaid balance under the agreement without incurring any additional charge.

SIGNATURE	Date	CO-APPLICANT SIGNATURE	Date of Birth (Co-App)
Laura B. Cooper	11/17/00		

CREDIT INSURANCE ENROLLMENT AREA – OPTIONAL

☐ YES — I wish to protect my Dawn's Department Store Account with Credit Insurance for the cost as Described on the enclosed insert. I understand the insurance is not required.

APPLICANT (SIGN TO ENROLL) ____________ Date of Birth ________

SPOUSE'S NAME ____________ Date of Birth ________

☑ NO — Do not enroll me for Credit Insurance at this time.

In signing the enrollment form above, I authorize that the premiums due for the insurance coverage enrolled for, be changed to my Dawn's Department Store credit card account. I agree to pay such amounts in full when billed.

For Store Use:

Picture I.D. Type (Store Call-In Apps Only)	Account Number	Date Approved/Disapproved

FIGURE 19-2
To apply for credit, you must fill out an application form.

FEDERAL AND STATE CREDIT LAW

Credit is governed to a great extent by state and federal laws. The main provisions of four federal laws that relate directly to credit appear in Figure 19-3.

ETHICAL ISSUES

IMPROVED CREDIT RATINGS CAN HURT!

Jonathan Allan worked as a computer specialist. He and his wife, Anita, often used the same bank credit card. For two years they had always paid the balance of their monthly credit statements on time. But six months ago, Jonathan lost his job because a larger firm purchased his employer's firm.

To get by, Jonathan used the credit card but was often not able to pay on time and even missed two months of making any payments. The credit card firm reported his recent poor record to the credit bureau. He was now a bad risk and could not get credit elsewhere.

Jonathan finally landed a better paying job. Within a few months, his credit record had greatly improved; but unknown to Jonathan and Anita, the credit card firm deliberately did not report this positive information to the credit bureau. Anita decided she would obtain her own credit card from another company, now that the family was doing so well. Her application was rejected.

Jonathan and Anita are not alone in facing this dilemma. A study reported by Experian, one of the three largest credit bureaus, found that one in four credit consumers do not always get as good a rating as they deserve. Some of the largest credit-issuing firms have been withholding information about their customers that competitors could get from the credit bureaus. In their search for new customers, the competitors then avoid people like Jonathan and Anita with poor ratings to focus on people with good ratings. The result is that Jonathan's credit card firm is preventing Anita from qualifying for credit with a competitor.

Competition for credit customers has caused the practice of not reporting updated information to credit bureaus to increase in recent years. Companies, however, have not changed their practices, in spite of warnings issued by bank regulators and strong complaints voiced by consumer groups. The credit card issuers seem to be ignoring the warnings. The association of credit card firms is trying to resolve this problem rather than have the federal government take action to stop it. However, to date, none of the card-issuing firms have stopped this undesirable practice of reporting primarily negative information to credit bureaus of consumers who have turned their credit lives around.

THINK CRITICALLY

1. Why should consumers occasionally check with a credit bureau like Equifax, Experian, or Trans Union before buying a house and obtaining a home mortgage?
2. Assume you are the CEO for a credit card company that refuses to withhold positive credit information, as your competitors are doing. How would your action help and hurt your company?
3. Do you believe the credit card companies can stop their undesirable practice voluntarily? Explain why or why not.
4. What action could a national consumers' group take to get the credit card companies to change their operating practice?

EQUAL CREDIT OPPORTUNITY ACT

This law makes it illegal to deny credit because of age, sex, marital status, race, national origin, religion, or public assistance. It requires businesses to notify credit card applicants of their application status within 30 days and give a reason for rejection, if requested.

TRUTH-IN-LENDING LAW

This law requires businesses to reveal on forms and statements the dollar costs of obtaining credit. Businesses must show the finance charge on statements as annual percentage rates (APR), to make comparing rates easier. If a credit card is lost or stolen and used by an unauthorized person, the card owner's loss is limited to $50. If a business advertises credit terms, it must include all information that a buyer might need to compare similar terms with competitors (down payment and number, amounts, and dates of payments).

FAIR CREDIT REPORTING ACT

This law gives cardholders the right to see their credit agency reports and to correct errors.

FAIR DEBT COLLECTION PRACTICES ACT

This law forbids debt collectors to use abusive, deceptive, or unfair collection methods. Under most state laws, if an account has not been paid within a specified number of years, collection efforts may not legally continue.

FIGURE 19-3

Federal laws help to regulate the credit card industry.

All 50 states also have laws that regulate credit transactions. The legal profession created the Uniform Commercial Code and the Uniform Commercial Credit Code to deal with matters not covered by federal legislation. Both national codes have been adopted by most states. These model laws cover credit conditions relating to credit terms and installment sales contracts. Because of the abundance of laws, firms often hire attorneys who are experts on state and federal credit matters.

CREDIT POLICIES AND COLLECTION PROCEDURES

Any business that extends credit to customers is concerned about losses from uncollectible accounts. Some firms have practically no bad debt losses. Others have rather high losses. Surveys show that the losses from uncollected debts can easily run 1 to 2 percent of net sales, even for well-managed businesses. However, when economic conditions are poor, bad debt losses will increase, causing some firms to go bankrupt. Effective credit policies and collection procedures can reduce the risk of business failure.

CREDIT POLICIES

Whether a business operates on a credit basis or not depends more on competition than anything else. A business almost has to offer credit if its competitors do. The chief disadvantage of offering credit is higher operating costs because of increased record keeping and bad debt losses. The chief advantage is that credit increases the volume of sales. With proper attention given to credit sales, the increase in sales volume should lead to increased profits.

COLLECTION PROCEDURES

Once a business establishes a credit system, it must decide how to collect from customers. This is an important function, since it involves the health of the firm. Managers try to meet two objectives when establishing collection procedures: (1) collect the amount due and (2) retain the goodwill of the customer.

The usual collection procedures include sending a statement at the end of the billing period, followed by impersonal reminders at 15-day intervals. Businesses often use letters, telephone calls, and duplicate copies of invoices with printed stickers on them to remind customers that their accounts are overdue. The final collection step is usually either to turn the account over to a collection agency or to bring legal proceedings against the customer. The longer the accounts are overdue, the less likely customers are to pay at all.

During the collection process, businesses should try to find out why customers are not paying their overdue accounts. Most people are honest and plan to pay. Besides, it is better for the business to get paid late than not at all. Therefore, it is important to learn why an account is overdue in order to work out a revised payment plan that the customer can meet.

Part of the reason for overdue accounts may be that the business extended too much credit too easily. Overextension of credit is as much the fault of the seller as it is of the buyer. Too often, businesses issue credit cards to unqualified applicants. These new customers sometimes get carried away by their new purchasing power. When they fall behind in making payments, some get new credit cards to pay off overdue balances on other cards. More cards just get the customers into further debt trouble. Young people are often poor risks, because they are inexperienced with managing money. Older people also experience credit difficulties when they lose their jobs or are involved in an accident or a lawsuit. Most cities offer credit counseling, such as that provided through the nonprofit American Consumer Credit Counseling, Inc.

Collecting bad accounts is time consuming and costly. In some situations, the credit manager may take no final action to collect, especially if the amount due is small or the customer is financially unable to pay. With installment credit plans, however, the final collection step may be to repossess (take back) the merchandise purchased on the installment plan.

ANALYZING CREDIT SALES

It is important for every business to watch accounts receivable (the debts or money owed to the business), so that the total does not get out of proportion to the amount of credit sales. For example, if credit sales are not increasing but accounts receivable are gradually growing larger each month, then the company is not collecting payments from customers quickly enough. Soon, the company may not have enough cash to pay its own bills. When accounts receivable get too large, the company must take action to collect accounts more efficiently.

The total accounts receivable may not show the true picture. For instance, an analysis of the accounts receivable record may show that most of the overdue accounts are only 30 or 60 days overdue, while only a few are 90 days or more overdue. In this situation, the problem lies with just a few customers. The company can take aggressive action toward those customers and may not have to change overall collection policies. On the other hand, if an analysis of the accounts receivable record shows that most of the accounts are 90 days or more overdue, the collection problem is more pervasive. In this case, the company may have to take stronger action to hasten the collection procedure for all customers.

One common method of studying accounts receivable is referred to as **aging the accounts**; that is, analyzing customers' account balances within categories, based upon the number of days each customer's balance has remained unpaid. The form in Figure 19-4 is an example of aging the accounts.

In the example, the amounts owed by the Adams-Jones Company and the Artwell Company are not overdue. However, Brown and Brown owes $82.23, which has been due for more than 60 days but less than 90 days; $120, which has been due for more than 30 days but less than 60 days; and $157.50, which has been due less than 30 days. The $228.18 owed by Custer Stores has been due more than 60 days but less than 90 days. And the amount due from A. Davis, Inc. has been due more than 90 days. The form shown in Figure 19-4 enables the manager to

ANALYSIS OF ACCOUNTS RECEIVABLE

DATE January 2, 20 --

NAME AND ADDRESS	1 TO 30 DAYS	31 TO 60 DAYS	61 TO 90 DAYS	OVER 90 DAYS	TOTAL	EXPLANATION
Adams-Jones Company Cincinnati, Ohio...	$705.00				$705.00	
Artwell Company, Chicago, Illinois..	$1279.53				$1279.53	
Brown and Brown, Gary, Indiana......	$157.50	$120.00	$82.23		$359.73	They wrote "will clear up account this month."
A. Davis, Inc. Detroit, Michigan..				$525.00	$525.00	Account in hands of attorney.
Custer Stores, Granville, Ohio....			$228.18		$228.18	Now on COD basis.

FIGURE 19-4

The aging-the-accounts method of analyzing accounts receivable shows the status of each account.

see clearly the status of the accounts receivable and to plan any necessary corrective action.

Another method of measuring the efficiency of collections is to compute the percentage of delinquent accounts in relation to the total outstanding accounts. For example, if 10 percent of the accounts in January are delinquent, 15 percent are delinquent in February, and 20 percent are delinquent in March, this indicates an unfavorable trend. One recent study revealed that if accounts are not paid within three months, the chance of collecting is 73 percent; and after twelve months, it is less than 30 percent.

By carefully analyzing credit sales, a business can learn which policies and procedures are most effective for increasing total sales while keeping uncollectible account losses to a minimum, so that net profits will increase. When bad debts increase, a firm's cash flow, profits, and credit reputation decline.

INSURANCE AND RISK REDUCTION

If you have $5 in your pocket, there is a risk that you might lose it. While you might not want to lose the money, its loss would not be a serious problem. However, if you own a $300 bicycle, you may not be able to afford to replace it if it is stolen. You may choose to buy insurance to protect against the larger loss.

If you own a business, you face uncontrollable events that could result in financial loss. A fire could destroy your building. Someone might steal your property or money. A customer or employee could get hurt at the business and sue you. Or, an important employee could quit or even die, leaving a gap in the skills needed to run the business. Some of these events could be minor (like losing $5) and so have little effect on the business. However, a major loss could result in the failure of the business. Consider the problem faced by Sandra Gilbert and her new jewelry business, discussed earlier. Without the proper type of insurance, she lost thousands of dollars of inventory with no way of recovering the cost. Most small businesses do not have the resources to survive a loss of that size.

Businesses face risks every day. Managers must determine the types of risk that the business is likely to face and find ways to reduce or eliminate the risk. If an important risk cannot be eliminated or reduced, the business may purchase insurance to protect against a loss that would result in its failure. **Insurance** is a risk management tool that limits financial loss from uncontrollable events in exchange for regular payments. As Figure 19-5 demonstrates, business losses can be very expensive.

MANAGING TO REDUCE LOSSES

Just as you would not buy insurance to protect against the loss of a $5 bill, businesses do not insure against every possible financial loss.

- **One-third of all small business failures result from significant business theft.**
- **Companies spend up to $10 million per year protecting against copyright losses.**
- **Companies lose $15-25 billion to employee theft each year.**
- **The average company loses $1.3 million each year to credit card fraud.**
- **Bad checks written by customers cost businesses an estimated $5 billion per year.**
- **The average cost to settle a liability claim brought against a company is $1 million.**

Source: *Business Risks International (www.businessrisks.com)*

FIGURE 19-5

Estimates of Annual Losses from Major Business Risks

As a normal part of operations, businesses will experience losses due to operational problems. Planning can anticipate those problems and prevent them from harming the business so much that it cannot continue to operate. Most businesses expect that a certain amount of shoplifting and employee theft will occur. Rather than insuring against that loss, they take steps to improve security. For example, if Sandra Gilbert had lost one inexpensive piece of jewelry, she might have been able to make up for the loss through additional sales. However, now that the large loss has occurred, Sandra probably wishes she had done more to emphasize and implement security procedures with her employees.

Businesses can also lose money if employees do not show up for work. An absent employee's work will not be completed unless the company takes some action to get the work done. Because large businesses expect a number of employees to be absent on any given day, they may have part-time workers available on short notice or have a contract with a temporary employment agency to provide replacements for absent employees. Some businesses may actually employ more people than necessary because of the expected absentee rates. Managers should watch absentee rates carefully and keep them as low as possible through policies, incentives, and penalties.

In most manufacturing processes, small amounts of materials are lost or damaged. To make sure that losses do not interfere with production, a company should keep a larger amount of those materials to have an adequate supply to complete production. Planning, training, and controls for production processes should also reduce the amount of material loss in the manufacturing process.

Many businesses, such as banks, investment firms, and insurance companies, base their operations on records. The records are so valuable that the businesses could not operate if the records were damaged or destroyed. In this case, insurance is not adequate protection.

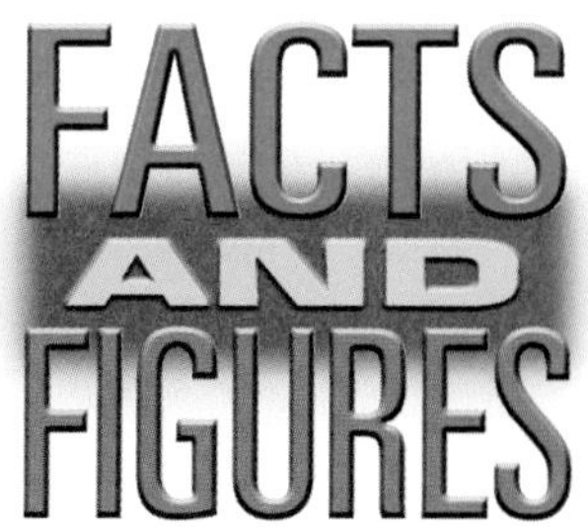

Under federal law, if a company fails to maintain accurate business records and to safeguard those records, the company may be held liable.

ILLUSTRATION 19-2

Why should a business prepare a disaster plan?

The businesses must rely on the safety and security of their records. They store them in well-protected, secure areas. They also keep duplicate records in a totally separate location, often in another city.

Another way businesses attempt to protect their vital operations is with a disaster plan. Businesses anticipate the types of disasters that could occur, the protection required, and ways to respond to the disaster. Each department in the company regularly practices the disaster plan. For example, without warning a manager may be asked to assume that an electrical problem has shut down all computers in a department. The department must recover and operate again as quickly as possible by following the procedures developed in the disaster plan.

In each of the cases described, the company is gathering information, making plans, and in some cases spending a smaller amount of money to prevent large losses. This may be a better strategy for the company than purchasing insurance for those losses, but it does not replace the need for insurance.

BASIC INSURANCE CONCEPTS

Even with effective management, companies need to purchase insurance to cover many types of risks. Figure 19-6 defines some basic insurance terms.

It is difficult for one business to predict whether it will have specific losses or the amount of those losses. However, many businesses face the same types of perils. Based on records kept over many years, insurance companies can estimate that a certain number of businesses will have fires each year and a percentage of merchandise will be shoplifted from retail businesses. By grouping the loss records of a very large numbers of businesses, insurance companies can estimate the probability of a certain type of loss and the amount of the loss. For example, using historical records on fire losses over many years, insurance

FIGURE 19-6
Common Insurance Terms

INSURER

A company that sells insurance.

POLICYHOLDER

The person or business purchasing insurance.

POLICY

The written agreement, or contract, between the insurer and the policyholder.

INSURED

The persons or organization covered by the insurance policy.

PERIL

The cause of a loss for a person or organization. Common perils are fire, accidents, sickness, death, and theft.

RISK

The uncertainty that a loss may occur.

PREMIUM

A payment by a policyholder to the insurer for protection against risk.

companies estimate the probable amount of fire damage that 10,000 businesses will suffer during a year. While the actual amount of loss in a specific year might be different from the estimate, over a number of years the estimates prove to be very accurate.

Insurance companies insure only against losses that are reasonably predictable. Since they cannot know which specific business will suffer the loss, they will spread the cost of the predicted losses across many businesses by selling many policies. Each policyholder pays a regular premium to the insurance company to insure against a specific type of loss. By paying a premium, the policyholder is paying a smaller amount of money for protection against a larger possible loss.

The insurance company uses the funds collected from policyholders in somewhat the same way as banks use deposits. With the funds, insurance companies make investments that earn an income. They then use the income to pay a loss suffered by an insured company. In order to make a profit, the insurance company must earn more from premiums and investments than it pays out in claims to policyholders.

Sometimes, insurance companies lose money because they do not make wise investments or because policyholders have many more losses than the company anticipated. For example, in a recent year, several large natural disasters (hurricanes, floods, and fires) occurred in several parts of the country at about the same time. Because of the number of disasters and the large amount of property in each area damaged or destroyed, insurance companies had to pay a much higher amount than expected. Some small insurance companies failed because of those events and larger companies increased their insurance rates in order to recover their losses.

INSURANCE RATES

An **insurance rate** is the amount the insurance company charges the policyholder for a certain amount of insurance. For example, a business may pay $40 a year for each $10,000 of property insured against fire loss. Rates vary according to the risk involved. For instance, if a particular type of business, such as convenience stores, has a large number of robberies, theft insurance rates are likely to be higher for that type of business than for, say, printing companies that have a lower rate of robberies. If fire protection is poor in a particular city or the building codes do not require inclusion of fire walls or sprinkler systems in buildings, the fire insurance rates will be high in that city.

Calculating insurance rates is a very scientific process completed by people known as actuaries. **Actuaries** review records of losses, determine the number of people or organizations to be insured, and then use statistics to calculate the rates insurance companies must charge to be able to cover the cost of losses and make a reasonable profit. Insurance companies compete with each other for business, so they must carefully set their rates. If rates are set too high, companies seeking to buy insurance will purchase from a company with lower rates. However, if rates are set too low, the insurance company may sell many policies but be unable to pay for the number of losses that occur among its policyholders. Insurance companies are very careful in setting insurance rates and have skilled and experienced people working to determine possible losses, total amounts of premiums to be collected, and the returns from investments the insurance companies will make. In many cases, states have divisions of insurance that review rates charged by insurance companies to make sure those rates are fair to the purchasers.

Regardless of the basic rates set by the insurance company, the charge made to a specific policyholder may be lower or higher than the basic rate, depending on certain circumstances. For example, a new building that has an automatic sprinkler system and is located where there is good fire protection can be insured at a lower rate than an older building that does not have a sprinkler system and is located where there is poor fire protection. In many states, automobile rates vary from the basic rate, depending on whether the driver has a good or bad accident record, the age of the person who drives the car, and the brand, model, and age of the car.

CANCELLATION OF INSURANCE

The insurance policy contains information about how the contract may be terminated. Most property or liability insurance contracts may be canceled by the insurer or may not be renewed when they expire if the insurer believes the risk has increased. If the insurer cancels the insurance, it must give enough notice to policyholders to allow them to find another insurer. Generally, states have passed laws that do not allow companies to arbitrarily cancel insurance without a good reason. Many states allow companies and individuals who have had insurance canceled to purchase insurance from a special state-sponsored fund, although often at a very high rate.

INSURABLE INTEREST IN PROPERTY

To insure any kind of property, the policyholder must have an insurable interest in it. An **insurable interest** is generally defined as the possible financial loss that the policyholder will suffer if the property is damaged or destroyed. For example, if a business owns a van, it has an insurable interest in that van. If the van were stolen or destroyed in an accident, the business would suffer a financial loss. People who use a building for storage have an insurable interest in their property housed in the building, even though they do not own the building. A fire could destroy their property in the building, causing financial loss. The amount of the policyholder's insurable interest in the property to be insured is usually specifically indicated in the policy and forms the basis for the insurance rates based on the possible loss.

DEDUCTIBLES

Many insurance contracts include deductibles. A **deductible** is the amount the insured pays for a loss before the insurance company pays anything. A deductible makes the insured responsible for part of the loss in return for a lower premium. For example, if a vehicle insurance policy has a $500 deductible and a $1500 loss occurs, the insurer pays $1,000 and the insured is responsible for paying $500 of the loss (the amount of the deductible). If the loss is only $400, the insured would bear the entire loss, and the insurer would pay nothing.

To reduce their premiums, people often choose to include a higher deductible in their policy if they can afford to pay the amount of the deductible in case of a loss. For example, the premium for a $200 deductible on an auto insurance policy may be $850 a year. The premium for a $500 deductible policy may be $600. Having the $500 deductible policy saves the policyholder $250 a year. Of course, if there is a loss, the policyholder must pay $500 rather than $200.

SELECTING AND BUYING INSURANCE

Most insurance contracts are purchased from insurance agents. **Insurance agents** represent the insurance company and sell insurance to individuals and businesses. Some agents represent several different insurance companies and can provide many types of insurance for a business. Other agents represent only one company or may sell only one type of insurance, such as life or auto insurance.

Most communities have reputable agents offering all types of insurance. There are often differences in the policies and services offered by insurance companies and agents. A businessperson should discuss insurance needs with two or three insurance agents before selecting a company and the type and amount of insurance. It is usually not the best business practice to select an insurance agent just because he or she is able to offer the lowest insurance rates. The service the agent and company provide if a loss occurs may more than make up for slightly higher insurance premiums. Figure 19-7 describes important factors to consider when choosing an insurance company and an agent.

The primary objectives when purchasing insurance are (1) to get the proper coverage of risks and (2) to make certain that the insurance company will pay the claim in the event of loss. For example, a business that needs fire insurance wants to be sure that the insurance company that issues the policy will pay a claim promptly so that business activities will not be interrupted. A business that buys liability insurance wants to be sure that if a person is injured, the insurance company will help to determine the business's responsibility and make a fair settlement with the injured person. A businessperson should consider the areas where major losses could occur when planning the purchase of insurance.

PROPERTY INSURANCE

A business may obtain various types of insurance to fit its needs in protecting its property. The major types of property insurance that a business might have are (1) fire insurance, (2) burglary and robbery insurance, (3) business income insurance, (4) transportation insurance, and (5) vehicle insurance.

Fire insurance provides funds to replace such items as buildings, furniture, machinery, raw materials, and inventory destroyed by fire. Fire insurance on a building may not cover the equipment, machin-

FIGURE 19-7

Important Factors in Selecting an Insurance Company and Agent

1. **Can the company that the insurance agent represents furnish the right kind of insurance?**
2. **Does the insurance agent have a proper knowledge of insurance?**
3. **Are the policies understandable?**
4. **Are the company's rates reasonable?**
5. **What kind of service does the agent furnish?**
6. **What kind of reputation does the agent have for helping when losses occur?**
7. **What reputation does the company have for settling claims?**
8. **Can the company help in reducing risks?**

ery, and materials in the building. Separate policies may be required to protect the contents as well as the building itself from fire loss. The owners of a building should be interested in insurance to protect their investment. The occupants of a rented building should be interested in insurance to protect their property inside the building. You should know exactly what the policy covers when buying fire insurance.

Some basic fire insurance policies may be extended to cover additional risks, such as wind, hail, hurricane, or flood. Additional protection beyond the primary peril is called *extended coverage*. It is obtained by paying an additional premium and by adding a special clause to the contract. Since extended coverage costs more, businesses generally buy it only if the additional perils are fairly common in their area. For example, West Coast businesses may buy earthquake insurance because earthquakes occur there, but Midwest businesses usually do not need this coverage. In some areas of the country, insurance companies will not sell extended coverage for some perils because the chance of loss is too high. For example, insurance companies may not be willing to sell flood insurance to cover homes built in an area where flooding regularly occurs. In such cases, businesses and individuals may be able to purchase insurance from the state or federal government.

Burglary and robbery insurance provides protection from loss resulting from people stealing money, inventory, and various other business assets. Because of the differences in types of businesses and methods of operating them, the risks vary considerably, as do premium rates. Burglary and robbery insurance does not cover losses of products and equipment taken by employees or shoplifted merchandise. Separate insurance is available to cover these losses, but it is often very expensive. Businesses usually spend a great deal of money on equipment and training for special security efforts to prevent these types of losses from occurring. However, they may still purchase insurance to protect against unusually large losses from shoplifting or theft.

Business income insurance (also known as *business interruption insurance*) is designed to compensate firms for loss of income during the time required to restore damaged property. For instance, after a hurricane, a damaged store suffers an additional loss because it cannot earn an income until its facilities are restored and it can start selling merchandise again. Some of its expenses continue in spite of the fact the business cannot operate. These are such expenses as interest on loans, taxes, rent, insurance payments, advertising, telephone service, and some salaries.

Transportation insurance protects against damage, theft, or complete loss of goods while they are being shipped. While the transportation company may be responsible for many losses during the shipment of goods, some losses may be the responsibility of the seller or buyer. The owner of the goods can purchase insurance, or the transportation company may provide insurance as a part of the cost of transportation. Anytime businesses ship products, they should find out if the goods are insured and who is paying the cost of the insurance.

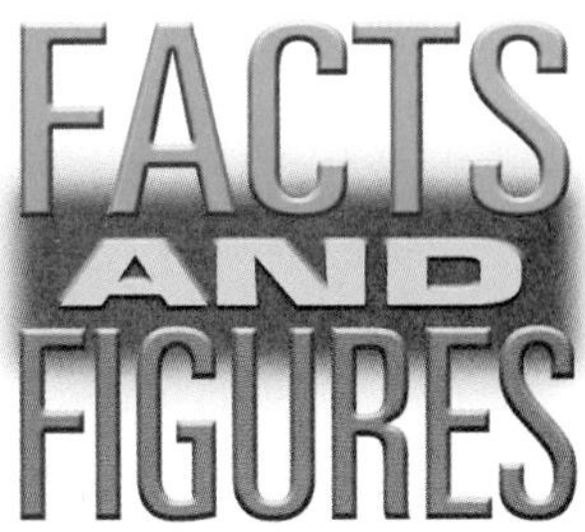

Flood insurance is administered through the federal government and can be purchased from an insurance agent or company under contract with the Federal Insurance Administration. Flood insurance is available only where the local government has adopted adequate flood plain management regulations.

VEHICLE INSURANCE

Many businesses own a large number of vehicles, including cars, trucks, and special vehicles for moving inventory and loading trucks, train cars, and airplanes. They will probably need to purchase several different kinds of vehicle insurance for protection against such losses as theft, property damage, or personal injury. Several common types of vehicle insurance policy are described next.

1. *Collision insurance* provides protection against damage to the insured's own vehicle when it is in a collision with another car or object.
2. *Comprehensive insurance,* included in most basic vehicle policies, covers loss caused by something other than collisions, such as rocks hitting a windshield, fire, theft, storm damage, or vandalism.
3. *Vehicle liability insurance* provides protection against damage caused by the insured's vehicle to other people or their property. Most states require all vehicle owners to carry a minimum amount of liability insurance.
4. *Medical payments insurance* covers medical, hospital, and related expenses caused by injuries to any occupant of the vehicle. These payments will be made regardless of the legal liability of the policyholder.

Normally, the insurance company of the person responsible for an accident must pay the costs of damages. However, some states have passed no-fault insurance laws. Under **no-fault insurance,** each insurance company is required to pay the losses of its insured when an accident occurs, regardless of who was responsible for the accident. The intent of no-fault insurance is to reduce the costs of automobile

ILLUSTRATION 19-3

What is the intent of no-fault insurance?

insurance that result from legal actions required in order to determine fault and obtain payment for losses.

INSURING PEOPLE

People are important to the success of all businesses. Owners and managers, employees, people working for suppliers or other businesses, and customers influence the financial success of the business. Because of this, there are economic risks that involve people. Insurance is available to protect businesses from those risks. The primary types of insurance related to employees of the business are health, disability, life, and liability insurance as well as employee bonding.

HEALTH AND DISABILITY INSURANCE **Health insurance** provides protection against the expenses of individual health care. Typically, businesses offer three categories of coverage to their employees: (1) medical payments, (2) major medical, and (3) disability. *Medical payments insurance* covers normal health care and treatment costs. *Major medical insurance* provides additional coverage for more critical illnesses or treatments that are particularly extensive and expensive.

Disability insurance offers payments to employees who are not able to work because of accidents or illnesses. Insurance companies will typically not pay disability claims unless the injured employee is unable to perform any work for the company. Then it will usually pay a portion of the salary the employee was earning before the disability.

Because the health and wellness of employees is important to both the business and the individual, both often share the cost of health insurance. Most businesses offer a group insurance policy. Under this type of plan all employees can obtain insurance at a reasonable cost, regardless of their health, and the cost is typically lower than if they purchased coverage individually.

Health insurance has become an important concern of American businesses, individuals, and government. Because of the high costs of medical care, insurance costs have increased to the point that many people and even companies cannot afford them. Alternatives have been considered to control costs and provide basic coverage to as many people as possible.

One alternative to health insurance for employees is a health maintenance organization. A **health maintenance organization (HMO)** is a cooperative agreement between a business and a group of physicians and other medical professionals to provide for the health care needs of the business's employees. The HMO receives a regular payment for each employee to pay for a complete set of medical services. To receive coverage, employees must obtain treatment only from the health care providers in the HMO. The goal of the HMO is to keep people healthy rather than waiting until they become sick and then treating the illnesses. Health services are planned and performed in a way that carefully controls health costs.

CAREER CONNECTION

INSURANCE CLAIM INVESTIGATOR

As people accumulate assets and take on family responsibilities, the need for insurance—including life, health, home, and automobile—increases. Insurance adjusters and investigators examine, analyze, and determine the validity of their firm's liability concerning personal, casualty, or property loss or damages and settle with claimants.

When a policyholder files a claim for damage or a loss, the claim investigator must initially determine whether the customer's insurance policy covers the loss and the amount of the loss covered. While minor claims are usually handled by telephone adjusters, more complex cases are referred to independent or company adjusters who investigate claims by interviewing the claimant and witnesses, consulting police and hospital records, and inspecting property damage to determine the extent of the company's liability. If the policyholder's claim is genuine, the claim investigator negotiates with the claimant and settles the claim. When claims are contested, adjusters may testify in court.

Most companies prefer to hire college graduates for claim investigator positions. Courses in insurance, economics, or other business subjects are helpful. In addition, many states require adjusters to be licensed.

For more career information about insurance investigators, check your library or the Internet for resources.

Some people prefer to receive health care services from a physician and hospital they select rather than from the assigned health care practitioners in an HMO. To fill this need, insurance companies offer another alternative health insurance program: the preferred provider organization. **Preferred provider organizations (PPOs)** are agreements among insurers, health care providers, and businesses that allow employees to choose from among a list of physicians and health care facilities. The insurance company negotiates with a number of physicians and hospitals for a full range of health care services. The contracts establish the costs that the insurer will pay for those services to control the costs of health care while still offering consumers a choice of providers.

The alternative health plans being used by many companies today, such as HMOs and PPOs, have not resulted in the anticipated cost savings. In fact, health care and health insurance costs are two of the most rapidly growing expenses of many businesses today. Most are looking for alternatives, and many are shifting more and more of the cost to employees or are reducing benefits. The cost and methods of health insurance are one of the most studied areas of employee benefits by both businesses and the federal government.

LIFE INSURANCE Another common form of insurance on people is life insurance. **Life insurance** is insurance that pays money upon the death of the insured to a person or people identified in the insurance policy. Those who receive the life insurance payment are known as **beneficiaries.** With life insurance, individuals can provide some financial protection for their families in the event of their death. Some companies provide a specific amount of life insurance as a standard part of employee benefits. Others offer the opportunity for employees to purchase life insurance, but the employee must pay most or all of the cost.

Many businesses insure the lives of the owners and key managers of the business because of their importance to the financial success of the business. In the case of sole proprietorships, the owners will usually find it easier to borrow money if they carry adequate life insurance on themselves. Life insurance has an especially important place in partnerships. Generally, a partnership is dissolved at the death of one partner. Each partner usually carries life insurance on the other partner, so that if one dies, the other will receive, as beneficiary of the insurance policy, sufficient money to buy the other's share of the business.

ILLUSTRATION 19-4

Why might a business insure the lives of the owners and key managers of the company?

OTHER BUSINESS INSURANCE NEEDS

In addition to insuring business operations and people, businesses often buy insurance to cover special types of risk. Two such special needs are liability insurance and bonding.

Businesses face many risks that result from the operation of the business. People may get hurt while on the job, products may cause damage or injury, and employees of the business may do things that damage people or their property. **Liability insurance** protects against loss from injury to people or their property that results from the products, services, or operations of the business. For example, if a toy injures a child, the child's parents may sue the toy manufacturer. Liability insurance would protect the company in such circumstances.

Clients sometimes sue professionals, such as lawyers and physicians, who provide personal services. **Malpractice insurance** is a type of liability insurance that protects against financial loss arising from suits for negligence in providing professional services. Malpractice claims are a major cost to professionals. Even if the businessperson is not guilty of malpractice, the legal fees can be very high.

Some businesses need a special type of insurance protection: bonding. **Bonding** pays damages to people who have losses caused by the negligence or dishonesty of an employee or by the failure of the business to complete a contract. Bonding is often required for contractors hired to construct large buildings, highways, or bridges, and for companies such as Wells Fargo that transport large sums of money between businesses and financial institutions.

INSURANCE FOR INTERNATIONAL BUSINESS

Many businesses operate or sell products in other countries. Insurance policies typically do not cover losses or liability resulting from those international operations. Special coverage may be available at additional cost within existing insurance policies. Business people need to remember that the insurance laws of the country where the business is operating must be applied. To encourage international business with developing countries, the U.S. government formed the *Overseas Private Investment Corporation*. The purpose of the corporation is to provide insurance coverage for businesses that suffer losses or damage to foreign investments as the result of political risks. While coverage is expensive, companies can even purchase insurance that covers losses suffered if the purchasers of exports do not pay for their purchases. Companies just beginning to engage in international trade or who have not worked with a specific international company before may want to consider that insurance. Businesses shipping products to other countries must also be aware of the need for special transportation insurance, because several companies and transportation methods may handle the products as they move from country to country.

NON-INSURABLE RISKS

Businesses are also concerned with risks for which there is no insurance. The discussion below focuses on some of these non-insurable risks.

1. Companies produce products because they expect to sell them. However, fashions, styles, and product features constantly change. If consumer tastes change, the business may suffer a loss when it can't sell its products or it must drastically reduce the price. A company that has a large stock of outdated products compared to their competitors will not only have trouble selling the products but will develop a negative image among consumers.
2. Old equipment and lighting can also cause customers to avoid a business. A store with a modern interior and new lighting may attract customers away from an old, established store.
3. Improved methods of transportation may give one type of business an advantage over another. For instance, private parcel services originally took a great deal of the parcel business from the U.S. Postal Service. The Postal Service now offers Priority Mail, Express Mail,

guaranteed delivery and other services to try to recapture some of the lost parcel business.

4. Changes in the weather can also cause serious business risks. For example, a long winter season may prevent manufacturers and retailers from selling spring clothing. A rainy summer may slow the business of resorts if people stay home. A lack of rain can result in crop failures for farmers who have invested large amounts of money in seed, fertilizer, and equipment. A lack of snow may reduce sales of skis and snowmobiles.
5. Changes in economic conditions present another serious risk. Increased unemployment rates cause people to be more careful when spending their money. This risk can be overcome to some extent by studying business forecasts and by planning carefully in anticipation of changes in the economy. Therefore, a knowledge of economics and business trends is valuable to business people.
6. Within any business community there are numerous local risks, such as the relocation of highways, which may cause customers to change their shopping behavior. The development of new highways may take customers to larger communities to do their shopping. Street improvements may make one location better than another and therefore draw customers away from an old location. Street repairs or the establishment of no-parking zones may have a bad effect on certain types of businesses. Population shifts in a community may make it necessary for businesses to move.

No insurance can protect businesses from these and similar risks. Unless business people recognize trends and take action, they may find their businesses totally or partially destroyed. Non-insurable risks pose a great challenge to managers.

CHAPTER 19 REVIEW

CHAPTER CONCEPTS

- To sell using credit cards, a business must establish a relationship with a bank and a credit card company, be approved as a business customer, obtain needed equipment, and follow the prescribed procedures for processing sales to credit customers. Some large firms offer their own store credit card as well as accept major credit cards, such as Visa and MasterCard. Businesses that sell high-cost, long-life products, such as cars, may also sell on an installment plan that allows monthly payments for an extended period of time.
- Unlike credit cards, debit cards are not loans. They are a means for paying bills electronically by immediately withdrawing cash from the cardholder's checking account and crediting the payment to the seller's account. Debit cards can be used to buy products online or at a store and to withdraw cash from ATM machines. Smart cards contain a memory chip that can store and process information. These cards can perform all the functions of credit, debit, and ATM cards.
- To decide whether to grant credit, businesses obtain information from the customer's application form and credit bureau ratings. Ratings are based on the person's character (financial responsibility), capacity (ability to earn enough to pay), capital (sufficient assets to pay), and the economic conditions that prevail at the time. Businesses apply a point system to these four credit factors by assigning them numerical values (points). The total score determines the applicant's creditworthiness. Credit agencies regularly receive and file information from businesses for use by consumers to check their own credit standing and by businesses to check on credit applicants.
- Four key federal laws that regulate credit practices are the Equal Credit Opportunity Act, Truth-in-Lending Law, Fair Credit Reporting Act, and Fair Debt Collection Practices Act.
- Effective credit management is critical to a business. Overdue accounts can hurt cash flow and reduce profits. Well-established collection procedures identify slow-paying customers early and encourage payment. Aging accounts receivable is one method for managing credit sales. Businesses may try to work out alternative payment plans with delinquent customers or take legal action to collect.
- Businesses face risks every day. Managers need to find ways to identify and reduce risks. One way of managing risks is to purchase insurance.
- Business people need to know what types and amounts of insurance to purchase. The major categories of insurance purchased by most businesses are property insurance, vehicle insurance, insurance on people, and other special insurance, such as liability insurance, bonding, and international insurance.

■ Businesses face many risks that cannot be insured. Consumers' needs and competitors change, equipment becomes outdated, and factors such as weather, economic conditions, and government decisions can affect the success of a business. Managers need to continuously study those changes and be prepared to respond to those non-insurable challenges.

BUILD VOCABULARY POWER

Define the following terms and concepts.

1. installment credit plan
2. revolving credit plan
3. debit card
4. smart card
5. creditworthiness
6. character
7. capacity
8. conditions
9. aging the accounts
10. insurance
11. insurer
12. policyholder
13. policy
14. insured
15. peril
16. risk
17. premium
18. insurance rate
19. actuaries
20. insurable interest
21. deductible
22. insurance agents
23. no-fault insurance
24. health insurance
25. disability insurance
26. health maintenance organization (HMO)
27. preferred provider organization (PPO)
28. life insurance
29. beneficiaries
30. liability insurance
31. malpractice insurance
32. bonding

REVIEW FACTS

1. What steps must a new business follow to set up a Visa credit card operation?
2. Why would a business want to create its own store credit card system?
3. What is the main difference between a credit card and a debit card?
4. Give three possible uses of a smart card.
5. What two questions do the four Cs of credit help a business answer?
6. What particular piece of information about an applicant do businesses consider most important in approving credit?
7. Which credit law helps consumers compare costs and terms when shopping for credit?
8. What two objectives should a credit manager try to achieve when collecting overdue accounts?
9. What are the two important ways managers can attempt to deal with the business risks they face?

10. Why do insurance firms group large numbers of businesses together when predicting the amount of losses that will occur in a year?
11. What are reasons that a particular policyholder may pay more or less for insurance than the basic rate established by the insurance company?
12. What are several important factors to consider when a business selects an insurance company and an agent?
13. What are the five major types of property insurance businesses should consider?
14. What is the difference between health insurance and life insurance?
15. What are several examples of non-insurable risks that businesses face?

DISCUSS IDEAS

1. Why could it be better for a small retail store to use a bank credit card system than to establish its own business credit card system?
2. If a business were not careful in managing its credit sales, what disadvantages might the business experience in terms of its relationship with the bank and the credit card company?
3. Discuss whether you believe the smart card will eventually replace credit, debit, and ATM cards. What might the advantages and disadvantages be?
4. Discuss the importance of character, capital, and capacity in a decision to grant credit to a young person who has just started a full-time job but has never had credit before. How can young people avoid getting into credit difficulty?
5. Although the use of credit usually leads to increased sales for retailers, when could credit sales actually lead to decreased profits?
6. Both Charm, Inc., and Cats Claws have $10,000 in accounts receivable, yet Charm has more trouble than Cats Claws in collecting accounts. Discuss how Charm, Inc., can find out more about its overdue accounts in order to improve its collection process.
7. Why might some companies choose to put their own money in a savings account to pay for possible losses rather than purchase insurance from an insurance company?
8. What is likely to happen to insurance rates if the amount of losses is much higher for several years than the insurance company predicted? What if the amount of losses is much lower than the company predicted?
9. What would you recommend that a company do if its insurance company notifies the company that its property insurance policy is going to be cancelled because the risk has increased from the previous year?

10. Do you believe it is better for a business to purchase the various types of insurance it needs from one insurance company or from several companies? Justify your answer.
11. Do you think a business should invest in burglary and robbery insurance, or spend the same amount of money on equipment and training to reduce the amount of merchandise losses? Defend your position.
12. Do you agree or disagree that no-fault insurance is a good idea? Defend your position.

ANALYZE INFORMATION

1. Assume you are the credit manager of a major retail store. A customer of several years, who has an excellent credit background, now has a $4,600 unpaid balance. The customer has made no payments in several months. You learn from your credit bureau that she lost her job, moved away from the area, and is hospitalized because of an auto accident. She should be back on her feet within several weeks. How do you handle this two-month overdue account? Under directions from your instructor, form a team of three students to propose three realistic ways you, as the credit manager, might handle this customer. To gather information, talk to small business managers or search the Internet.
2. Your local hardware store does business on a cash and credit basis. It uses a bank credit card system. Each week the store sends all credit card slips to the bank, and the bank credits the store's account for the proceeds after deducting a fee amounting to 3.8 percent of total credit sales. Cash sales last week were $4,575.87 and credit sales totaled $5,820.53. What is the amount of total sales for the week after deducting the bank credit card service fee?
3. Use the following information to prepare a credit report dated November 30 on the accounts receivable for a business that offers only 30-day credit terms. The report should contain (a) an analysis of accounts receivable, similar to the one shown in Figure 19-4, and (b) the percentage of delinquent accounts in relation to the total outstanding accounts receivable.

   Sykes purchased $600 of goods on November 15.
   Sanford purchased $1,500 of goods on November 19.
   Jenkins purchased $2,100 of goods on November 12.
   Sanchez purchased $900 of goods on October 17.
   Godowski purchased $600 of goods on October 10.
   Yamamoto purchased $300 of goods on September 25.

4. The following chart contains information on the amount of an insurance loss and the deductible amount included in the

insurance contract. On a separate sheet of paper, calculate how much of the loss will be paid by the insured and by the insurance company.

Amount of Loss	*Deductible Amount*	*Amount Paid by Insured*	*Amount Paid by Insurance Company*
$1,200	$100		
$400	$500		
$10,800	$1,500		
$200	$100		
$350	$1,000		

5. Find an Internet site that provides quotes for life insurance. Use it to determine what a $100,000 term life insurance policy would cost for a male, 45 years of age. Then determine the cost for the same amount of insurance for a female of the same age. Report the various costs of the insurance from several insurance companies. If you find that the costs differ for several companies and for males and females, join in a group discussion to identify possible factors that would cause those differences to occur.

6. Several companies have had to go out of business or stop producing products due to the cost of liability insurance or because of huge settlements they have had to pay as a result of lawsuits filed by consumers. Use library or Internet research to identify and report on one of those companies and products. As a part of your report, identify how you believe managers could have handled the situation differently to avoid the lost business or large liability payments. Also state whether you believe the business should be held responsible for the product liability problem you identified. Justify your belief.

SOLVE BUSINESS PROBLEMS

CASE 19-1

Alissa, a recent college graduate, has just been promoted from her part-time clerk's position to work in the credit department of a popular fashion-oriented clothing store. Alissa feels that even though most customers can pay for their merchandise immediately by cash or check, credit is very convenient. Alissa's friend, Tay-Von, works in the collection department of the same store. He has been involved in collections for some years and believes that a fashionable store with well-to-do customers does not need credit. Further, too many of the store's customers are always late in paying bills. They never give a reason for being late other than the typical "Oh, I just forgot."

Alissa always purchases items over $50 on credit herself, and Tay-Von has never purchased anything on credit. In fact, he does not have a single credit card. Tay-Von and Alissa usually avoid discussing credit, knowing they disagree. However, Tay-Von approached Alissa one day and told her that her uncle was now 30 days late in paying his bill for an expensive suit. Alissa, not being aware of the situation, was embarrassed and shocked.

"I'm sure it was just an oversight," she said.

"Not so," said Tay-Von. "We've sent him two notices 15 days apart by certified mail. It's no oversight." Tay-Von could not resist adding, "Now, do you still believe credit is so great for everyone? If the well-to-do can't pay on time, I bet half of the poor people are always in debt and unable to pay their bills. Credit should be outlawed. It encourages people to buy over their heads. Without credit, everyone would be better off. Stores wouldn't have to worry about collecting debts, and customers would buy only what they need."

By now Alissa was really angry. "And you and I wouldn't have jobs. Credit is good for the country and the people. Many customers wouldn't shop here without credit. Furthermore, anyone who doesn't like credit doesn't have to use it. Did it ever occur to you that my Uncle Henry might be away on a month's ocean cruise?" With that, Alissa left the room and slammed the door.

Think Critically:

1. What are possible advantages to credit?
2. What are possible disadvantages to credit?
3. Do you agree with Alissa or with Tay-Von? Explain.
4. What might account for Tay-Von's attitude toward credit?

CASE 19-2

Xavier and Olivia Sanchez are making final plans to open a small antiques shop. Most of their capital is tied up in inventory, display equipment, advertising, and a six-month advance payment on the rental of the store building. They plan to operate the shop themselves to save the cost of wages for employees. Olivia suggested that they consider buying a few insurance policies to protect themselves from various risks. However, Xavier believes that because their capital is so limited, they can do without insurance. "After all," he reasons, "we're renting the building, so we don't need fire insurance. If there is a fire, the landlord's policy will cover us. And we don't have any employees, so we don't need health or life insurance. Why should we waste money on unnecessary insurance?"

Think Critically:

1. Do you agree that if the owner of the building has a fire insurance policy, the Sanchezes would not need to purchase their own fire insurance for their antiques business? Why or why not?
2. What types of insurance policies would you recommend the Sanchezes seriously consider? Give reasons for your answers.

3. How can the Sanchezes reduce the cost of the insurance needed to protect the business?
4. What non-insurable risks might the Sanchezes face? How should they plan to reduce those risks and to deal with the risks in a way that won't force them to close their business?

PROJECT: MY BUSINESS, INC.

Credit and insurance decisions are important for every business. New businesses especially should consider whether to accept credit, whether they need credit to open and operate the business, and the types of insurable and non-insurable risks that the business will likely face. This project segment provides the opportunity for you to study and determine credit policies and insurance needs for your company.

DATA COLLECTION

1. Visit a bank and determine the differences between the credit and debit cards that the bank offers. Identify the cost to a business to accept each type of card from customers. Determine what information the bank will need from a new business in order to decide whether it will give the business approval to accept credit and debit cards.
2. Obtain a credit application from a business. Review it and determine the information that the business collects from the form. Categorize the information from the form within the 4 Cs of credit.
3. Interview an insurance agent to determine the types of insurance coverage available for small businesses, the protection provided, and the cost of each type of insurance.
4. Review newspapers for several days and identify the types of risks and reported losses suffered by businesses. Identify which companies appeared to be insured and which were not.

ANALYSIS

1. Many small businesses are beginning to accept debit cards in the same way they accept cash but do not accept credit cards. Decide whether you will accept debit or credit cards for sales in your business or operate on a cash-only basis. Develop a written justification for your decision and then develop one or more policy statements for the business, based on your decision.
2. A health club has approached you to provide large orders of juice drinks on weekends for their club. They will use the drinks for special promotions. They would like a 10 percent discount for orders of at least 50 drinks per week and a 15 percent discount for orders of 100 or more drinks per week. In addition, they would like you to extend credit that allows them to pay for the entire

month's order one week after the end of the month. Decide whether you will accept the offer described by the health club and defend your decision. Then develop specific credit terms you will offer to the health club and how you will determine whether the business meets the criteria for extending credit.

3. Prepare a list of the types of insurance you will need and the amount of coverage needed for each. Also list any insurable risks you have decided not to protect with insurance and a justification for each decision.
4. Identify all non-insurable risks that could affect your business. Suggest methods of avoiding or reducing each of the risks identified.

UNIT SIX

PRODUCTION and MARKETING MANAGEMENT

CHAPTERS

It is the fate of most companies to see a competitor come out with something new that they should have thought of. Worse, the idea may have been kicking around in their organization without ever surfacing at a level where it could have been seized and launched. Good ideas are in the air, and what separates the masters from the plodders is how well organized they are to capture and evaluate ideas, and then to develop and launch them successfully.
Phillip Kotler
Kotler on Marketing, 1999

PRODUCT PLANNING AND PRODUCTION MANAGEMENT

OBJECTIVES

- **20-1** Discuss the steps in new product development.
- **20-2** Discuss the differences among manufacturing processes.
- **20-3** Describe several important considerations in locating a manufacturing business and organizing the production process.
- **20-4** Describe the ways businesses maintain product and service quality.
- **20-5** Identify the characteristics of services that make them different from products and the challenges service businesses face in meeting customer needs.

PRODUCT PLANNING AND PRODUCTION MANAGEMENT

ADVENTURES IN SHOPPING

Laresa walked through the door of her home and collapsed on the couch. She and her friend, Desiree, had just returned from a shopping trip to a new store called Millennium. It was promoted as the "shopping experience for the 21st century," and the "alternative to the American mall." Although she was tired, she couldn't wait to tell her mother about the experience.

"It's the biggest store I've ever seen—bigger than the discount warehouses. The store seemed to have every product you could want and a lot of products I've never seen before."

Noticing how tired Laresa appeared, her mother asked, "With such a big store and so many products, do people really enjoy shopping there? I would think it would be confusing and exhausting."

Laresa replied, "It's really easy and fun. You don't have to walk. Instead, you can stand on slowly moving walkways just like you see in airports that move you up and down the aisles. There are huge video displays that identify the types of products in each area of the store as well as smaller computer screens you touch to find the products you want, see demonstrations of the products, and get answers to your questions. You don't have to carry any packages. If you see something you want to buy, you enter the information in the computer. They guarantee that if the product isn't in stock, it will be delivered to your home within 24 hours. All of your purchases are packaged and waiting for you when you're ready to leave. At the checkout, the clerk reviews your order, processes your payment, and even has the packages delivered to the curb so you can drive up with your car."

DEVELOPING NEW PRODUCTS

Laresa's experience demonstrates that businesses are constantly trying to find better ways to please customers. As consumers, we are offered a growing number of choices of products and services to satisfy our wants and needs. Businesses compete to develop and sell the products that consumers want. If consumers in Laresa's city decide that the new business offers them a better shopping experience, other stores will have to change in order to compete. As shown in Figure 20-1, before a business can offer new products to consumers, it must do the following:

1. Develop an idea for a new product that consumers want to buy.
2. Turn the idea into a workable product design.
3. Be able to produce the product and make it available to consumers at a price they are willing to pay.

If any one of the steps cannot be completed successfully, the product will fail.

Developing new products for sale is a very difficult and expensive task. For example, a national fast-food restaurant spent over a million dollars on research to develop a new sandwich for its menu. Then it spent additional millions of dollars developing a production process

FIGURE 20-1

The Steps in Product Development

1. Develop an idea for a new product that customers want to buy.
   - Conduct consumer research.
   - Conduct product research.
2. Turn the idea into a workable product design.
   - Build and test models of the product.
   - Determine what resources will be needed to produce large quantities of the product.
   - Determine the costs of producing the product and compare them to the product's price.
3. Be able to produce the product and make it available to consumers at a price they are willing to pay.
   - Build or remodel manufacturing facilities, if necessary.
   - Purchase raw materials.
   - Train employees.
   - Promote, distribute, and sell the product.

that would maintain a consistent taste and quality for the sandwich, no matter where the customer purchased it. In this case the sandwich was popular with consumers when it was introduced, so the company was able to recover all of its costs and make a profit. However, many times companies have spent that much money and more, only to find that not enough customers wanted the product. Their new product failed, and they lost all of the money they spent to develop it.

Only a small number of new product ideas ever reach the market. Even for those that do, over half will not survive in the market for five years. Therefore, a producer risks a large amount of money in buildings, equipment, materials, and personnel to provide the products that we consume.

Product development is the process of creating or improving a product or service. As a result of many factors, products are continuously changing—old products go out of use or are improved, and new products appear on the market. Most of the products you will be using in 10 years are not even available today. For a company to survive, it must continually search for ways to improve even its most successful products and regularly develop new products. Product development drives other business activities. Before a company can market, advertise, distribute, and sell a product, it must create and produce it. Think of the millions of dollars that were invested to develop the new store, Millennium, described at the beginning of the chapter. The investors in that business are excited by the new business idea, but to earn a return on their investment, the product must succeed.

CREATING PRODUCT IDEAS

The first step in product development is to come up with a good new product idea. You have probably seen a new product and said to yourself, "I could have thought of that." But developing successful product ideas is not easy. The process for coming up with the product ideas is both creative and scientific.

Ideas for new products can come from many sources. People inside and outside the company may suggest new product ideas. A company may get ideas from salespeople and production personnel, from other business people, and from research projects. Many companies employ people whose primary responsibility is to create and test new products.

CONSUMER RESEARCH Many companies gather information to help in product development by contacting the people who are likely to purchase the product. One of the best sources of ideas for product improvements or new products is a company's customers. They have used the company's products and know what they like and don't like, and what new products they would like to have. Companies can get this information from customers in many ways. Some companies send questionnaires to people who recently bought a product, asking for their opinions. Others have telephone numbers that customers can call or e-mail addresses they can use when they have questions or problems.

Salespeople can also gather information from customers. Since salespeople regularly talk to customers, they collect valuable information that can help the company improve its products. Managers should encourage salespeople to learn as much as they can about customer likes and dislikes. Many companies have specific procedures and forms

ILLUSTRATION 20-1

Why might a company use its customers to help in the process of product development?

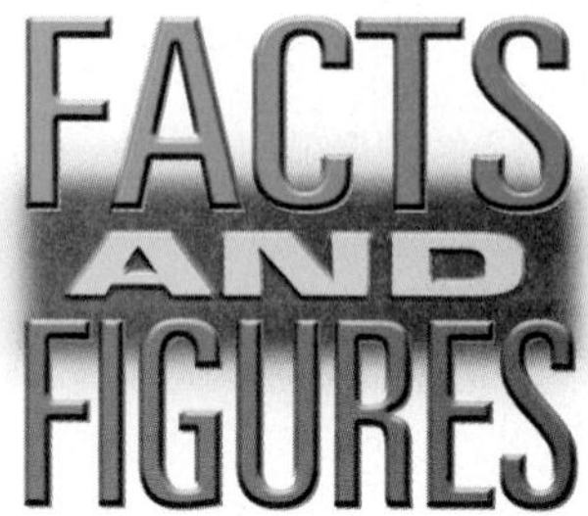

J. D. Power and Associates is an internationally recognized marketing information firm. Automotive studies are the product for which the company is best known. These consumer opinion studies measure customer satisfaction from vehicle purchase through five years of ownership. Automobile manufacturers are provided with information resources that help them anticipate and respond to changes in the time-sensitive automobile industry.

for salespeople to use when they gather important information from customers. The procedures ensure that the information is communicated to the people responsible for product development.

If a company wants to get a great deal of information from consumers about possible new products, it might form a **consumer panel**—a group of people who offer opinions about a product or service. The panel consists of several people who have bought or are likely to buy the company's products. The panel members meet with trained interviewers to discuss their feelings about new products and to tell the representatives what they think the company can do to improve its current products.

Have you ever been shopping in a mall when someone asked you to participate in a short interview or product review? Companies often conduct research in places where customers shop. The research may involve asking customers a short series of questions about their experiences with products or a more complicated process in which consumers are shown samples of new products and asked detailed questions about them. The developers of Millennium, the large store described earlier that was so exciting to Laresa, likely used a great deal of consumer research to design the best combination of products, services, and store layout to meet customer needs.

PRODUCT RESEARCH Product research is research completed by engineers and other scientists to develop new products or to discover improvements for existing products. There are two types of product research—pure research and applied research. **Pure research** is research done without a specific product in mind. Researchers in many companies are continually searching for new processes, materials, or ideas. They are experts in specific areas, such as biology, chemistry, robotics, electronics, or energy sources. They conduct experiments and tests in order to make discoveries that might lead to new products.

Many products we use today have been developed as a result of such research. The latest computer technology, life-saving drugs, energy-efficient appliances and homes, and improved food products have resulted from pure research projects. Many of the products we consume have been changed and improved through chemical research. Some examples are low-calorie sweeteners, meat substitutes made from soybean products, and vitamin-enhanced soft drinks. Insulation used in beverage coolers and non-stick surfaces on cooking utensils and razor blades are products that have been developed through research conducted by scientists involved in the space program.

Universities, medical research facilities, and government-sponsored research programs are heavily involved in pure research. Because of those efforts, we will likely see products developed in the near future that use energy more efficiently, apply laser technology, provide more effective treatments for diseases, and result in improved prediction and control of the weather.

Applied research is research that studies existing product problems or possible design improvements for current products. Improvements in electric battery storage and the mechanics of engines are resulting in a new type of fuel-efficient automobile that combines a small combustion engine with a battery that can recharge while you drive. Fiber optics research continues to increase the amount of voice and data communications that can move on the same transmission line while maintaining security and quality. Digital video technology improves the quality of the images we see on our television and allows us to select from among hundreds of channels of information to develop a personal viewing package at any time of the day or night.

To be successful for a long time, products must be constantly changed and improved. Many types of improvements result from product research. Changes can be made in the physical product, or new features can be added to existing products. Researchers may discover new uses for the product or ways to make the product easier to use. Sometimes changes in the package itself—without actual product changes—can improve a product.

DESIGNING NEW PRODUCTS

In planning and producing a new product, businesses should involve all major departments, including production, finance, human resources, and marketing. The product should be designed to meet customer needs. Customers should be able to identify features of the new product that are different from and better than those of competing products. Also, products need to be safe and easy to use. They must meet all state and federal laws for product quality and environmental and consumer safety.

If research results in a new product idea that has a good chance for consumer acceptance, the company will begin to design the product. In this step, engineers and researchers build models of the product and test them to be sure that the company can design a quality product. The design process should include factors such as durability, ease of use, and a pleasing appearance. Usually a great deal of testing will occur to be sure the product will meet all requirements for success before the company will make the large investment needed to produce it.

Once a model has been built and tested, the company must determine what resources it will need to produce large quantities of the product. It may have to buy production facilities and equipment or modify those it is currently using to produce other products. If the company can use existing facilities and equipment, it must develop a production schedule that shows how it can produce the new products without disrupting the production of current products.

The company will have to determine the costs of producing the product and compare those costs to the price it will charge for the product. It is possible that the product cannot be sold at a price that will cover all of the research, design, and production costs. In this case, the company will decide not to produce the product. If the company can make the decision to halt development at this point, it will incur less financial loss than if it produces a large quantity that goes unsold or must be sold at a loss.

PRODUCING THE PRODUCT

If the new product has survived the research and design process, the company can begin producing for sale. This is an expensive step. The company may have to build or remodel its manufacturing facilities. It must purchase raw materials and hire and train enough employees to produce the product. Then it must promote, distribute, and sell the product. However, if the company has carefully planned and produced the product, the product has a better chance of succeeding and earning a profit for the company when customers purchase it.

As you learned in Chapter 1, *production* is making a product or providing a service. **Manufacturing** is a form of production in which raw and semifinished materials are processed, assembled, or converted into finished products.

Manufacturing is a complex process, even when only one product is produced. Examine any product you purchased recently. Very likely, it is made of several parts. The company must either manufacture those parts or purchase them from other companies. The manufacturer must store the parts until it needs them. Then people and machinery must assemble the parts. Once assembled, the product must be packaged. Many products will be packed together for shipping and then stored in a warehouse for delivery to the businesses that will sell them.

In addition to the activities just discussed, the manufacturing process involves many other tasks. The manufacturer must maintain equipment, purchase supplies, and train people to operate the equipment.

As you can see, manufacturing just one product is a complicated process. Often, manufacturers produce many products at the same time. So you can see how complicated it can be to operate a manufacturing business.

When you think of a manufacturing business, you may have an image of a large factory with a long assembly line. Workers perform specific activities on the assembly line as the product moves past. Many products, all looking exactly alike, are produced on the assembly line each day. But while assembly lines are one way to manufacture products, there are many other ways (see Figure 20-2).

MASS PRODUCTION **Mass production** is an assembly process that produces a large number of identical products. It usually involves an assembly line where employees at each workstation continuously perform the same task to assemble the product. Many products you use are

TYPE OF MANUFACTURING	WHAT HAPPENS IN THE PROCESS
Mass Production	An assembly process produces a large number of identical products
Continuous Processing	Raw materials move through special equipment that changes their form to make them more usable for consumption or further manufacturing
Repetitive Production	The same thing is done over and over to produce a product
Intermittent Processing	Short production runs are used to make predetermined quantities of different products
Custom Manufacturing	A unique product is designed and built to meet the purchaser's specific needs

FIGURE 20-2

Different Types of Manufacturing

assembled through mass production. Automobiles, cameras, home appliances, and many brands of computers are mass-produced.

Mass production enables companies to manufacture products at a low cost and in large quantities. But many changes have occurred in mass production since Henry Ford first used assembly lines to produce cars in the early 1900s. Now, manufacturers often train assembly line workers to perform many activities. Workers can then switch tasks periodically to make the job more interesting. Teams of workers and supervisors meet regularly to identify problems and develop solutions. Computers monitor the assembly process to ensure that needed parts and materials are available at the right time and right place. Robots stationed at many places along assembly lines complete tasks such as painting, welding, and quality-control testing.

ILLUSTRATION 20-2

How has mass production changed since its first use in the early 1900s?

CONTINUOUS PROCESSING Raw materials usually need to be processed before they can be consumed. With **continuous processing,** raw materials constantly move through specially designed equipment that changes their form to make them more usable for consumption or further manufacturing. Steel mills, for example, convert iron ore into steel to be used by other manufacturers. Oil refineries change crude oil into a variety of petroleum products, including gasoline and oil. Cereal manufacturers process many different kinds of grain into the cereals you eat for breakfast. Production runs may last days, weeks, or months without equipment shutdowns.

REPETITIVE PRODUCTION Companies that use **repetitive production** do the same thing over and over to produce a product. The activity is usually rather simple and can be completed in a short time. The repetitive process may use modules (pre-assembled parts or units) in the assembly process. For example, the repetitive process is used to produce washing machines. First, the motor is assembled as a separate module. Then it is installed in the frame, which has been assembled separately. Controls, hoses, and other features may be added in yet another process. Mobile homes and recreational vehicles are often assembled using repetitive production. Individual sections are constructed and then brought together for final assembly on the frame or chassis.

INTERMITTENT PROCESSING **Intermittent processing** uses short production runs to make predetermined quantities of different products. The most common form of intermittent processing is the manufacturing or assembly of a specific product to meet a customer's order or specifications. An example of a business using intermittent manufacturing is a printing company. Each printing job varies in quantity, type of printing process, binding, color of ink, and type of paper. When the company receives an order, the printer assigned to the job assembles the necessary materials, selects the correct printing equipment, and completes the printing. A bakery uses intermittent processing, as does a company that roasts, blends, and grinds many varieties of coffee beans to order.

CUSTOM MANUFACTURING Often there is a need to build only one or a very limited number of units of a product. The product may be very large or complex and take a long time to build. **Custom manufacturing** is the process used to design and build a unique product to meet the specific needs of the purchaser. Buildings, bridges, and computer programs are all examples of custom manufacturing. If a company needs a special piece of equipment built, it hires a custom manufacturer.

A custom manufacturer must be able to work with a customer to develop a unique product. The company must be flexible enough to build a different product each time, and it may need to build part or all of that product at a new location each time.

PLANNING A MANUFACTURING BUSINESS

Establishing a manufacturing business requires a number of important decisions. The company must be able to get the materials it needs to build products. It must have buildings designed and built. The company must purchase specialized machinery and equipment and arrange it in the buildings so that it can produce quality products rapidly and at a low cost. The company must hire people with the skills to perform the many activities needed to produce the products. If it cannot find people with the needed skills, it must train others. Finally, after manufacturing the products, the company must store them until it can sell and distribute them to customers.

LOCATING THE BUSINESS

One of the first decisions of the manufacturing company is where to locate the business. While it might seem that a business could locate anywhere it wants to, it is a very complicated procedure to find the best location. As illustrated in Figure 20-3, several factors influence the decision of where to locate a manufacturing business.

AVAILABILITY OF RAW MATERIALS If a manufacturer needs to process raw materials as a part of the production process, it must have a reliable supply of those materials. Also, the cost of the raw materials must be as low as possible. The manufacturer, therefore, may choose to locate close to the source of the raw materials to make them easier to obtain and to keep the cost of transporting them as low as possible. Furniture and textile manufacturers, steel mills, and food-processing companies are examples of industries that locate close to the source of needed raw materials. Consider what the most important raw mate-

FIGURE 20-3

The Factors in Deciding a Manufacturing Facility's Location

ILLUSTRATION 20-3

What factors influence the location of a manufacturing business?

rials are for each of these manufacturers and where the manufacturers are likely to locate because of the need for these materials.

TRANSPORTATION METHODS The company must decide how to obtain the materials needed to manufacture the products and how it will ship the products to customers. The choice of transportation method can determine whether the company will receive materials and deliver products on time. The major transportation methods include air, rail, truck, water, and pipeline. Each has specific advantages based on time, cost, and convenience. Very bulky, fragile, or perishable products will need special transportation. Companies may decide to locate close to a railroad, an interstate highway system, or a major airport to be able to conveniently access the type of transportation needed. If the company is involved in international business, it may need to locate near a variety of transportation sources.

SUPPLY AND COST OF ENERGY AND WATER The costs and supply of energy that manufacturers use is an important consideration in production planning. The company must have an uninterrupted supply of energy (such as electricity, gasoline, or coal) at a reasonable cost. There have been times in recent years when several types of energy, including electricity and gasoline, have been in short supply. As a result, companies had to switch to other forms of energy or reduce operations. Energy prices can change dramatically in a short time, making it difficult to control costs. Water supplies are limited in many parts of the United States as well as in other countries. Governments tightly control access to water as well as the requirements for treatment and discharge of wastewater. Cities and states have passed environmental laws that regulate access to water and energy resources and where specific types of businesses can and cannot locate. A company must be sure to locate where it will have enough energy and water to be able to operate for many years in the future.

LAND AND BUILDING COSTS While some companies can operate in small buildings, others may need several hundred acres of land. Companies can purchase or lease land and buildings. Constructing a large manufacturing building will cost many millions of dollars. A company will need a source of financing for the construction and will normally pay the cost of the building over many years.

As a business grows, it must plan for possible future expansion. Many companies have had to expand several times since they started business. Expansion is easier if enough land is available close to the existing buildings, and buildings are designed to be flexible and allow for expansion.

Companies must carefully consider how the manufacturing process will affect other people and organizations located in the same area. Businesses with production processes that create odors or high noise levels may be severely restricted in where they can locate or may face lawsuits from adjoining neighborhoods.

LABOR SUPPLY Well-trained employees are an important part of most manufacturing operations. In selecting a location, a company should look at the available supply of workers, the training they might need, and the cost of the labor. The choice of location depends on whether the company needs highly skilled employees or unskilled labor. Few businesses can operate effectively today without well-educated employees. The days of easily available and inexpensive labor providing the skills a company needs are over. Businesses are working with government agencies, colleges, and universities to design training programs, so they will have a competitive workforce.

CYBER COMMUNICATION

E-mail is so easy to use that employees can be lulled into a false sense of security that results in the sending of overly blunt, abrupt, explicit, or careless messages. Although there are laws forbidding people to read others' postal mail, electronic mail has no such protection. In fact, an employee's e-mail is considered the property of the organization. As a result, businesses worried about lawsuits are using sophisticated tools to monitor employee e-mail. That, in turn, is raising concerns about the proper balance between employees' privacy and the employer's need to know.

Some privacy experts believe that private, interpersonal communication is an important human function in the workplace. Employees should be allowed to use e-mail without worrying about reprisals. However, some businesses fear complaints of computer harassment and possible lawsuits.

Businesses have responded to the problem in a variety of ways. Some say they limit monitoring to incidents when there is suspicion of wrongdoing. Other organizations warn employees each time they sign on that their e-mail isn't private. Meanwhile, the standard advice is for employees not to e-mail anything they wouldn't want to see on a company bulletin board with their signature.

ACTIVITY Conduct a debate in class on which is more important—employees' privacy or the employer's need to know. What arguments can be made in favor of and against each point of view?

LOCATION OF CUSTOMERS Just as some companies need to locate near the source of raw materials, others may consider the location of their customers. This is an important factor when most of the customers can be found in one part of the country, when they need products regularly and rapidly, or when transportation costs of the finished products will be very high.

Manufacturers that supply parts for the auto industry usually locate near the automobile production facilities. Some companies locate near seaports if they have important markets in other countries. Since soft drink companies must provide a regular, fresh supply of their product to many stores and businesses, they have bottling plants and distribution centers in most cities to reduce transportation costs.

Today some states are developing large airfreight centers. These are airports that are surrounded by efficient distribution centers and with easy access to interstate highways and rail lines. The airfreight centers are being created to attract to those locations manufacturing businesses that need to ship products quickly by air.

ECONOMIC AND LEGAL FACTORS A company also considers the type and amount of taxes it must pay in the location of its manufacturing facilities. Some cities offer reduced tax rates or may even remove some taxes for several years to encourage new businesses to locate there. Others have taxes on inventory and equipment that increase the costs of business operations. Most towns and cities use zoning laws to restrict where businesses can locate and how they can operate. Environmental regulations control the use of water and energy as well as require businesses to avoid polluting the water, air, and land.

PRODUCTION PLANNING

Developing a production plan can be compared to planning a meal. All ingredients must be available in the right quantities and at the right time. Cooking utensils need to be assembled. Since some foods require longer cooking times than others, preparation of each item must begin at the correct time. If scheduled and completed correctly, all foods can be served at the same time.

When planning production, the company identifies all of the resources required to produce the product and estimates when each will be needed and in what quantity. Because production occurs over a period of time and in a sequence, the company will not need all resources at once. If the company receives the materials before it needs them, it will have to use both space and money for storage. On the other hand, if the company can't get the resources when needed, it will have to delay production and spend money for employee time and materials that it can't use until the necessary materials arrive.

Three important activities are a part of production planning. **Inventory management** is planning the quantities of materials and supplies needed for production and the amount of finished products required to meet customer orders. **Human resource planning** is determining the types of jobs required for each part of production, the number of people needed for each job, and the skills each person will need in order to do the job. **Production scheduling** is identifying the steps required in a manufacturing process, the time required to complete each step, and the sequence of the steps. Managers use sophisticated planning systems to help them develop production schedules. Computers are very useful in scheduling production and monitoring progress toward meeting production schedules.

BUILDING LAYOUT

A manufacturer must organize its facilities, equipment, and materials to produce products efficiently. Products have to move through the building, parts must be added, and employees must be able to work on the product easily and safely. The manufacturer must have cost-effective methods for receiving and storing raw materials, parts, and supplies. Once products are finished, the manufacturer must store them or load them for shipment.

The type of layout a manufacturer uses will depend on the product and the assembly process. For example, one company that builds tractors has a continuous assembly line that is nearly a mile long. Many of the parts have to be stored long distances from the place they are needed. The parts are delivered to the assembly line with overhead conveyor belts and chains.

A small company that builds electric motors delivers all needed parts to each assembler's work area. The assembler puts the parts together to finish the motor. The motor then moves to the shipping area for packaging and storing for delivery.

A company that manufacturers desktop computers organizes its manufacturing employees in teams with their own work area. Each team orders the parts it needs and keeps them in easy-to-reach bins around its workspace. Then the entire team works on the assembly, tests the computer to be sure it works, and packages it for delivery. This procedure allows the company to quickly build a customized computer for each customer's order.

In addition to the type of product and the assembly process used, other factors influence the layout of the business. The layout should be designed to make product assembly easy and safe. Employees may need areas to test and repair products. Products and people must be able to move around the building. They will need food services and break areas. Other activities that support the manufacturing process, such as purchasing, information management, training, and administrative services, need space to work.

For most companies, the layout should be flexible so they can add new machinery and equipment. Also, companies may need to expand the layout as the company grows or change it to produce new products.

IMPROVING PRODUCTION PROCESSES

Improving quality and productivity has been one of the most important challenges facing businesses in the last decade. Increasing global competition has resulted in a larger number of products from which customers can choose. Businesses have found that customers will buy the best product available for the price they can afford, resulting in increased pressure to improve quality while holding down costs and prices.

As you learned in Chapter 1, for many years companies were more interested in production efficiency than in quality. As early as the 1950s, Dr. W. Edwards Deming was encouraging businesses to focus on quality as the most important company goal, but his ideas were largely ignored in the United States. However, because of the success of companies that have adopted Deming's ideas, most manufacturers use principles of quality management today. **Quality management** is a process for assuring product quality by developing standards for all operations and products and measuring results against those standards. For quality management to succeed, the company must believe that no defects are acceptable and that all employees are responsible for quality. Everyone must be able to identify problems and take responsibility for correcting them. Rewards need to be based on achieving the quality standards rather than meeting a certain level of production.

To encourage American companies to improve quality, Congress created the Malcolm Baldrige National Quality Award in 1987. To win the award, a company must demonstrate that it has implemented a program to develop and maintain quality in all of its products and activities. Companies compete for the award because customers are more likely to buy from companies that can prove their commitment to quality by winning this honor.

Technology has contributed to the improvement of manufacturing for many years. Computers have dramatically improved the quality and speed of production and have reduced costs. Robots now complete many of the routine and repetitive tasks previously done by low-skilled employees.

ILLUSTRATION 20-4

Technology has greatly contributed to the improvement of manufacturing. What effect have computers had on the employees of such companies?

GLOBAL PERSPECTIVE

ISO PROMOTES GLOBAL QUALITY

Global trade has created a variety of problems for companies, along with the opportunities to reach new customers with their products and services. One of the greatest challenges has been the lack of standardization among the products produced by different companies. Consider the problems that a company creates when it produces machinery that cannot be sold in another country because it is not compatible with the machinery that customers in that country already use. What if a company needs to make repairs and the available parts don't match the broken parts?

The International Organization for Standardization (ISO) was organized to deal with the standardization issue, which is a barrier to international trade. The two primary goals of this international organization are:

- to develop agreements on production designs to increase compatibility among products that are used with each other, and
- to establish standards to ensure quality and reliability when one company purchases the products of another company.

Over 130 countries participate in the voluntary organization. Because of the agreements developed by the ISO, products such as credit cards can be used in cash machines in any country and batteries produced in one country will work in a CD player produced in another country. If an airline needs to replace a bolt in an engine mount while the plane is in another country, it can be assured that the bolt produced in that country will fit.

Standards known as ISO 9000 establish very specific requirements for manufacturing processes and product specifications. Any business that works with another ISO-certified business can trust that the requirements have been met. A newer set of standards, ISO 14000, describes specific requirements for environmental management. A company that agrees to these standards assures that it will follow rigorous guidelines in the use of resources and protection of the environment.

Many government agencies and individual companies will not purchase products from a company that is not ISO certified. Companies spend a great deal of time and undertake expensive training programs to make sure that their products and processes meet the ISO requirements. The result is much more efficient trade among businesses and countries, plus increasing quality of products and operations in thousands of companies.

The International Organization for Standardization has had a big impact on the ways businesses interact with each other. It continues its work as new technologies emerge and as manufacturing problems are identified to make the process of international trade easier.

THINK CRITICALLY

1. What are some examples of products that are not standardized, resulting in problems using one brand with another?
2. Why would a company refuse to work with other companies that are not ISO certified?
3. Why might a company decide not to meet the standards established by ISO?
4. Use the Internet to locate companies that identify themselves as ISO certified. Find Web sites that provide additional information or that describe specific ISO standards.

Fewer people are now needed to accomplish the same level of production. However, the people needed must be skilled in computer operations and modern production processes.

In addition to routine tasks, computer technology can also accomplish very difficult and challenging tasks. Using a computer application known as **computer-aided design (CAD),** engineers can design and test products before they are even built. With a computer, engineers can view a design from various angles, study possible modifications, and test the products for strength and durability.

The most extensive use of computers in manufacturing is a system known as **computer-integrated manufacturing.** With this process, all manufacturing systems are designed and managed using computers. Design work, planning and scheduling, resource management, and control are all tied together through computers. When someone makes a change in one area, computers determine the impact of the change on other areas and communicate that information to the affected work units.

The Internet has now become a powerful resource in improving the speed and quality of manufacturing. Some of the uses of the Internet are very basic but have an amazing impact on how a business operates. As an example, it used to be a very expensive and time-consuming process for companies to get approval from the Food and Drug Administration in Washington, D.C., when they wanted to produce a new food product or drug. They had already spent months and often years developing and testing the product. Then they had to prepare, print, and ship volumes of reports to the FDA for approval. Today that entire process can be managed on the Web. Companies can transmit reports instantly, research questions online, send answers to the FDA by e-mail, and conduct meetings on computer screens. The time for obtaining approval has been cut in half, and the cost of approval has gone down substantially.

An automobile manufacturer with plants in many countries around the world is improving the automobile design process using the Internet. Product designers come together in cyberspace to share ideas and plan new products. If one factory identifies design or manufacturing problems, it can immediately share information about the problem with every other facility and cooperatively develop a solution. The system is resulting in cost savings because there are fewer design problems and good designs are now being used over and over in many locations. Also, the manufacturer benefits from greater creativity in developing new automobile models as people from around the world share their ideas.

FACTS AND FIGURES

E-commerce is creating new pressures on manufacturers for quicker response and shorter cycle times. "Lean manufacturing" is aimed at the elimination of waste in every area of production, including customer relations, product design, supplier networks, and factory management. Its goal is to incorporate less human effort, less inventory, and less time to develop products—while producing top-quality products in the most efficient and economical manner possible.

SERVICE BUSINESSES

Service businesses are the fastest growing segment of our society. Over two thirds of the U.S. labor force are now employed in service-producing businesses or service jobs. Over half of our consumer purchases are services. Therefore, the U.S. is changing from the world's leading manufacturing economy into its leading service economy. While many service businesses are quite small and employ only a few people, others have total sales of millions of dollars each year and employ thousands of people.

NATURE OF SERVICES

Figure 20-4 illustrates that services are very different from products. As you learned in Chapter 1, *services* are activities of value that do not result in the ownership of anything tangible. Traditional service businesses include theaters, travel agencies, beauty and barbershops, lawn care businesses, and insurance agencies. New types of services are emerging as well, such as Internet service providers (ISPs) that connect you to the Internet, comprehensive financial services providers, and companies that provide information management or human resource management services for other companies. Services have important characteristics that make them different from products. These differences in form, availability, quality, and timing result in unique operating procedures for service businesses.

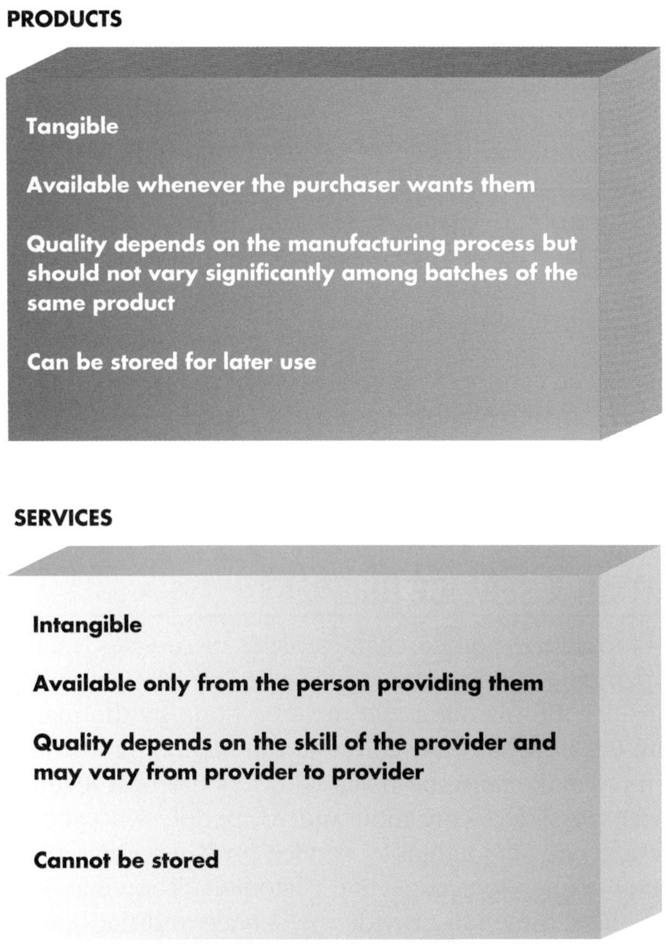

PRODUCTS

Tangible

Available whenever the purchaser wants them

Quality depends on the manufacturing process but should not vary significantly among batches of the same product

Can be stored for later use

SERVICES

Intangible

Available only from the person providing them

Quality depends on the skill of the provider and may vary from provider to provider

Cannot be stored

FIGURE 20-4

The Differences Between Products and Services

FORM Services are intangible. They do not include a physical product, they cannot be seen or examined before purchase, and they do not exist after the consumer uses them. When you go to a theater to see a play, you rely on a review in the newspaper or what you have heard from others to decide if it is something you want to attend. If a company hires a carpet cleaning business for its offices, it will need to bring them back again when the carpets must be cleaned again.

AVAILABILITY The service cannot be separated from the person or business supplying it. Dental care requires a dentist, a concert requires an orchestra, and tax preparation advice requires an accountant. People who purchase services are also purchasing the availability and the skill of the person performing the service. If a business or individual is unable to deliver a service, customers must go without. Trading in the stock market using the Internet has become popular as investors bypass traditional stockbrokers. However, in several instances, the business offering Internet stock trading had serious hardware or software problems that prevented customers from accessing accounts to buy and sell stocks.

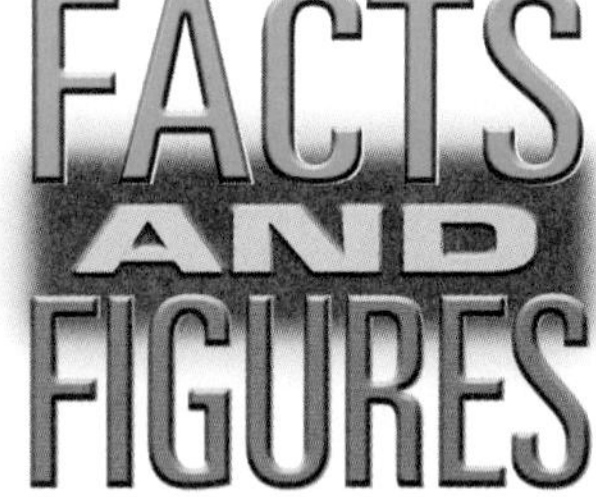

The Ritz-Carlton Hotel Company is the only two-time recipient of the Malcolm Baldrige National Quality Award in the service category. The Ritz-Carlton's strategy is to achieve 100 percent customer loyalty. The company set a target of "defect-free" experiences for guests, implementing a measurement system to chart progress toward elimination of all customer problems—no matter how minor. Any employee can spend up to $2,000 to immediately correct a problem or handle a complaint.

QUALITY The quality of the service depends on who provides it as well as on where and when that service is provided. Removing 10 inches of snow from a parking lot may be more effective with a tractor and a dump truck than with a small snow blower. A hairstylist who has not completed training recently may not be able to offer the latest hair designs. Knowing these factors makes it much easier for a business to control the quality of services and ensure that customers get the same quality time after time. A service provider who is tired, untrained, or unconcerned about the customer may not provide the same quality of service each time.

TIMING A service cannot be stored or held until needed. After a movie starts, it is no longer available in its complete form until it is replayed. If the courts in a tennis club are full, no one else can play tennis at that time. Likewise, the owner of a taxi company must have cars and drivers available, even if no one is using a taxi at a specific time.

OPERATING A SERVICE BUSINESS

By understanding the unique characteristics of services, managers in charge of planning services can do a better job of meeting customer needs. Consider the planning that must be done by the managers of Millennium, the new store described at the beginning of the chapter. The store must make sure the business offers the best level of customer service possible to the thousands of people who shop there.

Because a service is intangible, service providers must find ways to describe their service to prospective customers. They may have to demonstrate how they will provide the service and the benefits the customers will receive. To help overcome this problem, service businesses sometimes provide a product to customers as part of the service. Insurance companies provide policy documents and leather cases to hold the documents, tour services provide travel bags, and hotels provide small gifts in their rooms to remind their guests of the service and the service provider.

ILLUSTRATION 20-5

How can employees of service businesses do a better job of meeting customers' needs?

The service must be available and must be provided in an acceptable way to the customer. A client visiting a barbershop may want the services of a specific barber. A person completing a banking transaction may want to talk with a teller rather than use an ATM. Airline travelers may prefer not to stand in long lines to check their luggage and get a boarding pass for their flight.

The people providing the service must be well trained. They must be able to work with customers, identify needs, and provide the appropriate service. They must recognize that customer satisfaction is directly related to how well they perform. In turn, customers will expect the same quality of service each time they purchase it.

The supply of a service must be matched to the demand. If a bus company expects a large number of customers to ride its buses on the Saturday of a home football game, it may have to schedule more buses. If a snowstorm is anticipated, companies that clear parking lots and driveways may need to find additional equipment and operators. During a particularly cool and rainy summer, the operator of a swimming pool will probably need to schedule fewer lifeguards and pool attendants.

CHANGES IN SERVICE BUSINESSES

Just as manufacturers are constantly improving their products and processes to better satisfy customers, service businesses also look for better ways to provide services. Some of those ways include more careful hiring and training of employees, thoroughly planning how to maintain service quality standards, and using technology to improve the delivery and availability of services. The Internet is providing both opportunities and challenges for service businesses. For example, it is easier to get information to customers using the Internet. Pizzas, CDs, and videotapes can now be ordered online. However, when customers can download movies via the Internet or can place grocery orders at their favorite supermarket and have products delivered to their door, traditional businesses must consider the potential impact on their sales and profits.

Franchises for service businesses are becoming quite common. Franchising allows a service to be provided in a variety of locations while maintaining a consistent image and level of quality. Examples of franchised service businesses include car repair, video rentals, tax preparation and legal services, and house-cleaning businesses.

Service businesses are responding to the specific needs of customers. Extended hours, more service locations, a greater variety of services, and follow-up activities with customers to ensure satisfaction are all ways that businesses are attempting to meet customer needs. Managers of service businesses are learning that they must plan their service processes as carefully as manufacturers plan their processes. In both cases, customers expect a quality product or service delivered in a timely fashion at a fair price.

CHAPTER CONCEPTS

- Businesses are continually looking for new product ideas and ways to improve their current products. Only products that meet consumer needs are likely to succeed.
- Businesses use research to develop ideas for new products. Consumer research involves prospective and current customers in determining what new products and product improvements they prefer. Product research is done by scientists and engineers to discover new products and product improvements.
- The design process for new products begins with building and testing a model to be sure the company can manufacture a product that meets consumer needs and that will be safe and durable. Then the company determines the resources and facilities necessary to produce large quantities of the new product. Finally, the company decides if it can produce and sell the product profitably.
- Companies use different manufacturing processes, depending on the type of product and the needs of customers. Those processes include mass production, continuous processing, repetitive production, intermittent processing, and custom manufacturing.
- When deciding where to put their facilities, manufacturers consider the location and availability of raw materials, transportation methods, and supplies of energy and water. They also consider the costs of land and buildings, the labor supply, the location of customers, and any economic and legal factors affecting the business.
- Production planning involves three important activities—inventory management, human resource planning, and production scheduling. Also, the manufacturing facility should be designed to make production efficient, safe, and appropriate for the type of products and the production process to be used. Technology has influenced the way companies plan products and manage production.
- Service businesses are now the fastest growing segment of our economy. The characteristics of services that make them different from products are their form, availability, quality, and timing.

BUILD VOCABULARY POWER

Define the following terms and concepts.

1. product development
2. consumer panel
3. product research
4. pure research
5. applied research
6. manufacturing
7. mass production
8. continuous processing
9. repetitive production
10. intermittent processing
11. custom manufacturing
12. inventory management
13. human resource planning
14. production scheduling
15. quality management
16. computer-aided design (CAD)
17. computer-integrated manufacturing

REVIEW FACTS

1. What are the three steps a business must follow before it can offer new products to consumers?
2. Why are customers a useful source of information for new products or product improvements?
3. How is pure research different from applied research?
4. Why should a company produce a model of a new product before it begins to produce large quantities of the product?
5. What should a company do if it finds that it can't sell a new product at a price that will cover all of its costs?
6. What is the difference between mass production and continuous processing?
7. Why should some businesses locate close to sources of raw materials while others should locate close to their customers?
8. What economic and legal factors might affect the location of a manufacturing business?
9. How is production planning similar to planning a meal?
10. What are three tools that can be used to improve production management?
11. Why do companies compete for the Malcolm Baldrige Award?
12. Give four examples of service businesses.
13. What four characteristics make services different from products?
14. Why is employee selection and training so important to a service business?
15. In what ways has the Internet affected the operations of service businesses?

DISCUSS IDEAS

1. Why should a company use both consumer research and product research when developing new product ideas?
2. Some estimates suggest that at least five of every ten new products introduced will never succeed. In your opinion, what are several reasons for this high rate of failure?
3. Why would a company invest money in pure research rather than applied research?
4. Under what circumstances might a company decide to go ahead with the production of a new product rather than spend time developing and testing a model?
5. Use the Business section of a telephone directory, an Internet business directory, or another source to identify businesses that use each of the four types of manufacturing processes.
6. Of the factors that manufacturers consider in locating their facilities, which is most and least important in your opinion? Why?
7. Identify several ways that computers can be used to improve the manufacturing process.

8. Why are the number and size of service businesses increasing in the U.S. economy?
9. How does the concept of production scheduling apply to a service business?
10. How do you believe the Internet will affect the design and delivery of products and services in the next decade?

ANALYZE INFORMATION

1. The Neveau Corporation spent $8,937,250 on research last year. It spent 30 percent on consumer research, 25 percent on pure research, and the remainder on applied research. The company's annual sales for the last year were $297,550,000.
   a. What percentage of sales did the company spend on research?
   b. How much did the company spend on each of the three types of research?
2. A club you belong to has decided to prepare Valentine's Day baskets to sell in school as a fundraiser. The following items will make up the Valentine gift:
   - Small basket
   - Tissue paper for lining the basket
   - Fabric ribbon for bows
   - Three types of candies
   - Small artificial roses
   - "Be my Valentine" stickers
   - Personalized note card

   You plan to assemble the baskets on the afternoon of February 13th so they can be available for sale on the morning of the 14th. You will need to assemble 200 baskets.

   Using your classroom as the space for production, develop a plan for mass production of the Valentine's baskets. Complete a drawing that illustrates the assembly process. Make sure to allow space for the component parts while the baskets are being assembled and for the assembled baskets when they are completed. Consider how you will make the assembly process efficient and how you will ensure a quality product.
3. Participate in a debate with other students in your class. Your teacher will provide instructions on how the debate will be organized. Use research to gather information in support of your position. The two positions to be debated are:
   a. Cities and states should encourage economic development and provide better jobs for their citizens by reducing the amount of regulation on where manufacturing businesses can locate.
   b. Cities and states should increase the regulation of where businesses can locate to protect the environment and its citizens.

4. Join a team with several other students in your class. Your teacher may assign you to a specific group and topic. Use an Internet browser to gather information on one of the following topics: Dr. W. Edwards Deming; Malcolm Baldrige National Quality Award; ISO; Total Quality Management; Continuous Quality Improvement. Prepare an oral report. Include slides developed with computer presentation software. Provide at least three Internet addresses (URLs) where you found useful information on the topic.
5. Develop a chart that lists across the top the four characteristics of services that make them different from products. Then list five service businesses with which you are familiar in the left-hand column of the chart. Now complete the chart by describing how each business provides each of the characteristics listed.

SOLVE BUSINESS PROBLEMS

CASE 20-1

TaeMark, a major software development company, is facing increasing competition from many new businesses. It prides itself on staying in touch with its customers and carefully testing all new software products and upgrades to insure that they are easy to use and free of "bugs" before distributing them for sale. That process is both time-consuming and expensive. It often takes more than a year to get a new type of software on the market. The cost of the research and testing makes the company's software among the most expensive on the market.

TaeMark has noticed a new trend in software development in the past several years. Small and large competitors are flooding the market with new software. Many of the new products never achieve a high level of sales and often are removed from the market after a few months. However, it appears the competitors are willing to develop many products that don't sell with the hope that a few will be very successful and profitable. Also, most of the new software products are introduced without much testing to ensure quality. The new software developers believe that customers will put up with problems as long as the company quickly puts out a new edition of the software that corrects the problem. Competitors may put out two or three editions of a product in the time it takes TaeMark to develop and test one product. Because of the way the new software developers operate, they can price their software much lower than TaeMark can. TaeMark is also finding a change in customer attitudes about software developers. Customers express growing dissatisfaction with quality and say they are not willing to pay high prices for software when they know they will have to upgrade the software frequently.

Think Critically:

1. Why do you believe some companies are willing to forego the time and cost of research and testing in order to get products on the market faster?
2. Why do you believe customers appear to have negative attitudes toward software developers yet are still willing to purchase their products?
3. The new competitors are allowing customers to identify problems with their software. Then, they develop new editions that correct the problems. Is this really a form of research? Why or why not?
4. Would you advise TaeMark to change its product development process to be more like the new competitors or to continue the process it has used in the past? What are the advantages and disadvantages of each choice?

CASE 20-2

Rebecca and Jacob DeNucci vacation with their family each summer on an island just off the coast of North Carolina. The island is a popular tourist area with several large hotels and a ferry boat that brings people from the mainland to the island for day-long visits. Rebecca and Jacob began to think about ways they could use their time to make money during the summer. They thought about the needs of the tourists visiting the island, and they decided to begin a guide service for those people who wanted to explore the hills and forests of the island.

They spent some time planning two different tours. The short tour would last one hour. It would be for those people who wanted to see some of the beautiful spots on the island but were not prepared for extensive hiking. The long tour would take a half day and would include hiking over five miles. It was designed for the more experienced outdoors person who wanted to study the plants, trees, and wildlife unique to the island. They would provide the short tour to groups of 10 to 15 people at a rate of $2.00 per person. The long tour would serve four to eight people and would cost $10.00 per person.

After planning, Rebecca and Jacob developed small posters and some business cards that described their guide service, listed the days and hours the tours were available, and gave their home phone number. They distributed their materials to the hotels and restaurants on the island and the mainland.

Think Critically:

1. Do you think Rebecca and Jacob have done effective planning for their service business? What are some additional things they may want to consider before beginning the business?

2. Suggest ways that the DeNuccis can (a) help prospective customers understand the type and quality of their service, (b) ensure that customers get a high-quality service each time, and (c) provide the service to customers at an appropriate time and location.
3. During the second summer, the DeNuccis' business became extremely successful, and more tours were requested than they could personally lead. Now they are considering hiring other teenagers who also vacation on the island to lead the tours. What recommendations would you make on the qualifications and training of the new employees?

PROJECT: MY BUSINESS, INC.

Two important elements of product planning for a new retail business are (1) gathering information from potential customers about their attitudes toward the product and (2) scheduling the activities to be completed in organizing the business. You will complete those two activities in this section of the project.

DATA COLLECTION

1. Identify five people who represent potential customers for your business. They are your consumer panel, so select people who represent different ages, income levels, occupations, and interests. If possible, meet with them as a group. If that is not possible, then meet with each one individually. During the meeting, describe your business idea to them and ask for their reactions. Have them recommend what they would like to see in the products, prices, and location. They might also recommend some effective ways to promote the business. After you have met with the panel, write a report that summarizes its recommendations.
2. Identify and complete a detailed analysis of as many different juice drinks and related products as you can find in the town or city in which you live. For those that seem to be most popular, try to identify what product features (including factors such as the package) make them successful. Also identify any product features that you believe should be improved.

ANALYSIS

INTERNET

1. Search the Internet to find a list of the recommended steps for opening a new business. Then develop a schedule that lists the

activities in the order that you would complete them for your business. Prepare a time schedule for the completion of each activity. Make certain you allow enough time to complete each activity. Project the date you will be able to open your business.

2. Since your juice business relies on effective service, prepare a list of services you will provide to customers. Then prepare a step-by-step procedure for each service to ensure quality of service delivery each time.

NATURE AND SCOPE OF MARKETING

OBJECTIVES

- 21-1 Discuss the importance of marketing and its role in the economy.
- 21-2 List the activities that are a part of marketing.
- 21-3 Define basic marketing concepts and the four elements of the marketing mix.
- 21-4 Explain the four stages of the product life cycle.
- 21-5 Identify the consumer goods classifications.

THE SUPPLY VS. DEMAND DILEMMA

Tony Taylor looked back on the past week with amazement. He remembered that on Monday he sat through his economics class learning about the concept of supply and demand. As he listened, he thought, "This doesn't apply to me. At most, it might affect some very large businesses. I wonder why we're studying it." But what a week!

He and three friends had wanted to see a certain movie for several weeks but could not find a time when they could all go together. Finally, everyone was available after school on Tuesday to catch the 4:00 p.m. matinee. Tony rushed out of school and down to the bank to withdraw some money for the movie and snacks. When he entered the bank, he encountered a long line of customers waiting for the bank tellers. A computer problem had closed all of the ATMs, so everyone had to do their banking in person.

By the time Tony got his cash, he was already late for the movie. As he dashed up to the theater, he saw his friends standing outside. Because attendance for the movie they wanted to see had recently fallen off, the theater was no longer showing that movie.

Then Wednesday Tony heard that his favorite music group would be performing locally, and tickets would go on sale this weekend. Promoters announced that due to the expected high demand for tickets, a $15 surcharge was being added to the price of each ticket. Tony thought the tickets were already expensive and didn't see why he should have to pay more when several other, less popular groups had played with no surcharge added.

Finally, today had been the most frustrating. Tony's parents owned a small landscaping business, and Tony always helped them find high school students to work during the summer. He had never had problems getting enough applicants for the available jobs. However, few people he talked with today were interested. They told him that since the unemployment rate was so low, many jobs were available that paid more and were not as hard work as landscaping. Now Tony thought back through his week's experiences and remembered Monday's economics discussion. "Maybe supply and demand affects my life more than I realize," he reflected.

IMPORTANCE OF MARKETING

In our private enterprise economy, it is not always easy to match production and consumption. Individual business people make decisions about what they will produce, and individual consumers make decisions about what they want to purchase. For the economy to work well, producers and consumers need information to help them make their decisions, so that producers will provide the types and amounts of products and services that consumers are willing and able to buy.

Marketing activities, when performed well, help to match production and consumption. As you learned in an earlier chapter, *marketing* is a set of activities that gets products from producers to consumers. From that very basic definition, you may think that marketing is simply transporting products. However, it is much more than that. It includes packaging, developing brand names, and determining prices. Marketing even involves financing and storing products until customers purchase them. Also, most products require some type of promotion. Marketing is involved in all of these activities and many more.

A more detailed definition will provide a better description of modern marketing. The American Marketing Association defines **marketing** as the process of planning and executing the conception, pricing, promotion, and distribution of ideas, goods, and services to create exchanges that satisfy individual and organizational objectives. Because marketing is the key tool in matching supply and demand, it can be viewed in another way as well. If marketing is successful, businesses will be able to sell their products and services and consumers will be able to obtain the things they want to purchase. Therefore, the goal of effective marketing is to create and maintain satisfying exchange relationships between buyers and sellers.

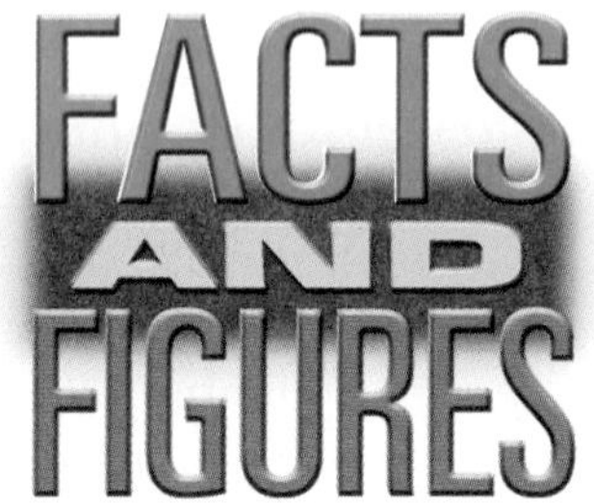

It is estimated that the average consumer sees about 1 million marketing messages a year—about 3,000 a day. One trip to the supermarket alone can expose you to more than 10,000 marketing messages.

Every consumer comes into daily contact with marketing in one form or another. Whenever you see an advertisement on television or on the Internet, notice a truck being unloaded at a warehouse, or use a credit card to purchase a product, you are seeing marketing at work. Each retail store location, each form of advertising, each salesperson, and even each package in which a product is sold is a part of marketing. A great deal of business activity centers on marketing.

Millions of businesses worldwide engage in marketing as their primary business activities. Those organizations include **retailers**—businesses that sell directly to final consumers—and **wholesalers**—businesses that buy products from businesses and sell them to other businesses. The thousands of businesses that sell services, rather than products, are also included. In addition, advertising agencies provide promotional services, finance companies offer loans and other financial services, and transportation companies handle and move products. All of these types of business as well as many others that support the marketing efforts of other businesses are directly involved in marketing.

Many manufacturers have marketing departments with employees who do marketing tasks. For example, marketing department employees do market research, design products, and sell the products. Other types of marketing jobs involve advertising and sales promotion, customer service, credit, and insurance. The many jobs range from clerk to vice president in charge of all marketing activities. Well over one third of all people employed in the United States work in a marketing job or a marketing business.

NATURE OF MARKETING

When many people think of marketing, they think only of advertising and selling. However, many marketing activities must occur before a product can be advertised and sold. To better understand marketing, we will examine the major marketing activities, the cost of marketing activities, and the role of marketing in business.

MARKETING ACTIVITIES

The most common marketing activities are listed below:

Buying Obtaining product to be resold. This activity involves finding suppliers that can provide the right products in the right quality and quantity at a fair price.

Selling Providing personalized and persuasive information to customers to help them buy the products and services they need.

Transporting Moving products from where they were made to where consumers can buy them.

Storing Holding products until customers need them, such as on shelves, in storage rooms, or in warehouses.

Financing Providing money needed to pay for the various marketing activities, such as by obtaining credit when buying and extending credit when selling.

Researching Studying buyer interests and needs, testing products, and gathering facts needed to make good marketing decisions.

Risk taking Assuming the risk of losses that may occur from fire, theft, damage, or other circumstances.

Grading and valuing Grouping goods according to size, quality, or other characteristics, and determining an appropriate price for products and services.

ILLUSTRATION 21-1

Storing is a common marketing activity. What are some others?

COST OF MARKETING

Whether the product is paper clips for offices or huge generators for utility companies, businesses must perform all eight marketing activities just described as the product moves from producer to customer. Because performing these activities requires many people and special equipment, the cost of marketing a product is sometimes higher than the cost of making that product. Therefore, perhaps half or more of the price you pay for a product may result from marketing expenses. Although this amount may appear high, the well-spent marketing dollar contributes much to the success of products and businesses as well as to the satisfaction of customers. Good marketing will make the product or service available to customers when and where they want it.

ROLE OF MARKETING

Marketing has not always been an important part of business. In the early 1900s, business conditions were much different than they are now. Customers had only a few products to choose from and a limited amount of money to spend. Usually only a few producers manufactured a product, and the manufacturing process was not very efficient. Demand for most products was greater than supply. As a result, most producers concentrated on making more kinds of products in greater quantities. Firms were **production oriented**; that is, decisions about what and how to produce received the most attention. Business people did not have to worry a great deal about marketing.

As production became more efficient and more businesses offered similar products, competition among businesses increased. Each business had to work hard to sell its products to customers when those customers saw they had many choices. Companies began to emphasize distribution to get their products to more customers. In addition, advertising and selling became important marketing tools as businesses tried to convince customers that their products were the best. Production was still considered the most important activity, but it was not enough for businesses to be successful. Businesses had become **sales oriented**; that is, they emphasized widespread distribution and promotion in order to sell the products produced.

However, with time, consumers realized that they had many choices of goods and services. Many businesses were competing with each other to sell the same product. Customers could demand products that met their needs, and a company would usually produce them. Companies began to realize it was not enough just to produce a variety of products; they had to produce the right products. Companies that produced what customers wanted and made buying easy for customers were more successful than those that did not.

Today, more and more businesses are focusing on customer needs. They have become **customer oriented**; that is, they direct the activities of the company toward satisfying customers. Keeping the needs

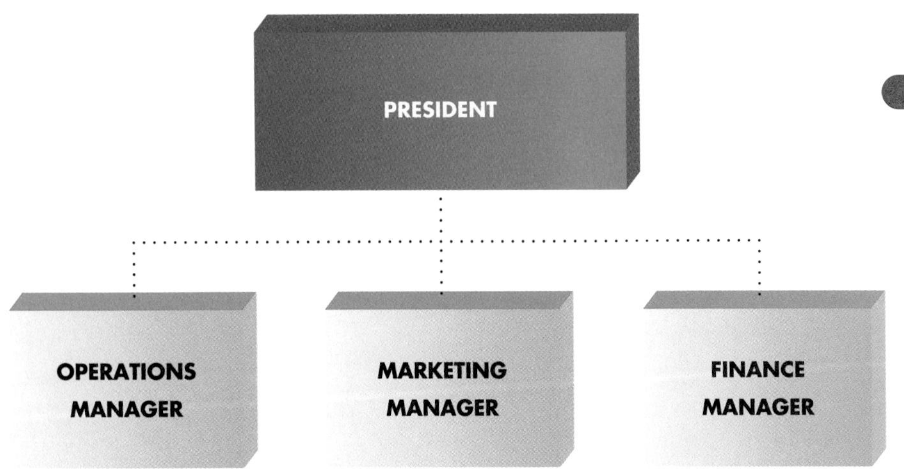

FIGURE 21-1

When a company is customer oriented, the marketing manager is part of top management.

of the consumer uppermost in mind during the design, production, and distribution of a product is called the **marketing concept**.

A company that has adopted the marketing concept will have a marketing manager who is part of top management and is involved in all major decisions, as illustrated in Figure 21-1. Marketing personnel will work closely with the other people in the business to make sure that the company keeps the needs of customers in mind in all operations. The company's success will be determined by more than current profits. While profit is important, long-term success depends on satisfying the customers.

MARKET DETERMINATION

Before a company decides to make and distribute a product to consumers, it must determine the market it wants to serve. Here, **market** refers to the types of buyers a business wishes to attract and where those buyers are located. All companies need to clearly identify their markets.

WHOM TO SERVE A company has many potential customers for every product. Some people may be searching for the product, while others do not currently want the product and will have to be convinced to buy it. Some people will be very easy to reach, while others are quite difficult to contact. For cost reasons, it is usually unwise to try to reach all potential customers. Therefore, a business identifies several groups of potential customers and then decides which group or groups will be the best markets for its product.

Marketers often use population characteristics, such as age, gender, family status, education, income, and occupation, to group consumers. A clothing manufacturer, for example, could handle women's or men's clothing, clothing for children or adults, casual clothing or the latest fashions, and so on. The producer of cellular telephones may want to attract families, people concerned about their safety, or business people.

ILLUSTRATION 21-2

How can a business identify potential customers for its product or service?

Businesses can decide to serve one or more markets. Companies choose a market based on the opportunities for success that the market presents. For example, an attractive market may have few existing competitors, a large number of customers with a need for the product, and customers with sufficient money to spend on such a product. If the business has the ability to produce a product that will satisfy the needs of that market, then it is a good market for the business to serve.

WHERE TO SERVE Producers often limit the scope of their business operations to certain geographic areas. Marketing managers study sections of a city, state, country, or continent to determine whether their product might sell more successfully in one area than another. Climate, for example, may cause a small producer of air conditioners to concentrate its marketing efforts on countries with hot and humid climates for its markets, whereas the maker of snow skis may concentrate on areas where there is an abundance of cold weather and mountains. Some products may sell better on the coasts than in the middle of the country, or in rural areas better than cities. Finding the best marketing locations enables a business to achieve the most sales for its marketing dollar.

IDENTIFYING TARGET MARKETS Companies can produce goods and services that meet consumers' needs better if they know who their customers are, where they are located, and what they want and need. Many companies spend a great deal of money on market research before they begin to develop products. **Market research** is the study of a company's current and prospective customers.

Companies use market research to identify their target markets. **Target markets** are groups of customers with very similar needs to whom the company plans to sell its product. If the company can find a group of people with very similar needs, it can more easily produce a product that will satisfy everyone in the group. On the other hand, if people in the group have needs that are quite different, it will be almost impossible to develop a product that will satisfy each of them.

Imagine developing a product like a bicycle. It can be made in a variety of sizes and shapes with a number of special features. No one bicycle will satisfy everyone's needs. Long-distance racers want something very different from what the weekend rider desires. However, if you could find a group of people with very similar needs, you could successfully design a bicycle for that group. If you identified the groups depicted in Figure 21-2, each with unique needs for your product, your bicycle company could choose to design a slightly different product for each group.

ELEMENTS OF MARKETING

Marketing managers have many decisions to make. These decisions center on four elements of marketing: (1) the *product,* (2) its *price,* (3) *distribution* (sometimes referred to as *place*), and (4) *promotion.* Planning each element involves answering some important questions. For example, assume that you want to market a new product. You must answer the following questions related to the four elements of

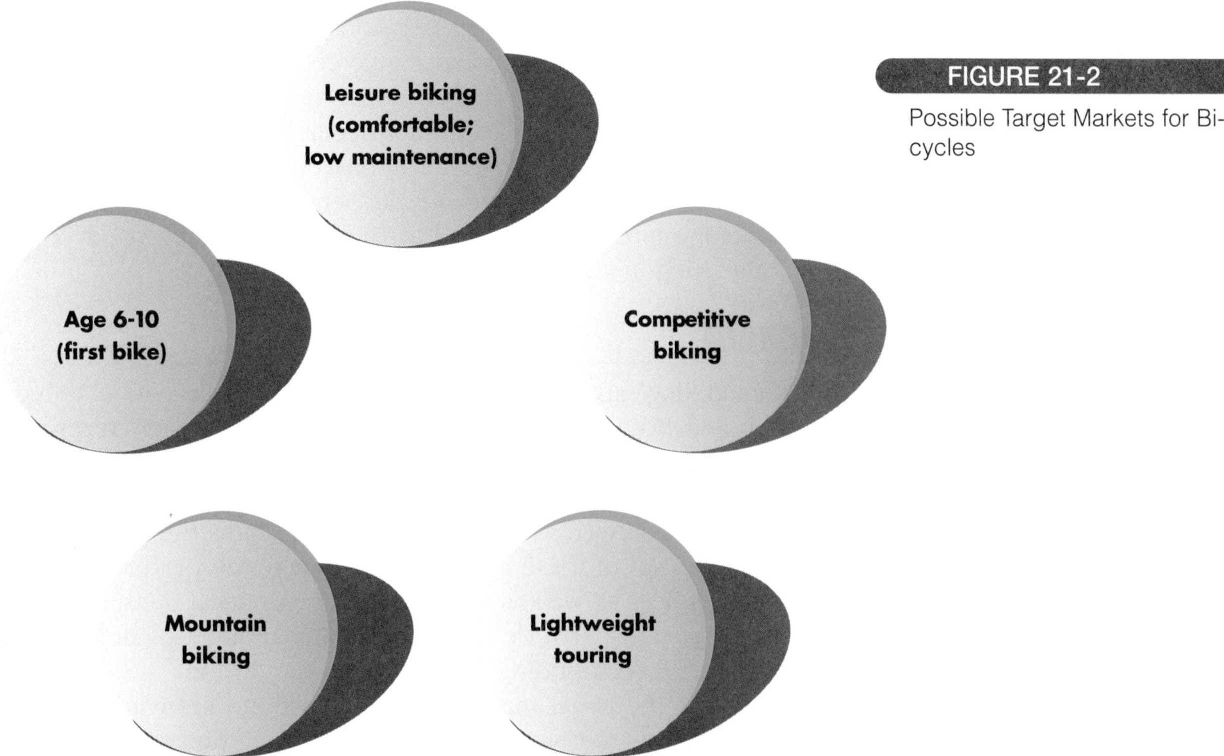

FIGURE 21-2

Possible Target Markets for Bicycles

CYBER COMMUNICATION

The world of e-mail has its own language. Regular users will quickly pick up its distinctive vocabulary.

- *Spamming* refers to sending mass, unsolicited messages or advertising (called *spam*).
- *Flaming* is the act of sending angry or insulting messages (called *flames*).
- *Emoticons* are icons, built by combining various letters or symbols, used to reflect emotion. Because they can be created with any keyboard, they are popular in e-mail messages to communicate meanings (such as sarcasm, surprise, confusion, sadness, or happiness).
- Abbreviations are frequently used in order to speed up keying. *BTW* means "by the way." *IMHO* means "in my humble opinion."

ACTIVITY Under what circumstances is it appropriate to use e-mail vocabulary and "tools," such as emoticons? Are there instances when it would not be suitable? Write a one-page article describing both kinds of occasions. If you have e-mail access, include any personal experiences you have had.

marketing: (1) Will you make the product in one size and color, or in several? (2) Will you price the product high, medium, or low? (3) Will you sell the product in retail stores or over the Internet? (4) Will you use newspaper, radio, television, or Internet advertising?

The blend of all decisions related to the four elements of marketing—product, price, distribution, and promotion—is called the **marketing mix.** The marketing mix for a new product may be to design the item for young adults, give it a low price, sell it through retail stores, and advertise it on the radio. Or it could be to produce a medium-priced item to be advertised on television and sold door-to-door to senior citizens. Can you identify the marketing mix for one of the businesses that Tony Taylor thought about in the chapter-opening scenario?

Several companies marketing the same product may use very different marketing mixes, because they made different decisions. Furthermore, they must review their decisions frequently, because conditions change constantly. Changes in general economic conditions, changes in consumer needs, and the development of new or improved products by competitors are factors that may require a change in the marketing mix. Next, you will learn about the decisions involved in each marketing mix element.

PRODUCT

The first marketing mix element is the product. **Product** can be defined as all attributes, both tangible and intangible, that customers receive in exchange for the purchase price. For example, when consumers buy a computer, they are also buying the company's customer service and technical support as well as other intangibles, such as the prestige of the brand name. All of these attributes are part of the product. Products include services as well as physical goods. A critical question relating to the product is: What do customers want? Product planning and development deal with finding answers to that question.

By identifying the target market for a product and knowing what customers in that market want, the company can design a product to fit those customers. Market information can help the people involved in product planning make such decisions as:

1. The *number* of items to produce.
2. The *physical features* the product should possess, such as the size, shape, color, and weight.
3. The *quality* preferred by the target market.
4. The *number of different models* and the *required features* of each model needed to serve the various markets the company wants to attract.
5. The *packaging features* of the item, such as the color and the shape of the package, as well as the information printed on the package.
6. The *brand name* to use.
7. Product *guarantees* and *services* the customers would like.
8. The *image* to be communicated to customers by the products, features, packaging, and brand name.

PRICE

The second mix element around which marketing decisions are made is price. **Price** is the amount of money given to acquire a product. The many decisions a company makes during product development influence the price. First, the price must be high enough to cover the costs of producing and marketing the product. If the company decided to manufacture a high-quality product, it would likely have to set a higher price to cover its costs than it would for a low-quality product. The number of competing products and their prices, the demand for the product, and whether the product will be sold for cash or credit are some of the many factors that influence price decisions.

When making price decisions, a company must do more than just set a price that customers will pay for the product. It must decide what price to charge other companies that buy and resell the product. Will the company offer coupons, discounts, or other promotional methods to attract customers? Will it allow customers to bargain for a lower price or trade in a used product for a new one? As you can see, pricing is not an easy marketing decision.

DISTRIBUTION

The third element around which marketing decisions are made is distribution. Distribution decisions relate to the economic concept of *place utility,* which you studied in Chapter 3. *Place utility* means that the product must be in a place where customers need or want it. **Distribution** (or **place**), therefore, is the set of activities required to transport and store products, and make them available to customers.

Marketing managers must select businesses to handle products as they move from the producer to the consumer. Many manufacturers prefer to use other businesses to sell their products rather than try to reach consumers directly. Therefore, they may sell their products to retailers or to wholesalers, which then sell to retailers. Choosing the various routes that products will follow as they are distributed and the businesses that will sell them to consumers are important marketing decisions.

Planning distribution also includes the actual physical handling of the products and the customer service provided in processing orders. Have you ever opened a product you purchased, only to find it damaged or missing pieces? Have you ordered something from a catalog or the Internet and have the order lost, filled with the wrong merchandise, or sent to an incorrect address? Each of these examples describes a problem with a company's distribution system and will result in dissatisfied customers as well as a loss of sales and profits for the company.

PROMOTION

The fourth marketing mix element for which decisions must be made is promotion. **Promotion** means providing information to consumers that will assist them in making a decision and persuade them to purchase a product or service. The major methods of promotion are advertising and personal selling. You will learn about other types of promotion in a later chapter.

Promotional decisions for a digital camera might involve selecting advertising as the main method to use and deciding whether to advertise in magazines or by mail directly to prospective customers. Marketing managers decide when to advertise and how frequently to show the ad. Then they must decide whether to use sales demonstrations in stores or to have product demonstrations at consumer electronics shows. Managers must also decide the type of information to communicate to consumers and whether to try to communicate directly with each customer or use more impersonal messages that can reach a larger audience at a time.

The type of product and its price influence promotional decisions. The strategy for promoting an expensive piece of jewelry will be much different from that for promoting tennis shoes.

While the product and its price provide general guides for promotion, marketing managers must consider many other factors before developing the actual promotions. For example, the company will budget only a certain amount of money for promotion. Managers must decide when to spend the money and how much to spend for advertising, displays, and other types of promotion. They must consider what promotions competitors are using and what information consumers need in order to decide to buy.

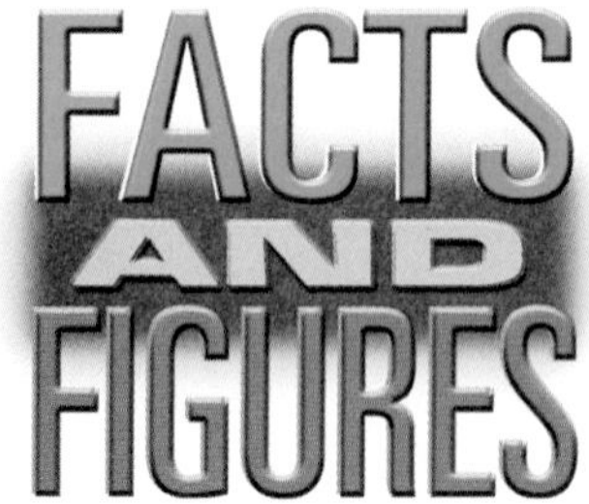

Eastman Kodak wanted to attract young consumers to its one-time-use cameras. Kodak developed a "Through Your Eyes" promotion by sponsoring a new teen rock band, Youngstown. The band played concerts at various U.S. malls, where souvenir pictures were snapped of the band members with their fans. In addition, "Through Your Eyes" retail packages were sold, featuring the band's CD and a Kodak one-time-use camera.

MARKETING PLAN

All the marketing decisions for a particular product must work together for the product to succeed. For example, marketing managers may want to time the advertising to coincide with the product's arrival in stores. To help coordinate marketing activities, businesses develop a marketing plan. The **marketing plan** is a detailed written description of all marketing activities that a business must accomplish in order to sell its products. It describes the goals the business wants to accomplish, the target markets it wants to serve, and the marketing mixes it will use for each product. It identifies the ways in which the business will evaluate its marketing to determine if the activities were successful and the goals were accomplished. The marketing plan is written for a specific time period (often one year).

The top marketing executive develops the marketing plan, based on information from many other people. Market research will be very important in developing a marketing plan. Once a written plan is completed, all of the people involved in marketing activities can use it to guide their decisions about each marketing mix element and to coordinate their efforts as they complete the planned activities.

THE PRODUCT LIFE CYCLE

Successful products move through rather predictable stages throughout their product lives. They are introduced, and then their sales and profits increase rapidly until a point at which they level off. Eventually, both profits and sales will decline, as newer products replace the old one. The **product life cycle** is the four stages of sales and profit performance through which all brands of a product progress: introduction, growth, maturity, and decline. Figure 21-3 is a graphical depiction of sales and profits at different stages of the product life cycle.

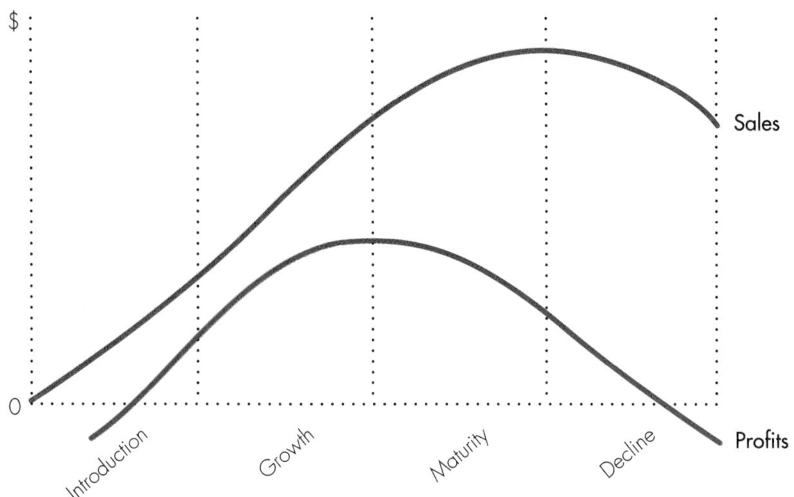

FIGURE 21-3

Sales and profits follow a predictable pattern as products progress through each stage of the product life cycle.

INTRODUCTION

In the **introduction stage,** a brand-new product enters the market. Initially, there is only one brand of the product available for consumers to purchase. The new product is quite different from, and hopefully better than, products customers are currently using. While every product has gone through the introduction stage at some time, examples of products that were recently in that stage include Web-ready cellular telephones, high definition television (HDTV), and portable audio players that can download digital music files from the Internet.

When a company introduces a product, it is concerned about successfully producing and distributing. The company needs to inform prospective customers about the brand-new product and its uses, since people will be unfamiliar with it. There is no competition from the same type of product, but customers will probably be using other older products. The company must show customers how the new product is better than the products they are currently using. Initially, only a few customers will buy the product, but their experience will often determine whether other people will want to buy it as well.

The costs of producing and marketing a new product are usually very high, resulting in a loss or very low profits for the firm initially. The company is counting on future sales to make a profit. If a product is successfully introduced, an increasing number of consumers will accept the new product, sales will start to grow rapidly, and profits will emerge.

GROWTH

When competitors see the success of the new product, they will want to get into that market as well. When several brands of the new product are available, the market moves into the **growth stage** of the life cycle. If customers like the new product, they will begin buying it regularly and telling others about it, so more and more customers are now regular purchasers.

In the growth stage, each company tries to attract customers to its specific brand. Companies attempt to improve their brands by adding features that they hope will satisfy customers. They also add to their distribution to make the product more readily available to the growing market. Most companies make a profit in this stage. Profits are likely to increase as companies sell enough of the product to cover the research and development costs. Examples of products that have been in the growth stage recently are digital video cameras, personal digital assistants (PDAs), and sports utility vehicles (SUVs).

MATURITY

A product in the maturity stage has been purchased by large numbers of customers and has become quite profitable. In the **maturity stage,** the product has many competing brands with very similar features. Customers have a hard time identifying differences among the brands but may have developed a loyalty to one or a very few brands.

ILLUSTRATION 21-3

How might a fast-food company respond to the maturity stage of the product life cycle?

In this stage, companies emphasize the promotion of their brand name, packaging, a specific image, and often the price of the product. Because there are so many customers, each business has to distribute the product widely, adding to their costs. Competition becomes intense. Companies must spend a lot on promotion and reduce prices, because customers have many brands from which to choose. Profits usually fall even though sales may still increase. Products in the maturity stage include automobiles, desktop computers, personal care products such as toothpaste and deodorant, and many other products that you use regularly and purchase without a great deal of thought.

One way that businesses respond to the maturity stage of the life cycle is to look for new markets. Businesses often begin to move into international markets as competition increases in their home countries. As fast-food companies found fewer and fewer attractive locations for new stores in the U.S., they began to open outlets in Canada, Europe, and Mexico. Now they are expanding into South America and even Russia and China.

DECLINE

Many products stay in the maturity stage of the life cycle for a long time. However, sooner or later products move into a decline stage. The **decline stage** occurs when a new product is introduced that is much better or easier to use, and customers begin to switch from the old product to the new product. As more and more customers are attracted to the new product, the companies selling the old product will soon see declines in profits and sales. The companies may not be able to improve the older products enough to compete with the new products, so they drop them from the market when declining profits no longer support their existence.

Some companies have been able to move old products out of the decline stage by finding new uses for them. For example, baby oil is now being used as a suntan product, and baking soda is used to remove odors from refrigerators and cat litter boxes. If companies cannot save a product from the decline stage, they will attempt to sell their remaining inventory to the customers who still prefer it. However, they will spend as little money as possible while marketing the product and will not produce any more.

TYPES OF CONSUMER PRODUCTS

When making marketing decisions, marketers need to understand how customers shop for and use products. Products can be classified as either industrial goods or consumer goods. **Industrial goods** are products designed for use by another business. Frequently, industrial goods are purchased in large quantities, are made to special order for a specific customer, or are sold to a selected group of buyers located within a limited geographic area. Examples of industrial goods include bricks purchased by a building contractor, aluminum purchased by an aircraft manufacturer, and computers and computer supplies purchased by accounting firms. Many, but not all, industrial goods are used to produce other products or are incorporated into the products being produced. Some are used in the operation of the business.

Consumer goods are products designed for personal or home use. Jewelry, furniture, magazines, soft drinks, and computer games are some of the many products used by consumers. Consumer goods require careful marketing attention, because there are so many products and brands available and so many possible customers located throughout the world.

Depending on who is making the purchase and how they will use it, however, a product may be both a consumer good and an industrial good. Gasoline and laptop computers, for instance, may be purchased by consumers in small quantities or by businesses in large quantities.

To look at the attributes of consumer goods more specifically, marketers group them into four categories: convenience goods, shopping goods, specialty goods, and unsought goods. The categories are based on (1) how important the product is to the customer and (2) whether the customer is willing to spend time to compare products and brands before making a decision to buy. Companies make different marketing decisions, depending on which category of consumer goods they are selling.

CONVENIENCE GOODS

Convenience goods are inexpensive items that consumers purchase regularly without a great deal of thought. Consumers are not willing to shop around for these products because they purchase them often, the many competing products do not differ much from each other, and they don't cost much money. Therefore, marketers will need to sell their convenience goods through many retail outlets that are conveniently located close to where people work and live. Products that are usually treated as convenience goods are candy, milk, soft drinks, pencils, soap, and many other inexpensive household items.

SHOPPING GOODS

Products that consumers purchase less frequently than convenience goods, usually have a higher price, and require some buying thought are called **shopping goods.** Customers see important differences between brands of these products in terms of price and features. Therefore, they are willing to shop at several businesses and compare products and brands before they make a purchase. Shopping goods do not have to be sold in as many places as convenience goods. They need effective promotion so customers can make informed decisions. Cars, furniture, large appliances, and houses are all examples of shopping goods for most people.

SPECIALTY GOODS

Specialty goods are products that customers insist upon having and are willing to search for until they find them. Customers who decide that only one product or brand will satisfy them will shop until they locate and buy that brand. Marketers place their specialty goods in fewer businesses within a shopping area, price them higher than competing

ILLUSTRATION 21-4

How are specialty goods different from other types of goods?

products and brands, and need not promote them as much as other types of consumer products. Examples of specialty goods are designer clothing, expensive jewelry, and certain brands of cameras, computers, or automobiles.

UNSOUGHT GOODS

Customers do not shop for some products because they do not have a strong need for them. Such products are known as **unsought goods,** and they present a difficult marketing problem. Life insurance, encyclopedias, and funeral services are unsought by most consumers. A company marketing unsought goods will usually have to go to the customer and use personal selling to discuss the need for the product. Unless the customer recognizes a need that the product can satisfy, the product will remain unsold.

SUCCESSFUL MARKETING STRATEGIES

Marketing managers cannot afford to guess about the types of marketing mixes to use. Marketing is too expensive and customers have too many choices for businesses to risk making mistakes. Marketers use concepts such as the product life cycle and consumer goods categories to plan effective marketing mixes. For example, if a product is in the growth stage, the mix will be quite different than if it is in the maturity stage. If consumers view a product as a specialty good, marketers will emphasize different mix elements than if it is a convenience good. Marketers study markets and competition and use their knowledge of marketing to make decisions that will satisfy customer needs and result in a profit for the company.

Many consumer complaints today involve marketing activities. Misleading advertisements, poor customer service, high prices, and poor delivery are all marketing problems. Businesses must be as careful in making marketing decisions as they need to be in producing a quality product. In the next two chapters, we will examine each part of the marketing mix in more detail. You will learn how businesses plan products and use marketing activities to satisfy customers and attract them away from competing businesses.

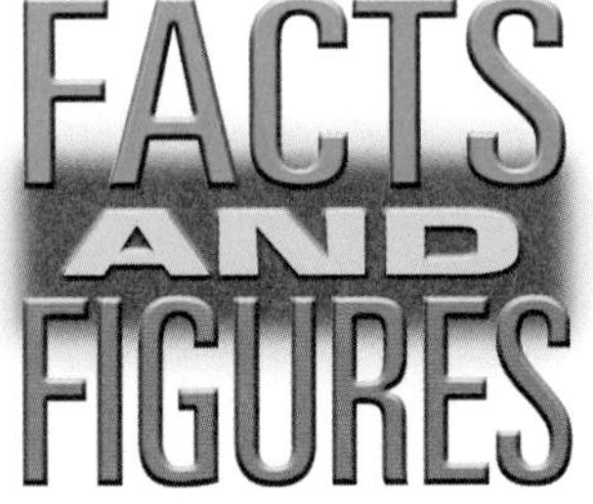

Marketing to children continues to be a controversial issue. The Federal Trade Commission's Children's Online Privacy Protection Act requires children's Web site publishers to post comprehensive privacy policies on their sites. In addition, the sites must notify parents about their information practices and obtain parental consent before collecting any personal information from children under age 13.

MANAGEMENT CLOSE-UP

RETAILERS THAT CHANGED BUSINESS

Most manufacturers of consumer goods rely on retailers to provide the connection with the customers who will purchase their products. The retailers purchase the products from the manufacturer, stock them in stores that are close to the locations where customers live, advertise and sell the products, and often offer delivery of the products and many customer services. Retailers provide these important marketing functions for manufacturers.

A few retailers have changed the way business is done. Because of their ideas, they forced their competitors to respond or risk going out of business.

One of the first was Sears Roebuck. In the late 1800s and early 1900s, some of the largest retailers reached their customers by mail. They sent catalogs to people all over the country and filled the customer orders by mail or by trucks and trains. Sears decided customers wanted faster service and the opportunity to examine merchandise before making a purchase. The company began building large stores filled with a large variety of products. Customers flocked to the stores, and Sears became the largest retailer in the world.

While Sears stores were located in large and mid-sized cities, Sam Walton saw opportunities in the thousands of small communities around the country. Wal-Mart grew because of its emphasis on carefully chosen locations, working with manufacturers to buy at the lowest prices, developing an efficient product distribution system, and creating a friendly shopping experience. Because of those efforts, Wal-Mart could offer lower prices than most other retailers. With this new philosophy of retailing, Wal-Mart replaced Sears as the world's largest retailer.

Today, a new form of retailing is developing, led by Jeff Bezos. Mr. Bezos recognized the new Internet consumers. By developing an easy-to-use Web site and offering customers secure online purchases, rapid product delivery, and effective customer service, Amazon.com developed into the largest e-tailer, with revenues approaching one billion dollars.

In each example, the success of the companies resulted from finding new ways to offer products and services to consumers. By performing marketing activities better than their competitors, each company has become a leading retailer.

THINK CRITICALLY

1. Why were major retailers using catalogs and mail order in the late 1800s and early 1900s to sell products to their customers? What changes were occurring in the U.S. that provided the opportunity for Sears Roebuck to change the way products were sold?
2. Review the eight marketing activities described in the chapter and suggest which of the activities were most important to the success of Wal-Mart. Why were many of Wal-Mart's competitors not able to offer the same low prices to customers?
3. Do you believe that an e-tailer like Amazon.com will ever replace Wal-Mart as the world's largest retailer? Why or why not?

CHAPTER 21 REVIEW

CHAPTER CONCEPTS

- Marketing helps to balance the supply of products produced with the demand for those products. The goal of effective marketing is to create and maintain satisfying exchanges between buyers and sellers.
- Every business is involved in marketing. Marketing is the primary activity for retailers and wholesalers. More than one third of all people employed in the U.S. complete marketing activities or work for a marketing business.
- Marketing is more than advertising and selling. It involves eight activities: buying, selling, transporting, storing, financing, researching, risk taking, and grading and valuing.
- During the 1900s, marketing approaches evolved from production-oriented to sales-oriented and finally to customer-oriented. Companies that operate according to the marketing concept keep the needs of consumers uppermost in mind during the design, production, and distribution of a product.
- Businesses must decide whom to serve and where to serve when planning marketing. They use marketing research to identify target markets—customers with very similar needs that the business wants to serve.
- Marketing managers make decisions about the four elements of marketing: the product, its price, distribution, and promotion. Together, these decisions form the marketing mix.
- Companies prepare a written marketing plan to coordinate the many decisions and activities involved in marketing. The top marketing executive usually prepares the marketing plan with information gathered from many other people.
- The product life cycle consists of four stages of sales and profit performance that products move through during their time on the market. The stages are introduction, growth, maturity, and decline.
- Products are classified as either industrial or consumer goods, based on who purchases them and how they will use the products. Consumer goods can be classified into four categories based on their importance to consumers and how much time consumers are willing to spend making the buying decisions. The categories are convenience, shopping, specialty, and unsought goods.

BUILD VOCABULARY POWER

Define the following terms and concepts.

1. marketing
2. retailers
3. wholesalers
4. buying
5. selling
6. transporting
7. storing
8. financing

9. researching
10. risk taking
11. grading and valuing
12. production oriented
13. sales oriented
14. customer oriented
15. marketing concept
16. market
17. market research
18. target markets
19. marketing mix
20. product
21. price
22. distribution (place)
23. promotion
24. marketing plan
25. product life cycle
26. introduction stage
27. growth stage
28. maturity stage
29. decline stage
30. industrial goods
31. consumer goods
32. convenience goods
33. shopping goods
34. specialty goods
35. unsought goods

REVIEW FACTS

1. In our economy, who makes decisions about what will be produced and what will be purchased?
2. What is the goal of effective marketing?
3. What is the difference between a retailer and a wholesaler?
4. What percentage of all U.S. employees work in a marketing job or for a marketing business?
5. How do customers benefit, even if more than half of the price of the products they purchase goes to pay for marketing activities?
6. Why did businesses change from a production orientation to a customer orientation during the last century?
7. What two questions must a firm answer about its customers when identifying a market to serve?
8. How does a target market make it easier for a company to produce a product that will satisfy customer needs?
9. What are the four elements of the marketing mix?
10. When marketing managers make decisions about distribution, what economic concept are they applying?
11. Why are the physical handling of the product and customer service important parts of distribution planning?
12. What are the two major methods of promotion?
13. How does the amount of competition change as products progress through the stages of the product life cycle?
14. How can the same product be both an industrial good and a consumer good?
15. What are the two factors that determine the categories of consumer goods?

DISCUSS IDEAS

1. In what ways are trucking companies, banks, and warehouses marketing businesses?

2. Explain how valuing and grading are used in the marketing of products you would purchase at a supermarket.
3. Why is it important for a business to conduct market research to determine the markets to be served before deciding what to produce and sell?
4. Identify several products for which you believe the cost of marketing would be well below half of the price customers would pay. Then identify several others for which you believe the cost of marketing would be well over half of the final price. What differences influence the cost of marketing for these products?
5. Do you believe that use of the Internet by businesses will increase or decrease the amount of marketing they must do? Do you believe it will increase or decrease the cost of marketing for those companies? Why?
6. What are some examples of goods or services that would sell well only in specific geographic locations?
7. How might customers know if a company has a customer orientation rather than a sales orientation?
8. How can a product's package be used to satisfy customers?
9. How do the other three elements of the marketing mix influence the price of a product? What could a marketing manager do with other mix elements to increase or decrease a product's price?
10. Why is a consumer willing to spend time shopping for some products but not for others?

ANALYZE INFORMATION

1. Select any product that you use regularly. Using the eight marketing activities listed in the chapter, give an example showing how each activity was completed between the time the company produced the product and the time someone purchased it.

2. Use magazines, newspapers, or the Internet to find examples that illustrate each of the four elements of the marketing mix—product, price, distribution, and promotion. Either by cutting and pasting the examples or by drawing the examples on posterboard (your teacher will give you specific instructions), create a collage illustrating the concept of a marketing mix.
3. On a separate sheet of paper, complete the following table for the four products listed by determining the total cost of the product and the percentage of the final product price that was spent on marketing.

	Product 1	***Product 2***	***Product 3***	***Product 4***
Raw Materials	$6.20	$28.00	$12,650.00	$ .78
Other Product Costs	3.80	56.50	2,500.00	.14

(continued)

	Product 1	*Product 2*	*Product 3*	*Product 4*
Operating Expenses	4.30	74.00	4,825.00	.32
Marketing Expenses	14.90	96.50	3,500.00	2.50
Total Cost	______	______	______	______
Retail Price	45.20	576.00	32,750.00	4.80
Marketing as a % of Retail Price	______	______	______	______

4. Participate in a debate with other class members. Your teacher will assign you to one side of the issue or the other and will give you specific instructions for the debate. The issue is: Marketing causes people to spend money for things they otherwise would not buy and do not need. Do you agree or disagree?

5. Interview 10 people to determine how they purchase jeans. Ask each of them the following questions:

a. Where do you usually buy your jeans?

b. What product features are important to you when you are deciding to buy?

c. How important is price in your decision to purchase your jeans?

d. Do you usually buy one brand?

e. Do you usually look in several stores before you buy a pair of jeans?

Based on each person's answers, determine whether he or she is treating jeans as a convenience, shopping, specialty, or unsought good. Write a short report discussing your findings and your conclusions. Include a chart or graph illustrating your findings.

SOLVE BUSINESS PROBLEMS

CASE 21-1

The personal computer market is becoming very competitive, and it is getting more and more difficult for computer manufacturers to make a profit. Technology changes rapidly, so if a company has not sold its inventory of one model of computer when a competitor introduces a newer, faster, more powerful model, it often has to sell its older model at a loss. Many computer purchasers are not brand-loyal and either look for a lower price or expect the manufacturer to include related products, such as a monitor, printer, scanner, or large amount of software with the new computer.

One computer manufacturer began a new marketing program that offered customers a free computer. The free computer was not the manufacturer's latest model. The offer also did not include a large monitor or additional equipment or software. Instead, the manufacturer required the customer to sign a contract to use the manufacturer's Internet service for at least three years at a cost of $25.95 a month. Typically, consumers could buy the same service for as little as $14.95 a month from other companies.

Think Critically:

1. Which stage of the product life cycle do you believe computers are in, based on the case information? Why?
2. In which consumer product category do you believe consumers classify computers, based on the case information? Why?
3. Describe the target market that you believe might be attracted to the manufacturer's offer of a free computer.
4. What are the advantages and disadvantages of offering consumers a computer that is not the company's latest model?

CASE 21-2

The Willomette Company manufactures small household appliances, such as toasters, blenders, and food processors. Ron Willomette started the company 20 years ago as a sole proprietorship. Initially, Mr. Willomette reconditioned and resold used appliances that other companies had manufactured. Now he has incorporated the business and has two manufacturing plants that produce his own brand of appliances. The Willomette Company has a full line of over 50 models of products that are sold throughout the United States.

In the past five years, competition from foreign companies in the small appliance market has increased. While the competition hasn't hurt Willomette yet, company executives don't want to wait until sales and profits start to decline before acting. One vice president recommended that Willomette begin a program of international marketing. Based on the traveling she has done, she believes that the demand for Willomette's appliances would be very strong in Europe and several countries in Africa and South America. Because there has been strong customer acceptance of the company's products in the U.S., she believes Willomette should have no trouble selling the same products in other countries.

Think Critically:

1. Which of the major marketing activities would Willomette have to perform to sell its products in international markets?
2. How does the marketing concept relate to the decision Willomette must make about entering international markets?
3. Do you agree that products that are successful in the U.S. will also be successful in other countries? Explain.
4. What would Willomette have to do if it wanted to try to increase the demand for its products in the U.S. by selling industrial products?

PROJECT: MY BUSINESS, INC.

To market your products effectively, you will need to identify the target market for your business. Then you must determine how customers will view your product as they make decisions to buy. The activities in this section of the project will help you understand your customers, so you can develop an effective marketing mix.

DATA COLLECTION

1. Locate books, newspaper and magazine articles, Web resources, and other information sources that describe people who are interested in healthy lifestyles and nutrition. Make a list of the sources of information that will help you describe possible target markets for your juice bar and provide brief descriptions of the information in each of the sources you list.
2. Review advertisements from other businesses that might compete with your juice bar. For each business, prepare a description of the target market it appears they are appealing to and the key part of their marketing mix that they are advertising.

ANALYSIS

1. Using the categories of consumer goods listed in the chapter, determine if customers will treat your product as a convenience, shopping, specialty, or unsought good. Describe how that decision will influence the way you market your products.
2. Develop a detailed description of one or more target markets that you can serve successfully. Make sure the description includes both an identification of the target market and their important needs related to your product. For the principal target market, prepare a general description of the marketing mix you believe you should provide to satisfy those consumers.

PRODUCT DEVELOPMENT AND DISTRIBUTION

OBJECTIVES

- **22-1** Identify why product development decisions are important to consumers as well as businesses.
- **22-2** Describe the three levels of product development and the types of product selection.
- **22-3** Discuss how packaging and branding improve product sales and customer satisfaction.
- **22-4** Discuss the important factors to be considered when selecting channels of distribution.
- **22-5** Describe the characteristics of major forms of transportation used to distribute products.
- **22-6** Give examples of product-handling procedures that improve product distribution.

DECISIONS, DECISIONS

Alexis Converse sat at her computer in the purchasing office late into the night. She was challenged by a crisis facing her company. A major piece of manufacturing equipment had failed today and could not be repaired. Each day that the equipment was not operational would cost the company several thousand dollars in lost production and sales.

The machine was over 10 years old, and it had worked well for most of the time the company owned it. In discussing its replacement with the production manager, Alexis agreed that they should replace the machine with the same brand. However, there were now two new models to consider. Alexis could purchase the equipment directly from the manufacturer from its location in Italy or from an equipment distributor located two states away. The manufacturer would take eight days to deliver, whereas the distributor could have one model available in two days and the other in four.

Alexis was concerned about installation and maintenance. She wanted to make sure the new machine would not break down again. The manufacturer had a specialist who would travel to the plant to install and make sure the equipment was working. That company also included a five-year warranty with onsite service, but it added 25 percent to the cost of the equipment. Alexis had heard that the distributor could help with the installation but did not provide an additional warranty or service. Delays or problems in installation would only add to the company's losses.

All Alexis wanted to do was to get the equipment replaced and the company back into production. Why did these decisions have to be so difficult?

You learned in Chapter 21 that companies develop a marketing mix to satisfy customers and make a profit. The marketing mix is made up of the product, distribution, price, and promotion plans. Offering products that meet the needs of customers would seem to be a company's most important responsibility. The product is important but must be carefully coordinated with each of the other mix elements. In this chapter, we will examine how companies plan products and make distribution decisions.

PRODUCT DEVELOPMENT

As you learned in Chapter 21, a *product* consists of all attributes, both tangible and intangible, that customers receive in exchange for the purchase price. It includes both physical goods and services. Some products are very simple and easy for the customer to understand and use, while others are very complex. Because of the variety of customer needs, the uses for products, and the number of competing companies producing and selling products, product development decisions must be made carefully. If companies produce the wrong products in the wrong quantities without the features and services customers need, they will have invested a great deal of time and money with no chance to sell

ILLUSTRATION 22-1

Why should a company make product development decisions very carefully?

the products at a profit. They will quickly lose out to competitors who make better product decisions.

Business people and consumers usually hold very different perceptions of a product. Business people think of their products as what they have to offer to customers. On the other hand, consumers are more likely to think of products as ways to satisfy their needs. The company that manufactures the machine Alexis needed to purchase at the beginning of the chapter designed a product to perform a specific production function. The company is expert in the technology of equipment design, so it builds what it believes to be a good product that customers will prefer, compared to alternatives. Alexis wants a good piece of equipment but is also very concerned about delivery, installation services, maintenance, and cost. If the equipment manufacturer does not carefully consider all of Alexis's needs, it probably won't make the sale.

Even the simplest products are made up of several components. An inexpensive handheld calculator consists of the operating unit to make the calculations, a case, display, and keys. It may be battery operated or use solar power or electricity. It could have a backlight to illuminate the display in the dark. It could be pocket- or desk-sized, and on and on. Also, it might come in a variety of colors and include special mathematical functions, a protective case, and an instruction manual. Given the combination of features, the price of the calculator could range from a very few dollars to as much as $50 or more. If you were the person responsible for designing a calculator to sell, what combination of design features would you include? This example shows that product planning can be very complex. Businesses have many choices in designing products but will make a mistake if they ignore the needs and wishes of consumers or believe they know more than the customers about their needs.

PRODUCT DESIGN LEVELS

There are three levels of product design—a basic product, an enhanced product, and an extended product. The **basic product** is the physical product in its simplest form. It should be simple in design and easy for consumers to understand and see how it can meet a need. The basic product of one company will usually be very much like that of its competitors.

The basic product will meet an important consumer need. However, most consumers are attempting to satisfy several needs at one time with a purchase or have very specific needs different from other consumers. In that case, the basic product will not be satisfactory. Therefore, a business will develop an enhanced product. An **enhanced product** is a product that offers different features and options for the consumer. For example, a basic computer can be produced in desktop or notebook form. It can have different screen and hard drive sizes, offer DVD, an advanced speaker system, and many other features. If you have looked at the Web site of an online computer manufacturer such as Gateway or Dell, you can see the many, many options available to prospective purchasers. Dell and Gateway group their choices by categories of customers, such as business, home office, education, and family, making it easier for customers to design the computer system they need.

The third level of product development is to plan extended products. An **extended product** is a product that includes additional features that are not part of the physical product but increase its usability. Examples are customer service, guarantees, information on effective use of the products, and even additional products that improve the use of the original purchase. If you purchase a new digital video camera, you will need tapes to begin filming. In addition, a tripod may be helpful to make sure the video images are not shaky. Editing software, instructional videotapes, and even lens filters to create special effects may be useful to some but not all customers. The right combination of choices allows customers to get just the right product to meet very specialized needs.

Each business will have to decide what basic, enhanced, and extended products to produce. That decision will be based on careful study of target markets and an analysis of the costs and possible sales and profits resulting from each choice.

PRODUCT SELECTION

After designing the product, companies must make another set of decisions to plan the product mix element. The first choice is to decide whether to offer a product line. A **product line** is a group of similar products with obvious variations in the design and quality to meet the needs of distinct customer groups. New and small companies may

CAREER CONNECTION

MARKETING MANAGER

The objective of any business is to market its products or services profitably. Marketing managers develop the business's detailed marketing strategy. They determine the demand for products and services; identify potential consumers; develop a pricing strategy; monitor trends in new products and services; and oversee product development and promotion.

For marketing management positions, some employers prefer a college or even a graduate degree in business administration, with an emphasis on marketing. Courses in business law, economics, accounting, finance, mathematics, and statistics are also desirable.

Persons interested in a marketing management career should be creative, motivated, flexible, decisive, and able to handle stress. The ability to communicate persuasively, both orally and in writing, is crucial.

For more career information about marketing managers, check your library or the Internet for resources.

begin by offering only one category of product to its customers. That product may have choices of features, options, and enhancements, but the basic product is the same for all customers. With more experience and resources, the company may decide to expand its product line.

One of the obvious ways to expand a product line is to offer different sizes of the product. That can be done with the serving sizes of food items as well as with the sizes of automobiles. As an example, automobile manufacturers have had a great deal of success in recent years with sports utility vehicles (SUVs). When SUVs were first introduced, most manufacturers produced one mid-sized model, such as the Chevy Blazer or Ford Explorer. As the popularity of SUVs grew, the manufacturers began to appeal to other market segments with smaller-sized models, such as the Toyota RAV4, and then very large models, including the Mercury Mountaineer and Cadillac Escalade. Some companies offer only one of those model sizes, while others have a model in each size category for a full product line.

Another way of developing a product line is to offer differences in quality and price. If you visit an appliance store, you will usually find low-, mid-, and high-priced choices for each type of appliance, such as refrigerators, dishwashers, and microwaves. The price differences are based on the construction, quality of materials, and available features and options. A person buying a microwave for a college dorm room probably does not want the most expensive, full-featured choices, and so will be drawn to the low-price level of the product line. On the other hand, a gourmet chef making a purchase for a new kitchen may want only the highest quality and latest features.

Once a company has made decisions about a product line, it should then continue planning by determining the product assortment. A **product assortment** is the complete set of all products a business offers to a market. A product assortment can have depth, breadth, or both. A company offering a deep product assortment carries a large number of choices of features for each product category it handles. Walk into a Bath and Body Works store and look at the variety of fragrances, colors, bottle sizes, and packages for any of the major products sold there. That is an example of a deep assortment. Compare that to the choices of bath lotions that you might find in a small drug store, where the assortment would be limited.

A broad product assortment means that a business offers a large number of different but often related products for their customers. If you visit a garden center, you may find many different types of products for lawns and gardens ranging from plants, shrubs, and trees, to lawn mowers, hoses, and patio furniture. While there may not be many choices within one of the product categories, the customers should be able to meet most of their outdoor home needs at one location. As shown in Figure 22-1, businesses can choose any combination of depth and breadth of their product assortment. Some will be very small and specialized, while others will offer a complete variety of many different products.

PACKAGING

Two important product mix decisions are packaging and branding. While neither decision is directly related to the actual physical product itself, each can be an important influence on purchase decisions.

Most companies package their products before selling them. The package can serve four different purposes. First, it protects the product while it is being shipped and stored. Products can easily be damaged when they are grouped together for shipment from the factory to the retail store. Boxes and containers are needed for protection. The actual

PRODUCT BREADTH

PRODUCT DEPTH	More (breadth)	Less (breadth)
More	A BROAD VARIETY OF MANY PRODUCTS	A LARGE VARIETY IN FEW PRODUCT CHOICES
Less	MANY PRODUCTS WITH LIMITED VARIETY	LIMITED PRODUCT CHOICES AND VARIETY

FIGURE 22-1

Businesses build product assortments to meet their customers' needs.

ILLUSTRATION 22-2

What different purposes could the packaging of this product serve?

container or wrapping in which the individual product is packaged also offers protection on the store shelf and even can offer security to keep the product from being lost or stolen.

Second, the package can provide important information to customers on product composition, special features, and proper use. Boxes and containers also provide information to shippers on appropriate handling, storage, and delivery.

A package can be designed to make the product easier to use. Soda pop in a plastic bottle is less likely to be broken if dropped. An easy-opening lid or a container design that fits the hands of the consumer makes product handling easier. Window cleaner that is premixed in a spray bottle is much more convenient than one that requires the consumer to pour the cleaner in a bucket and apply it with a sponge.

Finally, especially for consumer products, the package is often an important promotional tool. A well-designed, attractive package calls attention to itself on the store shelf, helps the customer recall previously seen advertising, and provides a reminder of the needs that the product will satisfy if purchased.

FACTS AND FIGURES

"Corporate identity" refers to a company's name or logo—its visual expression or its "look." "Corporate image" is the public's perception of a company. "Corporate branding," by contrast, is a business process—one that is planned, strategically focused, and integrated throughout the organization.

BRANDING

Can you name the brands of clothing, pizza, and toothpaste you prefer? Do you and your friends regularly shop at certain stores but not others? Product and store brands play a major role in buying decisions. A **brand** is a name, symbol, word, or design that identifies a product, service, or company.

Why are brands so important to consumers? Have you ever shopped in a store that had generic (non-branded) products or that sold only unfamiliar brands? Without any information to guide you, it is difficult to make a product selection with which you are comfortable. You and people you trust have had experiences with various brands. If you find a company's products consistently meet your needs, you will likely buy from that company again. However, a negative experience will usually result in avoiding a similar purchase. If you are satisfied with one product from a company, you are likely to have confidence in a different product sold under the same brand. Businesses recognize that brand recognition is an important influence in increasing sales. The levels of consumer brand awareness are shown in Figure 22-2.

PURPOSES OF DISTRIBUTION

Our economic system relies on the successful exchange of products and services between businesses and consumers. But no matter how good a product is, this exchange will not occur successfully unless the company fills orders correctly and delivers the product undamaged and on time to the correct locations. These functions are all part of effective distribution. Successful exchanges are not easy. In fact, most of the problems consumers and businesses face in our economy occur during the exchange process.

Economic discrepancies are differences between the business's offerings and the consumer's requirements. Marketers are concerned about four important economic discrepancies:

1. Differences between *types* of products produced and the *types* consumers want.
2. Differences between the *quantities* produced and the *quantities* consumers want.
3. Differences between the *location* where products are produced and the *location* where consumers want them.
4. Differences between the *time* of production and the *time* consumers want the products.

Producers manufacture large quantities of one or a very few products; consumers want small quantities of a variety of products. Producers

- **Consumers are unable to identify the brand.**
- **Consumers can identify the brand but it has little influence on their purchase decision.**
- **Consumers can identify the brand but will not purchase it because of its brand.**
- **Consumers easily recognize the brand and will choose it if it is available.**
- **Consumers view the brand as the most satisfying and will not purchase a different brand.**

FIGURE 22-2

The Five Levels of Consumer Brand Awareness

manufacture products at a specific time and in a particular location; that time and location do not typically match the place and time consumers need the product. Distribution systems are designed to get the types and quantities of products customers want to the locations where and when they want them.

CHANNELS OF DISTRIBUTION

The routes products follow while moving from the producer to the consumer, including all related activities and participating organizations, are called **channels of distribution.** Businesses that participate in activities that transfer goods and services from the producer to the user are called **channel members**.

Channel members are generally retailers and wholesalers. As you learned in Chapter 21, a retailer sells directly to the consumer. A wholesaler, on the other hand, buys from and sells to other businesses or organizations rather than to final consumers. Wholesalers, retailers, and other channel members serve important and specific roles in the exchange process.

Determining the number and type of businesses and the activities they will perform in a channel of distribution is an important decision. Adding businesses to the channel makes the channel more complex and difficult to control. However, using businesses that have particular expertise in transportation, product handling, or other distribution activities may result in improved distribution or actual cost savings. The activities that need to be performed as a product moves from producer to consumer will help to determine the number and types of businesses in the channel.

Customers influence the development of a distribution channel. When developing a channel, businesses must consider the location of customers, the number of customers wanting the product, and the ways in which customers prefer to purchase and consume the products.

Producers need distribution channels whether they make products for consumers or for other businesses. The channels that products follow may be quite simple and short or long and complex. The shortest path is for the producer to sell directly to the user; the longest path can include a retailer, a wholesaler, and even other businesses.

When producers sell directly to the ultimate consumer, it is called **direct distribution.** When distribution takes place through channel members, it is called **indirect distribution.** Figure 22-3 illustrates different types of distribution channels.

DIRECT DISTRIBUTION

Direct distribution (sometimes called *direct marketing*) is accomplished in a number of ways. One way is for sales representatives to call on users in person. This is the primary method businesses use when sell-

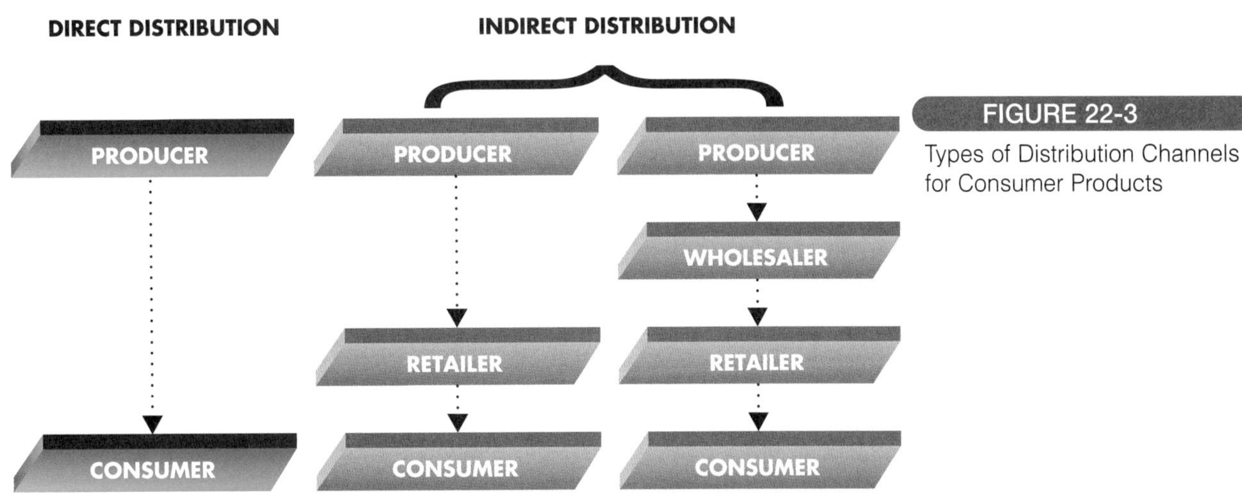

FIGURE 22-3
Types of Distribution Channels for Consumer Products

ing to other businesses. Another popular form of direct distribution is the use of the mail. Businesses send letters and advertising brochures or catalogs to prospective customers through the mail or e-mail. Customers can use a mail-order form, telephone, fax, or an online order form to make purchases directly from the manufacturer.

Today, one of the most popular methods of direct distribution is telemarketing. **Telemarketing** is marketing goods and services by telephone. It combines telephone sales with computer technology. Salespeople at computer terminals make and receive calls to and from prospective customers. Some telemarketing simply involves taking orders from customers who have seen merchandise advertised on television or through direct-mail advertising. When making a sale, the salesperson completes an order form displayed on the terminal screen. Then the salesperson routes the form to the company's distribution center for shipment. Telemarketing is an extremely efficient method of direct marketing, although its misuse by some consumer marketing companies has given it a bad name. Poorly prepared salespeople and calls placed at an inconvenient time for products that customers don't want are not effective business practices.

ILLUSTRATION 22-3
What are some of the positive and negative aspects of telemarketing?

An increasingly popular method of direct

ETHICAL ISSUES

TELEMARKETING—DOING IT RIGHT!

Telemarketing employs more people in the U.S. than any other form of direct marketing. Over 1 million people work directly in telemarketing, and their work creates over 8 million additional jobs in order processing, distribution, and related support positions. Companies spent $58 billion on telemarketing in the late 1990s compared to $37 billion on direct mail. However, telemarketing often has a negative image. Telemarketers sometimes bother people, act rude or unprepared, or mislead customers into thinking they are participating in a survey.

The responsibility for ethical business practices is shared by individual businesses, professional business associations, federal and state governments, consumer groups, and individual consumers. Each is responsible for enforcing laws and regulations when companies violate established fair business practices.

Business associations create codes of ethics that, while not enforceable by law, provide guidelines for ethical practices for member businesses. The association enforces the code of ethics by publicizing the information to consumers, asking customers to identify unethical businesses, and removing businesses from the association if they violate the code.

Here are some key features of the American Teleservices Association Code of Ethics for Telemarketing:

- Companies should not call people who are unlikely to be interested.
- Calls should be monitored by the company to ensure quality service.
- The product and delivery should be exactly as promised, and consumers should be informed of their options if service is unsatisfactory.
- All calls should clearly identify the name of the organization making the call and the purpose of the call.
- Guarantees and warranties should be clearly disclosed and copies made available on request.
- Merchandise should not be sent without clear customer permission.
- All calls should be made during reasonable hours.

THINK CRITICALLY

1. Why do you believe telemarketing is such a successful direct marketing tool yet continues to receive a large number of consumer complaints?
2. Based on your experience with telemarketing, do telemarketers generally follow the ethics statements listed above? Which are most often followed and which are not?
3. What responsibilities do you believe consumers have in dealing with ethical problems they encounter with telemarketing? Should they do anything when they encounter ethical treatment from businesses?
4. Prepare several statements of ethical practices that should apply to Internet marketing.

Source: *www.ataconnect.org (The American Teleservices Association, Inc.); www.the-dma.org (Direct Marketing Association's Telephone Marketing guidelines)*

distribution is through the Internet. A manufacturer can develop a Web site on which to feature its products. Customers order the products online from the site, and the company ships the products directly to the purchaser. Internet sales are expected to become a large part of sales for many companies because of the speed and efficiency of this distribution method.

INDIRECT DISTRIBUTION

When producers cannot or choose not to perform all marketing activities, they need an indirect channel of distribution. Manufacturers can simplify many of their marketing operations by selling to retailers. They will need fewer salespeople, because they sell to a small number of retail customers rather than to a very large number of final consumers. They can share advertising with the retailers, and the retailers will be responsible for much of the product storage, consumer credit management, and other activities. Retailers specialize in marketing activities, and this allows producers to specialize in manufacturing activities. As you learned in Chapter 1, specialization leads to improved efficiency, which benefits consumers through lower prices and added or improved services.

Retailers benefit consumers in several ways. Unlike producers, retailers can be conveniently located near consumers and can provide the products of many manufacturers in one place, thereby permitting consumers to make comparisons among a variety of types and brands of products. Furthermore, retailers can offer several kinds of products that consumers may need, making it possible for consumers to do all their shopping at one or a few locations. Retailers offer convenient shopping hours, credit terms, merchandise exchanges, and other special services to encourage customers to shop in their businesses.

Retail businesses range from large department stores that stock a broad variety of merchandise to small retailers specializing in a limited variety. Also, there is a growing number of non-store retailers. They sell products to customers in a number of ways that do not require a shopping trip to a store. Those ways include vending machines; direct marketing by retailers through telephone, catalog, or computer-ordering services; in-home parties and sales presentations; and shopping channels on cable television.

Producers prefer to sell products to retailers that buy in large quantities, such as department and discount stores and supermarkets. Smaller retailers are usually not able to deal directly with the manufacturer, so they must buy from other channel members. They turn to wholesalers, who consolidate the orders of a number of smaller businesses and then place the larger orders with manufacturers.

Wholesalers provide valuable services that producers may not provide. They sell to retailers in small quantities and can usually deliver goods quickly. Also, many wholesalers offer credit terms to retailers and provide help in planning promotions and sales strategies.

Wholesalers sell business products as well as consumer products. Many small businesses cannot purchase in the quantities required by large manufacturers or meet their terms of sale. These small businesses seek the service of a wholesaler, often called an *industrial distributor,* to purchase the products they need.

Wholesalers are an important part of international marketing today. Those that have developed international customers and distribution systems offer an effective way for companies to enter those markets. International wholesalers can also import products from other countries to sell to their customers.

INTEGRATED MARKETING CHANNELS

Usually the businesses involved in a channel of distribution are independent businesses. Those businesses make their own decisions and provide the activities they believe their customers want. It is not unusual for businesses in a distribution channel to have conflicts with each other. One of the challenges in distribution planning is to develop cooperative relationships among channel members.

One of the ways for channels to work more effectively is for a large business in the channel to take responsibility for planning, coordination, and communication. The business organizes the channel so that each participant will benefit and helps the other businesses complete their responsibilities successfully. A channel in which one organization takes a leadership position to benefit all channel members is known as an **administered channel**.

Cooperation is difficult among businesses that operate at different levels of a channel and have very different responsibilities. Some very large businesses attempt to solve that problem through channel integration. **Channel integration** occurs when one business owns the organizations at other levels of the channel. A manufacturer may purchase the businesses that provide wholesaling or retailing functions. A large retailer may decide to buy a wholesaler or even several small manufacturing businesses. Each business can still provide the specific functions needed for a successful channel, but having one owner for all businesses avoids the conflicts that occur in other channels.

DEVELOPING A CHANNEL OF DISTRIBUTION

From the available channels of distribution ranging from direct and simple to indirect and complex, producers must decide which channel or channels will best fit their needs. Producers generally prefer to use as few channels and channel members as possible. Sometimes producers need to use more than one channel to get the widest distribution for their product. Products such as books, candy, pens, and soap are purchased by many people in a variety of locations. Such items will require several channels to reach all of the possible consumers. The manufacturers may sell directly to national discount stores that can sell large quantities of the product. To reach other markets, the manufacturers may sell to large wholesalers that, in turn, sell to supermarkets, convenience stores, vendors, or other types of businesses.

Selling to different types of customers will result in varied channels of distribution. For example, a magazine publisher may sell magazines through retail stores, news agencies, newsstands, and magazine subscription agencies, as well as directly through the mail or Internet to subscribers. Figure 22-4 summarizes these different channels.

Producers must consider many factors when deciding which channel or channels to select for distributing the company's products. Some of the main factors are:

1. *Perishability of the product.* Highly perishable articles require rapid and careful handling. Those products, such as bread, fresh flowers, and ice cream, are usually marketed directly to the consumer or through very few channel members.
2. *Geographic distance between producer and consumer.* Many products are now sold internationally as well as throughout the country in which they are produced. If the market is very close to the point of production, there is less need for channel members. More businesses will likely participate in handling a product as the distance from producer to consumer increases.
3. *Need for special handling of the product.* If the product requires costly procedures or equipment for handling, it is likely to pass through as few channel members as possible. Gasoline, which requires pipelines, special tanks, and trucks for handling, is moved from the refiner to the retailer as directly as possible. Refiners own some gasoline retail outlets. Products that are highly complex and need experts to install

FIGURE 22-4

Five Possible Channels for the Sale of Magazines to Consumers

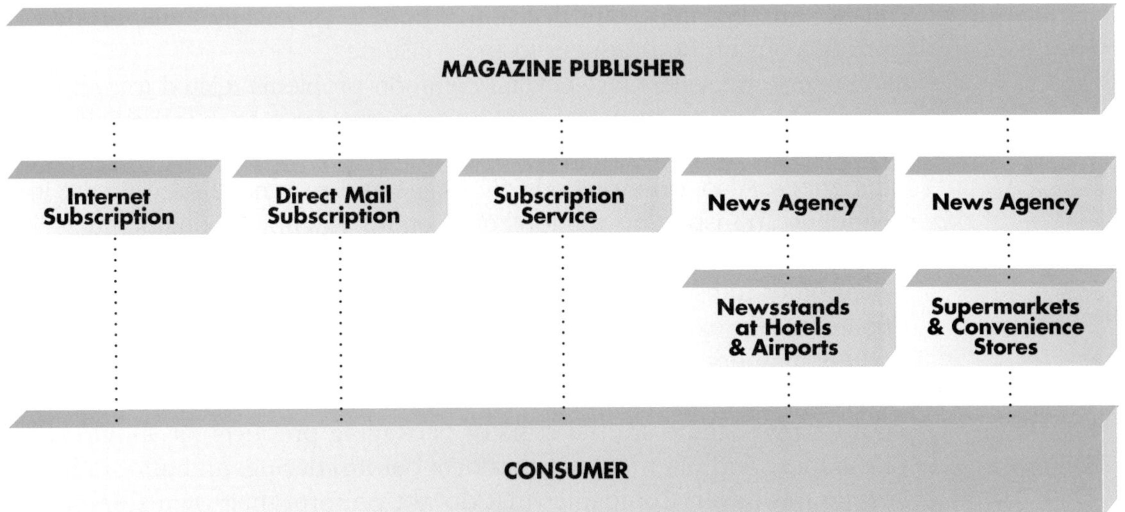

and repair also require short channels. Manufacturers of large computer systems, for example, sell directly to users.

4. *Number of users.* The greater the number of users of a product, the more channel members there probably will be. For instance, the manufacturer of steel is likely to sell directly to a few large users, whereas a shoe manufacturer may sell to wholesalers that then distribute to a variety of retail businesses.
5. *Number of types of products manufactured.* A producer that has only one product, such as pottery, will probably sell to a wholesaler. It is too expensive to maintain a sales force large enough to contact all retailers in the country. But if a producer has a large number of electrical products, such as coffee makers, clocks, heaters, and toasters, it might sell directly to large retailers that handle all of these products. The marketing costs can be distributed over many products.
6. *Financial strength and interests of the producer.* Large companies that are strong financially are better able to perform the marketing activities required to move goods from producer to consumer through the least number of channel members. They may find it more profitable to handle the marketing activities within the company rather than using other businesses. It also gives them more control over the channel rather than relying on others to perform many of the activities.

Channel decisions, like other marketing decisions, require careful study and are subject to change. Changes in technology, in transportation and storage facilities, and in retail methods are reasons why producers are constantly looking for more efficient ways to market their goods.

TRANSPORTATION DECISIONS

Selecting the channel members that will help sell the product to the consumer is only one of the distribution decisions a company must make. Another important decision is how to physically transport the products from the producer to the consumer.

Buyers and sellers face several common problems related to transportation. One problem deals with the types of products to be shipped. Factors to consider in shipping include the size, shape, and weight of the goods. Also, certain goods are fragile and may need special care in handling. Transporting 100 tons of steel, for example, requires much different treatment from that required for moving a carton of glassware.

Another transportation problem is the time needed for delivery. Some buyers expect or need shipment within a matter of hours, and others may not need or expect delivery for several weeks. Still another shipping problem is cost. In addition to the basic transportation charges, there are the costs of packaging products for shipment, insurance, and often storing products before, during, and after delivery to the buyer. Companies that do not perform their own shipping activities must first decide on their products' distribution requirements.

Then they can select the transportation method and companies that can meet these requirements.

Both consumers and business people are concerned about the quality of products at the time of purchase. They also want to have products available where and when they need them and at a reasonable cost. Since distribution activities affect all of these concerns, businesses plan them carefully.

United Parcel Service is the world's largest package distribution company. It transports more than 3 billion parcels and documents annually. The company uses more than 500 aircraft, 149,000 vehicles, and 1,700 facilities to provide service in more than 200 countries and territories.

COMMON TRANSPORTATION METHODS

The most commonly used methods of transporting goods are by railroad, truck, and airplane. A business may use more than one type of transportation, depending on the requirements for the shipment.

Railway transportation is one of the most common forms of shipping in the United States. Over a third of the volume of products shipped in the U.S. go by rail car. The principal advantage of rail transportation is low cost for moving heavy and bulky items long distances. However, products move slowly on long train routes because of the need to drop off cars that have arrived at their destination or are being routed in another direction or to add cars to the train. For bulky products or for shipping large quantities, the cost of shipping by rail is usually lower than for other methods.

Trucks are frequently used for short-distance shipping. Trucks are essential to smaller communities and rural areas that other transportation methods do not serve. Industries such as agriculture, mining, and lumber depend on trucks to move products from the source of production to the location of processing.

Much long-distance shipping is also done by truck. For products that need to be moved rapidly, in smaller quantities than can be economically shipped by rail, or where rail is not accessible, trucks are the typical transportation choice. Some transportation companies load truck trailers and place them on railroad cars to be shipped close to the final destination. This service is called **piggyback service.** Many trucking companies are now using computer systems to track customer orders and reroute trucks for rapid pickup and delivery. This flexibility is important for businesses that are trying to keep inventories low while maintaining high service levels.

Airplanes provide the most rapid form of transportation, but their rates are much higher than other methods. Airplanes can move products quickly over long distances. Items can move across a country in a few hours and around the world in a day, if necessary. The majority of air shipments involve items of relatively small bulk, high value, or quick perishability. Packages and mail are moved regularly on passenger airlines as well as through air parcel companies. Airlines are also used for shipping cut flowers, high-fashion clothing, seafood, film, and jewelry. Air shipments are very important for items needed in emergencies, such as medicine and blood, parts for machines needing quick repairs, or important documents.

Increasingly, businesses are shipping large and bulky items on special cargo planes. The planes have been designed for easy loading and unloading. Regional air freight terminals are being constructed so products can be moved rapidly into and out of airports without interfering with passenger travel. As rapid and efficient transportation becomes more important to businesses and consumers, more products are being shipped by air, even though the cost is higher. People pay more for the transportation that meets their requirements.

OTHER TRANSPORTATION METHODS

Water transportation (ocean, lake, and river) is the slowest method of transporting goods. However, it is also the cheapest for bulky goods, such as coal, iron ore, oil, lumber, grain, and cotton. Those are the principal items transported by water. Many products that are produced in large volume for international markets, such as automobiles and large pieces of equipment, are shipped across the oceans. At any large harbor on a coast you can see hundreds of types of products being loaded and unloaded from ships.

In the U.S., as well as in many other countries, networks of thousands of miles of pipelines have been built. Pipelines mostly transport petroleum and natural gas. In many countries, however, pipelines are important methods of moving water for irrigation and for human consumption.

One way of improving shipping services is through **containerization.** Products are packed in large shipping containers at the factory and are then shipped using a number of transportation methods before being unpacked. The containers can easily be loaded and unloaded from trucks to rail cars, ships, and cargo planes, and back to trucks. This reduces the amount of product handling and product damage.

ILLUSTRATION 22-4

How could containerization improve shipping services?

PRODUCT HANDLING

Lost, late, or damaged products are of little value to customers. Product handling is an important part of the distribution process. Most products are handled several times on their way from producer to consumer. Each time a product is handled adds to the cost of distribution, increases delivery time, and increases the opportunity for damage to occur. Businesses evaluate their product-handling procedures to find ways to improve the process. Improvements may include more secure packaging, more efficient procedures for packing and unpacking, and better equipment for handling and storing products.

TRACKING PRODUCTS

An important part of product handling is keeping track of the products. Businesses and customers want to know where products are in the distribution channel and when they will be delivered. The record keeping required is often a very time-consuming task. Businesses now use bar coding to track products during distribution. **Bar codes** are product identification labels containing a unique set of vertical bars that computer scanning equipment can read. Each product or container has a bar code. The scanning equipment can read the codes at any time during distribution to track the product's progress.

PRODUCT STORAGE

Manufacturers or channel members often must store products at points along the way from producer to consumer. Usually, consumers do not buy products as soon as they are produced. Producers and channel members may want to accumulate a large quantity of products to make shipping more efficient. Also, consumers buy some products more during one time of the year than another. Lawn mowers, air conditioners, snowmobiles, and skis are examples of such products. Most companies

ILLUSTRATION 22-5

How are bar codes used in product handling?

produce those products throughout the year to make production more efficient. They then store the products until they are ready to distribute them for sale.

Warehouses are buildings used to store large quantities of products until they can be sold. They are usually large buildings with racks, shelves, or bins for storing products. Warehouse operators may control temperature or humidity if the stored products need special protection. They must carefully handle and store the products to prevent damage. Warehouse personnel keep computerized records of where each product is stored in the warehouse. When they receive an order, the computer displays the quantity of the product available and its location in the warehouse.

Handling products and storing them for a long time is expensive. Also, moving them around increases the chances for damage. For more efficient handling with less risk of damage, many companies now use mechanical equipment and robots to handle the products in their warehouses. Computers control both the equipment and the robots as products are moved into storage and subsequently removed for shipment.

Large wholesalers and retailers that handle a variety of products and sell them through a number of outlets have replaced traditional warehouses with distribution centers. A **distribution center** is a large building designed to accumulate and redistribute products efficiently. A wholesaler or retailer usually buys products from a number of manufacturers. Each manufacturer ships these products to the distribution center in large quantities. Center workers then repackage the products into smaller quantities, combine them with products from other manufacturers, and ship them to stores that sell that bundle of products to consumers. Distribution centers can save businesses a great deal of money. They reduce transportation and storage costs and provide individual stores with the products they need quickly. Individual stores can order smaller quantities than if they had to order merchandise from each manufacturer, so products will not become outdated as easily.

ORDER PROCESSING

Customers place orders in person or by mail, telephone, computer, or fax machine. When an order reaches the business, employees must process the paperwork to fill the order and bill the customer. If customers have questions or problems with the order, employees must handle them in a friendly and courteous fashion. Some employees are responsible for tracking the order until it reaches the customers to make sure the customers receive what they expect.

Most companies have now automated some or all of the order processing system. Orders entered into a computer system can be easily tracked. Some companies now make computer records available to channel members and customers, so they can also track orders at any time from their own computers.

CHAPTER CONCEPTS

- Businesses think of their products as what they have to offer to consumers. Consumers are more likely to think of products as ways to satisfy their needs.
- Businesses develop products on three levels: a basic product, enhanced product, and extended product. Also, businesses must decide whether to offer product lines and product assortments.
- Packaging adds value by protecting the product during shipping and storage; providing information about product composition, features, use, and proper handling; making the product easier to use; and promoting the product.
- Branding gives customers confidence in making a purchase. If they recognize a brand name and have had good experiences with that brand, they will be more likely to buy the brand again.
- Effective distribution gets the correct products to customers at the right place and time and in the correct form.
- Channels of distribution can be either direct (from manufacturer directly to the purchaser) or indirect (using retailers and sometimes wholesalers to handle some of the marketing activities). Distribution activities include product handling and storing, transporting and tracking the product, order processing, and customer service.

BUILD VOCABULARY POWER

Define the following terms and concepts.

1. basic product
2. enhanced product
3. extended product
4. product line
5. product assortment
6. brand
7. economic discrepancies
8. channels of distribution
9. channel members
10. direct distribution
11. indirect distribution
12. telemarketing
13. administered channel
14. channel integration
15. piggyback service
16. containerization
17. bar codes
18. warehouses
19. distribution centers

REVIEW FACTS

1. What is likely to happen to consumers and to the business if the business makes poor product development decisions?
2. How does the consumer's view of a product differ from the business's view?
3. Why would a company want to offer differences in product quality and price as part of a product line?
4. What are several different purposes of product packaging?
5. How does a brand name help consumers make decisions about the products they plan to purchase?

6. What are the five levels of consumer brand awareness?
7. What are some examples of economic discrepancies that occur between producers and consumers?
8. Provide several examples of direct distribution.
9. List several benefits to businesses and consumers of using indirect distribution.
10. What are several important factors that producers should consider when selecting the channels of distribution to use for a product?
11. Provide an example of how timing and cost of shipping can affect the transportation method selected to distribute a product.
12. For each of the three commonly used transportation methods, describe a type of product that would most likely be shipped by each method.
13. Why is careful product handling important to both businesses and consumers?
14. In what ways can technology improve product handling?
15. What tasks do customer service employees perform after receiving a customer's order?

DISCUSS IDEAS

1. If a company believes in the marketing concept, it will try to provide products and services that its target market needs. Does that mean the company will not have to offer as many enhanced and extended products? Why or why not?
2. Identify a company with a product that has an extensive product line. Identify specific products that are part of the product line. Then describe the differences among those products and why they meet different customers' needs.
3. For a product with which you are familiar, describe ways that the packaging improves sales and usability. Now identify examples of packaging that interferes with sales and usability.
4. What are some reasons why consumers may reject a specific brand, even though they are very familiar with it?
5. Three producers make the same type and quality of cosmetics for sale. Producer A sells through wholesalers to retailers. Producer B sells directly to retailers. Producer C sells through door-to-door sales representatives. Why might the selling price be about the same, even though the channels of distribution are different?
6. Provide examples showing that the ways in which consumers purchase a product influence the type of distribution channel used.
7. Why might a manufacturer choose to sell products through a department store rather than a discount store?
8. Why would a company choose to use a truck to haul products from the East Coast to the West Coast when railroad shipping is available and is cheaper?

9. Make a list of products you purchased that were probably stored for a length of time before you purchased them. Then make a similar list of products that were not stored or were stored only a short time before you purchased them. Discuss the differences among the products.
10. Discuss the problems businesses and consumers might encounter with product distribution and order processing when the Internet is used for selling and buying.

ANALYZE INFORMATION

1. Most people are very aware of the brands of many of the products they use, but the brands they remember best may or may not be the ones they actually purchase. Form a team with other classmates to conduct a consumer survey. As a team, prepare a questionnaire for five product categories. Include some products with very familiar brands and other products with mostly unfamiliar brands. Each team member should use the questionnaire to interview a number of people representing various ages and interests. For each product, ask the person to list the brand names that are most memorable to them. Then have them identify the brand they most often purchase or use. When the interviews are complete, compile the results into a short report and draw conclusions about the importance of branding in influencing purchases.
2. A student organization to which you belong has decided to sell individual containers of bottled water at after-school activities, athletic events, and other functions as a fundraiser. Your organization made an agreement with the supplier that allows you to design a unique package for the water bottle. Prepare a diagram and description of the package you would recommend that will meet the four different purposes of packaging described in the chapter.
3. Bascagio's Bakery makes cookies, cakes, and pastries that it distributes directly to retail grocers within a 60-mile area with its own trucks. The company is considering doubling its baking facilities and marketing its products over a 200-mile area.
   a. If the distribution area is going to be much wider, will the bakery have to use an indirect channel of distribution? List the advantages and disadvantages of an indirect system.
   b. What outlets, other than retail grocers, can the company use for its products?
   c. Does the number of outlets help determine whether a direct or indirect channel is better? Explain.
4. An appliance store can purchase a certain brand of electric heater for $45.00 from a firm in City A or for $48.50 from another firm in City B. The transportation cost from City A is $3.88 per heater.

From City B, the transportation cost is $2.77 per heater. What is the difference in the cost of the purchase from each firm if the appliance store buys 500 heaters? What factors other than cost should the appliance store consider when deciding from which firm to make the purchase?

5. A company located in Utah manufactures children's toys and games. Its potential customers are located throughout the world. Identify ways in which it can use each of the following distribution methods to improve its customer service or profitability: (a) Internet sales, (b) containerization, (c) bar coding.

SOLVE BUSINESS PROBLEMS

CASE 22-1

Albany Muran has been a part-time photographer for many years. She has emphasized individual family portraits for most of her business. She primarily gets customers through word-of-mouth from people who see her portraits in people's homes. She enjoys the work but doesn't make enough money to do it full time. She has discussed the issue with several business advisors, who advised her to consider expanding beyond portrait photography. They recommended expanding into weddings and special events; taking photos of landscapes, buildings, animals, and such that would meet the needs of a broader audience; or purchasing and reselling home accessories that would comple-

ment the purchase of pictures and portraits. She is unsure of what direction to take with her business.

Think Critically:

1. Describe a basic product, enhanced product, and extended products that you would recommend to Albany for expanding her business.
2. If Albany decided to purchase and resell home accessories, how could she use the concept of a product line to effectively market those products?
3. Construct a grid like the one shown in Figure 22-1 for Albany, illustrating how she could develop a business that would fit into each of the four quadrants. Make sure to describe the types of products she would offer for each of the four positions on the grid.

CASE 22-2

The Elegant Affair is a specialty retail shop. It sells assorted gift boxes of various meats, cheeses, nuts, jams, and jellies. The business is located in a Midwest city and is facing declining sales due to the city's economic difficulties. One major manufacturing plant has closed, and layoffs from other businesses have caused many people to move from the area seeking new jobs.

The president of the company has been studying telemarketing as a way to increase sales without having to move the store or build a new store in an area with a more attractive economic climate. She believes that by using salespeople and a computerized telemarketing system, the company can sell the gift boxes to people throughout the U.S. She also believes that the cost of those sales will actually be lower than selling the products to people who come into the store.

Think Critically:

1. What types of activities would The Elegant Affair have to do to start a telemarketing system?
2. How can the company identify prospective customers in order for the telemarketing salespeople to call them?
3. Identify two distribution methods that The Elegant Affair might use for the products it sells through telemarketing. What are the advantages and disadvantages of each?
4. Develop a brief script for the telemarketing salespeople to use to introduce the company and its products to prospective customers.
5. Do you believe an online alternative for customer ordering might be a better method for the company than telemarketing? Why or why not?

PROJECT: MY BUSINESS, INC.

Two important marketing decisions for your new business are the type and assortment of products you will offer and how to distribute the products. Some new businesses have very limited product choices, while others offer an extensive set of enhanced and extended products. Most retail businesses purchase products and supplies from other channel members, so they are part of an indirect channel of distribution. An important part of distribution is to select a good location for the business that makes it convenient for customers to find the business and purchase your product. In this project segment, you will study the product development and distribution decisions for your new juice business.

DATA COLLECTION

1. Identify your basic physical product. Remember that it will be very similar to that offered by many competitors. Then study as many competitors as you can and identify the possible extended and enhanced product choices for this type of business.

2. Again, by studying competitors and collecting additional information about this type of business from magazines and the Internet, list possible product lines that seem appropriate for the juice products. Also identify possible product assortments.

3. Collect examples of the packages and brand names used by the primary competitors selling these products in your community.
4. Develop a simple map of the area of your town or city where you might locate your new business. Mark on the map the locations of the businesses that offer the same types of products you are considering.

ANALYSIS

1. Given your understanding of product development and the information you collected, identify the products, product lines, and product assortments you plan to offer during your first six months in operation. Justify your choices.

2. Review a business directory from your community or on the Internet. Identify at least four manufacturers or suppliers from whom you might purchase the products and supplies you will need for your business.
3. Design the basic juice cup or container you will use to package your product. If possible, contact a supplier and determine the cost of various sizes of cup or container. Identify any other packaging you will need.
4. Using the map you prepared in the Data Collection section of this activity, identify the three locations you prefer for your new business. Make sure that retail businesses can actually be located there. Rank your preferred locations with a short rationale for your decisions.

PRICING AND PROMOTION

OBJECTIVES

- **23-1** Discuss how businesses and consumers make their buying decisions.
- **23-2** Describe factors involved in establishing product prices and common pricing strategies.
- **23-3** Discuss ways that companies try to control costs that can lead to higher prices.
- **23-4** Discuss the purpose of promotion in meeting business and consumer needs.
- **23-5** Identify common promotional methods.
- **23-6** Explain the parts of the selling process and how each is used to help customers make effective buying decisions.
- **23-7** Identify important laws and regulations that apply to advertising and promotion.

WHY PAY MORE?

Michi and Arturo walked out of Windzors, a sporting goods store that had just opened in the new Regency Park shopping plaza. "I can't believe that store will be successful," said Michi. "I've never seen sports equipment priced that high!"

"The products really were expensive," agreed Arturo. "But it certainly isn't a normal sporting goods store. The salesperson said they would help design your own set of personalized golf clubs and that you would get five hours of lessons with the golf pro at the Regency Sports Centre if you purchased a set of clubs."

"Did you see the area where they sold downhill skis?" asked Michi. "They had a moving slide like an escalator where you could actually ski. They also had a machine that formed molds around your feet for custom-fitting ski boots. They sponsor a ski club and organize vacations to the mountains in the United States and even to other countries. I've never seen that in a sporting goods store."

"Why would people want to pay that much?" Arturo wondered. "Sure, they have the top brand names and unique services. But you can get the same type of products for 40 to 50 percent less at other stores."

"I don't know," said Michi. "They certainly have effective advertising, sales brochures, and customer service. And the store was filled with people. Maybe the owners are on to something."

A business is successful when it brings buyers and sellers together, and they are both satisfied with the exchange. To be successful, businesses must offer the type and quality of products and services that meet the needs of their customers. The products must be priced so that buyers consider them a good value for the money. Many consumers will have to view the high quality and extra services offered by Windzors sporting goods store as worth the higher prices if the store is to succeed.

Whether the buyers are businesses purchasing raw materials to use in manufacturing, equipment to operate the business, or products for resale, or consumers buying products for their own use, they must have information to make their decisions. Buyers must be aware of the products, how the products will meet their needs, and where they can buy them. Then buyers and sellers must agree on a price and method of payment. In this chapter, you will learn about the last two elements of the marketing mix: pricing and promotion.

THE BUSINESS BUYING DECISION

When planning a purchase, businesses actually make several specific decisions. They must decide what to purchase, when to purchase, from whom to purchase, and how much to purchase.

WHAT TO PURCHASE

To be successful, a business must keep the right kind of products in stock. Manufacturers buy products to use in producing products to

ILLUSTRATION 23-1

When planning a purchase, what decisions do businesses typically make?

sell to their customers. Wholesale or retail businesses purchase products for resale or for use in the operation of their businesses. In all cases, the most important consideration in making purchases is their customers' needs. Businesses that do not satisfy customers will not thrive. Businesses must consider both quality and assortment of products in deciding what to purchase.

Some buyers try to sell more products than their competitors by offering low-quality products at a low price. They believe that price is so important to customers that the customers will accept lower quality in order to save money. This strategy can backfire. Customer confidence is critical to the success of any business. While customers have different expectations of quality, they will not put up with inferior quality. When they find that a product is not as good as expected, they look for another product to buy. Customers compare price and quality to make the best possible decision. They will usually not select the absolute cheapest product if it is of inferior quality nor will they always pay the highest price even if quality is superior.

Two factors influence a business's selection of product assortment. The first is competition. A new store will have a hard time attracting customers if it carries only the same products or brands that are carried by local businesses that are already successful. A business needs to emphasize the products customers want but offer some differences from competitors' products.

The second factor in choosing a product assortment is the financial ability of the business. It costs a great deal to keep a wide selection of products available. Businesses can stock a limited variety of products while still offering customers a good selection. Product variety is a difficult decision. Businesses need to stock items that customers want, but their budget has limits.

Businesses have several sources of assistance in determining what to purchase. Catalogs and salespeople are valuable tools. Trade associations and their publications can also help. Businesses should listen carefully to their customers in determining what to purchase. They should also review company records of previous sales and regularly study what products sell well and not so well for competitors.

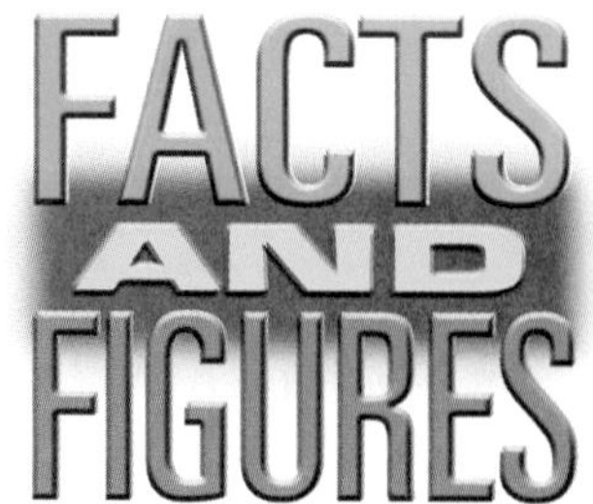

Ethics is an important issue in purchasing. A "kickback" is a payment from a vendor to a buyer for the purpose of improperly obtaining favorable treatment in the issuance of a contract or purchase order. Other actions that are considered unacceptable include the showing of excessive favoritism toward a vendor and the solicitation or acceptance of gifts from the vendor by the purchaser.

WHEN TO PURCHASE

The type of products, the types and locations of suppliers, and other factors such as style and price trends influence the decision about when to purchase. For a manufacturer, raw materials and component parts must be available when needed for production, or the business will not be able to maintain its production schedule. Wholesalers and retailers need an adequate supply of products when customers want to buy. Businesses often must place orders well in advance for products to be available when their customers need them. For example, retail clothing stores often order summer fashions in January or earlier. Whether a buyer believes the prices of products will fall or rise will also influence when product orders are placed.

FROM WHOM TO PURCHASE

Part of the purchasing decision is to choose the right suppliers. Businesses consider the reputation of each supplier in such areas as dealing with customers, filling orders rapidly and exactly as requested, and providing necessary services. Other considerations are the supplier's price and credit terms.

Businesses must decide whether to make purchases from only one supplier or to spread the orders among several suppliers. Most businesses concentrate their buying among a few suppliers. This practice usually develops better relationships between the suppliers and the purchaser. Better prices, credit terms, and service are also likely to result. However, relying on one supplier leaves the purchaser vulnerable when that business experiences problems.

HOW MUCH TO PURCHASE

A business should have sufficient products available to meet customer demand. If customers cannot purchase the products they want when they want, they will go elsewhere. If a manufacturing business runs out of the necessary raw materials and parts, they must delay production.

On the other hand, if businesses have a much larger inventory than they need, they are tying up large amounts of money in inventory that they could use in other ways to make a profit. The large inventory also requires extra storage space. If businesses keep only small quantities

Many car buying services are available on the Internet. For example, one service will research vehicle availability, negotiate a competitive price, verify the paperwork, and assist with delivery. The price for this service? $399.

in stock, they reduce the risk of loss from spoilage, changes in design, or changes in demand. Many suppliers are now able to fill orders quickly, making it easier for companies to carry lower quantities of many of the products they sell.

PAYMENT TERMS AND DISCOUNTS

Businesses establish a price at which they would like to sell a product. The original price that the seller posts on the product is the **list price.** Often, however, customers do not pay the list price. The terms of sale offered by the seller or requested by the buyer affect the actual price paid. The terms of sale identify delivery conditions, when invoices must be paid, and whether the buyer can receive credit or discounts.

PAYMENT TERMS

Companies that sell to other businesses often extend credit to their customers. They list their credit terms on the invoice. Invoices often state credit terms in a form such as *net 30 days,* which means that the buyer must pay in full within 30 days from the date on the invoice. Some businesses offer longer payment terms, such as net 60 days. The longer the terms, the better for the buyer, who will then have a chance to sell the goods by the time payment is due or can earn interest on the money that it otherwise would have paid to the supplier.

DISCOUNTS

Suppliers may offer discounts on products that their business customers purchase. **Discounts** are reductions from the price of the product to encourage customers to buy. Common types of discounts are trade, quantity, seasonal, and cash discounts. Discounts are subtracted from the list price.

A **trade discount** is a price reduction that manufacturers give to their channel partners, such as wholesalers or retailers, in exchange for additional services. For example, a manufacturer may give retailers a 30 percent discount but may give wholesalers a 45 percent discount from the list price (or 15 percent more than retailers). In this case, the manufacturer expects the wholesalers to perform additional marketing activities beyond those expected from retailers.

A **quantity discount** is a price reduction offered to customers that buy in quantities larger than a specified minimum. For example, a retail paint store that orders 200 gallons of paint from a wholesaler pays a certain price per gallon. However, the wholesaler may lower the price per gallon if the store orders at least 1,000 gallons at one time. The purpose of the discount is to encourage customers to buy in large quantities. The manufacturer can afford to sell the larger quantity for a lower price because that sale reduces the cost of inventory, the amount of storage space needed, the insurance costs, and the administrative costs

ILLUSTRATION 23-2

Why might a business offer a seasonal discount for its products?

of product handling. Quantity discounts may be based on the number of units purchased or on the dollar value of the order.

A **seasonal discount** is a price reduction offered for ordering or taking delivery of products in advance of the normal buying period. It encourages the buyer to purchase earlier than necessary or at a time when orders are normally low. An example is a discount on snowmobiles purchased in the summer. The seasonal discount is a way the manufacturer attempts to balance production and inventory levels throughout the year for products that are normally purchased at a few specific times during the year.

To encourage early payments, many businesses offer a cash discount. A **cash discount** is a price reduction given for paying by a certain date. A cash discount is usually stated as a percentage of the purchase price (for example, 2 percent). Businesses offer cash discounts with various dating and credit terms. For example, the terms of a purchase may be net 30 days with a 2 percent discount for payment within 10 days. If the invoice is dated May 1, the buyer can deduct 2 percent from the total price when paying on or before May 11. Otherwise, the buyer must pay the full amount by May 31. Businesses express terms like these in this form: 2/10, n/30.

COMPONENTS OF PRICE

The prices businesses charge can make the difference between success and failure of their products. Customers must view the product as a good value for the price. The price must be competitive with prices of competitors' products yet must be high enough for the business to make a profit on the sale.

The **selling price** is the actual price customers pay for the product. The selling price is determined by subtracting any discounts from the list price. Businesses often set list prices higher than the price at which they end up selling the products. To make a profit, businesses must plan for discounts when setting their list prices.

Figure 23-1 illustrates the components that marketing managers consider when setting prices. To make a profit, marketers must set prices high enough to more than cover all costs. The income remaining after deducting costs from the selling price is the net profit for that sale.

The largest cost that the price must cover is the cost of goods sold. The **cost of goods sold** is the cost to produce the product or buy it for resale. For manufacturers, the cost of goods sold is the total cost of the materials, operations, and personnel used to make the product. For wholesalers and retailers, it is the price they pay their supplier to buy the product plus the cost of transporting it to their location for resale to their customers. For example, if the invoice price of an item is \$55 and the transportation charge is \$5, the cost of goods sold is \$60.

Operating expenses are the costs of operating a business. They do not include costs involved in the actual production or purchase of merchandise, which would be a part of the cost of goods sold. Most costs involved in the day-to-day running of a business fall into this category. Figure 23-2 lists some common operating expenses.

The **margin** or **gross profit** is the difference between the selling price and the cost of goods sold. In Figure 23-1, the margin is 40 cents. Marketers think of the margin as the percentage of sales available to cover operating expenses and provide a profit. For example, a busi-

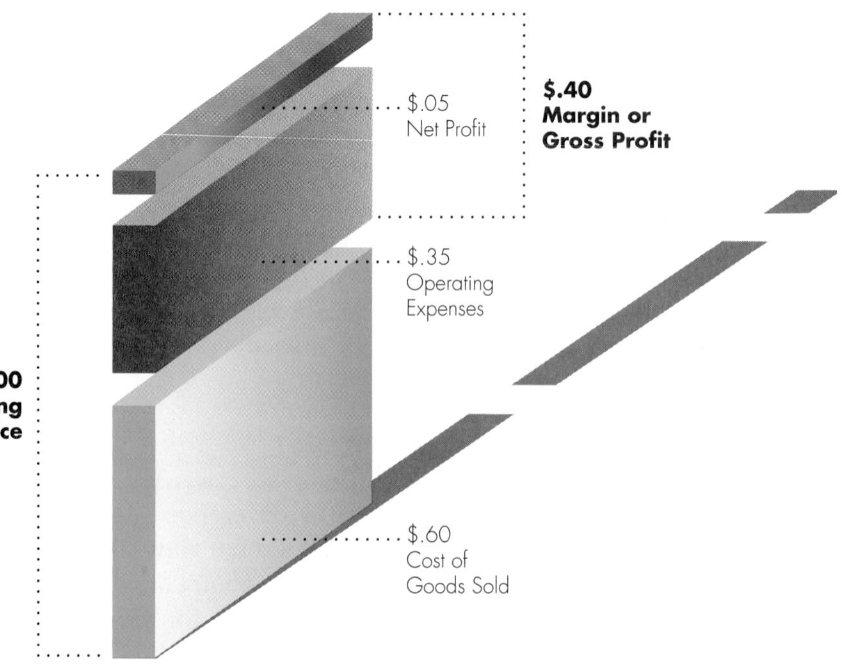

FIGURE 23-1

A product's selling price is made up of several components.

Rent	**Taxes**
Interest paid on borrowed money	**Repairs and maintenance**
Salaries, wages, and benefits	**Supplies**
Telephone service	**Inventory losses due to theft, spoilage, or breakage**
Depreciation expense	**Customer service expenses**
Furniture, fixtures, and equipment	**Advertising**
Uncollected accounts and collection expense	**Donations**
Delivery costs	**Utilities**
Insurance	**Cost of business services**

FIGURE 23-2

Businesses consider operating expenses such as these when setting a product's price.

ness may operate on a 25 percent margin. If operating expenses are more than 25 percent of sales, the company will lose money.

Net profit is the difference between the selling price and all costs and expenses of the business. Net profit can be calculated using the following formula:

Net profit = selling price − cost of goods sold − operating expenses

Markup is the amount added to the cost of goods sold to determine the selling price. It is similar to margin. When stated in dollars and cents, markup and margin are identical. For example, in Figure 23-1, the markup is also 40 cents. Often businesses express the markup as a percentage of the cost of goods sold or as a percentage of the selling price. Thus, the markup in Figure 23-1 is 66 2/3 percent (40 cents/60 cents) of cost. Expressed as a percentage of the selling price, it is 40 percent (40 cents/100 cents).

Some consumers confuse the markup percentage with profit. They believe that if a business has a 50 percent markup, it is making a profit of 50 percent of the selling price. However, markup must cover operating expenses. If the business with a 50 percent average markup on its products has operating expenses of 45 percent of sales, it will have a profit of 5 percent of total sales.

Markdown is any amount by which the original selling price is reduced before the item is sold. Companies use markdowns when their inventory is not selling at a satisfactory rate. Since the costs associated with the products remain the same, markdowns reduce profits, so companies want to avoid them.

PRICING STRATEGIES

Since businesses operate for profit, they must set prices that will entice customers to buy the products yet will still make a profit after deducting costs. Businesses can use different strategies to achieve this goal. For example, a business can establish a high price. Fewer customers will buy at a high price than a low price, but the company will make a greater gross profit per item sold. On the other hand, a business can choose to set a low price. More customers will buy at a low price than a high price, but the company will make less gross profit per item sold. In this case, the company hopes to make a satisfactory profit by selling a large number of items.

No one strategy is best in all cases. Either of these strategies can result in a satisfactory profit for the company. Consider the following example:

Business A buys a product for $500 and offers it for sale at $1,000. It sells four of these in a month, making a gross profit of $2,000:

$1,000 × 4 items = $4,000 revenue from sales
$500 × 4 items = $2,000 cost of goods sold
$4,000 revenue − $2,000 cost of goods sold = $2,000 gross profit

Business B, selling the same product, thinks it can make a better profit by setting a lower price and selling a greater quantity. It offers the item for $800. During a month, it sells six items, for a gross profit of $1,800:

$800 × 6 items = $4,800 revenue from sales
$500 × 6 items = $3,000 cost of goods sold
$4,800 − $3,000 cost of goods sold = $1,800 gross profit

In this case, Business A's strategy made the greatest profit. However, either strategy could result in the greatest profit. The challenge is to choose the strategy that works best for the situation.

While both of these companies made a gross profit, they still must deduct operating expenses to arrive at their net profit. If Business A's operating expenses are much greater than Business B's, then Business B might make the greatest net profit of the two competitors, even though its gross profit was lower.

Businesses must be careful about setting extremely high or extremely low prices. With extremely high prices, the business may not sell a sufficient quantity to yield a net profit. With extremely low prices, the business may not be able to cover its costs no matter how many products it sells. Between these two extremes is a reasonable price that satisfies customers and allows a reasonable profit. Next you will learn about some of the strategies marketing managers use for setting a reasonable price.

PRICING TO MEET COMPETITION

The amount of competition among companies handling similar products or services is an important factor in establishing prices. If one company has much higher prices than competitors for the same products, some of the company's customers are likely to buy from the competitors. Even similar businesses in separate locations may compete for the same customers. If prices are too high in one area, many people will travel to purchase goods or services. For example, if a service station in one neighborhood is selling a certain brand of gasoline for $1.89 a gallon and a station two miles away is selling the same brand for $1.59, customers may be willing to travel to buy where the price is lower.

ILLUSTRATION 23-3

Why has the Internet had a major effect on pricing?

The Internet has had a major impact on pricing, because it makes price comparison easy for customers. Some Web sites will search for the lowest prices for specific products. Customers who value low prices over service may buy from the lowest-priced competitor.

A business may need to offer some of its merchandise at a price that does not allow a profit because a competitor has established an even lower price. However, it is not always necessary to have a lower selling price than competitors. If a company has a loyal group of customers and offers a product with some distinct advantages, or provides services that customers want and other companies do not offer, the company may be able to charge a higher price without losing customers. Remember that the cost of providing higher-quality products or more services may be expensive, so profits may not be higher just because prices are higher. Windzors, the exclusive sporting goods store in the chapter-opening case, was relying on unique products, exclusive services, and an interesting shopping experience to justify much higher product prices.

When competition is intense, some companies may have to set some of their prices at or below the actual costs of doing business. In such a competitive situation, only the most efficient businesses make a net profit. Even when competition is not strong, if a company sets its prices too high, people will try to do without its products or find substitutes, rather than pay prices that seem to give that company an unduly large profit.

PRICING TO EARN A SPECIFIC PROFIT

When introducing a new product, many businesses base their selling price on a specific profit they want to make. The business first determines the costs of producing and marketing the product, and all related operating expenses. It then sets the price by adding the amount necessary to make the target profit. But even setting prices based on a target profit won't guarantee that the company will make that profit. Customers still must like the product well enough to buy it at that price. Also, competitors selling the same product might sell for less, luring away customers. In either case, the company may have to mark down its price to attract more buyers, reducing profit below its target.

PRICING BASED ON CONSUMER DEMAND

The owner of a business that carries fashion merchandise knows that at certain times the products will be in great demand, and at other times the demand will be very low. Swimsuits sell quickly early in the season, but slowly late in the season, unless the retailer greatly reduces the prices. Since a retailer cannot accurately predict the exact number of suits that it will sell, it will set a selling price at the beginning of the season that should ensure a net profit on the entire inventory of swimsuits, even though it may have to drastically reduce prices later in the season.

A manufacturer of a product that suddenly becomes popular may want to sell at a high price while the demand is great. When new competitors enter the market or customers tire of the product and the demand begins to decline, the manufacturer will need to sell the product at a much lower price.

The introduction of new products in the market presents an interesting study in price decisions. High definition televisions (HDTV) are just now coming onto the market. The few brands are priced extremely high—several thousand dollars—compared to standard televisions. Within a few years, customer demand will likely increase, many more competitors will enter the market, and prices will drop to between $1,000 and $2,000 or even lower.

PRICING TO SELL MORE PRODUCTS

Products that are priced higher usually sell more slowly than those that cost the same but are priced lower. For example, a product that cost $40 may be priced at $60, but may not sell for two months. A similar product that also cost $40 may be priced at $48 and sell in two weeks. If the second product continues to sell at that pace, the business will sell more of it and achieve a larger net profit from it for the year. The business must be careful that the lower price is high enough to cover operating costs and still contribute to profit. Otherwise, using the lower price is a poor decision. For example, if the product priced at $48 had a cost of goods sold of $40 and must cover $10 worth of operating expenses, then the business will never make a net profit on the product no matter how many it sells.

If a business has a low rate of inventory turnover, it must charge higher prices to cover the cost of the inventory and the operating expenses of the business. For instance, many items in an exclusive jewelry store may be sold and replenished at the rate of once a year or less. The jeweler, therefore, must mark the retail price of the products very high in relation to its cost in order to make a reasonable profit.

PRICING TO PROVIDE CUSTOMER SERVICES

A business that offers credit, free delivery, or 24-hour emergency service will have higher operating expenses than one that offers no services. Higher operating expenses require a higher selling price to yield the same net profit as that earned by a business with lower expenses. If a business's customers expect a high level of service, or if the business is using the extra service to appear different from competitors, it will have to set prices higher to achieve a profit.

CONTROLLING COSTS

Businesses are not always able to increase prices just because they are not making a profit. Costs of merchandise and operating expenses for the business often increase, while prices charged to customers cannot be increased due to competition. Businesses have to make careful purchasing and operating decisions to avoid unnecessary expenses. Three important areas that can affect costs are (1) markdowns, (2) damaged or stolen merchandise, and (3) merchandise returns.

MARKDOWNS

In many cases, businesses are forced to sell some products at lower prices than they had planned. This can happen because companies purchase products that customers do not want or go out of style. Businesses also have to sell products at lower prices when they overestimated demand and bought too many products or when competition increases or competitors lower prices.

Businesses cannot avoid markdowns totally, but they can usually control them. Careful purchasing can eliminate many markdowns. Proper product handling and marketing practices can also reduce the number of markdowns.

DAMAGED OR STOLEN MERCHANDISE

Some products may be damaged so much that they cannot be sold. Other products may be stolen through shoplifting or employee theft. These situations have a serious effect on profits.

Assume that a product with a selling price of $5.00 is damaged or stolen. The product cost the business $4.00, and operating expenses amounted to $.75 for each product. Expected net profit was $.25. In order to recover the cost of that one damaged or stolen product, the business will have to sell 16 more products than first planned (16 products × \$.25 = \$4.00). It will have to sell another three products to cover operating expenses. The business will not earn a profit on the sale of the 19 products if just one product out of 20 is damaged or stolen. To reduce the amount of damaged and stolen merchandise, companies may take actions such as employing security guards or installing surveillance cameras and training employees to handle merchandise carefully.

RETURNED MERCHANDISE

If customers are not satisfied with their purchases, they may return the products for a refund. This adds to expenses in two ways. If the business can resell the merchandise, it will have to sell it at a reduced price. Also, many expenses are involved in handling and reselling the returned merchandise, which increases operating expenses. Most likely, some returned merchandise cannot be resold.

To make a profit, businesses must consider their record of returned merchandise when buying and pricing merchandise. They must try to buy just the type and quality of merchandise that customers prefer in order to help reduce returns. Salespeople should be trained to sell products that customers need rather than attempting to convince customers to buy things they do not need. Offering customer service and support to help customers use the products properly and resolve their problems also reduces the amount of merchandise returned.

When managers give close attention to the three problem areas of markdowns, damaged or stolen merchandise, and returns, they can keep operating expenses at a minimum. As a result, they can maintain profits while lowering the markup percentage. In that way, both the businesses and their customers benefit.

PROMOTION AS MARKETING COMMUNICATION

To be successful, a business must interest people in buying its products and services. Even good products will not sell automatically. Consumers need to know the product is available and where they can purchase it. They must be able to easily see the differences among brands and determine which brand will best meet their needs.

Consumers generally follow five steps in progressing toward a purchase decision. Figure 23-3 summarizes the steps in the consumer decision-making process. While the five steps are common to all consumers, each consumer has different needs and gathers information in different ways to satisfy those needs. Some customers spend a great deal of time and consult many information sources before deciding to buy or not to buy. Other consumers might not be as careful or use the same methods. Therefore, businesses must provide appropriate infor-

PROBLEM RECOGNITION

The consumer identifies a need to satisfy or a problem to solve.

INFORMATION SEARCH

The consumer gathers information about alternative solutions for the need or problem.

ALTERNATIVE EVALUATION

The consumer weighs the options to determine which will best satisfy the need or solve the problem.

PURCHASE

If the consumer identifies a suitable and affordable choice, he or she makes the purchase.

POST-PURCHASE EVALUATION

The consumer uses the product or service and evaluates how well it met the need or solved the problem.

FIGURE 23-3

Steps in the Consumer Decision-Making Process

mation to help consumers move through the decision-making process to select the product that meets their needs.

Promotion is the primary way that businesses communicate with prospective customers. Businesses use promotion to inform consumers about the features and benefits of their products and services and to encourage them to buy.

Effective promotion is based on effective communications. You learned about the elements of a communications model in Chapter 10. In promotion, the company that develops the promotion is the sender. The

ILLUSTRATION 23-4

How do businesses communicate with prospective customers?

information in the promotion is the message, and the method of promotion (advertising, personal selling, sales promotion) determines the communication medium. The prospective consumer is the receiver. Feedback from the receiver will help the sender determine if the promotion was successful and to adjust the message, if needed. Forms of promotion that businesses commonly use to communicate with customers are advertising, personal selling, and sales promotions, such as coupons, sampling, and in-store displays.

ADVERTISING

Advertising is any form of paid promotion that delivers a message to many people at the same time. Because the message is designed to appeal to many people, it will be rather impersonal. However, since the message will reach thousands of people, the cost of communicating with each person is very low.

Organizations spend more money each year in the United States on advertising than on any other type of promotion. While the average business spends less than 2 percent of total sales annually on advertising, some businesses spend over 20 percent. Companies in industries such as beverages, cosmetics, and electronics depend on advertising and spend a significant amount throughout the year to keep their brand names in front of consumers.

In 1998, the U.S. corporation that spent the most dollars on advertising was General Motors, which spent almost $3 billion dollars.

ADVERTISING PURPOSES AND MEDIA CHOICES

Advertising is a powerful tool because it can help a business accomplish a variety of objectives. Companies need to consider carefully what they want to communicate to consumers and plan specific advertising to accomplish that communication goal. The major purposes of advertising are shown in Figure 23-4.

FIGURE 23-4

Advertising can accomplish many purposes. Businesses carefully plan each ad to focus on a specific purpose.

1. To inform and educate consumers.
2. To introduce a new product or business.
3. To announce an improvement or product change.
4. To reinforce important product features and benefits.
5. To increase the frequency of use of a product.
6. To increase the variety of uses of a product.
7. To convince people to enter a store.
8. To develop a list of prospects.
9. To make a brand, trademark, or slogan familiar.
10. To improve the image of a company or product.
11. To gain support for ideas or causes.

PUBLICATION ADVERTISING

newspapers, general and special interest magazines, business and professional journals, and directories

MASS MEDIA ADVERTISING

radio, network and local television, cable television

OUTDOOR ADVERTISING

billboards, signs, posters, vehicle signage, and electronic displays

DIRECT ADVERTISING

sales letters, catalogs, brochures, inserts, telemarketing, fax messages, and computer databases

DISPLAY ADVERTISING

window, counter, and aisle displays; special signage; self-service merchandising; trade show displays

INTERNET ADVERTISING

static banner, interactive banner, buttons, sponsored site, cooperative site listings, e-mail list development

FIGURE 23-5

Types of Advertising Media by Categories

Most businesses use some form of advertising to attract prospective customers. However, the methods of reaching consumers—the advertising media—vary a great deal. **Advertising media** are the methods of delivering the promotional message to the intended audience. The most widely used forms of advertising media are classified by categories in Figure 23-5.

PLANNING AND MANAGING ADVERTISING

Businesses have many choices of media to use to communicate information to customers. However, planning an advertising program involves more than selecting the media. Advertising should be planned to support other promotion and marketing decisions. Most businesses that spend a significant amount of money for advertising throughout the year develop an advertising plan. The plan outlines the communications goals and specifies a calendar of advertising activities, an advertising budget, and how the advertising will be evaluated.

Small businesses often need help in developing their advertising plans and in writing their advertisements. A printing company may have specialists who help in writing the copy and designing the advertisement for a direct-mail piece. The people who sell advertising space may offer suggestions in preparing newspaper advertisements. Radio and television station marketing people may also help plan advertising.

As the business grows, the owner has the option of hiring someone to handle the advertising or of placing all of the company's advertising planning in the hands of an advertising agency. Full-service agencies provide all of the services related to planning and producing advertisements for all media and buying the space or time for the ads in the media. Most agencies also offer research services to determine customers' product and information needs. For their services, advertising agencies usually charge a percentage of the total amount spent for the advertising, but may charge for the actual costs of developing and placing the ads.

Some very large companies have a complete advertising department that performs all of the functions of an ad agency. Because of the amount of advertising large companies do and its cost, it is more efficient for those companies to have their own advertising personnel than to pay an ad agency.

THE ADVERTISING BUDGET Companies allot an amount for advertising when they develop their overall company budget. Most businesses plan the advertising program for one year or less. Of course, emergencies may arise that require a quick decision, but planning helps avoid budget misuse. If the company is developing a new product, it will usually prepare an advertising budget to support the new product's introduction into the market.

Large businesses often develop separate advertising budgets for new products, product lines, customer groups, or regions of a market. Separate budgets make it is easier to determine the results of specific advertising on sales and profits.

The amount a business spends on advertising depends more on the characteristics of the product and target market than on the competition. A business with a loyal group of customers and a product that has been in the market for a long time may need to spend less than a business with a new or very complex product or one that is in an extremely competitive market. A business that relies on advertising for the majority of its promotion will, of course, spend a larger percentage of sales on advertising than a business that has a balanced promotional program of advertising, personal selling, and sales promotion.

TIMING OF ADVERTISING Advertising is more effective at some times than others. Companies determine the times when potential customers are most willing and able to buy the products or services advertised. Many products and services are seasonal, with the majority of sales concentrated in a few months of the year. Companies spend more advertising dollars during those times when consumers are considering the purchase of the product than during times when customers are less likely to buy. For example, advertising for ski resorts or ocean cruises increases during the winter months, while advertising for air conditioners and lawn mowers appears most in the spring and summer.

Occasionally, companies advertise to increase purchases at times customers do not traditionally consider buying the product. By emphasizing new product development and advertising, turkey producers and processors have increased the sale of turkey products throughout the year. Those businesses had previously sold almost all of their products near the Thanksgiving holiday and one or two other holiday times during the year.

A single advertisement may produce temporary results, but regular advertising is important in building a steady stream of customers. If advertising does not appear often enough, customers tend to forget about the business or product. To keep their name and brands fresh in consumers' minds, businesses often spread their advertising over the entire year. Only when the company wants an immediate impact, such as for a new product introduction or for a special event, would it consider a large, one-time expenditure.

PERSONAL SELLING

Personal selling is promotion through direct, personal contact with a customer. The salesperson usually makes direct contact with the customer through a face-to-face meeting. There are many types of customers, and a salesperson must be able to adjust to each. Some customers know exactly what they want, while others are in the early stages of decision-making. A critical sales skill is understanding the customer's motivations.

STUDYING THE WANTS OF CUSTOMERS

Individuals are motivated to buy for different reasons. **Buying motives** are the reasons people buy. Some common consumer buying motives are listed in Figure 23-6. To be successful, the salesperson must determine a particular customer's buying motive and then tailor the sales presentation to appeal to that motive. In many cases, the salesperson can appeal to more than one buying motive. For instance, a laundry company representative, in attempting to sell laundry services to a working couple with three children, may talk about the comfort and convenience of having the laundry done outside the home rather than doing it themselves. The salesperson may also explain that

Status	Ease of use	Affection
Appetite	Love of beauty	Wealth
Comfort	Amusement	Enjoyment
Desire for bargains	Desire for good health	Pride of ownership
Recognition	Friendship	Fear

FIGURE 23-6

Understanding common buying motives of consumers is an important selling skill.

GLOBAL PERSPECTIVE

CHAIBOL—THE SOUTH KOREAN CYBER-BUYING CLUB

Combine a unique cultural buying motive, the technology of the Internet, and effective pricing and you have a rapidly growing sales tool in South Korea. In 1998, the South Korean company Samsung tried to find a way to help its 185,000 employees through a difficult economic time by developing a group purchasing program using the Internet. Employees purchasing products offered by the company on their Internet "cybermall" known as Chaibol were given a 15 percent discount on the price of the products.

A unique aspect of the South Korean culture is that there is a strong commitment to group purchasing. Employee groups, groups of professionals, and even alumni of schools encourage each other to purchase from Internet sites set up specifically for their group. In addition to providing products for sale, the cyber communities offer chat rooms, bulletin boards, group information and news, and their own personal home pages. The cyber groups reduce the amount of promotion required and also allow companies to sell products at a lower cost because of the increased volume resulting from group purchasing.

Even Samsung was surprised by the success of the Chaibol. The Internet site increased its membership to 1.2 million customers within two years and expects to add at least another million in the third year. Sales are expected to top $1 billion dollars by 2005 with net profits of $45 million dollars.

For years, South Korean society has had many social networks formed around employee groups. So, it has been much easier to extend the buying club services to those existing groups. Samsung now establishes similar Internet services for many businesses. It has formed a partnership with Freechal.com to open a site called Samsung Mall that is available to anyone. However, it still uses purchasing clubs as the primary method of signing up customers, continuing to build on the cultural need to belong to a group. The next step for Samsung is to develop an agreement with one of South Korea's largest parcel delivery services to be able to guarantee 24-hour delivery of products ordered on the Internet.

THINK CRITICALLY

1. Why do you believe Internet shopping grew so rapidly among Samsung employees in the first two years of the new cybermall business?
2. What causes Internet sales to increase when Samsung develops specialized cyber communities and includes chat rooms, information services, and home pages developed specifically for a particular group of consumers?
3. Do you think the culture of the U.S. would support the same approach to developing Internet shopping groups as was done in South Korea? Why or why not? Are there examples of successful shopping groups in the U.S. that have developed without the use of the Internet? For those you can identify, what has made them successful?

Source: *BusinessWeek Online, March 20, 2000 (http://www.businessweek.com/2000)*

it is less expensive to send the laundry to a professional service because of all the expenses involved in doing laundry at home.

Suppose that this same salesperson calls on the owner of a barber shop or beauty salon. Here the salesperson can emphasize the special sterilizing treatment given to towels, capes, and uniforms and the speed of delivering the laundered items. Both the family and the business owner might find individually scheduled pickup and delivery services attractive. Providing customer satisfaction through a sale is the ultimate goal of a salesperson. This method of selling does not require high-pressure selling; it requires intelligent customer-oriented selling.

PRESENTING AND DEMONSTRATING THE PRODUCT

Customers are interested in what the product will do for them and how they can use it. Salespeople must have a thorough knowledge of the product, so they can provide accurate information and answer questions. For example, customers might ask the following questions: "How much paint will I need for a bathroom 12 feet by 8 feet?" "Which vinyl is best for a concrete basement floor?" "Why is this pair of shoes $68 and that pair $55?" Different customers will value different types of information about the same product. Salespeople should study the products they sell as well as the competition's products, so they can be prepared to answer any questions customers might ask. Nothing is more frustrating than to have a salesperson talk at length about product information that is of no interest to the customer.

In addition to giving customers information, salespeople should be able to demonstrate the use of the product, so that customers can determine whether or not the product will meet their needs. It is usually a good idea for salespeople to show the product and its uses at the same time that they provide information about it. The salesperson can then focus the customer's attention on the product while explaining its features and advantages. Whenever possible, salespeople should encourage the customer to participate. When a customer is directly involved and becomes comfortable with use of the product, initial interest can change to the desire to own the product.

In certain selling situations, such as selling very large or bulky products or selling services, salespeople demonstrate without having the actual product. They use items such as photographs, charts, catalogs, videotapes, or computer displays. Such situations make it more difficult for the customer to get a true feeling for the use of a product, so the salesperson will have to rely on effective communications to increase understanding and desire to purchase the product.

ANSWERING CUSTOMER QUESTIONS

A customer usually has many questions during the salesperson's presentation and demonstration. The salesperson should not be concerned by the questions but should view them as an opportunity to better understand the customer's needs and help the customer make the best decision.

When customers are not certain whether the product is suitable for them, they may raise objections. **Objections** are concerns or complaints expressed by the customer. Objections may represent real concerns. However, they may simply be an effort to avoid making a decision to purchase. It is difficult to try to second-guess a customer to determine if the objection is real or not. It is best for the salesperson to listen carefully to the objection, and then help the customer make the best decision.

CLOSING THE SALE

For many salespeople, the most difficult part of the selling process is asking the customer to buy. As you saw in Figure 23-3, a decision to purchase involves several steps, and each customer moves through those steps in a different way and at a different speed.

If the salesperson has involved the customer in the sales presentation and has listened carefully to the customer's needs, the customer's interest in buying should be rather apparent. Typically, effective salespeople give the customer the opportunity to buy several times during the sales presentation by asking for a decision on a specific model, color, price, or type of payment. If the customer continues to ask questions, the salesperson will answer the questions and continue the discussion until the customer appears satisfied. Then the salesperson will attempt to close the sale again.

Many sales, particularly for expensive products, take several meetings between the salesperson and the customer. In business-to-business selling, teams of salespeople and specialists from the company may meet several times with teams of buyers from the customer's company. Several people will likely make the final decision. Salespeople should continue to work with the customers until it is clear that they do not want the product or until the sale is made.

FOLLOW-UP

The selling process is not complete just because the customer agrees to purchase a product. Remember that effective marketing results in satisfying exchanges between a business and a customer. Therefore, selling is successful only when the customer is satisfied. After the sale, the salespeople should check with the customer to be sure the order is correct, the customer knows how to use the product, and that it meets the customer's needs. If the customer has problems with the product, the salesperson should correct them immediately. If the customer is satisfied, the salesperson's follow-up contact will remind the customer where the product was purchased, so that the customer may choose to buy from the same business again.

SALES PROMOTIONS

Sales promotions are any promotional activities other than advertising and personal selling intended to motivate customers to buy. Some sales promotions are designed to encourage customers to buy immediately. Others are designed to display the products in an attention-getting or attractive way to encourage customers to examine the products.

Coupons are a type of sales promotion used extensively to promote consumer products. Coupons are an effective method of increasing sales of a product for a short time. They are used principally to introduce a new product or to maintain and increase a company's share of the market for established brands. Coupons usually appear in newspaper and magazine advertisements, but they are also distributed by direct mail and are now even available on the Internet. A coupon packaged with a product the customer just purchased may encourage the customer to buy the same brand the next time. Or the enclosed coupon may be for another product from the same company, to encourage the customer to try it.

Manufacturers often cooperate with wholesalers and retailers by providing promotional materials. Some of these promotional materials, commonly furnished without cost or at a low price, include window displays, layouts and illustrations for newspaper ads, direct-mail inserts, display materials, and sales presentation aids.

When producers are introducing a new product, they may distribute samples through the mail. The purpose of this activity is to familiarize people with the products to create a demand for them in local businesses. Coupons often accompany the samples to encourage the consumer to go to a local store and buy the product.

ILLUSTRATION 23-5

How do businesses use coupons as a sales promotion tool?

CYBER COMMUNICATION

Free e-mail can be obtained over the World Wide Web at advertisement-based e-mail providers. As you can guess, advertising pays for the service. You don't need special software to use this type of e-mail; however, if you want to subscribe, you must provide personal information that is shared with advertisers on the site.

The best free e-mail systems will advertise to you by way of your e-mail account. As you visit their sites, you will see ads that you can click on or disregard. However, some free e-mail systems want you to provide your name and personal address and phone number. This information is then shared with advertisers or other users. Some systems even require a credit card number.

ACTIVITY Think about whether a free e-mail system is actually "free." Ask friends or family members if they have had experience with free e-mail. Discuss in class whether there are any rules that a person should follow when using such systems.

Producers and distributors also cooperate with retailers by arranging special displays and demonstrations within stores. For example, demonstrators may cook and distribute samples of a new brand of hot dog to customers in a grocery store. This practice usually helps the retailers sell the new product. The retailer, of course, gives this merchandise preference over other competing products because of this special promotion. Sometimes distributors pay merchants for the privilege of giving demonstrations or offer special prices for the opportunity.

Today, store designs, displays, labels, and packaging promote products so well that many stores let these promotions alone sell the products, rather than employ many salespeople. In **self-service merchandising,** customers select the products they want to purchase, take them to the checkout counter, and pay for them, without much help from salespeople. The display of merchandise in self-service stores attracts attention and makes it convenient for the shopper to examine the merchandise. The labels on the merchandise provide adequate information about the merchandise for the shopper to make a decision.

TRUTH IN ADVERTISING AND SELLING

Laws and regulations protect consumers from unfair promotional practices. Nationally, the Federal Trade Commission and the Federal Communications Commission are responsible for regulating promotion. False advertising is a violation of the law. **False advertising** is defined by federal law as "misleading in a material respect" or in any way that could influence the customer's purchase or use of the product.

To protect consumers, advertisers are required to use **full disclosure,** providing all information necessary for consumers to make an informed decision. They must also use **substantiation**—that is, be able to prove all claims they make about their products and services in promotions.

If businesses violate laws and regulations in their advertising, they may face three types of penalties from the regulating agencies: (1) The agency may impose a **cease and desist order,** which requires the company to stop using specific advertisements. (2) In situations where the advertising has harmed consumers, the company may be required to spend a specified amount of its advertising budget to run corrective advertising. **Corrective advertising** is new advertising designed to change the false impression left by the misleading information. (3) In unusual situations, the company may have to pay a fine to the government or to the consumers harmed by its illegal advertising.

Long-term business success is built on honesty and fair practices. A businessperson may occasionally be tempted to exaggerate or to imitate a competitor who seems to be stretching the truth. In the long run, however, it does not pay to destroy customers' confidence. If customers do not get what they believed was promised to them in advertisements or by salespeople, they will likely not return to the business. On the other hand, a satisfied customer is often an important source of promotion for a business.

CHAPTER 23 REVIEW

CHAPTER CONCEPTS

- Businesses as well as consumers must make careful buying decisions. In a successful exchange, the customer is satisfied with the purchase and the company makes a reasonable profit.
- Businesses must decide what to buy, when to buy, from whom to buy, and how much to buy. Mistakes in any of those areas will result in unsold products, dissatisfied customers, and losses rather than profits.
- When setting the price to charge for a product, businesspeople consider payment terms, discounts, and the elements that make up a product's price—the cost of goods sold, operating expenses, margin, and net profit. Price strategies include pricing to meet competition, to earn a specific profit, to sell more products, or to provide customer services.
- Businesses attempt to control costs by establishing practices that will help reduce markdowns, damaged or stolen merchandise, and the need for customers to return merchandise.
- Even good products require effective promotion. The most common methods of promotion are advertising, personal selling, and sales promotion. Well-designed promotion follows a model for effective communications.
- Advertising is paid promotion directed at a large number of people at the same time. While the cost of advertising is quite high, since it reaches many people, the cost of communicating with each person is usually very low. An advertising plan outlines the communication goals and specifies the timing, budget, and evaluation criteria for the advertising.
- Personal selling is selling through direct personal contact with a customer. It requires an understanding of buying motives. Salespeople study the wants and needs of customers, demonstrate the product, answer customer questions, and close the sale when customers are prepared to make a purchase decision. The sale is complete when the salesperson follows up with the customer to determine if he or she is satisfied with the purchase.
- The Federal Trade Commission and the Federal Communications Commission protect consumers from unfair and illegal promotion. Companies must be able to prove all claims made in advertisements and can be asked to stop using illegal advertisements, run corrective advertising, or even pay a fine. Businesses do not benefit from illegal advertising because it usually results in dissatisfied customers who will take their business elsewhere.

BUILD VOCABULARY POWER

Define the following terms and concepts.

1. list price
2. discounts
3. trade discount
4. quantity discount

5. seasonal discount
6. cash discount
7. selling price
8. cost of good sold
9. operating expenses
10. margin (gross profit)
11. net profit
12. markup
13. markdown
14. advertising
15. advertising media
16. personal selling
17. buying motives
18. objections
19. sales promotions
20. self-service merchandising
21. false advertising
22. full disclosure
23. substantiation
24. cease and desist order
25. corrective advertising

REVIEW FACTS

1. What four specific decisions do business buyers make when they plan a purchase?
2. What two factors affect a business's choice of product assortment?
3. What are the pros and cons for a business of buying from just one or a few suppliers?
4. What are some examples of terms of sale offered by suppliers?
5. Why is the price of a product important to both the customer and the business?
6. What is the result if operating expenses are higher than a product's margin?
7. What components make up a product's selling price?
8. How has the Internet affected the prices businesses can charge for their products?
9. While businesses cannot totally eliminate markdowns, how can they control them?
10. Why might a company have very good products yet not be able to sell them?
11. Compare promotion to the elements of effective communication.
12. What types of help are available to small businesses when planning advertising?
13. Why should companies spread their advertising throughout the year rather than spending most of their advertising budget at one time?
14. What is the advantage of having a salesperson demonstrate a product for a prospective customer?
15. Identify several promotional methods other than advertising and personal selling.

DISCUSS IDEAS

1. Why is it important for businesses to consider both the customer and the business when planning the sale of products?
2. Identify a product that you purchase regularly. For that product, review the four purchasing decisions that should be made

by a company that wants to sell that product to you and your friends: what to purchase, when to purchase, from whom to purchase, and how much to purchase.

3. Why would a company want to offer discounts to buyers rather than selling products at the list price?
4. Using the formula for calculating net profit, suggest several ways that a business can increase the net profit from the sale of a product.
5. How can a company actually sell more products yet earn less net profit or actually lose money from the sales?
6. Explain why high-technology products are often sold initially at very high prices, but then the price begins to drop rather dramatically.
7. Some companies have a policy of accepting returned merchandise with very few questions about why the customer is returning the product. Provide reasons for and against that policy. Consider both the customer and the business in developing your answer.
8. Your textbook states: "Promotion is the primary way that businesses communicate with prospective customers." Do you see communication as the primary goal of promotion, or do you believe promotion has a more important goal? Explain.
9. Which advertising media do you believe are most effective for the products you purchase? Why? Would the same media be most effective for advertising the products your parents buy? Why or why not?
10. Why do you believe that closing the sale is the most difficult step of the selling process for many salespeople? As a customer, what would you recommend to salespeople to make that step easier and more successful?

ANALYZE INFORMATION

1. A dress shop featuring prom dresses purchased 100 dresses at $125 each. The shop priced the dresses at $300 each and sold 50 dresses at that price. For the dresses not sold, the shop reduced the price to $225 and sold 30 dresses at that price. It then sold the remaining dresses for $100. What was the dollar amount of sales? What was the cost of goods sold? What was the gross profit?
2. A hobby shop has been selling an average of 10 model airplane motors each month that cost $20 each. The regular selling price has been $28. By reducing the selling price to $24, the shop increased the number of sales to 15 each month. If the average monthly operating expenses were increased a total of $10 by the change, how much was the monthly net profit increased or decreased by the change in price?
3. A book and gift store that has average annual sales of $700,000 spends 3 percent of its sales for advertising. The store's advertis-

ing budget is divided as follows: catalogs, 30 percent; calendars and other sales promotions, 7 percent; window displays, 15 percent; newspaper advertising, 15 percent; direct mail, 20 percent; and miscellaneous, 13 percent.

a. How much is the average annual advertising budget?

b. What is the amount spent on each type of advertising?

4. Go on the Internet and find examples of each of the following types of online advertising: static banner, interactive banner, button, sponsored site, cooperative site listing with another Internet site, e-mail list development. If possible, print each advertisement you find and prepare a display of the various types of Internet advertising.

5. Assume that you are a salesperson in a furniture store. Explain the buying motives you believe might be prompting each of the following types of customers to consider buying a sofa sleeper: (a) a college student who is buying furniture for a one-bedroom apartment, (b) a family that is outfitting a family room they are remodeling, and (c) a motel owner who is deciding between a less-expensive sofa and the sofa sleeper for 50 rooms.

SOLVE BUSINESS PROBLEMS

CASE 23-1

Kuen Young is planning to open a small convenience grocery store in a town of 50,000 people. Two well-known supermarket chains also serve the town. One chain is a cash-and-carry supermarket where customers must bag their own merchandise. The store offers no special services and stocks mostly private brands at relatively low costs but offers a wide variety of grocery and non-grocery items.

The second supermarket offers a selection of three or four national brands for most products. Its prices are much higher than the prices of the first chain, but it offers many customer services including an on-site branch of a community bank, a place to pay utility bills, and a package wrapping and mailing service. The supermarket is considering adding a service where customers can send in orders by fax or the Internet and then pick up the order within three hours.

Kuen's store will be located in a new housing development on the opposite end of town from the two supermarkets. At this point few homeowners live in the housing development, but it is expected to grow a great deal over the next three years. Right now, few businesses are located in the new housing areas, but that also is expected to change as more people move into the area.

Think Critically:

1. What types of grocery products and services should Kuen offer to compete with the two supermarkets?

2. What other products might Kuen carry in addition to grocery items to attract customers from the supermarkets?
3. How should Kuen decide on the prices to charge for the products he carries in his new business?
4. What effect do you think the planned growth in numbers of customers and possible new businesses will have on the decisions Kuen makes about his convenience store?

CASE 23-2

Peter and Torrie were discussing how companies use advertising. Their conversation follows:

Peter: *Companies spend too much money on advertising. If they would spend less, the prices of products would be a lot lower. I heard that companies that advertise on the Super Bowl program spend more than $1 million for one advertisement.*

Torrie: *I agree. It seems that companies advertise to get people to buy products they don't want. I know I've bought some things just because of the ad and regretted it later. I think companies with good products shouldn't have to advertise. People will find out about them from other people who try the products and like them.*

Peter: *The worst thing about advertising is that businesses can say anything they want to about products, even if the statements are untrue. They often criticize their competitors, making you think there's something wrong with the other product. After watching or listening to an ad, you're more confused than ever about what to buy.*

Think Critically:

1. Do you believe product prices would decrease if companies did not advertise? Explain.
2. Do good products need to be advertised? Why or why not?
3. What types of controls are there on what a business can say in its advertising? What can consumers do if they believe they have been misled by advertising?
4. Do you believe advertising results in more confusion than help for consumers? Justify your answer.

PROJECT: MY BUSINESS, INC.

One of the most difficult decisions for a new businessperson is to set prices on products that will provide a reasonable net profit. In addition, a new business needs to carefully plan promotion to introduce people to the business and its products and to encourage customers to visit the new business and try the products. The following activities will help you plan successful pricing and promotion strategies for your juice business.

DATA COLLECTION

1. Many Internet sites offer information on start-up expenses for small businesses in general and the type of juice business you are starting specifically. Locate sources of that information and develop a list of the common types of expenses and the range of costs you might expect to begin your business.
2. Interview one or two small business owners in your community. Ask them to explain the types of promotion they use, what assistance they get to help them with promotional planning, and how they estimate the amount of money they can spend on promotional activities.
3. Collect samples of advertising and promotion that small businesses in your area are using. Analyze their effectiveness in communicating with prospective customers.
4. Check with several media that offer advertising in your community (newspapers, television, radio, etc.). Obtain a price list that indicates the costs of advertising in each medium, based on the size, type, and frequency of the advertising.

ANALYSIS

1. Assume that, in an average month, your sales will include 700 small drinks, 800 large drinks, 900 supplement additions to the drinks (beyond any free supplements), and 2,000 high-energy snack bars. First, determine the price you will charge for each product, being realistic about what you believe customers are willing to pay. Then estimate your monthly expenses for each of the following items: cost of goods sold, inventory spoilage, taxes and fees, equipment expense, interest expense, supplies, repairs and maintenance, salaries, depreciation expense, insurance, advertising, and other expenses. Have several people review your estimates to determine if they are realistic. Then calculate your estimated monthly profit or loss.
2. Is your estimated monthly net profit adequate? If not, consider what changes you could make to improve it. (Do not make any price changes at this time.) Identify which of the possible changes are most likely to be successful and which are least likely to be implemented.
3. Being as creative as possible, list several ways of promoting your new business that would be (a) informative, (b) unique, and (c) affordable. Consider methods in addition to advertising.
4. Develop a three-month promotional plan for your new business. Include methods, media to be used, time schedule, budget, and samples of the promotions.

UNIT SEVEN

HUMAN RESOURCES MANAGEMENT

CHAPTERS

"People make change happen. Today's successful companies have recognized that only by investing in their most important assets –their people–can a true company transformation become a reality. People, using their knowledge and skills, are the only effective change agents for any company."

Daniel R. Tobin
Transformational Learning, 1996

HUMAN RESOURCES PLANNING

OBJECTIVES

- **24-1** Describe the types of activities that occur in a human resources department.
- **24-2** Outline the procedures to follow in identifying and selecting new personnel.
- **24-3** Identify factors to consider when employees are promoted, transferred, or released.
- **24-4** Compare three major systems that businesses use to pay employees.
- **24-5** Describe several common employee benefits.
- **24-6** Discuss how human resources management is changing in businesses today.

A HARD DECISION TO MAKE

Patrick Gomez was discussing job alternatives with his parents. He had two offers and was considering which would be the best choice. Both jobs were in marketing research, the area of business in which he wanted to work. One job was for a contract research organization, which accepted research projects from many other companies. The second job was in the marketing department of an international manufacturer, where all of Patrick's projects would be for that company. He thought he would enjoy the work he would do for either of the companies.

The major difference between the job offers concerned the rate of pay and benefits offered. In the first job, Patrick would be considered a contract employee. He would receive a rate of pay of $15 per hour. He would work a minimum of 35 hours per week and most weeks would work a full 40 hours. However, there were no benefits, such as insurance and paid holidays. Patrick could take time off between projects but would receive no pay for those days. He would personally need to pay for any insurance if he wanted coverage.

The second job paid a beginning salary of $21,000 per year. Patrick would work a minimum of 40 hours per week with occasional weekend work during particularly busy times. He would receive two full weeks of paid vacation plus five additional paid holidays. The company would contribute $150 per month and Patrick would pay $35 per month for a health insurance policy providing full health and dental care. He would also have a company-paid life insurance policy worth twice the amount of his annual salary. Each year the company would contribute an amount equal to 5 percent of Patrick's salary to a retirement plan. If Patrick stayed with the company for 5 years, he would become part of the retirement plan and would be entitled to the money upon retirement. If he left before that time, the money would go back to the company.

As Patrick considered the choices, he was impressed with the possibility of earning over $31,000 per year at the first company if he worked 40 hours per week for the entire year. He had a number of school loans to pay off, and the extra money would come in handy.

However, his parents reminded him that he was not guaranteed all of those hours and would not have any vacations if he expected to earn that much money. While he had not had any major health problems, any illness could be expensive and would be covered by the health insurance of the second company but not by the first. And, even though Patrick was only 22 years old, beginning to save for retirement at an early age was an important consideration. Patrick knew he had a difficult decision to make. He had never considered how salary and benefits could affect a job decision.

Of all the resources used by a business, probably the most important to its success is people. People are responsible for the effective use of all other resources in the business. People make decisions, operate equipment, maintain records, and deal with customers. Because of their value to the business, managing people is a critical function.

All managers work with people. However, **human resources management (HRM)** consists of all activities involved with acquiring, developing, and compensating the people who do the company's work. HRM is sometimes called *personnel management*. Employees' pay, training, benefits, work environment, and many other factors contribute to their productivity, performance quality, and willingness to stay with the company. The people who work in human resources management perform the tasks that help the business keep the skilled, productive, and satisfied employees it needs to succeed.

HUMAN RESOURCES ACTIVITIES

To begin human resources planning, companies must determine the number of people they will need in order to complete all of the tasks and the skills those people will need. Then they must recruit, hire, and train those employees. Once on the job, the employees will need the equipment and other resources to accomplish their jobs. Directions provided through descriptions of job duties, policies, and procedures help the organization operate effectively. Human resources employees take part in all of these activities.

Businesses must be sure that employees are satisfied with their jobs and motivated to perform well. They need to be concerned about employee safety and health, working conditions, wages, and benefits. Employees who are doing a good job need to be recognized and rewarded, while those who are not need to be given training and support to improve their performance. In some cases employees will need to be removed from their jobs if performance does not improve or if there are major changes in company operations. As you can see, working with people involves many responsibilities.

Most companies have a department that is responsible for human resources management. Large companies may have several specialized divisions within the department, each of which deals with a specific area in human resources. Some of the human resources activities may be performed in other departments across the organization but are planned and coordinated through the human resources (HR) department. Most managers regularly use the services of the HR department as they work with their employees. Employees also receive a variety of services from the people who work in human resources. The important HR services common to many businesses are illustrated in Figure 24-1 and are described next.

EMPLOYMENT

Employment is the one area most people associate with human resources management. The employment function of human resources involves all activities required to maintain an adequate number of qualified employees for the company. Employment activities include determining the need to hire employees, recruiting applicants, determining the qualifications of applicants, and hiring the most qualified to fill the available jobs. In addition, transfers, promotions, retirements, dismissals, and other job changes are part of the employment function.

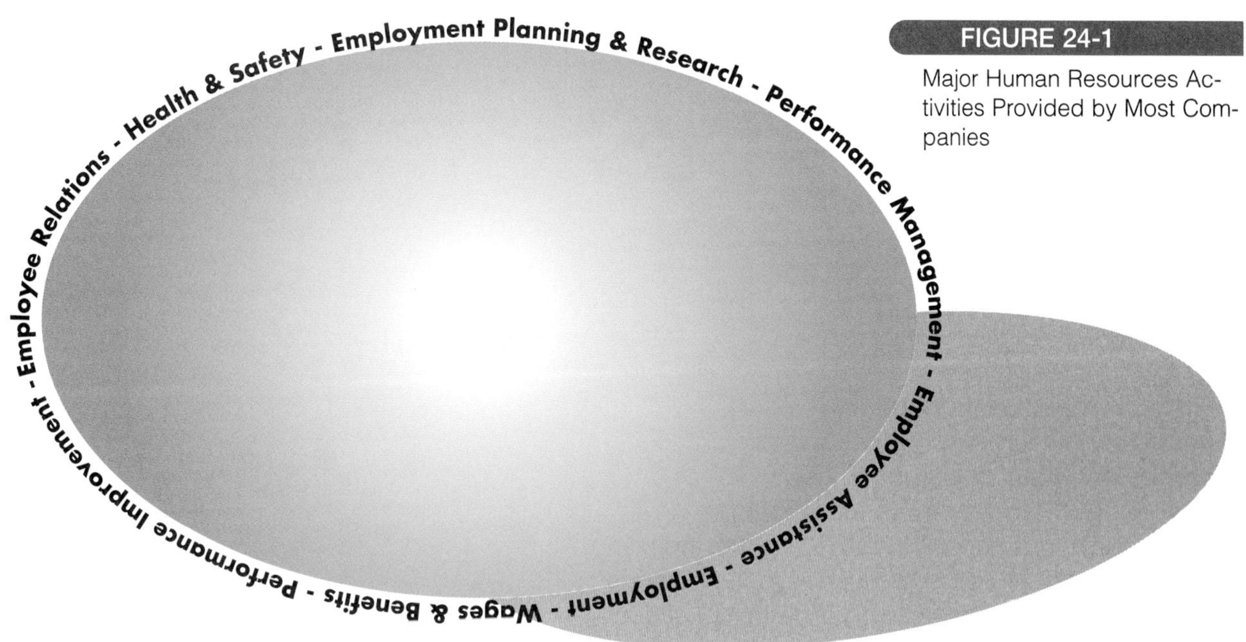

FIGURE 24-1

Major Human Resources Activities Provided by Most Companies

ILLUSTRATION 24-1

What are some of the activities involved in the employment function of human resources management?

WAGES AND BENEFITS

The amount a company pays employees directly and spends to provide employee benefits such as insurance and vacation time is a major part of its operating budget. The level of wages and benefits, especially when compared to competitors, helps to determine who will

CAREER CONNECTION

HUMAN RESOURCES SPECIALIST

Human resources specialists provide a link between top management and employees. They recruit and interview employees, and advise on hiring decisions in accordance with policies and requirements that have been established with top management. They also help their firms effectively use employees' skills, provide training opportunities to enhance those skills, and boost employee satisfaction with their jobs and working conditions.

Human resources specialists are employed in virtually every industry. Some are self-employed and work as consultants to public and private employers. The private sector accounts for about 80 percent of salaried jobs.

Employers usually seek college graduates. Many employers prefer applicants who have majored in human resources, personnel administration, or industrial and labor relations. Others look for graduates with a technical or business background.

For more career information about human resources specialists, check your library or the Internet for resources.

apply for job openings and whether they are likely to make a long-term commitment to the company or will be looking for higher-paying jobs. When performing the wages-and-benefits function, HR employees plan and manage the financial and non-financial rewards available to employees.

Wages and benefits must be carefully controlled. Employee productivity (the amount of work accomplished) compared to the pay and benefits will determine whether the company can be profitable or not. It is important that employees view the system for determining pay as fair and that there is a reasonable relationship between the amount paid to an employee and the value of that employee's work to the company. Human resources is typically responsible for developing a pay system that classifies jobs according to levels and pay ranges. When a person is hired, promoted, or given a pay increase, human resources completes or monitors the procedures to ensure that the employee gets paid the correct amount.

Companies offer benefits to their employees in addition to wages. Some benefits, such as social security and Medicare, are required by law. Others, such as insurance and vacations, are not legally required, but many companies provide them. Often benefit plans are different for full-time than for part-time employees or are based on the length of time the employee has worked for the company. People who work in HR study what benefits can be offered, determine the cost of each benefit, and help management develop the benefits plan. They also provide information to employees about each type of benefit and make sure that employees recognize the value of the benefits to them.

Some companies offer employees choices of benefits, so helping employees make the best decisions and keeping track of each person's choices can be quite complicated. Once employees make their decisions, HR employees complete the necessary paperwork or enter the data into the company's computer system. Each benefit program must be monitored to control costs and to make sure employees receive the benefits to which they are entitled.

PERFORMANCE IMPROVEMENT

Companies cannot thrive with employees whose skills are the same today as they were the day they were hired. Employees must improve their skills and learn new ones on the job. The role of human resources in performance improvement involves training and educating employees to ensure high quality and efficient work. Often the HR department plans and manages performance improvement programs in cooperation with managers and individual employees.

Most businesses conduct several types of training and education programs. Once hired, employees receive an orientation to the company and initial training to make sure they are successful in the new job. Then, as equipment or procedures change, the company must prepare employees for those changes. Finally, when evaluations indicate that an employee is not performing as well as expected, the company will provide support for the employee to improve his or her performance, so that the employee's performance does not result in poor-quality products or customer service.

Employees may be promoted or transferred to a new job in the company. Part of the process of preparing employees for possible promotions or to be able to use existing employees in new jobs is a continuing education and training program. Many companies also allow employees to participate in education programs for their own personal development, believing that such programs increase employee motivation and productivity. Companies sometimes reimburse employees for some or all of the costs of the education as an employee benefit.

Finally, if the company cuts back on the number of employees, eliminates a department, or has a major change in its business activities, it may help the discharged employees prepare for new jobs. Some of those jobs may be in other parts of the company that are adding employees, but the education and training may be for jobs in other companies. It may seem strange that companies would spend money to educate employees to work for other companies. However, progressive employers view these programs as a responsibility to employees who have contributed to the company's past success. They also believe that people are more likely to work for a company that demonstrates this level of commitment to its employees.

EMPLOYEE RELATIONS

Human resources plays a major role in employee relations by ensuring effective communication and cooperation between management and employees. If a labor union is organized within a company, a very formal set of relationships exists between employees and management. The HR workers responsible for employee relations assist in negotiating the labor contract with the union and deal with employee activities and problems that relate to the contract. If employees are not represented by a union, HR still performs the same types of activities, but usually in a less formal way.

Effective management/employee relations have become an important concern for businesses today. The flattened organizations of today mean fewer managers. Businesses expect employees to take more responsibility for their own work. Work teams made up of employees and managers are taking responsibility for many decisions once made just by managers. These decisions include hiring, determining how work will be performed, and improving work procedures. Human resources personnel help to prepare people for their new responsibilities and develop supporting materials, training, and computerized forms and procedures to help the teams successfully complete their new work responsibilities.

Another important area of employee relations is to assure that the company complies with all equal employment and affirmative action laws, such as the Americans with Disabilities Act (ADA). In addition, HR personnel work with employees and managers to prepare people for future job openings and promotions, as well as help them work cooperatively with each other despite individual differences. Companies are most successful when all employees have access to any job for which they are qualified and that discrimination is not a part of employment decisions or the daily work environment.

HEALTH AND SAFETY

Illnesses and injuries among employees are expensive for companies. If employees are unhealthy or injured, they may not be able to work. Other employees will have to complete that work, or the company must hire temporary employees to do it. Also, the cost of insurance and health care will increase when the number of employee illnesses and injuries go up. Expensive insurance is harmful to both the employee and the company. The HR department is responsible for maintaining safe work areas and work procedures, enforcing laws and regulations related to safety and health, and providing adequate education and training in health and safety.

Companies look to human resources to help employees be as healthy and productive as possible. Most HR departments provide regular safety training, place safety posters and materials in the work place to remind workers to follow safety procedures, and monitor procedures to identify and correct possible safety problems. They also collect and report data on work-related injuries and illnesses to be sure the company and employees are well informed about the level of safety in the company and each department. Companies often reward work units that operate for a specific amount of time without a job-related injury.

Companies sometimes promote good health by maintaining a smoke-free environment and offering help for employees to stop smoking through education programs, support groups, and even financial bonuses if they quit smoking. To reduce employee absences and to cut insurance costs, many companies organize wellness and fitness programs, build and staff fitness centers, and pay for employees to enroll in health education classes. Some even have medical personnel on staff to give physicals to employees, treat injuries and illnesses, and help to maintain a healthy workforce.

PERFORMANCE MANAGEMENT

Employees must be able to perform their jobs well. Managers regularly evaluate their employees' performance to determine how well it is meeting expectations. They identify their employees' strengths and reward them for superior performance. If they discover performance problems, they must help their employees improve and provide training, if needed.

Individual managers are responsible for evaluating the employees they supervise and using the results of the evaluation to improve performance. The role of human resources in performance management is to develop the evaluation system and materials and to educate managers and employees on the proper methods for evaluating and improving performance. Human resources personnel work with managers and experienced employees to design the performance management system and then prepare the forms and materials needed. They then train the managers to be able to evaluate employees objectively, complete the evaluation forms, and conduct evaluation conferences with the employees. They also help employees understand their role in the evaluation process. The HR department usually maintains the results of the evaluations in each employee's personnel file.

A newer method of performance evaluation, **360-degree feedback,** uses performance feedback gathered from a broad range of people with whom the employee works, both inside and outside the organization—rather than from just the employee's manager. People who are peers of the employee contribute performance feedback. For example, a manager gathers feedback from other managers who work at the same level; employees receive feedback from co-workers. In addition, the 360-degree feedback system includes information from people who report to the person being reviewed. Sometimes even suppliers and customers are asked for feedback.

In the 360-degree feedback system, people completing the reviews fill out a detailed questionnaire about the person's performance. The responses are anonymous, so the person evaluated does not know who specifically provided the information. Finally, the information is summarized, a report is prepared, and a performance improvement conference is held with an evaluation expert to ensure that the employee and manager interpret the information correctly and know how to use it to improve future performance.

EMPLOYEE ASSISTANCE PROGRAMS

Today, businesses recognize that employees have many important responsibilities in addition to their jobs. Personal and family concerns may interfere with an employee's work. Issues ranging from financial problems to marriage and family issues and alcohol or drug abuse are increasingly common among employees. **Employee assistance programs** provide confidential personal problem-solving, counseling, and support services for employees. For the most part, participating in the services is voluntary, and employees can choose to receive assistance whenever they need the help and support. For serious problems that are interfering with work, managers can refer employees to specific assistance services but, again, the employee can choose not to accept the assistance. For these types of employee assistance programs, the company hires specialists such as counselors, psychologists, and medical personnel to provide the services.

Some employee assistance programs have expanded to provide services needed by single-parent or two-working-parent families, employees in transition because of job changes or moving to a new location, and even special financial services such as short-term loans or financial assistance for education. HR personnel involved in employee assistance programs may arrange day-care services for children or elderly parents, help with short-term housing needs, plan for car pooling or other transportation services, and facilitate many other activities that help employees balance work and personal lives.

EMPLOYMENT PLANNING AND RESEARCH

You can see from the HR services described above that maintaining an effective workforce is very complex. Companies change rapidly, but it may take weeks and months to hire new people, design training programs, or complete performance reviews. Federal and state employment laws as well as company policies and procedures require a great deal of information about each employee to be collected and maintained.

A major HR function involves researching and maintaining the information that managers need in order to determine personnel needs and manage the workforce. The people working in this area of human resources gather information, use computer programs to analyze that information, and maintain and review employee records as well as company and competitive employment information. They then distribute this information to managers to alert them to problems, the need for changes, and ways to improve employee productivity.

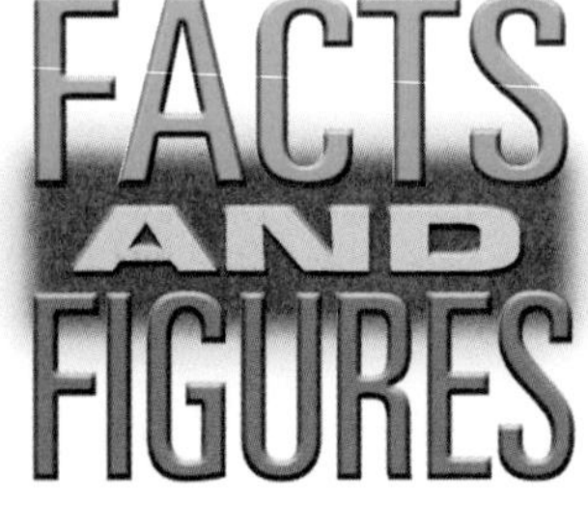

The Small Business Administration reports that for every $1 an employer invests in personnel screening, the employer saves $5-$16 in reduced absenteeism, productivity, turnover, safety, insurance, and in employer liability.

SELECTING PERSONNEL

Hiring new employees is one of the most expensive but important company activities. Effective selection means hiring people with the right skills for each job. Hiring people who do not meet specific job qualifications results in high training costs, dissatisfied employees, and poor performance. This section discusses some essential procedures for selecting personnel in a medium-to-large company.

ILLUSTRATION 24-2

Why is it important to hire employees with the right skills for each job?

ESTABLISHING A NEED

As a first step in the process of hiring a new employee, managers must establish that they actually need a new employee. Normally, the need develops to replace a current employee who has left the company, been promoted, or retired. If the company or department is growing, new employees will be needed to complete the extra work. Changes in the operations of a department or the use of new procedures or equipment may require that new employees be hired to perform those duties.

After identifying a need, the department manager typically will work with HR to complete the hiring process. The HR department must have detailed and accurate information about the position in order to screen applicants and choose only the most qualified people to interview. To compile the needed information, companies prepare a job description and job specification for each position in the company. A **job description** is a list of the basic tasks that make up a job. A **job specification** is a list of the qualifications a worker needs to do that job.

HR employees work with managers and employees who are currently doing each job to prepare job descriptions and specifications. This information is kept on file in the HR department and is updated regularly as job requirements and activities change. The data are used in a variety of ways, but in the selection process, the information is used to recruit a pool of qualified applicants and to help determine the best candidate for the job.

RECRUITING APPLICANTS

After the HR department has received a request to fill a position and reviewed the job description and specifications, it needs to identify applicants for the opening. An effective recruitment process will result in a number of applicants from which a well-qualified person can be selected. If the pool of qualified applicants is too small, the chances of finding someone who is well-qualified decreases. If the pool is too large, the process of selecting the most-qualified will take longer.

Many sources of prospective employees exist. The HR department must be aware of those sources and use those most likely to locate qualified applicants. Some of the most often-used sources of prospective employees are discussed next.

CURRENT EMPLOYEES Normally companies make information about all job vacancies available to everyone in the company and give current employees the first opportunity to apply. There are many reasons for using this source. The job may be a promotion for some employees, which can serve as an incentive to work harder. If it is not a promotion, allowing an employee to change jobs may provide better work hours or pay. The new job may match the employee's interests and abilities better. Placing a current employee in a job opening is also good practice for companies that are anticipating employment cutbacks.

Current employees may also recommend people they know for open positions in the company. Employees will need specific information about job openings and the procedures they should use to nominate people for openings. They must also know that the people recommended will be treated fairly and in the same way as other job applicants.

UNSOLICITED APPLICATIONS A business that has a reputation as a good employer is likely to have people applying for jobs at all times. Most large companies take applications regularly, even when they currently have no openings that fit the applicants. As applications arrive, human resources screens them for minimum qualifications and classifies them according to job categories in the company. Then they maintain the applications in an active file for a period of time, such as six months, and review them when openings occur.

EMPLOYMENT AGENCIES Employment agencies are businesses that actively recruit, evaluate, and help people prepare for and locate jobs. All states maintain an employment service supported by state and federal taxes. Public employment offices are usually located in several cities throughout each state. They offer testing services, job listings, and help in preparing applications and in developing interviewing skills. They will work with businesses to publicize available jobs and to identify qualified candidates for job openings.

OTHER SOURCES Colleges and universities, vocational and technical schools, and an increasing number of high schools have placement offices to assist graduates in obtaining jobs. Businesses can use those offices to obtain lists of potential employees and, in some cases, to obtain resumes and other information about the school's graduates.

The offices may provide assistance in scheduling interviews with a number of applicants to help the recruiting business.

Advertising is a common method of obtaining job applicants. Companies frequently advertise when they need a large number of employees or they must fill an opening quickly. HR employees carefully write employment advertisements to attract only qualified applicants, rather than large numbers of unqualified people.

The Internet has become a popular resource for recruiting personnel. Web sites such as monster.com provide thousands of job listings that job seekers can search by category of job, location, company, or salary expectations. Many employment sites on the Web also provide places where people seeking employment can post their resumes. Some sites provide services, such as help in resume preparation. Most major Internet employment sites make it possible for applicants to submit their resumes to prospective employers online. Today, companies that regularly hire employees place a link to employment opportunities on their home page, so that prospective employees can obtain an up-to-date listing of available jobs.

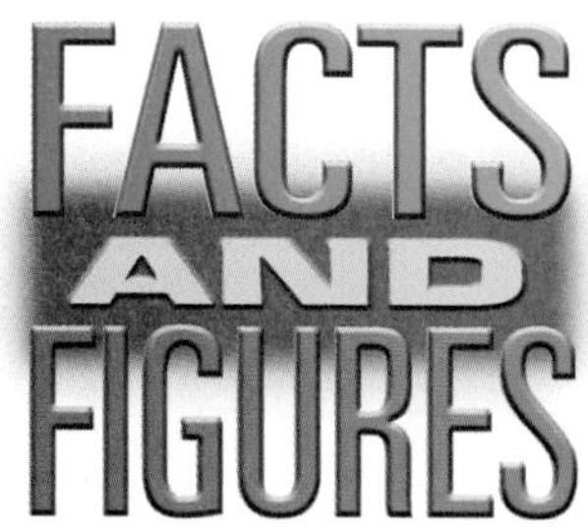

Employees regularly leave their companies for new jobs or even new careers, only to return when things don't work out. And employers, desperate for qualified employees and disenchanted with expensive candidate searches, are taking them back. They are called "boomerang" employees, and they compose as much as a third of the U.S. work force.

PROCESSING APPLICATIONS

Most businesses require applicants to fill out an application form. The form must ask only for information necessary to make the best selection for the job. The company must be careful that the form does not ask for discriminatory or illegal information.

After receiving applications for an opening, companies typically follow these procedures to narrow the pool to only the most qualified candidates and make their final selection:

1. HR employees review the applications to eliminate the people who do not meet minimum qualifications. Those qualifications would typically include level of education, specific training, certifications, or licenses. Applicants are often eliminated at this stage because they filled out the application form incorrectly, did not fully complete the application, or had very poor written communication skills.
2. An HR employee interviews the remaining applicants to confirm information on the application, to gather information on oral communications and human relations skills, and to provide more information to the applicants about the company and the job.
3. An HR employee checks the information supplied on the application form and through the interview for accuracy by contacting schools attended, previous employers, and listed references. Careful questioning of a reference can often reveal important information about an applicant's strengths, work habits, and human relations skills.
4. HR employees administer tests to the applicants remaining in the pool at this point to determine if the applicants have the needed knowledge and skills for the specific job. To be legal, the tests must measure only characteristics important for success on the job.

5. The manager or a work team of the department that has the opening then interviews the top applicants remaining in the pool. The interview allows more specific questioning related to the duties and qualifications for the job, can offer applicants detailed information about the job and the department, and give applicants the opportunity to ask questions. By understanding the job and its requirements, applicants will be in a better position to determine if the job would satisfy them.
6. The final selection is made by comparing information gathered with the job requirements. The decision should be made carefully and objectively to select the best applicant for the job. Many businesses require prospective employees to pass a physical exam, including drug screening.
7. When an applicant is hired, HR employees walk the new employee through filling out the necessary paperwork, such as tax forms and insurance enrollment forms. They then help the new employee get a good start by offering an orientation program and initial training. After the new employee has been at work for several weeks, the HR department may follow up to see whether the right person was selected, in order to improve employment procedures.

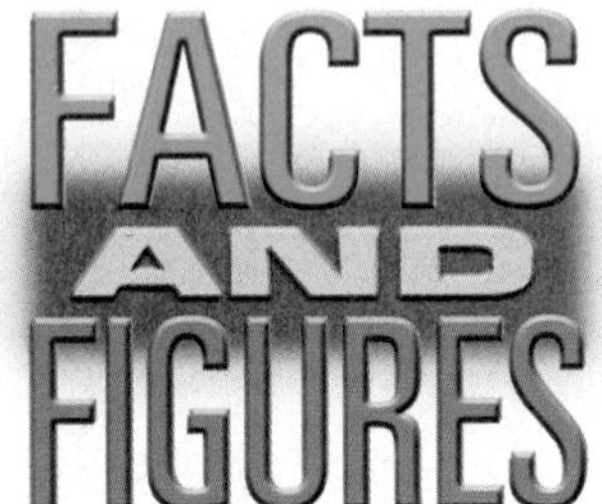

Assigning a buddy or mentor to a new employee can be extremely valuable. This person can educate the employee about whom to contact concerning different problems. The mentor can act as a resource if the new employee has questions or experiences difficulties in the first month or two on the job.

PROMOTING, TRANSFERRING, AND RELEASING EMPLOYEES

The amount of time and money invested in recruiting, hiring, and training a new employee is very high. Because of the expense, once the company finds a good employee, it should attempt to keep that person as long as possible. Offering employees opportunities for promotions and transfers can help retain good employees. The company also needs a procedure for dealing with employees who are not performing satisfactorily and for reducing the number of employees if changing economic conditions require downsizing.

A **promotion** is the advancement of an employee within a company to a position with more authority and responsibility. Usually, a promotion includes an increase in pay and may include greater prestige and benefits. Promotion opportunities occur when another person vacates a job (through promotion or retirement, for example) or when the company creates a new position.

Whenever possible, a business should fill vacancies by promotion. If the company has an effective selection procedure, it should have well-qualified employees who, with training and experience, could be promoted. Every employee should have an equal opportunity to receive promotions for which they are qualified. Employees need to know the job to which they can advance and the factors considered in promotion. Many companies now provide career counseling services for employees. Through career counseling, employees can plan career paths, determine the education and training required for the jobs in the career path, and develop plans to prepare for the jobs they want. You will learn more about employee development in the next chapter.

A **transfer** is the assignment of an employee to another job in the company that, in general, involves the same level of responsibility and authority as the person's current work. There are many reasons for transfers:

1. Employees being trained for management positions may be transferred among several positions to gain experience.
2. Employees may be transferred to give them a better opportunity for promotion.
3. Employees may be transferred to new departments or new company locations due to growth or reduction of the size of departments.
4. Employees may choose to transfer to jobs that better meet their current interests and needs.
5. Employees may be transferred to overcome difficulties resulting from poor performance or conflicts with other people on the job.

Some situations require employees to leave the company. Some employee separations are permanent, while others are temporary. They may result from a downturn in the economy or in the company's fortunes. Employees may also be released due to violations of company policies or continuing unsatisfactory job performance with no success in improving the performance.

A **discharge** is the release of an employee from the company due to inappropriate work behavior. In ordinary language, this means that the employee is fired. A **layoff** is a temporary or permanent reduction in the number of employees because of a change in business conditions. After a layoff, employees may be called back to work when jobs become available. When a company plans a large number of layoffs, the human resources department may be asked to help the employees plan for the layoff. The HR department may help in locating other jobs, offer personal and career counseling, or provide retraining for other jobs within the company.

EMPLOYEE TURNOVER

Employee turnover is the rate at which people enter and leave employment in a business during a year. The rate of turnover is important to a business because the loss of experienced employees means that new employees have to be hired and trained. New employees will not be as productive as experienced ones for some time. Between the time when an experienced employee leaves and a new employee is hired, the remaining employees will often be called on to get the work done. Most companies watch their employee turnover rate carefully and make every effort to keep it low. Two common formulas for computing the rate of employee turnover are shown in Figure 24-2.

FIGURE 24-2
Methods of Calculating the Rate of Employee Turnover

1. Number of employees who have terminated employment with the business ÷ Average number of employees = % of employee turnover

2. Number of employees hired to replace employees who have terminated employment with the business ÷ Average number of employees = % of employee turnover

An example will illustrate the difference between the two methods. Suppose that during last year 150 employees left their jobs in a company. The company hired 120 new employees to replace those who had left. The average number of employees during the year was 1,000. According to the first formula, the employee turnover was 15 percent (150/1,000). According to the second formula, it was 12 percent (120/1,000). To make it easier to study employee turnover trends, the company should use the same formula from year to year.

EXIT INTERVIEWS

Whenever an employee leaves the company, interviewing the person can gain some important feedback. An **exit interview** is a formal interview with an employee who is leaving the company to determine the person's attitudes about the company and suggestions for improvement. The exit interview provides an opportunity to learn about the causes of employee turnover and feedback about the company's policies and procedures, management, and operations. The interview procedure should be carefully planned to get important information in a way that is comfortable for the person being interviewed and to accurately record the information so it can be used to improve operations and employment procedures.

PAYING EMPLOYEES

While it is usually not the most important, one of the reasons people work is to earn money. But money is just one valuable benefit that employees receive for their labor. Other benefits include such things as paid vacations, company-sponsored health insurance, and employee assistance programs. The pay and other benefits employees receive in exchange for their labor are called **compensation.**

The method used to determine pay can be an important factor in attracting employees to the company, motivating them to give their best efforts, and retaining good employees. Therefore, the compensation system needs to offer a fair way to pay employees that encourages them to work for the company, while using the company's resources efficiently.

Many factors affect the amount of pay an employee receives. These include the skill required for the job, the work conditions, the amount of education and experience the person has, the supply and demand of that type of worker, and economic conditions.

WAGE AND SALARY PLANS

A **wage** is pay based on an hourly rate. **Salary** is pay based on a timeframe other than hourly, such as weekly or monthly. Salaries are most often paid to executives, supervisors, professionals, and others who do not have a fixed number of hours to work each week.

Because businesses vary a great deal in the types of work and the qualifications of employees, many methods are used to determine how employees are paid. Under some plans, employees with the same qualifications and experience are paid the same no matter what job they do or whether one is more productive than another. Other systems determine pay levels by the type of work, the amount produced, or the quality of the work.

TIME PLANS The most common payment method is to pay a certain amount for a specified period of time worked. Wages are a time-based plan. For example, an employee might earn $8.50 per hour. A salary is also based on time worked. For example, a company may pay an employee a salary of $2,800 per month, while another company may set an employee's salary at $43,800 per year. In either case, the employee will receive a regular paycheck, often on a semi-weekly or monthly basis.

Time plans are easy to administer, because pay is based directly on the amount of time worked. However, time plans do not reward employees financially who provide extra effort or do outstanding work.

ILLUSTRATION 24-3

What is the difference between a wage and a salary?

PERFORMANCE PLANS Two types of plans pay employees for the amount of work. A **commission plan** pays employees a percentage of the volume of sales for which they are responsible. For example, a salesperson may earn a commission of 5 percent on total sales. If the salesperson makes sales worth $10,000 during one week, the salesperson would earn $500 that week. The commission system provides a direct incentive to employees because their efforts directly determine their pay. Also, the business can control costs, because pay relates directly to the amount of sales. A negative result of the commission plan is that the salesperson will concentrate on activities that lead to the largest commissions. A salesperson may try to sell products a customer doesn't need, may concentrate on larger customers while ignoring smaller but important customers, and may not complete work that seems to detract from selling time.

A similar type of performance-pay system is the piece-rate plan. The **piece-rate plan** pays the employee a fixed rate for each unit produced. An individual employee's pay in this case is based directly on the amount of work the employee produces. For example, if an employee earns 30 cents for each unit and produces 250 units in a day, the employee will earn $75 for the day.

Although piece-rate plans were first used in factories to encourage employees to increase production, companies also pay other types of employees on the basis of units of work completed. They may pay billing clerks based on the number of invoices processed, data-entry personnel according to the number of lines of copy entered, order pickers based on the number of items they pull from inventory to fill orders, and market researchers based on the number of phone interviews completed.

Well-designed pay plans based on productivity usually result in increased performance, at least in the short run. However, performance plans can make it difficult for new employees to earn a reasonable amount, since they are inexperienced and can't work as efficiently as experienced workers. Performance plans may also encourage experienced employees to find shortcuts to increase their production, resulting in quality or safety problems.

Some companies are developing innovative ways to compensate performance on specific, short-term projects that motivate employees while not adding greatly to the organization's costs. The reward is often in the form of a product or service the employee values rather than a direct wage or salary payment. Under one such plan, managers reward employees who have performed well or have accomplished a specific, challenging goal. When an individual or work team achieves the established goal, the manager provides rewards such as tickets for an upcoming athletic event or concert, gift certificates for employees to take their family out for a night on the town, or some other reward that is meaningful to the employees in recognition of their efforts.

COMBINATION PLANS To get the advantages of various types of pay systems, some companies use combination plans. A **combination plan** is a pay plan that provides each employee a small wage or salary and adds incentive pay based on the person's performance. Such a plan assures the employee a specified amount of money but allows the person to earn an additional amount based on effort. It is particularly effective for jobs that require a number of activities that do not directly result in increased production or sales. Some companies provide the incentive based on the performance of a work team or group rather than on the individual's performance, in order to encourage cooperation and group effort.

A variation of the combination plan is the use of a bonus. A **bonus** is money paid at the end of a specific but long period of time (3, 6, or 12 months) for performance that exceeds the expected standard for that time. Bonuses relate employee rewards to organizational performance, so if the work unit or company does well, employees share in the profits.

FACTORS AFFECTING PAY LEVELS

Determining the amount of wages and salaries is an important business decision. In addition to the type of pay plan, companies consider other factors when determining wages and salaries. For example, employees who bring more skills to the job may be more valuable to the company and therefore receive greater pay than other employees in the same job. Also, some jobs may be more important to the company than others, justifying greater pay. The company may pay more for greater experience or more years worked for the company. The supply and demand of that type of labor, current economic conditions, and the prevailing wage rates in the community and in the industry also affect the rate of pay. Companies may choose to provide especially full employee benefits rather than pay high wages. Finally, federal and state labor laws, such as laws that set minimum wages, affect employee pay.

Usually HR departments of large companies employ economists and other specialists to develop pay plans and to help determine the total amount of money that should be spent on employee compensation, including benefits. Smaller companies usually attempt to compare the wages and salaries they offer to those offered by competitors so as not to lose valuable employees to other companies as a result of low wages.

EMPLOYEE BENEFITS

In addition to pay, employees often receive other valuable benefits from their employer as part of their total compensation. You will recall from the scenario at the beginning of the chapter that Patrick was deciding between two jobs. One of the factors he was considering was the amount of compensation. The first job appeared to pay significantly more than the second. However, the second job provided Patrick with benefits beyond the amount of money he would earn, including paid vacations and insurance. **Employee benefits** are all forms of compensation and services the company provides to employees in addition to salaries and wages.

Employee benefits can significantly increase the total compensation an employee receives. Many companies contribute between 20 and 40 percent of an employee's wages or salary to pay for benefits. Assume that a company employed 300 people at an average salary of $30,000. In addition to the $9,000,000 to pay the salaries, the company's cost of benefits may be as much as $3,600,000.

CUSTOMARY BENEFITS

Many businesses make it possible for their employees to obtain insurance at lower costs through group insurance policies. Life, health, dental, and disability insurance are common types of coverage provided. In many cases, the company pays part or all of the employee's insurance premium.

Some companies offer a **profit-sharing plan,** a benefit plan that pays employees a small percentage of the company's profits at the end of the year. Profit sharing encourages employees to do things that increase company profits in order to obtain the benefit.

As employees get older and begin to consider retirement, they become increasingly concerned about the income they will have once they stop working. Retirement plans are designed to meet that need. A **pension plan** is a company-sponsored retirement plan that makes regular payments to employees after retirement. Companies with a pension plan put a percentage of employees' salaries into a pension fund. The funds are invested and earnings are used to make pension payments to retired employees. In a few pension plans, the employer pays the entire cost of the pension, but in most plans the employee makes a contribution as well or pays the entire cost of the pension contribution. Figure 24-3 summarizes the differences among common types of retirement plans.

After employees have worked for a company for a specified time, often one year, they may begin to earn vacation days. Most companies pay the employees' regular salary during vacations. In addition to earned vacations, some companies are closed for holidays and may pay their employees for those days. Other common benefits are paid or unpaid absences for personal illness, the illness or death of family members, and the birth or adoption of a child.

HOURS OF WORK

To respond to the changing lifestyles of workers and the operating needs of businesses, some companies have experimented with changes in the standard 40-hour, five-day workweek. One such change involves

TYPE OF PENSION	DESCRIPTION
Pension Plan	A retirement plan in which the company invests a specific amount of money for each employee, based on his or her pay, and uses the earnings to make regular payments to retirees. The company owns and manages the investments.
401k Plan	A company-sponsored retirement plan in which employees may choose to have a percentage of their pay contributed to one of several alternative investment plans selected by the employer. Investment companies, rather than the employer, manage the investments, but employees own their accounts.
IRA Plan	A retirement plan that is not company-sponsored in which employees contribute a percentage of their pay, up to a specified legal limit, in any investment plan of their choice. The employer is not involved in selecting or controlling the employees' investments. The law allows only people who are not covered by an employer's retirement plan to have an IRA.
Keogh Plan	A retirement plan designed for self-employed people, who may contribute an amount of their earnings into an investment fund managed by an investment company. Keogh plans are open to people involved in sole proprietorships or partnerships.

FIGURE 24-3

Common Types of Retirement Plans

scheduling employees to work ten hours a day for four days per week. Another variation, **flextime,** lets employees choose their own work hours, within specified limits. **Job sharing** allows two people to share one full-time job. Each person works half the time, either half days or alternate days of the week.

Companies may also stagger the workweek by having some employees start their week on days other than Monday. In this way, the business can operate seven days a week without having employees work more than five days, thereby obtaining maximum use of facilities and equipment while controlling labor costs. It is also a way to reduce traffic congestion or demands on employee services, such as parking and food services, at a specific time.

OTHER BENEFITS

The benefits described above are most common and are available to employees in many companies. Increasingly, businesses are providing other types of benefits for employees. Many companies provide free or low-cost parking, food services and cafeterias, and discounts on the purchase of products produced or sold by the company. Many businesses contribute to the cost of college classes or other educational programs completed by employees. More and more companies are providing parents time off to visit their children's schools. Some companies

ILLUSTRATION 24-4

Why might a company provide a benefit such as exercise classes to employees?

today even offer unique services, such as hiring someone to do gift shopping or take clothing to a dry cleaner for busy employees and offering transportation for people who carpool but need to go home due to an emergency.

Some companies offer free or low-cost professional services to employees, including financial and investment advice, lawyers, accountants, and counselors. An increasingly important benefit for employees with young children is the availability of day-care facilities. That same benefit is being extended to families with elderly parents living with them. The company may offer elder-care programs as a benefit.

As you can see, the range of employee benefits is quite broad. Companies offer new benefits as employee needs change and as companies compete to attract and keep good employees. Since individual needs can be quite different, businesses have a difficult time providing the right set of benefits for each employee. Some companies have attempted to solve that problem by letting employees choose from among a number of available benefits. A program in which employees can select the benefits that meet their personal needs is known as a **cafeteria plan.** In this program, each employee can choose among benefits with equal value or give up certain benefits and receive their cost as additional compensation.

THE INCREASING VALUE OF HUMAN RESOURCES

Human resources management is very important in all types of businesses. Managers faced with improving the effectiveness and profitability of their business are increasingly looking at the ways that they can improve employee performance. As employees' needs continue to change and as the cost of providing employee services and benefits increases, all managers will have to emphasize building and maintaining effective employee relations. Several areas are of special concern to companies that value their employees. Those include legal responsibilities identified through employment laws, ensuring equal opportunity for all employees, and making changes to improve the way they provide and manage HR services.

EMPLOYMENT LAWS

State and federal governments have been concerned for years about employee/employer relationships and the protection of employees. They have passed several laws to protect employees, improve their health and safety, and provide minimum employee benefits. Figure 24-4 summarizes major employment laws. HR departments are responsible for understanding the laws and ensuring that the business complies with their requirements.

EQUAL OPPORTUNITY IN EMPLOYMENT

In recent years, many businesses have taken positive steps to correct discrimination in employment. Those steps include the development of written plans for fair employment practices, a review of recruitment and selection procedures, improved access to job training to qualify employees for promotions who may have been excluded in the past, diversity training for all managers and employees, and improved performance evaluation procedures that reduce bias. Companies that have taken a sincere and active interest in improving the diversity of their workforce and eliminating discrimination have found that diversity improves decision making by bringing a rich array of ideas and perspectives to company planning and problem-solving.

CHANGES IN PROVIDING HUMAN RESOURCES SERVICES

Companies are looking at ways to improve HR services while controlling the costs of providing those services. They are finding many ways to use technology to reduce paperwork and streamline the process of maintaining and distributing information to employees. Some companies are also employing outside companies to perform some HRM tasks.

USE OF TECHNOLOGY Managing human resources requires a great deal of information pertaining to every employee in the organization. Much of the cost of HRM goes into the paperwork needed to gather and update this information. Employees must fill out forms. Then HR employees must make copies, store them, and retrieve them when needed. Whenever a change occurs, the process must be repeated.

Computers have greatly improved the way companies gather and store employment information. Companies now store employment data electronically, making access and updates easy. When an employee

FIGURE 24-4

Laws Providing Benefits and Protection for Employees

LAW AND PURPOSE

OCCUPATIONAL SAFETY AND HEALTH ACT

The law developed very specific safety and health standards for businesses. The Department of Labor enforces those standards through inspections of businesses and investigations of accidents.

FAIR LABOR STANDARDS ACT

The Act established a minimum wage that must be paid to employees by those businesses included in the law. The businesses must pay employees 1 1/2 times their normal wage rate for any hours above 40 worked in a week. The law places limits on the number of hours and times during the day when teenagers can work. It also prevents businesses from hiring people under 18 years old to work in hazardous occupations.

SOCIAL SECURITY ACT

The portion of the Social Security Act that provides pensions to retired workers and their families and provides benefits to disabled workers is known as Old Age, Survivors, and Disability Insurance. Medicare is a broad program of hospital and health insurance for people who have reached retirement age.

UNEMPLOYMENT INSURANCE

Unemployment insurance provides a fund to pay an income to certain unemployed workers. The unemployment insurance program is administered by each state. To be eligible for unemployment benefits, a worker must not be responsible for losing the job and must be actively looking for new employment.

WORKERS' COMPENSATION

All states have workers' compensation laws that require employers to provide insurance for death, injury, or illness resulting from employment.

CIVIL RIGHTS ACT OF 1964

This act prohibits discrimination in hiring, training, and promotion on the basis of race, color, gender, religion, or national origin.

EQUAL PAY ACT

This act prohibits unequal pay for men and women doing substantially similar work.

AMERICANS WITH DISABILITIES ACT

This act prohibits discrimination on the basis of physical or mental disabilities.

FAMILY AND MEDICAL LEAVE ACT

This act permits workers to take up to 12 weeks of unpaid leave for the birth or adoption of a child and for personal illness or illness of an immediate family member.

MANAGEMENT CLOSE-UP

INCREASING EMPLOYMENT OPPORTUNITIES THROUGH THE ADA

Many companies search to fill increasingly technical and complex jobs with qualified applicants. Some employment divisions report screening hundreds of applications to find one person who meets the necessary job requirements. At the same time, businesses overlook millions of Americans who have necessary job qualifications for many jobs. Why? They have disabilities that many employers believe will prevent them from performing job duties effectively.

Because of misunderstanding, stereotypes, and discrimination faced by disabled Americans in the workplace, a new employment law was enacted in 1990. The Americans with Disabilities Act (ADA) prohibits employment discrimination against individuals with physical and mental handicaps or chronic illnesses, if the applicant is able to perform the basic functions of the job. Under ADA, employers must provide the opportunity for all disabled applicants who are otherwise qualified for the job to compete for available jobs. A qualified applicant is a person who has the required education and experience and can perform the work if the employer provides "reasonable accommodation."

Reasonable accommodation means that the employer must make facilities, equipment, procedures, and activities accessible and usable; restructure jobs and work tasks when possible; and provide access to the same benefits and privileges available to other employees. The word "reasonable" is used to ensure that employers do not have to make changes that result in a severe financial hardship for the business or that alter the job, so that required work cannot be completed. Studies done in businesses in preparation for implementing the ADA found that, with careful planning, many accommodations for disabled employees could be accomplished at no additional cost. Other changes could be made at relatively low cost by implementing creative solutions. While some organizations are concerned about the impact and cost of complying with the Americans with Disabilities Act, others have found that it has encouraged them to consider a group of productive employees they had previously ignored.

THINK CRITICALLY

1. Why do you believe it was necessary for the federal government to pass the ADA legislation?
2. If you were a businessperson, how would you respond to the ADA requirements?
3. Using your school as an example, in what ways have the facilities, equipment, and materials been modified to meet the needs of disabled students, faculty, and staff? Are there areas in the school where other reasonable accommodations can be made?

gets a raise or moves to a new home, HR employees can easily make these changes in the computer system. To keep records confidential, companies take security precautions, such as requiring a password to access employees' files.

The Internet has also made HR activities more efficient. The Internet provides a way for employers and job seekers to exchange information. Companies can use the Internet to communicate new policies or new benefit options to employees throughout the company and the world. Companies may even set up information kiosks in cafeterias and break rooms, so employees can easily check on benefits and other employment information. People participating in employee evaluation, such as the 360-degree feedback process, can complete their evaluation forms online.

OUTSOURCING OF SERVICES Some companies are now outsourcing some or all of the HR services. As you learned in Chapter 15, *outsourcing* is hiring an outside firm to perform specialized tasks. For example, a company may hire an outside employment agency to perform all of its employment activities, including recruiting, selecting, and even training. A second common use of outsourcing in HRM is to contract with an information systems company to administer all of the data required for managing human resources.

CHAPTER CONCEPTS

- Human resources management consists of all activities involved with acquiring, developing, and compensating the people who do the company's work. The HR department is responsible for maintaining an adequate number of employees and developing fair pay plans that will help keep them satisfied with their jobs and productive. HR managers work with all managers and employees in the company.
- The major activities of an HR department involve employment, wages and benefits, performance improvement, employee relations, health and safety, performance management, employee assistance programs, and employment planning and research.
- The HR department establishes procedures to recruit an adequate pool of qualified people from whom new employees can be selected. HR helps to orient new employees to the company and train them for their new jobs. HR then follows up in a few weeks to see if the selection process resulted in hiring the right person for the job and the person is performing well.
- Human resources plays a role in completing employee promotions, transfers, and releases. HR also helps establish objective criteria for determining who will be promoted, transferred, or released. The procedures must ensure that all employees have the opportunity to qualify for jobs in which they are interested. Replacing lost employees is expensive, so HR tracks employee turnover and tries to determine why people are leaving and attempts to help the company retain good workers.
- Human resources develops pay plans that encourage people to work for the company, while using the company's resources efficiently. Common types of plans are time plans, performance plans, and combination plans. Employees' total compensation includes benefits, such as insurance, vacation time, and pension plans, as well as wages or salaries.
- Computers and the use of the Internet have made information easier to gather, maintain, and make available to people when they need it. To improve services while controlling costs, some companies now outsource HR activities.

BUILD VOCABULARY POWER

Define the following terms and concepts.

1. human resources management (HRM)
2. 360-degree feedback
3. employee assistance programs
4. job description
5. job specification
6. promotion
7. transfer
8. discharge
9. layoff
10. employee turnover
11. exit interview

12. compensation
13. wage
14. salary
15. commission plan
16. piece-rate plan
17. combination plan
18. bonus
19. employee benefits
20. profit-sharing plan
21. pension plan
22. 401k plan
23. IRA plan
24. Keogh plan
25. flextime
26. job sharing
27. cafeteria plan

REVIEW FACTS

1. Why are people such important resources for businesses?
2. What must companies do to begin human resources planning?
3. What are the common human resources services provided by most companies?
4. How is a 360-degree feedback system different from the traditional way of evaluating employee performance?
5. Why are companies adding employee assistance programs to the benefits they offer employees?
6. What are several negative results of poor employee selection procedures?
7. What important sources should companies consider using in order to recruit applicants for a job opening?
8. What types of information should not be included in an employment application form?
9. What activities does the HR department perform when a new employee is hired?
10. Why should a company attempt to keep a good current employee as long as possible rather than hire a new employee?
11. What is the difference between a discharge and a layoff?
12. What are three common types of pay plans?
13. How do employee benefits affect a company's compensation costs?
14. What advantages does a cafeteria benefits plan offer to employees?
15. Why are some companies outsourcing some or all of their human resources tasks?

DISCUSS IDEAS

1. Of the human resources activities illustrated in Figure 24-1, which in your view are most and least important to a company's management? Which in your view are most and least important to a company's employees? Why?
2. Why should the HR department be involved in recruiting and hiring new employees rather than leaving it completely up to the department needing the new employee?
3. Why should applicants be eliminated if they do a poor job of completing the application form?

4. Why should the company consider alternatives to discharge for employees who are not performing well? Under what circumstances do you think that the company should discharge an employee immediately?
5. What problems may be indicated by a high rate of employee turnover? What are some common reasons that companies might experience a very high employee turnover rate?
6. What are the advantages and disadvantages of time and performance pay plans and what do combination plans do to emphasize advantages and reduce disadvantages of each type?
7. Offer some examples of jobs for which salaries have recently been affected by supply and demand for labor. How should a company respond when it finds that employees are leaving to obtain higher wages and salaries from other companies?
8. What do you believe would be the most important employee benefits to a young, beginning employee? To an experienced, married employee with children? To an older employee nearing retirement? Are there any benefits you believe all three types of employees would value?
9. What steps can a human resources department take to ensure that all people have an equal employment opportunity in the selection and promotion processes?
10. What kinds of protection do current laws afford employees?

ANALYZE INFORMATION

1. A telemarketing firm has a complex pay structure for its salespeople. Each person is given a base salary and a quota (minimum expected sales). In addition to the base salary, the company pays the following commissions on sales:

   4 percent for all sales up to $75,000
   5 percent for sales of $75,001 – $150,000
   6 percent for any sales above $150,000

   Any salesperson who exceeds the assigned quota is paid a bonus of $5,000. On a separate sheet of paper, complete the following table using the information given.

Salesperson	***Base Salary***	***Commission***	***Bonus***	***Total Salary***
Egan				
Ranelle				
Chen				

   Egan has a base salary of $20,000, sales of $80,000, and a quota of $75,000.
   Ranelle has a base salary of $28,000, sales of $140,000, and a quota of $150,000.
   Chen has a base salary of $31,000, sales of $220,000, and a quota of $200,000.

2. Cars-4-U is a new auto dealership owned by Fred Anderson and Julia Parente as a partnership. They are trying to decide what pay plan to use for their salespeople. They are aware that most auto dealerships pay salespeople commissions on sales volume. They know that some customers view salespeople negatively, believing they are willing to do anything to make a sale. Fred and Julia don't want to have dissatisfied customers based on the actions of their salespeople. However, they also know that they need sales to make a profit, so the salespeople must be able to convince prospective customers to buy cars. They are considering several options for paying the salespeople. The options are: (a) to offer an attractive hourly wage, which is not related to sales volume; (b) to offer a small weekly salary and a reasonable commission based on the number of cars sold; (c) to offer an attractive commission based on the total dollar sales generated by the salesperson with no additional salary; and (d) to offer a reasonable monthly salary, a small commission on each car sold, and a bonus based on the satisfaction level of customers after they have purchased a car.

   Discuss the four options with a small group of class members. Determine the advantages and disadvantages of each plan in meeting the goals of the partners as well as the needs of prospective salespeople. Consider other possible compensation plans, if appropriate. Report to the class on the plan that your team prefers and explain why.

3. Go to the Internet and locate an application form for a job. Print the form and fill it out. Which of the questions on the application do you think would be most helpful to the company in deciding whether to hire you? Are there any questions that do not seem useful or that could discriminate against some applicants? Describe the changes and improvements you would make in the application form to improve the selection process.
4. As the human resources manager of a large supermarket, you are responsible for hiring new cashiers. You normally hire two to five new cashiers each month, because this job category has a high turnover rate. Answer the following questions:
   - **a.** What sources would you use to find qualified applicants?
   - **b.** What procedures would you use to select the new person?
   - **c.** What would you do with a new employee to get him or her successfully started on the job?
   - **d.** What would you recommend to reduce the rate of employee turnover among cashiers?

5. Use the library or the Internet to find out more about three laws listed in Figure 24-4. Give the name of the law and the year the law was passed, and prepare a short written summary of what businesses and/or employees are required to do as a result of the law.

SOLVE BUSINESS PROBLEMS

CASE 24-1

Charles Morgan was hired five weeks ago to work in the mailroom of the Teletron Trading Corporation. His job was to collect mail twice daily from each office in the building, sort and process outgoing mail, deliver outgoing mail to the post office, and pick up incoming mail from the post office. He learned the job in one day by working with the outgoing employee, Tomika Williams. Tomika had been hired by another company and had only one day left with the company by the time Charles was hired.

After one month, Charles thought that he was doing rather well. While some of the first few days had been rather rough, things seemed to be going more smoothly now and he seldom had any complaints. He rarely saw his supervisor, but when he did the supervisor always had a pleasant greeting.

A week later he received notice that he was being discharged next week at the end of his six-week probationary period. There was no explanation for the discharge, and Charles was not aware of the probationary period. He went to the human resources office immediately. The employment manager pulled a folder from the file and began reading notes that had been placed there during the past month. Charles responded truthfully to each item:

a. An hour late to work on May 15: "My car wouldn't start, but I called to say that I would be in as soon as possible. I worked an extra hour at the end of the day to finish my duties."
b. Two offices complained that the mail had not been picked up on the second of the month: "It was my second day on the job, and I couldn't remember all of the stops. After the second day, I made a schedule and I haven't missed an office since."
c. The Research Department complained that an important document was sent by regular mail when it should have been sent by Express Mail: "I didn't know the policy for deciding when and how to send items until I was told I had done it wrong. I asked the supervisor, who gave me a procedures manual to study. Tomika Williams had not told me about the manual."

Several other similar complaints were included in the file. Charles readily admitted to but explained each one. According to the employment manager, Charles was being discharged in keeping with company policy. The policy stated that any employee who received five or more complaints about work procedures during the probationary period was automatically discharged.

Think Critically:

1. What is your opinion of the company's probationary and discharge policy for new employees? Justify your opinion.

2. Develop several reasons to justify the probationary and discharge policy of the company. Describe what you believe the company should do to improve the policy.
3. Why do you believe Charles was prepared for his job in the way he was? What role should the human resources department play when employees receive that type of training? What recommendations can you make to improve the company's training procedures?

CASE 24-2

Joanne Wilkens and Teresa Soto were exercising on the stationary bicycles in the health and fitness center of the Wainwright Company. As they exercised, they discussed an article that had appeared in the company's on-line newsletter.

Joanne: *The article said that the average employee in the company receives total compensation of $36,500 a year. I can't believe that. I think I'm close to the average in salary, and I'll only take home a little more than $28,000 this year.*

Teresa: *That's right. What they don't say is that we have a lot of money deducted from our checks each month for taxes, insurance, and the cost of the retirement plan.*

Joanne: *As a matter of fact, the article says the company contributes an additional $9,000 on the average for each employee to pay for benefits. That makes over $17,000 difference between what I take home and what the company says I receive in compensation and benefits. I can't imagine what benefits we get that cost that much money. There must be a mistake in those figures.*

Teresa: *Let's go past the Human Resources office when we get finished here. Maybe they can explain the difference.*

Think Critically:

1. If the newsletter information is accurate and if Joanne is paid about the average amount of all employees, how can you justify the difference between the compensation figures?
2. Should employees consider the amount that is taken out of their paychecks each month for taxes, insurance, and pensions as a part of their compensation? Why or why not?
3. Why do you believe that many employees are like Joanne and Teresa and don't recognize the total cost of employee benefits? What should a company do to avoid that problem?
4. If you worked in the human resources department, how would you explain the difference in the salary and benefits the company says it pays and the amount of money Joanne and Teresa take home in their paychecks?

PROJECT: MY BUSINESS, INC.

Because a small business has only a few employees, each employee is very important to the success of the company. When you begin to hire employees for your business, you will need procedures designed to hire excellent employees. You will also need to develop effective human resources policies and procedures that will encourage employees to be productive and help you keep them working for you.

DATA COLLECTION

1. Review the employment ads in your newspaper for several days. Identify ads for employment in small service businesses. Study the qualifications required and descriptions of duties listed.
2. Interview the owner of a small business. Discuss with the owner each of the human resources activities listed Figure 24-1. Identify the problems the business has in managing human resources.
3. Search the Internet to identify recommendations on benefit plans for small businesses. Sites such as the Small Business Administration and the Department of Labor are excellent starting points for your research.

INTERNET

ANALYSIS

1. Develop a job description and job specifications for an employee you would hire. Then write the copy for a newspaper advertisement you would use to recruit potential employees.
2. Develop a specific set of procedures to follow in hiring and orienting new employees.
3. Identify the advantages and disadvantages of two pay plans you would consider using for employees. Then select the plan you would use and establish the wage or salary rate for full- and part-time employees.
4. Identify the benefits you will provide for employees, including those required by federal and state law and any additional benefits, if any, you will provide. Attempt to calculate the cost of each benefit for one employee.

EMPLOYEE AND ORGANIZATIONAL DEVELOPMENT

OBJECTIVES

- 25-1 Define organizational development and discuss the two important components of an organizational development program.
- 25-2 Explain the components of a career development program.
- 25-3 Describe the value of performance reviews and training and development to businesses and employees.
- 25-4 Describe the variety of career opportunities in business, including international business careers.
- 25-5 Outline the steps in preparing a career plan.

THE END OF AN ERA AT ALLIANCE INDUSTRIES

James Lane had a good life. Since graduating from high school, he had worked for Alliance Industries, a company that produced steel and steel products for the auto industry. In the 23 years of his employment, he had enjoyed most days of work, had a great group of friends at the company, and earned a comfortable living for his family. His career had progressed at Alliance from a basic maintenance position, to machine operator, and then eight years ago to supervisor of machining. During that time he had completed a two-year technical degree at a community college and recently had enrolled again in two courses to be able to better use computers in his work.

James now faced an important decision. Alliance Industries was being challenged by competition and changes in the auto industry. The industry was changing from the use of steel to other metals and plastics. Changes in technology were requiring companies in the steel industry to acquire new equipment, and competition was forcing cost-cutting. Alliance was reducing its workforce, including the elimination of most supervisory positions. The company offered James the opportunity to go back to a machinist position, but it would require additional training and a slight reduction in pay. James didn't know how he would be accepted if he went back to work with the people he had been supervising and if he would be happy with that work. If he chose not to accept the job change, Alliance would provide career counseling and other services to help him find another job, but there was no guarantee that it would be the type of work James enjoyed.

THE NEW EMPLOYMENT ENVIRONMENT

In the last part of the 20th century, many companies faced global competitive pressures unlike those they had seen before. That competition forced companies to reconsider their organizational size, structure, and operations. Many were forced to downsize their operations by cutting the number of employees, reducing product offerings, or cutting costs in other ways. Other companies restructured their operations to work and use resources more efficiently. Some large companies reduced employment by thousands of people. Like the problem facing James Lane with Alliance Industries, employees who had spent many years with the same company (some nearing retirement) suddenly found themselves without a job.

Many former employees who lost their jobs when businesses cut back have been unable to find satisfying employment. Some have had to accept lower-level jobs or jobs that pay less or offer fewer benefits than those they held previously. Those who were able to keep their jobs are not certain of their **job security,** the likelihood that they will continue to be employed by the same company in the future. They may distrust their employer, believing that the actions of businesses demonstrate a lack of commitment to employees.

Now in the 21st century, the focus is on developing a whole new generation of businesses. The Internet has led to the creation of many new organizations that look quite different from traditional businesses. They may have only a few employees, and the employees may not work in the same building or even in the same city. The Internet companies may rely on other businesses to perform many of the traditional business functions, and the owners may have more skill and experience with technology than with organizing and managing a business.

Today, we see dramatic changes in both traditional and new businesses. Dealing with the result of those changes presents challenges to both employees and managers. Much of the pressure to maintain a strong organization falls on the human resources department. Whether it is a traditional business that has gone through a major restructuring or a new business attempting to build a unique type of organization, human resources personnel must help the organization be effective.

Two major responsibilities have emerged for the human resources department in today's organizations. **Organizational development** refers to carefully planned changes in the structure and operation of a business to adjust to a competitive business environment. **Career development** is a program that matches the career plans of employees with the employment needs of the business. This chapter focuses on these two human resources programs. You will learn how companies can make changes in the way the business is organized while maintaining positive management/employee relations. You will also learn about the roles of employee performance reviews and training programs in achieving business and employee goals. Finally, you will examine how individuals can take responsibility for their own career development through effective career planning.

ORGANIZATIONAL DEVELOPMENT

Consider all of the ways that employees can contribute to the success or failure of a business. Employees play a major role in product quality, customer satisfaction, equipment maintenance, and efficient use of materials to limit waste. You can probably think of many other ways that employees can help or hurt the business for which they work.

The ways businesses organize work and provide resources also affect their success. Inefficient work processes, delays in receiving needed resources, and problems within channels of distribution all hinder a business's ability to meet customer needs. Because of such problems, companies are now paying a great deal of attention to the way in which they structure their organization, how work flows through the business, and how employees work together and with their managers. Today, businesses are using organizational development programs to make sure they continue to be successful.

Two important elements of an effective organizational development program are making improvements in work processes and building effective working relationships. Improving work processes means improving the way work is accomplished in a business. The goal of work process improvement is to eliminate errors, improve quality, and reduce costs.

The focus of the second element of organizational development is on the people who complete the work. Studies have shown that employees who believe they are an important part of the organization will be committed to its success and will work to achieve the company's goals. Several important relationships contribute to an effective organization. They are the relationships among a company's personnel, including management-employee relationships, and relationships with people in other organizations with whom the company works and with the company's customers.

IMPROVING WORK PROCESSES

One of the focuses of organizational development is to improve the way work is accomplished. This includes the materials and resources used, the organizational structure and relationships among work units, the job duties assigned to individuals and groups, as well as work procedures and operations. Most of the emphasis on improving work processes is directed inside the company. But improving work processes also involves the way businesses work with each other as a part of product development and distribution.

Improving the way work is accomplished may require using new technologies, rearranging work space, changing relationships between departments and work groups, and modifying procedures for completing tasks. Remember the concerns James Lane had about the changes Alliance Industries was planning. The company was changing to new products, equipment, and procedures that would be quite different from what he and other employees had experienced.

It is not easy for any company to make these types of changes when people are used to the older ways of accomplishing work and are reluctant to use new technologies or to change the way they have been doing things for many years. It may even be difficult to identify new ways to organize and accomplish work, because people in the company are familiar only with the way things have been done in the past. Often organizational development programs will bring in experts from outside the company to help identify and study new work processes.

IDENTIFYING THE NEED FOR CHANGE

The history of business is filled with many organizations that experienced years of success, only to fall on hard times and ultimately fail. The cause of the business failure may be that competitors were able to make improvements in their products and services, customers did not receive the service they expected, costs were not controlled, or the organizational structure did not adjust to new conditions. No matter what the specific cause, the reason for the failure of previously successful businesses is most likely to be the inability to change. It

BUSINESS INNOVATION

IDEAS FOR SALE

Since most businesses are faced with the need to change, it is not surprising that people are starting new businesses to help other businesses manage change. One of the most unusual new businesses is one that sells ideas.

The BrainStore in Biel, Switzerland is one of those businesses. Its owners refer to their business as an idea factory. In fact, they believe companies can't rely on the typical way that new ideas are generated. The "great idea," a simple brainstorming session, or just thinking about a problem will not achieve the needed results when businesses are faced almost daily with problems and challenges. The BrainStore has moved the process of idea generation into a specific sequence of activities.

The process starts in the creativity lab. The lab is an open room with pens, paper, scissors, crayons, beads, and other "toys." These are the tools that support creativity. The room looks more like an elementary school classroom than a place where business people meet. The atmosphere encourages play, experiments, and "completely unrealistic thoughts." The result is usually a large number of creative ideas that can then be processed through the idea factory. The next step in the idea sequence is compression, where ideas are sorted, compared, and narrowed to the few judged as best. Then the idea moves through testing, where research is completed to determine if the idea will work and can be implemented. Often models or prototypes of solutions will be built for review and further testing. The final step is called finishing. Here the idea that has been successfully tested will be prepared for implementation. That may include developing marketing and communications strategies for the organization that will implement the idea or the actual development of products, services, or processes that will support the needed change or solve the problem.

Initially the BrainStore worked with large businesses to create new products, develop marketing programs, or solve challenging problems. However, the owners now believe their ideas can help individual consumers as well, so they have opened a retail version of the business. At a cost of under $20, they will provide help with home decorating ideas, improving personal relationships, or creative ideas for an important speech.

THINK CRITICALLY

1. Do you believe ideas can actually be developed in the same way that a company might manufacture a product? Why or why not?
2. What are the advantages of creating a room that looks like an elementary school classroom for the first step in idea generation? How do you think the results would be different if the company used a typical business office for that activity?
3. Why do you believe individuals would pay $20 to a business that only gives them help with ideas?
4. After working with the BrainStore, what other activities should an organization complete to implement the ideas that were developed?

Source: *Fast Company, April, 2000*

may be that the executives of the company did not recognize the need for change, believed the successful company did not need to change, or were unable to plan and manage the needed change.

Throughout this textbook you have learned that the environment faced by businesses today is very different from that in the past. Those differences occur both outside the business (the *external environment*) and inside the business (the *internal environment*). Today, the external factors that are most likely to result in problems for an organization are changes in workforce demographics, the nature of competition, customer expectations, and technology. Several important internal factors that affect a company's success are quite similar. They include changes in the makeup of the company's workforce, employee expectations, outdated work processes and technology, ineffective organizational structure, and poor management practices.

Figure 25-1 shows several key indicators that an organization may be experiencing problems requiring major change. Every organization should pay careful attention to its external and internal environment to identify changes in any of those indicators. Major changes in any of the indicators may suggest growing problems that should lead to plans for organizational development.

When a business tries to solve a problem, it often discovers that the problem results from a fundamental flaw in the operations of the business. Organizational development programs must identify and resolve the underlying operational problem in order to fix the original problem.

For example, one company found that production levels had declined significantly during June, July, and August. As company managers studied the problem, they discovered that employee absences were almost double on Mondays and Fridays than on the other days of the week. Production was delayed on both of those days because work teams were not full or temporary employees brought in on those

- **New competitors entering the market**
- **Introduction of new technologies by other businesses**
- **Changes in laws and regulations affecting the business**
- **Major changes in products and services offered or in markets served**
- **Rapid growth by the business**
- **Loss of market share**
- **Increasing customer complaints**
- **Poor relationships with business partners**
- **Increasing operating costs**
- **Decreasing revenues or profits**
- **Decline in employee morale and increasing employee turnover**
- **Conflicts among departments or other work units**
- **Participation in a merger or acquisition**

FIGURE 25-1

Important Indicators that Organizations Need to Make Changes

days were not as efficient. In order to solve the production problem, the employee absence issue had to be resolved. Working with employees, the managers discovered that the way vacation days were scheduled encouraged employees to use Mondays and Fridays to have short summer vacations. A revised policy allowed employees to schedule two- or three-day vacations in the middle of the week. This change reduced Monday and Friday absences and solved the production problem.

Another company experienced an increasing number of customer complaints regarding late deliveries of products. The company had used the same parcel delivery service to make deliveries to customers for over 20 years. A study of the problem revealed that the delivery company had changed its distribution procedures. It was using larger trucks and making few trips to many cities to cut its costs. To improve customer service, the company stopped using that parcel service and contracted with a new, smaller delivery company that used a computerized delivery scheduling system. This change allowed the company to schedule product delivery with customers when they made the purchase and reduced late deliveries by more than 80 percent. Fixing the underlying delivery service problem resolved the issue of customer complaints.

PLANNING AN ORGANIZATIONAL DEVELOPMENT PROGRAM

As soon as the company identifies a problem or need for change, it should plan and implement an organizational development program. Since almost all important changes in a business involve or affect employees, the human resources department should have an important role in the program. The changes may involve developing new employee skills or increasing or decreasing the size of the workforce. A change or major reorganization may affect management/employee relationships. The company may decide to change the pay or benefits plans to encourage employee participation or to reduce costs.

The major steps in planning and implementing an organizational development program are the following:

1. *Affirm the mission and goals of the organization.* There needs to be agreement within the company about the purpose of the business and the criteria to be used to determine if the company is successful. A company should not easily change its mission or goals but may need to change them in response to the external and internal environment.
2. *Identify the important markets that will be the company's primary focus and the products and services needed to serve those markets.* This step will require establishing customer service standards. In Chapter 13, you learned that a *standard* is a specific measure against which something is judged. **Customer service standards,** then, are measures against which the company judges its performance in meeting customer expectations. Those standards may include the mini-

mum acceptable levels of product quality, delivery speed, order-fulfillment accuracy, and customer support and follow-up.

3. *Determine the organizational changes required to achieve the company's mission, goals, and customer service standards, and prepare a plan for implementing the changes.* These will usually involve one or more of the following factors: work processes, the organizational structure, work relationships, and employee skills. Also, the plan should include **performance standards,** which are specific statements of the expected results from critical business activities. Most organizational development changes require a long time to achieve success. Implementation may take many months, and the company may not see results for a year or more.
4. *Build commitment within the organization for the changes.* Successful organizational change requires the understanding and support of managers and employees. That understanding and support will occur only if all employees are fully informed of (1) the change, (2) the reasons change is necessary, (3) the likely results if the changes are not made, (4) how they will be affected by the change, and (5) how the organization and its employees will benefit if the change is successful. Successful organizational development usually results when company personnel are involved early in the process and when they have a role in designing the plan.
5. *Follow through on the organizational development plans.* Employees are more likely to support the plans if they see that the organization is committed to them and that change is occurring. Managers should keep employees informed of results of the changes even if

ILLUSTRATION 25-1

How can a company build commitment within the organization for changes?

they are not always positive at the beginning. Unless something occurs that makes it clear that the plan will not work, the organizational development plan should continue until it achieves the goals.

6. *Make the new process part of the organization's culture.* If people believe the change is not important or is only temporary, they will not commit to its success. When the new process is implemented and supported, the organization has changed, and the old procedures are no longer appropriate, the organizational development program is complete.

Alliance Industries, discussed in the opening scenario, needed to implement an organizational development program for the major changes they were planning. Can you find evidence that Alliance used any of the six steps you just studied?

IMPROVING THE WORK ENVIRONMENT

The needs and expectations of workers today are very different from those of workers in the past. Work is just one part of an employee's life. Of course, employees want jobs that provide a reasonable wage or salary. But the amount of money earned is not always the most important thing. Today, employees are concerned about a variety of factors related to their work, including the work schedule and working conditions. Vacations, insurance, pensions, and other benefits are also important to most people. They also want an interesting and challenging job as well as recognition for their work. Both personal and financial needs are important to employees, and managers must recognize those needs in order to maintain an effective workforce.

Satisfied employees are more productive and more likely to want to stay with the company and contribute to its success. Therefore, managers spend considerable time working with employees to make the work environment as satisfying as possible. Studies have found that employees are most satisfied with their work when they (1) perform interesting work, (2) feel responsible for the work, (3) receive recognition for good work, and (4) have a feeling of achievement.

These results show that employees are concerned with many things other than the amount of their paycheck and benefits like vacation days. It is surprising to many managers that while the amount of compensation is important, it is not necessarily more important than other factors related to the job. Because of those studies, companies are directing their organizational development efforts toward the design of the work environment and jobs to better meet employee needs. **Job design** refers to the kinds of tasks that make up a job and the way workers perform these tasks in doing their jobs.

Organizations try to make work more meaningful and motivating for employees. One way to do this is through **job enlargement,** which means making a job more interesting by adding variety to the tasks. For example, three workers on an assembly line might be responsible for three separate tasks, each one performing one task over and over. With job enlargement, each worker is given responsibility to complete all three tasks. In this way they can perform a greater variety of tasks, making the work less monotonous and boring. Also, the company now has three people who can perform all of the work rather than three specialized employees who can perform only one part of a complex job.

Employees should be involved in making the decision to change the job and in redesigning the job. Employees also need training and adequate time and practice to develop the new skills. Companies should not enlarge jobs just to reduce the number of employees or to get employees to do more work. If employees believe that these are the real reasons for enlarging their jobs, they will not accept the changes willingly.

Another use of job design to increase employee effectiveness and motivation is cross training. With **cross training,** employees are trained to perform more than one job in the company, even though they typically perform only one. Employees can be rotated to other jobs when an absence or illness occurs, while a replacement employee is being trained, when a significant increase or decrease in the amount of work occurs for a specific job, or simply to provide change and variety for employees. Cross training makes an employee more valuable to the company since that person can perform a broader set of work tasks. Employees learn more about the work performed in the organization as they learn multiple jobs and increase their skills.

Another way to use job design to improve employee satisfaction is to involve employees in decision making. **Job enrichment** means giving employees the authority to make meaningful decisions about their work. For example, managers may allow workers to make choices about how to do their jobs. Managers may ask employees for advice on how to improve performance or how to reduce errors. Job responsibilities may be changed so employees can solve problems themselves, without checking with their supervisor. For example, in one major hotel chain, employees are authorized to immediately take the necessary steps to resolve a customer problem or complaint at a cost of up to $200 without consulting a manager.

As you learned in earlier chapters, some companies have work teams that are responsible for the entire assembly of a product, performance of a service, or operation of a small unit in the business. The team helps with goal setting, shares all tasks, and is responsible for the results. Companies using this system have found that team members develop a strong loyalty with the other members and take personal responsibility for the effective operation of the team and the quality of its work. An improved work environment and worker involvement are important goals of organizational development.

Improving management and employee relationships, making work more meaningful, and developing effective work teams are all important organizational development programs. They affect the internal

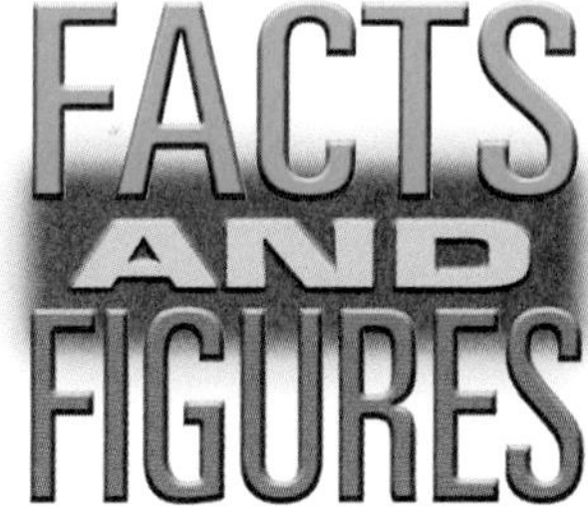

Employers who tap into their employees' need to grow in their jobs are more likely to retain talented people. An employer should *set a direction* for each employee that is in alignment with the firm's vision statement; *listen* to the employee's ideas about how he or she can help the company meet its goals; *guide* the employee in meeting the business's goals; and *measure and give feedback* through evaluations.

environment of the business. In addition, some organizational development programs work to improve relationships in the external environment, including the way employees interact with other businesses in the distribution channel and with customers. Many businesses involve personnel from cooperating businesses in solving problems and developing new procedures. They frequently consult customers in order to consider their needs and perceptions in planning organizational changes.

CAREER DEVELOPMENT

In the past, many companies were quite short-sighted when they planned for their employment needs. When a position was vacant, they would begin the recruitment and selection process. If they no longer needed employees, they might terminate those employees without considering future employment needs. Those procedures were based on the belief that companies could easily find the employees they needed. Those companies did not view employees as a particularly valuable resource.

Successful businesses view their relationships with employees very differently today. They realize that it is not easy to find employees with the qualifications required. It is also very expensive to hire and train a new employee. Companies invest in employees and want to get the greatest value from them. That occurs when companies hire employees with skills that closely match the needs of the job, train them, and then keep them happy, so they will stay with the company for a long time. The companies with this new philosophy recognize that the knowledge and performance of their employees are major factors in their success.

Changing technology requires employees to update their skills. For example, not many years ago, businesses processed most information manually, using typewriters and calculators. Today, companies process information with computers. Auto mechanics used to rely on hand tools and their own knowledge and observational skills to repair automobiles. Now they have access to a variety of electronic tools, machines, and computerized diagnostic equipment. Every business has similar examples of new skills that are required of employees. It is not possible to be successful with the old equipment and old skills. To get the needed skills, businesses offer training to current employees when new technology requires it and search for new employees with up-to-date skills to fill vacancies.

In the scenario at the beginning of the chapter, James Lane had been a very valuable employee to Alliance Industries for many years. Even though the company was undergoing major changes, it was attempting to include James in its plans by offering him another job and the needed training to prepare for that job.

ILLUSTRATION 25-2

How can businesses help their employees update their skills?

REQUIREMENTS FOR A CAREER DEVELOPMENT PROGRAM

A **career development program** is a plan for meeting the company's future employment needs by systematically preparing current employees for future positions in the company. While human resources personnel will be responsible for implementing the career development program, they will need the support of all parts of the company for the program to be successful. A career development program requires a long-term organizational plan, career paths, effective employee performance reviews, career counseling, and training and development for employees.

LONG-TERM PLANS Career development starts with the job opportunities in a company. Companies need to determine what jobs will be available in the future, how many people will be needed in each job, and the knowledge and skills those employees will require. In the previous section, you learned that companies study their external and internal environments to identify business opportunities and needed changes in the organization. One part of that study includes employment needs. Then the HR department can work with that information to project specific job opportunities in each part of the company and the requirements employees must meet for each job.

CAREER PATHS A **career path** is a progression of related jobs with increasing skill requirements and responsibility. Career paths provide opportunities for employees to advance within the company, to make additional contributions, and to receive increased satisfaction from their work.

Traditionally, career paths moved an employee from an entry-level position into management. However, companies also offer career paths that allow employees to advance into non-management positions. Some people do not want to be managers, and companies usually have relatively few management positions. Therefore, companies often make other opportunities available, so that employees do not get locked into one job if they choose not to become a manager or are unable to qualify for a management position. Examples of a management career path and a non-management path are shown in Figure 25-2.

Companies should identify a variety of career paths. Each job should be a part of a career path, and employees should be aware of the paths available to them from the job they currently hold.

PERFORMANCE REVIEWS Employees and managers need accurate information on the skills and abilities of each employee to make effective career decisions. When employees know how well they are performing, they can determine what skills they need to improve to meet the current job requirements or to qualify for another job in a career path. In an effective career development program, managers carefully evaluate employees' performance and regularly review the information with

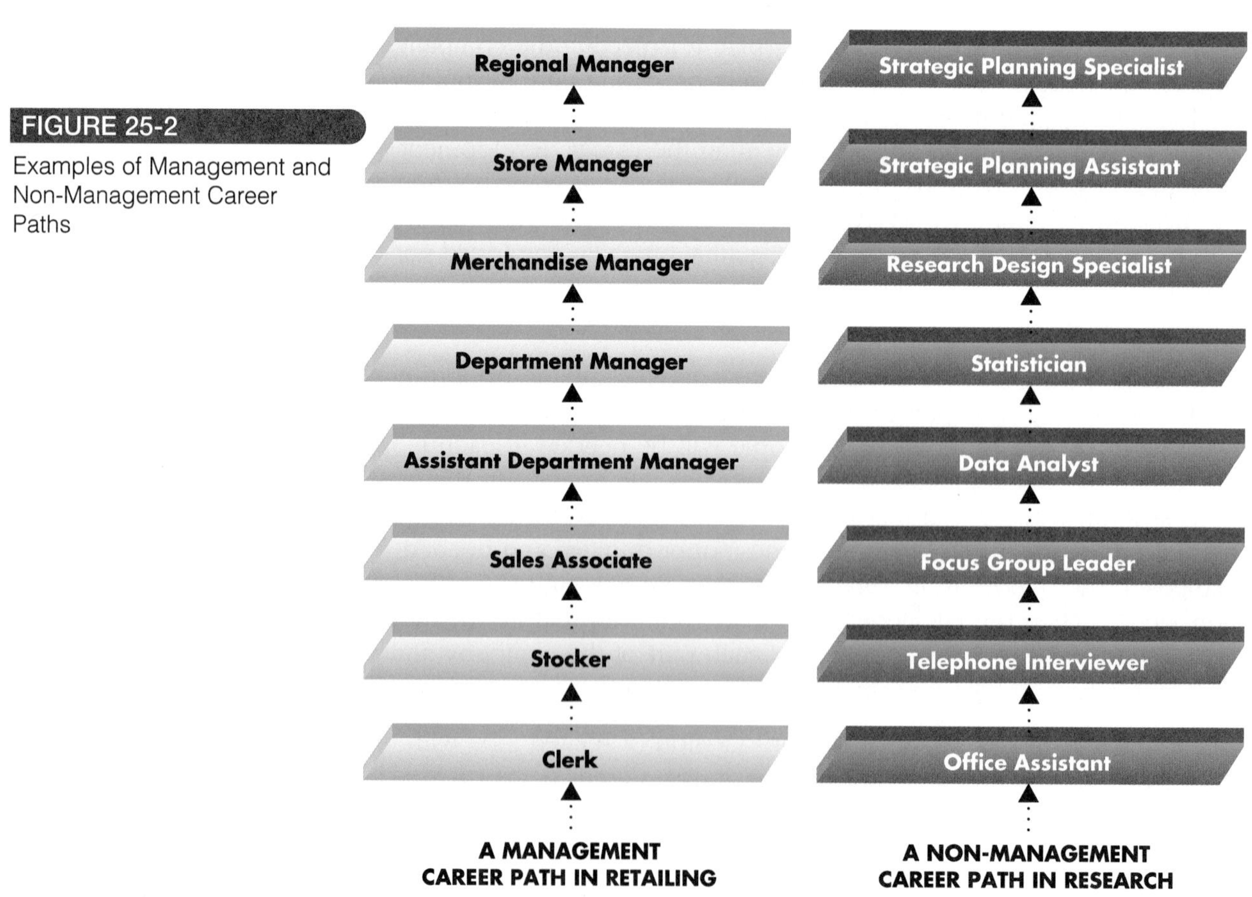

FIGURE 25-2
Examples of Management and Non-Management Career Paths

the employee. With that information, the manager and employee can determine whether the employee needs additional training to improve performance and to prepare to advance in the organization. The results of performance reviews should be compared to new job requirements as the company makes changes, so that employees know what is expected of them.

CAREER COUNSELING For career development to be effective, employees must be aware of opportunities and plan their career paths. The HR department offers career information and counseling services as a part of the career development program. Many companies have made career counseling part of every employee's performance review conference. Managers are often trained to provide career information to the employees they supervise.

Career counseling may result in an individual career plan. A **career plan** identifies the jobs that are part of the employee's career path, the training and development needed to advance along the career path, and a tentative schedule for the plan's activities. The plan is jointly developed by the employee, a human resources specialist, and possibly the employee's manager.

Some companies have career centers. **Career centers** are facilities where human resources employees manage career development activities. Employees can visit the center to obtain career information (computer programs, Internet sites, books, pamphlets, films, etc.), visit with career counselors, and schedule career planning workshops or testing as they prepare for new jobs.

TRAINING AND DEVELOPMENT The final part of a career development program is training employees in the skills needed for changing job requirements and new jobs. With careful planning, companies can develop training programs and other educational opportunities to prepare employees for new job requirements before the need arises. In that way, the business can be assured that it will have well-trained employees to fill job needs and employees will know they can get the training necessary for job changes.

IMPLEMENTING A CAREER DEVELOPMENT PROGRAM

Career planning does not just happen. It also cannot be considered the responsibility of employees alone. Businesses that want to match employees and jobs successfully must do several things to ensure that the career development program works well.

First, responsibility for organizing and managing the career development program must be assigned. Most companies assign the program to the human resources department. The HR department will put together the people, materials, and procedures needed for the program.

Second, everyone in the business must be educated about the career development program and his or her role in career planning. Managers need to identify career opportunities in their departments and work with HR personnel when changes are planned in their departments that will affect the career plans of employees. Managers also have specific responsibilities in a career development program. They evaluate employee performance and include career planning in follow-up conferences. They help identify employees who are ready for career advancement. They serve as coaches and mentors for their employees to help each worker make effective career choices.

Employees need to be aware of career development resources and how the career planning process works. They are responsible for much of their individual career planning and development but need to know where to get help when needed. Employees use performance reviews and evaluation conferences to gather information to make career plans. They can then schedule assessments, counseling, and training to prepare for career advancement.

SPECIAL CAREER DEVELOPMENT PROGRAMS

Companies that offer career development programs should make the services available to all employees from the newest to the most experienced. However, there are situations where specific individuals or groups of employees participate in programs designed to meet specific needs in the company. Those programs may not be available to all employees.

Most large businesses offer career planning, training, and counseling to employees selected to be managers. These employees receive testing services, obtain experience in all parts of the business, and often are assigned to an experienced manager who serves as a role model and mentor.

Non-management jobs can be targeted for specific career development programs as well. For example, many jobs are more frequently held by men than women or women than men. Companies may make extra efforts to encourage and prepare people from the underrepresented gender for those jobs. Some companies may have difficulty finding qualified candidates for certain jobs. Those positions may be targeted for career development attention. Employees who are interested in or have the knowledge and skills to qualify for hard-to-fill jobs will be encouraged to participate in the special programs. For example, if a company is having difficulty recruiting and hiring computer programmers, it may undertake a career development program to encourage current employees to complete the necessary training for the programming jobs.

Management experts believe that employees have a responsibility for their own performance management, and cite the following areas on which employees should focus: (1) committing to goal achievement; (2) soliciting performance feedback and coaching; (3) communicating openly and regularly with the manager; (4) collecting and sharing performance data; and (5) preparing for performance reviews.

IMPROVING EMPLOYEE PERFORMANCE

Companies depend on effective and satisfied employees. Just as a company cannot operate if equipment is outdated or regularly needs repair, it must have employees with up-to-date skills who perform their jobs accurately and efficiently. Two requirements for maintaining a quality workforce are an effective system for performance review and well-designed training and development programs.

PERFORMANCE REVIEW PROCEDURES

Companies must make sure employees are performing as well as they possibly can. A **performance review** is the process of assessing how well employees are doing their jobs. Companies use the information obtained from performance reviews for career planning, determining increases in wages and salaries, and planning training programs.

The first step in developing a performance review process is to determine what to evaluate. Each job should have a complete description of duties and performance expectations, and the review should focus on these duties and expectations. Next, the HR department prepares forms and procedures for performance reviews. Those materials should be designed to make the review process as easy and objective as possible.

Managers conduct formal performance reviews of all employees usually once or twice a year. The manager fills out an evaluation form about the employee's performance. The process in many companies also requires the employee to complete a self-evaluation using the same form. The manager and employee then meet to discuss the results in a performance review conference.

In addition to the formal reviews, employees can conduct self-assessments or ask managers, co-workers, or career counselors to provide feedback. These performance reviews are usually informal but can be very helpful to the employees in understanding how well they are performing their jobs and what needs to be done to improve performance or to prepare for new jobs in a career path.

ILLUSTRATION 25-3

What methods can a manager use to make the performance evaluation meeting a positive experience?

An upcoming performance evaluation

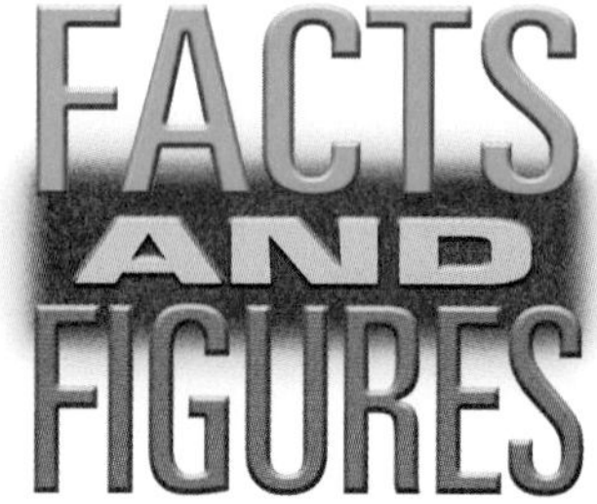

Like most hotel chains, Days Inn of America suffers tremendous employee turnover—around 120 percent a year for hourly employees. The chain has begun using an interactive Web-based training program that teaches the specific skills employees need and provides self-paced learning, testing, and tracking. Experts believe that such technology-based training can result in a 50 percent reduction in time and cost over classroom training.

meeting is often a source of anxiety for both managers and employees. However, if carefully planned, the evaluation meeting can be a positive experience. The following guidelines for managers can help in achieving that goal:

1. Schedule enough time for the discussion and plan for it in advance by reviewing the employee's job requirements and career plan.
2. Focus the discussion on the employee's performance, not on the employee. Feedback should be based on objective information, not opinions.
3. Discuss strengths as well as areas that need improvement. Identify how the strengths can contribute to the employee's career goals and specific ways the employee can develop needed skills and improve performance.

PLANNING TRAINING AND DEVELOPMENT

Businesses spend a great deal of money on activities designed to improve the productivity of their employees. Studies estimate that U.S. companies spend \$50–60 billion each year on formal training programs. Informal training (i.e., learning on the job, self study, coaching) may cost businesses as much as an additional \$200 billion each year. Beyond the costs of training, many companies pay some or all of the costs of college courses that employees take as part of career development programs or as an employee benefit. The large amount of money for training and development can be justified if the result is employees who are able to perform more and higher quality work.

As companies recognize the value of training, they are working to develop more effective training procedures. On the average, companies spend several hundred dollars on every employee each year for training. Therefore, they want to be sure the training is effective in improving employees' performance. Trainers use many techniques to improve employee performance. Figure 25-3 summarizes several characteristics of effective training.

An important activity for all companies is determining the need for employee training. Some training needs are quite obvious. When the company buys new equipment, begins new operations, or introduces improved procedures, employees need to be trained for the changes. Typically, when new employees are hired or experienced employees are promoted to new jobs, they do not have all of the skills needed to begin work immediately. In these cases, companies should offer the needed training.

Other training needs are not as obvious. In some instances, poor work performance can be a symptom of insufficient training. Conflicts among employees, areas of customer dissatisfaction, or work hazards and employee injuries signal the need for training. Unless companies are aware of problems and try to determine whether training can help solve them, the problems likely will not disappear.

TO BE EFFECTIVE, TRAINING SHOULD:

1. **Be interesting to the trainee.**
2. **Be related to knowledge the trainee already has developed.**
3. **Explain why as well as how something is done.**
4. **Progress from simple to more difficult steps.**
5. **Let the trainee learn complicated procedures in small steps.**
6. **Allow plenty of practice time.**
7. **Let the trainee concentrate on becoming comfortable with a new procedure before worrying about accuracy.**
8. **Provide regular and positive feedback to the trainee on progress being made.**
9. **Be done in short time blocks using a variety of activities.**
10. **Involve the learner in training activities as much as possible.**

FIGURE 25-3

Characteristics of Effective Training Programs

In some companies, each department has formed a problem-solving group made up of managers and employees. Those groups can be used to identify training needs in addition to their other responsibilities. Because they work regularly with the equipment and the procedures of the department, the groups are in a good position to identify performance problems and to help design training.

CAREER OPPORTUNITIES IN BUSINESS

Business careers are appealing because of the number and variety of jobs available and opportunities for advancement. No matter what your interests, skills, or level of education and experience, there is a job in business that matches. Once you have obtained your first job, many opportunities open up. You can advance with additional education or with continuing experience and training on the job.

You can identify career paths in almost any business. If you begin work in a clerical position, you may progress to more specialized jobs in information management or office administration. You can then advance from assistant manager to department manager or a highly specialized position in either area. Some people even progress to the very top of the company as executives. Similar career paths are available to people who begin as counter workers in fast-food restaurants, production workers in factories, or reservation clerks in hotels.

Because common areas of knowledge and skills are important to many types of businesses, you are not limited to one career path, one type of business, or one geographic area. People who begin in banking may change to an insurance career. Someone who is a salesperson for a computer-products company may decide to move to a building-materials company for an increase in salary or more responsibilities. If job prospects are not particularly good in one part of the country, a skilled businessperson can probably find employment in another region. Career paths in business are usually very flexible.

LEVELS OF EMPLOYMENT

When you first enter the workforce, you will most likely begin in an entry-level position. You may even get your first job when you are still in high school and have no experience and little understanding of business operations. The top positions in large corporations are held by people with many years of experience. Executives usually have worked in several areas of the business and often have experience in several businesses. Most business executives today have a college degree and, increasingly, graduate degrees.

Businesses have several levels of employment, based on the amount of education and experience required. Common levels are entry, career, specialist, management, and executive/entrepreneur.

Entry-level occupations usually involve routine activities and require little training. These jobs are open to people with little or no previous business education or experience. If you have not worked in business before, this is where you might begin. People hold entry-level jobs for only a short time until they have developed enough experience and skill for promotion. Examples of entry-level jobs are cashier, counter person, clerk, receptionist, and operator.

Career-level jobs require more complex duties. People in *career-level occupations* have the authority to control some of their work and make some decisions. To be successful, they should have a basic understanding of business and skills in the areas in which they are working. They usually view their work as more than a job and have an interest in the area of business as a potential career. Career-level jobs include sales associate, reservations agent, word processor, bank teller, and customer service representative.

Specialist occupations require a variety of skills in one or more business functions and extensive understanding of the operations of a specific company or industry. Specialists are the people considered the most skilled or expert in the activities they complete on the job.

CYBER COMMUNICATION

Besides e-mail, another important source of communication on the Internet is newsgroups. A newsgroup is formed by a group of people who are interested in a particular subject. These groups can be formal or informal. While some are created for entertainment, others are devoted to the exchange of knowledge about a topic.

As with the Internet in general, newsgroups are visited by all sorts of people. Sometimes, freedom of speech conflicts with common courtesy. Since postings can be read by thousands of participants, it's important to be concise and considerate in your messages. It's also wise to exercise caution when participating in newsgroups, and remember not to give out personal information that could cause problems for you later.

ACTIVITY Using library or Internet resources, research the topic of banning newsgroups that have "offensive" content. Is this censorship? Is it a violation of First Amendment rights? Prepare a one-page report on your thoughts about this topic.

Specialists in businesses include buyers, researchers, Web designers, programmers, analysts, professional salespeople, technicians, machine operators, and similar technical or skilled positions.

Supervisors/managers hold the first levels of management positions in companies. They must have a high level of knowledge in the parts of the organization that they supervise. They also must be effective decision-makers and have strong leadership ability. *Supervisor/management occupations* are responsible for specific units in a business and must make decisions about operations and personnel. The job titles associated with this level of employment are supervisor, assistant manager, and manager. The people who perform management tasks on work teams are often called *team leaders*.

Executives/entrepreneurs perform all of the management tasks associated with owning a business or managing a major function, a large unit in a company, or the entire company. People who work in *executive/entrepreneur occupations* are fully responsible for the success or failure of the company. They must possess a comprehensive understanding of business and management. They will spend most of their time planning and evaluating the work of the organization. The positions held by executives/entrepreneurs are vice president, president, chief executive, and owner.

CAREERS IN INTERNATIONAL BUSINESS

The growth of trade between countries and increasing global competition provide continuing evidence of the importance of international business. It has never been easier to travel to other countries, communicate with people around the world, buy products produced in other places, and sell products and services abroad. The Internet makes access to almost any business and millions of customers only a mouse-click away. We are members of a global community generally, and a global business community specifically. As businesses expand into international markets, so do the opportunities for international business careers.

International business careers have all of the advantages of a career in one country plus more. In addition to the excitement and challenges that accompany work in any business career, international careers usually offer additional job choices and the chance to develop new skills, travel, and interact with a wide variety of people from different cultures. You learned about many of the requirements to prepare for a career in international business in Chapter 4.

You will recall that the international businessperson needs to know something about the culture of the country in which the business will operate or to which the company's products and service are directed. The economic environment of countries is another important area of study. Currently, English is the international language of business. However, there is no substitute for understanding the language of the

ILLUSTRATION 25-4

What advantages do international business careers have?

country in which you will work. People are favorably impressed when you take the trouble to learn their language. It is difficult to predict which languages will be the most important in your future. Your commitment to study and learn a second language will impress employers as well as your international contacts. You will also find it easier to learn an additional language if needed later. Your selection of international courses in high school and college, travel opportunities, and interactions with people from other countries and cultures are all valuable experiences if you would like to work in international business.

PREPARING FOR A BUSINESS CAREER

Preparing for a career in business may seem like trying to negotiate a maze. People who are not familiar with business may have difficulty determining what preparation they need and how to obtain the job they want.

If you talk to people who have worked in business for many years, you will find that some did not plan or prepare for the job they currently hold. They often ended up there after starting in another part of the business or in an entirely different occupation.

Today, a person is less likely to enter a business career without specific preparation. In your study of business, you have seen that a business career requires a great deal of knowledge and skill in a number of areas. People who understand the requirements and carefully plan to develop the necessary skills are more likely to succeed in business. In some ways, preparing for a business career is complicated, but in other ways it is really quite simple. It is often a matter of matching your personal qualities, education, and experience with a career path in business.

Good business education programs exist in high schools as well as in community and junior colleges and vocational/technical schools.

Business is usually one of the largest degree programs in colleges and universities. You can complete a general business preparation or specialize in specific areas, such as accounting, computer science, marketing, or even e-commerce. Many businesses offer education and training programs for their employees or pay for some or all of the costs of college coursework. You can also attend conferences and seminars sponsored by businesses and professional associations.

Experience in business is always an advantage. Experience in working with people in any way can give you confidence and develop important communication and interpersonal skills. Even if you have not worked part time or full time in a business, other types of experiences are useful. Working on projects in an organization, writing for the yearbook or school newspaper, forming a Junior Achievement company, or helping in a parent's business are all examples of experiences that can develop skills important in business.

Most employers value experience when they hire employees. It is relatively easy to find an entry-level job if you are not particularly concerned about the type of work or working conditions. These entry-level jobs provide the work experience that will qualify you for the jobs you prefer. Even though the pay may not be as high as you would like and work schedules are sometimes difficult to manage with school and extracurricular activities, it important to have a good work record in your first jobs.

Beginning employees who stay with one employer for a length of time and receive favorable evaluations will find it easier to receive promotions or be hired by an employer offering a better job. Employees who take advantage of training, opportunities for leadership, or the chance to supervise other employees or contribute to team activities will have an excellent employment record to use when applying for promotions or advanced jobs in other companies.

DEVELOPING A CAREER PLAN

Many people do little planning, even for the things that are most important to them. You know from your study of business that planning is an important skill. Businesses that plan are much more successful than those that do not plan. Likewise, people who plan their careers are more likely to achieve their career goals than those who do not plan. By developing a career plan, you will be able to practice an important business skill. In addition, you can show your plan to potential employers to demonstrate your ability to plan.

The following steps provide an outline to follow in developing a career plan:

1. *Develop an understanding of business concepts and the types of business careers.* Study careers in depth to determine the industries, businesses, and jobs that most interest you and the types of career paths related to those jobs.

ILLUSTRATION 25-5

Why is it wise to develop a career plan?

2. *Complete a self-assessment of your knowledge, skills, and attitudes that are related to those needed in business careers.* Ask a counselor to assist you with appropriate interest and aptitude tests that can help you with your assessment. Get feedback from people who know you well (family, friends, teachers, and employers) about their perceptions of the important skills, knowledge, and attitudes you have identified.
3. *Identify the education and experience requirements for business careers that interest you.* Compare those career requirements with your current preparation, and determine the additional education and experience you will need to qualify for those careers.
4. *Discuss the education and experience you will need with people (counselors or businesspeople) who are familiar with education programs and employment opportunities.* Have them help you select those that fit your career plans and qualifications.
5. *Develop a career plan that identifies the knowledge and skills needed for the career you have chosen and how you will develop them through a combination of education and experience.* The plan can identify the jobs in a career ladder, the schools or educational programs you plan to complete, how long you expect to take in moving through each step of the career ladder, and the ultimate career goal you would like to achieve.

PREPARING A CAREER PORTFOLIO

Artists, models, and advertising people have used portfolios for many years to demonstrate their abilities and present examples of their work. A **portfolio** is an organized collection of information and materials developed to represent yourself, your preparation, and your accomplishments. You might want to develop a portfolio to help you with career planning and to represent yourself when you apply for jobs or for admission to an educational institution.

Your portfolio should provide clear descriptions of your preparation, skills, and experience. Those descriptions can include examples of projects you have completed in school and on the job or for organizations to which you belong. They can even be work you have done as a hobby that demonstrates an important business skill. You can include in your portfolio evaluations of your skills and work evidenced through tests, checklists of competencies you have mastered, and performance reviews from employers. Also, you might ask people who know you well to write recommendations that relate to your skills and abilities.

You can develop your portfolio over a long period of time. You might start it now and continue to add to it as you complete high school, go on for additional education, or move through jobs in your career ladder. You should prepare a portfolio that allows you to add and remove items. Put your materials in a binder or other protective covering to keep them in good condition. The portfolio should include your best and most recent materials. Many people are now developing a personal Web site that includes their career portfolio. You can scan printed materials and photograph objects to add to your Internet portfolio. If you decide to use the Internet for this purpose, be careful to protect personal and confidential information.

A portfolio is a good way for you to identify important materials that will help you with your self-assessment. It also keeps materials organized so you can show them to others to demonstrate achievement, or as you apply for educational programs and jobs. Because it needs to communicate your preparation and skills effectively, it should be well organized, understandable, and easy for others to review.

CHAPTER 25 REVIEW

CHAPTER CONCEPTS

- The dramatic changes facing both traditional and new businesses present challenges to both employees and managers. Human resources personnel can help businesses respond to those changes by establishing organizational development programs.
- Two important elements of an effective organizational development program are improving work processes and building effective working relationships. The goal is to make improvements to eliminate errors, improve quality, and reduce costs. Organizational development programs focus on management/employee relationships as well as relationships with people in other organizations with whom the company works and with the company's customers.
- Successful businesses value their employees. They realize that it is not easy to find employees with the right qualifications and it can be very expensive to hire and train a new employee. Companies develop programs to increase employee motivation and performance, so they can retain an effective workforce.
- Career development programs meet the company's future employment needs by systematically preparing current employees for future positions in the company. A successful career development program requires a long-term organizational plan, career paths, effective employee performance reviews, career counseling, and training and development for employees.
- Companies depend on effective and satisfied employees. Those employees need up-to-date skills so they can perform their jobs accurately and efficiently. Two ways companies can contribute to maintaining a quality workforce are an effective system for performance review and well-designed training and development programs.
- There are many opportunities for careers in business no matter what your interests, education, or experience. Careers paths exist in all types of businesses. International career opportunities are especially attractive to people who are well prepared for the special requirements of international business. Following career planning procedures will help you obtain a job that is both satisfying and rewarding.

BUILD VOCABULARY POWER

Define the following terms and concepts.

1. job security
2. organizational development
3. career development
4. customer service standards
5. performance standards
6. job design
7. job enlargement
8. cross training
9. job enrichment
10. career development program
11. career path

12. career plan
13. career centers
14. performance review
15. portfolio

REVIEW FACTS

1. What factor caused companies to make major changes in their organizational size, structure, and operations in the last part of the 20th century?
2. What are two important elements of effective organizational development?
3. In what ways can organizations make improvements in the way work is accomplished?
4. Identify factors in the external environment that are most likely to result in problems for organizations today.
5. What is the first step in planning and implementing an organizational development program?
6. Do most organizational development programs take a long or a short time to be successful?
7. What are four work factors that relate to increased employee satisfaction?
8. What is the difference between job enlargement and job enrichment?
9. Why do many businesses today view their employees as an important resource?
10. What are five components of an effective career development program?
11. How do performance reviews help employees make effective career decisions?
12. What are some examples of special career development programs?
13. Identify three guidelines that managers should follow in completing a performance review conference with an employee.
14. What are some situations that indicate a need for employee training?
15. In what ways can a portfolio help with career planning?

DISCUSS IDEAS

1. In what ways is the employment environment today different from the environment 10 years ago and in what ways is it similar?
2. Identify ways that the following levels of employees can most directly contribute to the success of a business: a beginning employee, an experienced employee, a supervisor, and the company's top executive or owner.
3. How can work processes be improved without changing the technology or equipment used to complete the work?
4. What are some valuable sources of information that managers can use to identify possible changes in the external environment?

5. What is the difference between a customer service standard and a performance standard? How can customer service standards influence performance standards?
6. The last step in developing and implementing an organizational development program is to make the new process part of the organization's culture. Why is that step important? Why do you believe it is often difficult to accomplish?
7. Using jobs with which you are familiar, suggest some ways organizations could use job enlargement and job enrichment to increase employee satisfaction and motivation.
8. What would be evidence that a company considers its employees to be a very important resource in achieving its goals? What would be evidence that the company does not value its employees?
9. Some companies believe that each employee should be totally responsible for his or her career development. Why is it likely that career development will not be successful in those companies?
10. There is evidence that some of the best-performing companies also spend the most for employee training. Why do you believe that a company that is already successful would want to devote more time and money to training?
11. In what ways would planning for a career in international business be similar to or different from planning for a career in a person's home country?
12. What do you believe are the most important resources for career planning? Justify your answer.

ANALYZE INFORMATION

1. With the rest of your classmates, identify one problem related to the "work" environment or "work" relationships of your school that you would like to study. Then divide the class into several teams of students (4–6 students per group). Discuss the problem to identify why the problem exists and how the school would be better if the problem were solved. Then propose several solutions and analyze each to determine its advantages and disadvantages. Select the one solution your group believes could be implemented and that would be acceptable to administrators, teachers, and students. Prepare a written report from your group that identifies the problem, the proposed solution, and the key steps to successfully implementing the solution. Share your report with the other teams.
2. Conduct a survey of five people who have been working full time for more than three years. Ask them to identify the three things they like most and the three things they like least about their jobs. Combine your results with those of other class members. Organize the individual responses into similar categories so the

result is 4–6 categories for each of the two groups of responses. Develop a chart that illustrates the findings of the entire class. Participate in a class discussion to identify how organizations could use the information your class collected.

3. A review of a report on the amount of formal training activities of Yarcho and Slayton, Inc., revealed the following data:

Date of Training	*Number of Participants*	*Cost of Training*	*Department*
2-4	45	$ 900	Marketing
7-26	26	3,120	Information
1-13	11	495	Management
4-05	58	870	
9-29	32	960	Operations
5-30	65	3,250	
11-08	29	435	Accounting
3-19	12	900	and Finance
7-12	38	760	
12-01	19	855	

a. Calculate the cost per participant of each training session.
b. Determine the average cost of training per participant for the entire company.
c. If Yarcho and Slayton has a total of 206 employees with 45 in Marketing, 58 in Information Management, 65 in Operations, and 38 in Accounting and Finance, determine the average amount spent on each employee for training for each department and for the entire company.

4. Obtain a copy of an employee evaluation form from a business or use one provided by your teacher. Fill it out as if you were the supervisor or manager of an employee. Make sure to identify both areas where the employee performs well and a few areas for improvement. Then use the form to role-play a performance review conference with another student in your class. Have a third student observe the conference. That student should make notes on the responses and reactions of the two students engaged in the role-play. When you have completed the role-play, participate in a discussion with the other two team members, noting what appeared to work well and how the conference could be improved. After the discussion, form another team and repeat the process until each student has completed each role.

5. Identify the title of a management job that interests you. Using career information from your school counseling center, a library, or the Internet, prepare a description of the education and experience requirements for the job. Now search the career information to identify an entry-level job and at least two other related jobs that have increasing requirements and responsibilities and

could form a career path for you if you wanted to obtain the management job. Write a complete job description for each of the jobs. Now begin to develop a career portfolio for the career path by developing clear descriptions of your relevant preparation, skills, and experiences. Identify projects or other materials you have developed in this class or from other sources that would make useful additions to your portfolio.

SOLVE BUSINESS PROBLEMS

CASE 25-1

The Orion Corporation recently implemented employee involvement teams as a part of an organizational development program. The employees in the customer support department of the engineering division were excited about the chance to participate in solving a problem they had been facing for some time. Fourteen of the twenty employees had school-aged children. Several times during the year, the employees needed to take time from work to attend parent-teacher conferences, help with projects in their child's school, or attend an important school activity involving their children. Orion had no policy that allowed employees time away from work. The employees either had to miss the school activities or call in sick. Most of the employees felt uncomfortable about taking a "sick-day" when they really were not sick.

The employee team worked carefully and developed the following plan: Each employee could have up to two half-day absences for school-related activities during the year. The absence would have

to be scheduled at least one week in advance and only one employee could be absent at a time. The other employees agreed to complete the work of the absent employee before they left for the day without additional pay. The department manager could cancel the absence with one day's notice if the department had special assignments or extra work.

The employee team submitted their plan to the department manager. The manager rejected the employee recommendation. She identified two reasons for rejecting the plan: (1) The company could not have different policies concerning employee absences for each department. (2) Since all employees in the department did not have school-aged children, the policy would be unfair to those employees.

Think Critically:

1. Do you believe the manager made the right decision about the team's recommendation? Why or why not? If you were the manager, how would you respond to the team's recommendation?
2. How do you believe the employees will feel about the organization, based on the manager's response to their proposal? What should the manager do now, based on her decision not to accept the team's recommendation?
3. How could the Orion Corporation improve the way it organized and used teams in the future?

CASE 25-2

Jacki Knox had just left her workstation when her supervisor, Dorothea Fernandez, stopped her.

Dorothea: *Do you have a few minutes, Jacki? I'd like to go over your performance evaluation with you.*
Jacki: *I'm just ready to go on break.*
Dorothea: *That's where I'm going, too. Let's get a table together in the break room and review your evaluation form. It shouldn't take very long.*

After they found a table in the corner of the break room, Dorothea removed an evaluation form from the folder she was carrying and handed it to Jacki.

Dorothea: *I think you're doing a very good job, Jacki. Your ratings have gone from four to five in three categories, and that's the top rating. You have maintained fours in four other categories. You need to pay attention to the two categories where I gave you a three and really work on the area where you received only a two. You're really a nice person, Jacki, and I'm happy to have you in my department. Do you have any questions?*

Jacki: *Well, I haven't had a chance to study the form, so I am not sure about questions. I'm obviously concerned about the areas where I received low ratings. Is this my formal evaluation that will determine if I get a salary increase?*

Dorothea: *No. We'll complete that in four more weeks. I just wanted you to see the form informally so we could discuss your performance before you had the formal evaluation.*

Just then a receptionist came to the table and told Dorothea that she had a visitor in her department.

Dorothea: *Jacki, why don't you spend some time reviewing the evaluation? Then we'll schedule some time in my office to discuss it completely.*

Think Critically:

1. Analyze the procedures Dorothea followed in discussing Jacki's evaluation with her. What were Dorothea's strengths and weaknesses?
2. Describe what Dorothea should do to improve the conference when she and Jacki meet again.
3. What should Jacki do to prepare for the next meeting with Dorothea? How should Jacki use the information she received from Dorothea and from the evaluation form during the next four weeks?

PROJECT: MY BUSINESS, INC.

Even new businesses must be concerned about change and maintaining an effective work environment and work processes. One of the serious problems faced by small businesses is being able to develop the skills of employees and then encourage them to continue to work for the business rather than changing jobs. The following activities will help you consider how to maintain an effective organization and develop effective, motivated employees.

DATA COLLECTION

1. Review magazine and newspaper articles about small business operations. Identify the types of problems small businesses face that often lead to major problems or failure of the business.
2. Identify a small number of people who have worked in a small business for a short time and then changed jobs due to dissatisfaction with the job. Also identify a small number who have worked in a small business and are satisfied with their jobs. Ask each group the reasons for their satisfaction or dissatisfaction. Ask them to identify which of the reasons are directly related to the size of the business and which are not related to the business's size.

3. Go to the Internet and gather information on the type of employee training that is currently being provided to employees by retail businesses. If possible, identify the amount of money small businesses spend on average to train employees compared to the amount spent by large businesses.

ANALYSIS

1. Prepare an outline of the training you would provide to each new employee of your business. Identify the training methods you would use, the materials or resources you would need, and the amount of time you would spend in training.
2. Develop a simple form to be used in reviewing the performance of your employees. Then outline the procedures you would follow to evaluate each employee's performance and to review the results of the evaluation with the employee.
3. Compile a list of things you could do as the owner of a new small business to develop a work environment that would be motivating for employees while encouraging effective performance. Try to list things that would not be particularly expensive to implement.

GLOSSARY

A

accountability: the obligation to accept responsibility for the outcomes of assigned tasks.

accounting equation: Assets = Liabilities + Capital

accounting records: financial records of the transactions of the business.

accounts payable: money owed for credit purchases.

accounts payable record: a record showing money owed and payments made by the business.

accounts receivable: the amount owed by customers.

accounts receivable record: a record showing what each customer owes and pays.

achievement need: take personal responsibility for work; set personal goals; want immediate feedback on work.

actuaries: persons who calculate insurance rates.

administered channel: a channel in which one organization takes a leadership position to benefit all channel members.

advertising: all forms of paid promotion that deliver a message to many people at the same time.

advertising budget: a plan of the amount of money a firm should spend for advertising based on estimated sales.

advertising media: the methods of delivering the promotional message to the intended audience.

affiliation need: concerned about relationships with others; work to get along well and fit in with a group.

aging the accounts: analyzing customers' account balances within categories based upon the number of days each customer's balance has remained unpaid.

application software: consists of instructions for performing various types of tasks.

applied research: studies of existing product problems or design improvements for current products.

assessed valuation: the value of property determined by tax officials.

asset book value: original cost less accumulated depreciation of an asset.

assets: things owned, such as cash and buildings.

authority: the right to make decisions about work assignments and to require other employees to perform assigned tasks.

autocratic leader: one who gives direct, clear, and precise orders with detailed instructions as to what, when, and how work is to be done.

automatic teller machine (ATM): a computer that enables bank customers to deposit, withdraw, or transfer funds by using a bank-provided plastic card.

B

baby boom: refers to the high birth rate period from 1945–1965.

baby bust: refers to the low birth rate period following the baby boom period.

balance of payments: an accounting statement containing the current account and the capital account.

balance sheet (statement of financial position): a financial statement that lists the assets, liabilities, and capital of a business.

bank: an institution that accepts demand deposits and makes commercial loans.

bank discount: interest deducted in advance from a loan.

bankruptcy: a legal process that allows selling assets to pay off debts.

bar codes: product identification labels containing a unique set of vertical bars that can be read using computer scanning equipment.

basic product: the physical product in its simplest form.

beneficiaries: persons who receive a life insurance payment on the death of an insured person.

board of directors (directors or **board):** ruling body of a corporation.

bond: a long-term written promise to pay a definite sum of money at a specified time.

bonding: provides payment of damages to people who have losses resulting from the negligence or dishonesty of an employee or from the failure of the business to complete a contract.

bonus: money paid at the end of a specific period of time for performance that exceeds the expected standard.

book value: the value of a share of stock that is found by dividing the net worth (assets minus liabilities) of the corporation by the total number of shares outstanding.

brainstorming: a group discussion technique that is used to generate as many ideas as possible for solving a problem.

brand: a name, symbol, word, or design that identifies a product, service, or company.

bricks-and-mortar businesses: businesses that complete most of their business activities at a physical location rather than through the Internet.

browser: a program that permits you to navigate and view Web pages.

budget: a financial plan extending usually for one year.

building codes: codes that regulate physical features of structures.

business: an organization that produces or distributes a good or service for profit.

business cycles: a pattern of irregular but repeated expansion and contraction of the GDP.

business ethics: a collection of principles and rules of conduct based on what is right and wrong for an organization.

business plan: (1) a written description of the business and its operations with an analysis of the opportunities and risks it faces. (2) a written guide that helps the entrepreneur during the design and start-up phases of the business.

buying: obtaining goods to be resold.

buying motives: the reasons people buy.

cafeteria plan: a benefit program in which employees can select the benefits that meet their personal needs.

capacity: earning power.

capital (net worth, owner's equity, stockholders' equity): what a business is worth after subtracting liabilities from assets.

capital account: an account that records investment funds coming into and going out of a country.

capital budget: a financial plan for replacing fixed assets or acquiring new ones.

capital formation: the production of capital goods.

capital goods: buildings, tools, machines, and other equipment that are used to produce other goods but do not directly satisfy human wants.

capital stock (or simply **stock):** the general term applied to the shares of ownership of a corporation.

capitalism: an economic-political system in which private citizens are free to go into business for themselves, to produce whatever they choose to produce, and to distribute what they produce as they please.

career centers: facilities where career development activities are managed.

career development: a program that matches the career planning of employees with the employment needs of the business.

career development program: provides a long-term focus on a company's employment needs combined with support for employees so they can prepare for future jobs in the company.

career path: a progression of related jobs with increasing skill requirements and responsibility.

career plan: identifies the jobs that are a part of the employee's career path, the training and development needed to advance along the career path, and a tentative schedule for the plan's activities.

cash budget: an estimate of cash received and paid out.

cash discount: given if payment is received by a certain date.

cash flow: the movement of cash into and out of a business.

cease and desist: requires that a company stop using specific advertisements.

centralized organization: all major planning and decision making is done by a group of top managers in the business.

certificate of deposit (CD): a savings account that requires an investor to deposit a specified sum for a fixed period at a fixed interest rate.

Certified Public Accountant (CPA): a person who has met a state's education, experience, and examination requirements in accounting.

channel integration: when one business owns the organizations at other levels of the channel.

channel members: businesses that participate in activities transferring goods and services from the producer to the user.

channel of communication: the means by which a message is conveyed.

channels of distribution (marketing channels): the routes products and services follow, including the activities and participating organizations, while moving from the producer to the consumer.

character: an indication of one's moral obligation to pay debts.

charter (certificate of incorporation): an official document granted by a state giving power to run a corporation.

check: a written order on a financial institution to pay previously deposited money to a third party on demand.

chief information officer (CIO): the top computer executive.

close corporation (closely held corporation): a corporation that does not offer its shares of stock for public sale.

coaching: regular observation of an employee by a supervisor or experienced employee with follow-up discussions on ways to improve performance.

code of ethics: a formal, published collection of values and rules used to guide the behavior of an organization toward its various stakeholders.

collateral: property a borrower pledges to assure repayment of a loan.

combination plan: a pay plan that provides each employee a small wage or salary and adds incentive pay based on the person's performance.

command economy: an economic system in which the method for determining what, how, and for whom goods and services are produced is decided by a central planning authority.

commercial bank: a financial institution that provides many services, such as handling time and demand deposits and commercial and consumer loans.

commercial businesses: firms engaged in marketing, in finance, and in furnishing services.

commercial loan: a loan made to a business.

commission plan: a compensation plan in which employees are paid a percentage of the volume of business for which they are responsible.

common stock: ownership that gives holders the right to participate in managing the business by having voting privileges and by sharing in the profits (dividends) if there are any.

communication: refers to the sharing of information, which results in a high degree of understanding between the message sender and receiver.

communication network: a structure through which information flows in a business.

communism: forced socialism where all or almost all the productive resources of a nation are owned by the government.

comparable worth: paying workers equally for jobs with similar but not identical job requirements.

comparative advantage theory: to gain a trade advantage, a country should specialize in products or services that it can provide more efficiently than other countries.

compensation: the money and other benefits people receive for work.

competition: rivalry among sellers for consumers' dollars.

computer: a machine that processes and stores data according to instructions stored in it.

computer integrated manufacturing: all of the manufacturing systems in a business are designed and managed using computers.

conditions: relate to economic and other matters such as the economic health of a community or nation and the extent of business competition that affects credit decisions.

conflict: a situation that develops when one person interferes with the achievement of another's goals.

consultant: an expert who is called upon to study a special problem and offer solutions.

consumer goods: products produced for sale to individuals and families for personal use.

consumer goods and services: goods and services that satisfy people's economic wants directly.

consumer loan: a loan made to an individual.

consumer panel: a group of people who offer opinions about a product or service.

Consumer Price Index (CPI): a measure of the average change in prices of consumer goods and services typically purchased by people living in urban areas.

containerization: products are packed in large shipping containers at the factory and then shipped using a number of transportation methods before being unpacked.

continuous processing: a process by which raw materials move through special equipment that changes their form to make them more usable for consumption or further manufacturing.

controlling: evaluating results to determine if the company's objectives have been accomplished as planned.

convenience goods: inexpensive items that consumers purchase regularly without a great deal of thought.

convertible bonds: bonds that allow bondholders to exchange bonds for a prescribed number of shares of common stock.

cookies: files of information about the user that some Web sites create and store on the user's own computer.

cooperative: a business owned and operated by its user-members for the purpose of supplying themselves with goods and services.

copyright: similar to a patent in that the federal government gives an author the sole right to reproduce, publish, and sell literary or artistic work for the life of the author plus 70 years.

corporation: a business owned by a group of people and authorized by the state in which it is located to act as though it were a single person.

corrective advertising: new advertising designed to change the false impression left by misleading information.

cost of goods sold: the cost to produce the product or buy it for resale.

creditors: those to whom money is owed.

creditworthiness: a measure of a person's ability and willingness to repay a loan.

cross training: employees are trained to perform more than one job in the company even though they typically perform only one.

culture: (1) involves the shared values, beliefs, and behavior existing in an organization. (2) the customs, beliefs, values, and patterns of behavior of the people of a country or group.

current account: an account that records the value of goods and services exported and those imported from foreigners, as well as other income and payments.

custom manufacturing: the process used to design and build a unique product to meet the purchaser's specific needs.

customer oriented: businesses that direct company activities at satisfying customers.

customer service standards: measures against which a company judges its performance in meeting customer expectations.

D

data: original facts and figures that businesses generate.

data processing center: a business that processes data for other businesses for a fee.

database: a collection of data organized in a way that makes data easy to find, update, and manage.

debentures: bonds that are not secured by assets but based upon the faith and credit of the corporation that issues them.

debit card: allows a person to make cash withdrawals from ATMs, pay bills by phone from bank accounts, and pay for on-site purchases such as foods and household items.

debt capital (creditor capital): capital loaned to a business by others.

decentralized organization: a business is divided into smaller operating units and managers are given almost total responsibility and authority for the operation of those units.

decision support system (DSS): a system that helps managers consider alternatives in making specific decisions.

decline stage: occurs when a product is introduced that is much better or easier to use, and customers begin to switch from the old product to the new product.

deductible: an arrangement that permits the insured to bear part of the loss in return for a lower premium.

demand: refers to the number of similar products that will be bought at a given time at a given price.

demand deposit: money put into a financial institution by depositors and which can be withdrawn at any time without penalty.

democratic leader: one who encourages workers to share in making decisions about work-related problems.

depreciation: decrease in the value of an asset due to wear and age.

depression: a long and severe drop in the GDP.

direct deposit: allows business to electronically transfer employees' paychecks directly from the employer's bank account to employees' bank accounts.

direct distribution: when producers sell directly to the ultimate consumer.

disability insurance: offers payments to employees who are no longer able to work because of accidents or illnesses.

discharge: the release of an employee from the company due to inappropriate work behavior.

discounts: reductions from the price of the product to encourage customers to buy.

distortion: refers to how people consciously or unconsciously change messages.

distraction: anything that interferes with the sender's creating and delivering a message and the receiver's getting and interpreting a message.

distribution (place): the set of activities required to transport and store products, and make them available to customers.

distribution center: a large building designed to accumulate and redistribute products efficiently.

dividends: profits distributed to stockholders on a per-share basis.

domain name: a Web-site owner's unique Internet address.

domestic goods: products made by firms in the United States.

dot-com business: a company that does almost all of its business activities through the Internet.

downsize: cutting back on the goods and services provided and thereby shrinking the size of a firm and the number of employees.

dumping: refers to the practice of selling goods in a foreign market at a price that is below cost or below what it charges in its own home country.

E

e-commerce: doing business online.

economic discrepancies: differences between the offerings of a business and the requirements of a consumer.

economic growth: occurs when a country's output exceeds its population growth.

economic system: an organized way for a country to decide how to use its productive resources; that is, to decide what, how, and for whom goods and services will be produced.

economic wants: the desire for scarce material goods and services.

economics: the body of knowledge that relates to producing and using goods and services that satisfy human wants.

effectiveness: occurs when an organization makes the right decisions in deciding what products or services to offer customers or other users.

efficiency: occurs when an organization produces needed goods or services quickly at low cost.

electronic funds transfer (EFT): transferring money by computer rather than by check.

electronic shopping carts: specialized programs that keep track of shoppers' selections as they shop, provide an order form for them to complete, and submit the form to the company through the Internet.

embargo: government bars companies from doing business with particular countries.

emoticons: facial expressions created with keyboard symbols and used to express feelings in e-mail messages.

employee assistance programs: provide confidential personal problem-solving, counseling, and support services for employees.

employee benefits: all forms of compensation and services the company provides to employees in addition to salaries and wages.

employee stock ownership: a benefit plan that gives company stock as bonuses or allows employees to purchase the stock at a discount.

employee turnover: the rate at which people enter and leave employment in a business during a year.

employment turnover: the extent to which people enter and leave employment in a business during a year.

empowerment: (1) letting workers decide how to perform their work tasks and offer ideas on how to improve the work process; (2) the authority given to individual employees to solve problems on the job with available resources.

endorsement: the signature—usually on the back—that transfers a negotiable instrument.

enhanced product: a product that offers different features and options for the consumer.

entrepreneur: a person who starts, manages, and owns a business.

equity capital (owner capital): money invested in the business by its owner or owners.

ergonomics: the science of adapting equipment to the work and health needs of people.

ethics: the code of moral conduct that sets standards for what is valued as right or wrong behavior for a person or group.

Euro: the currency of the European Union.

European Union (EU): a trading bloc consisting of 15 European countries as members.

exchange rate: the value of one currency to another.

excise tax: a sales tax that applies only to selected goods and services, such as gasoline.

executive: a top-level manager who spends almost all of his or her time on management functions.

executive information system (EIS): combines and summarizes ongoing transactions within the company to provide top-level executives with information needed to make decisions about company goals and direction.

exit interview: a formal interview with an employee who is leaving a company to determine the person's attitudes and feelings about the company's policies and procedures, management, and operations.

expert power: given to people who are considered the most knowledgeable.

exporting: when a company sells its goods and services to a foreign country.

extended coverage: additional insurance protection beyond the major peril.

extended product: a product that includes additional features that are not part of the physical product but increase its usability.

extranet: a private network that companies use to share certain information with selected people outside the organization.

F

401k plan: a company-sponsored retirement plan in which employees may choose to have a percentage of their pay contributed to one of several alternative investment plans selected by the employer.

factor: a firm that specializes in lending money to businesses based on the business's accounts receivable.

factors of production: land, labor, capital goods, and management—the four basic resources that are combined to create useful goods and services.

false advertising: advertising that is misleading in a material respect or in any way that could influence the customer's purchase or use of the product.

feedback: a receiver's response to a sender's message.

file server (or simply **server):** a computer in a LAN that stores data and application software for all PC workstations.

finance: deals with all money matters related to running a business.

financial statements: reports that summarize financial data over a period of time.

financing: providing money that is needed to perform various marketing activities, such as obtaining credit when buying and extending credit when selling.

firewall: a system using special software that screens people who enter or exit a network by requesting passwords.

fixed assets (plant assets): material assets that will last a long time.

flame: an electronic message that contains abusive, threatening, or offensive content that may violate company policy or public law.

flattened organization: one with fewer levels of management than traditional structures.

flextime: a plan that lets employees choose their own work hours, within specified limits.

foreign corporation: a corporation doing business in a state from which it did not receive its charter.

foreign goods: products made by firms in other countries.

formal communication network: composed of different levels of management with information flowing upward, downward, and across an organization in a prescribed manner.

franchise: a legal agreement between a company and a distributor to sell a product or service under special conditions.

franchisee: the distributor of a franchised product or service.

franchisor: the parent company of a franchise agreement that provides the product or service.

Frost Belt: the colder northern half of the United States.

full disclosure: providing all information necessary for consumers to make an informed decision.

G

Generation X: workers from the post-baby-boom generation.

glass ceiling: an invisible barrier to job advancement.

global competition: the ability of profit-making organizations to compete with other businesses in other countries.

goal: a specific statement of a result the business expects to achieve.

grading and valuing: grouping goods according to size, quality, or other characteristics, and determining an appropriate price for products and services.

grapevine: an informal communication system that develops among workers.

gross domestic product (GDP): the total market value of all goods produced and services provided in a country in a year.

growth stage: when several brands of the new product are available.

H

hardware: equipment that makes up a computer system.

health insurance: provides protection against the expenses of health care.

health maintenance organizations (HMOs): a cooperative agreement between a business and a group of physicians and other medical professionals to provide for the health care needs of the employees of the business.

high-context culture: a culture in which communication occurs through non-verbal signs and indirect suggestions.

home country: the country in which a multinational corporation has its headquarters.

host country: the foreign country where a multinational firm has production and service facilities.

human capital: the accumulated knowledge and skills of human beings—the total value of each person's education and acquired skills.

human relations: how well people get along with each other when working together.

human resource planning: determines the types of jobs that are required for each part of the production procedure and the number of people needed for each job.

human resources management (HRM): all activities involved with acquiring, developing, and compensating the people who do the company's work.

hygiene factors: job factors that dissatisfy when absent but do not contribute to satisfaction when they are present.

hyperlink: a Web page address embedded in a word, phrase, or graphic that, when clicked, transports users to that address.

I

identity power: given to people because others identify with and want to be accepted by them.

implementing: helping employees to work effectively.

importing: buying goods or services made in a foreign country.

income statement (profit and loss statement): a financial document that reports total revenue and expenses for a specific period.

income statement budget: a plan showing projected sales, costs, and individual expense figures for a future period.

income tax: a tax levied against the profits of business firms and against earnings of individuals.

indirect distribution: when distribution takes place through channel members.

industrial businesses: firms that produce goods that are often used by other businesses or organizations to make things.

industrial goods: products that are to be used by another business.

industry: a word often used to refer to all businesses within a category.

inflation: a rapid rise in prices caused by an inadequate supply of goods and services.

informal communication network: consists of unofficial ways of sharing information in an organization.

information: data that have been processed in some way that is useful to decision makers.

information liability: responsibility for physical or economic injury arising from incorrect data or wrongful use of data.

information system: a computer system used to process data for the purpose of generating information from that data.

initial public offering (IPO): the first time that a company sells stock to the public.

installment credit: credit used when a customer makes a sizable purchase and agrees to make payments over an extended but fixed period of time.

insurable interest: any interest in property that will suffer a possible financial loss if there is a loss of or damage to the property.

insurance: a risk management tool that limits financial loss from uncontrollable events in exchange for regular payments.

insurance agents: people who represent the insurance company and sell insurance to individuals and businesses.

insurance rate: the amount charged for a certain value of insurance.

insured: the persons or organization covered by the insurance policy.

insurer: a company that sells insurance.

intermittent processing: uses short production runs to make predetermined quantities of different products.

international business: business activities that occur between two or more countries.

international licensing: when one company allows a company in another country to make and sell products according to certain specifications.

International Monetary Fund (IMF): helps financially strapped countries pay for imports or repay loans.

Internet (Net): a worldwide network of linked computers that allows data and information to be transferred among computers.

Internet Service Provider (ISP): a service that provides Internet access.

interstate commerce: business operations and transactions that cross over state lines.

intranet: a private company network that allows employees to share resources no matter where they are located.

intrapreneur: an employee who is given funds and freedom to create a special unit or department within a company in order to develop a new product, process, or service.

intrastate commerce: business transacted within a state.

introduction stage: when a brand-new product enters the market.

inventory management: determines the quantities of materials and supplies needed for production and the amount of finished products required to meet customer orders.

investment bank: an organization that helps businesses raise capital through the sales of stocks and bonds.

investment company: an organization that specializes in the sale of a variety of stocks, bonds, and other securities.

IRA plan: a retirement plan that is not company-sponsored, in which employees contribute a percentage of their pay, up to a specified legal limit, in any investment plan of their choice.

job description: a list of the basic tasks that make up a job.

job design: the kind of work and the way the work is organized.

job enlargement: making a job more interesting by adding variety to the tasks.

job enrichment: encouraging employee participation in decision making.

job security: the likelihood that employment will not be terminated.

job sharing: an employment plan that allows two people to share one full-time job.

job specification: a list of the qualifications a worker needs to do a job.

joint venture: two or more businesses that agree to provide a good or service, sharing the costs of doing business and also the profits.

just-in-time (JIT) inventory controls: a method in which the company maintains very small inventories and obtains materials just in time for use.

K

Keogh plan: a retirement plan designed for self-employed people, who may contribute an amount of their earnings into an investment fund managed by an investment company.

knowledge workers: people who work with information.

L

labor: the human effort, either physical or mental, that goes into the production of goods and services.

labor force: most people aged 16 or over who are available for work, whether employed or unemployed.

labor participation rate: the percentage of the labor force either employed or actively seeking employment.

layoff: a temporary or permanent reduction in the number of employees resulting from a change in business conditions.

leader: a manager who earns the respect and cooperation of employees to effectively accomplish the organization's work.

leadership: the ability to influence individuals and groups to achieve organizational goals.

leadership style: the general way a manager treats and directs employees.

lease: a contract that allows the use of an asset for a fee.

liabilities: claims against assets or things owed—the debts of a business.

liability insurance: provides protection for risks involved in operating a business.

licensing: a way to limit and control those who plan to enter certain types of businesses.

life insurance: provides money that is paid upon the death of the insured to a person or people identified in the insurance policy.

limited liability company (LLC): a special type of corporation that is taxed as if it were a sole proprietorship or partnership.

limited partnership: restricts the liability of a partner for the amount of the partner's investment.

line organization: all authority and responsibility may be traced in a direct line from the top executive down to the lowest employee level in the organization.

line-and-staff organization: the addition of staff specialists to a line organization.

liquidity: refers to the ease of turning an investment into cash without significant loss.

list price: the original price that the seller posts on the product.

local area network (LAN): an electronic system that allows computer information to move over short distances between or among different computers.

long-term capital: capital that is borrowed for longer than a year.

long-term notes (term loans): loans written for periods of 1 to 15 years.

low-context culture: a culture in which people communicate directly and explicitly.

M

malpractice insurance: a type of liability insurance that protects against financial loss arising from suits for negligence in providing professional services.

management: the process of accomplishing the goals of an organization through the effective use of people and other resources.

management information system (MIS): integrates data from various departments to make it available to help managers with daily business operations.

manager: a person who completes all four management functions on a regular basis and has authority over other jobs and people.

manufacturing: a special form of production in which raw and semi-finished materials are processed and converted into finished products.

manufacturing firms: businesses that produce goods.

margin (gross profit): term used to indicate the difference between the selling price and the cost of goods sold.

markdown: any amount by which the original selling price is reduced before an item is sold.

market: the types of buyers a business wishes to attract and where such buyers are located.

market economy: an economic system that determines what, how, and for whom goods and services are produced by coordinating individual choices through arrangements that aid buying and selling goods and services.

market research: the study of a company's current and prospective customers.

market value: the value at which stock is bought and sold on any given day.

marketing: the process of planning and executing the conception, pricing, promotion, and distribution of ideas, goods, and services to create exchanges that satisfy individual and organizational objectives.

marketing concept: keeping the needs of the consumer uppermost in mind during the design, production, and distribution of a product.

marketing mix: the blending of all decisions that are related to the four elements of marketing.

marketing plan: a detailed written description of all marketing activities that a business must accomplish in order to sell a product.

markup: the amount added to the cost of a product to determine its selling price.

mass production: (1) an assembly process in which a large number of products is produced, each of which is identical to the next; (2) occurs when up-to-date equipment and assembly line methods are used to produce large quantities of identical goods.

matrix organization: combines workers into temporary work teams to complete specific projects.

maturity date: date on which a loan must be repaid.

maturity stage: when there are many competing brands with very similar features.

merchandise inventory: goods purchased to sell to customers at a profit.

merchandising budget: a budget that plans and controls the supply of merchandise to be sold to customers.

mid-manager: a manager who completes all of the management functions but spends more time on one of the functions or is responsible for a specific part of the company's operations.

mission statement: a short, specific statement of the purpose and direction of the business.

mixed economy: an economic system in which a combination of a market and a command economy is blended together to make decisions about what, how, and for whom goods and services are produced.

modem: an electronic device inside or outside the computer that enables it to send data over phone lines or cable.

money market account: a type of savings account in which the deposits are invested in short-term, government-backed securities.

monopoly: exists when competition is lacking for a product or service, or when producers are in a position to control the supply and price of goods or services.

Moore's Law: the prediction that the amount of data that can be processed by a computer chip will double about every 18 months.

mortgage bonds: bonds on which specific assets are pledged as a guarantee that the principal and interest will be paid according to the terms specified on the bonds.

motivation: the set of factors that cause a person to act in a certain way.

motivators: factors that increase job satisfaction.

multinational firm: a business that owns or controls production or service facilities outside the country in which it is based.

mutual fund: pools the money of many small investors for the purchase of stocks and bonds.

N

natural resources: anything provided by nature that affects the productive ability of a country.

Net Generation: those persons born between 1977 and 1997.

net profit: the difference between the selling price and all costs and expenses of the business.

no-fault insurance: each insurance company is required to pay the losses of its insured when an accident occurs, regardless of who might have been responsible for the loss.

nominal group technique (NGT): a process a leader uses to involve all group members to solve a difficult problem that may create conflicts among members.

non-bank bank (non-bank): an institution that offers only demand deposits or commercial loans, but not both.

non-economic wants: desired wants that are not scarce.

non-governmental organizations (NGOs): independent groups that influence businesses through lobbying, publicity, and pressure tactics.

nonprofit corporation: an organization that does not pay taxes and does not exist to make a profit.

non-tariff barriers: barriers other than tariffs that restrict imports.

non-verbal communications: delivering messages by means other than speaking or writing.

North American Free Trade Agreement (NAFTA): a trading bloc consisting of the United States, Canada, and Mexico.

O

objections: concerns or complaints expressed by the customer.

obsolescence: decrease in the value of an asset because it is out of date or inadequate.

officers: top executives who are hired to manage the business.

open corporation (public corporation): a corporation that offers its shares of stock for public sale.

open leader: a manager who gives little or no direction to workers.

open line of credit: authorization to borrow up to a specified amount for a specified period of time.

operating expenses: the costs of operating a business.

operating system software: a master control program that manages the computer's internal functions and file system.

operational planning: short-term planning that identifies specific activities for each area of the business.

organization chart: a visual device that shows the structure of an organization and the relationships among workers and divisions of work.

organizational development: carefully planned changes in the structure and operation of a business so it can adjust successfully to the competitive environment.

organizing: determining how plans can most effectively be accomplished; arranging resources to complete work.

output: the quantity, or amount, produced within a given time.

outsourcing: hiring an outside firm to perform specialized tasks for a business.

P

Pacific Rim: countries located on the western edge of the Pacific Ocean.

par value (stated value): a dollar value shown on a share of stock, which is an arbitrarily assigned amount that is used for bookkeeping purposes.

parent firm: a company that controls another company.

partnership: a business owned by two or more persons.

patent: an agreement in which the federal government gives an inventor the sole right for 20 years to make, use, and sell an invention.

pension plan: a company-sponsored retirement plan that makes regular payments to employees after retirement.

performance review: the process of assessing how well employees are doing their jobs.

performance standards: specific statements of the expected results from critical business activities.

peril: the cause of a loss for a person or organization.

personal digital assistant (PDA): a small, computer-like device that can send and receive messages wirelessly.

personal property tax: a tax on such items as furniture, machinery, and equipment.

personal selling: promotion through direct, personal contact with a customer.

piece-rate plan: a compensation plan that pays the employee a fixed rate for each unit of production.

piggyback service: a distribution method where truck trailers are loaded and placed on railroad cars to be shipped close to their final destination.

pixel: one or more dots that act as the smallest unit on a video display screen.

planning: analyzing information and making decisions about what needs to be done.

point-of-sale terminal: cash registers that are connected to computers.

policies: guidelines used in making decisions regarding specific, recurring situations.

policy: the written agreement, or contract, between the insurer and the policyholder.

policyholder: the person or business purchasing insurance.

portfolio: an organized collection of information and materials that represents a person's accomplishments.

position power: comes from the position the manager holds in the organization.

power: the ability to control behavior.

power need: desire to influence and control others and to be responsible for a group's activities.

preferred provider organizations (PPOs): health care available from a selected set of physicians and health care facilities through negotiated contracts between the health care providers and the insurer.

preferred stock: ownership that gives holders preference over the common stockholders when distributing dividends or assets.

premium: a payment by the policyholder to the insurer for protection against a risk.

price: the amount of money given to acquire a product.

price discrimination: setting different prices for different customers.

prime rate: the lowest rate of interest; the rate at which large banks loan large sums to the best-qualified borrowers.

private property: items of value that individuals can own, use, and sell.

privatization: when a state or country transfers its authority to provide a good or service to individuals or businesses.

problem: a difficult situation requiring a solution.

procedure: a list of steps to be followed for performing certain work.

process improvement: efforts to increase the effectiveness and efficiency of specific business operations.

producer: anyone who aids in creating a utility.

product: all attributes that customers receive in exchange for the purchase price.

product assortment: the complete set of all products a business offers to a market.

product development: the process of developing or improving a product or service.

product life cycle: (1) predicts the sales and profit performance of a given product; (2) the four stages of sales and profit performance through which all brands of a product progress.

product line: a group of similar products with obvious variations in the design and quality to meet the needs of distinct customer groups.

product research: research done to develop new products or to discover improvements for existing products.

production: involves making a product or providing a service.

production oriented: businesses that emphasize decisions about what and how to produce and then how to sell the products.

production scheduling: identifies the steps required in a manufacturing process, the time required to complete each step, and the sequence of the steps.

productivity: producing the largest quantity in the least time by using efficient methods and modern equipment.

profit: the incentive, as well as the reward, for producing goods and services.

profit-sharing plan: a benefit plan that pays employees a small percentage of the company's profits at the end of the year.

progressive tax: tax based on the ability to pay.

promissory note: an unconditional written promise to pay a certain sum of money, at a particular time or on demand, to the order of one who has obtained the note.

promotion: (1) providing information to consumers that will assist them in making a decision to purchase a product or service. (2) the advancement of an employee within a company to a position with more authority and responsibility.

property tax: a levy on material goods owned.

proportional tax (flat tax): tax rate remains the same regardless of the amount on which the tax is imposed.

proprietor: the owner-manager of a business.

prospectus: a version of registration statement for the Securities and Exchange Commission that contains extensive details about the company and its proposed sale of securities.

proxy: a written authorization for someone to vote in behalf of the person signing the proxy.

public franchise: a contract that permits a person or organization to use public property for private profit.

pure research: research done without a specific product in mind.

Q

quality management: involves developing standards for all operations and products and measuring results using those standards.

quantity discount: used by sellers to encourage customers to buy in large quantities.

quasi-public corporation: a business that is important, but lacks the profit potential to attract private investors, and is often operated by local, state, or federal government.

quotas: limits placed on the quantity or value of units permitted to enter a country.

R

real property tax: a tax levied on land and buildings.

recession: a decline in the GDP that continues for six months or more.

recycle: the reuse of products or product packaging whenever possible.

regressive tax: taxation wherein the actual tax rate decreases as the taxable amount increases.

repetitive production: when the same thing is done over and over to produce a product.

researching: studying buyer interests and needs, testing products, and gathering facts needed to make good marketing decisions.

responsibility: the obligation to do an assigned task.

retailers: businesses that sell directly to final consumers.

retained earnings: profits that are put aside to run a business.

revolving credit: a credit plan that combines the features of regular charge credit and installment credit.

reward power: based on the ability to control resources, rewards, and punishments.

risk: the uncertainty that a loss may occur.

risk taking: assuming the risk of losses that may occur from fire, theft, damage, or other circumstances.

Rust Belt: the north central and northeastern states where major manufacturing centers were once dominant.

S

salary: compensation paid on other than an hourly basis, such as weekly or monthly.

sales budget: a forecast of the sales for a month, a few months, or a year.

sales finance company: specializes in purchasing installment sales contracts at a discount from businesses that need cash or that do not care to handle collections.

sales oriented: businesses that emphasize distribution and promotion in order to sell the products that have been produced.

sales promotions: any promotional activities other than advertising and personal selling intended to motivate customers to buy.

sales tax: a tax levied on the retail price of goods and services at the time they are sold.

sanctions: a milder form of embargo where specific business ties with a foreign country are banned.

savings account: an account that allows customers to make deposits, earn interest, and make withdrawals at any time without financial penalties.

schedule: a time plan for reaching objectives.

search engine: a program that assists in locating information on the Internet.

seasonal discount: given to the buyer for ordering or taking delivery of goods in advance of the normal buying period.

secured loan (collateral loan): a loan that requires the borrower to pledge something of value as security.

securities: stocks and bonds.

self-directed work team: a team in which members together are responsible for the work assigned to the team.

self-service merchandising: customers select the products they wish, take them to a cashier or checkout counter, and pay for them.

selling: providing personalized and persuasive information to customers to help them buy the products and services they need.

selling price: the actual price paid for a company's products by the customer.

seniority: the length of time an employee has been with the company.

service firms: business that provide assistance to satisfy specialized needs through skilled workers.

services: (1) activities of value that do not result in the ownership of a physical product. (2) intangible products that result from a high degree of labor input and that satisfy consumer needs.

shares: equal parts of the division of ownership of a corporation.

shopping goods: goods that are bought less frequently than convenience goods, that usually have a higher price, and that require some buying thought.

short-term capital: borrowed capital that must be repaid within a year, and often in 30, 60, or 90 days.

situational leader: one who understands employees and job requirements and matches actions and decisions to the circumstances.

small business: the term applied to any business that is operated by one or a few individuals.

smart card: a credit and debit card with a memory that stores financial, health, credit, and other kinds of data that can be read by computers.

social responsibility: the duty of a business to contribute to the well-being of society.

socialism: an economic-political system in which the government controls and regulates the means of production.

software: special instructions computers are provided to perform tasks.

sole proprietorship (proprietorship): a business owned and managed by one person.

spam: unsolicited advertising over e-mail.

span of control: the number of employees who are directly supervised by one person.

specialty goods: products that customers insist upon having and are willing to shop for until they find them.

stakeholders: the owners, customers, suppliers, employees, creditors, government, the general public, and other groups who are affected by a firm's action.

standard: a specific measure by which something is judged.

sticky-floor syndrome: the inability of workers to move up from low-paying jobs requiring little skill and education.

stock: a share of ownership in a corporation.

stock index: a kind of average of the prices of selected stocks considered to be representative of a certain class of stocks or of the economy in general.

stock rights option: a contract that allows stockholders to buy additional shares for less than the market price for a specified period of time.

stockbroker (broker): a professional who buys and sells corporate securities for customers through a stock brokerage firm and gives investment advice.

stockholders (shareholders): owners of a corporation.

storing: holding goods until needed by consumers, such as on shelves, in storage rooms, or in warehouses.

strategic alliances: when firms agree to cooperate on certain aspects of business while remaining competitors on other aspects.

strategic planning: long-term planning that provides broad goals and directions for the entire business.

subsidiaries: the name for foreign operations that are branches or are separately registered as a legal entity.

substantiation: being able to prove all claims made about products and services in promotions.

Sun Belt: the warmer southern half of the nation.

supervisor: a manager whose main job is to direct the work of employees.

supply: refers to the number of similar products that will be offered for sale at a particular time and at a particular price.

SWOT analysis: an examination of an organization's internal strengths and weaknesses as well as opportunities and threats from its external environment.

symptom: a sign or indication of something that appears to be the problem.

T

360-degree feedback: a method of performance evaluation that uses performance feedback gathered from a broad range of people with whom the employee works, both inside and outside the organization.

target markets: groups of customers with very similar needs to whom the company can sell its product.

tariff: a tax on foreign goods to protect domestic industries and earn revenue.

team organization: divides employees into permanent work teams.

telecommunications (data communications): a system involving the electronic movement of information from one location to another location.

telecommuting: allowing employees to work at home using computers rather than at the business.

telemarketing: marketing goods and services by telephone.

third world nations: countries that are underdeveloped, have few manufacturing firms, and have large numbers of poor people who possess few goods.

total quality management (TQM): a commitment to excellence that is accomplished by teamwork and continual improvement.

trade discount: a special deduction from the list price that is given to certain types of buyers, such as wholesalers or retailers, because the buyers perform certain functions for the seller.

trademark: a distinguishing name, symbol, or special mark placed on a good or service that is legally reserved for the sole use of the owner.

trading bloc: an arrangement between two or more countries to remove all restrictions on the sale of goods and services among them while imposing barriers to trade and investment from countries that are not part of the bloc.

transfer: the assignment of an employee to another job in the company that involves the same type of responsibility and authority.

transporting: moving goods from where they were made to where consumers can buy them.

treasury bill (T-bill): short-term security sold by the federal government to finance the cost of running the government.

treasury bonds: securities sold in $1,000 to $1 million amounts with maturities ranging from 10 to 30 years.

treasury notes: securities sold by the U.S. government in amounts of $1,000 up to $5,000 that generally mature in one to ten years.

U

underground economy: income that escapes being recorded in the GDP.

unity of command: means that no employee has more than one supervisor at a time.

unlimited financial liability: indicates that partners are responsible for their share of the business debts.

unsecured loans: a loan that is not backed by collateral.

unsought goods: products that many customers will not shop for because they do not have a strong need for the product.

utility: the ability of a good or service to satisfy a want.

V

variance: the difference between current performance and the standard.

vendor: the company from which goods are being ordered.

venture capitalist: an investor or investment group that lends large sums of money to promising new or expanding small companies.

virtual organization: a network of companies that form alliances among themselves to take advantage of fast-changing market conditions.

W

wages: compensation paid on an hourly basis.

warehouses: buildings used to store large quantities of products until they can be sold.

Web-hosting service: a private business that maintains the Web sites of individuals and organizations on its computers for a fee.

wholesalers: businesses that buy products from businesses and sell them to retailers or other businesses.

wholly-owned subsidiary: when a firm sets up a business abroad on its own without any partners.

wide area network (WAN): a network of linked computers that covers a wide geographic area.

work rules: regulations created to maintain an effective working environment in a business.

work team: a group of individuals who cooperate to achieve a common goal.

working capital: the difference between current assets and current liabilities.

World Bank: provides low-cost, long-term loans to less-developed countries to develop basic industries and facilities.

World Trade Organization (WTO): creates and enforces rules governing trade among countries.

World Wide Web (WWW, Web): makes the Internet accessible to the average person.

Z

zoning: regulations that specify which land areas may be used for homes and which areas may be used for different types of businesses.

INDEX

C

D

H

I

J

K

L

M

N

PHOTO CREDITS

Chapter 1 2, 4, 6, 8, 14, 17 © 2000 PhotoDisc
Chapter 2 30, 33, 37, 42, 46, 47 © 2000 PhotoDisc
Chapter 3 56, 58, 62, 66, 68, 76 © 2000 PhotoDisc
Chapter 4 84, 86, 90, 93, 101, 102, 103 © 2000 PhotoDisc
Chapter 5 112, 114, 120, 124, 128, 134, 135 © 2000 PhotoDisc
Chapter 6 138, 141, 149, 152, 155 © 2000 PhotoDisc
Chapter 7 164, 167, 170, 172, 176, 178, 183, 189 © 2000 PhotoDisc
Chapter 8 194, 195, 201, 205, 208, 210 © 2000 PhotoDisc
Chapter 9 218, 220, 222 © 2000 PhotoDisc; 225: Netscape Communicator browser windows © 2000 Netscape Communications Corporation. Used with permission. Netscape Communications has not authorized, sponsored, endorsed, or approved this publication and is not responsible for its content; 227, 230, 235 © 2000 PhotoDisc
Chapter 10 242, 245, 249, 255, 256, 258, 265, 267 © 2000 PhotoDisc
Chapter 11 272, 274, 275, 276, 280, 284, 289 © 2000 PhotoDisc
Chapter 12 296, 298, 302, 303, 305, 311, 314, 318, 319 © 2000 PhotoDisc
Chapter 13 322, 324, 327, 331, 335, 337, 348, 349 © 2000 PhotoDisc
Chapter 14 352, 354, 358, 362, 368, 370 © 2000 PhotoDisc
Chapter 15 382, 383 © 2000 PhotoDisc; 384, QuickBooks® by Intuit; 387, 394, 398, 404, 405 © 2000 PhotoDisc
Chapter 16 408, 409, 417, 421, 422, 426, 428 © 2000 PhotoDisc
Chapter 17 430, 432, 434, 437, 443, 444, 446 © 2000 PhotoDisc
Chapter 18 454, 456, 461, 464, 466, 474, 475 © 2000 PhotoDisc
Chapter 19 478, 480, 494, 500, 503 © 2000 PhotoDisc
Chapter 20 516, 519, 523, 526, 530, 535, 536 © 2000 PhotoDisc
Chapter 21 544, 547, 550, 557, 559 © 2000 PhotoDisc
Chapter 22 568, 570, 574, 577, 584, 585, 590, 591 © 2000 PhotoDisc
Chapter 23 594, 596, 599, 603, 607, 615, 617 © 2000 PhotoDisc
Chapter 24 626, 629, 635, 641, 646, 650 © 2000 PhotoDisc
Chapter 25 658, 665, 669, 673, 678, 680, 681, 686, 687 © 2000 PhotoDisc